Reference Key to the Writing Process

(continued)

W9-AOB-503

ORGANIZING

WRITING (DRAFTING)

PARAGRAPHS

REVISING

(continued on back end paper)

The Writing Commitment
Fourth Edition

The Writing Commitment
Fourth Edition

Michael E. Adelstein
University of Kentucky

Jean G. Pival
University of Kentucky

HARCOURT BRACE JOVANOVICH, PUBLISHERS
San Diego   New York   Chicago   Austin   Washington, D.C.
London   Sydney   Tokyo   Toronto

Preface

Revising a textbook for a Fourth Edition is akin to caring for a mature plant. In order to stimulate new growth, it may be necessary to prune, to enrich, to graft new material. So it is with our Fourth Edition of *The Writing Commitment*. The basic "plant" of our original edition remains. As always, it leads the student from writer-oriented personal papers to reader-oriented expository and persuasive ones and finally to the research paper and other types of writing for specialized audiences. However, this progression is considerably clearer and smoother as a result of our pruning and grafting.

The Fourth Edition also retains the integrated, "spiral" approach that has been basic to our philosophy of composition: We discuss prewriting and rewriting tactics, organization, sentence and paragraph structure, and language concerns not once but several times, each time focusing on the special aims and requirements of the particular kind of discourse being studied. The chief advantages of such an approach are that (1) as in the act of writing itself, the student encounters these topics in the context of specific writing situations, and (2) the student can grasp the essential concepts far better by returning to them again and again than by encountering them "once and for all" in a single chapter, isolated from purposeful applications.

Also retained and strengthened is the emphasis of previous editions on the writing process. In the Fourth Edition our discussions of the process have been considerably clarified, and we have taken special care to stress that the process is both recursive and highly individualized and that the writer needs to stay flexible, *using* rather than being constrained by what is now known about how writers write. At the same time that we have improved our discussions of process, we have also clarified and added to our discussions of the rhetorical strategies most suitable for particular writing purposes. Instructors familiar with previous editions will find throughout our discussions of both process and form a greater emphasis on audience considerations.

Perhaps the most radical change is the pruning out of Part Two of our previous editions, Descriptive Writing, and the grafting of its concepts into the preceding and following parts on personal and expository writing. This change allowed us to eliminate much repetition and also to structure the book closer to the three major aims of nonliterary discourse as espoused by James L. Kinneavy and others: expressive, referential, and persuasive. Subjective description is now in Personal Writing, along with three other writer-based forms: autobiographical narrative, the personal essay, and the character sketch. Objective description, because of its referential emphasis, is now discussed in Expository Writing.

In response to many requests from students and instructors, we have added Chapter 25, Writing for Business and Business Courses, in Part Five, The Academic Voice: Writing across the Curriculum. This chapter deals with the résumé and application letter, the memo, and the report — all forms that may be useful for class assignments and for applying for part-time and summer jobs as well as career-related positions.

Throughout, we have enriched the text with new — and more numerous — writing examples. We have used well-written student pieces when available. When not, we have selected professional writing within the reach of freshman students. In deference to the increased enrollments of mature students, we have been careful to choose topics of general interest.

Other specific changes in the Fourth Edition include the following:

- **The journal:** Previously treated separately as a "form" of personal writing, the journal has been moved to a chapter on prewriting and is now more integrated throughout the text as a useful prewriting aid for any kind of writing.
- **The paragraph:** Added to Part One is a new chapter — Chapter 3 — on the essentials of the paragraph (previously not introduced until Chapter 15), with special emphasis on paragraphs in personal narration and description. Additionally, as in previous editions a comprehensive treatment of expository paragraphs is included in the section on expository writing (in what is now chapter 10). The findings of Francis Christensen — always essential in our treatment of the expository paragraph — have been made more accessible than before, and there is greater emphasis on parallelism as a device for signalling the various levels of modification.
- **Sentences:** The discussions of sentences emphasize sentence-combining even more than before, and combining exercises have been added to later sections of the book.
- **Checklists:** All the checklist questions in the chapters on rewriting have been changed to call for substantive answers rather than merely yes or no. This change should encourage students to think more specifically about what they need to do to improve their writing.
- **Process explanations:** The treatment of writing about processes (in Chapter 8, The Forms of Expository Writing) has been expanded to include both instructions ("how to do it") and descriptions ("how it works or is done").
- **Cause-and-effect and comparison-and-contrast:** The discussions of both these rhetorical strategies have been expanded, and full-length examples of both have been included.
- **Rogerian argument:** Formerly treated as a separate form, Rogerian argument is now treated as a strategy pertinent to all persuasion. An essay by William Raspberry arguing the advantages of language proficiency has been added as a model of skillful Rogerian strategy.

- **Peer evaluation:** Both the text and the instructor's manual, *The Teaching Commitment,* give greater attention than before to the uses of a workshop approach — peer evaluation — in teaching writing.
- **Documentation styles:** In the discussions of research-paper documentation, which include both the current style of the Modern Language Association of America (MLA) and that of the American Psychological Association (APA), the addition of APA examples comparable to all those provided for MLA style enhances the Fourth Edition as a resource for writing across the disciplines.
- **Reference Guide:** The Reference Guide (pages 529 through 590) has been reorganized and includes convenient revision symbols throughout so that it can truly function as a reference handbook to help students correct grammar, usage, punctuation, spelling, and other problems in their papers. A key to the revision symbols — now greatly expanded — is printed inside the back cover.
- **Other reference aids:** To enable students to draw together related materials from throughout the text — particularly important with our integrated approach — a new reference chart, Reference Key to the Writing Process, printed inside the front cover provides a convenient synoptic view. For example, some seventeen discovery techniques are presented in four prewriting chapters on personal, expository, and persuasive discourse and research writing. Each technique, however, while especially productive for a particular type of discourse, may be useful for other types as well; so the student will find all seventeen listed in the Reference Key under the single heading "Discovery Techniques." Additionally, the index (page 593) is much fuller and more detailed than in any previous edition and allows the user to go quickly to every significant mention of any topic.

Acknowledgments

As in our Second and Third Editions, we have incorporated suggestions from numerous instructors who have used the text — composition specialists, literature specialists who occasionally teach composition, linguists, graduate students beginning their academic careers, and our colleagues at the University of Kentucky — as well as, of course, our own students. In particular, we are grateful to our colleagues who sifted through hundreds of student essays to help us with model papers — James Wyatt, Gurney Norman, Patrice Mayo, Chris Cetrulo, and Thomas Blues — and of course we are deeply indebted to the student authors of these papers as well.

As always, we are obliged to the many scholars on whose research and theory we have freely drawn. Aside from those mentioned in the text, the following have especially influenced our thinking and teaching: Edward P.J. Corbett, Peter Elbow, Linda Flower, James L. Kinneavy, Erika Lindemann, Donald M. Murray, Frank O'Hare, Joseph M. Williams, W. Ross Winterowd, and Richard Young.

We owe much to our fellow composition teachers across the country for sharing their experiences with us in response to our questionnaires: Richard Boudreau, Ellen Bourland, Carol Breslin, Thomas A. Brethauer, Richard Costner, Michelle Dabel, Sister Mary Delaney, Robert Gerye, James L. Jolly, Jr., Joyce V. Jolly, Anne

Kaler, John H. Knight, Frank Knittel, Joseph J. P. Linzmeier, Linda Maik, William J. Martin, Thomas C. McCall, Marilyn Monaghan, Betty Nave, Peter Nettleton, Marietta Patrick, Charisse Richarz, Brenda S. Ryan, Raymond G. Schoen, Ann K. Schwader, JoAnn Seiple, John K. Sheriff, Lana White, and Elizabeth Sue Willey. A few respondents preferred not to be named, but their comments were no less valuable.

We particularly appreciate the help of the following reviewers, whose detailed critiques have been priceless to us: Lil Brannon, Richard Costner, Martha Kay, Arlene E. Kuhner, Raymond G. Schoen, Peter Nettleton, and Jeffrey L. Spear. We, of course, take full responsibilities for imperfections.

To our editor, Tom Broadbent, and his colleagues at Harcourt Brace Jovanovich, especially Lesley Lenox, Fran Wager, and Eleanor Garner, go our heartfelt thanks for valuable advice and careful supervision of our work from beginning to end.

Finally, we thank our families and friends for their patient toleration of our periods of self-imposed exile.

M.E.A.
J.G.P.

Contents

5 Language in Personal Writing   89

6 Special Topics: Grammar, Usage, and Language Varieties   105

23   Writing in Literature Courses   457

24   Writing in Science and Social Science Courses   481

Introduction:
Writing Well

As a student in a writing course, you deserve answers to certain frequently asked questions:

Why learn to write?
Can I learn to write well?
How will I learn to write?
What is good writing?

As a reader of this textbook, you are entitled to the answers to other questions as well:

What is this book about?
How can I best use this book?
What does the title mean?

First questions first.

WHY LEARN TO WRITE?

At the moment, you may view writing as an activity that occurs mainly in English classes. But as you continue through college and pursue your career, you will find that you have to write effectively to succeed. For example, in other courses during your college years you will have to write reports, essay examinations, and term papers. Often your academic success will depend upon how well you can express your ideas. Then there may be applications for jobs (summer, part-time, or regular), scholarships, and perhaps admission to graduate and professional schools. Once again, your ability to write will be crucial. And after graduation, whether you go into business, industry, government, or the professions, your success will often be determined by your writing ability. Peter Drucker, a nationally recognized management consultant, points out that "as soon as you move one step up from the bottom, your effectiveness depends on your ability to reach others through the spoken or written word."

Today, as you begin college, you may not realize how often you will be represented by your writing. You will be known, evaluated, admitted, awarded jobs, promoted—achieve success or not—on the basis of how well you write. Professors, registrars, deans, award and admissions committees, personnel managers, and others ordinarily cannot take the time to become well acquainted with you in person. You must make yourself known in writing. What you say is you.

There are other reasons for learning to write—less practical, perhaps, but no less meaningful. Writing is one of the best ways for you to discover who you are and what you think. What, *exactly,* are your views on the appropriate response to terrorism, on abortion, on compulsory drug tests, the death penalty, or subsidized student loans? Committing yourself on paper about such subjects—even if you are to be the only reader, as in a diary or journal—requires you to probe your mind, reexamine your assumptions, reach into your subconscious to find out what you really think and why. As you write out your thoughts, their appearance on paper often stimulates other ideas that have been lurking vaguely in your mind. In this process, you may very well change your opinions, and you may even decide to take action on them. At the least, you will discover what you know, what you think, what you believe, what you feel.

Of course, you can discover much about yourself and your knowledge, understanding, and values in talking about them. But speech is slippery, words disappearing in air. Writing, because it stays right there on the page where you put it, allows you to see your thoughts, grasp them, clarify them, and check and recheck them, working out contradictions, adding qualifications, making distinctions. Only writing enables you to discover yourself fully and accurately. E.M. Forster the novelist, stated it well when he said, "How can I know what I think till I see what I say?"

You also learn better as a result of writing. Remember that high school paper you wrote about the Civil War or *Jane Eyre* or the possibility of life on Mars? Whatever your subject was, you probably understand and remember that subject much better today than any others you studied at the same time. One reason for this is that, while writing, you were actively participating in the learning process instead of passively reading about a subject or listening to your teacher talk about it. Thus, writing is a learning tool, helping you to understand and remember.

Still another reason for learning to write is that writing can be a pleasure—a means of self-expression comparable to painting, sculpting, or composing music. As an effective vehicle for sounding off, writing may furnish emotional relief or ego satisfaction. There is something fulfilling about expressing your ideas and feelings on a subject. Writing may be compared to other creative acts: cooking a meal, taking photographs, designing a house, making pottery—all contain the signature of your personality. If the result is something that will interest and appeal to others, so much the better. But that isn't really necessary for the creative act of writing to give you self-fulfillment. What you create is *you*. You may think, however, that you cannot. You may wonder, "Can I learn to write well?"

CAN I LEARN TO WRITE WELL?

Of course you can. Every college freshman can learn to write. We are not talking about writing stories, poems, or plays—though you may wish to try your hand at these, too. We mean learning to write the clear, concise, effective prose required in college and the working world. Skill in writing may come more slowly to some than to others, but with interest and effort it can be learned.

Learning to write, like learning practically any other skill, involves three components: instruction, practice, and criticism. Let's apply them to learning how to play a sport—say, tennis. A book, a coach, or an experienced player provides instruction about how to hold the racquet, how to stand, how to swing, and the like. Then come hours of practice, hitting a ball against a backboard, volleying with friends, and finally, perhaps, entering tournaments. During this time, your coach or friend often provides criticism, pointing out that you're not throwing the ball up properly on your serve or not getting your racquet back far enough on your backhand. So you practice throwing the ball up properly or getting your racquet back. Instruction, practice, criticism. That's how you learned to swim, read, play the piano, or drive a car, and that's how you will learn to write well.

HOW WILL I LEARN TO WRITE?

You can probably guess the answer. This textbook and your instructor will teach you the principles. For practice—and, we hope, pleasure—you will write papers, the more the better. Your teacher and perhaps your classmates—your "coach" and fellow "players"—will criticize the results of your efforts, praising what you are doing well, suggesting how you can improve. You can learn to write and improve your writing only by writing. There is no other way.

Like athletes who spend hundreds of hours on the court or field practicing, you need to spend many hours writing and rewriting. It would be simple if you merely had to read this book or listen to your instructor, but nothing can replace practice in the process of writing.

WHAT IS THE PROCESS OF WRITING?

Just as you can improve your technique by imitating experts in such fields as sports, music, theater, or dance, so you can profit by trying the ways experienced writers work. Generally, they follow a three-stage composing process somewhat as illustrated in Figure I-1. As the arrows looping back from later steps to earlier ones indicate, the process is not simple and straightforward, as we shall see. First, however, let us consider what is involved in each stage.

Prewriting, the first stage, involves <u>discovering a subject and restricting,</u> developing, and organizing it—all according to the purpose and for the audience you have in mind. Generally, you engage in all these activities to some extent before you formally start to write. We say "formally" because, from the beginning, you may actually be making notes and scribbles and perhaps doing some "free" writing, as we shall discuss later.

The second stage, *writing,* consists of getting the composition down on paper in a rough (or first draft) form. Some writers do this by working straight through the composition from beginning to end. Others find that they work best by writing in "chunks" that are out of sequence—whatever parts happen to come most easily—and then assembling them. But however you work, this stage involves translating the ideas in your mind into words, sentences, and paragraphs on paper. In this drafting stage, writing perfection is not the goal. Instead, you should try mainly to set your ideas down on paper to see what you have to say, bothering

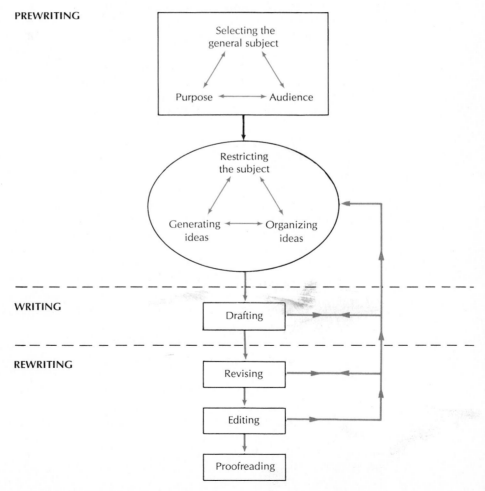

Figure I-1. The Writing Process.

little about selecting precise words, crafting crisp sentences, and following the conventions of printed English.

A hint: you will work best if you are comfortable and have your preferred writing materials conveniently at hand. Such physical details as where you sit when you write and whether you use pen, pencil, typewriter, or word processor; listen to music and what kind; and write in the morning, afternoon, or evening are all important in helping you to feel in the right mood to write well.

The third stage, *rewriting,* comprises three sub-steps (which, like the main stages, can overlap in practice). In the first—*revising*—you reconsider all the major, or overall, aspects of your first draft: its organization, development of ideas, unity of thought, completeness of discussion, and so forth. Among the questions you might ask yourself are the following:

Is there irrelevant material that should be deleted?

Should more examples, details, reasons, or facts be added?

Do the ideas follow one another logically?

How could the introduction and conclusion be improved?

When you have reviewed your paper in light of these and other questions concerning content and arrangement, making the necessary changes, you are ready to move to the next step—*editing.* Here you focus your examination—as with a magnifying glass—on smaller elements, making your paragraphs more coherent, your sentences more effective, your choice of words more precise. And you also check to make certain that you have carefully followed the conventions of written English, such as grammar, spelling, and punctuation.

Finally, after you have prepared the last draft of your paper, but before you submit it, you should complete the third step—*proofreading.* This requires you to go over your paper more closely still, searching for typing errors, word duplications, omissions, and other careless mistakes.

As we have described it, the composing process may seem to be an orderly, step-by-step procedure. Not so, as the arrows pointing in different directions in Figure I–1 are meant to indicate. While writing a draft, for example, writers may think of additional ideas or even choose a different subject entirely. They may stop occasionally to edit their work as they write—checking on a spelling, searching for a better word, or redesigning a sentence. And they may well decide to rewrite whole sections as they edit.

However, even though the stages of the composing process are far from orderly, being aware of them enables you to approach a writing task in a somewhat systematic way that works for other writers. By understanding the process and following it, modifying it to suit your inclination and purpose, you should be able to improve your writing. We will return to the discussion of the process at various points throughout this book.

WHAT IS GOOD WRITING?

Because good writing is one of those ideal abstractions that are seldom pinned down—held in high esteem but rarely defined—let us list some of its characteristics.

- *Good writing is clear.* Its ideas have been organized so logically, its words selected so carefully, and its sentences crafted so skillfully that the designated readers need not guess at, struggle with, or reread the material to understand what the writer means. Good writers provide details, examples, reasons, and facts to support their ideas.
- *Good writing is concise.* It contains no unnecessary words, phrases, or sentences. Consequently, readers will not feel that their time is wasted.
- *Good writing is effective.* It conveys a message to its readers in such a way that they will respond as the writer intended. Good writers choose their words, sentences, and paragraph structures wisely in order to have the desired impact on their readers. They unify their writing by eliminating irrelevant material and by providing continuity, linking sentences to sentences and paragraphs to paragraphs. And they abide by the conventions of standard English usage and of spelling, punctuation, capitalization, and the like.
- *Good writing projects the authentic voice of the writer.* It conveys the personality of an individual human being talking to other humans, unlike the impersonal, often mechanical prose found in government publications and many textbooks. However, good writers adapt this "speaking voice" to suit the audience, purpose, and occasion.
- *Good writing is interesting* regardless of whether it is designed to amuse, inform, or persuade a reader. Writers generally stimulate interest by offering the reader some information or insight that is new or at least freshly stated. Writers need not always be experts on the subject, but they should avoid boring readers by stating what is obvious.

WHAT IS THIS BOOK ABOUT?

The composing process does not in itself communicate your ideas to your reader. The ideas must be presented to the reader in some *form:* a narrative, explanation, or argument, for instance, depending on the situation. Because writing involves not only practicing the composing process but also gaining control of these written forms, *The Writing Commitment* is concerned with both.

Underlying everything we say in the book is a key concept: Not all writing is the same. Everything you write—a letter home for money, a newsy note to a friend, an application for a job—is written for a particular purpose to a particular audience in a particular situation. The purpose of the money request is to persuade; the audience is friendly (we hope), the situation serious. The newsy note aims to inform and entertain; its audience is friendly, the situation casual. The job application aims to persuade, but the audience is unknown, the situation formal. This book will provide you with different strategies and structures for various writing assignments.

HOW CAN I BEST USE THIS BOOK?

Essentially, your use of this book will be dictated by your instructor, who will assign chapters according to a course syllabus. But you can use the text profitably in other ways. As you work your way through it, you will note that it is organically structured, dealing with various writing concerns where they are especially relevant to a particular kind of writing. You will not find all kinds of paragraphs or sentence structures in a single chapter, nor is there one chapter that discusses all the aspects of language or all organizational tactics. For example, because writers tend to use many simple and compound sentences in personal writing, we discuss those sentence basics in that section. We are well aware, however, that in this form of writing you may need to use more complex sentence structures. If you need help with them, you should check the table of contents, the index, or the reference chart inside the front cover for the appropriate pages.

Even though we have discussed the forms of writing in the first chapter of each section, we suggest that, before you actually start to write in those forms, you study the following chapter on prewriting tactics, then employ the tactics most effective for your particular assignment and your individual needs.

In the writing and rewriting stages, you may need help with language or grammatical usages. In that case, you can turn to a chapter on language or use the Reference Guide at the end of the book.

We also suggest that, after you have finished a first draft, you go through the rewriting checklists in the last chapter of each section. These contain specific questions tailored especially to the forms presented in the section. Even though you may have rewritten some sentences or paragraphs and corrected errors while writing the draft, you will benefit from these questions as you work through the three steps in the rewriting stage. Also, if your instructor encourages peer evaluation of papers in your course, you can use these rewriting questions as guidelines for helping your classmates with their writing problems. For references to all the book's checklists, as well as other helpful information, see the reference chart inside the front cover.

To give you quick access to all the various sentence, punctuation, or usage conventions and other writing concerns, we have provided a substantial Reference Guide at the end of this book. There you will find an alphabetical listing and discussion of grammatical terms, as well as explanations of the most common usage problems and of punctuation and other conventions. If you are plagued by nonstandard usages or poor spelling, you will find valuable suggestions and exercises there to help you overcome your problems.

On the inside covers are concise reference charts. You may use them or the index in the back pages to locate all the references to any subject that interests you. Like a dictionary or an encyclopedia, a composition textbook is a reference tool. You don't have to wait for an assignment from your instructor to make good use of it.

WHAT DOES THE TITLE MEAN?

We chose *The Writing Commitment* as our title to impress upon you that every time you write, you commit some portion of yourself to paper, and you also enter into a commitment with readers. When you turn in a well-organized, logically reasoned, adequately developed, and carefully written paper, it reflects well on you as a person. So your primary writing commitment is to yourself: to work hard, to do your best, to set high standards for yourself. Remember, your message is you—you are what you write.

You also have a commitment to your readers. In a sense, it is a moral commitment: Write for your readers as you would have them write for you. When *you* read, you don't want to be bored, so you have an obligation to your readers to be interesting. *You* don't want to struggle to understand a passage, so you have an obligation to your readers to be clear. Also, *you* don't want to be distracted by misspellings, faulty punctuation, or inappropriate usages, so you have an obligation to your readers to follow the conventions of written English. This is the Golden Rule of writing—your writing commitment to your readers.

PART ONE

The Intimate Voice: Personal Writing

The special pleasure and challenge of personal writing is the freedom it affords for self-expression and self-discovery. Whatever you may happen to be writing "about," the real subject of personal writing will be your own ideas, feelings, and impressions—your own experience. This is true whether you write for your own use, as in a diary or journal, or to share with others. You may choose to *re-create* the experience so that you or your readers may relive it in the way it happened, as we'll see writers doing in the sections that follow on autobiographical narrative and personal description. Or you may prefer to *reflect* on your experience, to draw some significant meaning from it, as the writers do in our examples of the personal essay and the character sketch. But whatever form your personal writing takes, it is unlike literary writing that is set in a fictional universe peopled by imaginary characters. Personal writing is a self-portrait—a slice of *your* life, set in *your* personal world, inhabited by people *you* know.

Reading what you have written about a past experience is much like looking at a snapshot of the event, but it is also different: Although a photograph may remind you of how places and people *looked,* the memory of how you *felt* about the occasion may be dulled by time or sweetened by nostalgia. In contrast, a written personal account can recapture exactly how the experience affected you. You may remember an exciting outing, a relative's wedding, a tragic accident, or your first day on a challenging job, but if you have written about it, capturing its special quality on paper, you will almost certainly find that it retains a sharper, more vivid reality for you, and perhaps greater meaning.

The very act of writing helps us to become more aware of life itself, as Anne Morrow Lindbergh says of her own voluminous journal writings:

> I must write it all out, at any cost. Writing is thinking. It is more than living, for it is being conscious of living.
>
> —*Locked Rooms and Open Doors*

Personal writing may also be a therapeutic process of self-analysis that helps you to understand yourself better and to work your way through difficult and painful experiences. It affords you the opportunity to understand your failures as well as your successes, your weaknesses as well as your strengths, your disillusionments as well as your dreams. The reward for such understanding can be increased self-mastery and self-confidence.

Personal writing is also fine preparation for more rigorous and structured writing assignments. As you explore various arrangements for presenting your experiences and ideas, you will learn some basic techniques of organization. Your descriptive powers will increase as you experiment with words and become more aware of the various effects you can create with differing shades of meaning. Practicing with a variety of sentence techniques will give you a versatility that enlivens not only your personal writing but all your writing, whatever form it takes.

This first section of our text focuses on two major purposes of personal writing: re-creating the experience of an event, place, or person and reflecting on the meaning of such experience. We will consider four forms—the autobiographical narrative, the personal description, the personal essay, and the character sketch. In discussing each, we will point out its particular purpose, its characteristics, and the special writing problems it entails. To help you write better, we will provide specific instructions, as well as student and professional examples to show you how others have handled such personal writing tasks.

As you work your way through this section, you should come to understand more fully the nature of the commitment writers make when they write—both to themselves and to their readers.

1

Forms of
Personal Writing

This chapter focuses on two aims of personal writing as noted in the introduction: *re-creating* experience, as in autobiographical narrative and personal description, and *reflecting* on experience, as in the personal essay and character sketch. You should bear in mind, however, that in practice these aims are not strictly separate. Generally, writers pursue both, but giving greater emphasis to one than to the other. For example, an autobiographical narrative may include reflections on the events narrated, even though the writer's main purpose is to retell and share the experience itself. On the other hand, a personal essay or character sketch may include descriptive details that re-create experience, even though the main emphasis is on the writer's reactions to it.

Although each kind of personal writing discussed in this chapter can be satisfying in itself, each develops skills that you can apply to other writing tasks. For example, autobiographical narrative—the retelling of an event in your life—requires some skill in organization and in providing details. You can't jump randomly from one episode to another; you must tell your story in some orderly fashion, providing appropriate "signposts" when necessary to help your reader follow the time sequence. And you must decide what to include and what to omit, culling out irrelevant details to avoid boring your readers. The ability to organize information clearly and to use details effectively is important for all writing tasks.

Personal essays, personal descriptions, and character sketches—the other forms in this chapter—will give you practice in identifying a central theme or idea to give your writing the direction and focus necessary for all writing. And you will further develop your organizing skills because these forms, like the explanatory essays and the argumentative writing we'll consider in later chapters, usually require tighter organization than the chronological sequence common to narrative.

Finally, in working with all the forms of personal writing here, you will become more aware of the importance of word choice and how words can be used to create the effect you wish to achieve—whatever your writing purpose may be.

AUTOBIOGRAPHICAL NARRATIVE

To be effective, a short autobiographical narrative should have a central incident or event, as well as a time framework, believable characters, and a setting. Once you have an incident in mind, you may find that the other elements fall naturally into place as you write. As in most endeavors, however, success in writing rarely results from lucky accidents. A look at some of the characteristics of narrative, therefore, should help you in both planning and writing.

- *Interest.*   The incident should be interesting to *you.* If you choose a significant event in your life, one that has made a difference to you, the chances are that readers, too, will find it interesting. The following narrative from a student's journal illustrates how a single small event can have significance and interest.

> I ran over a possum last night. I have never run over any animal before. It gave me a very nervous feeling. You don't necessarily feel bad about it. Just nervous. And a little angry. We were downtown and it just ran out from between two parked cars and I hit it. I didn't stop. People don't stop for a possum.
>
> Later, I got out the picture I took of one in our backyard last summer. She was digging a hole and I walked right up to her. Bravery or friendliness kept her there. She didn't run. The photograph is hilarious—or at least, it was. Now, I look at her differently. Perhaps it was a relative of hers—an aunt or brother—that I killed. Perhaps, as a child, I was influenced too much by Beatrix Potter's story of the possum.
>
> So I look at the picture. Possums have the kindest eyes. The eyes seem alien to their bodies. Brown, brown eyes.
>
> Next time, I think I'll stop.
>
> *—Shelly Slatin*

- *Central action.*   A short narrative should focus on a single event and include only those details that are pertinent to the action. Everything in the narrative should be closely related to your story's purpose.
- *Time framework.*   The narrative should be limited to a brief period of time. Long, drawn-out events or periods (a vacation, a long trip, a semester in college) do not lend themselves to the kind of detailed, concrete writing that brings an experience to life for readers.
- *Believable characters.*   Like the event itself, any people involved—including yourself—should be made "real." You need not describe characters fully; focus instead on significant features that contribute to the development of your story. Although a few carefully chosen physical details are often necessary,

concentrate on portraying what the characters say and do, how they interact with others.

- **Setting.** The setting, too, should contribute to the narrative. For instance, if you are writing a narrative about a humiliating request for a bank loan, then you should describe the plush surroundings if they contributed to your embarrassment. But remember, *unnecessary* details slow down the action and distract or even confuse the reader.

Discourse Techniques of Autobiographical Narrative

Often, telling a story requires close attention to the conversation of the characters because people's speech reveals their attitudes and personalities. Dialogue can also be useful in creating a sense of action moving the plot along or in explaining the situation.

Writers can choose between two major approaches to reproducing conversation. The first, called direct discourse, reproduces exactly what each character says in the character's own words, presenting the conversation as in life or in a play. The second—indirect discourse—describes or summarizes what characters say rather than attempting to reproduce the conversation exactly.

The following two examples, taken from Maya Angelou's autobiography, *I Know Why the Caged Bird Sings,* demonstrate the difference in the two approaches.

Direct Discourse: No recriminations lay hidden under the plain statement, nor was there boasting when he said, "If I'm living better now, it's because I treats everybody right."

Indirect Discourse: He told me that they made Negroes sleep in the street in the North and that they had to clean out toilets with their hands in the North and even things worse than that.

Note that direct and indirect discourse require different conventions of punctuation. (For a more detailed discussion of the punctuation conventions for direct discourse, see pages 59–60.) Also, in the direct discourse example, Maya Angelou realistically portrays the speaker's dialect, while in the second example, she makes no attempt to show the speaker's idiosyncratic speech habits.

Each approach has its advantages. Writers generally use one throughout a short narrative; in longer works, they may combine the two.

In the essay that follows, the student writer chose to use direct discourse. As you read, consider what is added by this choice.

An Autobiographical Narrative

The Encounter
Catherine Ross

Preoccupied with thoughts of the peace demonstration I was about to attend, I walked quickly toward the 24-hour banker. There was a chill in the air and it looked as if rain might fall within the hour, so I intended to be well prepared and have plenty of money for coffee or any other chill-lifting beverage that might be available at the demonstration site. Hurriedly, I jammed my bank card into the slot and pressed the "quick cash" button as the familiar greeting appeared on the screen. The machine clanked and whirred, and I pulled open the cash window and withdrew my thirty dollars. "Enough money for all the participants to get toasty," I thought to myself.

As I withdrew my card and receipt, a light rain began to fall. It was mid-October, and darkness seemed to come all too quickly. As the rain became a steady drizzle, I turned to the parking lot and the warmth of my car. I had gone only a few paces when I was startled by a loud voice from behind; the proximity unnerved me.

"Hey, bitch, you give me that money now!"

As the command registered, I felt a tingly rush of adrenaline. My hair stood out from the back of my neck.

"Give it," the voice demanded.

I looked over my right shoulder at the same instant that he grabbed my arm and whirled me around. I was face to face with a snarling young stranger with whiskey-laden breath. I jerked my arm from his grip, took an instinctive step backward. My assailant was a boy of about sixteen, a scowling youth about an inch shorter than I.

Suddenly, I perceived my predicament as humorous. The kid took an unsure step toward me and opened his mouth to speak. I brought my knee up—hard. He let out a howl, grabbed his groin, and doubled over. In a flash, I locked my hands together and brought them down upon his bent figure. He crumpled to the ground with me on his back. He struggled and flipped over so that he was face up beneath me. Still enraged, I lifted his head by the hair and pounded it on the concrete several times. It was then that I noticed him peering intently over my shoulder, almost oblivious to the punishment I was inflicting.

My breath caught in my throat. "Oh, God! Does he have a partner somewhere?"

I leapt to my feet and whirled around, ready. The sidewalk was bare, deserted. I turned back just in time to see my "attacker" struggle awkwardly to his feet and bolt. I grabbed for him, but caught only his jacket. He slipped free of the loose garment and yelled, "Leave me alone, you crazy bitch!"

With his jacket hanging limp in my grasp, I watched him sprint the length of the parking lot and disappear into the shadowy drizzle. I dropped my shoulders and sighed wearily. My mind whirled in confusion.

How could a sixteen-year-old punk redefine my whole identity? For years I had thought myself a pacifist, had walked away from even the most blatant dare. Tonight, however, I had fought. I had struck back with vengeance and felt exhilaration at recognizing my own prowess. When threatened, I can be fiercely combative.

The student vividly and realistically re-creates the event. She accomplishes this by a number of narrative devices: (1) direct discourse; (2) action-packed verbs, such as *jammed, leapt, whirled, sprint;* (3) short, simple sentences in describing the struggle: and (4) vivid, concrete details relevant to the action: "the warmth of my car," "tingly rush of adrenaline," "snarling young stranger," "whiskey-laden breath," "unsure step," "shadowy drizzle." Observe, too, that although the writer's emphasis clearly is on re-creating the event, the essay ends on a note of reflection.

PERSONAL DESCRIPTION

Personal description can be an end in itself. For example, a whole essay might be devoted to describing a place, an object, a person, or perhaps a pet, important in some way to the writer. But often personal description is integrated in other forms of writing: in narrative, as you have seen, and frequently to serve as an example in an explanatory essay or to support a point in an argumentative one (as we'll see in later sections of this book).

In this section, however, we'll focus on personal description as a kind of writing engaged in for its own sake. Personal description relies on images that appeal to the five senses—what we see, hear, small, taste, or feel—to convey the writer's own reactions, responses, impressions, or feelings. In writing personal description, we are likely to reveal as much about ourselves as about our subjects. The personal description proclaims: This is the way it was to *me*, the writer.

The following paragraph from Jean Henri Fabre's captivating essay on the praying mantis vividly demonstrates the writer's attitudes toward his subject.

> Apart from her lethal implement [the forelegs], the Mantis has nothing to inspire dread. She is not without a certain beauty, in fact, with her slender figure, her elegant bust, her pale-green coloring and her long gauze wings. No ferocious mandibles, opening like shears; on the contrary, a dainty pointed muzzle that seems made for billing and cooing. Thanks to a flexible neck, quite independent of the thorax, the head is able to move freely, to turn to right or left, to bend, to lift itself. Alone among insects, the Mantis directs her gaze; she inspects and examines; she almost has a physiognomy.
>
> —*Edwin Way Teale, ed., The Insect World of J. Henri Fabre*

The purpose here is to convey an impression of the insect, particularly how this writer feels about it. To most people, the mantis looks sinister; to Fabre, the mantis resembles an attractive, slender woman with an elegant bust, a dainty mouth, a head that turns to inspect and examine. An objective description would refer to a mantis as *it;* here the mantis is *she.* Fabre provides his readers with a fresh, distinctive way of thinking about and visualizing the mantis. This personal description is distinctive, individualistic, interpretative, although it includes some facts, as do nearly all personal descriptions. And, in language that is rich and suggestive (*elegant, ferocious, like shears, billing and cooing*), the description contains elements of both irony and humor as it points out the contrast between the appearance of the gentle beauty and the reality of the lethal forelegs.

Organization

Unlike autobiographical narratives, which are generally organized chronologically from past to present, personal descriptions are usually organized spatially, moving from one location to another. In the paragraph on the praying mantis, for example, Fabre moves from a general description of its body to the head, which he then treats in great detail. The opening paragraphs of narratives and descriptions also differ: Autobiographical narratives usually start with some event; personal descriptions usually begin with some statement of the writer's main impression of the item to be described. Again, in the praying mantis example, Fabre begins his description of the insect with the statement that she "has nothing to inspire dread." Then the writer, through careful choice of details, attempts to maintain and build that impression throughout.

In the following sentences, Annie Dillard creates an atmosphere of fear in her description of nightfall at Tinker Creek:

> But shadows spread and deepened and stayed. After thousands of years we're still strangers to darkness, fearful aliens in an enemy camp with our arms crossed over our chests. I stirred. A land turtle on the bank, startled, hissed the air from its lungs and withdrew to its shell. An uneasy pink here, an unfathomable blue there, gave great suggestion of lurking beings. Things were going on. I couldn't see whether that rustle I heard was a distant rattlesnake, slit-eyed, or a nearby sparrow kicking in the dry flood debris slung at the foot of a willow. Tremendous action roiled the water everywhere I looked, big action, inexplicable. A tremor welled up beside a gaping muskrat burrow in the bank and I caught my breath, but no muskrat appeared. The ripples continued to fan upstream with a steady, powerful thrust. Night was knitting an eyeless mask over my face, and I still sat transfixed.
>
> —*Annie Dillard, Pilgrim at Tinker Creek*

With the words "strangers to darkness, fearful aliens in an enemy camp," Dillard establishes the main impression—an impression that becomes a recurring theme in the description. Stating a main impression in your opening paragraph can make your first attempts at description easier to organize; later, you may wish to experiment by placing such a statement in your conclusion to give the effect of a summary.

In addition to stating the dominant impression, you must consider point of view, whether you wish to be a static or moving observer. If static, then you should select and consistently follow some clear order. If moving, then you must clearly signal readers with phrases or sentences that mark the shift from one location to another. As an illustration, here are some of the introductory sentences from paragraphs in John Ruskin's description of St. Mark's Cathedral in Venice:

> And now I wish that the reader, before I bring him into St. Mark's Place, would imagine himself for a little time in a quiet English cathedral town, and walk with me to the west front of its cathedral.
> Think for a little while on that scene. . . . And then let us quickly recollect that we are in Venice. . . .
> We find ourselves in a paved alley. . . .
> A yard or two farther, we pass the hostelry of the Black Eagle. . . .
> Let us enter the church.
>
> *—John Ruskin, The Stones of Venice*

Whether static or moving, description is generally organized spatially—moving from top to bottom, left to right, head to toe, far to near, and so forth—as the eyes might move in regarding the object. Chronology, or time order, may also be involved, however, especially if you are a moving observer (as Ruskin is in the example just given) or if you are stationary but the object is moving, as when you describe a race or a parade. As in all writing, the topic or subject often dictates your organizational decisions.

Ways to Arouse and Maintain Interest

Throughout, we have emphasized that personal descriptions can gain direction and focus from an introductory statement of the central impression or theme. But such a statement can serve an additional purpose—to catch the readers' interest—if the writer has taken care to make the statement fresh, dramatic, intriguing. In *Particularly Cats,* a book about the cats she has owned, Doris Lessing captures her reader's interest by describing a kitten as a "fairy-tale cat."

> The kitten was six weeks old. It was enchanting, a delicate fairy-tale cat, whose Siamese genes showed in the shape of the face, ears, tail, and the subtle lines of its body.

Once the reader's attention is engaged, the challenge for the writer is to sustain it. One effective way is to make sure that key sentences—especially the opening ones in paragraphs throughout the description are also couched in provocative language. Here are a few such sentences from Henry David Thoreau's *Walden.* Consider what it is about each that might motivate readers to continue.

> This is a delicious evening, when the whole body is one sense, and imbibes delight through every pore.
> I rejoice that there are owls.
> The scenery of Walden is on a humble scale, and, though very beautiful, does not approach to grandeur, nor can it much concern one

who has not long frequented it or lived by its shore, yet this pond is so remarkable for its depth and purity as to merit a particular description.

Whatever the technique used, try to interest your readers, arouse their curiosity, and compel them to want to share your experience. If you've chosen a subject that genuinely interests you, you've made a good start. Now build on it. Record the small, individual sense impressions that combine to create vivid images in readers' minds. Be alert to the sights, sounds, odors, tastes, and textures of the world around you and include those in your writing when relevant. In the following paper, written by a student, note how vivid details graphically depict the scene:

A Personal Description

Pond Creek
Lucy Lubbers

Walking through a hazy, warm October afternoon, in my mind I could see Pond Creek in the July sun as clearly as if I had been there only yesterday instead of years ago. Now, in another year, another season, and another place, the memory of Pond Creek comes sharply into focus and once more I feel that I'm ambling along its banks on a warm, redolent, unhurried midsummer afternoon.

It seems that days were never anything but beautiful at Pond Creek, or at least my memories always picture them so. It was always warm, but in a special way. I don't recall it being uncomfortably humid. Rather, there was a dry enveloping kind of heat that wrapped itself around you and seemed to dispel all memories of winter chills with its gentle pervasive warmth. It used to come in soft, sweet-smelling breezes that would tousle you like huge children ruffling up a puppy's fur and then swirl you about lethargically. All this glorious warmth seemed to be confined within a tent of sky that was perpetually the color of chicory blooms, a clear, soft, unobtrusive blue that seemed to have absorbed some of the warmth of the day into itself. The sky was an important part of Pond Creek and is prominent in my memories of the place. I can see it now, vaulting high above the whole scene, glowing in the warm July sunlight, and gathering the whole valley under its buttresses.

I could never quite figure out whether this sky held the hills about Pond Creek with its edges to keep them from undulating away like benign green sea monsters or whether the hills reached up and clung to the skirts of the sky to hold it and keep it from lifting away. At different times both have seemed appropriate. These hills about the creek weren't really outstanding as far as hills go, but they always seemed to have a personality. Their green rounded forms always reminded me of old, old creatures who have seen, experienced, and understood much life and who are patiently waiting for whatever the future has to distribute over their sinewy, weathered coils. These long, low-lying giants were always marked by a soft blue haziness that perhaps hid many scars that were evidence of their having existed eons ago.

Bound among the coils of these ridges were the wide, rocky, grass-covered fields through which wound Pond Creek. Sloping from the hills to the very water line of the creek, the land as I remember it teemed with things that stimulated every sense. I can remember vividly the sweet dusty fragrance of hot dry grass; the acrid, alive smell of sweating horses and cattle; the sharp tang of wood sorrel and the blandly sweet taste of honeysuckle nectar; the whipping of the blowing grass against my jeans; the playful snatching of the matted blackberry vines at my hands and ankles; and the exhilarating loss of balance as I trip in some hole or over a root; the warm contented chirring of the cicadas, the rustle of the tall grasses and the squeaky munching of the horses—all in a world of golds, browns, and greens interspersed with the brilliant flowers of later summer that are just beginning to bloom.

But most of all, I remember Pond Creek itself, flowing in a long, lazy, almost unvaried curve through these grassy fields. Even now I hear it babbling like a small baby as it trundles busily among the round brown stones of its bed, a kind of clear sparkling brown in color that catches the gold colors of the grass and reflects them back brightly. A coolness always seemed to rise off its waters as they'd pass beneath an overhanging bank, bringing with it the peculiar odor of mossy stones and water reeds and the suggestion of hidden crannies where miniscule animals cling in the dark to cool wet rocks, safe from the sun's intrusion. The creek then deepens in the sunshine and takes on a more majestic flow, or rather a slower one, for Pond Creek was always a bit of a baby and never able to summon the dignity necessary for majesty. It then disappears around the bend, under the single-laned bridge and out of memory.

It's strange how real Pond Creek's memory is. I haven't seen it in a long while but the day, the season, the hills, the grass, and especially the creek are recalled whenever I experience the warm, hazy afternoons similar to those at Pond Creek.

Much of this description's effectiveness stems from its wealth of detail. Note how the writer has relied on all the senses:

Sight
clear, soft, unobtrusive blue sky
green rounded hills
wide, rocky, grass-covered fields
round brown stones

Hearing
the warm contented chirring of the cicadas
rustle of the tall grasses

squeaky munching of the horses
babbling of the creek

Smell
soft, sweet-smelling breezes
sweet dusty fragrance of hot dry grass
the acrid, alive smell of sweating horses and cattle
the peculiar odor of mossy stones and water reeds

Touch
the dry enveloping heat with its pervasive warmth
the whipping of the blowing grass
the playful snatching of the matted blackberry vines

Taste
the sharp tang of wood sorrel
the blandly sweet taste of honeysuckle nectar

In addition to this abundance of detail, the description gains its effectiveness from its rich language. The writer's feeling for Pond Creek is conveyed in large part through similes (the breezes "that would tousle you like huge children ruffling up a puppy's fur," the hills that might undulate away "like benign green sea monsters,"); through metaphors ("heat that wrapped itself around you," "long, low-lying giants"); and through the alliterative repetition of initial sounds ("the soft, sweet-smelling breezes," "the contented chirring of the cicadas," and "trundles busily among the round, brown stones of its bed"). The richness of the language adds not only vitality and interest to the description but evokes feelings of pleasure, enabling readers to share the joyful mood of the author as she describes memories of Pond Creek.

Also contributing to this effect are the sentences that often ramble lazily like the creek itself. Many flow on to great length, adding phrase upon phrase, packing in details, pointing out specific sights, impressions, sounds, and smells, all suggesting how meaningful and moving were the writer's summer days at Pond Creek and how poignant are her recollections of it.

Such well-developed sentences, along with the evocative language, the sensory details, and some attempt to create and maintain reader interest, are stylistic qualities of personal descriptions. This is not to say that every personal description must contain all these elements (note, for example, that "Pond Creek" does little initially to attract reader interest); but most of these characteristics may be found in effective personal descriptions—and all can help you in your writing.

THE PERSONAL ESSAY

As in the forms discussed earlier, the writer of a personal essay deals with personal experience and reveals a personal attitude toward the subject, but the emphasis is different. Although personal essays may include some narration and description, they emphasize reflection. That is, the focus is on some generalization or conclusion about the experience, its meaning or its effect on the writer's life. Narrative elements—for instance, anecdotes—serve as examples to support this central idea. Similarly, any descriptive details are related to the writer's reflective purpose.

Opening Devices and Thesis Statements

Often, a personal essay opens with a brief anecdote or description to introduce its subject. Or it may start with a summary of a situation that has triggered the writer's desire to write. Whatever the opening device, the writer not only introduces the subject but also sets the essay's tone or atmosphere—flippant, humorous, ironic, and so on. Here are two openers, the first an anecdote, the second a brief description of a situation.

> When my son entered the first grade, his teacher asked to see me. She began our meeting by telling me, "He verbalizes during class, periodically engages in excursions up and down the aisle, has no viable goals and seemingly no definitive conception of his role expectations. Peer pressure seems advised at this time."
> "Are you trying to tell me my son is goofing off?"
> "I would not have expressed it in the vernacular, but you are correct."
>
> —*Erma Bombeck, "Se Habla English?"*

> I am, as most people in Washington know, a very patient man. But there are times when even I lose my cool, and it usually happens in the winter when everyone is giving galas and benefits for some worthy cause.
>
> —*Art Buchwald, "The Man Who Hated Benefits"*

Bombeck's anecdote introduces a series of similar incidents she experienced throughout her son's school career—encounters with a professional jargon. She sets the humorous tone by exaggerating the teacher's language and by countering with her own slangy response. Buchwald's opening lines both suggest a recurring situation irritating to him and set a tone of impatience that he sustains throughout the essay.

All of us have had experiences such as those in our examples. They might involve our relationships with other people or everyday misadventures with the products of our machine age, such as encountering uncooperative vending machines, starting the car on cold mornings, or trying to decipher confusing messages given by our personal computers. As a result, we start to formulate attitudes, to generalize about them. A series of such personal experiences might be summed up in a generalization such as: "That vending machine in the lobby is a con artist" or "The world desperately needs computer translators." Even comparatively minor situations—repeated warnings to be careful with the family car—can make an interesting topic for a personal essay. If such things bother you, chances are they also bother others, and readers will be interested.

Personal essays should contain a thesis statement—a generalization about the subject—which sets forth the central idea and also reinforces the tone and attitudes established by the opener. Generally, writers place the thesis statement in the opening paragraphs, but may wait until the final paragraph, offering the thesis as a conclusion. In either case, the thesis reflects both the subject and the writer's attitude toward it. Note how the following statements achieve all these ends: clearly stating the subject, helping to establish the tone, and adding interest.

> Surely nothing in the astonishing scheme of life can have nonplussed Nature so much as the fact that none of the females of any of the species she created really cared very much for the male as such.
>
> —*James Thurber*

In this beginning statement, Thurber introduces his subject, the universal indifference of females toward males. In addition, this sentence establishes the tongue-in-cheek tone that is sustained throughout the essay. The words "astonishing" and "nonplussed" contribute to this end, as does the ironic suggestion that this indifference is not what Nature intended.

> There is a book out called *Dog Training Made Easy* and it was sent to me the other day by the publisher, who rightly guessed that it would catch my eye. I like to read books on dog training.
>
> —*E. B. White*

Here again, in his opening statement the writer introduces his subject and establishes his sympathetic point of view toward it. Note, too, how the first-person pronouns and the commonplace vocabulary help to establish a conversational, familiar tone.

> I'm wild about walking. . . .
>
> —*Leo Rosten*

In this succinct statement, Rosten introduces his subject, walking, and establishes his enthusiasm for it by using the word *wild*. To make yourself aware of how one word can make a difference in tone, try substituting different adjectives for *wild*. "I'm *fond of* walking," for instance, has a markedly different tone.

From these examples, we see that the opening sentence—whether or not the thesis statement—acts as a direction pointer and a barometer: it sets the essay off in a particular direction and indicates its climate, the writer's attitude about the subject—sympathetic, sardonic, hostile, or amused. Sustained throughout the paper, this attitude is largely what gives the personal essay its unity. In the following personal essay, even though the explicit thesis statement appears at the end as the conclusion, the opening paragraph establishes the subject and focus—the writer's grudging admiration for people who do things right.

A Personal Essay

There's a Mouse In the Bluebird's Box
M.R. Montgomery

Our local weekly newspaper reports that a lady has succeeded in attracting the Eastern bluebird to her property by putting up special nesting boxes. I admire this sort of ingenuity much as a tone-deaf person admires someone who can play the trombone.

Ah, it seems only yesterday that I was out there, nailing up birdboxes, hoping to bring the elusive bluebird of happiness into our yard. The whole trick, according to the literature I skimmed, is to make a nesting box with a hole too small for the revolting starling.

Bluebirds, according to this theory, will be happy to move in, while starlings, which are slightly larger, will go away.

This does not account for the house wren, which can fit into a bluebird house the way a subcompact automobile fits into a parking space. The house wren is a very small bird with a loud, irritating song and an inexhaustible desire to build one nest after another as fast as you can open up the birdbox and throw out the old one.

Not every bluebird house was filled with wrens. There is also the wild mouse, which has bigger ears than the house mouse, and can climb trees like billy-be-damned. Wild mice do not give up easily. First you can rap on the birdbox with a stick, and the mouse will poke its nose out the hole and look at you. Open up the birdbox and the mouse will come out.

This is fairly interesting, if you are standing on a ladder and your right hand is the beginning of the quickest way for the mouse to get from the birdbox back down to the ground.

The other common occupant of the birdbox is the yellow jacket hornet, which comes in two sizes, too small and too big. Everything about a hornet is too something.

It turns out I was misinformed. You do not put bluebird houses on tree trunks. The successful lady puts them on fence posts, far away from the wild wet woods filled with mice and wrens and hornets. She never has to climb on ladders to evict mice. House wrens avoid her. Hornets like to build nests in cool shady places, like underneath the bushes by the front door.

She read all this in a book. It had directions for building houses and putting them up in a "bluebird trail."

Sometimes I think the world is divided into two kinds of people: some of us read the directions on the box and some of us don't. This lady probably puts tricycles together without ending up with four or five left-over nuts and bolts. Her cakes don't fall, her souffles rise, her dandelions die and her grass grows green.

Montgomery establishes a light, sardonic tone in the opening paragraph with the simile "much as a tone-deaf person admires someone who can play the trombone." The tone is maintained throughout by such phrases as "Ah, it seems only yesterday," "elusive bluebird of happiness," "revolting starling," "billy-be-damned." The writer uses another popular device of humorous personal essays—exaggeration or hyperbole—as exemplified in the following: "an inexhaustible desire to build one nest after another as fast as you can open up the bird-box and throw out the old one," and "the yellow-jacket hornet, which comes in two sizes, too small and too big." Amusing use of real or implied comparison is also found throughout: "the way a subcompact fits into a parking space," "Her cakes don't fall, her souffles rise, her dandelions die and her grass grows green." This final set of contrasts implies that the writer's cakes and souffles fall, and dandelions flourish. The contrasts help to sustain the tone and to amplify the thesis sentence which opens the last paragraph. Note that narrative summary is also employed with the account of the mouse in the bird nest.

Like Montgomery's, many modern personal essays are light in tone and subject matter, dealing with the minor, petty joys and discomforts of human existence; more formal and serious treatment is reserved for weighty problems. Writing a personal essay should be fun, reflecting your individuality and personality. So be experimental. Just keep in mind that the point is not only to explore your experience but to share your reflections with the reader. Anecdotes and descriptive details, a good opener, a thesis statement, and a sustained tone throughout the essay can all contribute to that sharing.

THE CHARACTER SKETCH

As its name indicates, a character sketch delineates a person's main personality traits. In the process, it may include some descriptive details about a person's appearance, but it does more than tell what people *look* or *seem* like; it shows what they *are*.

Another use of the character sketch is to write about a type, rather than an individual. Such character sketches reveal the characteristics common to the members of a group, such as campus jocks, avid fishermen, irascible tennis stars, snippy sales-clerks. In such sketches you should treat the subject as a composite of most members of a particular group. For example, in writing about "The Avid Fisherman," you would include only those characteristics shared by most of the avid fishermen you have known. Descriptions of types, therefore, require more generalization than do descriptions of individuals, but both rely on essentially the same rhetorical techniques.

These techniques include not only narrative and descriptive but also expository devices. Important in vividly portraying a person or a type are personal narrative and dialogue; one anecdote demonstrating a person's stubbornness is far more effective than a flat statement that the person is stubborn. But the writer may also explain an action or show how certain personality traits were developed—both expository devices (which we'll consider in detail in Part Two).

Generally character sketches are organized in three parts: an introduction, a body, and a conclusion.

Introduction

Like the opening paragraphs of a personal essay, a provocative introduction serves both to interest readers in the subject of the character sketch and to present the subject's most striking characteristic, as in the following examples:

> Tough and mean. That's the best way to describe Bill Evans. When babies are born, they're sweet, soft, and cuddly. Not Bill Evans. He was probably fighting and clawing and scrapping from the start.
>
> *—student essay*

> It is Friday night at any of ten thousand watering holes of the small towns and crossroads hamlets of the South. The room is a cacophony of the ping-pong-dingdingding of the pinball machine, the pop-fizz of another round of Pabst, the refrain of "Red Necks, White Socks, and Blue Ribbon Beer" on the juke box, the insolent roar of a souped-up engine outside and above it all, the sound of easy laughter. The good ole boys have gathered for their fraternal ritual—the aimless diversion that they have elevated into a life-style.
>
> *—Bonnie Angelo, "Those Good Ole Boys"*

The key idea in each of these introductions commits the writer just as "I've got a funny story to tell you" commits a speaker. Each writer has created a clear assignment: to show Bill Evans' toughness and meanness, and to delineate the characteristics of "good ole boy" as a type. Note that the final sentence in the Angelo opening serves as a thesis statement.

Body

The second part of the character sketch—the body—can be organized according to either a chronological or an analytical pattern. If the introduction describes an initial encounter with the subject of the description, then it would be logical to show how this first impression was supported, modified, or reversed in subsequent encounters. A flashback—a device common in films—taking the reader back to an earlier situation is sometimes appropriate, as when the paper begins with a later meeting or situation and then shows what led to it. For instance, in a personality sketch of one of your teachers, you could start with the first day of class and proceed in a straight-line chronological fashion, or start with the last day and flash back in time to the first day. Or you could start with a striking anecdote and then go back to the first day and move forward from that point. Be careful, however, not to let anecdotes "take over" the sketch. Like anecdotes in the personal essay, they should *support* the idea you are trying to convey—in this case, the traits of the character you've chosen. The danger of using a chronological approach is that the paper may take on the characteristics of a story rather than of a character sketch centered on personal traits. In using narratives, the writer must show a close relationship of the events to the character's personality.

The second option for organizing a character sketch, the analytical pattern, consists of dividing the paper into parts, each elaborating on a trait that contributes to the main impression you want to convey. Bonnie Angelo's sketch of the "good ole boy," for instance, goes on to divide the character traits into paragraph units which make up the body of the paper—his unique frame of mind, his light-hearted approach to life, his need for fraternizing with buddies, and his love of automobiles.

Conclusion

Although it may consist of only one or two paragraphs, a conclusion to your character sketch is necessary to give readers a sense of completion and a final glimpse of the character's main trait. Keep this need in mind while planning your paper. Perhaps you will want to save an apt quotation, a short anecdote, or a brief observation for the conclusion. Here's an illustration from the end of a character sketch about Donald W. Nyrop, the highly active chairman of Northwest Airlines:

> Recently, a clear-plastic plaque appeared on Nyrop's desk. A gift from a compatriot at another airline, it reads: "Along the way . . . take time to smell the flowers." The recipient does not appear to be heeding the sentiment. The plaque faces those seated in front of him.
>
> —*Hugh D. Menzies, Fortune*

Other popular techniques consist of a reference to the subject's future, or to the introduction of the sketch, thereby bringing it full circle. For example, the opening sentence about Nyrop relied on a cowboy metaphor: "Like a bronco rider of old, Donald W. Nyrop . . . is willing to dig in his spurs and take his lumps in order to stay on top of everything that affects his beloved bottom line." A full-circle ending might have taken this form: "Despite labor problems, increasing competition, and the lure of fishing, Don Nyrop enjoys being in the saddle and gives little evidence of giving up the rough ride to settle back in the comfort of the old corral."

Whatever technique you use in your wrap-up, strive for an appropriate last glimpse of your subject and a clear signal of the ending. Difficult to achieve, the conclusion probably requires as much work as your introduction. But readers usually remember your final words, so they are important. The following example, written by an older student, illustrates the characteristics of an effectively written character sketch. As you read it, note the student's adept use of narrative to exemplify character traits.

A Character Sketch

The Hunter
Paul Prather

Donnie rarely talks, not even with his eyes. They sit deep and shadowed beneath bushy brows, hidden from long practice behind thick, half-closed eyelids, the skin drooping until there is just enough openness to let him see you.

I remember when he talked, or tried at least, when his eyes could shine. He was no more than a boy then, still growing joints and sinews, still awkward, his dark brown hair shorter than most boys', blown back at times by a fall wind, his face perhaps broken out. But like most people now, it is the voice I remember most, deepening, occasionally cracking, the words not understandable in his rush to get them out, the tongue thickened by some flaw—a minor problem it would seem, but in an age of life when words are everything, what can it mean not to talk well? And so the words slurred, and the harder he tried the worse it got, and the more we all laughed.

He went to the army right out of school, and that must have been the best time of his life—he could shoot so well. He'd spent most of his life alone in the woods with a gun or a bow. The first time he came back from basic training he was so ecstatic he needed no words; his face told it all. And his father, who runs a hardware store, looked as if it had been he who won the expert's badge, who took a company trophy. At the half-time of a high school basketball game, standing beneath the backboard drinking a Coke, watching a pudgy teenage manager sweep the floor free of paper cups, his dad told us, "I think Donnie's going to make it in the army. He just loves it, you know, not like some guys who bellyache all the time. He might even turn out to be a career soldier." But the army didn't work out, either. They don't shoot rifles much after basic training in peace-time. And he came back home, but he kept the clothes, and he wore the fatigues, and all he talked about—when you could understand it—was army, army, army. He went through five or six jobs then, never liked the jokes, most jokes still on him.

He bow hunts often, deep in the woods, where there is no strong light, where there is no visitation except the slinking, soundless moving of animals, the wary, invisible vision of the hunter, who is the hunted as well. Donnie threads an arrow silently, hardly moving, hardly breathing, draws back the string, the tendons of his taut fingers aching with it, so smooth, so rapid. He pulls through the string and slides the arrow faster than sight into the heart of a deer. And even then he does not speak, does not cry out with jubilation or remorse. It is what he has to do.

Once in a patch of woods, I was out for a Sunday walk. It was early fall and damp, not too long ago. Leaves were soggy on the path, the ones still in the trees had turned, and it was quiet out there, though close to town.

And sliding down a bank, getting mud on my shoes and grabbing a sapling to stay on my feet, I felt someone, no sound. My breath jerked and I slid around, clenching my fists, ready for I don't know what. It took me a second to find who it was—Donnie—in his camouflaged fatigues. Off in the distance he sat, on a large boulder, legs outspread, loose, the strung bow resting beside him, his eyes black slits gazing right at me, not acknowledging my presence. For some reason I ducked behind a tree, a small tree that couldn't hide me. He just sat there. So, feeling stupid, at last I threw up my hands and yelled a greeting. But he just gazed on, silent.

Then, glancing away, he picked up the bow and in one smooth motion drew up on a knee—even from where I was I could see the boniness of the thigh beneath his pants. I flinched. I could almost feel the stark steel arrowhead's point sliding into my chest, crushing my breastbone, ripping my lungs. He looked back at me, that same drooped-eye emotionless stare. The corners of his mouth turned up almost imperceptibly. "You hunting with me again?" he shouted very clearly.

I did not answer him. He grinned, just for a moment, not expecting any reply, as if he already knew a much deeper answer than I would have given him anyway. His face returned to its impassive set, and he scooted off the rock on the other side. When I thought he had disappeared into the dense, shadowy forest, I heard him, just beyond the boulder, laugh.

The first two paragraphs introduce the subject—Donnie—by describing only those physical characteristics necessary to establish his alienation and his inability to communicate, both intensified by the ridicule of his peers. The opening sentence, "Donnie rarely talks, not even with his eyes," not only attracts our attention, but introduces us to one of his most significant character traits.

The thesis idea of his lonely hunting is introduced in the third paragraph—at the beginning of the body section. Here the writer gives background material relevant to Donnie's alienation and his growing neurosis: his failures to succeed in the army, to live up to his father's expectations, and to keep a job. The description of his bow-and-arrow hunting both exemplifies his ability to kill without emotion and prepares the reader for the final anecdote.

The ending of the narrative encounter serves also as the conclusion of the character sketch. Donnie is thereby established as a weird loner and a compulsive hunter—the main traits of his character.

Throughout, the student writer effectively uses narrative and descriptive techniques to bring vividness and life to his character.

SUMMARY

This chapter has dealt with several forms that personal writing can take according to the purpose of the writer. If a writer chooses to re-create an experience so that readers can relive it as it was, then autobiographical narrative or personal description might be the result. If the goal is to react to an experience, to show the reader how the writer felt about an event or an encounter with some person or type of person, then the paper may take the form of a personal essay or a character sketch.

Even though all are satisfying writing experiences in their own right, they also help the writer develop skills applicable to all forms of writing. Retelling an experience in an autobiographical narrative strengthens your abilities to add color and life to any writing. In presenting your impressions in descriptions of a place or object, you learn the discipline of establishing a main impression and of choosing relevant details. And you experiment with words to create a dominant atmosphere or tone.

Learning the organizational skills of the personal essay and the character sketch, should help you make the transition to the more complex structures of expository and persuasive writing.

Perhaps most important, the chapter introduces you to the act of writing about your individual experiences, thus making you more "conscious of living" (in Lindbergh's phrase), and alerting you to the fact that *you* have much to write about.

ASSIGNMENTS

For Discussion

1. This autobiographical narrative is a first draft, written as an in-class assignment. Read it in light of the questions that follow it, and be prepared to respond in a class discussion.

> I drove down the road in my large, cantankerous Chevy station wagon. Although solid steel and cumbersome, it could literally fly at times. One of the many trivial pursuits my friends and I had was to see if we could get this car airborne, and we did on occasion.
>
> On this particular day, however, I was proceeding down the road at a safe speed (airborne cars are best attempted at night), the radio on loudly and the windows down.
>
> As I approached an intersection, I saw a car coming towards me; it was one of those new plastic models. What struck me immediately about this on-coming vehicle was its hood ornament—not an insignia, not a chrome horse or a bizarre bird, but a live girl.

There she sat, legs hanging in front of the car's grill, arms holding her school books, slowly coming towards me in the opposite lane.

Now live ornaments are not that unusual; I myself have perched on the front of a car. But what made this experience particularly exciting was that at the last possible instant when the car could have swerved in front of me, it did. Just as we were passing the plastic car with the flesh ornament, it cut into my lane and bang! A head-on crash for the record books.

After the crash, I found myself looking up at all the wires which dangle just out of the driver's vision. I was soon overwhelmed by an image of the girl's legs dangling just prior to the impact. Ghastly images of smashed legs and a blood-covered hood filled my head, which were only strengthened when I found that the wailing I heard was not from my radio, but from the hood ornament.

Hesitantly, I lifted myself up to peer out the shattered windshield (the result of having too hard a head) and spotted, over the crumbled hood of my own car, the ornament girl on the lawn of a house just off the road. Her ankle was all that was broken, luckily.

—Bill Brymer

a. Where in the paper has the student vividly re-created the experience and where only told about it?

b. What details could be omitted to make it a more vivid and suspenseful re-creation?

c. How could he use dialogue in his revised version?

d. Comparing this attempt with the narrative on pages 15–16, discuss the differences in the ways the two students handled their writing tasks. From what characteristics of "The Encounter" could this paper benefit?

2. Read these two personal descriptions and use the questions that follow them as the basis for class discussion.

a.   One tour around the island before the last ferry to Anacortes and the drive home. And I might as well admit it, I've got to check out that view from Mount Constitution. The road winds up the mountainside through dense woods, pops out into rocky clearings for quick, postcard previews of the panorama to come, ducks back under a canopy of delicate maple and alder. A parking lot. A trail leading to the stone lookout tower built during the Depression by the Civilian Conservation Corps. It's like a little cairn on the highest point of the summit, the highest point in the archipelago, up above the tiny island, above the treetops, above everything, a 360-degree cinerama, sense-surround, worldscape that is . . . well, it's a vast, interminable, unimaginable space without fore or middle ground, without point of reference, nothing but whirligig distance and the sound of wind in my ears. To the east, the white cone of Mount

Baker towering above the mainland haze; to the south, the Strait of Juan de Fuca and the Olympic Range, snow-capped peaks jutting above the purple wash of mountain wall; to the west, islands, water, islands, water, islands; to the north, Canada, Vancouver, the Queen Charlottes.

—Page Stegner, "Orcas Island, Washington"

b.   A young flying squirrel is clumsy at first. He makes all his flights from low altitudes and often drops onto the ground, until after a few months he learns the trick. The launching: on a high bough, with his feet close together, his sharp little nose stretched far out and his eyes on the distant goal, he rocks back and forth, faster and faster, gathering strength and perhaps courage, then *springs* into the air. At once his legs spread to the sides, opening his chute, and he drops fairly level. If a big bough is in his way, he can maneuver around it, but he cannot turn fast enough to glide through dense leaves and he therefore must land on the trunk of a tree under the lowest branches. At the end of the glide he makes a quick upward flip with his rudderlike tail and catches onto the trunk with his head towards the top, ready to scramble aloft if an unsuspected enemy should be there on the ground. His skill is almost an art and, as he is soon to discover, it is a wonderful way to play.

—Sally Carrighar, "The Creative Spirit"

1) Which of these descriptions is primarily organized spatially, which chronologically? Identify in each where both kinds of organization are used. What influence did the subject matter have on the organization?

2) How does each writer express personal impressions of the subject?

3) What is the dominant impression in each? How is this developed or sustained?

3. The following are opening sentences from students' personal essays. Discuss whether each is effective in identifying the subject and establishing the paper's tone and purpose. Suggest examples of incidents that might be used in a paper written on each subject. Which could serve as thesis statements?

a. Mother's school days were not *my* school days.

b. Let's face it. I'm a hypochondriac. I know because I immediately develop the symptoms of any new disease that I hear about.

c. Why am I the only one who doesn't understand football?

d. Hiking in the woods is a healthy activity?

e. It isn't only the three-year-olds who can't open the child-proof packages.

4. Discuss each of the following essays by students, pointing out the strengths and weaknesses of each in terms of organization; descriptive techniques such

as use of vivid details; establishment of atmosphere or tone, and so on. Indicate what the writers might work on when they rewrite.

a. My roommate is definitely a unique character. He has a life style strictly limited to one human being—Jim Beard. I think no other person has such a combination of peculiarities as Jim does. Since I've know him, I've become accustomed to being prepared for anything. From my experiences of the last few weeks, there is nothing he could do that would shock me.

In appearance he seems to be average enough—six feet tall, straight blond hair and blue eyes. However, quite often his actions are to the contrary.

For example, the average college student living in a dorm normally sleeps on a bed, but not my roommate! Instead, he prefers to sleep on the floor without a mattress. He uses his mattress for lounging around in the daytime but not for sleeping.

Another peculiarity I'm becoming accustomed to is to see him walking down the corridors of the dorm at all hours of the night doing John Wayne imitations while dressed only in his underwear and cowboy boots. On our floor we have people from all over the country, but no one but Jim walks around at midnight in such attire!

Jim has a variety of odd eating habits to go along with his unusual clothing styles. He seems to be the only person I know who combines sweet pickles and beer, herb tea and pizza, and bananas with black coffee.

In addition to strange eating habits he constantly redecorates the room. He changes posters so often I barely have time to become accustomed to one before he changes it. His latest addition to the room is a black light which he uses to send Morse Code to the girls in Donovan Hall.

Jim may have some odd personal habits, but he is a decent person to have for a roommate. Very seldom is he unhappy, and he's one of the best-liked fellows on Haggin Hall's B-3. In spite of some of his more distinguishable habits, I feel I couldn't have found a better person with whom to share such close quarters.

b. In a student's lifetime, hopefully he will be fortunate enough to have one teacher who dedicates his whole being to his pupils. In high school, we were blessed with a man like this. Mr. Fiorucci taught biology and chemistry, and he made the whole realm of these courses come alive for every student. He made each class hour a fascinating new discovery into a world of science none of us knew or understood before. Mr. Fiorucci sincerely loved the students and wanted them to realize the total value of education. His influence certainly changed the lives of many teenagers. Many students went eagerly on to college because he had touched their lives. I myself am here today with inner thoughts of someday teaching students with that same thrill for learning Mr. Fiorucci always gave.

5. Discuss the following questions about the Montgomery essay on page 25.

   a. What is the writer's main purpose in relating the birdhouse experiences?
   b. Besides those mentioned on page 26, what other devices of comparison and exaggeration are used? How do they contribute to the tone and to the thesis idea?
   c. Since Montgomery withholds the thesis statement until the end, what devices are used to maintain the focus throughout the essay?

For Practice

1. List chronologically all the incidents that occurred on your pre-registration day at college, your first day on campus, or your first day of classes. If you were writing a narrative about the frustration you felt on one of those days, which incidents would you delete?

2. Following the suggestions on pages 14–15 for writing an autobiographical narrative, select two possible subjects and decide on the techniques to use. Prepare to discuss your ideas with your classmates to see which subject they would prefer reading about and how they respond to the way you plan to write about it.

3. Using any of the following, or similar, sentences as your opening statement, write a descriptive paragraph:

   a. My town springs to life on Saturday.
   b. For the first time, I was truly stirred by the beauty of nature.
   c. People's disregard for the environment was evident everywhere.
   d. The _____ was out of place in those surroundings.
   e. Bedlam broke loose after the game/concert.
   f. The old neighborhood looks different.
   g. On my first day of class, Professor _____ was the most terrifying/sympathetic teacher I had ever met.
   h. _____ is the most important person in my life.

4. Choose one of the following and write paragraphs according to the instructions.

   a. You probably had or have some toy, object, or other "security blanket" that you were or are attached to. Write a personal description that conveys your attitude toward the object. Then write an entirely objective description, one that accurately depicts the item without revealing any feelings.
   b. Write a paragraph-length objective (purely objective description of your doctor's or dentist's office; then write a personal description of how it looked to you as a nervous patient.
   c. If you have ever been in an automobile accident, write two descriptions of it; first, a detailed account that you might write to a friend; second, an account that you might write to your insurance agent.

5. Write opening statements or opening short paragraphs for two possible personal essays. Prepare to discuss them in class to determine which opening, and which hypothetical essay, would be more effective.

For Writing

Autobiographical Narrative

1. Write about some past event that your memory has probably distorted. At the time it occurred, it may have caused you embarrassment, anguish, despair, or fear, but now you can laugh about it. Or perhaps you thought highly of yourself on that occasion but now can view your achievement in proper perspective.
2. Reminisce about some fascinating, unusual, significant, or memorable incident in your life. Try to avoid beginning with a sentence like "It all comes back to me now."
3. Write about the tension between you and your parents that was caused by your attempt to assert your independence.
4. Write an action-focused narrative about some personal experience that had lasting significance for you:
    a. An episode that contributed to better understanding of someone in your family.
    b. An incident or series of related incidents that changed your outlook on human nature, your school, parental authority, or whatever.
    c. An incident that helped you decide on a different course of action—for example, a change in career plans, college or summer plans, marriage plans.

Personal Description

1. Write a personal description of a place where a lot of activity occurs, recording all the sights, sounds, smells, and other sense impressions. Among subjects you might choose are a country fair, rock concert, church or other picnic, high school dance, the locker room after a game, lunch hour in the school cafeteria, Saturday night at the high school hangout, a day at the mall, or a popular time at the video arcade. Assume that you are writing the description for a contest run by the *Reader's Digest*, which has requested articles about "A Place and Its Activities."
2. Write a personal description of a place. If one does not come quickly to mind, perhaps the following questions will help. If you could spend the next few hours anywhere, what place would you choose? What is the most beautiful place you've ever been? The ugliest? The most disturbing? Most peaceful? Noisiest? Happiest? Most inspiring? Most terrifying? Most ornate? Dingiest? Oldest? Most charming? Most comfortable? This description is to be submitted to a contest run by *America,* a newpaper distributed on college campuses.

3. Most of us are creatures of routine, walking or driving the same way from our room to class every weekday. Write a personal description of what you see, hear, smell, touch, and experience as you proceed from door to door. Assume you are writing the description for your college newspaper.

4. As a child, you probably had some favorite hideaway where you could be all alone. Describe it, reflecting on your feeling of comfort and seclusion. Plan to submit it to *Parents* magazine.

Personal Essay

1. Write the personal essay decided on with the class in For Practice assignment 5.

2. Write a personal essay on coping with some fairly insignificant, everyday, recurrent activity that you find frustrating or annoying, yet which has amusing or ironic aspects. The following suggestions may be helpful:

> Dialing wrong numbers
> Commuting
> Church experiences
> Trying to make a good impression
> Applying for a job
> Finding a campsite or motel
> Borrowing the family car
> College meals
> Opening plastic and cardboard packages
> Receiving junk mail
> Finding a parking space

Character Sketch

1. Write a character sketch either of a favorite relative, teacher, neighbor, minister, friend, employer, or of someone you dislike or detest. Be sure to provide sufficient evidence to support your opinion. Your audience consists of a committee of faculty members on your campus, who have been asked to select the best character sketches written by six freshmen for an annual fund left by a wealthy business executive interested in stimulating interest in writing.

2. Write a description of the most unforgettable character you have ever met. It might be someone you have encountered only once—on an airplane, perhaps, or at a concert. Assume that your character sketch is being written for a contest, sponsored by a local women's club, offering five prizes of $100 each for the best papers on "The Most Unforgettable Person."

3. From your experience in a summer or other job, write a character sketch about some person or type. For example, if you worked as a waiter or waitress, you might want to describe your boss or someone you worked with, or such customers as The Big Spender, The Indecisive Individual, The Wine Connoisseur, or The Spoiled Brat. Plan to submit the description to a

student publication on summer jobs, which is planning to publish a collection of student essays about work experiences.

4. Write a character sketch about a certain type of person at high school—student, teacher, administrator, or other employee. Be certain to discuss at some length the appearance, interests, mannerisms, likes, and dislikes of such a composite individual, and to portray him or her in some characteristic incident or situation. Plan to submit your paper, which may be serious or satirical, to a new magazine like *People*, assuming that the magazine is offering a prize of $1000 for the best sketches.

2

Prewriting Tactics for Personal Writing

PREWRITING AND THE COMPOSING PROCESS

We suggested in the Introduction that writing can be viewed as a three-step process: prewriting, writing, rewriting. These are not necessarily isolated steps. For instance, during the actual writing stage, you may discover that what is really your main idea is buried inconspicuously in a late paragraph, or that the plan you developed isn't working out for some other reason. You may change a word or a sentence structure or correct a misspelling while you write—using techniques more often reserved for the rewriting step. But in the early stages of learning to be a good writer, it often helps to consider these steps as separate and to approach the writing task by consciously practicing them as such.

In the prewriting stage, you act as an explorer and a tactician. As explorer, you search out a topic, discover what you know about it or what you need to know, and identify your purpose in the writing task. As tactician, you plan your approach, analyze the audience you wish to reach, and devise the writing strategies you think will work best.

Any technique that gets you started is a good one. But you should remember that some of the techniques we suggest throughout the text will be more useful for certain kinds of writing than for others. The prewriting tactics discussed in this chapter are especially applicable for personal writing, but may work as well for other writing tasks.

JOURNAL WRITING

If used purposefully, one of the most valuable prewriting tools is the journal. Unfortunately, journals are too often used merely as diaries to record daily events; they become little more than annotated calendars, as this example shows:

May 2, Tuesday. Met this neat guy today. He walked home with me after class. Then we talked for about an hour. He asked me to go out with him on Friday night. I think I'm really going to like him.

Even though such a diary entry may once have served an important purpose for you, it is not very useful as a prewriting tool. In keeping a prewriting journal, although you write primarily for yourself, about your experiences with other people and your reactions to new situations or ideas, you write differently. You try to re-create an experience, adding the descriptions and sensory impressions that recapture it as you lived it. You experiment, try different approaches. Since the journal is for you, it doesn't matter if you stub your toes occasionally. You will also make discoveries. Finally, you may want to rewrite favorite entries, polishing them into pieces of writing you can be proud of and share with other people. Used in this way, the journal is a practice book or a learning log—an effective device for helping you learn to write well enough so that you can let your private thoughts go public.

Why Keep a Journal?

Once you have acquired the journal habit, you may find that it has many uses. Other than as a prewriting tool, why would anyone want to keep a journal? The answer to that question is both simple and complex. Many people keep journals to help them remember the details of events that might otherwise be forgotten. But journals do more than that. They provide a concrete record of not only what happens to us, but how we react to what happens and why. The human mind is not a computer that simply stores facts. Intentionally or not, we alter facts according to our continuing perceptions of the world. Being able to refresh our memories on how and why we acted or reacted in the past enables us to live more effectively and perceptively in the present.

There are secondary reasons for keeping a journal as well. The journals of Lewis and Clark were begun to keep a careful record of the previously unexplored Northwest, but they also created a vivid historical document of an exciting expedition. In writing only to "support and comfort" herself through the frightening and dehumanizing experience of hiding from the Nazis during World War II, a Jewish teenager, Anne Frank, left a record that would move millions of people after her death. The journals of Leonardo da Vinci record observations about birds and flight dynamics as well as important events in his life. The journals of novelists, poets, and journalists often serve as the basis for books or articles; sometimes the journal itself appears in print.

Keeping a journal, then, can be more than a composition class assignment to give you writing practice. You may be inspired to keep a journal for the rest of your life, thus acquiring an extremely valuable personal history that will help you record, assimilate, and enrich your experience in a way that photographs, tape recordings, films, and souvenirs cannot. According to Anne Morrow Lindbergh, a journal is kept "not to preserve the experience but to savor it, to make it more real, more visible and palpable, than in actual life."

Re-creating an experience in this way requires putting down on paper its specific details. When this is done effectively, the writing becomes vivid, alive, colorful, and authentic—as this excerpt from Anne Frank's journal shows:

> Continuation of the "Secret Annexe" daily timetable. As the clock strikes half past eight in the morning, Margot and Mummy are jittery: "Ssh . . . Daddy, quiet, Otto, ssh . . . Pim." "It is half past eight, come back here, you can't run any more water; walk quietly!" These are the various cries to Daddy in the bathroom. As the clock strikes half past eight, he has to be in the living room. Not a drop of water, no lavatory, no walking about, everything is quiet. As long as none of the office staff are there, everything can be heard in the warehouse. The door is opened upstairs at twenty minutes past eight and shortly after there are three taps on the floor! Anne's porridge. I climb upstairs and fetch my "puppy-dog" plate. Down in my room again, everything goes at terrific speed; do my hair, put away my noisy tin pottie, bed in place. Hush, the clock strikes! Upstairs Mrs. Van Daan has changed her shoes and is shuffling about in bedroom slippers, Mr. Van Daan, too; all is quiet.

Anne Frank's details about the restrictions of movement and time—"not a drop of water, no lavatory . . . noisy tin pottie . . . shuffling about in bedroom slippers . . . the clock strikes . . ."—give her readers the opportunity to become involved in the experience, not simply read about it. Suppose Anne Frank had described the experience in this way:

> We were always anxious about the time and whether our daily activities would be detected.

You can see that without the specific details most of the urgency of her situation would be lost.

Hints for Writing a Journal

In order to use journal writing most effectively as a writing aid, follow these suggestions:

- Buy a wide-lined, stiff-backed notebook that is small enough to carry with you.
- Write something every day, even if it must be only a few sentences. The entries can be on any subject: an experience of the day or a memory triggered by it.
- Restrict each journal entry to only one major or unusual subject. A chronological listing of the day's activity is not much more exciting than a bus schedule.
- Keep the words flowing: write without looking up words or stopping to edit. Try to capture every significant detail of the event. You can edit later.

- Tell it in your own language. Try to translate your natural speaking voice to the written page.
- Read your entries a day or two later. You may wish to rework and polish some that you feel are of special interest.

Expanding Journal Entries

So far, we have discussed journal writing as an end in itself and as a tool for improving writing skills. But one of its important uses is in generating ideas for writing longer pieces. The following excerpt, taken from a student's journal, illustrates a method for doing this. As you read the example, keep in mind that the student did not revise or polish this first-draft entry.

> Halloween, the night of witches, ghosts, goblins, and trick or treaters, is one of my favorite days. It was always best when my mom and dad didn't tag along and I could go around with my friends. The first time I went out, I was ten and for two weeks my friends and I planned where to go, what pranks to pull, and what costumes to wear. Halloween night, I dressed up as a hobo, using my father's ragged work clothes and using pillows for a stomach. I painted my face completely white with a big red mouth and black eyebrows. Then us frightening kids started on my street and went about twenty blocks, soaping windows, smashing pumpkins and collecting candy. After being out for four hours from 8—12:00 p.m. and going past the scariest house we could find, we decided to go home. The next morning, waking up and trying to get the makeup off my face, I was glad Halloween was on Friday and not Sunday so I had two days to get off the makeup and eat all my candy.

You can see that the student has the germ of a longer essay. In this case, the opening sentence provides the thesis for a paper dealing with the student's most memorable Halloween experiences. "Halloween . . . is one of my favorite days." But in developing the thesis for a longer paper, the student must decide whether to use examples of many Halloween adventures—both chaperoned and unchaperoned—or to restrict the focus indicated in the second sentence, using only those times when Mom and Dad did not go along. If restricted to unchaperoned times, the examples should illustrate clearly that no adults were along—a clarity lacking in this first draft example. Questions that the student writer needs to ask about the material include:

What is the main idea?
How should I limit the focus?
Do my examples fit? If not, how can I rework or add to them?
What do I want my readers to gain from reading this essay?
In responding to these questions, the student with the Halloween journal entry might have made these decisions:

1. Main idea: Halloween is one of my favorite days.

2. Limit focus: Restrict paper to the first Halloween I went out without Mom and Dad.

3. Examples: Provide details about soaping the windows on the O'Hare's car and the Dailey's sun porch. Smashing pumpkins in front of unlit houses. Tell about scary, old, empty house, different ways (soap, cold cream, dishwasher liquid) to get make-up off, types of candy received.

4. Readers: I want readers to relive the thrill and excitement of that Halloween with its peculiar mixture of glee, vandalism, fear, fun, bravery, and freedom.

By making use of questions such as these and of the discussion on personal essays in Chapter 1, (pages 22–24), you should be able to select and develop topics from your own journal entries.

FREEWRITING

Freewriting is probably the most commonly used prewriting tactic in journal writing, but it is not restricted to journals. To get started on any writing assignment, you can practice freewriting almost anywhere, anytime—on scrap paper, at a typewriter or word processor. Freewriting is simply a means of coming up with a possible subject by writing down whatever enters your head. Many professional writers use it as a warming-up exercise, as a stimulus for the composing process. Poet-essayist William Stafford says this about freewriting:

> To get started I will accept anything that occurs to me. Something always occurs, of course, to any of us. We can't keep from thinking. Maybe I have to settle for an immediate impression: it's cold, or hot, or dark, or bright, or in between! Or—well, the possibilities are endless. If I put down something, that thing will help the next thing come, and I'm off. If I let the process go on, things will occur to me that were not at all in my mind when I started. These things, odd or trivial as they may be, are somehow connected. And if I let them string out, surprising things will happen.
>
> —"A Way of Writing"

Most advocates of freewriting advise writing without pause and without corrections for a preset period of time, usually about ten minutes. Remember that the purpose of freewriting is not to produce a finished paper; freewriting is merely a problem-solving device that serves as a catalyst or stimulus for finding a topic and ideas about that topic.

How easy it is to say, "Write without pause for ten minutes." It is not so easy to do. But if the freewriting technique is to work, you must keep the pen flowing. If you block, write anything—your name, messages to yourself, anything at all, even if you have to repeat sentences over and over again. There seems to be some magical power in keeping the pen flowing or the typewriter clicking. Sooner or later, the ideas will flow again.

Suppose you were given the assignment of writing a paper about someone or something you feel strongly about. Here's what a piece of freewriting might look like:

> Someone or something I feel strongly about. The draft? Too heavy. I can't write. Why did I come to college anyway? Nothing has ever happened to me. Can't think of anything intresting—any thing intresting, interesting. Spelling? Don't stop. Don't stop. The night I got stopped by a cop? No. Nothing really happened that I could write about. Can't write, can't think of anything. Who has meant a lot to me? I guess I loved Matt more than anyone. My brother and the car. I can do that—write about him and what a great guy he was. Other people liked him a lot so my teacher and the other students in my class might like to read about him. I can write about Matt and how he got killed.

This example follows the "rules" of freewriting—random thoughts were written down as they popped into the writer's head. There was no pausing to check punctuation or spelling and certainly no concern about arrangement of ideas; consequently, the paragraph is far from a finished piece of writing. But the exercise has achieved two goals of freewriting: *The writer stopped staring at a blank page and started to write, and the writer discovered something to write about.*

In your own freewriting, don't be discouraged if your first attempt doesn't generate an interesting topic. If nothing germinates on the first try, take a break for a few hours and have another go at it: let your subconscious work. Often a second try will be productive. However, freewriting may be a method that will not work for you. Then try another of the methods described in this book. No one method succeeds for everyone.

FOCUSED FREEWRITING

Focused freewriting differs from freewriting in that you begin with some topic, if only a hypothetical one, arbitrarily chosen just to get you started. Such a topic, even one that seems absurd, may generate a chain of associations that leads to a topic which you find interesting. Once you have a topic you like, you can use focused freewriting to develop it—that is, to generate ideas about it. You can also use focused freewriting for practice in your journal or for expanding an entry created earlier by freewriting.

Using Your Freewriting as a Basis for Focused Freewriting

To develop and expand a freewritten journal entry, first read it over and then write *about* it nonstop for about ten minutes, using the same procedures as for freewriting and adding more details. Read what you have newly written, looking for ideas, events, or descriptions that you might develop even further. This process can be repeated for as long as it continues to be productive.

To see how this method works, consider the following focused-freewriting paragraphs developed from the freewriting example on page 44.

I loved Matt, my older brother. He was the greatest guy you'd ever meet. He was friendly, easy to get along with, and would do anything for you.

During the summer he worked with the recreation department helping little kids. He'd teach them how to play baseball, football and other sports. He got paid about a dollar an hour, but he liked the job so he didn't care what he was making.

Mom was really crazy about him. She was proud of raising such a "good boy." In her eyes he could do no wrong. Matt was killed in a wreck almost two years ago. A drunk ran into him and killed them both. Mom almost died too, from the shock, sadness, and everything else. She never could understand why it had to be Matt hit by that drunk. Neither could I.

Although this still unpolished expansion of a freewriting journal entry leaves too much out to be entirely clear to a reader who did not share the experience described, it serves its prewriting purpose: the student has generated additional ideas about the subject.

The student's next step is to decide what approach to take. For example, this germ of a paper generated by the two freewriting sessions could grow into a more detailed story or narrative of the accident that killed Matt; or it could develop into a personal essay about the special relationship that brothers share, building on the statements in the first paragraph. Or, if the material in the second paragraph were expanded, it could become a character sketch of Matt. Lurking in the third paragraph, there is even the germ of a paper arguing for stronger controls on drunken drivers—evidence that this prewriting technique can be useful for other kinds of writing.

QUESTIONING

Questioning, a popular device among newspaper writers, is especially useful for narrative writing, but it also works well for personal essays and for other kinds of writing in which you wish to describe an event or procedure. The key is a systematic set of WH-questions—*who, what, where, when, why, and how.* Before you write, ask yourself these questions:

WHO are the people involved?
WHAT happened?
WHERE did it happen?
WHEN did it happen?
WHY did it happen?
HOW did it happen?

Listing answers to each of these questions will provide a stock of ideas and details to use in an autobiographical narrative or character sketch, probably many more than you need. Some of the information may not be relevant. For instance, if your purpose is to develop a main character, such as Matt, then you don't need an elaborate description of the place where the action occurred, although you may wish to set the scene with a few carefully chosen details. Instead you will emphasize Matt's actions and statements, the *who, what,* and *why* taking precedence over *where* and *when.* In an autobiographical narrative, however, in which your main purpose is to re-create events, *where* and *when* might take on greater importance. The discussions in Chapter 1 can help you decide which questions would be most pertinent for your purposes. Here is an example of how you might use the questions:

> WHO: mother, Matt, Peggy, student writer (I)
> WHAT: auto accident, hospital operation, Mom's faith in doctors, the surgeon's sad news.
> WHERE: accident on I-75, 3 miles south of Richmond; phone call at home; drive to hospital; wait in visitor's lounge.
> WHEN: November 21, 9-12 p.m.
> WHY: high alcohol content in driver's body.
> HOW: Matt driving home after seeing Peggy; other driver mistakenly enters exit ramp, heads wrong way on one-way lanes, head-on collision; passing driver in other lane called police, who arrived about fifteen minutes later.

Like freewriting and the other prewriting tactics described throughout this book, these questions will not work equally well for every paper. But they should help you much of the time, providing a systematic method with which you can generate ideas and details, recognize the special writing problems involved, and so eliminate false starts in early drafts.

CHARTING

Charting is another systematic method you can use for all kinds of personal writing, particularly when searching for a topic. Draw up a chart similar to the one in Figure 2–1 with four columns headed "Occasions/Locales," "People," "Places," and "Objects." Then fill in the first column with words or phrases referring to general scenes and situations in your life, somewhat like those in the illustration. Next, for each entry in the first column, go across the chart and fill in the blank in each of the other columns with one or more items related to the first. Consider each group of items for a few minutes, trying to trigger something specific from your memory. If necessary, leave some blanks empty; if possible, write several ideas in some. Finally, after working your way through the chart, review all the possible subjects, circle the appealing ones, and then choose the one with the most possibilities for your paper.

Figure 2-1 Charting

OCCASIONS/ LOCALES	PEOPLE	PLACES	OBJECTS
Home	my brother	attic	kitchen table
Home town	barber	shopping mall	courthouse statue
College	psychology teacher	cafeteria, lab	totem pole
College community	pizza waiter	movie theater	historic statue
High school	janitor	locker room	
Work (paid or volunteer)	boss		stove
Trips—routine to stores, school, church	bus driver	busy intersection	altar
Trips—vacation (car, bus, plane)		O'Hare Air Terminal	pilot's instrument board
Ball games— player, participant	basketball referee tailgaters	state tournament hotel lobby	RV's, vans
Visits—homes of friends, relatives other	Aunt Gert	Jean's garden	daughter's re-decorated bedroom
Visits—offices, malls, public buildings	librarian	department store	bank safe
Other	auctioneer	country auction, flea market	old car, player piano

CHANGING PERSPECTIVE

Sometimes you can generate ideas about a subject or an event simply by changing the way you think about it. Although shifting the perspective can be adapted to the prewriting needs of many kinds of writing, it is especially valuable in developing details for a description. Here are some ways to go about it:

Division   Divide the place or object into its separate parts so you can concentrate on each. A college cafeteria, for example, might be divided into the entrance, food line, chairs and tables, surroundings, and exit. By observing or recalling each part of your subject individually, you will generate more details than you would by considering it as a whole.

Angle   View your subject from different angles. How does the place or object look from near, far, above, below, on all sides? Or, how would different people perceive the person you wish to describe? By looking at your subject from different angles—top to bottom, left to right, front to back—you should see more than you would have otherwise.

Time   How would the person, place, or object appear at different times of the day, seasons of the year, or years of life? For instance, in writing about a shopping mall, you might wish to portray how the scene changes from morning to evening.

Note how each of these different perspectives is exemplified in the following short passage from E. B. White's essay, "Once More to the Lake."

(angle)

(division)

(time)

> In those other summertimes all motors were inboard; and when they were at a distance, the noise they made was a sedative, an ingredient of summer sleep. They were one-cylinder and two-cylinder engines, and some were jumpspark, but they all made a sleepy sound across the lake. The one-cylinders throbbed and fluttered, and the twin-cylinder ones purred and purred, and that was a quiet sound too. But now the campers all had outboards. In the daytime, in the hot mornings, these motors made a petulant, irritable sound; at night, in the still evening when the afterglow lit the water, they whined about one's ears like mosquitoes.

TWO PREWRITING TACTICS FOR DESCRIPTION

Because the aim of descriptive writing is closely related to that of the visual arts—to re-create an image of a place, object, or person—these two tactics for generating useful details call upon some of the devices a landscape or portrait painter might employ.

Sketching

Begin by drawing a sketch of the person, place, or object. Even though you may have little artistic ability, the challenge of reproducing your subject in a drawing will force you to concentrate on observing or thinking about it as you strain for details, trying to include everything. In the process, you'd be surprised at how seemingly forgotten particulars come to mind.

Using Individual Senses

Next, using only one of your senses at a time, list whatever details you can about how your subject looks, feels, smells, sounds, and, if appropriate, tastes. Obviously, not all of the senses will be involved with some topics. But by considering those that do, you will discover details that you might have overlooked.

RESTRICTING THE SUBJECT

A major concern in all prewriting is determining how to limit or restrict a subject so that it can be covered effectively. Many of the tactics suggested in this chapter and elsewhere in this book are useful for such limiting and focusing. But a final word of caution is needed. If a subject would allow you to generate an almost endless list of details, it is probably too broad. Unless it is further limited, writing on it will result in a paper consisting of uninteresting generalizations, or one flawed by poorly related details.

Too broad a subject can be undesirable in another way: It may actually cause a writing block similar to that described in Robert M. Pirsig's *Zen and the Art of Motorcycle Maintenance.*

A student of Pirsig's found it impossible to write a five-hundred word essay about her home town or its main street. Pirsig suggested that she describe one building there, the Opera House, starting with the upper-left brick. She returned at the next meeting of the class with a five-thousand word essay, explaining how "I sat in the hamburger stand across the street . . . and started writing about the first brick, and the second brick, and then by the third brick it all started to come and I couldn't stop." Pirsig concluded that the student couldn't write on the other assigned subjects because she was not involving herself, her own reactions, her own ideas. Instead, she was trying to rely on what others thought or felt. By limiting the subject to a simple object, she saw it afresh and gained confidence in her own abilities to write about it.

A vast subject—say, Washington, D.C.—might be effectively described in a book, but not in a five-hundred word theme. To avoid having on rely on stale generalities, narrow the focus. Ask yourself the following question: What is it about this subject that most interests me? (Another version of the same question is: what is it about the subject that most annoys me?) If your fascination with Washington revolves around the attractiveness of the streets, you may have the basis for a good short essay. But you should ask yourself the same question about this new subject: What is it about the attractiveness of the streets that interests me? You may find that only when you have focused on one aspect of one particular street have you found a subject that can be described in a short essay full of concrete, interesting details. In a sense, the object of this focusing is not so much discovering what you want to write about as it is blocking out everything that might detract from what you really want to say.

SUMMARY

Recent studies of the writing process indicate that prewriting is probably the most crucial step. In this chapter, we have introduced you to several prewriting tactics that are especially adaptable to the needs of personal writing. However, none is limited to personal writing; include them in your bag of prewriting tricks, to use whenever the need arises. The journal, for instance, is a valuable writing tool for a variety of purposes, and journal entries can often be expanded into longer works.

If you can't think of anything to write about, try freewriting or focused freewriting. Or experiment with charting or questioning. If you have a subject, generate details about it with such devices as sketching, relying on your individual senses, and changing perspectives. Always consider whether your subject is too broad; if it is, narrow it. Then decide which details are most relevant for your writing purpose. Before you tackle your first draft, formulate a statement that expresses the central idea or main impression you wish to convey to your reader.

As we introduce various kinds of writing throughout this book, we will suggest other prewriting tactics that writers use to discover and refine topics and to plan their writing tasks.

ASSIGNMENTS

For Practice

1. Jot down two possible journal subjects based on experiences that have occurred within the past twenty-four hours. Then list at least five significant details for each that would make the entries vivid and authentic.

2. Find a quiet spot free of all distractions. Then write for ten minutes without stopping about anything that comes to mind. The thoughts do not necessarily have to be all related to a single subject; just keep writing. Then, after laying what you have written aside for at least 30 minutes, study it. As we did for the "Matt" example, jot down the possible topics it suggests; then briefly describe the kinds of papers that might arise from each.

3. For a journal entry, write about some emotional reaction to one of your day's activities. When you have decided on a subject, write more about it for ten minutes without stopping. After resting, use questioning or the changing perspectives approach to generate more details on the subject. Then write a paragraph explaining how you could use the material to write an autobiographical narrative, a personal essay, or a character sketch.

4. Walk around the campus or through a college building with your journal in hand, noting several places that you think help make the campus distinctive. Then make a sketch of one such place and, as a prewriting exercise for a personal description, list the sensory perceptions you experienced.

5. Draw up your own chart and practice charting to find a subject for a personal description or a character sketch.

3

The Paragraph
and its Use in
Personal Writing

Unlike sentences, paragraphs are units primarily restricted to written language. In speaking or listening, we are aware, either consciously or subconsciously, of the structure of the individual sentences: we sense when sentences begin and end. But this is seldom true of paragraphs, perhaps because they vary so greatly in length and purpose, particularly in a give-and-take conversation. And paragraphs, unlike sentences, have no clearly defined intonational features such as lowering the pitch of the voice to signal the end.

Even in written discourse, the structure of paragraphs is more arbitrary than that of sentences, varying greatly according to the writer's purpose—whether it is to narrate, to describe, to explain, to compare, to persuade. But other factors, such as the nature of the audience and the print medium, influence the variability of paragraphs as well. For example, in books, magazines, and newspapers, paragraph length varies greatly. Newspaper paragraphs tend to be short, because newspaper articles typically give only the essentials about an incident or situation. Moreover, because newspaper columns are narrow, lengthy paragraphs would be difficult to read.

If you examine a variety of magazines and books, you will find that their paragraph length often reflects the nature of the reader for whom the material is intended. Magazines written to reach a general audience with varying education levels, such as *Time* and *Newsweek,* tend to have many short paragraphs. Magazines like *Smithsonian* and *Atlantic,* written mostly for college-educated people, generally have longer paragraphs. To say much more than this about paragraph length is impossible, for in most writing, short paragraphs are interspersed among longer ones to provide special emphasis or transition from one paragraph idea to another.

MEANING IN PARAGRAPHING

In spite of its elusive character and its infinite variety, the paragraph is a recognizable unit in written discourse. The obvious visual clue, of course, is the indentation of the first line. But this visual aid for the reader is not arbitrary, determined by the whim of the typesetter; it reflects the writer's meaning and is created by the writer, on the basis of conventional paragraphing signals within the writer's own text. A simple experiment can help you become aware of some signals that writers (and their readers) respond to in deciding where paragraphs should begin and end. In the following passage, from a paper written by a freshman, we've run the paragraphs together. After reading the passage, decide where you would indicate paragraphing. Then check your results with those of your classmates *before you read the five paragraphs of commentary after the passage.*

1. To a speleologist the excitement of cave-exploring seldom grows stale. 2. There are thousands of sights and variations in the underworld and each trip below entices a new adventure. 3. Although every cavern is different, it is possible to classify most caves. 4. The most inspiring type of cave to "spelunkers" is the virgin cave. 5. It is a cave that is still in its natural state and has never been explored. 6. Its interior is alive with the wonders of the Dark Frontier; untouched and unmarred by the searching hands and trudging feet of curious visitors. 7. The virgin cave is delicately beautiful, walls covered with brilliant crystaline gypsum flowers and onyx streaks, ceiling draped with stalagmites and stalactites, ice-water pools filled with mysterious life forms. 8. Probably the rarest type is the ice cave. 9. It is usually nothing more than a large hole in an iceberg or a crack in the frosty Arctic land formations. 10. But for the dedicated spelunker who is willing to cope with the severity of the sub-zero weather, it offers a wide variety of sights and adventures not found in other caverns. 11. A third type is the "living" cave—one that is actively affected by flowing water that enlarges its passages, or by seepage water that leaves deposits. 12. In this evolving cave is found the widest variety of formations and wild life and usually it presents the most difficult exploring passages known to spelunkers.

Chances are that you and your classmates agreed on where to begin each new paragraph. Similar experiments have been tried successfully so many times that there is considerable evidence that readers generally respond to certain signals that mark the paragraph as a unit.

We can now analyze the example to infer why the student paragraphed as he did. Since most definitions of the paragraph emphasize meaning as an important element in its structure, we'll examine the passage first for meaning clues. The student's first paragraph includes sentences 1–3, which introduce the subject of the paper—different types of caves. Since sentence 4 introduces a specific type, *the virgin cave,* the student started a new paragraph here. This paragraph also includes sentences 5-7, which describe the virgin cave. The third paragraph begins at sentence 8, which introduces the *ice cave* and includes descriptive sentences 9 and 10. A fourth paragraph starts with the mention of the *living cave* in sentence

11 and includes sentence 12. Thus, in paragraphing, the student responded to the influence of meaning, as you probably did.

Each of these meaning units comprises a separate paragraph; each deals with a particular subject or topic, as introduced in sentences 4, 8, and 11. Such sentences that introduce the subject of a paragraph are traditionally referred to as *topic sentences.*

Using our findings from this series of paragraphs, we can construct a definition, based solely on meaning relationship: A paragraph is a unit of written discourse, made up of a topic sentence and a cluster of sentences that immediately relate to it.

But meaning alone is not a sufficient criterion for determining what a paragraph is. By examining printed paragraphs, you could find numerous examples of a single idea or theme discussed throughout several paragraphs instead of being confined to a single one. Nor is meaning always sufficient to provide cohesive unity of ideas within a paragraph. Other devices, therefore, must help to signal the scope of a paragraph and to give it cohesion by "gluing" the ideas together.

LINKING STRUCTURES AND PARAGRAPH UNITY

In addition to cohesive meaning relationships, well-constructed paragraphs are characterized by devices we might term linking structures—words and phrases that signal the relationships of ideas or that link the information in one sentence to that in the next. The most obvious of these are transitional words and phrases, such as *however, therefore, in other words, but.* However, other items—nouns and pronouns used as synonyms, words that connote time or place, even verb tenses— not only link the sentences within a single paragraph, but often serve as well to signal when different information is introduced and thus to indicate a new paragraph.

In our cave example, even though the writer does not yet have the skill to supply the number and variety of structural devices employed by more experienced writers, you can still isolate some that you responded to, perhaps subconsciously. Words like *most* and *rarest,* for instance, signal ranking, often used to show relationships between ideas or items; pronouns such as *it* (sentences 5, 9, 10, 12) and *one* (sentence 11) make clear reference to the specific type of cave being discussed. Words like *its* (sentence 6) and *this* (sentence 12), in positions commonly occupied by the less specific articles *a* or *the* establish a close relationship between the material in these sentences and that in the sentences preceding them. Reordering of elements, as in sentence 12 ("In this evolving cave"), helps to hook the sentence ideas together.

Before we discuss in greater detail those devices that help to "glue" ideas together within the paragraph, try another simple experiment. By listing the sentences in an order that seems natural and logical to you, try to reconstruct this scrambled paragraph as the student writer originally might have written it.

1. This erosion removes precious topsoil, making the ground unfit for anything to grow—not rabbit's tobacco, not sassafras, not corn, not beans.

2. But now the pasture is filled with boulders from the strip mine up the hill, and never again will cattle graze nor meadow birds nest there.

3. I have seen creeping soil banks topple towering oak trees and cover the lush shrubs and vines carpeting the ground.

4. The land dies.

5. Finally, I know of a pasture where partridges once nested after the cattle were removed.

6. Not only the waterways but the land itself has been a victim of strip mining.

7. And because there is no ground cover, erosion occurs.

8. Rabbits also lived there, as did many other ground creatures.

9. Erosion, in the form of monstrous land slides, resulting from locating strip mines close to highways, blocks the roads and makes it impossible for school children and workers to reach their destinations.

10. Because the trees are toppled, squirrels, birds, and possums can't nest there and the habitats of the wildlife are crowded; more squirrels must nest in fewer trees.

You should not have had too much trouble unscrambling this paragraph. Except in sentence 4, the student writer has provided you with many structural signals. Here is the original paragraph with the signals marked to show how the various elements are linked to chain the sentences together.

6 Not only the waterways but the land itself has been a victim of strip mining. **3** I have seen creeping soil banks topple towering oak trees and cover the lush shrubs and vines carpeting the ground. **10** Because the trees are toppled, squirrels, birds, and possums can't nest there and the habitats of the wildlife are crowded; more squirrels must nest in fewer trees. **7** And because there is no ground cover, erosion occurs. **1** This erosion removes precious topsoil, making the ground unfit for anything to grow—not rabbit's tobacco, not sassafras, not corn, not beans. **4** The land dies. **9** Erosion, in the form of monstrous land slides, resulting from locating strip mines close to highways, blocks the roads and makes it impossible for school children and workers to reach their destinations. **5** Finally, I know of a pasture where partridges once nested after the cattle were removed. **8** Rabbits also lived there, as did many other ground creatures. **2** But now the pasture is filled with boulders from the strip mine up the hill, and never again will cattle graze nor meadow birds nest there.

Note that the circled words are synonyms for or refer in some ways to *land* in the topic sentence; these are then woven throughout the paragraph, creating a unifying chain. Rectangles enclose words that tie together clusters of sentences having significant relationships: *erosion* in *7* to *erosion* in *1* to *erosion* in *9*, for example. Both circles and rectangles indicate words generally equivalent or related in meaning. We will refer to these signals as *meaning links.*

The underlined words in the paragraph provide transition from one idea to another (*not only . . . but, and*) or allow the reader to move from one relationship to another (*because, also*) or act as signals of time or place (*there, now, never again, finally*). These linking devices help to give the paragraph *continuity*—allowing the ideas to flow from one sentence to the next and helping the reader to follow the writer's trend of thought.

In summary, we can classify structural signals of paragraph cohesion according to their function:

1. Meaning links.
    a. Repetition of words or phrases, such as the repetition of *land* in the sample paragraph.
    b. Series of words having equivalent meanings: synonyms, pronouns, and the demonstratives (*this, these, that, those*) are most commonly used.
2. Transitional words.
    a. Subordinate conjunctions such as *because, if, when, thus, although.*
    b. Coordinate conjunctions: *and, or, either . . . or* are most common.
    c. Transitional phrases or adverbials such as *furthermore, for example, in other words, on the other hand.*
3. Signals of time or place.
    a. Time: *now, then, later, sooner, previously.* Also prepositional phrases such as *at that time, in the past, in the future, last week.*
    b. Place: *Here* and *there.* Also hundreds of prepositional phrases such as *over the hill, in that place, outside the window.*
4. Verb sequences
    We did not discuss this category in reference to the student example, but frequently a shift in verb tense is a signal that a new paragraph is needed. In our sample paragraph (except where the student writes about the past condition of the meadow), all the verbs or auxiliaries of the main clauses are in the present tense: "*has* been," "*is,*" "*blocks.*" But suppose the student had added this sentence at the end of the paragraph: "Strip mining *was* outlawed in Illinois." You as the reader would have immediately responded as much to the shift to past tense as to the abrupt shift in content; you would have been disturbed that the writer included this statement as part of the paragraph. This may help to explain why English professors react to such instances in student papers by writing "tense shift" in the margins.

The omission or skimpy use of these signals is an easy trap for any writer to fall into, but it is especially hazardous for inexperienced writers. Because you as the writer are aware of the relationships you intend, you may not feel compelled to supply helpful signals to your reader. But to do so is part of your commitment to your readers. You have an obligation to help them quickly grasp your meaning, unhindered by the seeming illogic and the fuzzy references that so often result from omitting these signals.

THE TOPIC SENTENCE

As we have said, the topic of the paragraph is generally, though not always, stated in a single sentence. As the thesis statement does for a whole paper, this topic sentence summarizes the information in the paragraph. The topic sentence, then, contains the most general information in the paragraph. The other sentences expand or develop the topic idea and so are usually more detailed, more specific. Typically, the topic sentence is the opening statement, as in this student's description of a wildlife sanctuary:

> Raven Run is not a recreation park; it is a sanctuary for wildlife and people. It is a place for quiet walks, for unwinding from the tensions of everyday life. It is a place to teach your children that there is more to life than sidewalks and shopping malls and MTV. It is a place to sit on 460 million-year-old rocks, once the lime muds of vast tidal flats, and to follow with your finger the tracings of ancient, tidal-flat animals, themselves long gone, but their burrows preserved in limestone; a place to dabble your fingers in the water that over tens of thousands of years has uncovered these rocks, and to listen as it splashes and swirls over the ledges and down into the old mill pond below.
>
> —Ann Watson

Occasionally a writer may place the topic sentence in the last sentence of the paragraph, a useful strategy when, for instance, the writer wishes to make a description or a reference to some action or event serve as a lead-in to the topic. This pattern is common in opening paragraphs in which the topic sentence of the paragraph also serves as the thesis statement for the paper. Here is an example:

> For about a month I spent most of each day either on the Peak or overlooking Mlinda Valley where the chimps, before or after stuffing themselves with figs, ate large quantities of small purple fruits that tasted, like so many of their foods, as bitter and astringent as sloes or crab apples. Piece by piece, I began to form my first somewhat crude picture of chimpanzee life.
>
> —Jane van Lawick-Goodall, "First Observations."

As is generally the case, in both examples the topic is clearly and explicitly stated. On occasion, however, particularly in narrative and descriptive writing, the topic idea is implicit in the whole paragraph rather than openly stated. In the following paragraph from Helen Keller's autobiographical work, the blind and deaf writer does not state her topic—that she must experience life through the sense of touch; this idea is implicit in her examples.

> When I think of hills, I think of the upward strength I tread upon. When water is the object of my thought, I feel the cool shock of the plunge and the quick yielding of the waves that crisp and curl and ripple about my body. The pleasing changes of rough and smooth, pliant and rigid, curved and straight in the bark and branches of a tree give the truth to my hand. The immovable rock, with its juts and warped surfaces, bends beneath my fingers into all manner of grooves and hollows. The bulge of a watermelon and the puffed-up rotundities of squashes that sprout, bud, and ripen in that strange garden planted somewhere behind my finger tips are the ludicrous in my tactual memory and imagination.
>
> *—Helen Keller, The World I Live In.*

Whether the topic sentence is at the beginning or end of a paragraph, it is an integral part of well-constructed paragraphs, acting as a focusing point for the ideas in the unit. The form that the topic sentence takes—indeed, the form of the whole paragraph—is determined by the writer's subject and purpose, and the audience. As we progress through this text, we will discuss paragraph conventions in relation to these factors. Here we'll consider paragraphs in personal writing and the special organizational considerations they entail.

NARRATIVE PARAGRAPHS

Because narrative paragraphs are integral units of longer narratives which move in time, they too are organized in chronological order. And they appear in a sequence dictated by the narrative's overall organizational scheme—generally, past to present, though, as we've noted, there may be departure from a strict chronology—as when flashbacks are used.

Like other paragraphs, those used in narrative are unified around a central idea or theme, but it may sometimes be implied, rather than stated in a sentence. When a topic sentence is present, often it indicates a shift in the action or the time. The first of the following two narrative paragraphs indicates a movement in time; the second points a new direction in the continuing action involving a sleep-walking family:

> One hot night, four Lundbergs took a hike, aroused by thunder and lightning, aroused but not awakened. Their neighbor Mrs. Thorvaldson, widow of Senator K.'s brother Harry, called the constables. Carl, Jr., had pitched into her marigolds and the other three were moving around on her lawn. "They're having dreams, and I don't want to be part of it," she said.

Gary and LeRoy hauled Carl, Jr., out of the flowers and herded the others to their own yard and, rather than wake them, tied clothesline to their ankles and tethered them to a tree. Of course, when Carl walked to the end of his rope, he fell like a load of bricks. He awoke then, mad about the rope, the light in his face—"This isn't right," he said, as LeRoy untied him. "You got no *right* tying up people in their sleep. We were *asleep*. You woke us up. *You* can't do that."

—*Garrison Keillor, Lake Woebegone Days*

In the first paragraph the opening sentence acts as the topic sentence, in this case starting a new action and signalling the shift in time by the opening phrase, "One hot night." In the second paragraph, the first sentence again serves as the topic by starting a new action involving the constables. Note how the verb sequence—*"hauled," "herded," "tied," "tethered*—establishes the order of the constables' actions.

One device peculiar to narrative situations is dialogue, which has special paragraphing conventions. As a rule, each person's statement is placed in a separate paragraph, as in this example from Ernest Hemingway's autobiographical account of a trip he took with F. Scott Fitzgerald:

Scott did not come up and I met him down at the dock.

"I'm terribly sorry there was this mix-up," he said. "If I had only known what hotel you were going to it would have been simple."

"That's all right," I said. We were going to have a long ride and I was all for peace. "What train did you come down on?"

"One not long after the one you took. It was a very comfortable train and we might just as well have come down together."

"Have you had breakfast?"

"Not yet. I've been hunting all over the town for you."

"That's a shame," I said. "Didn't they tell you at home that I was here?"

"No. Zelda wasn't feeling well and I probably shouldn't have come. The whole trip has been disastrous so far."

—*Ernest Hemingway, A Moveable Feast*

Note that in the third paragraph of this passage Hemingway includes a two-word "tag"—"I said"—that is not spoken by either character, but he does not then start a separate paragraph because the "I" continues speaking. Also, he does not use such tags—"I said," "he said"—in each dialogue paragraph because the indentation itself signals the change in speaker.

Such paragraphing is used only with direct discourse, as in our example, and not always then. And, as in the Keillor example, writers occasionally include a conversation written in direct discourse within a single paragraph—especially when the conversation contributes closely to the action being described.

If written in indirect discourse, a whole conversation is normally included in a single paragraph, thus treating it as any cluster of closely related sentences. Here's an example from the same Hemingway work:

> Scott had obviously been drinking before I met him and, as he looked as though he needed a drink, I asked him if he did not want one in the bar before we set out. He told me he was not a morning drinker and asked if I was. I told him it depended entirely on how I felt and what I had to do and he said that if I felt that I needed a drink, he would keep me company so I would not have to drink alone. So we had a whisky and Perrier in the bar while we waited for the lunch and both felt much better.

Although indirect discourse usually lacks the freshness and vitality of direct discourse, it is extremely useful in compressing conversation intended merely to provide information or a transition between two scenes.

Special Problems of Dialogue

As is obvious in our first Hemingway example (page 58), direct dialogue presents special problems with punctuation, needing to be set off with quotation marks. In addition, three special devices are used:

1. Speaker identified by speaker tag:

"That's a shame," *I said*. "Didn't they tell you at home that I was here?"

Note that here the comma and the question mark are both inside the quotation marks. Commas and periods always go inside. Other devices of punctuation—question and exclamation marks, colons and semicolons, and dashes—go inside if they are part of the quotation.

2. Speaker unidentified:

"Have you had breakfast?"

This treatment is possible only when just two speakers are involved, and then only if who is speaking is clear from the context.

3. Other narrative information included in paragraph along with quoted dialogue.

"That's all right," I said. We were going to have a long ride and I was all for peace. "What train did you come down on?"

This device gives a writer many advantages: showing the speaker's thoughts during the conversation, as is done here; indicating the passage of time; making a smooth transition between bits of conversation; and adding descriptive materials.

Although indirect discourse involves no special punctuation, it presents its own problem: the word order of questions starting with question words (*who, what, when, where, why, how*). The word order for indirect questions is as follows:

He asked me *where   I   had   been.*
Wh-word + Subject + Auxiliary + Verb

Wh-questions in direct discourse follow the normal word order of all such questions, the auxiliary verbs coming before the subject.

He asked me, "Where   have   you   been?"
Wh-word + Auxiliary + Subject + Verb

This example demonstrates another peculiarity of indirect discourse questions, that of verb accord. In the indirect sample, *had* is required to follow the same tense as *asked;* in direct discourse, this kind of tense accord is not necessary and *have* is the auxiliary permitted.

DESCRIPTIVE PARAGRAPHS

Just as narrative paragraphs usually involve time, descriptive paragraphs usually involve space. A new paragraph frequently marks a move from one location to another or from one aspect of the thing described to another. Normally this shift is signalled by the topic sentence. The topic sentence of a descriptive paragraph may also state the writer's general impression of a person or place or may summarize the writer's emotional response, as in these examples:

General impression: "The stovepipe hat he (Lincoln) wore sort of whistled softly, "I am not a hat at all; I am the little garret roof where he tucks in little thoughts he writes on pieces of paper." —Carl Sandburg

Emotional effect: "But most of all, I remember Pond Creek itself, flowing in a long, lazy, almost unvaried curve through these grassy fields. —Lucy Lubbers

Governed by the topic sentence, the other sentences of the paragraph then move in some appropriate order, frequently spatial. Sandburg's paragraph, for instance, moves from a general description of the whole hat, to the inside band with its tucked-in notes, to the lining and the things printed on it. Lubber's paragraph (page 21) follows the creek as it flows into the distance.

In this paragraph describing a member of a sharecropper family, James Agee mixes detailed, objective description with emotional and imaginative impressions which help determine the choice of details.

She is a big girl, almost as big as her sister is wiry, though she is not at all fat: her build is rather that of a young queen of a child's magic story who throughout has been coarsened by peasant living and work, and that of her eyes and demeanor, too, kind, not fully formed, resolute, bewildered, and sad. Her soft abundant slightly curling brown hair is cut in a square bob which on her large fine head is particularly childish, and indeed Emma is rather a big child, sexual beyond propriety to its years, than a young woman; and this can be seen in a kind of dimness of definition in her features, her skin, and the shape of her body, which will be lost in a few years. She wears a ten cent store necklace and a Sunday cotton print dress because she is visiting, and is from town, but she took off her slippers as soon as she came, and worked with Annie Mae.

—*James Agee and Walker Evans, Let Us Now Praise Famous Men*

Even in a paragraph like this one which moves from one of the writer's reactions to another, there is still a spatial progression: general body build—head—hair—features and skin—dress.

Often writers combine movement in time with movement in space, particularly when their purpose is to describe something in terms of "then and now," or to describe a moving scene. In the following example, the writer takes the reader on a ride in Spain, moving forward in time from one site to another, as evidenced in phrases such as "as you reach" and "climb becomes." But the actual descriptions are spatial—presented as the eye sees.

You'll find yourself on a two-lane road that winds past a power station, pastures grazed by drowsy cows, a few white farm houses with smoking chimneys, tethered burros, cork trees and olive groves. As you reach higher altitudes, pine forests and clumps of cactus take the place of farmlands. The climb becomes increasingly steep, with shear drops alongside the road. Behind, the blue Mediterranean sprawls to the horizon and Gibraltar looms in the westward haze.

—*Tom Bross, "A Spanish Hill Town"*

As you are probably beginning to realize, descriptive paragraphs do not follow any prescribed pattern, but are organized according to the writer's wishes and purposes and the needs of the readers. They should generally, however, follow the basic rules of any well-unified paragraph by containing a topic sentence and details which are closely related to the topic. And they should contain the appropriate structural signals to link the sentences together (see pages 53–55).

SUMMARY

Paragraphs are recognizable units of discourse, but, unlike sentences, paragraphs are conventions only of written discourse. Paragraphs have a subject or topic, generally explicitly expressed in a *topic sentence*. When all of the other sentences in the paragraph are closely related in meaning to the topic sentence, the paragraph has *unity*. A number of linking devices provide *cohesion* and flow. Some of these are synonyms, transitional words and phrases, and signals of time and place. We'll consider others, such as parallelism, in later chapters. Certain kinds of paragraphs, such as those in dialogue, include special punctuation or—in the case of indirect discourse—special word order in sentences.

ASSIGNMENTS

For Discussion

1. Why is it easier to determine sentence structures than to recognize paragraphs in spoken discourse?

2. What are some of the factors, even in written discourse, that make paragraphs difficult to define?

3. In constructing paragraphs, why can you not rely solely on meaning relationships?

4. What is the function of a topic sentence in a paragraph? Using narrative and descriptive paragraphs as examples, discuss how the writer's purpose helps to shape the topic sentence?

5. Why might you expect to find many time signals in narrative paragraphs? Many place signals in descriptive paragraphs?

6. Break this lengthy paragraph taken from Mark Twain's *Autobiography* into several shorter ones. Be able to justify your paragraphing by meaning and structural clues.

> I can call back the solemn twilight and mystery of the deep woods, the earthy smells, the faint odors of the wild flowers, the sheen of rain-washed foliage, the rattling clatter of drops when the wind shook the trees, the hammering of woodpeckers and the muffled drumming of woodpheasants in the remoteness of the forest, the snap-shot glimpses of disturbed wild creatures scurrying through the grass—I can call it all back and make it as real as it ever was, and as blessed. I can call back the prairie, and its loneliness and peace, and a vast hawk hanging motionless in the sky with his wings spread wide and the blue of the vault showing through the fringe of their endfeathers. I can see the woods in their autumn dress, the oaks purple, the hickories washed with gold, the maples and the sumachs luminous with crimson fires, and I can hear the rustle made by the fallen leaves as we plowed through them. I can see the blue clusters of wild grapes hanging amongst the foliage of the saplings, and I remember the taste of them and the smell. I know how the wild blackberries looked and how they tasted; and the same with the pawpaws, the hazelnuts, and the persimmons; and I can feel the thumping rain upon my head of hickory-nuts and walnuts when we were out in the frosty dawn to scramble for them with the pigs, and the gusts of wind loosed them and sent them down.

a. To what signals did you respond in breaking the paragraph into smaller units? How much influence did the repetition of the sentence opener "*I*" + *verb* have on your decisions?

b. How do you think Twain's topic sentence may have influenced his decision to put this whole description into one paragraph?

For Practice

1. Write a short anecdote in which you include dialogue. Write it first with direct-discourse dialogue, then with indirect. Which was more effective for your purposes? Why?

2. Write a paragraph descriptive of a place, organizing it as your eye might move from one part of the place to another.

3. Write a paragraph descriptive of a person that includes your emotional responses to that person. Use those responses as Agee did in the paragraph on pages 60–61 to supply its organizational scheme.

4. Making sure that you supply the necessary time signals, write two or three paragraphs narrating some everyday activity, such as a walk from a classroom to the library. You need not include dialogue.

4

Sentence Strategies

The police did not come. In my agitation I found myself beside Ruth First whose article I had not written. She didn't seem to mind at all. Time passed and the knots began to shred away slowly. I joined the head-shaking people making their way to the Anglican Mission in Proes Street, shaking my head as I went. I looked back. There was no one on the pavement outside the old synagogue. The police had also left.

—*Alfred Hutchinson, Road to Ghana*

This passage is taken from an autobiographical narrative describing the release of a number of black political hostages after two years in prison. If you read it aloud, you will find that the short sentences encourage fast reading, thus heightening the sense of action and urgency, a common use of such sentences in narrative. With the exception of a few sentences in the passage, most are what we traditionally call simple sentences.

SIMPLE SENTENCE STRUCTURE

Actually, the term *simple* is a little misleading because it connotes short, simple-minded sentences, and simple sentences are not always that simple. In the sample paragraph, there are some short examples: "I looked back," "The police did not come," and "The police had also left." But what of "I joined the head-shaking people making their way to the Anglican Mission in Proes Street, shaking my head as I went"? Although not short, it too fits the traditional definition of a simple sentence—it consists of only one subject and one main verb.

To understand simple sentences and their usefulness to personal and other kinds of writing, let's look first at some general characteristics of the sentence.

Traditionally, a simple sentence is defined as having a single thought or idea. But in conversations, short phrases or even single words can imply a complete thought, as in this example where John relies on Helen's question to supply the missing information in his answer:

Helen: "Where are you going after class?"
John: "Home."

Because Helen's question supplied "are going," John did not need to repeat the verb to express that idea. If spoken without the context supplied by the question, however, an isolated "home" would be incomplete and make little sense to a listener. Even in conversation, missing sentence parts must be implied by a previous reference in order to convey a complete thought. As you can see, defining a sentence as a complete thought is not adequate; it is more accurate to define the sentence as a language structure having two main parts or components, a *subject* and a *predicate* (and containing no word, such as *if* or *because*, that makes it grammatically dependent on another structure).

The first component of the sentence—usually in initial position—is the *subject*. Generally a noun, a noun phrase, or a pronoun, it identifies the sentence topic: the someone or something central to the situation established in the sentence. A noun phrase is made up of a noun with modifiers: *the sky, an interesting question*.

The second component of a simple, basic sentence—the predicate—contains a verb and other words closely tied to the verb in meaning; together they make a comment about the topic stated in the subject. The comment frequently takes the form of an action, as in the final sentence of our opening paragraph, "The police *had also left*." Or it can be descriptive, as in "The grass *is green*." In any case, the predicate states or "predicates" something about the subject.

If we make a frame to show the underlying components of a simple, basic sentence, it might look like this:

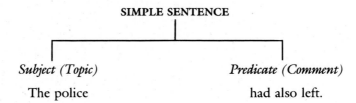

SIMPLE SENTENCE

Subject (Topic)   *Predicate (Comment)*

The police   had also left.

As you can see, the form of a sentence is closely related to its meaning; both the subject and the predicate are needed to express a "complete thought"—to supply the basic information in the sentence. And both are necessary to establish the relationships between the topic and its comment. Certainly, you would not employ simple sentences containing *only* these essential components for every writing purpose, but they can be extremely useful in some situations. In a personal narrative or character sketch, for instance, they can be used in dialogue to emulate natural speech, and in the telling of a story or anecdote they move the action quickly along. Also, they are effective in all kinds of writing for making a statement in a direct, straightforward manner. Placed among longer, more complicated' sentences, they can give special emphasis to an idea.

BASIC SENTENCE PATTERNS

In addition to having such uses as we have noted, the basic subject–predicate sentence patterns supply the raw materials to build *all* sentences—simple, compound, and complex. To form compound and complex sentences, we can join these basic sentence patterns in various ways. Because they are the building blocks of all sentences, and because we will use them later in showing you how to combine sentences, basic sentence patterns deserve some background discussion.

As in all languages, the basic sentence patterns in English are limited in number—less than ten. And all of them contain the two essential components discussed above: *subject* (topic) and *predicate* (comment). The predicate must always include a main verb in present or past tense form—for example, *wash, was, seems, gave, had gone*. Occasionally, the verb alone makes up the entire predicate, as in Julius Caesar's famous declaration that strings together three basic sentence patterns: "I *came*, I *saw*, I *conquered*."

Generally, however, the comment made by the predicate requires more information than the verb alone can supply. In these cases, we add a *complement*—a word or group of words that are closely related to the meaning and function of the verb in its role of commenting on the subject.

Complements take several forms, depending upon their relationship to the verb and subject. For example, a complement may be a noun phrase which receives the direct action of the verb, as in "Victor washed *the baby*." Or it may be an adjective that describes the subject in some way, as in "Felicia was *happy*."

In other sentence patterns, the complement is an adverb—a word such as *well* and *there*, or an adverbial phrase like *in the oven* or *at nine o'clock*. Some adverbs indicate the manner (*how*) of the verb's action: *vigorously, by sheer will power*. Others tell *when* or *where* the action occurs: *now, at ten o'clock, there, at the student center*.

Now that we have briefly discussed the components of all basic sentence patterns, we can look at the different types of basic patterns. These are determined mainly by the relationship between the verb and its complement. The kind of complement that a verb can take and the complement's function in the sentence are both determined by whether the verb is *transitive, intransitive,* or *linking*.

Patterns with Transitive Verbs

A transitive verb transfers its action to one or more of three possible kinds of objects which are nouns or pronouns:

1. *Direct objects* directly and immediately receive the verb's action, as in *hit the ball, run the rapids, play the piano*. In some sentences, the direct object is the only object.

2. *Indirect objects*, on the other hand, rarely occur without a direct object present. Whereas the verb transfers its action directly to the direct object, the indirect object "benefits" indirectly from the verb's action: pass the ball [direct object] *to me* [indirect object]; buy the piano [direct object] *for me* [indirect object]; ask a question [direct object] *of me* [indirect object]. In these examples, the indirect object follows the direct object and so must be preceded by a preposition. But when indirect objects occur between the verb and the direct object, no preposition is necessary: pass *me* the ball, buy *me* the piano, ask *me* a question. Only indirect objects have this flexibility. Note that the preposition used for the indirect object is determined by the verb; *to* and *for* are the most commonly used.

3. The *objective complement* is most closely tied in meaning to the direct object, further identifying or defining it; for example, in this sentence, "Rene called Mario a fool," *Mario* is the direct object; *a fool* is the objective complement because it refers to the direct object, describing Mario in some way.

This chart of the most common basic sentence patterns created by transitive verbs and their objects should help you remember them better.

1. | *Subject* | *Transitive Verb* | *Direct Object* |
   | Joan | bought | the suit. |

2a. | *Subject* | *Transitive Verb* | *Direct Object* | *Indirect Object* |
    | Carlos | sent | a letter | to his mother. |

2b. | *Subject* | *Transitive Verb* | *Indirect Object* | *Direct Object* |
    | Carlos | sent | his mother | a letter. |

3. | *Subject* | *Transitive Verb* | *Direct Object* | *Objective Complement* |
   | She | considered | Tom | a clown. |

Patterns with Intransitive Verbs

Verbs that have no object are *intransitive*. In such cases, the verb may either stand alone as the predicate or be followed by an adverb that is optional, not a grammatically necessary part of the sentence pattern.

4a. | *Subject* | *Intransitive Verb* |
    | The dog | howled. |

4b. | *Subject* | *Intransitive Verb* | *Optional Adverb* |
    | The dog | howled | piteously. |

Patterns with Linking Verbs

Linking verbs—such as *be, seem, become, feel*—show little or no action to be completed; instead, they point to the status or condition of the subject. Accordingly, rather than receiving or benefiting from the action of a verb, as direct and indirect objects do, the complements of linking verbs supply the predicate's comment about the subject. For example, in the sentence, "The weather is warm," it is the adjective *warm* that adds the information rather than the linking verb *is*. Mainly, that is, linking verbs serve to link the subject with a complement. Complements that follow linking verbs may be predicate nouns, predicate adjectives, or occasionally (with verb *be* only) adverbs.

5. *Subject*   *Linking Verb*   *Predicate Noun*
   Rosario   became   a lawyer.

6. *Subject*   *Linking Verb*   *Predicate Adjective*
   Ivan   was   happy.

7. *Subject*   *Linking Verb (be)*   *Adverb*
   The train   is   on time.

These seven patterns comprise almost all of the basic sentence patterns in English. As we have indicated, sentences are rarely employed in this basic form. But they are important to understand because they are used to create the wide variety of sentence structures you will need for effective writing.

ALTERING BASIC SENTENCE PATTERNS

One way to create sentence variety is to alter the composition of a basic sentence in some way: by adding and reordering optional adverbs; by changing the sentences to questions; or by deleting materials to form sentence fragments.

Adding Optional Adverbs

Without changing their basic form, all these sentence patterns can be expanded by adding adverbs at the end, as we did with pattern 4. Such adverbs are not tied to the predicate components—verb and complement—and can be moved to other positions in the sentence, as we will show later. Here's how the basic patterns look after an optional adverb is added at the end of each.

Pattern 1:   Joan bought the suit *yesterday*.
Pattern 2:   Carlos sent a letter to his mother *last week*.
Pattern 3:   She considered Tom a clown *at the dance*.
Pattern 4:   The dog howled *piteously*.
Pattern 5:   Rosario became a lawyer *last year*.
Pattern 6:   Ivan was happy *every day*.
Pattern 7:   The train is on time *every day*.

Reordering Optional Adverbs

Because these adverbs are optional and therefore movable, they are useful in giving simple sentences some variety or in providing transition from one sentence to the next. In the following example, a student reordered some optional adverbs (shown in italics), placing them first in the sentences to provide transitions and thus to help move the narrative along swiftly and clearly in both time and space.

Suddenly we heard a scream. *Ahead* a man was pulling a young child into a car. We started to run towards it. He slammed the door and started the car. The child continued to cry. *As* we reached the car, we banged on the window. *Then* the car moved away.

Even this brief example shows how effectively the series of simple, basic sentences aided the student in re-creating the sense of haste, panic, and immediacy she had experienced.

Too many subject-verb-complement optional adverb sentences become monotonous for the reader. Varying this pattern can remedy the monotony, although variety should never be pursued at the expense of clarity. Because optional adverbs are more freely movable than other sentence components, they afford the writer an especially convenient means of creating sentence variety.

Let's examine some of the effects that can be achieved by reordering. As we saw in the student example, moving optional adverbs to a frontal position can often create a smooth transition from one sentence to another. The following example is from John Steinbeck's "The Chrysanthemums." Note that Steinbeck moves the place adverb "on every side" to the front of the second sentence. Because the information supplied by the adverb is pertinent to both sentences, it works very well as a bridge between them.

> Steinbeck's version: The high gray-flannel fog of winter closed off the Salinas Valley from the sky and all the rest of the world. *On every side* it sat like a lid on the mountains and made of the great valley a closed pot.
>
> Contrast: The high gray-flannel fog of winter closed off the Salinas Valley from the sky and all the rest of the world. It sat like a lid on the mountains *on every side* . . .

As you can see, Steinbeck's ordering breaks the monotony of two consecutive sentences starting with a subject, and it also provides transition from the first sentence to the second. Further, the position of the place adverbs at the beginning gives emphasis to the location of the fog.

Place adverbs are not the only optional adverbs that can be used for transition, variety, and emphasis. These examples employ adverbs of time and manner reordered to the frontal position.

> *On Monday*, you report to the Marine Corps office. (*Time* adverb, *on Monday*, receives special emphasis and importance.)
>
> *Gingerly*, he scraped the egg off his shirt. (Draws attention to the *manner* in which he scraped off the egg.)

Optional adverbs have other reordering possibilities. Sometimes you may wish to place an adverb of time, place, or manner after the subject or the verb. These placements are desirable when you need to set the subject in the beginning position to retain focus and clarity. However, the special emphasis and transition advantages are lessened. Here are the last two examples rewritten so that you can see the different effects.

> You report *on Monday* to the Marine Corps office.
>
> He *gingerly* scraped the egg off his shirt.

In reordering optional adverbs, we are moving only one element in the sentence pattern. Other situations may demand reordering several components.

Inverting Sentence Order

Inverting the order of basic sentence components is occasionally a useful device for creating special emphasis. Unlike moving optional adverbs, which maintains the basic sentence order, inversion reorders other, less moveable elements. Here are three of the most common inversions:

Subject and verb exchanged: Up *came the diver* to the surface.)
Object moved to initial position: *Hypocrisy* he detested.
Predicate adjective moved to front position; subject and verb exchanged: *Particularly nasty was* the letter from the IRS.

As with all devices used for special emphasis, inverted sentences should be used wisely and sparingly so that they do not lose their effectiveness.

Questions and Their Use in Writing

In personal writing, questions can be valuable in achieving a natural voice when writing dialogue. Generally, as in speech, questions in dialogue will be short and direct. Occasionally, they may be no more than a "huh?" or a brief "How come?" "Why not?" or "So what?" Usually, however, questions in written dialogue include more information than there is in actual conversation, since the principal use of dialogue is to reveal something about the people speaking. Because you know intuitively how to form questions, we offer here only a brief review of their structures, primarily to make you aware of different types of questions, the reordering processes involved, and how their forms differ.

Basically, there are four types of questions in English: those starting with an auxiliary verb; those starting with a question word such as *when* or *what*; those that are statements with a question tagged on; and those used in indirect discourse. Because we discuss indirect questions on page 60, we will not give space to them here.

1. Questions starting with an auxiliary verb.

In forming these questions, we reorder the subject and an auxiliary verb of the basic sentence. If there is no auxiliary present, a form of *do* is substituted for it.

Subject	Auxiliary	Verb	Direct Object	Optional Adverb
Harry	will	see	his mother	on his trip.
Harry		saw	his mother	on his trip.

Auxiliary	Subject	Verb	Direct Object	Optional Adverb
Will	Harry	see	his mother	on his trip?
Did	Harry	see	his mother	on his trip?

Here the auxiliary verb *will* or *did* was moved to the initial position and the subject, *Harry*, placed after it. Other auxiliaries used in questions include all the forms of *be* and *have* as well as *might, will, can,* and others. Note that all questions in this category can be answered simply with yes or no.

2. Questions starting with question words

When we wish a more informational answer than a mere yes or no, we keep the same format as for *yes/no* questions, but add a question word in initial position. Here are examples of reordered questions again based on the sentence pattern "Harry will see his mother." We have repeated the yes/no format so that you can see the contrast.

Auxiliary	Subject	Verb	Direct Object
Will	Harry	see	his mother?

Question Adverb	Auxiliary	Subject	Verb	Direct Object
When	will	Harry	see	his mother?

When we wish a "who" or "what" answer, the appropriate pronoun is substituted for the object and moved to frontal position, as in:

Question Pronoun	Auxiliary	Subject	Verb
Whom (who)	will	Harry	see?

3. Statements with questions tagged on

Frequently used in conversation and mainly reserved in writing dialogue, these statements with an added-on question are fairly complex in their structure and use, so we will deal with only the most common forms. As you look at these examples, notice the typical patterns of negative statement with positive questions and vice versa:

Positive Statement	Negative Question

Harry will see his mother on his trip, won't he?

Negative Statement	Positive Question

Harry won't see his mother on his trip, will he?

Although there are other kinds of tag questions, generally they follow this rule: a positive statement is tagged to a negative question; a negative statement takes a positive tag.

Except in dialogue and in a few restricted uses to be discussed later, questions should generally be avoided in writing. Readers read your writing to find out what *you* know, not to question their own knowledge. Like expensive perfume or champagne, questions lose their novelty and effectiveness if used too often.

Sentence Fragments

In the preceding discussions about altering simple or basic sentences, we have retained all or most of the sentence components, simply reordering them for a specific purpose. In creating sentence fragments, however, we delete parts of the sentence, leaving it incomplete.

Rarely used in other kinds of writing, sentence fragments can be effective in personal writing, particularly in narrative and personal essays. Starting with a capital and ending with terminal punctuation, but often lacking a subject or a verb that shows tense, these non-sentences can add color and vigor to personal writing. In the following passage from Dick Gregory's autobiography, *Nigger*, note Gregory's skillful use of sentence fragments (italicized):

> The teacher thought I was stupid. *Couldn't spell, couldn't read, couldn't do arithmetic. Just stupid.* Teachers were never interested in finding out that you couldn't concentrate because you were so hungry, because you hadn't had any breakfast. All you could think about was noontime, would it ever come? Maybe you could sneak into the cloakroom and steal a bite of some kid's lunch out of a coat pocket. *A bite of something. Paste.* You couldn't really make a meal of paste, or put it on bread for a sandwich, but sometimes I'd scoop a few spoonfuls out of a paste jar in back of the room. Pregnant people get strange tastes. I was pregnant with poverty. *Pregnant with dirt and pregnant with shoes that were never bought for me, pregnant with five other people in my bed and no Daddy in the next room, and pregnant with hunger.* Paste doesn't taste too bad when you're hungry.

The fragments here are all effective. In the first, the omission of the subject (I) shifts the emphasis from the writer to the reasons for the teacher's opinion of him and achieves a free, natural effect that would have been lost in the traditional counterpart:

> The teacher thought that I was stupid because I couldn't spell, read, or do arithmetic.

The emphatic summary fragment ("Just stupid"), by picking up the last word in the first sentence, adds a decisive note of finality. The next two fragments ("A bite of something" and "Paste") pick up the word "bite" in the preceding sentence, amplifying and focusing on the boy's hunger. The final fragment ("Pregnant with . . .") is a lengthy one that repeats "pregnant" from the preceding paragraph. The series of fragments with their ironic repetition of "pregnant," allows Gregory to give specifics about his poverty in a very effective way.

Like Gregory's, sentence fragments, if they are to work for a writer, must in some way repeat and amplify what was said earlier. Also, the missing sentence components should be easily recoverable by the reader, as in our rewritten version of Gregory's first sentence. Although such fragments can be dramatic, attention-getting devices, they should be used sparingly—even in personal writing.

Some kinds of fragments, however, should be avoided in all writing: those that do not repeat a word or share a sentence component from an earlier sentence. Here are some examples of common unacceptable fragments (italicized):

1. I had a perpetual clash with my mother. *A woman who was as stubborn as I was.*

Unlike the Gregory examples, this noun phrase modifier of *mother* detracts from the close relationships involved, rather than emphasizing them. It does not repeat in some way what went before; instead it is a dangling, isolated unit. A comma or a dash after *mother* is needed, joining the fragment to the preceding sentence.

2. He felt that he was capable of making his own decisions. *Being of sound mind and body.*

This common culprit involves an *-ing* participle, sometimes mistaken by student writers for a main verb which has tense. Verb phrases introduced by an *-ing* participle or a past participle ("possessed of sound mind and body") are integral parts of a sentence, and generally set off by a comma.

3. The airport police arrested John. *For drunk and disorderly conduct.*

Here an isolated prepositional phrase is the problem. Functioning as an adverb, it is an essential part of the whole sentence. However, it could become a potentially effective fragment if *arrested* were repeated: The airport police arrested John. Arrested him for drunk and disorderly conduct.

4. John's wife bought a mink coat. *Which he thought was extravagant.*

Considered unacceptable by many, this fragment involves a relative clause—a dependent clause introduced by a relative pronoun, *who, which, that.* Replacing the period with a comma after *coat* reestablishes the clause's close relationship as a modifier of the noun.

5. He wore a raincoat. *Although it was not raining.*

This unacceptable fragment is a subordinate clause, dependent in meaning on the preceding sentence. Such a clause is introduced by a subordinating conjunction (*because, whether, although*), and thus is an integral part of a sentence. See pages 76–79 and the Reference Guide for further discussion of these clauses and their punctuation requirements.

Like other language devices, fragments can be highly effective, but they require that you understand their structure and their limitations. Fragments are certainly helpful in personal writing as another means of adding the spice of naturalness to your prose. But like other spices, they should be applied sparingly.

Exclamations

Exclamations are short sentences, sentence fragments, or single words that are punctuated with an exclamation point: "You can't mean that!" "What a guy!" or "Wow!" Common in conversation, they are avoided in most writing. They can add naturalness to narratives and personal essays. But practice moderation! Repeated exclamations lose their impact.

COMBINING BASIC SENTENCES BY JOINING

Combining sentences is a creative process. We can form *compound* sentences by joining two or more simple sentences with a coordinating conjunction (*and, or*). We can make *complex* sentences by joining two or more simple sentences and subordinating all but one with a subordinating conjunction (*because, while, although*, etc.). And we can create an infinite variety of sentence structures by inserting modifying elements from one sentence into another.

Creating Compound Sentences

In combining sentences to create a compound sentence, the basic structure of each of the simple, subject-predicate sentences is retained. They are simply joined with a coordinating conjunction:

        S   P   S   P
The wind shifted to the North, *and* the snow started.

Compound sentences consist of two or more such subject-predicate structures joined by a coordinating conjunction—*and, but, or, nor, for, so, yet*—or occasionally a semicolon. Generally, a comma precedes the conjunction, although the comma is occasionally omitted if the two joined sentences are short. When a semicolon is substituted for the conjunction, no comma is needed.

Structurally, a compound sentence looks like this:

$$SP, \begin{bmatrix} \text{and} \\ \text{but} \\ \text{or} \\ \text{nor} \\ \text{for} \\ \text{so} \\ \text{yet} \\ ; \end{bmatrix} SP$$

The SP structures can also be linked by a pair of conjunctions—*either/or, neither/nor, not only/but* (*also*). In such cases, the first conjunction precedes the subject of the first sentence:

[either] SP,   [or] SP

Either we mow the lawn, *or* we go to the movies.

When the negative pairs are used, however, the auxiliary verb is placed after the negative conjunction and (as the questions) before the subject.

Not only *did* we mow the lawn, *but* we also went to the movies.
Neither did we mow the lawn, *nor did* we go to the movies.

Because compound sentences are common to oral narrative, their use in writing helps to create a natural voice. They also tend to focus a descriptive passage, or to move the narrative along. Richard Bradford, in this opening paragraph of *Red Sky at Morning*, uses compound sentences to achieve these effects:

> We were using the old blue china and the stainless steel cutlery, with place mats on the big oval table and odd-sized jelly glasses for the wine. *The good stuff was all packed and stored, and the Salvation Army was due the next day for the leftovers. My mother called this last dinner a picnic, but she didn't wear her overalls to it.* She had on the blue hostess gown with the purple flowers.

Despite their usefulness in personal writing, compound sentences joined by *and* should be used sparingly in other kinds of writing because *and* is a vague conjunction: it can signal more than one kind of relationship. In the following example, for instance, the reader must decide whether the conjunction signals a causal relationship (because he did it) or a temporal one (after he had done it):

> He cut a full cord of birch, *and* his wife called him into the house.

Even in personal writing, however, too many sentences joined by *and* may sound juvenile, as shown in this account by a child:

> I was walking to school and a bird hit a tree. I ran to it and it tried to fly away. It could not move and I carried it to school. My teacher made me take it to the principal's office, and he called someone on the phone. He told me the bird would be taken care of, and I went back to class.

Creating Complex Sentences

When we combine two sentences with *and* or *or*, there is little change in the relationship between them. But when subordinating words are the linking devices, one sentence becomes dependent upon or subordinate to the other. Here's an example, using the subordinating conjunction *because* as the joining device. The term *base* identifies each of the original sentences and *result* identifies the new sentence that results from the joining.

Base 1: He hurried to open the door for them.
Base 2: It was cold outside. (BECAUSE)
Result: He hurried to open the door for them *because* it was cold outside.

As you can see, the conjunction *because* signals a cause-effect relationship between the two sentences: the second contains the cause for the action in the first. Used alone, the dependent clause would be an incomplete sentence—a fragment: *Because it was cold outside.*

But *cause* is not the only relationship established by subordinating conjunctions; so before you work with them in combining sentences, it is useful to understand what some of those relationships are. Here is a partial list of these joiners and the relationships they signal:

Cause:	because, since, as
Purpose:	so that, in order that
Limitation or restriction:	though, although
Time:	when, after, as soon as, while, before, until
Special condition:	if, whether, unless

Using this list, you can combine sentences in such a way as to make their implied relationship clear. For instance, in the following example, *weather conditions* seems to be the cause for the situation in the first sentence. If we use the word CAUSE as our combining signal, then we could choose the most appropriate conjunction from the list to show that relationship. Here's how it works:

Base 1:   The controller delayed the airplane's takeoff.
Base 2:   The weather conditions were threatening.   (CAUSE)
Result: The controller delayed the airplane's takeoff

$$\left\{ \begin{array}{l} \textit{because} \\ \textit{since} \\ \textit{as} \end{array} \right\} \quad \text{the weather conditions were threatening.}$$

Because is the best choice here, although *since* would also be possible. Note that *as* would not work in this example because it could refer to time rather than cause. The same problem often exists with *since*, as in the following ambiguous sentence:

I haven't seen him since he's been living in Springville.

We have created complex sentences by placing the base clause first, followed by the subordinate clause. But for some purposes—for special emphasis or as a transition from the previous sentence—we can reverse the order, placing the subordinate clause at the beginning:

Base 1:   The weather was very bad.   (LIMITATION)
Base 2:   The men did not hesitate to go fishing.
Result: *Although* the weather was very bad, the men did not hesitate to go fishing.

Although complex sentences are used in personal writing, they occur with much higher frequency in explanatory and persuasive writing, where it becomes important to show various logical relationships. For that reason, we will expand in later chapters the discussion started here.

COMBINING BASIC SENTENCES BY INSERTION

Creating new, expanded sentences by insertion involves combining two or more sentences containing some words that are the same. In such cases, we delete the duplicate or "old" information from one sentence, retaining only the "new" information or descriptive material. Then we insert what is left into the sentence chosen as the *base sentence*. To demonstrate, we'll use this descriptive paragraph in which a student writer has supplied many specific details.

> **1.** The sparkling water rolls up against the beach. **2.** The water is crystal clear as I take my usual morning stroll. **3.** The morning air comes alive with the fresh, crisp smell of the ocean breeze. **4.** The ocean breeze creates a coolness like that of an autumn day. **5.** It makes wearing a warm jacket necessary. **6.** My toes sink into the oozing wet sand as I walk close to the water's edge. **7.** The cool brisk water gives my feet a chill. **8.** The tossing, turning water is turquoise-colored and churns up huge waves. **9.** The waves reflect the sun. **10.** Foam surrounds the edge of the waves as they splash on the beach.

As you can see, the paragraph is flawed by too many short, simple sentences. The result is not only a "choppy" effect but also the unnecessary repetition of obvious information. A paragraph with these characteristics is always a good candidate for sentence-combining. Let's look at some common sentence-combining techniques as we revise the paragraph.

Inserting Relative Clauses

One way to combine sentences by insertion is to change one sentence into a relative clause and add it to another (the base sentence). To be combined in this way, both sentences must contain some reference to the same person or thing, whether by a noun, a noun phrase, or a personal pronoun (*it, they, them, he, him, she, her,* etc.). The reference in the insert sentence (the sentence to be added) is then replaced with a relative pronoun, *who, whom, which,* or *that.* Let's use sentences 1 and 2 to demonstrate the technique:

Base Sentence: The sparkling water rolls up against the beach.
                         which
Insert Sentence: ~~The water~~ is crystal clear as I take my usual morning stroll.

Adding the newly created relative clause "which is crystal clear" after *water* in the base sentence and retaining the remaining material yields the following sentence:

Result: The sparkling water, which is crystal clear, rolls up against the beach as I take my usual morning stroll.

Sentences 3, 4, and 5 all refer to the "morning air" in sentence 2, and repeat material unnecessarily. In fact, sentences 3 and 4 indicate a need for combining, since 3 ends and 4 begins with the same material: "the ocean breeze." Using sentence 3 as the base sentence, let's combine them:

Base: The morning air comes alive with the fresh, crisp smell of the ocean breeze.

which
Insert: ~~The ocean breeze~~ creates a coolness like that of an autumn day.
which
Insert: ~~It~~ (the ocean breeze) makes wearing a warm jacket necessary.
Result: The morning air comes alive with the fresh, crisp smell of the ocean breeze, *which* creates a coolness like that of an autumn day and *which* makes wearing a warm jacket necessary.

Using the same technique, we can combine sentences 8 and 9 by changing sentence 9 into a relative clause:

Base: The tossing, turning water is turquoise-colored and churns up huge waves.
that
Insert: ~~The waves~~ reflect the sun.
Result: The tossing, turning water is turquoise-colored and churns up huge waves *that* reflect the sun.

Here's the revised paragraph:

1. The sparkling water, which is crystal clear, rolls up against the beach as I take my usual morning stroll. 2. The morning air comes alive with the fresh, crisp smell of the ocean breeze, which creates a coolness like that of an autumn day and which makes wearing a warm jacket necessary. 3. My toes sink into the oozing wet sand as I walk close to the water's edge. 4. The cool brisk water gives my feet a chill. 5. The tossing, turning water is turquoise-colored and churns up huge waves that reflect the sun. 6. Foam surrounds the edge of the waves as they splash on the beach.

Although the sentence combining has eliminated the primer-like style of the original paragraph and has solved part of the repetition problem, much unnecessary material remains. In addition, too many relative clauses make the passage cumbersome and difficult to read. Using the revised paragraph, let's examine another technique that can eliminate excessive relative clauses.

Inserting Adjective Phrases

In sentence 1 of the revised paragraph, the descriptive material in the relative clause is "crystal clear." By deleting the unnecessary "which is," we leave only the adjective, gaining further compression. Generally, in such cases, we place the adjective before the noun, as in:

Result: The sparkling, *crystal-clear* water rolls up against the beach as I take my morning stroll.

But there are other possibilities of placement, particularly when two or more words are involved. We could, in this instance, place the adjective phrase at the beginning of the sentence or leave it after the noun, setting it off with commas or dashes.

Result: *Crystal clear,* the sparkling water rolls up against the beach . . .
Result: The sparkling water—*crystal clear*—rolls up against the beach . . .

As you can see, different placements give different emphasis to the descriptive material; you decide which emphasis is best on the basis of your purpose in writing the sentence.

Not only single adjectives but also adjective phrases can be created by deleting unnecessary information and inserting the rest into the base sentence. For example, in sentence 2 the verb *comes* adds little to the descriptive imagery. Thus, we eliminate it, setting the remainder of the predicate off with commas:

> Original: The morning air ~~comes~~ alive with the fresh, crisp smell of the ocean breeze . . .
>
> Revised: The morning air, alive with the fresh, crisp smell of the ocean breeze, which creates a coolness like that of an autumn day and which makes wearing a warm jacket necessary . . .

This change has created a fragment by deleting the main verb, requiring us to eliminate the relative pronoun *which* and use *creates* as the main verb. Now let's move to the relative clause "which makes wearing a warm jacket necessary." By deleting *which* and *wearing*, and changing *makes* to *making*, we have created "making a warm jacket necessary." Here's the resulting sentence:

> Result: The morning air, alive with the fresh, crisp smell of the ocean breeze, creates a coolness like that of an autumn day, making a warm jacket necessary.

In this sentence, the slight change in meaning is not important because *air* and *breeze* are practically synonymous. But you do need to test meaning constantly as you experiment with sentence-combining. It is better to have several short, simple sentences than a complex one that distorts your intended meaning.

The sentences in our sample paragraph lend themselves to still other kinds of adjective phrase invention. For instance, sentence 6 could be made passive and the verb could then be deleted to produce an adjective phrase that could be added to sentence 5:

> the edges of the waves ~~are~~ surrounded by foam as they splash on the beach.

But we note that repetition of *the waves* offers a further opportunity for compression, and so we change "the edges of the waves" to "their edges." Putting all these elements into sentence 5 and reordering some of them, the final version might look like this:

> Result: Tossing and turning, the turquoise-colored water churns up huge waves that reflect the sun, their edges surrounded by foam as they splash on the beach.

Following similar techniques to combine sentences 3 and 4, let's see how our paragraph looks (and sounds) now:

1. The sparkling, crystal-clear water rolls up against the beach as I take my usual morning stroll. **2.** The morning air, alive with the fresh, crisp smell of the ocean breeze, creates a coolness like that of an autumn day, making a warm jacket necessary. 3. As I walk close to the water's edge, my toes sink into the oozing wet sand, my feet chilled by the cool brisk water. 4. Tossing and turning, the turquoise-colored water churns up huge waves that reflect the sun, their edges surrounded by foam as they splash on the beach.

Although our final revision seems more descriptive than the original, no details were added. The sentence-combining techniques of deleting, inserting, and reordering eliminated the unnecessary, non-descriptive words, thus focusing attention on the rich detail the student had provided.

The Cumulative Sentence

Our discussions of sentence combining have suggested techniques for creating complex sentence structures and for inserting rich descriptive details from one sentence into another. There are, however, pitfalls to this process. Although carefully considered insertions may result in effective description by appealing to the reader's senses—sight, hearing, taste, touch, and smell—too many modifiers can produce sentences that are almost unreadable:

All the ten thousand "catch-as-catch-can" spectators, old and young alike, standing with their heads thrown back and their mouths dropped in awe, emitting not a sound, not even the shuffle of feet nor the rustle of clothing, watched in frozen silence, a silence that seemed almost an entity in itself, the drama of life and death, of hesitation and despair, being enacted on the bridge.

As you can see, this sentence is *too* rich in detail; it contains so many inserted modifiers between the subject and the predicate and between the elements of the predicate that the base sentence—*all the spectators watched the drama being enacted on the bridge*—almost gets lost. When you wish to add this much detail, you would do well to choose the *cumulative* or loose sentence. In a cumulative sentence, the base sentence is *followed* by the inserted modifiers, as in this example using *-ing* structures:

Writing is often a frustrating task, demanding long hours of thought, requiring us to sharpen both wit and pencil, forcing us to discipline ourselves to inevitable criticism.

Unlike the modifiers in the previous, "muddy" example, the insertions in this sentence do not interrupt the elements of the base sentence. They follow after it, leaving the base sentence intact and clear. At the same time, the cumulative sentence structure allows the writer to add modifiers and thus move from general to more and more specific. Structurally, the cumulative sentence looks like this:

BASE SENTENCE, modifier a, modifier b, modifier c, etc.

We can see how this pattern applies to the example above, in which each modifying phrase refers directly back to the base (italicized here):

Writing is often a frustrating task,
> demanding long hours of thought,
> requiring us to sharpen both wit and pencil,
> forcing us to discipline ourselves to inevitable criticism.

In this sentence, we move through only two levels of generality—from the general statement in the base to specifics in the series of modifiers—in this case, three parallel *-ing* phrases. Note that any of the modifiers can be rearranged or omitted without destroying the basic meaning of the sentence. But such a sentence can be expanded further by adding descriptive or explanatory details to the modifying phrases, as one student did in the next example. Again we will use indentation to indicate increasingly specific details and to show what they modify.

The Berlin street was alive with activity—
> everywhere people walking or riding, (modifies BASE)
> Volkswagens swarming like flies, (modifies BASE)
>> black and noisy, (modifies *Volkswagens*)
> young children with red cheeks playing on the sidewalk, (modifies BASE)
> elderly women walking slowly, (modifies BASE)
>> huddled in their woolen coats (modifies *women*)
>>> clutched tightly against the bitter wind, (modified *coats*)
> all ages riding bicycles. (modifies BASE)

Because the student uses a number of modifying levels, he makes use of *parallelism* to make clear to readers which modifiers refer directly to the base. Parallelism involves the repetition of similar structures, words, or ideas. In this case, the student uses a series of *-ing* phrases: *walking or riding, swarming, playing, walking.* When you combine and expand sentences, parallelism is an effective device to help your readers follow your meaning. To test whether you have provided such clues for your reader, you may find that the analytical method discussed here is useful.

SUMMARY

In this chapter, we have approached sentences with an eye to both their form and the writing process: indicating the characteristics of different types of sentences and suggesting strategies for creating more complex structures from basic, simple sentences. The reordering, joining, and combining techniques discussed here suggest only a few of the possibilities. Although these procedures are not limited to personal writing, some are especially useful in narrative and description.

Reordering simple sentences and joining basic patterns to create compound sentences are especially common techniques in personal narratives. Expanding sentences with modifying structures is particularly useful in any writing that involves description. Sentence-combining techniques can enhance all kinds of writing. Writing is most effective when the sentences are varied and tailored to the purpose of the writer and the needs of the reader.

ASSIGNMENTS

For Discussion

1. Using the frame on page 66, identify the subject and the predicate components of the following simple sentences. Which have reordered adverbs? Which have inverted sentence order?

    a. Emotions play a large part in dancing.

    b. Next came the railroads.

    c. About three houses down on the opposite side of the street lived a cute little girl named Kathy.

    d. The present population of the world is four billion people.

    e. Balance is the key factor in skiing.

    f. The following year I dropped math.

    g. One night I rode my bicycle on the fraternity house roof.

    h. Clarke gives us a picture of a world that is similar to today's society.

    i. I was in the senior band that winter.

    j. Overnight he became a big star.

    k. An Albert Einstein he isn't.

    l. Up the ladder came Tom.

2. Identify the simple and compound sentences used in the following student narrative of an adventure on a railroad bridge. What advice about sentence choice could you give the student to make the descriptions even more exciting? Can fragments be used to advantage anywhere?

High Bridge

We parked the motorcycle on the side of the highway and climbed up. The hill was covered with limestone gravel, glittering in the bright sunlight. The loose stones rolled down the incline as our feet sought firm footholds. Finally, my hand grasped the rusted steel railing at the top and I pulled Robin up behind me. We were at High Bridge after a half hour of hard riding and climbing.

We looked all around us and tried to take in the beauty below us. There was even beauty and grace in the old, black and rusty railroad bridge spanning the open distance between two high rising cliffs. We could see the muddy water of the river below us, moving slowly in its sluggish course. The tall oaks and their neighbors in the river valley tried in vain to reach up to us. We were almost higher than the birds in their own territory.

I held a small rock over the edge and released it. We started to count, one, two, three . . . nine . . . ten, splash! In that brief span of ten seconds the small missile seemed to hang motionless in the atmosphere. I didn't see it move; it just shrank until it crashed into the water. All this time Robin held her breath and ended up just saying, "God!"

It all seemed so serene; we were just suspended in space by a network of steel. Whomp! WH OO MP! As soon as my ears picked up this deep bellow, I experienced a sickening realization. There was a train coming and we were both in the middle of the bridge. The diesel engines were thundering as it came churning ever closer. It was too late to get off the bridge, so we sat down on the catwalk clutching the handrail. Now came the monster. The bell was clanging constantly as his white eye flashed back and forth. The bridge began to shake violently to and fro. The metal struts were singing like telephone lines. I wondered if that structure of rusted steel could hold such weight on its back.

I looked around at Robin as if nothing was happening, but I really felt sick. Robin was still there—staring wordlessly at me. The cars rolled by as the caravan of steel picked up speed. All I could see was a blur of colors, letters, and numbers posted differently on every one. The wheels clicked monotonously over the small breaks where the rails had been joined. The springs on the cars creaked as they were pitched from one side to the other. Will this never end? How long have we been hanging here? Then we saw the red caboose. It looked like a small house on wheels chasing after the iron serpent ahead of it. We both knew that our ordeal was finally over. As the fire-breather snake wound back into the hills from where it came, the bridge became quiet and stable. We stood up and made our way back to the motorcycle. Neither of us spoke.

3. Identify the fragments in the following student examples. Be able to provide a possible explanation (other than punctuation) as to why the students may have confused each one with a complete sentence structure.

   a. The people are moving out of the cities to own homes with lawns. Places away from the bustle of the cities. Good farm land is being bought up and subdivided. Thousands of new homes are built every year. More and more mouths to feed with less land to produce necessary crops.

   b. But if some parents think married students should be on their own and need help financially, then the young couple will have to work, but not make enough money to live adequately and save money, too. Which they will need desperately in the future.

   c. If we have disagreements about where to go or what to do. My wife does not insist that we do what she has planned.

   d. The great awakening started back in the 1950s when a mild form of violence make its way into films. For example, the Bogart movies of the 50s.

   e. The Puritans also had crime and mental disease among their ranks. Disease being the biggest problem they had.

f. College athletic recruiters are as bad as advertising agents; they both have something to sell. The advertising agent selling his product, the college recruiter selling his school.

g. The amateur golf player and the professional both have their own unique character and style of playing. Such as their clothes: one could be fancy and flashy, the other not so colorful. The individual way they swing and hit the ball.

h. As I look over the green lush grass of the meadows and fields, I am aware that there are many beautiful things going on. There is new life and excitement everywhere. Rabbits crawling out of their winter homes in the ground. Rabbits taking their first breath of crystal-clear spring air. Also, the trees and flowers trying desperately to show their new beauty.

4. In the following descriptive sentences, identify first the base sentence, then the modifiers. Reproduce, if you can, the underlying insert sentence for each modifier.

a. The water skier, his life-jacket a bright orange band, swerved suddenly.

—student paper

b. Disgusted with the turn of events, the cyclist propelled her machine toward the hills, purple in the distance.

—student paper

c. The silent birds sat motionless in the sand.

—student paper

d. He felt the impact of the blow throughout the length of his arm, jarring his flesh lightly.

—Richard Wright

e. Silently we unlatch the door, letting the drift fall in, and step abroad to face the cutting air.

—Henry David Thoreau

f. They are feeding it on to the conveyor belt, a moving rubber belt a couple of feet wide which runs a yard or two behind them.

—George Orwell

g. It had an amber tree against a blue-green background, resplendent with fruits and flowers and the all-important roots.

—Jane Howard

h. During the climb, I had seen the moss-covered boulders mottled by the shafts of bright sunlight which fell through the canopy of green leaves overhead.

—student paper

i. Porch lights cast long streamers of light and shadow over the flooded yards, revealing through the rain a picnic table submerged to its bench; a child's swing set, the seats covered, the chains swaying eerily back and forth in the current; a large rubber ball caught in an eddy between trees and chasing frantically around and around.

—student paper

For Practice

1. Rewrite the sentences in exercise 3, working the fragments into complete sentences.

2. Rewrite the following student paragraphs, making use of short simple sentences or compound sentences to add a stronger air of immediacy. Add details if you feel they would make the narrative more effective.

    a.   I got a taxi and headed for the National Airport in Washington, D.C. I figured it to be about five miles away—it was more like thirty. "Damnation" was all I kept saying. The driver had been covered with perspiration from waiting outside the cab, but he was cooling off now in the air-conditioned cab, and loving it. I asked him to step on the gas and he did, quite readily. I think that he must have been drunk.

    When I arrived at the National Airport, I ran up and down stairs to get to my terminal, dragging my bicycle behind me. A man asked me when I made it there what flight I was to be on. "Eastern Flight 547," I replied. "There she goes!" he said as he pointed out the window at the red tail-lights of my plane disappearing into the black sky. I was only five minutes late.

    b.   Sunday morning at ten o'clock, Tony, Albert, and I were in the canoe ready for the "Great Canoe Race." The gun went off and we were on our way down the river. The first part of the race we were in the lead, but someone had drilled a hole in our canoe. I had to take my shoes off and start bailing the canoe. As we neared the finish it was obvious we would not win so Tony decided to tip the canoe. At which time I lost my shoes and car keys. The water was thirty-six degrees Fahrenheit. My skin turned a pale blue and I thought I was dying. We came in fourth in the "Great Canoe Race" and won absolutely no prize at all, but we did get our picture put in the school newspaper.

3. Create an expanded sentence from each of the following sets of sentences. Change the insert sentences into the structures signalled in parentheses before inserting them into the base sentence. Experiment with rearranging sentences that can be reordered, making sure that you use appropriate punctuation.

    a. Base: The beach is backed by lofty pine trees.
    The pine trees create a cathedral interior of the north woods. (relative clause)

    b. Base: The eyes cover nearly the entire width of the owl's head.
    The eyes are a hundred times more sensitive to light than man's. (relative clause)

    c. Base: The Chippewa Indians called it Gitchegome.
            The Chippewa Indians lived on the shores of Lake Superior. (relative clause)

    d. Base: The river water is stained with tannic acid from the dead leaves of the forest.
            The water is tea-colored. (relative clause)

    e. Base: I wearily carried the last load of clothing to my dormitory room.
            The load was heavy. (adjective)
            The clothing was rumpled. (adjective)
            The dormitory room was cluttered. (adjective)
            The dormitory room was lonely. (adjective)

    f. Base: The porcupine lay beneath a tree.
            The porcupine was still. (adjective)
            The porcupine was cold. (adjective)
            The porcupine was warm a moment ago. (adjective)
            The porcupine was alive a moment ago. (adjective)

    g. Base: The river carries tons of water into the lake.
            The water is foaming with white froth. (*-ing* adjective phrase)
            The water is booming through caves. (*-ing* adjective phrase)
            The water is roaring through walls of rock. (*-ing* adjective phrase)

4. As in the example on page 76, join each sentence group into a complex sentence. Using the combining signal given, refer to the list on page 77 to choose an appropriate subordinator. Then experiment with reordering each subordinate clause. (Examples are adapted from sentences in Wendell Berry's *The Unforeseen Wilderness.*)

    a. Base: There is nothing to be found.
            I slip up and examine the spot. (TIME)

    b. Base: You would hardly notice that it is water.
            There were not shadows and ripples. (CONDITION)

    c. Base: Some of the duller trees are already shedding.
            The slopes have not yet taken on the bright colors of the maples. (LIMITATION)

    d. Base: I no longer had the faintest shadow of a wish to go any farther.
            My pride held on to my intentions a while longer. (LIMITA-TION)

    e. Base: It was my own strangeness that I felt.
            I was a man out of place. (CAUSE)

5. Using the sentence-combining techniques studied in the chapter, expand the following base sentences in as many ways as possible, being sure to match up the nouns you modify with the subjects in the insert sentences. (You may use structures other than those studied in this chapter if they suit your needs.)

    a. Base: Mountains surround the lake.
            The mountains are high.

The mountains rise in peaks.
The mountains are gray granite.
The peaks are snow-covered.
The lake is blue.
The lake is cold.
The lake is deep.

b.   Base: The two people pitched their tent.
The two people were young.
The two people were intent on their task.
The two people were pounding in the stakes.
They (the two people) were pulling on the ropes.
They were adjusting the poles.
They were building a shelter.
A shelter protects them from the weather.
The weather is cold.
The weather is rainy.
The weather is windy.

c.   Base: The spectator becomes expert in the ritual.
The ritual is of insult.
The ritual is of provocation.
The ritual is of braggadocio.
The spectator boasts of the prowess of his team.
The spectator (he) exaggerates the prowess.
He belittles the skill of the other team.
He develops feuds.
The feuds are long-standing.
He carries on a war with the umpires.
The war is a guerilla war.
He consumes mountains of hot dogs all the while.
He drinks oceans of soda pop all the while.

6.   If you have not already done so, combine the sentences in **3b** to create a cumulative sentence. Then analyze the expanded sentence to determine whether each added modifier modifies the base sentence directly or some word in the preceding structure.

5

Language in Personal Writing

"Watch your language!"

You may have heard this warning from your parents when you were a child. Here it is again, this time referring not only to avoiding offensive language but to recognizing the importance of selecting all words thoughtfully and carefully. Particularly in personal writing, writers reveal much about themselves through the words they use. For example, they can disclose their real attitudes about eighteen-year-olds not only by what they say about them but by how they refer to them: *kids, teenagers, adolescents, juveniles, youngsters, young men and women*—terms that reflect disdain, tolerance, or respect.

Consequently, you must make sure your language says what you want it to say and reveals what you want it to reveal. Language is distinctive and personal. Often you can characterize your friends by their pet expressions or favorite words. Just as you can recognize them on the phone by their speaking voice, you can tell who they are by their use of language. Likewise, language is an important part of your writing voice, distinguishing your papers from those of your classmates.

This writing voice should be similar to your speaking voice to reflect your personality. Naturally, you cannot write exactly as you speak because conversations are cluttered with fragments, repetitions, "uh's" and "er's," faulty sentences, and "you know's." However, in writing, you can clean up and polish your speech so that it still sounds like you but is cleaner, clearer, brighter, more acceptable, more attractive, and more effective.

NATURAL LANGUAGE

Why keep your language natural, particularly in personal writing? Think of how you react to people. Most of us prefer those who seem real, unaffected, not pretending to be more cultured, educated, or important than they are. We like people to be friendly and informal. We even expect our Presidents to act this way except on ceremonial occasions. How do we distinguish between natural and affected people? We judge them mainly by what they say. When they talk in artificial, flowery, pompous, or stilted language, we react adversely. The same is true when they write. We respond favorably to natural language, unfavorably to artificial.

Of course, there is a time and place for formal language. We expect it in legal papers, government documents, scholarly articles, and scientific reports, but not in personal writing.

Yet some students think that all writing should be stilted and "impressive," characterized by long words like those used by doctors and lawyers. Probably the student writer of the following paper felt that way in describing her return from a party when she was fifteen:

> I recall well one night when, due to my own stubbornness and ignorance, I came prancing home an hour late. Naturally, my parents were awake and waiting anxiously for my return. I interpreted their anger as distrust of me. A young person does not always comprehend how parental love is shown. I grew bitter that they would be so protective of me. My bold attitude as I answered their queries stirred greater anger with them. The gap of misunderstanding spread wider and we were soon unable to communicate with each other. I felt unfairly treated because they weren't giving me a chance to exert my independence. My attitude towards my parents at this time was hostile.
>
> My parents were at a loss as to what should be done about this situation, which was progressively growing worse. A total lack of understanding existed between us. I felt completely alienated from my parents and tears of frustration overwhelmed me. Well-intentioned discussions resulted in further upsets. There seemed to be no reasonable solution to calm the fires that flared between my parents and me. The tension was not resolved overnight. Only time dissipated the turmoil.

No doubt this paper was written by an intelligent student who selected an interesting experience that was important to her. The passage starts well with the colorful phrase, "I came prancing home." But from that point on, the language fails to capture the feelings of a fifteen-year-old girl being shocked, angered, and hurt. Certain words and phrases seem written mainly to impress an English instructor: "stirred greater anger," "the gap of misunderstanding spread wider," "tears of frustration overwhelmed me," "to calm the fires," and "time dissipated the turmoil." The experience is not re-created in language that allows us to see, hear, and feel how bitter the girl became, how angry her parents grew, or how unbearable the situation seemed. Instead, we sense that the writer is trying to impress others, attempting to be a Great Author. The paper misses because the language is not natural.

In contrast, here's a passage from a paper by a student who describes her desire to be a loner.

> There was that party for me when I was seven. (I have no recollection what the occasion was, probably my birthday.) All I remember of the trial was a superdesire to barricade myself in my room. So I did. Mom was upset later that evening when one of her friends remarked that I was a loner. It was true. But for a seven-year-old, it appeared to be a crime.
> Later I developed an even stronger need to dart from the throng. During high school I slowly dropped out of attending parties and dances. Whether in a bustling pep rally or a tightly packed school assembly, I felt strangled. Finally, it came to the point where only a long walk alone out of the sight of the school could enable me to face another busy event. I recall always being the first to my locker in the morning and then up to homeroom so that I could avoid the clamor.

The language is natural to the writer. We can hear her saying, "a superdesire," "So I did," "It was true," and "I felt strangled." As readers, we can feel her sincerity and conviction. We can visualize her looking us straight in the eye as she chats about herself in relaxed and easy tones. Her voice is distinctive, lively, and natural. But being natural in writing may seem to you about as difficult as relaxing in a dentist's chair. To help you, we offer two suggestions:

1. Rely on short, simple words. Don't search for words to impress people. Remember that simple words are used in the most memorable statements in our language. President Kennedy did not say:

> Do not interrogate government officials about what your homeland can execute for you—query what you can transact for it.

Instead, he said:

> Ask not what your country can do for you—ask what you can do for your country.

2. Don't write it if you wouldn't say it. If you want your papers to sound like you, then write them the way you would sound. Here's an illustration from a student paper:

> It was on the day following high school graduation that I commenced the task of locating employment.

When asked if he would talk that way, the student grinned embarrassedly, admitting he would probably say:

> The day after graduation I started looking for work.

The improvement is obvious. The writer sounds natural, not affected, someone like us, not a pompous stuffed shirt.

In personal writing, where the written language should resemble relaxed conversation that has been touched up for print, natural language is desirable, appropriate, and effective.

SPECIFIC LANGUAGE

Describing an experience or conveying ideas or feelings requires more than using natural language. It also demands that you express yourself in specific terms, using concrete words that refer to what you see, hear, touch, taste, or smell. Obviously, *camping* does not fit in this category; *tent* does. Yet although the word *tent* is specific, it is only relatively so, being less so than *pup tent, nylon tent,* or *green tent,* and much less than *green nylon pup tent.*

Assuming that readers know these terms, they evoke exact images not conveyed by the more general term *tent.* By allowing readers to see precisely what you mean, you more vividly re-create an experience, describe a place, or convey ideas. Note how this works in the following example from a student paper:

First draft: I became aware of sounds after returning from vacation. (General)

Second draft: I became aware of city noises upon returning from vacation. (More Specific)

Third draft: I became aware of the sirens of police cars, the clang of fire engines, the ringing of telephones, the clatter of garbage cans, and the hum of traffic after returning from vacation. (Most specific)

The more specific you are, and the more concrete information you convey, the more clearly readers can perceive the experience you are writing about.

How can you be more specific? One way is to revise your sentences as the student did, trying to provide precise details whenever they would be effective. Another is to stay alert for overworked verbs, worn-out nouns, and tired adjectives, removing them from your first drafts. And a third is to use figurative language to create images that make abstractions concrete. We have already discussed using precise details, so let's look at the other methods.

Overworked Verbs

The verb is the quarterback of the sentence, directing the flow and movement of the other words. By substituting specific, lively verbs for general, overworked ones, you can more clearly convey your thoughts, as these examples illustrate:

The professor *looked* at the student.
The professor *gazed* at the student.
The professor *glanced* at the student.

The professor *peered* at the student.
The professor *stared* at the student.

Looked is the most general word in the list, suffering therefore from the weakness of all generalizations. *Looked* has the added disadvantage of being used so frequently and in so many different senses that it no longer arouses interest. The other verbs, because they are more unusual, command more attention and convey more information. *Stared* suggests a lengthy look, perhaps at some wrongdoing; *gazed*, a steady look, maybe of admiration or appreciation; *glanced*, a quick look, probably as a check; and *peered*, a searching look, probably through glasses or with squinting eyes.

Aside from *look*, the most deadly of all the overworked verbs are the members of the *be* family. Like termites, they swarm everywhere, gnawing away at the foundations of sentences:

am	be
is	being
are	been
was	were

Here's how these termites work and how they can be exterminated:

FIRST DRAFT	**REVISION**
His typing was poor.	He typed poorly.
He is the pitcher for the Cincinnati Reds.	He pitches for the Cincinnati Reds.
I am a worker on the assembly line.	I work on the assembly line.

In each of these simple examples, the overworked, worn-out form of *be* has been replaced with a livelier verb (*typed, pitches, work*), thus tightening the sentences and transferring the action where it belongs—to the verb. But remember that *be* functions not only as a main verb but also as a helping verb. When used alone, it may be avoided; when used as an auxiliary, it may not. For example:

He is used to helping me.

The *is* form of *be* in *is used* functions as a necessary auxiliary in this sentence. In other words, there are auxiliaries that can help your sentences, and main verbs that may hinder them.

Other worn-out verbs can weaken sentences. A few of the more common feeble verbs are listed here:

do	hold
give	make
get	put
have	take

Here they are in action, or more appropriately, inaction, along with *be*:

First Draft: The professor *is* in the habit of being late, but on Thursday, he *got* to class on time.

Revision: The professor habitually arrives late, but on Thursday, he reached class on time.

First Draft: After *making* a rough diagram of a part of the human body on the board, he *gave* a glance at his watch, *made* a statement that we should *put* a label on each part, and then *took* his leave of the astonished class.

Revision: After roughly diagramming a part of the human body on the board, he glanced at his watch, stated that we should label each part, and then left the astonished class.

Worn-Out Nouns

Let's admit it, most of us are basically lazy! If avoiding work is not too difficult, painful, costly, or embarrassing, we'll do so. For example, in selecting nouns, we often rely on the same worn-out few, instead of struggling to find the precise one to explain exactly what we mean. Here are some other catch-all words you should try to avoid:

area	fashion	nature
aspect	field	process
case	kind	situation
factor	manner	type

Please don't misunderstand: You cannot always avoid these worn-out nouns. They are particularly necessary when referring to concrete objects, people, or qualities (a *case* of bourbon, the latest *fashion*, the *type* for the newspaper). But often you can eliminate them:

First draft: In most *cases*, freshmen are not interested in attending the concert and lecture programs.

Revision: Usually, freshmen are not interested in attending the concert and lecture programs.

Tired Adjectives

Just as we overuse certain nouns and verbs, so we overwork certain adjectives. In talking, this practice is common because we have little time to search for the precise word, we can use our voice inflection to convey meaning, and we can elaborate on the subject if we see that the listener frowns or looks perplexed. In writing, lacking this feedback from our readers and unable to use our speaking voice, we should take the time in rewriting to replace such tired adjectives as the following with more specific, fresher ones or with more details:

fantastic	nice	terrific
good	pretty	terrible
great	super	funny

First draft: It was a good class.
Second draft: It was a stimulating class with bright students and a dynamic instructor.
First draft: It was a fantastic party.
Second draft: It was a delightful party with attractive Hawaiian decorations, a lively rock trio, gourmet food, stimulating and attractive people, and a cordial host and hostess, who quietly saw to it that all their guests were enjoying themselves.

FIGURATIVE LANGUAGE

You've been using figurative language all your life! But if you're like most of us, too often you turn to trite but true phrases that once may have been as pretty as a picture but now are as old as the hills. You may have thought that you were being as sharp as a tack, but these expressions, to make a long story short, are as dead as a doornail and as ugly as sin, being much the worse for wear. It goes without saying that it is penny wise but pound foolish to let them rear their ugly heads in your writing. If you do, you may even bore your own family, although blood is thicker than water. Truer words were never spoken!

Once fresh and striking, hackneyed phrases or cliches, like the ones in the preceding paragraph, have lost all their sparkle. They pop into our mouths when we talk, and in our haste to express ideas, we find them handy. But in writing we have an advantage: the time to search for other words.

Devise your own fresh similes and metaphors when they may be appropriate to illustrate abstract concepts. Here are some examples:

Simile: He looked as innocent *as a first grader*.
Metaphor: Excessive team loyalty can be *a disease* that destroys good sportsmanship.

Both similes and metaphors function like analogies, providing an illuminating comparison. A simile signals the comparison explicitly with a word such as *as* or *like* ("as/like a first grader"). A metaphor suggests the comparison indirectly ("can be a disease" = can be like a disease).

Of the two, metaphor is the more common, often slipping unnoticed into our daily speech (*the light at the end of the tunnel, a foot in the door, break the ice*). The test of a metaphor is to determine whether the statement is *literally* possible. For example:

He is the captain of our team.

Captain is not a metaphor because its literal meaning is not violated.

He is a rock in times of trouble.

Rock is a metaphor because a human being cannot literally be a rock.

Metaphor allows a writer to inform readers about something unknown or unfamiliar in terms that are easy to grasp and enjoyable to consider because of their imaginativeness and originality. Unfortunately, in straining for metaphors, writers sometimes produce outlandish or mixed ones:

> He thought he had a key to the problem, but he found he did not get to the heart of it.

In the first clause, the problem is treated like a lock; in the second, like a human being. The resulting mixed metaphor is disconcerting and confusing.

Similar to metaphors are similes, explicit comparisons signaled by *as* or *like*. The metaphor "He is a rock" becomes a simile when the form is changed to "He is like a rock." Perhaps because they are more obvious and less compressed than metaphors, similes are as easy to write as cars with automatic transmissions are to drive and are therefore more popular.

But be wary. In addition to avoiding trite similes ("busy as a bee"), watch out for far-fetched ones except in humorous writing. Anything that seems exaggerated may detract from the mood of serious writing:

> When she laughed, it felt like an 8 on the Richter scale.

> His booming voice exploded in our ears like a hydrogen bomb.

Of course, you should feel free to use figurative language because it adds color, life, and vividness to your writing, but avoid trite or exaggerated expressions and mixed metaphors.

A SPECIAL PROBLEM IN PERSONAL NARRATIVES: THE "I"

Two eyes are natural; a third would be distracting. We can't be as precise about what number of "I's" would distract readers, but you should be aware that in all writing, unless you are cautious, too many "I's" in your sentences may make you sound pompous and egotistical. And because we write about ourselves, personal writing is especially vulnerable to excessive "I's." Look at this passage:

> I took up the first layer of sod, which I planned to use for a bare spot on the other side of the house, and I began to dig in earnest. As I found that the ground was not frozen, I began to fill the wheelbarrow with dirt. With my spade, I picked up several large stones, most of them no bigger than eggs. Then I hit a rock—distinguished from a stone, I suppose, because I needed several minutes of chipping dirt and prying to dislodge it. I realized that it was as big as a good-size lunch pail.

The numerous "I's" in the paragraph make the writer seem self-centered. Contrast it with the following paragraph by David G. Stout:

> I took up the first layer of sod, to be used for doctoring a bare spot on the other side of the house, and began to dig in earnest. The ground was not frozen and the wheelbarrow began to fill with dirt. The spade

picked up several stones, most no bigger than eggs. Then the blade hit a rock—distinguished from a stone, I suppose, because it took several minutes of chipping dirt and prying to dislodge it. It was as big as a good-size lunch pail.

—*David G. Stout, "Solid Rock"*

In the first example, there are ten "I's"; in Stout's version, two. The superiority of the latter is apparent.

How to reduce the number of "I's"? The best advice is to realize that because they are sure to clutter your sentences in a first draft, you must try to delete many of them in revising. By scrutinizing every "I" and tinkering with your sentences, you should be able to reduce the number, thus improving your personal writing.

A SPECIAL PROBLEM IN DESCRIPTION: CONNOTATION VS. DENOTATION

A man was killed and his son seriously injured in an automobile accident. The boy was rushed to a hospital. The surgeon took one look at him and said, "That's my son! I can't operate on him." How could the boy have been the surgeon's son?

The answer: The surgeon was the boy's mother!

Most people have difficulty with this problem because the word *surgeon* suggests to them a man, not a woman. They do not think of the word's denotation, its literal or dictionary definition, which defines *surgeon* as a physician who diagnoses and treats injury, deformity, and disease by manual and instrumental operative procedures. Instead, most think of a male, dressed in a white gown, perhaps even with covered shoes, and a surgical cap on his head and a surgical mask around his neck. This connotation of the word is its implied meaning, one that stems from the emotions, feelings, attitudes, and associations that a word arouses in the reader.

Writers, therefore, must be aware not only of the denotation of a word but also of its connotation. To understand this point, compare the following passages. One, taken from a newspaper ad, relies heavily on the connotations of words; the other, on their denotations. Decide which is which.

Copy A

Come to stately Spain, land of mountains, plains, castles, and palaces. See the old bridges and aqueducts constructed centuries ago by the Romans, as well as the mosques built by the Moors. And you won't want to miss the cathedral at Seville, the largest Gothic building in the world. Of course, you'll visit Toledo's Gothic cathedral, too, with

Copy B

Awesome, inspiring, breath-taking. All these words describe the grandeur of Spain. Come and see these superlatives actually come to life in countless castles silhouetted against clear blue skies, in ancient Roman ruins, in precious Moorish palaces, in historic Sephardic monuments, in stately Christian cathedrals . . . .

Copy A	*Copy B*
its many famous paintings. And then there's also the famous monastery on Montserrat standing on a mountain cliff nearly 3,000 feet above sea level.	In Spain, what man could not build, nature generously supplied: sweeping plains, cloud covered mountains, golden beaches and fjord-filled coasts. To see Spain is to see the unbelievable. The Monastery of Montserrat rising up from the edge of a jagged cliff. The sharp contrast of Barcelona's Gothic cathedral and Sagrada Familia Church with the incredible creations of Gaudi's genius. The Roman monuments of Tarragona. It's grandeur defined.

As you can see, Copy A adequately describes many of the sights and scenes in Spain; Copy B—the actual ad from the *New York Times*—depicts these sights and scenes as they will affect visitors, using emotional terms with attractive connotations. Compare the opening words used about Spain. In Copy A, *stately* refers to something dignified, suggesting esteem and formality. In Copy B, *grandeur* creates richer images of greatness, splendor, nobility, and majesty. Note also the difference between *old* and *ancient* in the references to Roman ruins. *Old* is a common word, overused so much that it often carries little connotation of age (for instance, "old man" can refer to a teenage boy). But *ancient* creates an image of distant historical places that existed long ago and far away. Or compare the description of the Montserrat monastery: Copy B's "rising up from the edge of a jagged cliff" appeals more to the visual senses than Copy A's "standing on a mountain cliff."

How do you find words rich in connotation? They may not pop into your mind as you write your first draft; but as you go over it, search for other words that will more accurately portray what you are describing. Try not to settle for bland statements like "There was a *bad* smell in the room." Instead, hunt for other words that will evoke your experience in readers' minds. Any of the following would be more effective:

stale	smoky	fishy	rancid
musty	fragrant	foul	burnt
greasy	cloying	pungent	sour
damp	heavy	dusty	acrid

Naturally, it takes extra time to rack your brain for the right word, which often is located in your passive vocabulary, the one composed of words you know but seldom use. If the appropriate word does not come to mind, check the dictionary for a synonym. For instance, if you are referring to a heavy person, the *American Heritage Dictionary* would provide the following synonyms and discussion of them:

Synonyms: *fat, obese, corpulent, fleshy, stout, portly, pudgy, rotund, plump, chubby.* These adjectives mean having an abundance of flesh, often to excess. *Fat* always implies excessive weight and is generally unfavorable in its connotations. *Obese* is employed principally in medical usage with reference to extreme overweight, and *corpulent* is a more general term for the same connotation. *Fleshy* implies an abundance of flesh that is not necessarily disfiguring. *Stout* and *portly* are sometimes used in polite terms to describe fatness. *Stout,* in stricter application, suggests a thickset, bulky person and *portly,* one whose bulk is combined with an imposing bearing. *Pudgy* describes one who is thickset and dumpy. *Rotund* suggests roundness of figure in a squat person. *Plump* is applicable to a pleasing fullness of figure, especially in women [note that dictionaries are not immune to sexism]. *Chubby* implies abundance of flesh, usually not to excess.

You might also consult a book of synonyms or a thesaurus, although there is some danger in using the latter, which only lists words, not explaining how they differ in meaning. Under *fat,* for example, the following words appear: *corpulent, fleshy, gross, heavy, obese, overblown, overweight, porcine, portly, pursy, stout, upholstered, weighty.*

Unless writers are familiar with these words and their connotations, they may use them inappropriately. And, because inexperienced writers often like to impress readers, they might select the most unfamiliar word, one like *porcine,* which is associated with swine and pigs and would therefore be misleading when used in describing a stout or plump person (unless the writer really means pig-like). So be careful when using a thesaurus; a synonym book is usually more helpful because, like the dictionary, it explains the different meanings.

While a dictionary, synonym book, and thesaurus are all valuable tools to have when you write, most helpful is to cultivate an interest in words and their connotations, to acquire a taste for them, to struggle and play with them. If you do, you will be better able to make your readers see and feel and hear and smell what you are describing.

SUMMARY

Effective written language requires effort. Natural expression does not necessarily come naturally. It takes time and thought, usually in the rewriting process. Consider your draft from the point of view of someone who knows you well—a close friend, perhaps—and replace any language that such a person would say "isn't you." Look instead for the short and simple words that make up much of your own everyday speech. However, in this process, you must also be aware of the need to be specific and concrete, which often requires your substituting fresh words for the overworked verbs, the worn-out nouns, and the tired adjectives that we all tend to fall back on in speech and that may have cluttered up the first draft of your paper. Be imaginative in your search for appropriate similes and metaphors that will give life to abstractions. And always in your personal writing, listen to the voice that you are projecting in your paper, being aware of the personality you are conveying to your readers.

This conveyed personality may be adversely affected by the overuse of "I's." Especially in personal writing, they can take over a paper if you are not careful, distracting readers and causing them to view the writer as conceited and self-centered.

In personal descriptions especially, choose your words with their connotations in mind so that they accurately and richly portray the scene or person you are describing. Such words not only tell readers what you have seen but arouse in them many of the same sensations and feelings you have experienced; thus you can paint a word picture that will not only inform but delight.

In this chapter of words about words, we hope that you will realize that your commitment to your readers in personal writing requires that you take special care with your language. By your words shall your readers know you and your subject. In a sense, your writing is only as good as your words.

ASSIGNMENTS

For Discussion

1. What is your reaction to the language in the following letter written by a college freshman to his aunt?

Dear Aunt Gert,

It is with utmost gratitude that I wish to express my appreciation to you for the splendid dictionary that you gave me. I shall cherish this gift of great utility during my college career and afterwards. I truly hope that this epistle finds you in excellent health and in full and complete enjoyment of life.

Sincerely,

Albert

How would you reword this letter?

2. What words would you change in the following passage to make it more natural?

When my husband ascertained that I was in a family way, he communicated to me that he hoped the offspring would be a female. You see, he wasn't gifted at sports, being, in fact, quite inept at all of them. And he was cognizant that he would have to engage in football and baseball catches with a male heir as well as escort him to Fenway Park to view the activities there. Well, we had a baby girl. But my husband had not been prescient. As soon as she was about four or five, she pursued him to play ball with her. And a few years later, she kept requesting that he accompany her to the Red Sox encounters.

3. Read through the following paragraph. Then go back and select the words in parentheses that would be most appropriate, and explain your choice:

First an (insane, loud) noise of violence in the nozzle, then the (still, quiet) sound of adjustment, then the (regulating, smoothing) into steadiness and a pitch as accurately tuned to the size and stream as any (violin, musical instrument). So many qualities of (sound, noise) out of one hose, the almost (noiseless, dead) silence of the release, and the short still arch of the separate big drops, silent as a (mouse, held breath), and the only noise the flattering noise on leaves and the (slapped, bent) grass at the fall of each big drop. That, and the intense hiss with the (intense, forceful) stream; that, and that same intensity not growing less but growing (more quiet and delicate, less noisy and heavy) with the turn of the nozzle, up to that (extreme tender whisper, soft spray) when the water was just a wide (bell, circle) of film.

—James Agee, "Knoxville: Summer of 1915"

4. Fill in the blanks and point out the connotation of each added term:
   a. When you tell me to do it, it's nagging; when I tell you to do it, it's _____.

   b. When you talk to your friends, it's idle chatter; when I talk to mine, it's _____.

   c. When you don't like something, you complain; when I don't like something, I _____.

   d. My dog is playful; yours is _____.

   e. I offered helpful suggestions; you offered _____.

   f. Our basketball team plays an aggressive game; your team plays _____.

   g. I am broad-minded; you are _____.

   Can you make up any additional sentences?

5. Create new similes to replace the following:

   brown as a berry   drunk as a lord
   cool as a cucumber   poor as a churchmouse
   fit as a fiddle   sick as a dog

For Practice

1. Rewrite the following sentences, trying to enliven the language by avoiding overworked verbs, worn-out nouns, tired adjectives, and trite phrases.
   a. Her uncle, who is friendly in manner, was able to give her advice about the driving situation in New York.

b. She is one of those terrific types of people who are willing to make a donation at the drop of a hat.

c. Students have the desire to make decisions about the process of selecting their electives.

d. A comparison of various colleges cannot be done by most people in the area of faculty quality.

e. Her fantastic nature was the factor that had the result of her being elected class president.

f. The instructor made use of his knowledge of the field of psychology.

g. She made a good suggestion that the faculty give consideration to making a change in the regulations.

h. My father had the ability to make an analysis of a situation of the type that would have had the effect of placing most people in confusion.

i. Her mother was a definite influence on my decision to put an application in for a scholarship in the field of mathematics.

2. In the following sentences, substitute each of the verbs in parentheses for the italicized one. Jot down the resulting difference in meaning as we did with the verb *looked* on page 93, consulting a dictionary or synonym book if you wish.

a. When the door opened, she *cried out*. (screamed, shrieked, yelled, shouted, roared)

b. He *turned down* the offer to settle the insurance claim. (refused, declined, rejected, repudiated, scorned)

c. She *saw* her mother getting into the car. (noticed, observed, watched, witnessed)

d. He *fixed* it in about two days. (repaired, corrected, mended, remedied, renovated)

e. The noise *frightened* me. (scared, alarmed, terrified, terrorized, startled)

3. Rewrite the following sentences, eliminating as many *I*'s as possible but preserving most of the original wording.

a. Because I am not accustomed to agreeing with Bill, I would like to point out that I do agree with him on this subject.

b. I had dolls that talked and cried and opened their eyes, but I never had a doll that I loved as much as I did the Betsy doll.

c. As I think back on the incident, I can realize now that I was being arrogant.

d. When I consider how my Sundays were wasted, I know that I could have studied more and I could have gotten higher grades.

e. I can remember vividly how I felt when I first drove off in the car alone.

f. I had not seen Terry for several weeks and as I thought about meeting her in an hour, I realized that I was worried about what I would say to her.

   g.   One night as I was returning from the library, I looked in the Chemistry Building and I saw a dog on the lab table, sniffing at the test tubes.

   h.   I felt I was too weak to continue. I thought I was going to pass out. I was afraid that I would not be found until it was too late.

4.   In *Language in Thought and Action*, S. I. Hayakawa points out that, connotatively, words can be neutral, can "purr" (have a favorable effect), or can "snarl" (be insulting to the audience). These three sentences, all describing the same church breakfast, demonstrate how word choice can add different emotive color to description.

     Neutral: Every Sunday, between the church services, the women of the congregation serve a breakfast of scrambled eggs, bacon, grits, biscuits, juice and coffee for $1.25.

     "Purr":   Every Sunday, between the inspiring services, the untiring ladies of this charming congregation offer an appetizing brunch of fluffy scrambled eggs, crisp bacon, butter-laden grits, light, hot scones, fresh frothy nectar, and steaming *café au lait* for a reasonable $1.25.

     "Snarl":   Every Sunday, between the deadening services, the female do-gooders of this sleepy congregation ladle out a nauseating mess of leathery scrambled eggs, limp hogback, soggy hominy, heavy, cold buns, stale, flat, juice-flavored water, and tepid java for a presumptuous $1.25.

   Write three paragraphs describing something from your own experience—a place, a person, something that has special meaning to you—describing it first in neutral language, then with "purr" and "snarl" connotations. As in the examples, make use of colorful verbs, adjectives, and synonyms to accomplish your purpose.

5.   Write two descriptive paragraphs of an eyesore on your campus: one for inclusion in a letter to a friend or relative; the other to be included in a letter to the president of the college. In writing to the college president, use the dictionary to find more formal synonyms for words used in the paragraph for a friend. Be aware of the tone required in each letter. Be sure that you know the full meaning of each word you choose, and be especially careful with connotations!

6.   Rewrite the following student anecdote, adding specific details and verbs that contribute to the action.

After the collision, when we finally stopped moving, I opened my eyes. I was alive and so was my mother. I tried to get out of the car but my door was jammed. So I had to crawl out the back window. My mom got out finally when someone got her door open, but she couldn't really do anything for herself. The condition of the cars after impact made me feel small and powerless. Our car was not badly damaged, because we had a much heavier car; still the front left side was completely crushed. There was broken glass everywhere, but when I looked at the other car

I was completely horrified. It was about half the weight and size of our car. The remains of the vehicle looked like someone had taken parts of it and crumbled, crushed, and thrown these parts into the air to land wherever they pleased. The battery was on one side of the road and the radiator on the other.

6

Special Topics: Grammar, Usage, and Language Varieties

Language is the primary tool of human communication—a skill that we learn subconsciously at a very young age. By the time we have reached adulthood, we have proficiency not only in the myriad varieties of our native tongue, but also in discerning when it is appropriate to use specific varieties. Although we innately know how to use language, we may not be able to explain how it works. The purpose of this chapter is to give you a conscious, basic knowledge of the structure, usage, and varieties of English, particularly American English. The chapter also emphasizes the appropriate occasions for applying the various language styles available to you. Through such knowledge, you should become a more effective writer.

GRAMMAR, USAGE, AND APPROPRIATENESS

In what special situations would you expect the following examples to be used?

1. Youse guys ain't got no sense.
2. Gonna eat with us or not?
3. a. Who did you go to the movies with?
   b. Whom did you go to the movies with?
   c. With whom did you go to the movies?
4. I might could go.

Certainly, all are possibilities in English, but you would not find all of them appropriate for all occasions. Even though sentence 1 would be considered "bad" grammar in most situations, it could be highly appropriate in a "bull session" with friends or in written dialogue. "Gonna eat" is a spelling of the relaxed, conversational pronunciation of "Are you going to eat." The questions in 3 represent three different levels of language: 3a is appropriate for common, everyday use, while 3b and 3c would be reserved by most people for formal occasions. As a spoken form, sentence 4 is perfectly acceptable in certain regions of the United States or in written dialogue, but rarely found in writing addressed to a general audience.

Language usages, then, are similar to clothing styles; some are more acceptable than others in a given circumstance. For instance, the language in examples 1 and 2 is appropriate on occasions when old jeans, ragged T-shirts, or stringy cut-offs would be worn. The options in 3, on the other hand, are analogous to the clothing you wear for public occasions: 3a for everyday school or work; 3b and 3c for formal affairs when you need a tuxedo or formal gown. In example 4, the regional *might could* is as fitting in Tennessee or Mississippi speech as wearing a muu-muu and lei in Honolulu, but both the regional usage and apparel would be out of place in a New York City office.

Like contemporary clothing styles, the grammar of the English language gives us many choices. But can you say that any one choice is innately more correct than another? Certainly our example *Youse guys ain't got no sense* would not be "correct" for a formal party; but the formality of *with whom* in 3c might seem out of place at a beach party.

Adopting a definition of *grammar* from current language study, we use the term to refer to the whole language system, including all general patterns such as sentence word order, the rules that govern word formation, and all the possible choices or usages available, even those often viewed as "bad" or "incorrect." All the examples at the beginning of this chapter, therefore, are part of that total system and represent only a small number of the choices available to us. The term *usage*, then, refers to the individual choices we employ in a given situation, such as choosing between *who* and *whom*.

But how do we make such choices? What influences us to make decisions about which option to use and whether it is appropriate for the occasion?

LANGUAGE USE AND SOCIAL INFLUENCES

As with mode of dress, one major influence on language choice is *custom*. For everyday purposes, we tend to use the language structures that we encounter most often at home, work, or play—the ones that seem most natural or comfortable.

Another influence involves both the *situation* in which we use language, and our *purpose* in using it. Language, like other forms of human interaction, is tempered by certain forces, such as the seriousness of the occasion, the demands of etiquette, the ritualistic nature of the event, the roles of the participants. Society demands a different kind of behavior at a funeral, for instance, than at a Saturday night dance. If we switched these behavioral and language patterns, our social audience would be uncomfortable or offended.

A major influence on language usage is the *audience*. When you go to work, you probably leave your comfortable, faded jeans and shapeless T-shirts in the closet and wear more acceptable clothes. Perhaps, without realizing it, you also tuck away your comfortable wardrobe of language usage and don a more respectable garb. For the easy, slangy vocabulary of your peers, you substitute more generally used words. You change from looser, more relaxed sentence structures to tighter, more concise sentences, substituting complete sentences for the short idiomatic phrases and sentence fragments spoken when conversing with close friends. You consciously avoid usages that your employers would find crude or unacceptable, just as you avoid clothing that might be offensive to them.

Let us now consider in more detail the various social influences on language usage. Much of our discussion here centers—and will center—on the spoken language; some attention is given to the written in the last part of the chapter. Since the spoken form is the primary source of your language usage, it is important to know and understand the subtle influences it has on your writing habits.

As a speaker of English, you have a natural ability to use the language easily in writing, especially when you are not cramped by concern about form or about the social acceptability of your usages. However, if you are to communicate effectively, you must consider your reader's reaction. Students often lose sight of this necessity. Instead, they view their particular way of speaking or writing as something not to be tampered with or questioned. It is true that language usage is highly personal and individualized: Each of us has a distinctive way of speaking and writing, just as we have a unique set of fingerprints or a special style of handwriting. In a real sense, your language is *you*—an integral part of your identity and personality.

On the other hand, language is not simply for self-expression. As the most complex of all human communication, it necessarily demands the use of conventional structures and usages shared by all members of the language community. You might amuse yourself by greeting your friends with "Dirky ratafratch" or "Morning to good you." But if you want genuine communication, you would do better to use one of the conventional greetings of English, "Good morning."

The demands of comprehensibility, however, are not the only social influences on language use. Certain usages may be given greater value than others, even though the preferences may be arbitrary, shifting from one generation to another. An example of this is the double negative used for emphasis. The modern English community frowns on negatives like "I won't go nowhere with you," even though the usage was perfectly respectable in Shakespeare's time.

Usage changes, and so eventually does the grammar of a language. But unlike usage options, the grammar of a language requires centuries to change perceptibly. The grammar system of modern English required almost a thousand years to evolve from that of Old English, while the loss of the subjunctive *be* usage in structures like "If that be wise" has occurred over a span of several decades.

Always, your language communication will be shaped by two major forces, sometimes without your awareness: (1) your subconscious, built-in knowledge of the restraints and demands of English *grammar* (the system); and (2) the usage or choice dictated by a particular social *situation* (which includes the occasion and purpose of the communication, the topic, and the audience). If you wish to communicate effectively, your choice of language must not only fit the patterns possible to English, but must be acceptable to your social community. As a college student, one of your social communities is the college or university you attend. It will place its own special demands on your English usage. And as you become a successful participant in this new language community, you will fashion yet another garment to hang in your usage closet and you will be able to don it comfortably when the situation demands it.

VARIETIES OF SPOKEN ENGLISH: DIALECTS

As we have indicated, although the grammar of a language is fairly static, usage is flexible. We all speak our own brand of English, which is as it should be. But in writing to a general audience, we must continually decide which of our particular usages will aid or interfere with communication. A knowledge of the forces shaping our language patterns and the usages peculiar to the different varieties of American English can help us make those choices. In this discussion, we will briefly examine the geographical and social varieties of spoken English that skillful users of the language must be able to recognize.

Like all languages, English is composed of many varieties of speech called *dialects*. These dialects differ in pronunciation, vocabulary, and sentence structures, but because they share most of the features of the language, speakers of one can understand the speakers of another with little difficulty. If these dialects are a result of geographical location, they are called *regional* dialects; if they are a result of social differentiation, they are called *social* dialects. Other dialects may be ethnic in origin; that is, they result from the immigration of another language-speaking group, so that some aspects of their native language become fused with the adopted language. Pennsylvania Dutch, the dialect spoken in some areas of Pennsylvania by German immigrants, illustrates such a fusion: Aspects of German pronunciation, word order, and vocabulary have become a part of their English as illustrated by their well-known saying, "We grow too soon old and too late smart."

Occupational fields, such as music, coal mining, railroading, the television industry, and professional sports, may produce other interesting language varieties. But these varieties are not generally considered dialects, since they do not vary in all aspects of language, only in vocabulary (jargon).

Each of us is influenced by all these sources. Our speech bears the stamp not only of our home geographical region, but of our social and ethnic backgrounds, and it may also include elements of specialized jargon. Your own speech may contain slang words derived from the particular jargon of your high-school or home community.

Geographical Dialects: Three Main Regions

The English language is rich in regional dialects because of the massive migration of its speakers to many parts of the world. Today, because of separation from the English spoken in Britain and the influence of local languages, many varieties of English exist throughout the world. In the United States, where English became the dominant language despite the many early French and Spanish settlers, three main geographical or regional dialects have evolved. Their distribution and peculiar characteristics are closely tied to the history of the British settlement of the New World and the geographical barriers the settlers encountered. The settlers of New England and the central Atlantic coastal states came largely from the eastern and southern parts of England, whereas later immigrants to the Piedmont areas came from north and northwest of London. The differences in their original dialects account for many of the present variations we encounter in these three major regional dialects: Northern, Midland, and Southern. Let's take a brief look at their geographical distribution and at a few of their differences.

—Adapted from Roger Shuy, *Discovering American Dialects*

Northern Dialect Regions Northern dialect includes both Northeastern Northern (spoken in the New England area north of New York City) and Great Lakes Northern (spoken in the area surrounding the Great Lakes and extending north and west to areas in the Northwest). The division of Northern into two subclasses results primarily from the difference in the pronunciation of *r*. Northeastern Northern speakers pronounce a word like *party* as *pahty*, whereas those in the Great Lakes region say *party*, pronouncing the *r* sound after the vowel. Some Northeastern speakers also have an intrusive *r*; that is, they include an *r* sound between two vowels. Although the west coast states are mostly North Midland, the area around San Francisco has many characteristics of Northeastern Northern.

Midland Dialect Regions Like the Northern, the Midland region is subdivided into two dialect areas, North and South Midland. As the map shows, the Midland region extends from the east coast across the central part of the United States, including the Appalachian region, the Midwest corn belt, and the states west of the Rockies. The dividing line between North and South Midland roughly approximates Interstate 70. The Midland area has been subclassified into North and South Midland mainly because of variant pronunciations in words like *greasy* (North Midland: greasy; South Midland: greazy) and in whether there is a *pin/pen* distinction. South Midlanders tend to pronounce the latter two words exactly alike so that they often must be asked whether they mean "stickin' pins" or "writin' pins." In both Midland dialects, *r* is pronounced after vowels.

Southern Dialect Regions   The Southern dialect area not only manifests the most variation within a speech region in the United States, but it is also the smallest geographical area. During the nineteenth-century westward migration, Southern settlers were more limited by the laws prohibiting slavery in the new territories than by geographical barriers. If Southern families wished to move west, taking their slaves with them, they were confined to those areas where slavery was legal. The Southern dialect shares the pronunciation of *greasy* as greazy, the lack of *pin/pen* distinction, and similar vowel sounds with South Midland dialect, but lacks the *r* sound after vowels characteristic of Midland varieties.

Differences in Pronunciation, Vocabulary, and Syntax   Whether or not the speakers of a region make a *pin/pen* distinction is only one of the specific ways in which dialects vary. Following is a chart listing a small but significant sampling of dialect differences:

PRONUNCIATION FEATURES	NORTHERN	MIDLAND	SOUTHERN
r after vowels	deleted in N.E. present in G.L.	present	deleted
intrusive *r*	between vowels in some N.E. varieties	absent	absent
vowel contrast in *on/not*	no contrast (both rhyme with *hot*)	*on* pronounced as in *pond; not* rhymes with *hot*	same as Midland

VOCABULARY ITEMS			
animal with strong scent	skunk	skunk	polecat
nocturnal insect	firefly (urban) lightning bug (rural)	lightning bug fire bug	lightning bug
large sandwich	hoagie, hero	submarine, sub, poor boy (S. Midland)	poor boy

SYNTACTICAL STRUCTURES	NORTHERN	MIDLAND	SOUTHERN
nauseated	sick *to* my stomach	sick *on/in* my stomach	sick *at* my stomach
plural of *pair*	two *pair* of	two *pairs* of	two *pair* of
fifteen minutes before the hour	quarter *to,* quarter *of*	quarter *till*	quarter *till*

Significance of Regional Differences   Obviously, this discussion of American dialects has touched on only a few of the pronunciation, syntactical, and vocabulary differences in regional speech. But even from this small sample of socially acceptable features, it is clear that in the United States there is no one "correct" way of speaking. Instead, each geographical dialect has its own norm; each has its own cluster of pronunciations, and its own syntactical and word usages that the majority of that region's people, including the most educated and influential, consider respectable English. In their spoken language, Americans do not impose a single "standard" dialect upon their speakers as people in other countries, such as France and England, have attempted to do. True, some Americans training for the stage or national broadcasting may adopt a leveled-off form of American English, sometimes referred to as "CBS" or "network" English, which avoids regional characteristics. But most cultured Americans talk in the voice of their home region, thereby helping to preserve the flexibility of speech and the individuality that are so highly valued in our country.

Social Dialects

However strong a factor in language variety it is, geographical variety can account only in part for the complexity of speech patterns in the United States. A second influence, on both spoken and written English, comes from the many social dialects: clusters of language usages that become associated with social prestige and approval. In the preceding discussion of language, we emphasized that speakers place social values on certain usages: Some are greatly respected and viewed as standard; others, less respected, are therefore viewed as nonstandard. For instance, "Ain't nobody see nothin'" and "Nobody has seen anything" communicate approximately the same message to all Americans because both are possibilities in the grammar of English. But many people would automatically stereotype the "Ain't nobody see nothin'" speaker as uneducated.

Each geographical dialect has several social varieties, one that is the most prestigious, that becomes the norm or *standard* of the region; the others are considered less prestigious or *nonstandard.* Many critics of this nonegalitarian classification refer to standard dialects as "Establishment English," that spoken by the educated and socially influential people in the community. Nonstandard varieties, on the other hand, are usually spoken by people less educated, less affluent, and generally less influential in the "power structure" of the community.

Language use, then, whether or not we approve of such an interpretation, reflects social position. The standard dialects, like a large estate in the country, indicate a more respected social position. The fact that the nonstandard forms, like a three-room house, are just as functional as the standard forms is often obscured by highly emotional factors. Since "nonstandard" carries such snobbish connotations, linguists prefer to call such forms *community dialects*—subdialects within a regional variety that are limited to tightly integrated, close-knit social groups. The community dialects most thoroughly studied to date are those in the large urban centers settled largely by southern blacks who migrated north for economic reasons. Because of their social isolation in the northern city ghetto, they have retained many of the features, both standard and nonstandard, of their Southern and South Midland origins.

The findings of such studies should help dispel some of the misconceptions about community dialects. Far from being "verbally deficient" as claimed by some, speakers of such dialects, whatever their language characteristics might be, communicate fully and effectively with each other. It is only when a community dialect is used outside the group that certain usages might interfere. Just as some regional forms can temporarily impede communication and social interaction, so too can specialized community usages. The broader our personal social base becomes, the more "voices" we need. When we attempt to inform or persuade a widely divergent audience, then we should strive for a voice free of usages that would confuse or irritate some of those people.

FROM SPOKEN TO WRITTEN ENGLISH

In this section on personal writing, we encourage you to write *close* to the way you speak in informal situations. But you should be aware that the written language is never an exact transcription of the spoken. The first and most influential reason for this is that when you write, you lose all the nonverbal advantages of face-to-face contact that you have in conversation. As speakers, we use facial expressions, body movements, hand gestures, changes in voice quality, and the intonational features of language to aid our communication. A frown, a wave of the hand, or a change in voice pitch often substitutes for a dozen words. In addition, we "catch" our listeners by literally touching them or by involving them in the conversation through such question devices as "isn't that so?" or "don't you agree?"

Another difference in spoken and written English is in the grammatical structures we employ for each. Spoken conversational English is characterized by short sentences, sentence fragments that are often single words, and omission of structural "clues," such as prepositions, sentence subjects, parts of verb phrases. In speaking, we tend to use contractions—*I've, he's, you'd*—and often the sounds represented by *'ve, 's,* and *'d* disappear entirely. In writing, because we cannot rely on visual and vocal aids or the closeness of our audience, we must replace many of the missing parts to make communication work.

To note some of the differences between spoken and written English, let's look at a transcription of an interview with a professional tennis player taped by Studs

Terkel for his book *Working*. Next to it is a version rewritten to demonstrate the characteristics of informal English written to a general audience. Note the differences indicated by the italicized words and the omissions indicated by the caret (∧).

<table>
<tr><td>

ORIGINAL

If I go out with *guys* that aren't sports-minded, I feel like a *jock*. ∧ The whole conversation, there's nothing to go on. ∧ *You* go out with a baseball player or something, *you* carry on a normal conversation. But *this one guy* can't get it out of his mind. A female athlete is just so new. It's just like a *kid* growing up to be an astronaut. This *was* never before . . . . I meet *these* fantastically weathly people I would never have ∧ a chance to meet before. A dentist, *he goes* to a cocktail party, who's gonna talk about *your* teeth?

</td><td>

REVISED

If I go out with *men who* aren't sports-minded, I feel like an *athlete*. Through the whole conversation, there's nothing to go on. If *I* go out with a baseball player or something, *I* can carry on a normal conversation. But *other men* can't get it out of their minds. A female athlete is just so new. It's just like a *child* growing up to be an astronaut. This never *happened* before. I meet *some* fantastically wealthy people I would never have *had* a chance to meet before. A dentist *goes* to a cocktail party and who's going to talk about teeth?

</td></tr>
</table>

Even though Terkel probably edited out many characteristics of the real conversation, such as repeated words, pauses, false starts, the *uh's* and the *y'knows*, his version deliberately retains many characteristics of relaxed, informal conversation. As you can see, the spoken version is rich in slang: *guys, jock, kid*. Omissions include the preposition *through*, the conjunction *if*, a subject (*they*), and part of a verb phrase (would never have *had*). The repeated subject ("A dentist, *he*"), although common to spoken English, occurs only in realistic dialogue in written English. The impersonal *you* ("*You* go out with a baseball player") is another common feature in speech, but one that should be used sparingly, even in informal writing.

Obviously, Terkel's version demonstrates more of the authentic flavor of relaxed speech than the revised one. If you wish to write realistic dialogue, you should imitate the devices of casual speech. Otherwise, you need the tighter conventions of written English.

When you write, remember that all usages are relative to the writing situation and to the audience. Just as some standard speakers might be offended by usages they consider nonstandard, so might speakers of a community dialect view some standard usages as pretentious. In highly personal inter-relationships, by all means tailor your spoken language to the personal occasion and the familiar audience. But in speaking or writing to a general audience, you will better achieve effective communication if you avoid unacceptable usages and the special vocabulary of your community dialect, just as many network announcers change their regional pronunciations to avoid antagonizing a national audience.

Just as you vary your speaking styles according to the situation and audience, you adopt a different voice when you shift from writing about personal experience to more public matters. Your written voice then moves even farther from your natural, speaking voice and closer to the one you reserve for strangers. Written English, like spoken English, permits a choice of styles, which are employed according to the occasion for writing. As with spoken English, the levels of written discourse can be viewed as a continuum—moving from informal and casual to highly formalized.

STYLISTIC VARIETIES OF LANGUAGE

When talking to friends or in writing personal papers, you address an audience that is either participating in the event or that can relate to it because of their own experiences. You can, therefore, expect that they share much in common with you. But in writing to a less familiar audience about less personal experiences, you need to be aware that more "distant" readers, having less familiarity with your topic, will require you to employ varieties of language usages other than those discussed so far—those influenced by social situation, by dialect variation, or by differences between spoken and written English. Even in spoken English the distance from the audience can be an influence. If speaker and listeners are close in age and interests, the speaker shifts to a different level of language than that used when talking to parents, teachers, or strangers. But in written English, this separation is not only generational and social, but physical. Gone is the face-to-face contact of speaking; your concrete, live audience is replaced by an abstract, hypothetical one. What you write is the only contact you will have. Because it is hard to address someone who is not there, you need to imagine an audience, one that may be as sympathetic as your friends, as indifferent as a stranger, or even as hostile to your ideas as the registrar when you ask for an extension of fee payment. Consequently, you should tailor your language levels and your word choice so that your writing is acceptable to a particular audience, appropriate for your purpose, and suitable for the writing occasion.

Casual, General, and Specialized English

An analysis of three examples can help to clarify the relationship of audience, purpose, and occasion in determining appropriate usage.

1. Well, you just sour your dough. You start it off with a little yeast and flour and water, and you set it up close to the stove with the lid off, 'cause they say there's so much wild yeast in the air. Then you just set it up there and you leave it sit for thirty-six hours or so. And it gets a tang to it. And then when you get ready to make your pancakes, you pour a little bit of this in a bowl, the way I do it. Now most of the people don't do it this way. I keep quite a little sour dough on hand. Most of the people, just a cupful.

   —*Quoted in Carol Hill and Bruce Davidson, Subsistence U.S.A.*

Even out of context, this paragraph contains clues to its social situation. The purpose is to convey a general idea of how sourdough is made. The highly conversational tone suggests a face-to-face relationship between writer and audience; the choice of everyday, simple vocabulary and the use of the personal pronouns *I* and *you* add to the intimate tone. In the statement, "You pour a little bit of this in the bowl," the use of *this* indicates that the speaker is pointing to the mixture—speaker and listener are almost sharing the experience. This close relationship is additionally signaled by the simple sentence structure throughout and the fragment at the end, which convey only minimal information. Sentence introducers, such as *now, well,* and the clipped word *'cause,* also bear witness to the informal, conversational quality characteristic of close social contact. All of these combine to produce a distinctive style of writing: a written variety that we'll call *Casual English.*

2. Sourdough ranks among the world's most controversial foods. Like fried chicken or spaghetti sauce, it has its factions and fanatics, each of whom knows more about it than the next fellow, or thinks he does. There is the old-fashioned type who believes that the only real and effective starter is made from hops, water, and flour, and must be at least a couple of decades old—a kind of eternal flame that should never be extinguished. And then there is the type of aficionado who is convinced that potato water makes a better starter . . . with a boost from today's active dry yeast, and, though he will concede that a starter *can* improve almost indefinitely as it ages, he tosses his out at the end of each year. About the only point on which Phil and the others agree is that a starter should not be kept in a metal container, for its ingredients corrode almost all metals; thus Phil's kitchen boasts the ubiquitous earthenware crock of the true sourdough devotee.

—Dale Brown, *American Cooking: The Northwest*

Again on the subject of sourdough cookery, this paragraph has markedly different characteristics from the preceding one. The purpose is still to inform the audience about the topic, but the writing situation is obviously not similar. Here, the writer speaks to a distant audience: a stranger not in the room. He can't point to one sourdough batter and then another. Instead, he is forced by the situation to supply additional information, and in doing so must use more precise language. And in order to convey details, the sentence structure takes on complexity and length. The longest sentence in the previous example of Casual English contained 23 words, but, with the exception of the first, all sentences in paragraph 2 exceed that—the longest having 44.

Further evidence of the writer's distance from his audience is in his use of the neutral third-person pronouns, resulting in a more formal tone than was projected by the *you* of the first example. However, some writers prefer to use the second-person impersonal *you* to establish a more intimate relationship with a general audience than is possible with the third person.

Other features of the second example that add formality and distance are the choice of words and the lack of conversational sentence openers such as *Well.*

Although most words in the passage are suitable for a general audience, others are addressed to one with a fairly high level of education (note especially the words *aficionado* and *ubiquitous*). Formal grammatical structures such as *each of whom* also point to an educated audience.

Taken together, all these factors create a style of writing distinctively different from that of Casual English, one we call *General English.*

> 3. For the manufacture of yeast, most authorities have recommended that subsequent to the treatment with malt the mash should be "soured" by the action of lactic acid bacteria, a culture of which is added in the final stages of the process and allowed to act for a period of 12 to 15 hours at a temperature of 59°C. The precise effect of this treatment is obscure. It is claimed on the one hand to bring about a hydrolysis of the proteins present in the grain extract and thus render them more readily available for yeast growth.
>
> —*Magnus Pyke, "The Technology of Yeasts"*

Again, essentially the same topic is dealt with, but purpose, audience, and occasion are drastically changed. The purpose of this excerpt from a scientific text is not to give a practical, general description, but a detailed technical explanation of the process. The social context is a classroom or laboratory. The audience is not general, but highly specialized, familiar with the scientific jargon. Note that the writer expects his readers to understand *59°C* and *hydrolysis*. In addition, the writer usually separates himself from the audience as much as possible: *authorities* recommend, not the author; his quotation marks around *soured* almost apologize for the near-casual tone of this commonplace usage; impersonality is also conveyed by introductions such as "It is claimed" instead of "I have observed." In such writing, *I* is used sparingly, if at all.

To convey precise information, the sentences are long and involved: The first sentence alone contains fifty-eight words. Most of the verbs are passive—"should be soured," "is added . . . and allowed," "is claimed"—contributing not only to the complexity of sentence structure but adding an even greater tone of impersonality by removing any human agents.

This paragraph represents a variety of written English different from the other two, one that we call *Specialized English.* Most writing that relies heavily on a special vocabulary (as in this example) fits this category.

Mixing Styles

Not all writing falls neatly into these three categories; human nature and language usage do not permit such simplicity. But these are convenient starting points of classification. Little writing will be purely one variety or another. Instead, like regional and social dialects, the three varieties tend to overlap.

This overlapping occurs when a writer who is using predominantly one style or variety dips into another for a special purpose. Particularly in dialogue sections, many autobiographical narratives are predominantly written in Casual English, but may exhibit some characteristics of General English in expository passages. Personal essays written to a general audience, like the Montgomery essay on page 25, are basically in General English with a few features borrowed from Casual. Many quasi-scientific articles written for magazines with popular appeal, such as *Psychology Today* and *Scientific American*, are in General English, interspersed with some vocabulary items of Specialized English. This textbook, for example, is mostly in General English, with some characteristics of Casual—the use of the impersonal *you* and the occasional direct references to you as audience. Because we are writing to a general audience, we avoid technical jargon as much as possible, being careful to define any technical terms that are necessary.

SUMMARY

In this chapter, we have distinguished the *grammar* of a language from its *usages*—grammar as it refers to the whole language system, usage as the ways we use the pronunciation, vocabulary, and structural options available. The usages consistently chosen by a community of people can create a separate dialect—regional or social. However, some usages can become more or less socially acceptable than others, resulting in favorable or unfavorable attitudes toward them. Some usages acceptable to a limited group of people may be criticized by the larger community.

Also, we have indicated differences between spoken and written English— even when both are informal and relaxed. The following list summarizes these characteristics:

INFORMAL SPOKEN ENGLISH	INFORMAL WRITTEN ENGLISH IN PERSONAL WRITING
1. Large number of regional and social usages (vocabulary and syntactical)	Vocabulary and syntactical usages closer to those recognizable to a larger audience.
2. Many single words and short sentence fragments	Fragments used sparingly—complete enough to avoid reader confusion
3. Omission of "function" words, such as *at, with, be, have, the, a, because*	Careful inclusion of function words to provide meaning clues for readers
4. Heavy reliance on tone of voice, intonation features, and body gestures	Substitution of more complete syntactical structures and punctuation devices for speech features
5. Numerous repetitions and pauses	Careful choice of words to avoid distracting repetitions
6. Choice of words—slang, profanity, specialized jargon—suitable to a limited peer group	Word choice tailored to a broader audience

Of course, in free, personal writing and in written dialogue, written English is close to spoken and is characterized by regional and social usages. But in communicating with a wide, diverse audience, writers adopt a new dialect, somewhat different from their spoken one—a dialect that has universal features rather than those of a particular region and social group. Because of their commitment to being understood by as wide an audience as possible, writers do this even if it means sacrificing some of the individual flavor characteristic of their spoken language.

In this chapter, we have also tried to make you aware that there are many influences on the language you use and that some features of regional and social dialects are inappropriate when you are speaking or writing to a general audience. In addition, we have indicated that the audience, purpose, topic, and occasion influence the language you choose, and that even in personal writing, the written language is different from the spoken—in a sense, a separate dialect.

As a student of writing, you should be aware of the characteristics of each of the stylistic levels of written English—Casual, General, and Specialized—so that you can switch to whichever will best fit your own needs and those of your readers. Feel free to mix styles when it suits your purposes, but learn to judge when the interchanging of styles benefits communication and when it does not. Strive for consistency. A few slang words in a paper primarily written in General English may add life and interest, but an excess may seriously detract from the style and tone you wish to establish.

Strive also to project your own voice—the intimate one you use for close friends and loved ones, the informal one you reserve for a friendly but less familiar audience, and the more formal one saved for strangers. You have already learned how to make these switches in speaking; you need now to apply this skill to writing.

ASSIGNMENTS

For Discussion

1. What distinctions does this chapter make between grammar and usage?

2. Referring to the discussion on grammar and appropriateness, indicate the language situations in which the following might be most appropriate:

   a. Dja eat yet?
   b. Where's he at?
   c. Ask him where is he.
   d. Ain't nobody seen nothin' around here.
   e. The question is, who's fooling who?
   f. At what are you looking?
   g. What are you looking at?
   h. He's never at home when I call.

3. Analyze the following three passages. How would you characterize the usage in each? The "dialect" in each? Which passage is the most formal? Why?

   a.   I like the spring of the year the best because everything looks as if it is coming to life. In the fall of the year, it looks like it's done everything it is going to do. You see these here things jumping up out of the ground. The trees turning green, like life is coming into things. In the fall of the year, the cold winds begin to blow and the leaves look like they are dying away, don't it?

—*Craig Evan Royce, Country Miles Are Longer than City Miles*

b.   "Well, naturally, I canned that guy. But the next broker was no better. First he touts me into a couple, they barely move, he touts me out again. Then I give him one I heard at the country club, United Fruit isn't making bananas any more, something like that. The stock is twenty-eight, at thirty-five the lousy tout makes me sell. The stock goes right on to fifty-five, but the lousy tout makes me sell. Then he makes me buy some piece of junk he's touting."

—*Adam Smith, "What Are They in It For?"*

c.   And so, my fellow Americans: ask not what your country can do for you—ask what you can do for your country.

My fellow citizens of the world: ask not what America will do for you, but what together we can do for the freedom of man.

Finally, whether you are citizens of America or citizens of the world, ask of us here the same high standards of strength and sacrifice which we ask of you. With a good conscience our only sure reward, with history the final judge of our deeds, let us go forth to lead the land we love, asking His blessing and His help, but knowing that here on Earth God's work must truly be our own.

—*John F. Kennedy, Inaugural Address*

4.   Compare slang terms for the following items with other members of your class or friends on campus:

a.	an automobile	h.	an unpleasant person
b.	a policeman	i.	money
c.	a party	j.	a broken down car
d.	an attractive male	k.	marijuana
e.	an attractive female	l.	being drunk or high
f.	an unattractive male	m.	a conceited male
g.	an unattractive female	n.	a conceited female

Did you find differences that might be accounted for by regional variation? By social dialect?

5.   Look up the listed items in any two of these three books (available in the reference room of the library). Do they agree? Discuss

Bryant, Margaret M. *Current American Usage* (1962).
Evans, Bergen and Cornelia. *A Dictionary of Contemporary American Usage* (1957).
Follett, Wilson, *Modern American Usage* (1966).

     a. *the reason is because*   **e.** *can* and *may*

     b. *ensure/insure*   **f.** *lie/lay*

     c. *hangs, hung/hanged*   **g.** *sit/set*

     d. *dive, dove/dived*

6. Using the *Dictionary of American Regional English (DARE)*, Volume 1 (1985), as your reference, look up the following terms, noting the dialect regions for each.

     a. *belly-bump*   *belly-bumper*   *belly-bunt*   *belly-buster*
     b. *catercorner*   *cattycorner*   *cattacorner*
     c. *baby buggy*   *baby carriage*   *baby cart*   *baby coach*

Compare the term or terms most common in your dialect area with those of your classmates. (There may be other terms that emerge in the discussion. If so, document the region where they occur and check in the *DARE* to see if they are included.)

For Practice

1. In the following selections are usages appropriate to natural dialogue but inappropriate for other writing purposes. Rewrite the passages, replacing questionable usages with standard forms more appropriate for other kinds of writing. From your results and from comparing the two versions, what argument could you make about the use of such dialect characteristics in personal writing?

     a. The father grunted. "I'll be bound. If there was trouble there, I'll be bound he was in it. You tell him," he said violently, "if he lets them yellow-bellied priests bamboozle him, I'll shoot him myself quick as I would a reb."

                           —*William Faulkner*, Light in August

     b. "Oh, yeah, I tole her ever'thing about ever'thing, from now on back to I don't know when—to when I first started goin' out," said Leota. "So I ast Lady Evangeline for one of my questions, was he happily married, and she says, just like she was glad I ask her, 'Honey,' she says, 'naw, he isn't. You write down this day, March 8, 1941,' she says, 'and mock it down: three years from today him and her won't be occupyin' the same bed.' There it is, up on the wall with them other dates—see, Mrs. Fletcher? And she says, 'Child, you ought to be glad you didn't git him, because he's so mercenary.' So I'm glad I married Fred. He sure ain't mercenary, money don't mean a thing to him. But I sure would like to go back and have my other palm read."

                           —*Eudora Welty*, "Petrified Man"

c.   "There was her hens," suggested Mrs. Fosdick, after reviewing the melancholy situation. "She never wanted the sheep after that first season. There wa'n't no proper pasture for sheep after the June grass was past, and she ascertained the fact and couldn't bear to see them suffer; but the chickens done well. I remember sailin' by one spring afternoon, an seein' the coops out front o' the house in the sun. How long was it before you went out with the minister? You were the first ones that ever really got ashore to see Joanna."

—*Sarah Orne Jewett,* The Country of the Pointed Firs

2.   Specify the written variety of each of the following passages and identify the word usage, sentence structures, the intended audience that led you to your choice of Casual, General, or Specialized English.

a.   Before I had gone that 50 yards, I noticed an uneasy feeling. Then, just as I realized I was getting dizzy, I fell. Sitting there in two feet of water, I couldn't get up. The world seemed to be moving back and forth. What I had not noticed before I began to walk was that the entire sheet of water was moving—mostly out, but with small undulations, unrippled. The moving water and the still land around had collided in my eyes and bounced off the ear balancers, so all I could do was fall. I sat there several moments, smiling into the sea, relieved to know why I was soaked.

—*Charles Jones, "A Place Apart"*

b.   In children the infection [obsteomyelitis] is caused by organisms such as the staphylococci and less commonly by streptococci or pneumococci. The germs usually reach the bone through the bloodstream from a focus elsewhere in the body. Osteomyelitis can also be caused by direct spread from infected tissue in the vicinity of bone, or as a result of a wound or open fracture.

—*Adrian E. Flatt, "Bones and Muscles and Their Disorders,"*
Family Medical Guide

c.   Acute osteomyelitis of children starts as a localized infection of the yet uncalcified ends of the shaft of a growing bone. This infectious process rapidly extends to the medullary cavity of the shaft whence it may perforate through the cortex to the periosteum separating the latter from the bone by formation of a subperiosteal abscess; or it may dissect through the epiphysis (the end of the bone, developed separately as part of a joint, and which later unites with the shaft) into the near-by articulation, causing a purulent arthritis.

—*Charles Phillips Emerson and Jane Elizabeth Taylor,*
Essentials of Medicine

d.   *What* and I had an unpleasant time of it during my childhood. Like many of us I was told never to respond with "What?" "Tommy?" "What?" was to be replaced by "Tommy?" "Yes, sir?" or "Tommy?"

"Yes, Ma'am?" or to my peers, "Tommy?" "Yes?" "What?" meaning "What did you say?" was another no-no. I was told to say, "I beg your pardon?" I never understood why I should beg the pardon of someone if *he* was mumbling.

—*Thomas H. Middleton, "What's What"*

For Writing

1. Write a paragraph about an activity common to your geographical region or social group, such as dating practices, wedding ceremonies, or a christening or bar mitzvah, and use the regional or social dialect vocabulary terms for such activities.

2. Rewrite the paragraph done for assignment 1, changing the special dialect terms to more generally used ones.

3. Describe an event typical of your home region that attracts many kinds of people, such as an arts and crafts fair, a drag race, a state or country fair, a street fair or festival. Use words and expressions you hear at home but not in other places. Before writing, practice the prewriting tactic of focused freewriting discussed in Chapter 2.

4. Your local school board has questioned the educational value of literature written in community dialects. Using the examples in the assignment under "For Practice," write a letter justifying such uses when they occur in narrative dialogue.

5. Using the knowledge you gained from your research and discussion concerning Assignment 6 under "For Discussion," write a brief personal narrative or essay on your experiences with this activity.

6. Using the examples on sourdough as models, write two contrastive descriptive paragraphs—one in Casual, the other in General English—about a person or place that impressed you.

7

Rewriting Personal Writing

WRITERS AND REWRITING

Good writing results from careful, thoughtful rewriting. Although it is probably the most important step in the writing process, most students overlook the rewriting stage, apparently feeling that papers can be dashed off at one sitting and then copied in a neat final draft. Experienced writers know better. The American essayist James Thurber has told of rewriting a short piece fifteen times. James Michener never even writes an important letter in one draft, because he considers himself "not a good writer" but "one of the world's great rewriters." Innumerable other professional writers testify about the importance of rewriting.

Why then do most students fail to rework their papers? It may simply be that they do not realize the importance of rewriting. They may not think of writing as a process, a system of achieving an objective through a series of step-by-step operations much like other processes, such as performing a lab experiment or preparing a meal. As we mentioned previously, the writing process consists of three such steps: (1) prewriting—creating and developing ideas about a subject and planning their presentation; (2) writing—translating ideas into words, sentences, and paragraphs designed for intended readers; and (3) rewriting— revising, editing, and proofreading what is written. We will discuss here rewriting in general, as well as its application to personal writing.

BLOCKS TO EFFECTIVE REWRITING

The main obstacles to effective rewriting are practical and psychological. In practice, you usually have little time for it. Normally, you write at the last minute, postponing Monday's paper until late Sunday night or early Monday morning.

The result: About all you can do is write a skimpy first draft, then copy it over. Obviously, there's no time for rewriting.

But even if you finish your assignment early, say by Saturday afternoon or Sunday morning, chances are that you will be so psychologically relieved at completing the paper you won't want to fuss with it any longer. How wonderful to be rid of that nagging worry about writing it! Why not copy the paper neatly, then dash off for a pizza or a film?

Added to this euphoria is the satisfaction derived from the act of creation. We all experience a special pleasure in creating something with our own mind and hands, whether it is a sandcastle, a candle, an omelet, a sketch, or a writing assignment. But often, in our enthusiasm, we fail to see our creation's imperfections. Blinded by pride, we turn in the unrevised paper—an incomplete, imperfect product.

APPROACHES TO EFFECTIVE REWRITING

To overcome the practical and psychological obstacles to rewriting, you must understand and accept the fact that effective writing requires completing the three stages of the process, none of which can be omitted, least of all rewriting. The first draft is simply a rehearsal, much like one for a concert, game, wedding, or drama. It is probably full of errors, omissions, and unforeseen problems. So you must allow ample time not merely for copying the first draft, but for completely redoing it: rearranging ideas to clarify them for readers, adding details, omitting irrelevant information, changing and deleting words, polishing sentences, improving flow, and attending to such conventions of the written language as spelling, punctuation and mechanics, and, finally, proofreading.

Ideally, you should plan your writing so that a day or two will elapse between your first draft and your review of it. In that way, you will gain some "distance," allowing you to read what you've written as others will. Like pie just taken hot from the oven, its value can't truly be judged until it cools. If you can't organize and discipline yourself to start early, at least take a break for an hour or more after completing the first draft to get away from it. Make a phone call, watch TV, take a walk, or work on an assignment for another course. By getting away from your paper for a while, you can read it critically, aware of what you actually wrote, not what you thought you wrote.

As a critic, you must look for trouble—searching for weaknesses, hunting for problems, seeking ways and places to improve what is written—in sum, trying to transform a rough first draft into a polished paper. If you review your draft simply to admire rather than to improve it, you are wasting your time.

As you can see, effective rewriting requires that you have enough time and the proper attitude to demand the best of yourself. Only then can you succeed.

STRATEGIES FOR REVISING PERSONAL WRITING

Rewriting consists of three steps—revising, editing, and proofreading. Revising, the first stage, requires you to read through your paper, focusing on major concerns. As you proceed, answer the following questions about your personal writing. Because each form discussed in this section has its own distinctive characteristics, we have provided a different revising checklist for each.

Revising Checklist—Personal Narrative

1. How can I improve the interest-catching effect of my opening sentences?

2. What other organizational plan might I have used for presenting the order of events? Which is best for my purposes?

3. What dramatizations and descriptions work best? How can I improve others less effective?

4. Where have I failed to use realistic speech and action to portray my characters?

5. What details can I omit? What do I need to add to re-create the episode so that it is as real to my readers as to me?

6. How can I make the ending more effective?

Revising Checklist—Personal Essay

1. What readers did I have in mind when I started? Where might I have strayed from my awareness of my audience?

2. Can I find a more interest-catching way to open my essay?

3. What is my main idea or thesis? Where does it first appear?

4. What order did I use for organizing my ideas? Might another order work better?

5. What examples, illustrations, or anecdotes could be added or further developed?

6. What material seems parenthetical or irrelevant?

7. How does my ending relate to my opening thesis? To the tone I tried to establish?

Revising Checklist—Personal Description and Character Sketch

1. How can I improve the introduction so that it better establishes an overall impression? What information could I add?

2. What organizational plan have I followed—spatial, chronological, or a mixture of the two? How can I rewrite to make my reader's job easier?

3. Where can I add sensory details—of sight, sound, smell, touch, taste—to make my description more vivid?

4. What can I change to make the writing closer to my own voice? To convey the tone I wish to establish?

5. How can I improve the ending so that it relates more closely to my introductory paragraphs and better establishes a sense of finality?

These are the kinds of questions you should keep in mind in revising. Often you may have to delete some sentences or passages, a heroic act requiring you to sacrifice your favorites to the waste basket. On other occasions, you may have to return to the drawing board to provide a new introduction or conclusion, or to add several sentences or paragraphs elsewhere. Sometimes, you may even discover that you have started poorly and must begin anew. We know what it's like. We've revised practically every page of this book, reworking third and fourth drafts—deleting, adding, changing, touching up here and there. It's all part of the commitment that good writing requires.

The following first draft, written as a focused freewriting exercise, shows the marginal comments the student writer made after considering the questions just given for revising a personal description.

Jekyl Island

Every afternoon at Jekyl Island, the beach comes *I need an intro. telling something about the place and why I was there.*

alive with people. People sunbathing or just

hunting for seashells. The sun shines its bright

glow of sunlight on the many different bodies of

people. The tide goes out really far. The cool

water is really appreciated because of the

hotness of the sun's rays [Afternoon time on the *Place this sentence earlier, deleting "on the beach"?*

beach is the time to gather a lot of sun]

   I started laying out on the beach about 11:30 *Redo next 3 paragraph for better organization.*

or 12:00 p. m.. The glare of the sun beat down

upon me. My suntan lotion felt sticky or like glue,

underneath the sun's rays.

   The excitement happens on the beach during

the afternoon. People fly kites, have volleyball

games and swim. I decided to brave it and went

into the icy-cold water. Waves splashed around

and around. The saltwater smell was everywhere.

I love to take a swim in the ocean.

   At night the ocean is quite peaceful until *Reorganize the sentences in this paragraph; it seems disjointed.*

the tide comes in. The *dark* blue ocean brings

reflections off in the moonlight. Nightime on the

beach is calm. After the tide comes in, people in
the beachhouses can hear the roar of the water
hitting the rocks. The tide brings in various
ocean life and stores it on the beaches. [In the   *Move this sentence to*
mornings people search for seashells and   *paragraph about*
sanddollars.] Early at night, is a good time to ride   *mornings.*
your bike, jog, or just walk down the beach.

    Morning on the beach is the best time to be   *Put this paragraph*
out. It's deserted enough, to do anything you   *first. Organizational*
want to do. The scenary during the morning is   *plan centered around*
beautiful. But a sunset cannot compare with it.   *different times of the*
                                                          day. It needs more
                                                          DETAILS.

    All the times, whether it be morning,   *Not a very strong*
afternoon, or night are memorable. The ocean   *ending — seems*
and its life are wonderful to look at. Jekyl Island   *disjointed.*
is so much fun to enjoy.   *Combine the*
                                                          sentences.

STRATEGIES FOR EDITING PERSONAL WRITING

    Often, at this second stage, you might profit from writing a second draft before you don your editor's visor. If you catch some spelling or mechanical errors as you look at the major concerns raised by the revising questions, you can incorporate these corrections into this second draft. Or you can use your original draft for the whole process, first going through the revising step, then looking for editing concerns such as word usage, appropriate punctuation, grammatical problems, and so on, before you write a second draft. If you use this time-saving tactic, however, you will need to analyze the rewritten material carefully and critically before going to the last step—proofreading. As you edit your personal writing papers, consider this checklist of questions.

Editing Checklist

1. What words seem awkward, inappropriate, misleading, or unnecessary?
2. Where have I used imprecise or vague words, such as *good, nice,* or *this*? What words can I substitute?
3. How can I revise so that I eliminate any outworn verbs, petrified phrases, and unnecessary passives?

4. How can I revise my sentence problems: fragments, run-ons, dangling modifiers; short, repetitive sentences that need combining; long confusing sentences that need to be broken up?

5. What words may be misspelled? Have I checked all of them in a dictionary?

6. Have I used too many *I*'s or *we*'s?

7. Have I checked doubtful capitalizations, abbreviations, punctuations, numbers, and underlinings in the Reference Guide?

Although all these editing matters are important, you should know that many university professors and people in business and the professions feel that your spelling indicates how well you write, and even how intelligent you are. Nothing—absolutely nothing—irritates these readers more than poor spelling. So spend ten or fifteen minutes checking every questionable word in a dictionary or spelling handbook. You needn't be a good speller. Simply realize that because correct spelling is important to many readers, you must look up any word that you would not be willing to bet five dollars on. Use the suggestions in the Reference Guide if you have serious problems. But our best advice for everyone is—look it up! Don't be lazy.

As we've just discussed revising and editing, they may seem like two distinct processes to be performed in a definite order. That's not necessarily so. We do feel that generally you should attack major matters first so as not to lose sight of the forest for the trees. Naturally, as you revise your first draft, looking for places to add, delete, or change ideas, you may note a questionable spelling, a faulty punctuation mark, or a weak word. If so, check or change it. Or as you edit, you may spot some revision problem—a point that needs more details, or sentences that might be omitted. Moreover, as you rewrite the first draft, new ideas may come to mind about major or minor matters.

For illustrative purposes, we will skip the second draft stage, editing the original before showing the rewritten version. Here is how the new draft of "Jekyll Island" looks with the editing comments in the margins.

Jekyl Island   *sp? Check*

Every afternoon at Jekyl Island, the beach comes
alive with people. People sunbathing or just   *← fragment needed?*
hunting for seashells. The sun shines its bright   *better verb?*
glow of sunlight on the many different bodies of   *awkward*
people. The tide goes out really far. The cool
water is really appreciated because of the
hotness of the sun's rays. Afternoon time on   *omit   right word?*
the beach is the time to <u>gather</u> a lot of sun.   *Can I capitalize on gather?*

I started laying [*lying?*] out on the beach about 11:30 [*needed?*] or 12:00 p.m. The glare of the sun beat [*better verb*] down upon me. My suntan lotion felt sticky or like [*omit?*] glue, underneath the sun's rays.

The excitement happens [*appropriate?*] on the beach during the afternoon. People fly kites, have [*play?*] volleyball games [*omit*] and swim. I decided to brave it and went [*tense shift — fix*] into the icy-cold water. Waves splashed around and around. The saltwater smell was [*omit?*] everywhere. I love to take [*omit?*] a swim in the ocean.

At night the ocean is quite peaceful until the tide comes in. The dark blue ocean brings reflections off in the moonlight Nightime [*sp? omit*] on the beach is calm. After the tide comes in, people in [*awkward — rewrite*] the beachhouses can hear the roar of the water hitting the rocks. The tide brings in various ocean life and stores it on the beaches. In the mornings people search for seashells and sanddollars. Early at night, is a good time to ride my [~~your~~] bike, jog, or just walk down the beach.

Morning on the beach is the best time to be out. It's deserted enough, to do anything you want to do. The scenary [*sp?*] during the morning is beautiful. But [*logical?*] a sunset cannot [*too formal*] compare with it.

All the times, whether they [it] be morning, [*needed? try dashes here*] afternoon, or night are memorable. The ocean and its life are wonderful to look at. Jekyl Island is so much fun to enjoy.

STRATEGIES FOR PROOFREADING

After all that work on your paper as critic and editor, write the final draft that you will turn in, confident you've done your best. But you can't turn it in just yet; you have another job to do, another role to play. It's now time to don your visor as proofreader and prepare for the last step in the rewriting process.

Proofreading a paper prior to turning it in is like glancing in the mirror before an important date to make sure that you look your best. Yet good proofreading requires more than a glance. It calls for a slow, deliberate, critical scrutiny of your paper.

It's difficult to decrease your reading speed to about five miles an hour to inspect your final copy, making sure that no words are missing, no letters omitted or transposed, no words accidentally repeated at ends and beginnings of lines and pages, and so on and on and on. It's easy to race through a paper, skim it quickly, and think that it is proofread. Proofreading requires that you inch through your paper patiently and painstakingly. You may find it helpful to read it aloud again slowly to yourself, or start at the end and go through the paper backward, sentence by sentence, as some professional proofreaders do, or redot every *i*. Also, even though you may have proofread your paper the previous night (or early morning!), do it again when you get to class. Instructors will generally accept a few neat, last-minute, inked-in corrections. But no one excuses careless mistakes, even when they occur in the most informal personal writing. These checklist items may help refresh your memory as you work through this last, but important, step.

Proofreading Checklist

1. Have I proofread the final draft slowly and carefully, looking for omitted or repeated words?
2. Have I double-checked for typos or wrongly copied words?
3. Have I made sure that the words at the top of a new page follow those at the bottom of the preceding page?
4. Have I double-checked punctuation and capitalization?

Here is the final draft of "Jekyll Island," illustrating how the student benefited from following through these three steps in the rewriting process. Again, we have provided marginal comments to show the major changes.

REWRITING A STUDENT'S PAPER: THE FINAL DRAFT

Jekyll Island

Every summer my family and I vacation at Jekyll Island. Located a few miles off the coast of southern Georgia, it is a small

Introduction is added.

island with vacationing facilities that range from primitive camping to luxury hotels. Although it offers such tourist features as fishing, tennis, golf, and tours of Millionaires' Village, the main attraction is the beach. It is there that time is best spent.

I always find that morning is the best time on the beach. Then it's practically deserted and I can do anything I want to do--walk barefooted in the oozing sand along the water's edge or sit in solitude watching the waves crash against the beach. Sometimes a mist rises from the ocean or the rising sun halos the waves with miniature rainbows. The morning scenery is always beautiful; even a sunset can't compare with it. Later in the morning, a few people venture out to gather seashells and sanddollars left behind by the tide.

Morning paragraph is placed first and developed with details. Sentences are reorganized and some combined.

In the afternoons, the beach comes alive with people--people swimming or bathing in the bright glow of the sun, people flying kites, people playing volleyball. As I lie there watching the activity and excitement, the sun's rays beat down on me, turning my suntan lotion to glue. When I get too hot, I decide to brave the icy-cold water. Once in, I love to swim in the ocean, feeling the waves splash around my body and savoring the smell of the saltwater. Afternoons are definitely the time to gather sunshine.

Paragraphs on afternoons are reorganized and some sentences combined.

At night, the ocean is quite peaceful and
calm until the tide comes in. Then people in
the beachhouses can hear the roar of the water
hitting the rocks. The tide brings in its
treasure of ocean life--conches, sanddollars,
sea urchins, and tiny crabs. Early at night, I
ride my bike, jog in the sand, or take a
leisurely walk on the beach.

All times on Jekyll Island--morning,
afternoon, or night--are memorable. Both the
ocean and its life are wonderful to look at
and to enjoy.

Some sentences are combined. "Tide" sentences are placed together.

REWRITING AS A RECURSIVE PROCESS

Although it is convenient to discuss rewriting as a step-by-step process, we repeat that writers often combine steps. For instance, they may find poorly constructed sentences or misspelled words as they skim through a paper in the revising stage. And they may discover ways to improve the organization or flaws in tone or logic as they edit. Even at the proofreading stage, it is not uncommon for a writer to become aware of reference problems, malformed sentences, or faulty transitions.

Remember that although, as a novice writer, you will be concentrating on one step at a time to train yourself to be a careful rewriter, rewriting is really a continuous process. As you become more proficient at writing, you will probably telescope many of the suggestions offered here into one stage—learning to look for many problems at once.

REWRITING FROM PEER EVALUATION

In this chapter, we have emphasized the rewriting skills you should develop from self-evaluation. But you may find that your instructor makes peer evaluation available to you through workshop sessions or that you have access to a writing center in your college. If so, you should not abandon self-evaluation exercises, but consider evaluations by others as supplementary to them. Remember, you will not always have a reliably critical friend available to read and criticize your work, but *you* yourself are always at hand.

How can you best use writing aid from others? If your composition course is workshop-oriented. then your instructor will organize the rewriting activities. In your writing center, you will need to adjust to whatever procedures are followed.

Here are some suggestions for making peer evaluation most beneficial to you:

- Be sure to take a fairly neat and legible draft with you to the workshop session.

- Encourage your peer readers to ask you questions similar to those listed under Revising Checklist (page 125), or you can ask them to respond to your questions.

- Ask them to point out sections that they think represent effective writing.

- Ask them for suggestions about how you might improve the paper.

- Show the same interest in evaluating their papers as you expect them to show in criticizing yours.

- Take notes during the discussion, or make notations in the margin of your draft.

One word of caution: Don't expect peers to rewrite your paper for you. They are playing the role of critical reader, not your writing coach or coauthor. You may accept or reject their suggestions, always aware, however, that when readers question the meaning of what you have written, some rewriting is necessary.

And leave your ego at home! You will not benefit from peer criticism if you become hurt or defensive. Remember that good writing is always a product of constructive criticism, whether it comes from you or someone else.

PART TWO

The Explanatory Voice: Expository Writing

You've been writing and speaking exposition all your life! Of course, you haven't called it that. You've probably thought of it as informing, explaining, advising, instructing, analyzing, or considering. These are all forms of exposition.

Look at the word *exposition* itself. In a general sense, it means "a setting forth." A world's fair is often referred to as an exposition, a place where nations set forth their artistic or industrial works. In fiction, the author sets forth the background of the characters in the exposition. In a fugue or sonata, the composer sets forth the themes in the exposition. In your papers, when you set forth your ideas or information about a subject, you are writing exposition.

You may be wondering: Why not simply refer to expository writing as informative writing? Why not use the common word instead of the specialized one? Is there some distinction, and does it matter?

There is a distinction, and it does matter. Nearly everything you write could be classified as informative: an account of your attending the wrong class the first day of college, a poem expressing your feelings toward a loved one, a letter describing your dorm room to your mother, or a handout urging students to vote for your friend in a campus election. Exposition differs from these informative writings because its purpose is not primarily to narrate or persuade, but to explain. It does so in numerous ways: by classifying, defining, analyzing, exploring, interpreting, and evaluating, to mention a few.

Now that you understand what exposition is, you should realize why it is important to master this prose form. In college, whether in English, history, psychology, business, engineering, or other courses, most of your written assignments will be expository. After college, whether you work in law, sales, teaching, medicine, banking, or insurance, you will undoubtedly be expected to write exposition in letters, memos, or reports. In a sense, exposition is the writing of the working world and the writing that enables the world to work by providing answers to such questions as the following:

What is the meaning of _____?
How can someone do _____?
How does _____ work?
What are the causes of _____?
What are the effects of _____?
What are the facts about _____?
What are the parts, divisions, or components of _____?
In what way are _____ similar or different?

In answering such questions as these, you will be providing facts or opinions, or both, for the benefit of your readers. Whether writing directions to your home, instructions about assembling a toy, comparisons of new car prices, or definitions of income tax terms, you will deal mainly with facts. On the other hand, when explaining why high school students are poorly prepared for college, how future computers will be better, what the best films of the present year are, or the easiest way to start a car on a freezing morning, you will be dealing mainly with opinion. No matter. In writing exposition, you are free to provide facts or opinion, or both.

But you should remember that your primary purpose is not to convey what you did or heard or saw or felt. Your purpose in expository writing, unlike that in personal writing, is not writer-focused but topic-focused. You are not setting forth facts and ideas to show what you know but to make readers understand your topic. Thus in expository prewriting, you must understand your readers: what they know about the topic, what they need to know, and what they want to know. And when writing or revising, you must constantly consider whether you are explaining your topic clearly, completely, and effectively to your readers.

To help you achieve this purpose in expository writing, we will discuss the characteristics of its various forms, provide various strategies for you to use, indicate ways to develop effective paragraphs, consider language problems, and examine several other matters.

Naturally, in these chapters as in our earlier ones, while explaining these points, we will be writing exposition.

8

The Forms of
Expository Writing

Jack: Had any time to watch TV lately?

Jim: Just *Miami Vice*. I love their wild car chases. They remind me of the old Steve McQueen and "Dirty Harry" movies.

These two students are starting a discussion that could involve some common expository forms used in explanatory, informative writing. Jack might provide a factual description of the main characters or of the cars used. Or, if he is knowledgeable about the way a car chase is filmed, he might explain the process to Jim. Jim might divide movie auto chases into several kinds, classifying them according to their function in the plot: building suspense, illuminating character, or satirizing the American preoccupation with fast cars. During the conversation, Jack might mention a trucking shot, a term unknown to Jim, and then be called upon to define it, to tell what it means in this context. Or Jim might briefly describe the steps in producing an effective chase scene, then show the relationship of the chase scenes to the plot, or he may make a comparison with chase scenes in other movies.

Even in such an everyday discussion, Jack and Jim are using expository forms that their subject and purpose naturally require. In describing *who* the characters are or *where* the scenes were shot, Jack may use *objective description*. In dealing with *how* scenes are shot, Jack analyzes a *process;* when he explains *what* a term means, he uses *classification* or *definition*. When Jim talks about *why* people are interested in chase scenes or why chase scenes are similar, he may analyze *cause-and-effect* relationships or use *comparison-and-contrast*.

In all these expository forms—objective description, process, classification, definition, cause-and-effect, and comparison-and-contrast—you will be called on to perform a dissecting task, to divide your subject into parts so you can inform your readers about the subject. You will explain how those parts operate, what relationships they have to each other and to similar phenomena, why they function as they do, or why they result in a particular effect. Unlike your aim in personal writing, you will be mainly concerned with your reader's needs, not your own.

OBJECTIVE DESCRIPTION

In contrast to personal description where a writer's subjective impressions are paramount, objective description assumes that people, places, animals, buildings, objects, and scenes can be accurately and factually described as they truly are, regardless of a writer's perceptions, associations, and ideas. What is important in such descriptions is fidelity to the subject. As a writer, you try to present the subject not as it seems to you alone, but as it appears to any objective observer. An objective description of toads, for example, enables readers to recognize and learn about them. It would not include your squeamishness about them or any other of your emotional reactions.

As you'll recall, personal description is different. It is primarily concerned with the viewers' minds and senses. In personal description, therefore, we can portray our own reactions, impressions, or responses about anything we see, hear, smell, taste, or feel. In so doing, we may reveal as much about ourselves as about our subject.

In a nutshell, personal description proclaims, "This is my experience of it"; objective description says, "This is the way *it is*."

At this point, you might find the following table useful in helping you determine the differences between these two approaches to description.

	OBJECTIVE	**PERSONAL**
Purpose	To present information	To present an impression
Approach	Objective, dispassionate	Subjective, interpretative
Appeal	To reason	To the senses
Tone	Matter-of-fact	Emotional
Coverage	Complete, exact	Selective, some facts
Language	Simple, clear	Rich, suggestive
Main uses	Writing in science, industry, government, professions, business	Personal narratives and essays, character sketches, literary writing

Organization

To understand how objective description is usually organized, let's look at this opening paragraph from a scientific description of a praying mantis:

The praying mantis, a member of the family Mantida, order Orthoptera, derives its name from the prayerful position it assumes with front legs raised while the mantis is waiting to attack its prey. A full-grown mantis varies from 2 to 5 inches in length, resembles in color the plants on which it rests. Behind the small, freely movable, triangular head with a biting mouthpiece is a long and thin prothorax, which is held almost erect. The rest of the body is thicker, although the general shape is long and slender. The wings are short and broad. The forelegs have sharp hooks for capturing and holding the prey, which consists mainly of injurious insects.

Because the purpose is to present scientific information objectively and clearly, the writer's tone is matter-of-fact, the language simple, clear, exact. The writer's attitude about the insect is not revealed; any trained observer could have written this description. It has no flavor, nothing personal or distinctive.

Because the primary purpose is informative and readers are assumed to be already motivated by their desire to learn, the writer places the thesis statement first. Note that it contains much background information, giving the insect's family, group, and the reason for its name. The description then moves spatially, from overall length, to color, to the head and its mouthpiece, to "neck," to body, to wings, and finally, to the forelegs.

Sometimes an objective description is organized to follow a sequence of senses—beginning with what the readers see, proceeding to what they hear, and so moving on to other sense impressions that will help identify the subject.

Style

Generally, you can assume that readers of objective description are already interested in the subject and wish to be informed about it accurately, clearly, and completely. Background information should be kept to a minimum—to inform, not to create interest.

In most instances, the language, too, should be simple and specific, particularly when addressed to a broad audience as in the mantis example. Of course, an account of a breeder reactor for producing plutonium would be couched in more technical terms for nuclear physicists than for less informed readers. Sentences also are relatively simple and short, the verbs mainly forms of *be* or *has*. Most sentences begin with subject-verb combinations and avoid the first-person *I*.

Gras Rifle

The French Model 1874 (Gras), caliber 11 mm. (.433), bolt-action single-shot rifle was designed by Captain Basile Gras (1836–1904), who presented it to the Commission at Douai in May 1873. The Model 1874 was a modification of the Chassepot rifle adopted in 1866. The general lines of the Chassepot were retained, while the barrel and breech mechanism were modified to take a center-fire metallic cartridge, which replaced the "self-consuming" one formerly used. The overall length of the Model 1874 without bayonet is 51.25 inches, and of the four-grooved barrel 32.5 inches. The weight without bayonet is 9 lb. 11 oz. The Model 1874 épée bayonet has a brass pommel, wooden grips and a straight 20½-inch blade T-shaped in cross section. The scabbard is steel. The musketoon Model 1874 has a turned-down bolt handle. The trigger guard, butt plate and three bands are brass. Its total length is 27.25 inches. No bayonet was provided for the musketoon. A carbine Model 1874 was also produced. The Model 1878 Kropatschek rifle, caliber 11 mm., incorporated the Model 1874 breech assembly with a tubular magazine fitted in the stock under the barrel. This arm, used by the French Navy, served as the prototype for the Model 1886 (Lebel) rifle.

—*Harold L. Peterson, Encyclopaedia of Firearms*

As you can see, the sentences are mostly short and simple, the main verbs are "is" and "has," the adjectives are precise, the nouns concrete. Most sentences are active. Passives are used sparingly, and only to eliminate unimportant subjects and emphasize details of the description: for example, "No bayonet was provided for the musketoon." No wordiness distracts readers from the relevant details.

Tone

Tone in writing refers to the overall atmosphere that a writer creates. In our discussion of personal description in Chapter 1, we pointed out that writers can create a subjective tone—dread, sympathy, irony, and so on. In objective description, however, the tone must be appropriate to the factual, straightforward presentation of the material. Readers should be unaware of the writer; no judgments should be rendered, no opinion stated, no personal impression exposed. For instance, a writer may mention the fact that a driver smells of alcohol, but not that he or she is drunk (a judgment). It might help in your own writing if you remember that you should project the voice that you would use in describing to a policeman an accident that you have witnessed.

An objective description—whether of an eye, a rock formation, a television tube, or an engine—may be quite formal, even dull and dry. But otherwise it may not be trusted. The voice heard in the writing should be that of an authority speaking soberly and calmly, not that of an average person expressing opinions and emotions. Perhaps objective descriptions, as a result, do not make for exciting reading, but they do serve important, useful functions when readers need reliable information. And generally because readers want to learn about the subject, they will be interested in any intelligent, clear, carefully written description of it. Consequently, in this form of description, which implies "Here are the facts," only a sincere, straightforward, matter-of-fact tone is effective.

ANALYZING A PROCESS

Certainly one of the most common kinds of writing in the contemporary world is the "how to." Literally hundreds of books have been published on every topic imaginable—how to bring up children, how to succeed in business, how to improve your physique, even how to write a successful novel. Pick up almost any popular magazine and you will find articles on how to lose weight, how to survive an accident, how to photograph a bird, and so on. Process writing is also prevalent in the professional world; step-by-step directions, instructions, and descriptions are common in almost every professional field.

Process papers are of two major types. *Directional* papers explain step by step how the reader can follow a procedure, such as putting a child's bicycle together or operating a personal computer. *Informational* papers explain a process that the reader cannot or need not duplicate, for example, an earthquake or the pumping of blood through the human circulatory system.

In both types of paper, however, the organization is essentially the same—a chronological, sequential progression from one step to the next. However, spatial organization may also be used to describe some individual steps—equipment used, the nature of the phenomenon involved. For instance, in a recipe setting forth the chronological steps in creating an omelet, the writer might include a spatial description of the pan recommended for use.

As in objective descriptions, the tone of a process paper is factual and straightforward. Occasionally, however, it can be subjective and personal, according to the writer's purpose. Directional process papers, utilizing second person pronouns, may seem more personal than informative process papers written in third person. To a large extent, the tone depends on the subject, the audience, and the purpose for the writing. For instance, telling someone how to avoid a blind date or how to learn to love a cat might call for a personal, even humorous, approach, using your own experiences as examples. But if, as is usually the case, you seriously set out to tell someone how to do something or to explain how something is done, then an objective, factual approach is best.

Directional Process: "How to Do It"

In writing a process paper for informing readers how to follow a procedure, you need to consider the steps involved, making sure that you don't leave out any crucial information and that you haven't placed a step out of sequence. Always assume that the reader knows nothing about the procedure and needs careful instructions. For example, directions on how to light a gas heater may be useless if the location of the hard-to-find pilot light is omitted.

Even simple operations need careful scrutiny of the steps involved. In explaining how to use a screwdriver, for instance, you would need to consider the following steps:

1. Choose the right size screwdriver for the job.
2. Make a hole where the screw is to be set in order to hold the screw secure.

3. Grasp the screwdriver in one hand while holding the screw steady with the other.

4. Insert the flat end of the screwdriver into the slot in the head of the screw.

5. Turn the screwdriver in the direction of the threads of the screw until the screw head is flush with the surface.

Every process, even one as simple as using a screwdriver, involves a unique set of steps. Describing how to change the oil in a car, for example, requires a different approach than describing how to choose a tennis racquet or how to select a mate. But there are some general questions that can help you to organize your thoughts before you begin to write a process description. Throughout, remember that your primary purpose is to answer the question *how,* because a process paper is a how-to-do-it description. Here are some questions to ask yourself before writing:

1. Do I need to interest readers in the process?

2. What must they know about the process before attempting it?

3. What special equipment will they need? Tools or materials?

4. What preparations should they make?

5. What essential steps must they take to complete it?

6. In what order should they take these steps?

7. What is the purpose of each?

8. What results should they expect?

Like the outline for using a screwdriver, most process explanations are arranged chronologically: First this is done, then that, and so on. Determining the logical starting point is important. In describing an effective tennis serve, for example, you would not need to describe the racquet or explain how to obtain a court. You would, however, need to indicate how one step relates to the next—hand grip on the racquet, ball toss, swing, and follow-through.

In writing about the steps involved in a process, you will need to decide whether you will list and number the steps or integrate them as regular paragraphs. In recipes or directions for specific tasks, numbers are frequently used, as in these steps taken from a computer manual:

Step 1. Turn on or reset the computer.
Step 2. Insert the working copy of your DOS diskette in drive A.
Step 3. Type: COPY
         Press the RETURN key.

A more common method of handling steps, however, is to include them in regular discourse, not numbered, as in the following example written by Katie Daugherty, a student. As you read through it, make yourself aware of the devices Daugherty uses to show chronology.

A Flag Captain's Handbook
Katie Daugherty

It's nine o'clock on Saturday morning. Everyone on campus is sleeping soundly, right? Wrong. Not everyone—especially not the captain of a marching band's flag corps who has to be ready for a pregame rehearsal at ten. In order to prepare for a halftime show, a flag captain must perform certain tasks every Saturday before rehearsal. If she routinely follows certain steps, the procedure is actually quite painless.

The first step in this process concerns you as the captain. Immediately after showering, assemble your uniform on the bed and inspect it thoroughly for tears, stains, or other possible irregularities. When you are certain everything is in top shape, stop. Clear your mind. Now mentally dress yourself from head to toe. Do you have the hat and bobby pins to secure it? The T-shirt for under your uniform? The uniform jacket, pants, silver cummerbund, and bow tie? What about white opaque hose, white oxford-type shoes, white gloves and safety pins to secure them? If you answered yes to these questions, place everything *but* the hat in your uniform bag. The hat goes in a box to avoid being crushed. Next, check if your flag is securely attached to your flagpole and then place the entire ensemble on top of your garment bag, so that everything goes with you when you leave—there will be no time to run back to the dorm between rehearsal and the game. During that brief period, you must wait in the band's dressing room, located next to the stadium, recovering from the rehearsal and preparing for the performance. Knowing this, you stock a small shoulder bag with make-up, pin money, curling brush, comb, towel, deodorant, and any other vital personal effects. Add the bag to the growing pile on the bed.

Now that you have yourself together, you can begin to worry about the other women who make up the flag corps. At this point, it is wise to believe in Murphy's Law and be the eternal pes-

Introduction

Step 1

Step 2

Step 3

Step 4

Explanation of need for steps

Step 5

Step 6

simist. Imagine the worst thing that could possibly happen and plan for it.

This planning involves preparing the "Flag Captain's Survival Kit." Its components are as follows: (1) field placement charts in case one of your "sheep" continually wanders and needs to be reminded of her place in the fold; (2) velcro for flags that refuse to stay on poles; (3) safety-pins, bobby pins, masking tape, a needle and thread for on-the-spot uniform repairs; and (4) extra flags, gloves, hats, and cummerbunds to replace the inevitably forgotten ones.

Enumerates supplies needed for emergencies

After stocking the survival kit, add it to the pile and then spend a few minutes mentally reviewing the marching drills and the flagwork. Are there moments during a drill when the corps is uncertain about where to march or what to do with the flag? Do the corps members form curves instead of corners? If so, make a mental note to worry about these problems during rehearsal.

Step 7

Now concentrate for a moment on the flags themselves. Does every person have one? Are there any additional props needed for the show-streamers or extra flags? If such props are to be used, *who* is responsible for getting them to the stadium and onto the field? If you have any nagging doubts about any of these matters, contact the appropriate person to set the record straight.

Step 8

Satisfied that you are ready for all emergencies, you may now dress for the rehearsal. Check the weather and dress accordingly. Then brace yourself for all the last-minute panic calls you will receive from the corps members about a lost jacket or whether to bring rain gear.

Step 9

By the time you have solved these problems, it is time to start out. Run quickly through one final check of the now huge pile on the bed, strategically place the various bags and boxes in your arms, and head for the rehearsal field. As you stifle a stray yawn and shift the garment bag that is cutting off the circulation in your arm, keep thinking, "Being captain is a dirty job, but somebody has to do it."

Final step

Notice how the writer uses such chronological signals as *now, then, next, by the time.* She uses enumeration only in the paragraph that lists the items for the "Survival Kit," but the steps of the process are not obviously numbered as in the computer directions preceding this example.

The format you choose for analyzing a process will be mainly determined by the complexity of the process itself and by the needs of your audience. Because learning to use a computer is a new and frustrating task, the reader who is a novice will benefit most from the simplest possible outline of the steps. Packing for an important event, on the other hand, is a process everyone is familiar with, even though the specific occasion portrayed here is unfamiliar.

In both examples, the writers use sentence structures common to process writing—the imperative sentences of the computer example that omit the unnecessary "you," and predominantly short, simple sentences providing mainly basic information. In both examples, figurative language is generally avoided.

Informational Process: "How It Works"

As we have seen, directional process papers give explicit, step-by-step instructions about how to do a specific procedure. Informational process papers, on the other hand, explain to readers how something is done, created, or achieved, but it is not intended that readers will duplicate the process. Instead, as the name implies, such papers merely inform the reader, explaining the process and its steps. In this type of process writing, therefore, writers need not be so concerned with strict chronology. Also, because the reader will not duplicate the procedure, the writer may make greater use of examples without fear that the digression might hamper the reader's understanding of the process.

In the following illustration, a general explanation of how a computer is programmed, the writer does not expect the readers to be able to adapt the process to a particular computer or a specific computer language. Our marginal notes indicate how the essay follows the form of an informational process paper.

How to "Write" Computer Programs

Hardware is not difficult to understand. It is nuts and bolts and microchips. But what is software? Perhaps the easiest way to think of it is in terms of a simple analogy: hardware is to software as a television set is to the shows that appear on it. Computer programs, rather like those aired on TV, are a man-made effort to turn lifeless hardware into something one might want to spend some time with.

Background knowledge needed

Definition of software

Programs, like television scripts, are "written"—not in English, but in English-like commands that vary from machine to machine. BASIC, for example, is a "language" most desktop computers are wired to understand.

Definition of
language

In the past, computer owners had to write their own software. Today thousands of prewritten programs are on the market, ranging from games to accountants' tools. Running these software packages, as opposed to writing them, is no more difficult than playing a record or a videotape. Just find the appropriate disc, put it in a disc drive and push a button. In a matter of seconds the computer is programmed and set to do the job at hand—from balancing the books to finding misspelled words to playing a video game.

Introduction of
process

Making the programs, however, involves grueling and painstaking work, most of it done by a software engineer, also known as a programmer. Just what is it that a programmer does and how does he do it?

The first step is to decide what you want the computer to do—play blackjack, manipulate text, juggle figures? Once the task is clearly defined, the programmer lays out a step-by-step procedure for executing that task. Think of these procedures as roughly akin to cookbook recipes. The recipe for playing blackjack, for example, might go something like this: "Get a deck of cards. Shuffle the cards. Deal two cards to each player. Ask the first player if he wants another card. Did the face value of that third card put his total over 21? If not, ask if he wants another card. . . ."

Steps in the
Process:
1. Define the task

Once the task is set and the recipe spelled out, the programmer sits down at a computer and translates each step into commands that the machine can understand. A typical command might say: PRINT "DO YOU WANT ANOTHER CARD?"

2. Translate task
into commands

The computer, interpreting commands one word at a time, recognizes the word PRINT and the quotation marks that follow it. It has been wired to gather up messages that appear between quotation marks and translate them, character by character, into sequences of numbers. These numbers, in turn, are translated into a corresponding sequence of electrical signals. These signals are sent to an electron "gun" housed in the vacuum tube behind the computer's video screen. This gun, following the sequence of signals, fires bursts of electrons at the back side of the screen. The electrons strike bits of phosphor that coat the screen and energize them, lighting up a pattern of dots. These dots form the shape of alphabetical characters, spelling out the message: DO YOU WANT ANOTHER CARD?

Thankfully, the programmer does not have to worry about how the computer does its job. He has enough on his hands typing his commands into the computer and testing them to see if they do what he meant them to do. Even a program for playing blackjack can quickly grow to be hundreds of lines long, each line densely packed with convoluted commands and alphanumerical characters. If there is even one character out of place in those hundreds of lines, chances are the program will not work properly. These software "bugs," as programming mishaps are called, can take weeks to find. One bug in an AT&T program knocked out all long-distance telephone service to Greece in 1979. It was months before Ma Ball's programmers pinned down the problem.

3. Test the commands

When the programmer has thoroughly tested and corrected his work he stores it on a magnetic tape or disc, much as someone might use a tape recorder to store a noteworthy speech. A particularly useful or entertaining computer program might be accepted by one of the growing number of software publishers. They will copy the program onto blank discs and send them to computer stores around the country.

4. Store program

When a user slips his brand-new blackjack program into a disc drive and turns on his computer, the drive starts spinning the disc at a rate of hundreds of revolutions per minute. As the disc spins, a record-playback head moves

across its surface, picking up the original programmer's typed instructions and loading them
into the computer's memory. When the disc
stops spinning—presto!—an exact replica of
the program will be imprinted on the machine's temporary memory, all debugged and
ready to deal the cards. Or, depending on the
disc, proofread the term paper, balance the
books or tell you to sell the hogs.

—*Time Magazine*

Unlike the previous example on how to format a disc, this process explanation
defines terms ("hardware," "software," "language"), gives examples ("BASIC,"
finding of bugs), and digresses with information about the internal workings of
the computer. Because most of the readers of *Time* are not computer experts, the
writer defines the few technical terms used and, to make the process more understandable, uses analogy and figurative language ("cookbook recipes," comparison
to videotapes and recordings, jargon metaphors such as "gun" and "bug").

CLASSIFYING

Just as analyzing a process demands that you divide the procedure into steps,
classification requires that you divide a broad subject into the groups or categories
it is composed of. Take, for instance, *chair* as a subject. In order to treat *chair*
as a species, or *class*, you would first need to determine what kinds of furniture
have general chair characteristics. Then you would divide these into subspecies
or *subclasses* by the ways in which they differ—straight-back, rockers, upholstered,
and so on.

Although often included within another type of expository paper, classification
can be an end in itself. For instance, an agriculture student might write a paper
classifying the corn plants available to farmers; a business executive might prepare
a report that lists and describes the company's various copiers. In both projects,
the main purpose is classification; no other rhetorical form is needed.

Classification is often an important aspect of definition (pages 157-58). In
defining *investments*, for example, it would be informative to include a breakdown
and brief description of the various kinds, such as savings accounts, CDs, Treasury
bills, stocks, and bonds.

Classification can also be useful in papers in which evaluation is the objective.
If you were rating cars, you might first classify them according to such shared
features as price, engine type, gas mileage, aerodynamics, and safety devices. Here,
as in definition, the classification would not be a separate form, but a means to
some other rhetorical end.

The Techniques of Classification

Suppose you plan to write a paper that will classify addictive substances (*class*). Before you divide this general class into its subclasses, however, you should consider your purpose for writing. If the paper is for a psychology class, intended to emphasize the psychological effects of these substances, you may wish to restrict the *class* to addictive, mind-altering substances. In this case, you would not include tobacco, which, though usually considered addictive, is not mind-altering.

If, on the other hand, you are writing for a biology class in order to classify only those substances that frequently lead to medical problems, then you would certainly need to include tobacco as a subclass. As you can see, the writing purpose strongly influences the classification process.

In planning your classification scheme, keep these suggestions in mind:

1. Have a clear-cut basis for establishing *class*. For instance, "addictive substances" can be clearly separated from "nonaddictive substances."

2. Be able to divide the *class* into several *subclasses*. Obviously, if there were only one addictive substance in the world, then it could be not be divided into subclasses.

3. Include all pertinent subclasses. For example, it is distressing that many articles on addictive substances omit the most widely abused one, alcohol.

4. Be sure that your subclasses are mutually exclusive—that is, that they do not overlap. For instance, "snow" and "crack" could not be treated as separate subclasses, since both are essentially the same substance, cocaine. Cocaine, then, would be the subclass, further divided into snow and crack.

5. Determine subclasses according to the subject matter and the purpose of the paper.

It is sometimes helpful to create an organizational scheme before you write a classification paper and then test it against these five suggestions. Here is such a scheme for classifying bike carriers for cars to inform potential buyers about available models.

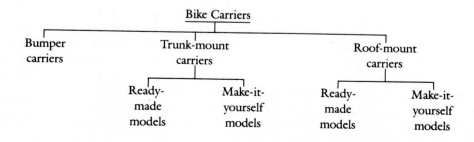

Now to apply our tests:

1.   Is there a clear basis for establishing class? Bike carriers could include only devices used specifically for bicycles. Boat or trailer carriers could not be included.

2.   Is each class divided into at least two subclasses? In the diagram, the class *bike carriers* is divided into three subclasses, two of which are divided into at least two subclasses. If the student wished to include information about chrome and aluminum models, then each subclass could be further divided.

3.   Are all pertinent subclasses included? All types of bike carriers available on the market have been included.

4.   Are the subclasses mutually exclusive? Obviously, they are; bumper carriers are not likely to be mounted on the trunk or roof.

5.   Are the subclasses determined by the subject matter and the purpose of the paper? All subclasses include types that students might consider buying.

Although the following essay has some weaknesses, it successfully follows classification form. The student divides the class *students* into six subclasses, sufficient for his purposes. However, a technical classification for a science or history assignment might require the inclusion of all possible subclasses.

Students in Action
Bradley Myers

Whenever I think of a classroom, I get a mental image of about six rows of solemn students who all give their undivided attention to the teacher. They listen intently to the lecturing, then dutifully write down every word. Not for them is the wasteful habit of doodling or daydreaming—they're there to learn.

But in the real world, a typical classroom is quite different. True, there are some students like the ones described above, but the majority are considerably more diversified in their classroom activities. It is interesting to note, too, that there is somewhat of a grouping pattern. If you observe what different students are doing in different areas of the classroom, this pattern will become apparent.

In the front row, or sometimes in the second, is located the intense student. He is the one that hunches over his desk and scribbles away at ninety miles per hour, trying to catch everything the teacher says. He seems like a butterfly catcher, snagging the words as they come out and pinning them to his paper. At periodic intervals he curses under his breath as he makes a mistake. He furiously scribbles it out, not taking the time to erase it. Then he writes the thing correctly—but now he's behind. He dives into a flurry of writing. He must get the words down before he forgets them. He finally catches up; then oops, he makes another mistake. Scribble, scribble.

While this is going on in the front row, the complete opposite is occurring in the back row. Here is where we find the talker and the sleeper. The sleeper is self-explanatory; she had a long night, studying for an exam or typing an English paper, and now she is catching up on her sleep. Sometimes the sleepiness is drug-induced, such as from too many medications. Sometimes it stems from pure boredom: the student enters the classroom bright-eyed and awake; then as the teacher drones on and on about Medieval European history or How to Fill Out Accounting Forms or The Many Uses of Maple Syrup in Modern Industry, certain changes occur in her. Her eyes glaze over, her head starts to droop, and the desktop takes on the softness of a down pillow. Instantly she is asleep and drooling on her desk.

The talker, on the other hand, is constantly alert. He even takes notes to a certain extent. But his brain is buzzing with activity not concerned with notetaking. He is constantly comparing phrases, experimenting with word groupings, and readjusting spelling. His mission is immediate and purposeful: to make a joke out of everything the teacher says. Then, of course, he must tell it to someone. In a large lecture hall, he whispers it to his neighbor, or just tosses it into the air for all to enjoy. In a small informal class he usually shares it with the teacher, accompanied by exaggerated groans from most of the class. The teacher, if she is good-natured, returns a token laugh, while if she is not she presents the talker with a cold stare. Whatever the result, the talker soon busies himself with the formulation of his next joke.

In the middle of the room, perhaps for the obscurity it offers, are located the doodler and the looker. The looker is called such because she looks at everything: at the ceiling, at the floor, in her backpack, at her neighbor—anywhere but at the teacher. She is the most informative type of student. She can tell you how many cracks there are in the walls, the location of all the electrical outlets, the condition of the weather outside. She is not the person, however, to question about the lesson. She is so concerned with looking at things that she doesn't hear the teacher give the lesson.

The doodler, the other student who sits in the middle, is another type that tends to miss most of the lecture. He usually starts out attentive, or at least partly so, but by various degrees he starts to lose touch. His pen drifts off into the margin and starts to draw circles and squares, or sometimes it connects the rings in a spiral notebook, or even sketches people. Then the doodler notices what his pen is doing and starts absent-mindedly to expand on it. He turns squares into boxes, puts faces on the people, or just draws strange designs. Then he really starts to take an interest and begins to connect his doodles, sometimes drawing arrows, or putting curly lines around his pictures, or shading them. Unfortunately, by this time he has missed most of the lecture. I am this type of student, as can plainly be seen from the drawings on almost every page of my notebooks.

The last type, which doesn't really have a definite location, is what I call the space cadet. She sits in a different place every day, so it is hard to assign her to a specific area. She just wanders in, plunks her books down, and slumps in the chair with legs outstretched. Usually, she doesn't even bother to open her notebook; she just stares off into space for the entire class. At the end of the class she picks up her books and wanders out, as though she had never been there. It is very interesting to observe this type of person and I have often marveled that a person could sit and do nothing, slouching at a desk with a vacant look on her face, for such a long time.

Of course, all the other types are interesting to watch, too. It is fascinating to watch the different things people do when it is assumed that they are all doing the same thing, in this case paying strict attention to what the teacher is saying. It totally destroys my initial mental image of the solemn, monkish classroom. But that is a small price to pay for the enjoyment of observing human beings in action, doing nothing.

Compare the following outline of "Students in Action" with the one on bike carriers (page 151). Which is more likely to include all possible subclasses? Why?

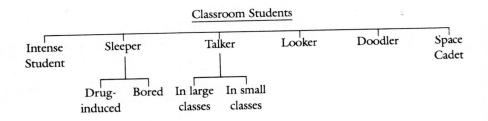

DEFINING

As the preceding section indicated, classification is a relatively uncomplicated process when there is general agreement about the scope and meaning of a term; in such cases, the term as a *class* has already been determined. But often a term has several possible meanings, depending on the situation and the audience. In that case, the writer or speaker must isolate and clarify the meaning intended. For instance, a professor in a psychology or education course might frequently use the term *exceptional children*. Without knowledge of the specialized definition, you might assume that the term refers to highly intelligent or gifted children. Other students might think the children are mentally retarded. Because neither assumption would be accurate, the professor would be obligated to explain that the specialized definition applies to *any* child who does not meet the criteria for "normal." True, the term *exceptional children* does include both bright and mentally retarded children. But its specialized meaning in education and psychology also includes children with birth defects, children with acquired physical handicaps, and emotionally disturbed children.

The definition of a term, then, is often crucial to clear communication. And, as our examples and earlier discussion implied, the connotative meaning of a word depends on numerous factors: context, age of the user, geographical dialect, use in specialized language. To write clearly, especially in exposition, you will often have to define your terms, particularly abstract, technical, and key words. So you should be aware of the different ways of handling definition. Your choice depends on your purpose and the complexity, or difficulty, of the word.

Synonym Definition

We used synonym definition in the preceding sentence by adding *difficulty* to indicate our meaning of *complexity*. This simple method of defining by adding one or more similar terms can clarify an unfamiliar word quickly and easily. For instance, in a paper pointing out the many difficulties of classroom teachers, the writer may simply add a synonym definition to a term like *exceptional children* in order to establish the meaning to be used: A particular problem that taxes the energies and resources of many classroom teachers is meeting the needs of exceptional (gifted) children. Synonym definition is particularly useful to supply a brief explanation for readers who need it without boring or offending those who do not. Avoid synonym definition, however, with key words or those with multiple meanings. Our brief definition of *exceptional children* would not suffice for a paper dealing only with the classroom problems attendant to such children. A more detailed definition would be required.

Another caution in using synonyms to define is to make sure that the synonym is as close as possible to the meaning you intend. Remember that the connotation of a word may differ from its denotation (see pages 97–99). For instance, defining a *blooded horse* as a thoroughbred nag would create unfavorable connotations not suitable for your purposes.

Illustrative Definition

Illustrative definition relies on examples. Often it consists of naming or pointing to a specific person, place, or thing to illustrate the meaning: "The 110 pocket cameras, such as the Kodak Instamatic, are convenient." Writers sometimes use illustrative definition to explain an unfamiliar concept by referring to a familiar one, as in mentioning the classic television series *M*A*S*H* as an example of *war satire*. Another use of illustrative definition is to cite an example of behavior associated with the term, as in Leo Rosten's "A shlemiel is a man who is always spilling hot soup. . . ."

Negative Definition

It is often easier to define a term more accurately by indicating what it is not, as in "An open classroom is not one in which children do exactly as they please.

Nor is it one where no discipline is exacted." Rarely is negative definition the sole method used, but it can be beneficial in eliminating those features that separate the term from other similar ones or in dispelling common misconceptions about it. For example, in a paper about equal employment opportunities for minorities, you might define *minorities* as referring not to religious minorities (Jews) or ethnic minorities (Japanese-Americans), but to those minorities most often deprived economically (blacks, American Indians, Hispanics).

Formal Definition

Frequently, in writing a paper, you will need a more accurate and precise definition of a term than the ones just described. This is particularly true when you use a word in a very special or limited sense. Let's select as an example our previous term, *exceptional children*, this time to refer to highly intelligent or creative children. In such a situation, a formal definition would be helpful.

If you were classifying *exceptional children*, you would subdivide it into its parts—the gifted, the handicapped, and so forth—and further subdivide them. In definition, however, although you classify, you begin by describing your term as part of a larger group and then indicate how it differs from other members of that group. Exceptional children, therefore, are members of a group of children who are not ordinary or average. As you plan to use the term, exceptional children differ from other members of that group by possessing such qualities as high IQ, unusual problem-solving ability, a high degree of creativity, and mature motor-development. Thus you have first related the term to be defined to a larger classification (non-average children); then you have explained how your use of the term excludes certain characteristics of that classification. You have performed these two steps:

1. Related the term to its larger group or class.
2. Indicated how it differs from that group or class.

Here's another example to show you how formal definition works. Suppose you wish to define the term *university* accurately in a paper. First, you should determine the larger class the term belongs to, in this case *institution of higher learning*. However, there are other institutions of higher learning; you must now determine what distinguishing features of a university are not shared by other members of its larger class—four-year colleges, junior colleges, community colleges—all of which, like universities, award some kind of undergraduate degree or diploma. An organizational scheme for a formal definition that includes these differences could look like this:

1. Item to be defined: *university*
2. Larger class: *institution of higher learning*
3. Distinguishing features that make it different from other members of the class:
   a. Includes a number of colleges.
   b. Awards degrees at the master's and doctoral levels.

c. Awards advanced professional degrees (such as law, medicine, engineering).

d. Places great emphasis on research.

The following brief formal definition, which clearly establishes *university* as a class, could be written from this scheme:

> A university is an institution of higher learning that is made up of not one, but many colleges. A university awards degrees at three levels: bachelor's, master's, and doctor's. In addition, it trains advanced professional people in such fields as law, medicine, and engineering. Unlike other institutions of higher learning, it places a high premium on research in all fields.

Note that the writer of the example follows the conventions usually recommended for writing a serious, formal definition:

1. Uses a form of the verb *be:* "A university *is—*." (Occasionally, verbs such as *means* or *refers to* are used.

2. Makes positive statements. (See discussion on negative definition)

3. Does not repeat the term or use a close synonym. Taboo: "A university is a *university* of higher learning." or "A university is a *multiversity* of higher learning."

4. Avoids figurative language. Defining a university as "a haven where dreams are realized" makes for colorful writing, but does not accurately explain what a university is.

5. Shows no personal bias, as would a statement such as, "A university is allegedly an institution of higher learning."

Although figurative language and subjective attitudes may characterize humorous or satirical definitions, more accurate and objective writing is required in serious definitions. It may be fun to write comic, caustic, or witty definitions, such as "Love is a warm football date." And it may be easier to dash off inaccurate generalizations like "A university is a social club" than to search for more accurate characteristics. But formal definition requires logical thinking and precision of word choice.

Extended Definition

Occasionally you will need to develop a more complete, detailed explanation of a term than you can achieve with a synonym, an example, or even a brief formal definition. Let's say you are asked in a history course to write about the legislative branch of the American government. For such an assignment, you might choose to write an extended definition.

As in formal definition, your first task would be to identify the larger, general group it belongs to: *legislative branches of governments*. Then you would need to examine the differences between the American variety and other legislative branches, such as the British, Canadian, and French, to determine what features the American version has that distinguish it from the others. At this point, having established the American legislative branch as a separate class, you can expand the formal definition you have created by subclassifying the term into its component parts: legislative branches of the federal government, the state governments, and local governments. The resulting paper would be an extended definition, a rhetorical form with two main parts:

1. *Establishment of class.* As we have said, this involves the methods of formal definition, introducing the term and setting up its distinguishing features. Two common methods of separating a particular meaning of a term from other possibilities are to examine the historical origin and meaning of a word (its derivation), and to examine some crucial aspect of the item in great detail. For instance, in your extended definition of the American legislative branch of government, you might include the derivation of the word *legislature* from the Latin *lex,* meaning "law."

2. *Extended discussion of the term.* A term can be more fully explained in a number of ways: subclassification, discussion of the history of the word, extensive comparison with a similar item, historical or sociological analysis of the term, or examples. Any one or combination of these can be used in an extended definition.

   a. *Subclassification.* This involves subcategorizing the members of the class, as in classification. You can simply enumerate them, compare and contrast them, furnish an extensive description of them, or subdivide them into more subclasses.

   b. *History of the word.* This will involve using a dictionary with information about the origin and history of a word, as we suggested earlier for *legislature.* Such information not only clarifies the definition of a term, but adds interest and life to the essay as a whole.

   b. *Comparison.* This device is especially useful when defining a new term or one that has many connotations. In defining *detective story,* for example, you might pinpoint your definition of the term by comparing it to other kinds of mystery stories.

   d. *Historical or sociological analysis.* This approach would be especially applicable to subjects like our legislature example. Giving a brief history of the development of legislative forms of government, starting perhaps with Greek and Roman forms, could help explain the peculiar characteristics of American legislatures.

AN EXTENDED DEFINITION

Many of the techniques discussed in this section are exemplified in the following essay—an extended definition written by a student.

Hollers
Benita Joy Riley

First-time visitors to southern Appalachia are often left perplexed when told that someone lives "two miles up the holler" or that to reach their destination they must "go to the mouth of the holler and turn right." Directions such as these only leave strangers asking themselves and others, "What's a *holler?*" or "What's a *mouth?*"

Introduction:
Introduces the term to be defined

The word *hollow* would have little meaning to most native mountaineers in a region where the colloquial pronunciation and spelling are so prevalent that they are assumed to be correct. So for the purposes of this paper, the more familiar word "holler" will be used.

Explanation of the word form

To say that a holler is simply a narrow valley between two hills completely denies the true essence and life of the term. Hollers reveal social standing, exemplify voluntary social segregation, represent family clans, and provide a sense of community. In physical fact, a holler is a very narrow valley beginning at the part known as the "mouth" and terminating at the "head." Usually the mouth of the holler is closest to one of the small towns scattered throughout the hills, or is found leading onto a main, paved road. Also, many times, a small branch of a creek, or "crick," runs into a larger body of water at the mouth of the holler. The source of the smaller creek usually can be found at the head of the holler where the water trickles slowly and constantly out of the hills behind. At the head, the holler abruptly ends and fades into the wooded mountains.

Formal Definition:
States distinguishing features of a holler as a social entity and as a physical place

To the people who populate the hollers, the location of their homes is very important. Almost always the more affluent families occupy the larger, nicer homes found at the mouth of the holler, closest to the store, post office, and main road. Farther up the holler, visitors find the more poverty-ridden and substandard living conditions. The mountain phrase,

Sociological Analysis

"she acts like she comes from the head of the holler," has definite negative connotation in Appalachia.

But frequently the holler population represents a family clan with numerous relationships spanning several generations. In such cases of social segregation, the family name is almost always given to the holler and fierce loyalties flourish within these clannish groups. It is very doubtful that a stranger could make it to the head of "Hall Holler," for example, without meeting up with several Halls inquiring about the nature of the visit.

Subclassification:
a. Family clans
b. Diverse but close-knit
   communities

Even people in a holler filled with diverse, unrelated families are united by a sense of belonging together. It's hard to keep a secret in a holler, especially since there is only one road and it goes by everyone's house. All comings and goings are noticed by neighbors who sit on their front porches during the evening hours.

Comparison

There are no signs in the mountains saying "This is a holler." But the hollers are there, at every turn—narrow valleys of life and lore, a part of the lifeline that is Appalachia.

ANALYZING CAUSES AND EFFECTS

We said earlier in the chapter that analyzing a process requires a concern with *how* and that classifying and defining deal mainly with *what*. In handling these expository methods you should be mainly objective—reaching outside your personal observations to the public domain of facts and knowledge. In analyzing the causes and effects of a phenomenon (*why*), you will rely on your personal domain as well—drawing inferences, making judgments, finding relationships, and sometimes expressing your opinions about the subject.

Like analyzing a process or classifying the types, or categories, of an item, analyzing the causes and effects of a subject is a dividing and sorting task. For instance, in classifying student organizations on your campus, you would merely list and describe the different types—social fraternities and sororities, religious clubs, service-oriented groups, academic societies, and so on. In writing a cause-and-effect paper on the same subject, however, you might explore such concerns as the reasons for their existence, why they are or are not important, and what effects they have on students and on campus life.

Cause-and-effect is often used in scientific, technical, and business writing—for example, in analyzing why animals behave as they do under certain circumstances, in explaining why a nuclear reactor malfunctioned, or pointing out why a certain management program could benefit a company. But it is also used when writers set forth their opinion about something or when they try to persuade readers to adopt a proposal; essentially the writer is saying "I hold this opinion because. . . ," or "Accepting my proposal will result in _____ because. . . ." The persuasive use of cause-and-effect is discussed in Part Three of this text.

Of course, writing a paper that explains causal relationships requires careful organization. In one organizing scheme, the writer expresses the effect (result or opinion) in the opening paragraphs and then devotes the remainder of the discussion to causes or reasons (EFFECT → CAUSES). It is sometimes rhetorically effective, however, to present all the causes first, building up to the effect as a climactic conclusion (CAUSES→EFFECT). In long papers dealing with complex subjects, both schemes may be incorporated—using the first in one section, the second in another.

As a writing assignment, you might wish to explore the causes and effects of the sense of alienation experienced by many college freshmen. The alienation would be the *effect* and you would then set forth possible *causes:* the impersonality of large classes, the inaccessibility of teachers and administrators, an elitist student government or fraternity system, and others that in your opinion are contributing causes. Once you have determined what these causes are, you would need to decide which organizational scheme would best suit your purpose.

A CAUSE-AND-EFFECT PAPER

The following example—a cause-and-effect paper written for a general audience by an older student—first explores some causes for many people's reluctance to volunteer for community service, and then points out the benefits of volunteerism. Thus, she incorporates both organizational schemes, as our marginal comments indicate:

Why Volunteer?
Marie Gregory

Why should we volunteer to work for a worthy cause when we could be pursuing self-interests and increasing our chances in the All-American game of getting ahead? Self-help gurus across the country tell us that looking out for "number one" is the way to fulfillment. Their philosophy is projected daily from nation-wide talk shows and the best-seller lists. Femi-

"Why" question paves way for causal analysis.

Reasons for not volunteering

nists tell us that women who volunteer are exploited because they work without pay. Even the military has a standard motto that is passed on to new recruits—"Never volunteer for anything." Certainly, it doesn't make sense to do something for nothing when inflation and taxes make it so difficult to get ahead.

Still, volunteering is deeply ingrained in the American character. Today we donate more time and effort than ever before. According to a recent Gallup poll, 31 percent of America's adults are involved in organized, structured volunteer work on a regular basis. These volunteers include college students, senior citizens, auto mechanics, doctors, and housewives.

In the June 1983 issue of *Health* magazine, Sara Berkman tells about some ordinary citizens that have made enormous contributions to society. Homer Fahrner of Sacramento helped found Gleaners Statewide in California because he saw a need for the food wasted in that state. Now, many low income families and senior citizens benefit from his efforts. Bon Eulert of Wichita transcribes school texts into braille and gives the blind new opportunities to learn. These two are making a profound impact on the world through volunteer service.

Certainly, the main purpose of volunteer work is to advance a worthy cause. But what's in it for you as a volunteer? Skills learned through volunteer training may become the experience you cite on a future résumé. Or, you may gain the opportunity to obtain special insight into careers you are considering. And there is always the possibility of making new friends and expanding your horizons. Most important, you will be doing something worthwhile and gaining a sense of self-worth.

Imagine a world with no volunteers. Suppose there were no blood banks to rely on when a medical emegency arises. What if you called a hot line, desperate for help, and nobody answered? Who would help flood victims, and senior citizens in need of fuel to heat their homes, if Red Cross volunteers or Scout leaders decided to pursue some personal goal rather

Background information:

Statistics

Examples

Effect: **Benefits**

Effect: **Results of no volunteerism**

than commit themselves to unprofitable service? Volunteers keep the country moving. We
rely on them to provide assistance in time of
need, to protect the environment, and to preserve historic treasures.

Effect:
**Results of
volunteerism**

Those who advocate fulfillment through
pursuit of selfish personal goals at the expense
of volunteer service are mistaken. *It is through
our acts of unselfish aid to those in need that we
gain true fulfillment.*

Conclusion:
Thesis statement

Note that the student writer has organized the paper so that the cause-and-
effect analysis is used to lead climactically to the overt statement of the thesis
at the end. The opening question introduces the subject, but only hints at the
thesis idea. Also, although the writer makes much use of questions, she does it
masterfully: first to set up the discussion, and then to challenge her readers with a
series of thoughtful questions in the closing paragraphs. This questioning strategy
allows her readers to respond from their own experience and knowledge—but the
questions are posed only after the writer's own points are thoroughly developed.

COMPARING AND CONTRASTING

In comparison-and-contrast papers, writers analyze the ways in which two
or more subjects are similar and dissimilar. On occasion, such papers may be
restricted to similarities alone, or to differences. Like the other expository methods
discussed in this chapter, comparison-and-contrast can be used as an end in itself
or merely as a writing tactic in a paper with some other overriding purpose—for
instance, persuasion, description, or definition.

There are several ways to go about the task of comparing and contrasting. One
method is to deal thoroughly with one subject and then to move to discuss the
second. This method can be very effective when you wish to develop a complete
picture of each subject without interruption. For instance, in comparing two
extreme opposites such as Hitler and Ghandi, you might be able to make a more
striking contrast of their personalities and philosophy by dealing with each figure
separately. This method is also effective in short discussions; readers can remember
the characteristics of the earlier comparison.

A second method is to devote one part of the paper to the likenesses of the
two subjects and the other part to the differences. This is most effective when
you wish to place the greatest emphasis on one or the other. For instance, you
probably would view the differences between Ghandi and Hitler as much more
significant than their likenesses; in that case, you could deal quickly in the opening
paragraphs with their similarities and then move to a fuller discussion of their
differences.

A danger in both these approaches is that they can result in what seem like two separate papers, not carefully related to each other. Using either strategy requires that you take great care with the introduction and conclusion of the paper to ensure that the readers are made aware of the relationships you intend.

A third, perhaps more common, form of comparison-and-contrast is to sort out the specific points of comparison you wish to make and discuss each in reference first to one of the subjects and then to the other—a point-by-point comparison.

Perhaps a schematic outline can clarify the differences in the three approaches and help you in organizing your own papers.

SUBJECT-BY-SUBJECT	LIKENESS-DIFFERENCE	POINT-BY-POINT
I. Camera A	I. Likeness	I. Price
A. Price	A. Price	A. Camera A
B. Focus	B. Focus	B. Camera B
C. Flash	C. Flash	
D. Prints		
E. Weight		
II. Camera B	II. Difference	II. Focus
A. Price	A. Prints	A. Camera A
B. Focus	B. Weight	B. Camera B
C. Flash		
D. Prints		
E. Weight		
III. Conclusion	III. Conclusion	III. Flash
		A. Camera A
		B. Camera B
		IV. Prints
		A. Camera A
		B. Camera B
		V. Weight
		A. Camera A
		B. Camera B
		VI. Conclusion

Each plan has strengths and weaknesses other than those already mentioned. The subject-by-subject organization is usually the simplest to write, but it can be the most difficult for readers, particularly if the comparisons are lengthy. The likeness-difference method is easy for readers to follow, but requires that the writer use care in organizing it. Although the point-by-point approach is perhaps the most difficult for writers to organize, it is the easiest for readers to follow.

A COMPARISON-AND-CONTRAST PAPER

The following article, written by a senior journalism student, is organized point-by-point. In comparing and contrasting students who commute with those who live on campus, the worker discusses in turn various aspects of the college experience, dealing first with one group of students and then the other before moving to the next point.

Be Kind to Commuters
Christopher M. Bellito

You may think that those of us who live at home and commute to school have it easy. There's a washing machine with no wait, a new tube of toothpaste in the medicine cabinet and, most important, a fridge stocked with food someone else has paid for. Not only that, but the phone bill is usually taken care of and dinner's sitting in the microwave even late at night. That's not college, you sneer, that's permanent adolescence.

So maybe we look like pampered kids, but it's not that simple. The college student living at home leads a paradoxical life. Like you [campus dwellers], we came to college to learn about ourselves; self exploration is as much a part of our education as organic chem. Yet it's hard to maintain our independence when Mom or Dad can't shake the parental instincts for surveillance. Nor can family obligations be avoided easily. What do I do, for instance, when my parents' anniversary falls the day before finals? The truth is, being a student who hasn't left the nest can be just as difficult as trying to get along with a roommate you don't like.

Our problems can be complex. To some extent, we're second-class citizens in the social world: it's tough to enjoy clubs, frat parties and dances when you have to drive back home or catch the last bus. Thus, we lose out on the results of those activities: a sense of camaraderie that springs from nights spent cramming for industrial psychology, gossiping about who's sleeping with whom and, after most of the favorite topics of both George Will and Dear Abby are exhausted, sharing the heart-to-heart realization that graduation is closer than we think. True, we commuters can join in every

Introduction:
Stimulates interest in subject

Begins comparison-and-contrast

Point 1:
Loss of social advantages

now and again, but we can't fall into the day-and-night rhythm of collegial introspection. There's a whole group of us who'll never be able to appreciate the lifetime bonds of "The Big Chill" as much as our dorming peers.

Then there's the issue of budgeting time. Commuters have much more structured days than dormers; we have to. Many of us live as we do to save money, and we devote a lot of hours to jobs that can help defray tuition. Of course, working out our convoluted schedules may teach more about efficiency than all the freshman workshops on note-taking. Who else but a commuter could perfect the art of plotting discrete-probability distribution on a train hurtling through a dark tunnel while some sleaze with Mick Belker breath hulks down over the textbook?

Point 2:
Time budgeting

There's a myth that commuters are lucky because they can leave the jungle of school and go home. Actually, you dormers may have it easier here: at least you can get away with screaming out the window and working off tension at a party that's never hard to find. When we have a bad stretch, there's no escape; the end of a frustrating day is just the beginning. First there's the long ride home where, on public transportation, the heaters and air conditioners seem to operate on Argentina's schedule of seasons. Then there are reminders from parents which, however well intentioned, are still nagging. How can we feel "on our own" when we're constantly told: "*Call* if you'll be late"?

Point 3:
Handling tension

And when the breakaway point does come, leave-taking is more painful for those who've never really left. Students who move out of the house for college can enjoy a separate peace; they build another base of operations on campus. True, all families have a hard time saying goodbye to the child who goes off to school at 18, but by graduation they've gotten over it and come to view you as an adult with your own life. Commuters are not nearly so detached.

Point 4:
Achieving maturity

We are a special breed: young adults who are enthusiastic about the independence of

Conclusion:
Brief summary of main point of comparison

being in college yet remain to some degree children in our family's eyes—and to some extent, perhaps, in our own. So don't think of commuters as lesser beings or as softies who are taking the easy way out. We're just caught between the rock of academia and the sometimes hard place at home, struggling with the age-old problem of serving two masters.

SUMMARY

In the previous pages, we have looked at the most commonly used methods of exposition: the ways that writers explain and order knowledge and experience so that an audience can receive the message clearly. We have compared objective description with personal description discussed in Chapter 1, pointing out the differences in purpose, language choice, and tone. The outlines that we supplied for those forms of exposition that are mainly explanatory—process explanation, classification, definition, cause-and-effect, and comparison-and-contrast—can also serve as organizational patterns—"game plans"—for writing your own papers.

Throughout the chapter, we have emphasized the special problems involved when you set out to explain something lucidly and precisely to readers who are strangers, when you move from writer-based to reader-based writing. Among these were determining how much your audience needs to know and how best to organize the information for your writing purpose. More will be said about these and other pertinent matters in subsequent chapters.

You should realize, however, that many expository tasks require a great deal of prewriting—using tactics that enable you to think through the often complex relationships involved. Before writing an expository paper, you should explore the methods (discussed in Chapter 9) for doing this.

ASSIGNMENTS

For Discussion

1. Writers of objective descriptions are sometimes faced with the problem of providing a great deal of statistical information in an interesting manner. How does Ted Morgan try to accomplish this in the following paragraphs? Which details do you think best indicate the enormity of the luxury liner *S. S. France*? To what extent is the description objective? To what extent personal? Discuss its organization, tone, style.

> "To give you an idea of the size of the *France*," a ship's officer said, "it is the only ship in the world where you can travel with your wife and your mistress with the assurance that they will never meet."

The *France* is 1,035 feet long, almost as long as the Eiffel Tower, and 110 feet wide. It weighs 66,348 tons, can do better than 30 knots, and can carry up to 2,044 passengers. It has eight boilers that develop 90 tons an hour of steam pressure and four propeller shafts driven by a set of turbines that can deliver up to 160,000 horsepower. Each propeller weighs 27 tons. It has two autonomous engine compartments, with 14 watertight bulkheads—so that no damage can deprive the ship of more than half its propulsion machinery—and two pairs of antiroll stabilizers. Its red and black smokestacks, with fins that drive soot away from the ship, weigh 45 tons each.

All the fresh water, including the water for the boilers, is produced in four distillery plants capable of converting 300 tons of sea water in 24 hours. The ship has long lines and a terraced silhouette like the *Normandie*. The curves of her hull are so graceful that below the water line there is not a single flat plate. The plates are welded, not riveted. There are 22 elevators serving 11 decks, and telephones in each cabin, linked by 18,000 miles of wiring. There are 46 miles of sheets, cut up into useful lengths; two padded cells; one prison cell; a hospital; a refrigerated morgue; a printer who stocks 80 different models of engraved invitations; 13 fulltime firemen, and stainless steel kennels with wall-to-wall carpeting and five-course meals, and imitation fire hydrants for homesick American dogs.

On the two-class North Atlantic run, the segregation is horizontal. First-class passengers use the upper decks. The passengers in tourist class, which is called *Rive Gauche,* are spared the humiliating barriers with "first class only" signs as they take their turns around the deck.

2. For the following topics, discuss the steps necessary to write a directional ("how to") process paper that would address an audience with little or no knowledge of the subject. Also discuss each in reference to the questions suggested on page 144.

   a. Getting a date
   b. Getting a good grade
   c. Washing clothes at a coin laundry
   d. Repotting a plant

3. Choose one of the following topics to determine the chronological steps, the special equipment, and information needed to write an informational ("how-it-was-done") process paper for readers uninformed about it.

   a. Buying a car
   b. Making a dress
   c. Tuning up a car
   d. Programming a VCR

4. Discuss the different classification schemes that might be used for the following:

   a. Fast-food restaurants
   b. Campus jocks

    c. TV situation comedies

    d. Rock or country music

    e. Sports announcers

5. Consider the following statements about war to determine their adequacy as formal definitions and also to note whether they contain anything that would be helpful to you in writing an extended definition of the subject.

    a. War, more ancient than any history, is the outcome of passions, follies, fallacies, misconceptions, and defective political institutions common to the great mass of men. They are not incurable misconceptions, not incurable follies. But they may well become so if we persist in assuming that they don't exist.

—Sir Norman Angell

    b. For a war to be just, three conditions are necessary—public authority, just cause, right motive. . . . But those wars also are just, without doubt, which are ordained by God himself, in whom is no iniquity, and who knows every man's merits.

—St. Augustine

    c. War is a racket.

—Smedley Butler

    d. To my mind, to kill in war is not a whit better than to commit ordinary murder.

—Albert Einstein

    e. War is delightful to those who have had no experience of it.

—Erasmus

    f. Warfare is the means whereby the members of a parasitic ruling class of alien origin endeavor, while exploiting their own subjects, to dominate those surrounding peoples who produce wealth in a tangible and desired form.

—Havelock Ellis

    g. We have no adequate idea of the predisposing power which an immense series of measures of preparation for war has in actually begetting war.

—William E. Gladstone

    h. I have never advocated war except as a means of peace.

—Ulysses S. Grant

    i. War is a science, a series of mathematical problems, to be solved through proper integration and coordination of men and weapons in time and space.

—George Zhukov

    j. War alone brings up to its highest tension all human energy, puts the stamp of nobility upon the peoples who have the courage to meet it.

—Benito Mussolini

6. The following extended definition of sexual harassment was formulated at the University of California at Berkeley. Which of the steps recommended in this chapter does it include? What step is omitted?

> Sexual harassment occurs within an academic community when one person, in a position to affect the academic career of another, subjects an unwilling individual potentially so affected to sexual attention and advances or attempts to coerce that individual into a sexual relationship, and when punishment or reprisals are reasonably perceived as possible for failure to comply. Sexual harassment can range from subtle forms of pressure which affect the academic environment to verbal abuse to physical aggression. Punishment or reprisals include but are not limited to: inappropriate grades or recommendations; limitations or refusals concerning job referrals, research appointments or collaborations; sponsorship in formal academic societies and organizations; and exclusion from informal gatherings. Such behavior is clearly distinct from the strong and valuable bonds that should develop between faculty and students based on intellectual sharing and trust and controlled by normal standards of acceptable behavior.

For Practice

1. Choose one of the following topics and write an objective description that will allow readers to see it "as it is."
   a. Write a paragraph about some toy, object, or "security blanket" that you were or are attached to.
   b. Write a paragraph describing your doctor's or dentist's office.
   c. If you have ever been in an automobile accident, write three paragraphs describing it: 1) your own view of it as you might write it to your insurance company; 2) the other driver's account to an insurance company; and 3) the policeman's report.

2. Choose one of the discussed topics from assignment 1 in "For Practice" and write a directional process paragraph.

3. Choose one of the topics from assignment 2 in "For Practice" and write an informational process paragraph.

4. Select one of the following topics and develop an appropriate organizational scheme that could serve as the basis for a classification paper.
   a. sports cars
   b. sports shoes
   c. TV cop shows
   d. camping vehicles
   e. word processors
   f. academic advisors

5. Write a one-sentence formal definition of one of the following:
   a. A blind date
   b. A dunkshot
   c. A pushover
   d. A nerd
   f. A dormitory
   g. A blooper
   h. Punk rock
   i. Spaced out

For Writing

Objective Description

1. Write a factual description of a stereo-radio, the attire worn for some sport, or your English classroom.

2. Write a factual description of something you know about from a hobby or activity that interests you: for example, a tropical fish, a breed of dog or cat, a musical instrument, a make of automobile or motorcycle, jogging shoes.

Process Explanation

1. Selecting a topic from those listed in item 2 in "For Discussion" or a similar one of your own, write a paper explaining step by step how to do it.

2. Choosing a topic from item 3 in "For Discussion" or a similar one of your own, write a step-by-step, informative explanation of the process involved.

Classifying

1. Using an organizational scheme you developed for a topic in assignment 4 in "For Practice," write a paper that divides the topic into its various subclasses. Be sure to establish a reader audience and the purpose for the classification.

Defining

1. Choose one of the following terms or one of your own and, using the method recommended in this chapter, write an extended definition. Before writing, list the distinguishing features that you will need to include and decide what kind of readers will be your target audience.

   a. Terrorism
   b. Cheating
   c. Reagan Economics
   d. Sexism
   e. Condominium
   f. Pass-Fail grading

2. A ninth grade teacher has asked you to be a guest speaker for his political science class. He would like you to define freedom of speech, constitutional government, or civil rights. Being apprehensive that you might talk above the heads of his students, he has asked you to submit a draft of your talk, which should run about 750 words. You agree to write it for him.

Analyzing Causes and Effects

1. Because the local newspaper editor is interested in the views of college students, she is offering $25 to any student submitting a publishable article on one of the following subjects: 1) an explanation for the popularity of video game arcades, 2) an analysis of the poor academic preparation of college students for college work, 3) the causes for divorce among young couples, and 4) the effect of increasing the age by a year or two for obtaining a driver's license. After consulting your instructor about the advisable length of the article, write it.

2. Assume that your college is considering one of the following: 1) abolishing basketball; 2) raising tuition; 3) decreasing dormitory visitation hours; 4) increasing parking fees by 50%. On behalf of a student group (you name it), write a statement that will be sent to the president, members of the board of trustees, and the college and local newspapers, pointing out the effects of such a decision.

3. To obtain permission to enroll in a highly popular course next semester, you must write a paper analyzing the causes or effects of some recent economic, political, or cultural occurrence. Because you hope to get in the class, you decide to write the paper for the professor.

Comparing and Contrasting

1. You have been asked to write an article for a handbook that will provide consumer information to students on your campus. Write a paper that will provide comparative information about one of the following:

Hair Styling Salons	Laundries or Laundromats
Student Housing	Video Stores
Book Stores	Night Spots
Clothing Stores	Restaurants
Dry Cleaners	Sporting Goods Stores
Grocery Stores	Pizza Places

2. You have lately become upset at an offensive, tasteless television commercial, so you decide to write to the sponsor, pointing out why the commercial should be removed and comparing it to an acceptable commercial of a similar product.

3. A PTA committee for the improvement of teaching at your high school has asked graduates to write a statement of about 500–750 words comparing the skills of high school and college teachers. Your parents have implored you to write because the head of the committee is a good friend of theirs. Write the statement.

4. A local sports magazine is offering a $50 prize for a comparison paper about sports. It has suggested such subjects as high school versus college football, men's versus women's basketball, or high school soccer versus high school football. You may, of course, select other sports subjects. Submit an article of about 750 words to the magazine.

9

Prewriting Tactics for Expository Writing

As you know from previous chapters, the art of writing consists of more than the act of writing. True, a few writers are inspired just by picking up a pen or sitting down before a typewriter or word processor, but most begin with some preparation in the form of thinking, planning, and organizing. Because exposition usually deals with more complex writing topics than those in personal writing, these prewriting steps are even more important. Also, because exposition requires that you write for readers you may not know at all, you must be more concerned about their possible interests, knowledge, background, and taste. Finally, unlike personal writing which generally requires only time or space arrangement, expository papers demand more complicated organizational patterns.

Because expository writing is usually more difficult and demanding than personal writing, you need to spend more time and energy in prewriting than you did formerly. To help you understand what is involved, we have organized the rest of this chapter according to the six steps of expository prewriting.

1. Selecting a subject
2. Generating ideas about the subject
3. Limiting the subject
4. Adapting the subject to readers
5. Formulating a thesis sentence
6. Developing a plan

SELECTING A SUBJECT

Quite often, both in college and at work, your writing topics will be assigned. Your history, sociology, or psychology instructor will suggest certain ideas or problems; your boss at work will ask you to get out a memo or report about a specific matter; your English instructors may assign topics from this book or another source. But what if the assigned subject leaves you blank, or if no topics are suggested?

You can wait for an inspiration. If one comes while you are daydreaming or searching the ceiling, fine. But—as usually happens—what if it doesn't? Then you might try one of the previously discussed techniques—freewriting, focused freewriting, noting, charting, or questioning—or the following new technique: viewpointing.

Viewpointing

Similar to the changing-perspective technique discussed in writing descriptions (pages 47–48), viewpointing requires that you consider a general subject from different points of view. Using the viewpoint wheel in figure 9–1, select some broad topic of interest, such as cars, camping, travel, or television. After writing it in the hub, approach your subject from the various viewpoints indicated around the rim. As ideas for essays come to you, write them down along the connecting spokes.

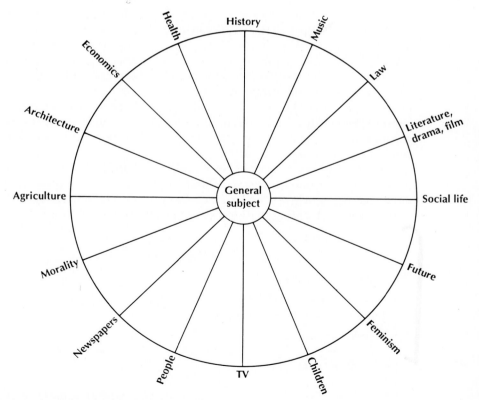

Figure 9-1 Viewpoint Wheel

Note in Figure 9-2 how we have done this with the general subject of football. Sometimes, as in the example about football and law, you may be unable to generate any ideas. In most instances, however, you will produce some by going around the wheel and asking yourself such questions as the following:

Considering my subject from a historical perspective, what could I write about?

Considering my subject from the perspective of the future, what could I write about?

Considering my subject from the perspective of morality, what could I write about?

And so on. However, do not expect answers to these and similar questions to pop immediately to mind. Think about each one for several minutes. Write all ideas down, no matter how silly or irrelevant they may seem at the time because later they may look better to you or they may spark other ideas. Only after you have considered your general subject thoughtfully from one perspective should you move on to another.

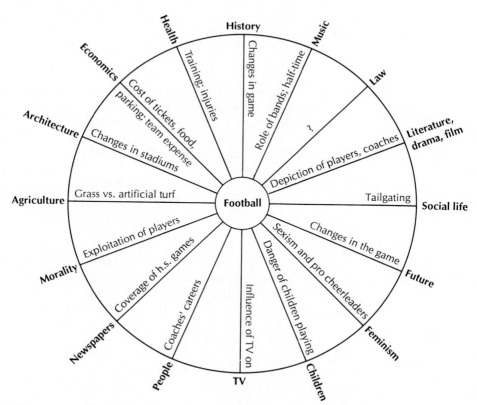

Figure 9-2 Filling In the Viewpoint Wheel

Viewpointing should help you, but don't expect miracles. You may strike many blanks. You may even decide that your general subject in the hub isn't fruitful. Then try another. The point to realize is that this technique or some of the others mentioned previously will generate more ideas than waiting for an inspiration, wringing your hands, or moaning about your plight.

Also, nothing is sacred about these methods. Use them in any way you wish. They are there to help you when you feel helpless.

GENERATING IDEAS ABOUT A SUBJECT

Before selecting a subject, consider whether it appeals to you, whether it would interest readers, and whether you know enough to write about it. Determining its appeal to you and its interest to readers is a judgment only you can make, although you could test your subject on some friends. If they are curious about it, chances are that others will be. But if they say, "So what?" or look bored, try to find something else or realize that you will have to work hard to stimulate reader interest.

Once you have selected your subject, you may have some ideas, but you may need to generate others about it. Here we suggest several brainstorming techniques for you to try.

Listing

You can reasonably determine whether you know enough about your topic by listing ideas on paper. For example, if you decide to write about football and architecture, you might list such points as the following:

Games can be held in domed stadiums despite the weather.
Domed stadiums are expensive to build.
Artificial turf must be used in domed stadiums.
Natural grass may be used in bowl stadiums.
Watching football played in a bowl stadium is more invigorating than seeing it in a domed stadium.

Unless you can think of other points, you might conclude that you do not have much to say about the subject. And what you have to say will be obvious to most readers. So you could try another category, such as football and people. Here, you might write about the arduous lives of coaches, pointing out the following:

Football coaches work hard all year.
They have no tenure.
Alumni insist that they produce winning teams.
Coaches stay in touch with players in the summer, plan for the fall, and do PR work.
Businessmen want winning teams.

Contracts can be broken easily.
Coaches are busy in the spring with practice.
They must make certain that players remain academically eligible.
Coaches either win or leave.
Students want winning teams.
Recruiting takes much time in the winter.
The media blame a coach for a losing team.
In the fall, coaches work a seven-day, seventy-hour week.

After examining this list, you should feel that you have something interesting and appealing to write about. In addition, as you think about your subject, write your paper, and revise it, other ideas will probably come to mind.

DECCEC

What if you have a subject but would like to generate additional ideas? In this instance, you may try a technique we call by its acronym—DECCEC (Definition, Effect, Cause, Classification, Examples, Comparison). This technique requires that you try to answer a series of questions keyed to the letters of the coined word DECCEC.

Definition:	How would you define, describe, or characterize the subject?
Effect:	What effect or result does it produce?
Cause:	What has immediately caused it? What are its underlying causes?
Classification:	How would you classify or categorize it? Is it part of a larger group? Can it be divided into parts, types, kinds?
Example:	What illustrations can you provide?
Comparison:	What is it similar to? In what respects? Different from? In what respects?

Applying another perspective, the economic, to the general subject of football, you might generate the following ideas by answering the DECCEC questions:

Definition:	The nature and characteristics of big-time college football: national recruiting, TV exposure, huge crowds, plush training facilities, schedule of major football powers, alumni in pro football.
Effect:	Increased alumni contributions and support; large income from gate receipts, TV appearances, bowl games; student recruiting help from name recognition and appeal; contribution to school spirit.
Cause:	Desire for local, regional, and national recognition; greater revenue; alumni and student satisfaction.

Classification: Expenses. Player expenses: room, board, tuition. Staff expenses: coaches, trainers, others. Equipment expenses: uniforms, shoes, jackets, exercise machines, training and medical supplies; Administrative expenses: accounting, publicity, tickets, secretarial. Travel expenses: away games, recruiting.

Examples: Revenues received by Penn State from football during the past five years; Michigan's sell-out attendance at its 101,000 seat stadium; rise and fall of alumni support at Notre Dame.

Comparison: Comparison of basketball and football expenses. Football at major schools vs. those that subsidize the sport by paying for it with funds from the academic budget.

By asking yourself questions based on the six DECCEC categories, you should find your memory stimulated and your mind probing for answers. To use this method effectively, you must respond to the questions slowly and thoughtfully, writing down your ideas before you move to the next category. Later, you can review your notes to select whatever looks most promising for your paper.

Perspective Approach

This technique for generating ideas by viewing a subject from different perspectives is loosely related to the viewpoint wheel on page 174. Adapted from a prewriting method developed by several writing experts[1], the perspective approach is especially useful for expository assignments in natural and social science courses. In fact, it draws from a systematic way that scientists explore an object or phenomenon: as a single item or subclass, as a dynamic process, and as a system. Each perspective, besides serving to generate ideas about a subject, helps to determine the rhetorical form that the paper can take—an objective description, a process explanation, a cause-and-effect analysis, or others, depending upon the group of questions you choose to write about. In using this prewriting tactic, remember that not every perspective or question may be relevant to a given subject.

Perspective I—Viewed as a single item (object or event):

1.   What is it?
2.   What happens or what is involved?
3.   What features characterize it? Make it distinctive?

Perspective II—Viewed as one (subclass) of a class:

1.   In what ways is it the same or different from other members of its class?
2.   In what ways is it the same or different from members of related classes?
3.   How does it relate to the whole?

Perspective III—Viewed as an on-going process:

1. How did it come into being?
2. How is it changing—from earlier manifestations to present?
3. How does it interact with its environment?

Perspective IV—Viewed as a whole system or part of a system:

1. How are the components organized?
2. How do they relate to each other?
3. What are the dynamics that govern its behavior or that result from it?
4. What is its role in a larger system?

Let's see how you might make use of this problem-solving device. Suppose that in a sociology course dealing with criminology, you have been assigned a paper on the general topic of plea bargaining. From your readings and class discussions, you have a lot of knowledge about the subject but don't know how to limit it or what approach to take. Exploring the subject from these different approaches might elicit clusters of ideas such as these:

Perspective I: Definition of the subject (system for settling out of court); involves a deal by lawyers and judge, by-passes jury trial; by-passes the normal judicial procedure.

Perspective II: One type (subclass) of judicial procedure; similar in that lawyers and judge are involved; differs in that the accused is involved in the decision and loss of jury. Similar to other negotiation procedures, such as divorce settlements and collective bargaining agreements.

Perspective III: Originated as a means to expedite handling of minor offenses; extended to more serious crimes, used as a bribe for informants, has become more prevalent.

Perspective IV: Its role in the judicial system is destructive; undermines the criminals' respect for the law; interacts with the pressures on the court system; tends to undermine society's respect for law; threatens civil rights.

These are only a few of the ideas that can be elicited on this subject. Clustered around a certain perspective, they comprise an informal organizational scheme for a particular kind of expository paper. Perspective I could result in either an objective description or a definition paper, depending on the subject. The material gleaned from Perspective II leads naturally to a classification or a comparison-contrast approach. From Perspective III comes a need for analyzing causes and effects or showing the steps of the process involved. Handling the ideas from Perspective IV may require a combination of expository tactics, perhaps picking up some ideas generated from other perspectives.

LIMITING YOUR SUBJECT

Just as you may have too little material, so you may have too much. It's always tempting to select a broad subject for a writing assignment because then you feel confident you will have enough to say. For example, it may seem safer to write about cooking than about a limited subject like baking bread. But remember, the purpose of writing an expository paper is to explain something in detail, making it as clear and informative as possible to the reader. In a short paper, no writer can do justice to a topic as vast as cooking.

This conclusion may not be as apparent with other topics. So you should test your subject by listing the points that you would discuss. If you can come up with only one or two ideas, forget about that topic. On the other hand, if you find many, watch out. You may have selected a subject that is too broad for your purposes. When this happens, chop it down to size.

The need to limit your subject is particularly necessary in many college papers because instructors usually assign broad topics, leaving it to you to limit it to a workable subject. For example, here are some topics you might be assigned and some papers you might write:

ASSIGNED TOPIC	LIMITED SUBJECT
World War II	A Comparison of the Allied and the German Air Forces
	The Effect of Twenty Million Casualties on the Russians
	The Failure of the Italian Campaign
Divorce	The Economic Plight of Divorced Women
	Children and Stepparents
	Second Marriages

As mentioned, a broad subject may seem safer because it offers more to write about. However, your essay will be doomed to failure; your points will be much too general to be informative or useful to readers. A limited subject, on the other hand, can be fully developed with specific and informative details, resulting in an effective paper. Consequently, by thinking small when selecting a subject, you are more likely to write successfully.

ADAPTING THE SUBJECT FOR READERS

Assuming that you've completed the first three steps—selecting a subject, generating ideas about it, and limiting it—then you're ready to adapt it to the needs of your readers. Realize that when you speak to people, you can usually tell from their reaction whether they understand you or not. In addition to this feedback, you can use your voice, gestures, or facial expression to clarify what you are saying. These advantages are unavailable in writing. Consequently, you must be more concerned about who your readers are and what they already know.

For example, let's assume that you've decided to write a paper evaluating your high school. You've jotted down numerous notes about its teachers, programs, facilities, sports, administration, students, and activities. Now consider which of the following possible readers you're writing for:

Junior high school students entering a strange high school
High school students transferring to the high school
Parents of high school students
Teachers and administrators interested in improving the high school
College education majors considering a teaching position at the high school
College freshmen who do not know the high school

Many of these readers might be interested in the same information, such as the quality of the teaching. But in some instances, what you write for one group would be inappropriate for another.

And the way you write would differ from group to group. You would be careful not to use difficult words or complex concepts with junior high school students. With high school students, you would be informal; with parents, more formal. With teachers and administrators, you would need to be tactful and respectful, concerned about not antagonizing them when criticizing. With college seniors thinking about teaching at the school, you could assume a highly interested and motivated audience. Not so with college freshman, who may have little interest in learning about your high school.

In similar ways, you adapt the information and style of any subject to your readers' needs. You can make this process easier by considering the following questions in your prewriting:

1. What do the readers want or need to know about the subject?
    a. What do they already know about it?
    b. How important is the subject to them?
    c. Are they interested in it? Why or why not? Why should they be?
    d. How complete an explanation do they need?

2. Who are the readers?
    a. What is their social, political, and economic background?
    b. How well educated are they?
    c. What are their expectations and needs as regards style and vocabulary?

Of course, you cannot always answer all these questions accurately or completely. But by asking and trying to answer them, you will reach some general conclusions that will make your essays reader-focused. As a result, you will write more interesting, more effective papers.

That point brings us to another one about readers. Don't take them for granted. Follow the Golden Rule by writing for others as you would have them write for you. Be as clear and interesting and informative as you would like writers to be when you read.

FORMULATING A THESIS SENTENCE

read

In exposition, the thesis sentence is a statement of the writer's main idea. In a way, it functions as a summary, encapsulating the entire paper in one sentence. Like any sentence, the thesis sentence consists of two parts—a subject and a predicate that comments on the subject. Each serves a specific function: typically, the grammatical subject provides the general topic of the paper; the predicate indicates the way that topic will be approached, limited, or modified. Therefore, the thesis sentence plays a crucial role and requires careful consideration, usually taking some time and trouble to write. The following two questions should help you write an effective thesis statement:

read

What person, place, thing, or idea am I writing about? Your answer is the subject of the sentence.
What do I want to say about it? Your answer is the predicate of the sentence.

By applying these questions to various subjects, you can formulate a number of thesis sentences, as the following examples illustrate:

SUBJECT	PREDICATE
Citrus fruits	can help people lose weight.
Older students	usually study more than younger ones.
Noise, visits, and phone calls	make it difficult to study in the dorms.
Morality	is a major concern in the study of literature.

Each of these thesis sentences limits the subject of the paper to the specific idea expressed in the predicate. For example, in the paper about how citrus fruits are helpful in dieting, a discussion of sugar substitutes would obviously be out of place. Consequently, formulating a thesis sentence helps writers by limiting and restricting the subject.

General Suggestions about Thesis Sentences

In some situations, you may be unable to write a thesis sentence before writing your essay. Like many writers, you may be uncertain about exactly what you want to say. If you use a freewriting approach, preferring to work out your ideas in a first draft, you can then discover what you have in mind and formulate your thesis sentence to guide you as you rewrite.

But keep in mind that this thesis sentence is not set in concrete. You can change it as you develop new ideas. Your thesis sentence will function like a rudder to help keep you on the course you have chosen, but you may discover a new course that is more promising. If so, formulate a new thesis sentence as soon as you can.

1. A grammatically simple sentence is usually best for a thesis statement. A complex sentence can lure a writer into emphasizing subordinate ideas too much. Here's an example:

> Because fast-food restaurants are inexpensive, attractive, convenient, and save people the labor of cooking, they are popular and contribute greatly to the weight problems of many Americans.

With this thesis sentence, the writer might mistake several ideas for the real subject of how fast-food restaurants are responsible for people's being overweight. The writer might drift away from this main idea by dwelling on (1) the popularity of fast-food restaurants, (2) the decor of these restaurants and their appeal to children; (3) their convenience; and (4) the changing life styles that result in people's eating out more often.

With complex thesis sentences like the one in the example, writers too often get mired in a long discussion of subordinate material and then, as an afterthought, dash through the real subject in the last paragraph or two. A simple declarative statement that clearly expresses the main idea of your paper can usually keep you from going astray. Here, for instance, is a clearly focused simple sentence:

> Fast-food restaurants contribute greatly to the weight problems of many Americans.

2. Specific, concrete words are also helpful in formulating a good thesis sentence. Figurative or emotional language is often so inexact that it may prevent you from focusing your paper clearly. Consider this example:

> Emotional: The high murder rate in the United States is criminal.
> Specific: The high murder rate in the United States could be caused by the easy access to guns, the large number of them possessed by people, the survival of the frontier spirit, and the influence of violence in the media.

As you can see, the first of these two thesis sentences provides no clear sense of purpose or direction. Emotional or figurative language may be appropriate in the paper, but not in the thesis statement. In contrast, the specific language of the second thesis sentence helps the writer by stating the precise idea to be developed in the paper—some possible causes of the high murder rate.

The Thesis Sentence and Expository Form

So far, we have been discussing thesis statements in general—the overall sentence structure and the most appropriate language. But you need to be aware that the writer's purpose is crucial in determining the form that a thesis statement takes for a particular paper. A paper that tells a reader how to put something together needs a thesis statement different in form from one analyzing cause-and-effect relationships. Even for papers with the same expository approach, the writer's purpose may dictate very different kinds of thesis statements.

Process Analysis: In a process analysis, where the writer's purpose is merely to tell readers how to do something or explain how something is done, the thesis statement may simply indicate the topic (the process to be explained) and perhaps outline the steps:

> Letters to members of Congress should follow five simple rules. (indicates number of steps)
>
> Writing poor papers is an art that can be mastered by choosing a broad subject, ignoring readers, refusing to revise, and failing to proofread. (outlines the steps in the process)

Classification: If the purpose of a classification paper is not to express an opinion but simply to divide something into categories for purposes of explanation, then the thesis statement may have much the same form as for a process analysis, stating the subject to be classified and indicating the method of classification. For example, you might write an essay, not to deplore the high cost of a college education, but merely to classify for prospective students the expenses involved in earning a college degree. Then a simple purpose statement would suffice:

> Many kinds of expenses are inherent in attaining a college degree.

If, however, you were expressing an opinion by means of your classification, you would probably need a fuller thesis statement—one that named the categories, as the following does:

> People's body build often determines their personalities: thick people tend to be "digestion-minded"; wide people, "muscle-minded"; thin people, "brain-minded."

Definition: Papers whose whole purpose is to define a term usually begin with a single-sentence logical definition: "A _____ is. . . ." But papers drawing some conclusion or making a judgment usually start with a thesis statement that triggers an extended definition. For example, in defining plea bargaining, if part of your purpose is to show that it varies from case to case, you might have a thesis statement like this:

> Plea bargaining takes many forms, depending upon the nature of the individual cases.

Cause and Effect: In a paper analyzing cause and effect, your thesis statement is usually an inference, a generalization you have formulated from considering examples or observation and perceived logical relationships. An inference thesis can take several forms and usually contains such "causal" words as *effect, cause, result* or *because.* For a paper showing the impact of television on political news, you might construct a succinct thesis statement like this:

> A political issue gains importance because of the way it is covered on television.

A more specific thesis statement that sets forth the main points to be covered is another possibility:

A political issue gains importance according to its coverage on television, especially its treatment by the anchormen and its selection as the subject of late evening or Sunday "in-depth" news analysis programs.

Comparison and Contrast: In comparison-and-contrast papers, the thesis statement identifies the items to be compared and indicates something about the method to be used. In the following example, an emphasis on likenesses is indicated:

> Despite their differences, the leading sports cars all offer approximately the same benefits to their buyers.

In the next example, the writer even more clearly suggests the direction the paper will take:

> Standard cars are superior to subcompacts in passenger comfort, safety features, and durability.

The advantage of thesis statements like this one is that they not only summarize the main idea and indicate the purpose of the paper, but they also provide a mini-outline. However, they impose two requirements:

1. The points should be expressed in parallel structure. Example: passenger comfort . . . safety features . . . durability.
2. The order in which the points are named should be the same as the order in which they are discussed. Example: first, comfort; second, safety; third, durability.

Once again, remember that in prewriting, formulating a thesis sentence helps you to pull your thoughts together before you begin to write (perhaps after you have used freewriting to develop some ideas). A thesis sentence helps your readers, too, by informing them what you are writing about and suggesting what approach you will take.

DEVELOPING A PLAN

Many travelers with a specific destination like to draw up a plan before leaving on a trip. Others with only a general idea where they are going prefer to plan as they go, keeping flexible for side trips. So with writers. Those with definite ideas often find it helpful to start with a fairly detailed plan; those with only general ideas may start off in the right general direction and organize their material later.

The Topic Outline

When you know your subject well and have a clear idea of your thesis, you would be wise to draw up a tentative plan or rough outline first so that as you write, you need not worry about your overall organization and can concentrate on other important matters, such as structuring paragraphs and sentences as effectively as possible and choosing words that will convey your exact meaning. Here's how you might develop a plan around this thesis:

The status of American women is still low.

First, you need to generate ideas to support this point, realizing that later, as you write or revise, you may add other ideas. Let's say that at first you have jotted down the following:

1. Women's wages are 67 percent of those of men.
2. Few women in Congress.
3. Many men fail to pay child support.
4. Few women executives.
5. Financial losses due to no-fault divorce.
6. Few women in major positions of political power.
7. Difficulty of single women working and parenting.

From this first step of listing your ideas, you move to the second step—categorizing. Here you group related ideas. Items 1 and 4 deal with women and work; 2 and 4, with women and politics; and 3, 5, and 7, with women and the family.

Ordering, the third step, involves deciding on the best sequence. Consider the possible impact of each point on your readers. If you need to gain their attention, begin with the most startling point: here perhaps the significantly lower earnings of women. If you need to convince an indifferent or antagonistic audience, start with the most appealing point: here perhaps the plight of single women with children. To avoid alienating your audience, save the most controversial point until last. As you can realize, people who become initially annoyed or upset when reading articles may not proceed further.

Depending on the audience then, the final topic outline might look like this:

Thesis: The status of American women is still low.
   I. The job market
      A. Lower pay than men receive
      B. Few women in executive positions
  II. Politics
      A. Few women in Congress
      B. Few women in national political positions
 III. Family
      A. Suffering from no-fault divorce laws
      B. Failure of many men to pay child support
      C. Burdens of working and parenting

Although we have used the standard outline form here of designating main points by Roman numerals and minor ones by capital letters, you are free to omit them or use any other form unless your instructor specifies a particular one. The outline is for you; write it as you wish.

The Sentence Outline

For long papers, you may wish or be required to write a sentence outline. If so, you may develop one from your topic outline. Or you may build one from scratch, following the same procedure of listing, arranging, and categorizing, except that you should write complete sentences instead of phrases.

Thesis: The status of American women is still low.
  I.   Women fare poorly in the job marketplace.
       A.   They receive 33 percent less than men for their work.
       B.   They hold few executive positions.
 II.   Women have little political power.
       A.   Few members of Congress are women.
       B.   Few women hold prominent national political positions.
III.   Women suffer hardships in family affairs.
       A.   They do poorly in no-fault divorce cases.
       B.   They often do not receive child-support payments.
       C.   They are burdened by the responsibilities of working and parenting.

Using the Outline

An outline usually deals only with the ideas presented in the body of the paper, not those in its introduction or conclusion. The introductory and concluding paragraphs (discussed on pages 246–57) serve special functions. However, in long papers, you may find it helpful to include your introduction and conclusion in your outline.

Here are some other points about outlining:

- The outline can help you even when you are uncertain about your thesis statement and ideas. After writing a draft to discover what you have to say about the subject, outline it to see whether the draft is unified, whether it is logically organized, and whether ideas should be added, changed, or deleted. This use of the outline as a help in reviewing what you have drafted is most valuable.

- The outline should have the thesis sentence at the top, where you can refer to it often. In the paper, however, it should be worked at whatever place is most appropriate (usually in the introduction), as we will discuss in the next chapter.

- The outline is only the substructure of your final paper. A paper that goes no further than the skeletal outline is about as interesting and informative as someone else's botany notes. Provide plenty of examples and details to support your points.

- The outline should not hamper or restrict you. As you are writing, for example, if you are smitten with some inspiration, feel free to add the new idea. But do check the outline carefully to see that such a change fits logically into the organization of your paper.

SUMMARY

In this chapter, we have discussed the prewriting of expository papers, suggesting how you might select a subject, generate ideas about it, limit it, adapt it to your readers, formulate a thesis sentence, and develop a plan. These prewriting techniques will help you write a variety of papers, ranging from a humorous discussion of how to diaper a baby to a serious consideration of the acid rain problem. Although each writing assignment requires individual consideration, each usually necessitates some search for a subject, development of ideas about it, restriction of subject, adaptation to readers, and concern about a plan of presentation.

But these six steps are not cut and dried; they need not all be followed, and certainly not in the order discussed. You may start by developing an outline or end by drawing up one as a check after you have written your paper. You may limit your subject before you begin or after you have written a first draft, or both. You may generate ideas while planning or while writing. Stay loose and be flexible. Consider your options and then decide how to proceed. Whatever works best for you is best.

ASSIGNMENTS

For Discussion

1. In writing about one of the following subjects, what different perspectives might you select for a viewpoint wheel?

Advertising	Drugs
Animals	Magazines
Automobiles	Teenage pregnancy
College	Travel
Crime	

2. Assume that you've decided to write a paper for an automobile manufacturer about why people fail to buckle their safety belts in cars. How would you adapt your paper differently for each of these groups of readers: 1) junior high school students who do not drive; 2) senior high school students who do drive; 3) parents of young children; 4) college students; and 5) senior citizens?

3. Using a concrete thesis statement, limit one of the following subjects to a topic that could be covered in a 500–1,000 word paper:

Education	Foreign Affairs
Entertainment	Hobbies
Fashion	Vacation

4. Why is each of the following sentences inadequate as a thesis statement for an expository paper? Reword each to make it an effective, workable thesis.

    a. The pollution caused by our technology has had an effect on everyone.

    b. Classes are the toys of college freshmen, and drop–add is the traumatic procedure they must go through to purchase their toys.

   c. Sports are a deciding factor in the actions and behavior of many people.

   d. There has been a great need for organized labor because working conditions were bad, with long hours, low wages, and few vacations.

   e. Should we grant amnesty to all, or should we grant amnesty with punishment, and who should make the final decision on amnesty.

   f. Riding a bicycle to, from, and in the park can be disastrous.

   g. Bread and pasta are alike in many ways.

   h. In selecting a college, students consider academic reputation, social atmosphere, and costs.

   i. Because college freshmen have a hard time adjusting, they need to live in a dormitory and be forced to attend class.

   j. The registration system at this college is lousy.

5. Design a viewpoint wheel for a subject of your choice.

6. Write a topic or sentence outline for your restricted subject.

Notes

[1]The perspective approach on pages 178–79 is adapted from Richard Young, Alton L. Becker, and Kenneth L. Pike, *Rhetoric: Discovery and Change* (New York: Harcourt, 1970) 126–129, and from Barbara E. Fassler Walvoord, *Helping Students Write Well: A Guide for Teachers in All Disciplines* (New York: MLA, 1982) 88–90.

10

Expository Paragraphs

In chapter 3, we introduced the paragraph as primarily a unit of written discourse that is made up of a topic sentence and a cluster of sentences immediately related to it and to each other. We also pointed out that in personal writing the structure of paragraphs is comparatively loose.

Expository paragraphs usually are more tightly structured, the information arranged according to the writing purpose and the relationships demanded by the subject matter. A paragraph explaining how something works, for instance, requires chronological, step-by-step organization. One objectively describing some item needs the kinds of spatial organization discussed for personal description on pages 60–61. Paragraphs explaining cause-and-effect relationships or showing comparisons and contrasts rely chiefly on a logical structure determined by the relationships involved. Because such paragraphs move from idea to related idea, from fact to related fact, from cause to effect, or from the comparison of one thing to that of another, they require sufficient linking devices necessary so that the reader clearly understands the intended relationships.

However organized, then, expository paragraphs must be more tightly structured than those in personal writing. If one paragraph is poorly organized or inadequately developed, the whole paper may suffer. And even though expository paragraphs may vary in length, purpose, function, or arrangement, they tend to share a common underlying skeletal structure or internal form. Knowledge of this basic structure can help you in writing and revising expository paragraphs.

THE COMPONENTS OF THE EXPOSITORY PARAGRAPH

A.L. Becker's research indicates that expository paragraphs most often consist of three components: *topic* or *subject* (S), *restriction* (R), and *illustration* (I). Becker and his colleagues concluded that a paragraph is a unit characterized by the presence of certain kinds of "slots": one that introduces a topic, one that limits or restricts it, and a third that illustrates or develops the restricted topic.

These correspond to two main parts of an expository paper: the introduction, which restricts the subject of the paper to a workable scope, corresponds to the subject and restriction slots of the paragraph; the body of the paper, in which the supporting and illustrative ideas are presented, is analogous to the illustration slot of the expository paragraph.

Expository Essay	*Expository Paragraph*
Introduction ———————————	{ Subject { Restriction
(statement of thesis)	
Body ————————————————	Illustration

Now let's examine the paragraph itself. Earlier in the chapter, the paragraph was defined as a unit of discourse containing a series of sentences and having as a central, focal point a topic or main idea, generally an explicitly stated topic sentence. How then does this definition relate to a paragraph *form*? Let us examine the following paragraph from the middle of a *Time* magazine article about current marriage experiments.

> Versions of the 50–50 marriage are cropping up all over the country. In Detroit an industrial relations specialist does all the cooking and his social worker wife keeps the family books. In Berkeley a research economist quit his job so his wife could continue working as a radio program coordinator while he takes care of their two children. A Boston lawyer feeds and dresses his children each morning because his wife often works late for the National Organization for Women.

(Subject / Restriction; Illustration)

In this paragraph, the opening sentence is the topic sentence, establishing both the subject—"50-50 marriage"—and the restriction of the subject—"versions . . . are cropping up all over the country." As is often the case, the paragraph subject refers back to the subject of the whole essay—in this case, co-operative marriages. The restriction is directed toward the paragraph itself. In longer, more complex paragraphs, the writer may use two or three sentences to establish subject and restriction, as in this example from an article whose general subject is competitive sports.

The competitive-sport experience is ⎫ Subject
unique in the way it compresses the selec- ⎭
tion process into a compact time and space. ⎱ Restriction
There are few areas of human endeavor that ⎰
can match the Olympic trials or a professional training camp for intensity of human
stress. A young athlete often must face in
hours or days the kind of pressure that occurs in the life of the achievement-oriented
man over several years. The potential for
laying bare the personality structure of
the individual is considerable. When the
athlete's ego is deeply invested in sports   Illustration
achievement, very few of the neurotic pro-
tective mechanisms provide adequate or
sustaining cover. Basically, each must face
his moment of truth and live with the consequences. The pro rookie usually gets only
three or four chances to demonstrate ability
before he is sent home. What sort of personality structure supports the person who
can face this blunt reinforcement of reality?

—Bruce D. Ogilvie and Thomas A Tutko,
*"Sport: If You Want to Build Character
Try Something Else"*

Both preceding paragraphs provide examples in the illustration slot to develop the topic idea set forth in the beginning. This creates a discernible progression from general to specific: the material in the paragraph moves from a general statement of the topic (subject) to a more specific restatement of it (restriction) and then to a concrete discussion that often includes examples (illustration). But some paragraphs reverse this order: They begin with a series of sentences containing specific material, move to a general statement about the content, then close with an indication of that statement's relationship to a more general topic. Here's an example:

Under a canopy of hickory and oak trees
file people of all ages and sizes, some neatly
dressed in street clothes formal enough
for lunch at the Tavern, others in sloppy
jeans and fringed jackets, with huge, floppy
hand-crafted leather hats on their heads,
and here and there, some older women in
the long gingham dresses and sun-bonnets   Illustration
characteristic of the Appalachian farm wife.

They file past booths topped with red, yellow, and blue-striped canvas and filled with
the handcrafts traditional to this fair: thin,
beautifully polished wooden trays, brightly
colored enamelware, rainbows of cornstalk } Illustration
flowers, and macramé wall hangings shar-
ing the limbs of trees with sandcastle can-
dles. Near the gate the loud clatter of
a corn-meal grinder can be heard, interspersed in the quiet pauses between customers with the plucking of dulcimer strings
and the soft crooning of mountain singers.
This Mardi Gras scene, greeting the newcomer to the Berea Arts and Crafts Fair, is)
an annual rite of spring. This gentle orgy, } Restriction
one of several in the area, is a reaffirma-)
tion that traditional craftsmanship is alive } Subject
and well and still flourishes in Appalachia.)

Such an IRS paragraph (specific to general) can be used effectively to break
the monotony of a long series of SRI paragraphs and often provides an interesting
way to structure opening or closing paragraphs.

Other possibilities for ordering these components exist. You can restrict,
illustrate, and then state your subject (RIS); or you can restrict, state the general
subject, and then illustrate (RSI). You can follow the pattern of the sports
paragraph on page 193 (SRI plus transition to the next paragraph); or you can
restate the subject at the end (SRIS). Besides the SRI forms, other discernible
but less frequently used paragraph types occur: problem—solution, obviously,
describes a paragraph that opens with a statement of a problem and then proceeds
to suggest solutions; question—answer follows a similar pattern. However, the
SRI form seems most favored by modern writes. The most important thing to
remember about any paragraph form is not that the components are restricted
to any particular order, but that you must include all the components if your
paragraphs are to be complete and well developed.

The workhorse paragraphs in your expository papers—that is, the informative
and explanatory paragraphs—should be especially well developed. If any of the
slots is empty or only half-filled, your paragraphs will be anemic. However, at
times, like other writers, you may deliberately delete some parts of the paragraph
for specific purposes. We will have more to say about these possibilities later.

Using Parallelism to Achieve Clarity

In our discussion of cumulative sentences on pages 80–81, we pointed out that
in expanded sentences modifiers are inserted at various levels of modification,
moving from the general information stated in the base sentence to more and

more specific details. Paragraphs frequently work in much the same way—the most general statement appearing in the topic sentence, the specific details provided by the other sentences. In a sense, the latter act as modifiers, either referring directly to the topic information or referring to a word or idea in a preceding sentence.

As in complex cumulative sentences, the modification relationships in a lengthy, involved paragraph can become confusing or vague to readers. When writing cumulative sentences, writers often help to prevent such confusion by using parallel structures. This device helps readers follow the writer's train of thought more easily.

In the following student's paragraph, all the sentences following the topic sentence modify it, referring back to John Kennedy and the growth of the hero cult. We have indented these supporting sentences to indicate the level of modification—in this case only one; all the sentences serve as examples of how Kennedy built the legend.

> But the John Kennedy legend and the hero cult grew. (Topic, most general)
>> *He* told the nation to help itself, when he said "Ask not what your country can do for you; ask what you can do for your country."
>> *He* went to Berlin and proclaimed to the world, "Ich bin ein Berliner," identifying himself as a man with a strong desire to establish interrelationships with the world community.
>> *He* went sailing on his yacht with family and friends, portraying the role of gentleman and father for all to see.
>> *He* stood firm as a leader when Russia attempted to expand her political and military influence in the Western Hemisphere.
>> And, on November 22, 1963, *he* became the ultimate hero as an assassin's bullet ended Camelot in a Dallas political parade.
>
> *—Brad Kutchens*

Note that except for the last, all the sentences following the topic sentence begin with *he* and all open with subject-verb structure. Even though some opportunities for special emphasis are sacrificed by such a device, writers often provide such parallelism of sentence structure to sort out meaning relationships for readers. The device serves also as a linking structure to improve paragraph cohesion.

Paragraphs such as this, with only one level of modification, are usually fairly general, providing a minimum of detail. But in paragraphs where several levels of modification are added, parallelism may be even more important to help readers sort out the modification relationships. The following example is such a paragraph; here the writer classifies the characteristics of a farmer who is his "own boss." In addition to indentation, we have italized the opening words of the sentences containing characteristics:

> A competent farmer is his own boss. (Topic, most general)
>> *He has* learned the disciplines necessary to go ahead on his own,

as required by economic obligation, loyalty to his place, pride in his work. (Refers to "own boss" in topic: second level)

His workdays require the use of long experience and practiced judgment, for the failures of which he knows he will suffer. (Example of "discipline": third level)

His days do not begin and end by rule, but in response to necessity, interest, and obligation. (Further amplification of "workday": fourth level)

They are not measured by the clock, but by the task and his endurance; they last as long as necessary or as long as he can work. (Refers back to length of workday idea in preceding sentence: fifth level)

He has mastered the intricate patterns in ordering his work within the overlapping cycles—human and natural, controllable and uncontrollable of the life of the farm. (Another characteristic of "own boss" in topic sentence: second level)

—Wendell Berry, The Unsettling of America

In this multileveled sentence, besides using parallel sentence structure, the writer also provides many linking clusters (see pages 54–55) to give the paragraph cohesion: the pronouns *he* and *his,* repetition of words such as *obligation* and *necessary.*

Thus, parallelism can outline the levels of modification and enhance clarity, particularly when combined with other linking structures. It also adds an elegance of style. Certainly it is a worthwhile device to keep in mind as you develop your paragraphs with greater and greater detail.

DEVELOPING PARAGRAPHS

Earlier in the chapter we hinted that a variety of fillers can occupy the functional slots—subject, restriction, and illustration—of the SRI workhorse paragraph. The nature of these fillers and their relationship to the overall structure of the expository SRI paragraphs might be diagrammed like this:

Subject: General subject matter of both the paragraph and the paper. May be mentioned in a transitional sentence or in a topic sentence that takes the form of a generalization, a statement of opinion, or an inference.

Restriction: The main, specific point of the paragraph. May be included in the topic sentence with the subject or restated in a generalization, opinion statement, or inference.
Definition of terms used.
Clarifying materials—background, history, orientation information.

Illustration: Supporting material to demonstrate the validity of the restriction:

Example	Classification
Statistics	Definition
Reasons or causes	Comparison
Authority	Anecdote

We have emphasized throughout the chapter that "workhorse" paragraphs should be well developed with numerous sentences to expand the topic sentence. Even though skimpy paragraphs may lack adequate development in any of the three slots, generally the illustration slot is the puniest in student writing. True, one of the most frustrating writing tasks is deciding how much development is enough. Usually, complex or controversial material requires more supporting details than generally accepted facts. As always in writing, the writing context, the nature of the material, and the needs of your readers will influence the amount and kind of information you should provide. But by using devices available for generating information in the illustration section, you can write solid, strong paragraphs.

Developing by Example

Perhaps the most common method for developing the *illustration* slot is by providing examples that expand or support the ideas presented in the *subject* and *restriction* components. In the following paragraph, we have italicized the S and R statements and indicated the location of each slot.

> The Korean tragedy is only the latest in a long series of events that have helped fix *overhead surveillance* in the mind of the American public *as crucial to military security,* but also as *a possible cause or cure of many an international confrontation.* In 1960, it was the shooting down over the USSR of an American pilot and his ultra-high-level aircraft that produced the abrupt close of a top-level East-West peace meeting. The event also provoked some of Soviet Premier Nikita Krushchev's most bellicose antics, including shoe pounding at the United Nations. In 1962, aerial photographs offered the first sure proofs of Soviet offensive missile installations in Cuba, leading to President Kennedy's "quarantine" and subsequent deadly showdown with the Soviet Premier. Months before the recent U.S. landing in Grenada, President Reagan presented the TV public with eye-in-the-sky images from his own daily CIA briefing that showed one cause of U.S. and Caribbean uneasiness: the 10,000-foot runway being built on the tiny island by armed Cuban work gangs.

> *S*
> *R*
>
> *I*

> —Dino Brugioni, *"Aerial Photography:
> Reading the Past, Revealing the Future"*

As you can tell from the title, the general topic of the paper is "aerial photography"; the term "overhead surveillance" is a synonym for it. "International confrontation" restricts the use of overhead surveillance to incidents involving conflict between nations. Note how the writer achieves parallelism by introducing each event with a time reference: "In 1960, . . ." "In 1962, . . ." "Months before. . . ."

Developing with Statistics

Although a highly effective device for establishing your knowledge of a subject, statistics can be deadeningly dull to read. They will be most effective and interesting if you incorporate them somehow into your discussion, as is illustrated in the following example from a paper discussing sexual harassment:

> The *coercion level appears to be even higher at some prestigious* S, R
> *universities:* Harvard's 1983 Sexual Harassment Survey Project, for
> example, found that 34 percent of the 1,000 female undergraduates
> polled had experienced sexual pressures in some form, ranging
> from lewd jokes and suggestive comments to threats of poor grades I
> to rape. Only 9 percent of the women reported the incidents to
> a university official. On rare occasions the impersonal numbers
> become public accusations; in one incident a tenured professor left
> the faculty after a female student filed a sex-harassment complaint
> against him.
>
> —*Newsweek on Campus, "Coed Coercion on Campus"*

Note that, although numbers are used, *percent* is spelled out rather than shown by the mathematical symbol (%). For further discussion on handling numbers in a written text, see the Reference Guide.

Development by Authority

On occasion, particularly when dealing with controversial or specialized material, writers cite authorities in the field. Like the injudicious use of statistics, this practice loses its effectiveness unless the citations are woven carefully into the general discussion—to amplify a point or to give validity to an example. Also, some form of credit or documentation must be provided. This ranges from a formal citation, in which complete information about the source is furnished, to an informal mention of the authority and the article, book, or study in the text of the paragraph. In much popular writing, the latter method is used, whereas full documentation is expected in more formal writings such as scientific reports, term papers, and scholarly studies. Your instructor will inform you about the documentation required in your composition course. (Chapter 20 of this text deals extensively with formal documentation.) In the following paragraph, taken from a magazine article, informal documentation is used. As you read through it, notice its organization—from specific to general (IRS)—and the graceful way in which the quotation is incorporated.

A weakness of the present laboratory methods for identifying carcinogenic substances is the fact that the compounds which probably should be tested are too numerous and the testing procedures too slow, cumbersome, and expensive. New, quicker, cheaper techniques are being devised and may bring some relief. However, leaving aside the massive problem of analyzing the hundreds of thousands of compounds and contaminants already in our environment, we presently are not able to keep up with testing the new ones being produced. *It is this situation that has led many to speculate that we are casually creating environmental health problems—creating an environment different from any the world has had before.* We are doing so, says Dr. Samuel Epstein, of the University of Illinois School of Public Health, and one of the nation's leading environmental toxicologists, "by the introduction into the universe of potent chemical agents which are largely untested for adverse public health effects."

I

R, S (Topic Sentence)

I (Authority)

—*Bil Gilbert, "All in Favor of Cancer, Say 'Aye'"*

Developing with a Narrative Incident

A device that not only develops the topic idea of a paragraph, but also adds interest and color, is the inclusion of a brief narrative—with or without dialogue. Frequently such narratives are summarized for the sake of economy, as in the citation of case studies. Most commonly employed in opening paragraphs to catch readers' attention, narrative can be effective elsewhere in the paper, as long as the story is relevant to the subject. Paragraphs developed by narrative very often lend themselves to IRS form, as in this example that opens a student writer's paper.

(I) Four boys were driving home from the Kentucky State Fair one summer night. They were all a little drunk. About three miles from their homes they were pulled over because one of the headlights was out. Immediately the police detected the alcohol and quickly called another patrol car. Then began a series of incidents which convinced me that (R-S) *some of the "rumors" about police treatment of teenagers are true.* (thesis statement)

In this example, the narrative leads up to the thesis idea, moving from specific to general.

Occasionally, the paragraph division required by dialogue forces the writer to devote several paragraphs to the brief narrative and to state the topic idea in the last one. At other times, a writer may summarize an event in one paragraph, then in a subsequent paragraph establish its significance to the topic idea. Whatever strategy you choose, remember that the narrative must be concise and somehow enhance the subject of your paper: Include only those details and actions that are relevant.

Developing by Classification

When used to develop paragraphs, classification follows the same patterns as those discussed in reference to a classification paper (see pages 150–52). Here is an example with SRI organization, taken from an article on the exile of Tibet's Dalai Lama.

> *During the next two decades more than 100,000 Tibetans fol-*   S
> *lowed him into exile;* the *exodus encompassed virtually the entire*
> *spectrum of Tibetan society:* government officials—both monastic   R
> and lay, businessmen and traders, high lamas and ordinary monks,
> farmers and nomads. A like number may have perished en route.
> From the far eastern province of Kham the people of several villages
> and monasteries, with 5,000 of their yaks and sheep, fought their
> way for two years across a thousand miles of Tibet into Nepal. Oth-   I
> ers went as far as Europe and America. But most crossed hundreds
> of miles of roadless, turbulent country into India—individually, in
> family bands and large groups.
>
> —E. Richard Sorenson, "To Tibet's Dalai Lama,
> Exile is a Haven—and an Opportunity"

Here the writer sets up two different classification systems: the first on the subclasses of people who followed the Dalai Lama into exile, the second on the destination of different population groups.

Developing by Definition

Although the most common uses of definition in paragraphs are by synonym, to clarify a term used in the *subject* slot, and by substitution of a single-sentence formal definition for the restriction (R) of the paragraph, occasionally a writer uses a brief extended definition. Generally, such development occurs in opening paragraphs, although it may appear in the body of a paper that includes a number of unfamiliar terms. The example here immediately follows an opening paragraph that has introduced the paper's thesis; the writers now pinpoint their specialized meaning of a widely used and ambiguous term.

> *Household hazardous* waste is any material discarded from the   S
> home that may, because of its chemical nature, *post a threat to*
> *human health or the environment when handled improperly.* These   R
> wastes can be solids, liquids, or gases. They differ from other house-
> hold wastes in that they are toxic, corrosive, caustic, flammable, re-
> active, or explosive. Hazardous substances are often found in such   I

common products as pest strips, mothballs, insect and roach sprays, motor oils, antifreeze, wood preservatives, rust removers, metal polishes, batteries, deodorizers, degreasers, weed killers, drain cleaners, paint thinners and strippers, disinfectants, battery and pool acids, hobby products, bleaches, gasoline, kerosene, oven cleaners, nail polish remover—even car waxes.

—David Galven and Sally Toteff, "Toxins on the Home Front"

Here, in addition to the SRI form we have indicated, the paragraph follows almost exactly the format discussed on pages 197–98. The writers use examples both to extend the definition and to develop the *illustration* slot.

Developing by Cause-and-Effect

Individual paragraphs that embody cause-and-effect relationships follow the principles of organization discussed on pages 160–61 for cause and effect papers. The topic sentence can state an effect (S) followed by causes (I), or a major cause (S) may open the paragraph and be followed by a series of effects (I).

In the first example, the topic idea is incorporated into an opening question— the survival of the panda (*effect*). The paragraph is then developed by a series of *causes* that resulted in that survival, ending with a possibility that leads into the next area of discussion.

One question obtrudes: Since such *die-offs* have occurred for   S
millennia, *why did the panda not become extinct long ago?* There
are two answers. First, although much bamboo in an area may die,   R
remaining patches provide pandas with enough food to survive
the crisis. Second, several bamboo species often grow at different
altitudes on a slope. When a species died, pandas could move up
and down the hillsides to find an alternative bamboo to eat. But   I
in recent years farmers have pushed fields so far up valleys and
slopes that now often only one bamboo species caps a mountain
top. When it dies, so may the pandas there.

—George B. Schaller, "Secrets of the Wild Panda"

In our second example, the writer opens with a major cause that includes both S ("weapons-related research") and R ("will end up classified as secret"). The effects then serve as the specifics in the ILLUSTRATION slot.

What Aftergood and other critics of *weapons-related research*   S
on campus now fear is that an *increasing amount of college research*
will end up classified as secret or requiring approval before publica-   R
tion, impinging on academic freedom and inhibiting the exchange
of information that is necessary to allow scientists to build on each
other's work. Another major concern is that federal grant dollars   I

are being drained from other fields to support weapons-related research. If this fear is borne out, graduate students can be expected
to follow the money, emptying the talent pool for other fields like
medicine or nonmilitary computer science.

—*Sheila Kaplan, "Big Man on Campus"*

Developing by Comparison-and-Contrast

Single paragraphs used primarily for comparison may follow any one of the
patterns discussed in chapters 8 and 9. The following paragraph illustrates the
point-by-point arrangement shown on page 164, comparing the similarities (I) of
two famous sports stars (R) in handling anger(S).

Swedish tennis star Bjorn Borg was a master at *converting anger to
his own purposes.* "When something went wrong," Tutko says, "Borg
became even more efficient and more intense. He was truly a model who
absolutely did not respond to outside provocations. He had the maturity
and the ego strength to accept the setback and use the emotion to
make himself even keener. Jack Nicklaus is similar. Instead of becoming
emotional in a situation that might provoke another golfer to anger, he
simply concentrates more on the task at hand. Athletes who have learned
that do marvelously well under pressure."

—*Edwin Kiester Jr., "The Uses of Anger"*

In the next example, two subjects (women and blacks) are compared on
a number of points in a subject-by-subject pattern. In this case, the writer is
discussing only the similarities, not differences:

Comparison between women and blacks sheds new light on the   R
handicaps they both face in *the job market.* Both are fired before   S
white men and hired after them. Both are arbitrarily limited to
the lower-paying, least productive, less-skilled jobs and sometimes
the same ones. For many years, for instance, Southern textile mills
reserved for white women those jobs that were filled in the North
by black men. It is not surprising to learn from the Bureau of Labor
Statistics that women average 2.4 years less than men on the jobs
they hold, while the black men average two years less than white   I
men. The gap between the races in job tenure is similar to the
gap between the sexes. The similarity is worth noting because
it suggests reasons why neither blacks nor women gravitate to
steady work. Both are fired before white men, of course, but both
are also more apt to quit because they move away or can't get
transportation to the job. Women and blacks often do not have as
much control over where they live as white men.

—*Caroline Bird with Sara Welles Briller, Born Female*

Another common use of comparison-and-contrast paragraphs is to point out paradoxes or contradictions between two subjects or within a single subject. In this example, the writer points out some contrasts or contradictions in Thomas Jefferson's character:

> Perhaps the heads of bison don't go with the gilt-daubed French Neoclassical or the parquet floors or the Sky Room's soup-tureen dome and Mars-yellow walls. But *Jefferson* was himself a bundle   S
> of *contradictions*. Mild-mannered and meticulous in speech, he   R
> could also be hyperbolic and boastful. He disliked institutions of
> all kinds, because they shackled the mind, but he founded many of
> them, including the United States Military Academy at West Point. A
> sophisticated cosmopolitan, he was also down-home American. An
> aristocrat, he was also a democrat. Though he reviled slavery and
> promoted legislation outlawing it, he kept as many as 200 slaves
> himself. He was outspoken about free speech but wished to censor   I
> reading and was keen to prosecute seditious talk. A gourmet, he
> kept himself on a tight puritanical rein. He didn't always follow
> due process of law. A hardheaded, practical politician, he was also
> dreamy, idealistic and visionary. He most often seemed unruffled,
> the soul of reason, but there was a violent, eruptive streak in him
> that led him to suggest we "burn the city of London" during the
> War of 1812, hang Aaron Burr (his own Vice President) out of hand
> and sidestep the Constitution at times.

> —*Diane Ackerman, "The Man Who Knew Almost Everything"*

Such a series of contrasts can be extremely effective, providing an economical way to present many details.

Developing by Analogy

Closely related to comparison-and-contrast, analogy also compares two items (see also pages 163–64). Writers of expository papers most often use analogy to explain a difficult concept or process by comparing it to a simpler, more familiar one. In the following example, a scientist compares a theory of language variation—specialized knowledge—to another one more familiar to his readers: Darwin's theory of evolution.

> The separate *languages* of the Indo-European were at one time,   S
> perhaps five thousand years ago, maybe much longer, a single
> language. The separation of the speakers by migrations had *effects*   R
> *on language comparable to the speciation* observed by Darwin on
> various islands of Galapagos. Languages became different species,
> retaining enough resemblance to an original ancestor so that the
> family resemblance can still be seen. Variation has been maintained   I
> by occasional contact between different islands of speakers, and
> perhaps also by random mutations.

> —*Lewis Thomas, The Lives of a Cell*

Although analogy is often quite effective for clarification, there are dangers in its use. These are discussed on pages 276–77 in reference to persuasive writing.

In this discussion, we have presented each type of paragraph development as a single possibility for use in any given paragraph. You should realize, however, that writers often combine several methods, such as including an example with a comparison, citing statistics to explain a causal relationship, or quoting an authority in definition.

FUNCTIONAL VARIETIES OF PARAGRAPHS

As you become more aware of paragraph structure and are exposed to more college-level prose, you will realize that there are several varieties of paragraphs besides the previously discussed "workhorse" paragraph, in which all the component slots—subject, restriction, and illustration—are filled.

As we have indicated, sometimes writers employ a short, isolated paragraph to emphasize an important point that might be buried if it appeared within a fully developed paragraph. Writers occasionally use short paragraphs to signal an important transition, particularly when moving from one major idea to another in a lengthy paper. Such paragraphs can also give special emphasis to a significant statement. And sometimes writers break up a long enumeration paragraph into short, more readable paragraphs, each containing a reason, cause, or other enumerated item.

Transitional Paragraphs

A transitional paragraph has an empty illustration slot. It usually performs two functions: it summarizes or evaluates previous material, and it foreshadows subsequent material.

A transitional paragraph introduces both subject and restriction, as this example shows:

> And that's why welfare is a women's issue. For a lot of middle-class women in this country, Women's Liberation is a matter of concern. For women on welfare, it's a matter of survival.
>
> —*Johnnie Tilman, "Welfare is a Women's Issue"*

The first sentence summarizes the reasons presented in preceding paragraphs. The phrase "women on welfare" in the last sentence picks up the overall subject of the article. And "a matter of survival" introduces the restriction to be discussed in the paragraphs to follow.

Sometimes a transitional paragraph takes the form of a question, which moves readers from one idea to another and has the added advantage of making readers confront the material. Two examples follow:

How real and how general does the confusion seem actually to be?

—Joseph Wood Krutch

This one-sentence paragraph bridges the writer's preceding discussion of the subject, "confusion," and the restriction of the discussion to follow, indicated by "how real" and "how general."

In the next sample, the writer asks a question and then indicates the nature of the subsequent discussion by observing that no answer has been previously sought.

What happens inside the mind of a woman struggling with such a conflict? Since it has not been properly acknowledged until now, the question has remained unaddressed.

—Vivian Gornick

Our final example of a transitional paragraph states a value judgment pertaining to the previous discussion and then introduces the subject of the forthcoming paragraphs, indicated by the italicized words:

But not even those wonderful clergymen who pray in behalf of Congress, expressway ribbon cuttings, urban renewal projects, and testimonial dinners would pray for a demolition derby. *The demolition derby is, pure and simple, a form of gladiatorial combat* for our times.

—Tom Wolfe, The Kandy-Kolored Tangerine Flake Streamline Baby

Emphatic Paragraphs

A paragraph of emphasis consists of short declarative sentences (sometimes only one sentence) generally intended to shock readers, elicit a gut reaction from them, or ensure that they get the message, clear and unadorned. This example from a student publication probably accomplishes all three:

The last frontier is indeed gone—but this time it's not the dinosaur or the buffalo who are in danger of extinction, it's man himself, and at his own hand.

—Linda Hanley

Sometimes the emphatic paragraph effectively ends a paper, providing an impact not easily achieved by a longer paragraph. Here, from a student paper, is an effective two-sentence final paragraph that also serves as a general summary:

The Greek system has grown up, moving from a "teenie-bopper" mentality to a seriousness of purpose more appealing to young adults. Because of all the changes in the system, more students are choosing to be Greeks than freaks.

Introductory and Concluding Paragraphs

Paragraphs that serve as openers and closers of a paper have many of the formal characteristics of the other kinds of paragraphs discussed in this section. Because they present unique problems, they are treated separately and at length in chapter 13.

Enumerative Series of Paragraphs

Frequently in papers with complex subject matter, you may have to deal with several aspects of a problem, such as a recital of the factors that contributed to United States involvement in Southeast Asia. Or you may be faced with a situation like that of one student writer whose final paragraph was reprinted above: listing the reasons for the recent renewal of interest in fraternities and sororities. If you discuss each factor or reason in detail, the resulting paragraph with its many items will be too long to be read easily. What to do? The most common device is to divide the paragraph material into a series of paragraphs. For instance, the subject and restriction can be introduced in a short paragraph that is followed by a series of paragraphs, each dealing with separate aspects of the illustration materials. Here's how one student, writing on America's use of the atomic bomb, solved the problem:

> In spite of much information from reliable intelligence sources that Japan's defenses were rapidly weakening, President Truman listened to the pro-bomb advocates and went ahead with the bombings. There were several major factors which were considered by the pro-bomb factions as over-whelming reasons for the use of the bomb.

First paragraph in the series introduces subject and restriction

> The first was that the entire research and building projects had been geared toward their eventual use. [Factor 1: supported in the rest of the paragraph.]

Second paragraph in the series: illustration 1

> The second factor was the cost in money and resources which the production of the bombs had required. [Factor 2: developed in the rest of the paragraph.]

Third paragraph in the series: illustration 2

In this section of the book we have explained some of the ways in which the various paragraph forms can be used. Paragraphs in which only one or two of the function slots are filled can serve important rhetorical functions—to provide a bridge from one idea to another, to emphasize an important point, to enumerate a list of items, to summarize, or to introduce a new aspect of the paper. But remember, good writers do not use these shortened paragraphs indiscriminately;

they place them carefully, next to fully developed ones. Remember, too, that they design every paragraph to serve a purpose.

SUMMARY

In this chapter, we have examined the characteristics of expository paragraphs, moving from the underlying form to ways of developing and using paragraphs. Like a complete essay, a well-developed expository paragraph normally contains three "slots": one that introduces the general subject (S); another that states the way in which the subject is restricted in the paragraph (R); and a third that develops or illustrates (I) the restricted subject.

We have also pointed out that by using parallel sentence structures, writers can help readers to grasp the meaning of the paragraph.

Paragraph development is accomplished mainly by adding details and discussions to the *illustration* slot. Many devices are available to expand paragraphs, including the use of examples and brief narratives, the citing of statistics or other authority, and analysis by classification, definition, causal relations, comparison-and-contrast, or analogy. Often a combination of these methods is used.

Not all paragraphs in an essay function the same way: Some serve as opening or concluding paragraphs; some may provide transitions from one major point to another; some may give special emphasis to a major idea; and others may appear as a series enumerating related points.

Expository paragraphs are the building materials for an effective explanatory paper. Like weak girders that lead to the collapse of a bridge, underdeveloped paragraphs can fatally weaken an expository paper.

ASSIGNMENTS

For Discussion

1. Use the following student paragraph to discuss the questions that follow it:

    Another asset of solar energy is its economical benefits for every family income. Inflation has attacked our escalating utility bills, until low to lower-middle income families are finding it difficult to afford heating for their homes. Installation of solar panels with maintenance equipment is the only initial bulk cost (sometimes referred to as an "investment") to the consumer. Once properly installed, the system begins paying for itself. There are no monthly heating bills to pay, and maintenance costs are minimal. Homeowners literally have a "monopoly" on their own personal utility company. The possibilities are innumerable: solar water heaters, household heating systems, cooling systems, solar laundries, solar kitchens, solar cars, and so on. Back-up systems can store up to ten days of heating energy when sunlight is unavailable.

a. Where are the *subject-restriction-illustration* sections?

b. Is parallel structure used effectively? What suggestions would you give to the student about using it more effectively?

c. Discuss the devices the writer uses to "glue" the paragraph together. How could it have been given better continuity?

d. What kinds of information could be added for development?

2. Identify the underlying organization of each of the following paragraphs. Is it SRI, IRS, SRIS—or is one slot missing? Which method(s) of paragraph development discussed on pages 69–77 does each exhibit?

a.   To some his [Calvin Coolidge's] aphoristic self-confidence represented homely folk wisdom; to others, intolerable smugness. To some his inaction was masterly restraint; to others, it was the complacent emptiness of a dull and lazy man. To some his humor was innocent fun; to others, it was sadistic meanness. To some his satisfaction with his purpose represented "character"; to others, it seemed a bankruptcy of mind and soul. To some he was the best in the American middle class. To others he was almost the worst.

—*Arthur M. Schlesinger, Jr., The Crisis of the Old Order*

b.   However, one important aspect of the college that is often considered early in the planning stage is the particular college's general reputation. This general reputation is made up of the picture one sees of the college in academics, sports, and social life. The image that is thus presented of what the school is like is quite often a prerequisite to trying to find out more about the college. For example, perhaps a young man in junior high school read an article in a sports magazine about the outstanding athletic program at college "X." After reading it, he decided that this school was one that interested him. So, he then tried to learn about other aspects of the college. In a similar manner, what a student has read or heard about a school's academic, athletic, or social life can be the initial factor in his beginning to select a college.

c.   The grading system also contains penalties and rewards, but that's what makes people tick. Would any student write a term paper, read a textbook, or attend a lecture in a field outside his interest if he were not motivated by grades? Because studying and learning are hard work, students need penalties and rewards. Of course, this results in pressure. Certainly, this produces competition. But without them, few people would strive to let their learning exceed their intellectual reach. Oh yes, there are a few students who are highly self-motivated and are genuinely interested in learning. But most students would rather see a basketball game, rap in the Grill, or watch a movie. Let's face it—that's why we need the present grading system. Anything else would result in a lowering of the standards and a fifth-rate university.

d.   Seaward-moving ice in Antarctica sometimes becomes blocked and pushed up against mountains largely hidden below the surface. Because of low temperatures the blocked ice cannot melt, but, scoured by high winds, it sublimes, escaping as vapor. Meteorites trapped in the icy conveyor belt are thus exposed on the surface, and gradually they accumulate. There is astonishingly little snowfall on the continent, so with diligent searching, the black objects from space may be spotted against the pale blue ice.

—Kenneth F. Weaver, "Invaders from Space"

e.   Courts often need the precise time and nature of death to settle manslaughter charges, inheritance claims, insurance proceeds, tax problems, and the disposition of jointly held money and property. One often quoted case involves a 1958 auto accident which claimed the lives of an Arkansas couple. The man died instantly, but his wife remained in a deep coma for 17 days before her heart stopped beating. In a legal disagreement over their two wills, an attorney contended that the man and wife had died simultaneously because both lost the power to act in the same instant. The court denied this, and ruled that the woman's beating heart delayed her legal death for the 17 days.

—Leonard A. Stevens, "When is Death?"

f.   For educational purposes, there are at least three distinct groups of mentally retarded children. . . . Each group has its unique characteristics and problems requiring a distinct educational program. These groups are the *trainable mentally retarded, the educable mentally retarded,* and the *slow learners.* A fourth group not considered for educational purposes are those children who are so intellectually deficient that they require constant care and supervision. Many of these persons can never learn to communicate or to provide for their most simple, personal needs such as eating, dressing, and toileting. Others can accomplish these but little more.

—William M. Cruickshank and Orville G. Johnson, Eds.,
Education of Exceptional Children and Youth

3. Identify the various kinds of structural signals (discussed on pages 54–56)—meaning link clusters, transitional words, signals of time or place—employed in the paragraphs in "For Discussion" item 2. Also identify instances of parallelism.

4. Following is a paragraph in which the sequence of sentences has been scrambled. Try to put it back together as the student wrote it. State what form the paragraph takes (SRI, IRS, or whatever) and arrange it on the page with indentations to show the levels of modification as we did on pages 67–69. If you find that, like Humpty-Dumpty, it can't be put together again, analyze the weaknesses of the paragraph that prevent the reassembly.

1. The members of the group all go to a designated place and sit in a circle around the fire.
2. Each member then partakes of the peyote and goes through his "experience."
3. These ceremonies always follow a set pattern.
4. This was described in a brief statement on how the ceremony is set up.
5. Peyotists do not deviate from this pattern, unless absolutely needed, and then only rarely.
6. He starts the group through by chanting songs and prayers to Mescalito, who is the god of peyotism.
7. These experiences or "trips," as the modern drug culture terms them, are how a peyotist learns from his religion.
8. There is a leader to guide the group through the ceremony.
9. The ceremony usually breaks up in the morning when the ceremonial feast is eaten.

5. Outline the definition paragraph on toxins (pages 73–74). Then compare your result with the outline for extended definition on page 158.

For Practice

1. Using the following as opening sentences that contain the subject and restriction of the paragraph, add illustration, using the method of paragraph development indicated in parentheses.

   a. In our society, automobiles are both a delight and a curse. (comparison)
   b. Purses serve many important functions in women's lives. (classification)
   c. Most colleges and universities require freshmen to engage in orientation activities. (definition)
   d. Surely something can be done to make college registration less traumatic to students. (anecdote)
   e. Clean air can become a reality if industry is economically affected by an irate citizenry. (examples; perhaps statistics or authority)
   f. Many freshmen withdraw from my college during the second semester. (reasons or causes)
   g. Many buildings on campus are in serious need of renovation. (examples)

2. Using the skills learned earlier for sentence combining (see chapter 4), combine the following clusters of sentences, using whatever combining tactics seem appropriate. Then construct an SRI paragraph that exhibits a logical progression of ideas.

   a. Classification paragraph—add transitional devices where needed.

      Many people now have smoke detectors in their homes.
      Many people now have fire detectors in their homes.
      Not many vacationers include one in their camping equipment.
      It can hang in a tent.

It can hang in a cabin.
It can hang in a recreational vehicle.
Campfires are a dangerous fire hazard there.
Lanterns are a dangerous fire hazard there.
Camp stoves are a dangerous fire hazard there.
Heaters are a dangerous fire hazard there.
Several kinds are available for campers.
One is enclosed in a carrying case.
One includes the smoke detector.
The detector has a test button.
The detector has a weak-battery signal.
The detector has a hanger to hook on any kind of door.
One device is also an anti-intrusion alarm.
The device can fit into the crack of a door.
The device can be attached to a board.
The board is across the entrance of a tent.
The device warns about intruders.
The device warns about smoke or fire.

b. Cause-and-effect paragraph. Use some of the CAUSE conjunctions listed on page 76 or transitional adverbs such as *therefore* and *however.*
The telephone has affected our society in many ways.
The telephone was invented about one hundred years ago.
The telephone has saved lives.
Lives have been saved by speedy messages.
The messages are of emergencies.
The messages are life saving.
The telephone has increased the speed for disseminating information.
The telephone has accelerated scientific research.
The telephone has accelerated technological growth.
The telephone has replaced letter writing.
Letter writing is an art.
The telephone has contributed to the growth of the nuclear family.
The telephone makes keeping in touch with family members easier.
The telephone has made war more efficient.
The telephone may have prevented wars.
The telephone avoids the misunderstandings.
The misunderstandings can result from written messages.
The telephone permits instant personal contact.
This saves personal energy.
This saves man-made energy.
Man-made energy is used for transportation.

11

Sentence Strategies in Expository Writing

In chapter 4, we described the sentence as a patterned language structure, introduced some techniques of sentence reordering and combining, and discussed those sentence types most common in personal writing. In this chapter, we deal with reordered and combined sentences that are frequently used in expository writing. Obviously, however, the sentence types previously discussed are also used in expository writing; simple, coordinate, subordinate, and cumulative sentences are the principal building blocks of all kinds of writing. But, as in other fields of activity, particular tasks call for specific tools. And the special tasks of explaining an operation, classifying something, comparing several items, or showing causal relations often require sentence structures different from those previously covered.

REORDERING AND DELETING SENTENCE ELEMENTS

As you recall, reordering involves a rearrangement of the essential sentence elements. In chapter 4, we concentrated on the reordering of simple sentences; in this chapter, we expand the reordering techniques to compound or complex sentences. Previously, we spoke of deleting to create intentional sentence fragments; here we discuss it as a device to create imperative sentences, a form commonly used in writing instructions.

Changing Active Sentences to Passive

In our earlier discussions of basic sentence patterns (chapter 8), we have focused on sentences in the active voice—that is, with the subject placed before the verb to emphasize that the subject-actor initiated the action expressed in the verb. But sentences with the pattern *Subjective—Transitive Verb—Direct Object* (see page 67) can be made passive. As in the following example, the subject moves to a new position after the verb, deemphasizing the action relationship between the two sentence elements. The result is that the immediacy of the action is diminished:

Active: Jonas Salk developed the first polio vaccine.
Passive: The first polio vaccine was developed by Jonas Salk.

Although passive sentences should not be extensively used in narrative and descriptive writing, they do have a place in explanatory writing, especially in scientific and technical writing. Unlike narrative and descriptive writing where action, immediacy, or suspense are primary concerns, much expository writing deemphasizes action, concentrating more on results, explanations, relationships, or causes. For such purposes, passive sentences are sometimes more effective than active ones.

Understanding the structural differences between active and passive sentences will help you to use both more effectively. When we make an active sentence passive, a number of changes take place.

1. We move the object to the subject position and place the subject in the object's place after the verb. Note that we now supply *by* to indicate the subject's function in the sentence.

    Active: Jonas Salk developed the first polio vaccine.
         (subject)   (object)
    Passive: The first polio vaccine was developed *by* Jonas Salk.
         (object)   (subject)

    Although *Jonas Salk* remains the *logical* subject in the passive, the subject's repositioning sometimes confuses readers about who the subject-actor is—one of the problems involved in using passives.

2. We change the active verb by adding a form of *be* in front of the main verb, now changed to a different form (a participle):

    developed changes to *was developed*

    As you can see, the addition of the auxiliary verb *be* lessens or dilutes the sense of action.

3. A third possibility in creating passives is to delete the subject-actor altogether, thus eliminating entirely the initiator of the action and diluting the action even more:

    The first polio vaccine was developed.

A good rule of thumb is to use active sentences as much as possible in all forms of writing. On occasion, however, when the subject is obvious or unimportant, passives can prove useful. In describing the steps taken in an experiment, for instance, a scientist may choose passives to avoid the distracting repetition of the *I* or *we* subject. Passive sentences are also beneficial when the subject is obvious or unknown, as in "Eternal life *is accepted* universally," or "The window *was broken*."

On other occasions, a shift from active to passive can be used to maintain parallelism, as in the following example, where the shift from active in the first sentence to passive in the second allows the writer to use "I" as the positional subject in both.

> I hope with some fervor that we can learn a lot more than we now know about the human mind, and I see no reason why this strange puzzle should remain forever and entirely beyond us. But I *would be deeply disturbed by any prospect* that we might use the new knowledge to begin doing something about it—to improve it, say.
>
> —*Lewis Thomas, "The Art of Teaching Science"*

Passive sentences are also useful for maintaining focus throughout a paragraph. In the following example, the passive in the second sentence continues the main focus ("the fact") of the preceding sentence:

> The fact that you arrived in this building half an hour ago on foot, or on a bicycle, or in a car, is just as much a fact about the past as the fact that Caesar crossed the Rubicon. But it will probably be ignored by historians.
>
> —*Edwin Hallet Carr, "The Historian and His Facts"*

Even though passives are often appropriate in expository writing, they should be used with care. Too many result in dull, lifeless writing, and sometimes blur meaning. Later we will discuss the uses and abuses of passives in persuasive writing.

Rhetorical Questions

Although they take the same forms as other questions (see chapter 4), rhetorical questions have a different purpose. While other questions request an informative response, rhetorical questions are used to evoke readers' interest in the subject, to jolt them into a new approach, or to get their active participation. In such cases, the writer sometimes supplies no answer. Rhetorical questions are generally most effective, however, when serving as a springboard to an explanation or as a transition from one idea to another. With this brief transitional paragraph, Elizabeth Kübler-Ross moves from a previous discussion of scientific advances in psychology to an explanation of the reasons that we fear death:

> The more we are making advancements in science, the more we seem to fear and deny the reality of death. How is this possible?
>
> —*On Death and Dying*

In this example, we see one of the most beneficial uses of the rhetorical question in expository writing—to point out causal relationships. Note that the question could be answered with "This is possible *because.* . . ."

Student writers often use rhetorical questions too liberally and indiscriminately, and tend to forget that in exposition such questions should normally be restricted to introducing explanations, especially explanations of causes. Like passives and fragments, rhetorical questions should be used sparingly and wisely. Don't you agree? How long would you maintain interest in a list of unanswered questions?

Using Imperative Sentences in Expository Writing

Imperative (command) statements delete the subject, *you*. Because writers must use many instructional "You do so-and-so. . ." sentences in explaining a process, they find imperatives useful in eliminating the obvious subject, as you can see from this example describing how to make a holiday table wreath:

> First, force some branches of boxwood into a wreath shape. Then fasten colored ornaments, foil-wrapped plastic-foam squares, and strings of gold balls to the wreath. Secure inexpensive glass candle holders to the branches, covering them with greens. Finally, place votive candles in the holders.

By using imperative sentences in this way, you avoid distracting the reader with the repeated "you," and give greater emphasis to the instruction itself.

One caution, however, in employing imperatives: Too many, particularly in writing that is not intended to give instructions, can create an authoritarian or condescending tone that will offend your readers.

SENTENCES CREATED BY COMBINING

In chapter 4, we discussed how two or more simple sentences can be combined to produce an expanded sentence. In addition to explaining how to form coordinate and subordinate structures, we suggested ways to add detailed modifiers. Although in expository writing you will continue to make use of the sentence types we discussed there, you can add others to your store of writing tools.

Periodic Sentences

The periodic sentence has a form opposite that of the cumulative sentence discussed earlier. As you recall, cumulative sentences state the base clause first and then tack on a series of modifiers. Periodic sentences have the reverse pattern:

Modifier, Modifier, Modifier, BASE

Such sentences with a large number of modifiers can be very effective for creating a climactic effect: placing the base at the end of the sentence gives the information there special emphasis and importance, as in this example (the base is italicized):

> Not a communicable disease treatable by antitoxins (Modifier 1), not a congenital trait passed on in the genes (Modifier 2), not a product of a weak character (Modifier 3), *nicotine addiction is an acquired, treatable habit.*

Note how suspense is created in this example: The reader's curiosity is aroused by the modifiers, then satisfied by the information in the base.

Another use of periodic sentences is to make the added details serve as a transition from a preceding sentence. In the following example, the second sentence (periodic) does just that:

> Thus baseball's most delicate and detailed aspects are often, to the spectator, the most interesting. *The pitcher's windup, the anticipatory crouch of the infielders, the quick waggle of the bat as it poises for the pitch*—these subtle miniature movements are as meaningful as the home runs and the strikeouts.
>
> —Murray Ross, *"Football Red and Baseball Green"*

Conditional Sentences

Conditional sentences are created by joining two basic sentences by paired coordinating conjunctions (*either . . . or; neither . . . nor*) or by subordinating conjunctions paired with *then* (*if . . . then; when . . . then*). These pairs set up some kind of relationship—usually that of an alternative, condition, or result—between the two sentences. Because all conditional sentences involve logical relationships, the writer must take special care to avoid faulty reasoning (see chapter 18).

1. **either . . . or; neither . . . nor:** This sentence type sets forth a pair of alternatives (*either . . . or*) or negates two related conditions (or causes, effects, actions).

    > *Either* the challenged person will retreat from the problem *or* he will start a problem-solving procedure to solve it. (sets forth two alternative effects)

    > Washington *neither* had ambitions to rule *nor* was he eager to serve a third term. (negates two related characteristics).

2. **if . . . then; when . . . then:** Both these conditionals set up a first situation and a second situation that may result from it, thus making them useful tools for showing cause-and-effect relationships and sequential results in explaining a process. Frequently, *then* is omitted.

    > *If* the glue is applied at the wrong temperature, [*then*] bonding will not result. (cause-and-effect)

    > *When* you have kneaded the bread for ten minutes, [*then*] it will be smooth and shiny. (process)

On occasion, the order of conditionals may be reversed for special emphasis, for smoother transition, or for climactic effect. In such cases, *then* is always omitted.

> Bonding will not result *if* the glue is applied at the wrong temperature.

The dough will be smooth and shiny *when* it has been sufficiently kneaded.

Note: Some *if* clauses require a special verb form when *be* is the main verb.

If I *were* you, I would resign.

If you are unsure about which verb form to use, check "subjunctive" in the Reference Guide.

Balanced Sentences

Balanced sentences are created by joining two sentences having parallel structure, length, and content. Generally, the two are separated by a semicolon. Because they provide an emphatic device for showing contrasts, they occur frequently in comparison-and-contrast writing. Our two examples illustrate the most common forms: The first retains all the elements of both sentences; the second deletes the verb in the final clause (showing the omission with a comma).

To be French is to be like no one else; to be American is to be like everyone else.

—*Peter Ustinov*

Lee was the last of the great old-fashioned Generals; Grant, the first of the great moderns.

—*T. Harry Williams, Lincoln and His Generals*

FAULTY SENTENCES

As you create more complex sentence structures in your writing, you may encounter problems not inherent in simpler sentences. Adding modifiers indiscriminately can result in faulty sentences that are ambiguous or downright baffling. Learning to prevent these problems is part of your commitment to your readers—writing as clearly as possible.

Modification Booby Traps

Is there anything peculiar about these sentences?

1. The mayor is a dirty street fighter.
2. A girl with a flag that was waving at us looked very familiar.
3. Rodolphe sent Emma Bovary a note that he was leaving town in a basket of apricots.
4. Pedaling frantically and watching the bus barrel down on you from behind, a raucous voice pierces the air: "Don't you know what bicycles are for?"

You're right. They're all a little weird. In 1, the mayor could fight dirty streets or fight dirty in the streets. In 2, either the girl or the flag could wave at us. In 3,

Rodolphe may have discovered a new way to travel—in a basket of apricots. And 4 presents the mind-boggling possibility of a raucous voice pedaling a bicycle down the street, dodging buses.

Although these sentence problems can be humorous, we rarely set out to create them; in fact, we often find them embarrassing—slips of the pen, so to speak. These ambiguous structures are not only disconcerting, they also seriously interfere with clarity of meaning. Therefore, we try to avoid these kinds of booby traps, all of which involve ambiguous or dangling modifiers. But they often occur accidentally, especially because, as writers, we tend to place modifiers in sentence positions natural to *spoken* English.

Ambiguous Noun-Phrase Modifiers

As in examples 1 and 2 above, a very common source of ambiguity is the expanded noun phrase. The kind of double meaning illustrated in example 1 ("The mayor is a dirty street fighter") would not cause problems in spoken English. The speaker's intonation would clearly indicate the meaning intended. In writing, however, to clarify such structural problems, we must either rewrite the phrase or use punctuation devices to substitute for the intonation. The hyphen, creating a compound word, is useful for this purpose:

The mayor is a dirty street-fighter.

As you can see, the hyphen indicates which compound the writer intended. Any remaining ambiguity stems from the multiple meanings of *dirty*, rather than from the structure.

This kind of ambiguity booby trap awaits the unwary writer in the process of adjective insertion because the resulting expanded noun phrase can often be interpreted in more than one way. When you insert an adjective into a noun phrase you should be especially wary when two nouns are present: Adjective + Noun + Noun (*dirty + street + fighter*).

Another pitfall in noun phrases is possessive nouns. The ambiguity in a statement like "Smith is an old women's college" arises from two structural possibilities:

(Adjective + Possessive) + Noun
   (old women's)   (college) = a college for old women

Adjective + (Possessive + Noun)
  (old)   (women's college) = an old college for women

Here, rewriting can solve the problem.

Modifiers following the noun can also cause trouble. In the noun phrase of example 2, "A girl with a flag *that was waving at us*," the italicized relative clause could have been derived from either of these insert sentences.

A girl was waving at us.

                  → that was waving at us

A flag was waving at us.

The proximity of the relative clause to *flag* and the use of the neutral *that* exaggerate the ambiguity. A more careful choice of relative pronouns solves this problem:

> A girl with a flag *who was waving at us.* (*who* is used to refer to humans)
> A girl with a flag *which was waving at us.* (*which* is used to refer to non-humans and inanimate objects)

Ambiguity Created by Movable Modifiers

If such a strong risk of ambiguity lurks in noun modifiers that are not movable, imagine the dangers inherent in those that are. One of the tricks that adverbial modifiers can play on unwary writers is illustrated in example 3:

> Rodolphe sent Emma Bovary a note that he was leaving town *in a basket of apricots.*

In many instances, a place adverb can be put at the end of a sentence without causing ambiguity, as in:

> Rodolphe sent Emma Bovary a note that he was leaving town *in a stage coach.*

No problem here. Logically, only Rodolphe will use the stage coach as a conveyance. But if another sentence element is placed between the base sentence and the adverb, a different modification meaning could result:

> Rodolphe sent Emma Bovary a note that he was leaving town *to stay with his mother* in a stage coach.

Now there is confusion: Is he leaving in the coach or planning to live in it? In both examples, the problem is basically the same: The place adverb could have come from the original base sentence or from the insert sentence. Here are the two possibilities for our original example:

> Rodolphe sent Emma Bovary a note *in a basket of apricots.* (base sentence)
> Rodolphe was leaving town *in a basket of apricots.* (reconstructed insert sentence)

You can use this device of breaking down sentences (*decombining*) as a test to spot ambiguity. Then solve the problem by placing the modifier closer to the main clause:

> Rodolphe sent Emma Bovary a note *in a basket of apricots* that he was leaving town.

Dangling Modifiers

Perhaps the structural booby trap that most jeopardizes writers is the dangling sentence modifier, the culprit in example 4:

> *Pedaling frantically and watching the bus barrel down on you from behind,* a raucous voice pierces the air: "Don't you know what bicycles are for?"

Unlike the modification problems discussed earlier, where the modifiers were tied in meaning to a single sentence, the dangling modifier in this example results from the student writer's attempt to make a transition from the preceding sentence:

> Motorists will actually vie for the honor of having you and your machine entangled in their front grills as trophies of a good day's work. *Pedaling frantically and watching the bus barrel down on you from behind,* a raucous voice. . .

The use of *motorists* as the subject of the first sentence sets up the expectation that *pedaling* and *watching* will refer to it. Indeed, structurally they seem to do so, but logically they cannot; instead, they dangle.

Traditional grammar dictates that, with the exception of such transitional adverbs as *moreover, on the other hand,* and *incidentally,* any modifiers placed at the beginning of a sentence must be logically tied to the subject. However, language scholars now realize that some movable modifiers may relate to the sense of the whole sentence, not simply to the subject. In many cases, the information the reader needs in order to relate the modifier correctly is implicitly included in the rest of the sentence as in this example:

> *Excepting the medical school, all colleges in the university follow the same schedule.*

Because the reader recognizes that the medical school is one of the university colleges, all of which follow some kind of schedule, there is no ambiguity. Your common sense tells you that the modifier does not dangle. But that test does not always work. Another test, perhaps more reliable, is to decombine the sentence, changing the *-ing* structure into a possible insert sentence that supplied the modifier. To do this, you simply supply the possible deleted elements. Let's see how it works, using this example:

> *Driving down the interstate,* the moon followed us at the same rate of speed.

Obviously, the moon is not driving down the interstate. Now that you have learned some of the principles of sentence-combining (chapter 4), you should be able to reconstruct an insert sentence from which the *-ing* phrase was derived. You simply reconstruct the underlying sentence by supplying the possible missing elements.

> Reconstructed insert: *We were* driving down the interstate.
> Base sentence: The moon followed us at the same rate of speed.

Now we see that *We* is the subject of the insert sentence and *moon* of the base sentence; therefore, deleting *we* creates a dangling modifier. In this case, combining the sentences by using the *-ing* phrase was an unfortunate choice; better to have changed the insert sentence to a subordinate clause, retaining *we:*

> *As* we were driving down the interstate, the moon followed us at the same rate of speed.

Note that both of the ambiguous examples involve *-ing* phrases, the guiltiest structure in dangling modification—so guilty that it is often set apart by a special label: dangling participle. Writers need to be especially vigilant about these and other subjectless verbal phrases. In most cases, if the subject of the insert sentence is different from that of the base sentence, the modifier dangles.

In many instances when the subjects in the base sentence and in the inserted sentence are different, no ambiguity results because some other grammatical device signals the relationship. Look at this example.

When John was twenty-one, his father decided to retire.

Here, the possessive pronoun *his* shows an unambiguous relationship to *John.* But in the next example, we can't be sure whether *he* refers to John or to his father.

When he was twenty-one, his father decided to retire.

Many times ambiguity can be eliminated by very simple devices. Here are a few additional tips that may help you.

- You can add gender signals (*his, her, its*):

  Ambiguous: The boy on the horse with a patch over one eye
      Clear: The boy on the horse with a patch over one of *his/its* eyes

- You can change the verb form to show singular or plural (*is/are; was/were*):

  Ambiguous: one of the football players who seemed exhausted
      Clear: one of the football players who *was/were* exhausted

- You can add a coordination signal (*and, but, or*) or repeat a key structure signal

  Ambiguous: a car that was parked in front of a garage that needed paint
      Clear: a car that was parked in front of a garage *and* that needed paint

All this does not mean that you should avoid using certain structures just because they may result in ambiguity; they are much too valuable for that. If you are alert to ambiguity and apply the suggestions given here, you can avoid these modification booby traps.

FAULTY SENTENCE STRUCTURE IN EXPANDED SENTENCES

Although ambiguity is troublesome, it is not the only cause of unhealthy sentences. Such sentence blights as poorly joined sentence elements, illogical relationships, or inept ordering of sentence modifiers can also plague readers. Sentences such as the following are not necessarily ambiguous, but they are faulty and therefore confusing to readers.

1. Henry for years has never made it to class on time, who on the night of his graduation from high school was getting a haircut, who at his dear uncle's funeral arrived as they were carting the casket to the hearse, who procrastinated so about his term paper that he handed it in a week after it was due.

2. People are constantly hustling by, mumbling under their breaths, planes thunder in the exits and entrances of the airport with a booming sonic sound, and vehicles are constantly buzzing around the grounds.

Although the students who wrote these sentences were probably not consciously aware of it, both resulted from sentence-combining tactics. Understanding what went wrong with them can help you to avoid similar problems or to identify and correct them when they do occur in your own writing. Since such sentences result from faulty sentence-combining, one way to fix them is by following the decombining technique we have been using—breaking down the expanded sentence into its base and insert sentences. Not only will you discover the sources of awkwardness in the sentences you have written, but the practice you gain from analyzing the structure of sentences and from recombining them should make you a more proficient writer of sentences in the future.

Faulty Use of Relative Clauses

Although the student who wrote example 1 is to be commended for creative effort, closer attention to the arrangement of the relative clauses would have produced a clearer and more stylistically pleasing sentence. First, we'll look at the student's version, then revise it by decombining, reconstructing the basic underlying sentence patterns that might have supplied the modifying materials.

Henry for years had never made it to class on time, who on the night of his graduation from high school was getting a haircut, who at his dear uncle's funeral arrived as they were carting the casket to the hearse, who procrastinated so about his term paper that he handed it in a week after it was due.

Although the student reordered some adverb phrases, the basic combining technique produced a series of relative clauses. Let's decombine, using the relative pronouns as signals for the underlying insert sentences.

Henry has never made it to class on time in years.   (Base sentence)
Henry was getting a haircut on the night of his graduation.   (*who*)
Henry arrived at his dear uncle's funeral as they were carting the casket to the hearse.   (*who*)
Henry procrastinated so about his term paper that he handed it in a week after it was due.   (*who*)

Before recombining, let's ask these questions about the insert sentences: Which contains material most closely related to that in the base sentence? Which contains the most startling information—information that could serve as climax of the series of modifiers? Obviously, arriving late at a loved uncle's funeral seems a more serious example than being late to class. Benefiting from such an analysis, we can then recombine the sentences. Note that we placed material most closely related to Henry's behavior near the beginning of each relative clause.

For years, Henry has never made it to class on time—Henry, who *procrastinated so about his term paper* that he handed it in a week late, who *was getting a haircut* on the night of his graduation, who *arrived at his dear uncle's funeral* as they were carting the casket to the hearse.

In our revision, we have applied two principles of effective writing—using vocabulary (repeating "Henry" and substituting "late") to tie ideas together and provide focus, and creating an effect of climax if possible. We achieved the latter by reordering the relative clauses, placing all the information about school behavior first, then moving to more shocking instances of procrastination.

Faulty Parallelism

As we suggested in our discussion of sentences in chapter **4**, grammatical parallelism is important not only as a stylistic device, but also as an aid for sorting out the modification. Example 2 fails as a well-written sentence because the parallelism is faulty:

> People are constantly hustling by, mumbling under their breaths, planes thunder in the exits and entrances of the airport with a booming sonic sound, and vehicles are constantly buzzing around the grounds.

Using the commas as signals of coordination, let's reconstruct the insert sentences:

> People are constantly hustling by.   (Base sentence)
> People are mumbling under their breaths.   (*-ing* phrase)
> Planes thunder in the exits and entrances of the airport with a booming sonic sound.   (*and*)
> Vehicles are constantly buzzing around the grounds.   (*and*)

With reordering of adverb modifiers, deleting or changing repeated words, and replacing commas with semicolons, here's a possible revision (the changes are italicized):

> *Mumbling under their breaths,* people constantly *hustle by in the airport;* airplanes, with a booming sonic sound, thunder in the exits and entrances; vehicles *buzz busily* around the grounds.

Because the information is more closely tied together, the sentence is tighter. Also important was making the verb forms parallel; the present-tense forms, in addition, create a sense of haste and urgency.

Decombining sentences you have written without consciously using sentence-combining techniques is often difficult. Consequently, the following steps may be useful:

1. Before decombining, circle any sentence-combining signals: commas, dashes, semicolons, conjunctions, relative pronouns, or *-ing* verbs.

2. Break the sentence into its underlying base and insert sentences, using the circled elements as a guide.

3. Examine the sentences for grammatical and structural problems, such as verb parallelism, dangling modifiers, pronoun reference, subject—verb agreement. Correct them. There is nothing to gain from recombining the same mistakes.

4. Recombine the sentences, avoiding the problems of the original. Don't hesitate to change the combining techniques, to rearrange materials, to add new material, or to reject existing information that you realize is useless or insignificant.

5. Realize that some sentences can't be fixed, in which case, a complete rewrite is needed. Sometimes your information is too involved for a single sentence, no matter how expanded; in such cases, don't hesitate to create several sentences from the original.

SUMMARY

In this chapter, we have expanded our discussion of sentence combining, presenting a variety of sentence structures particularly adaptable to specific needs in expository writing. We have recommended using passive sentences primarily for situations when the doer of the action is unimportant or when a passive helps maintain continuity or focus. Rhetorical questions, when used sparingly, are effective attention getters. Imperatives eliminate the need in a process analysis for a repetitive and distracting subject (*you*). Periodic sentences can provide variety, effect transitions, and create suspense by withholding the base clause information until last.

We have also pointed out some traps created by adding modifiers and have suggested ways both to test for ambiguity of meaning and to repair the damage. We have introduced you to the reverse of sentence combining—decombining, or breaking an expanded sentence into its component parts so that you can discover the source of ambiguity or awkwardness.

All these techniques are valuable additions to your box of writing tools. Mastering all the possible sentence types in the language takes much conscious practice and an awareness of their stylistic significance. But no other aspect of writing is more important to becoming an expert writer.

ASSIGNMENTS

For Practice

1. Combine the clusters of sentences below, creating the appropriate sentence types. Delete or add words to form well-constructed sentences.

   Active to Passive

   a. The committee had originally amended the bill.
   The committee sent it to the Senate for consideration.

   b. The light of the sun passes through the glass.
   The plants inside the greenhouse absorb it.

c. Someone blew up the warehouse.
Someone burned all the contents in the warehouse.
The contents were valuable.

Imperative Sentences

You should choose a quiet workshop.
You should stock it with reference books.
You should spend a few minutes at a prewriting exercise.
You can start to write a first draft.

Periodic Sentences

a. Base: She exhibited all the symptoms of a panic attack.
   She was shaking.
   The shaking was violent.
   She was gasping for breath.
   She was sweating profusely.
   She was unable to speak.
   She was unable to focus her eyes on her book.

b. Base: These are the challenges.
   The challenges face many Third World countries.
   Religious hostility is a challenge.
   Class hostility is a challenge.
   Population growth is a challenge.
   Inadequate schools are a challenge.
   Poverty is a challenge.
   The poverty is desperate.
   Hunger is a challenge.
   The hunger is pervasive.
   The government is a challenge.
   The government is corrupt.

Conditional Sentences

a. I read the advertisments in the magazines.
I realize that they are lies.

b. I hunt for a property to buy.
I find the land.
Someone had purchased the land long ago. (change to passive)

c. (Create a short paragraph)
Some people would pick a man's pocket in the street.
Some people did not have anything else to do.
Some people needed the money.

Other people rob me all the time.

I light my house.
I light my office.
The electric company holds me up.

I ride on the subways.
The transportation system holds me up.

The robbery is legal.
The thief goes free.
The robbery is against the law.
The thief goes to jail.

Balanced Sentences

a.   Men are expected to age.
     Women are not expected to age.

b.   Women need to be ambitious for themselves.
     Women do not need to be ambitious merely for their children.

c.   Men choose a mate.
     Someone chooses a woman. (change to passive)

2.   Try to identify the problems caused by these passives taken from students' papers. Either correct each problem or change the sentence back to active.

a.   Ships were the first form of transportation shown in the film as people were brought to America.

b.   One wonders if all the campus activities are only carried on during the week.

c.   The bow and arrow has been replaced by the gun for protection purposes.

d.   Also, John Lennon is constantly seen barefoot in these pictures and on their album "Abbey Road," which is the way they bury the House of Lords, which all Beatles are a member of.

e.   Because of the fear one would experience in coping with such extraordinary circumstances, emotions would be stirred.

f.   The paper must be written by him by tomorrow.

3.   All of the following sentences are ambiguous. Explain the source of the trouble in each and rephrase to clarify. Use decombining where appropriate.

a.   They are now experimenting on food to be shot with atomic rays that can stay under water as long as the submarine.

b.   Reminiscing about 1964, my father had a heart attack and was taken to the hospital.

c.   In its concentrated form, a teaspoon could kill 30 million people.

d.   Since the magic ring was devised by an evil power, it inevitably corrupted anyone who used it in the end.

e.   A woman was petting a horse with a big cartwheel hat.

f.   While a small child, my grandfather carried me on his shoulder.

g.   Driving through the Smokies, a bear stopped our car at a garbage can.

h. He didn't see how a woman had the ability to run the office without someone helping her like a man.

i. I sit here writing my autobiography, weighing two hundred and forty-five pounds.

4. All of the following sentences have faulty or awkward structure. Using the decombining technique, recombine the sentences to correct the problems.

a. I watch as the cat readies to spring at my bare toes, its facial expressions, its ears, and its body movement which is a swaying movement.

b. In the magazine there is a full page ad for cigars with a picture of a sexy blonde sitting on a horse staring meekly but passionately at the reader with a large bared bosom clearly visible under a nylon suit.

c. Frank was manly, mature, and an intelligent man.

d. He has not and will not master fundamentals.

e. Capsules, space platforms, and figures clad in spacesuits were available included Batman art toys, games, costumes, wheel toys, model kits, and a Batman walkie-talkie.

f. Inside the home stand eight pianos every girl over twelve can play, and twenty-five guitars.

5. From one of your recent papers, choose several sentences that your instructor marked as "awk" or "syn" and revise, using the decombining-recombining method.

12

Language in Expository Writing

Good ideas, organization, paragraphs, and sentences are not the only keys to a successful expository paper. The effective use of language is also essential. In this chapter, we discuss ways to achieve clarity, accuracy, economy, and appropriateness in the use of words.

CLARITY

Clarity—the word should be uppermost in your mind as you search for language to express your thoughts in expository writing. After all, the main purpose of this kind of writing—to explain—cannot be achieved if your language is murky or misleading. Although that statement is practically self-evident, some other questions remain about clarity. Specifically, the word *clarity* itself is unclear. Just what does it mean?

The great English letter writer Lord Chesterfield provided some help when he advised his son in the mid-eighteenth century to write *clear* business letters. He explained that "every paragraph should be so clear and unambiguous that the dullest fellow in the world may not be able to mistake it, nor obliged to read it twice in order to understand it." We don't agree with that statement about "the dullest fellow in the world," but we do like two concepts that Chesterfield advocates. The first is that clarity is defined in terms of readers. The second is that clarity may be determined by readability, the ease of the reader's ability to understand the writer's meaning.

Naturally, what you write is always clear to you. You know what you mean. For example, college students are so familiar discussing grade point averages in terms of a four-point scale that they fail to realize some readers do not understand what a 2.5 GPA is. Doctors, lawyers, and scientists are so accustomed to talking to their own colleagues that they often cannot communicate to people outside their special fields.

The following true example illustrates what can happen when writers do not tailor their language to their readers. A plumber wrote to a Washington government department asking whether any damage was done to sewer pipes that he had cleaned with hydrochloric acid. He was informed that "The efficacy of hydrochloric acid is indisputable, but the corrosive residue is incompatible with metallic permanence." The plumber thanked the department for letting him know that no damage had been done. The department replied in dismay: "We cannot assume responsibility for the toxic and noxious residue of hydrochloric acid and suggest you use an alternate procedure." Again the plumber thanked them for approving. Finally, the department wrote the plumber, "Don't use hydrochloric acid. It eats hell out of the pipes."

As you can infer from this example, when you are uncertain whether or not readers will understand a term, it is better to err on the side of simplicity than complexity. To avoid offending other knowledgeable readers, however, you might consider the following devices:

1. The explanatory *such as.*

   Critics of business assert that it is stacked in favor of private goods, *such as* food, cars, cigarettes, hair sprays, soaps; and against public goods, *such as* parks, libraries, beaches, clean air.

2. The explanatory *or.*

   Passive restraints (*or* air bags, as they are commonly called) may add hundreds of dollars to the price of retail cars.

3. The flattering *which, as you know.*

   Plea bargaining—which, as you know, is the practice of pleading guilty to a less serious offense instead of being tried for a more serious one—is increasing in our overburdened courts.

You might ask whether the simpler words could not always be used. Why such specialized terms as *private* and *public goods, passive restraints,* or *plea bargaining?* Sometimes such terms are necessary because no suitable synonyms exist. For instance, we use *fair catch* in football to refer to the receiver's signal that he will not return the kick, thereby notifying opposing players that they will be penalized for interfering with him. Imagine having to write this explanation instead of the specialized term!

But using such terms poses a problem—specifically, deciding whether to define them or not. When informing experienced do-it-yourself carpenters how to frame a basement or attic wall, you could assume that they would be familiar with such terms as *studs, plumb line, toenailed, joist,* and *lag screws.* You could assume that camera buffs would understand such terms as *XL cameras, reflexes, automatic metering, zoom lens, fixed-focus lens,* and *built-in exposure meters.* But if you were writing for beginning carpenters or photographers, you would need to clarify these words by defining them as discussed on pages 154–57.

You may argue that all these examples are about real people in the real world and have little to do with you in class, writing composition assignments for your

English instructor. But your papers are evaluated by your instructor according to how effectively they communicate to an audience of your classmates or some other specified group. Your task, therefore, is real in the sense that your grade depends upon it, just as on the job your performance evaluation, salary increase, or promotion may depend on some written assignment. And in every instance, you will need to consider your readers: their backgrounds, needs, interests, values, and other characteristics mentioned earlier (see pages 180–81). By doing so, you will increase the chances of your readers' understanding clearly what you have written.

Of course, you can't explain everything to every one of them. But you can try to make your ideas clear to most. This means being careful about specialized terms, particularly those that could be misleading. For example, if you were writing a paper about choosing a computer, you might state: Software determines hardware. But do your readers know these specialized terms? Might they think of hardware as consisting of nails, screws, and bolts? Note how the article on pages 147–50 handled this problem.

To write clearly, you should be aware of such problems. Solving them generally involves using synonyms or short definitions, as the following passage from the *New York Times Magazine,* revised here for high school readers, illustrates:

Original	*Revision*
Although the beaver is an air breather, it is beautifully adapted to an *amphibious* life. Its oversized liver and large lungs enable it to hold its breath for as long as 15 minutes. Its ears and nose are *valvular* and can be shut off at will. A *transparent membrane* protects its eyes when it dives. Its mouth is constructed so that fur flaps close behind its front *incisors,* allowing it to chew wood underwater without choking.	Although the beaver is an air breather, it is beautifully adapted to a *life in the water as well as on land.* Its oversized liver and large lungs enable it to hold its breath for as long as 15 minutes. Its ears and nose work *like valves* and can be shut off at will *like a faucet.* A *thin transparent layer of tissue* protects its eyes when it dives. Its mouth is constructed so that fur flaps close behind its front *cutting teeth,* allowing it to chew wood underwater without choking.

Some of these changes might be unnecessary for high school students. The important point to remember is that you should write to your readers and for them. This requires that you develop a sixth sense, an awareness not only of what your words mean to you but also what they mean to your audience. Then you can adapt your language to your readers either in drafting or in revising.

ACCURACY

Words may fail to communicate clearly for reasons other than that they are difficult or specialized. Sometimes we fail to use words accurately, selecting not the exact one but one almost like it. This is often done deliberately by comedians who mangle the language for comic effect. However, when students write *raised* for *razed, granite* for *granted, respectively* for *respectfully,* or *accept* for *except,* it is no laughing matter. The trick in avoiding such errors is to check every word in your essay that you have any doubt about. The few seconds spent checking a word in a dictionary may save you embarrassment and perhaps a lowered grade.

Flaubert, the great French novelist, relates how he spent hours searching for *le mot juste* (the precise word) when writing. Although you probably have neither the time nor the inclination for that, you can strive for accuracy. Particularly in revising, try to substitute a more precise term for the one that popped into your head while you were writing your first draft. Consulting a thesaurus, a synonym dictionary, or a college dictionary may be helpful. But be careful about using a thesaurus: It merely lists words and does not distinguish their connotations or different shades of meaning. A dictionary or synonym dictionary is safer and more helpful.

ECONOMY

Most Americans hurry. Whether driving, eating, shopping, dancing, vacationing—or reading—we seldom do it slowly. Although we may slow ourselves down as we read personal narratives and descriptions, savoring the experiences they convey, we generally speed through exposition. When Americans look for information about assembling a bicycle, buying insurance, or enrolling in summer school, they want it to be to the point.

To the point is what we mean by economy. In our writing and teaching, we used to try to convey this concept with words like *conciseness* and *brevity.* The trouble with these terms is they may suggest that all sentences should be short, simple sentences, rather than the expanded ones we have discussed. That's not what we mean by economy. Your writing must be complete enough to communicate everything necessary to help your reader understand the subject fully; on the other hand, it should not include unnecessary words or information. Achieving economy is like dieting: The purpose of both is to remove fat. What's left should be strong, firm, and muscular. Remember this: Omit any and all words for which you do not have any use. Or economically stated: Omit useless words!

Here are some questions to ask yourself while revising to achieve economy:

1. Can I omit the relative pronouns *which, who,* or *that*? These three little words—*which, who, that*—are likely to clog your sentences unless you are alert. Note that one or two words are saved in the revised version of each of the following sentences, making each that much more economical:

Original: The fumes *which* come from millions of cars fill the air with pollutants.
Revision: The fumes from millions of cars fill the air with pollutants.

Original: Some people *who* own sports cars keep them for more than ten years.

Revision: Some people keep their sports cars for more than ten years.

Original: Many automobile parts *that* are now made overseas were formerly produced in this country.

Revision: Many automobile parts now made overseas were formerly produced in this country.

Note that when we deleted the relative pronouns, we also removed part or all of the verb phrase in the clause. Of course, you cannot always delete *which, who,* and *that;* sometimes they are essential to your desired effect. But when you can remove them, do so. Your writing will be more economical and more vigorous.

2. Can I remove the introductory *there is, there are,* or *it is?* Just as inexperienced writers often lead up to the subject of their papers slowly, so they do with the subject of sentences, resulting in the unnecessary introducers—*there is, there are,* and *it is.* Although they are sometimes needed, generally you can delete them:

Original: *There is* an increase in membership in sororities and fraternities this year.

Revision: Membership in sororities and fraternities has increased this year.

Original: *It is* a new policy of student government to encourage civic projects.

Revision: A new policy of student government is to encourage civic projects.

Look out for *it is* expressions such as *it is necessary that* and *it is possible that, it might happen that.* The word *must* should replace the first; *may, might, can,* or *could* the others:

Original: It is necessary to spell correctly.

Revision: You must spell correctly.

Original: It is possible that taxes will be increased.

Revision: Taxes may be increased.

3. Can I delete prepositions? Prepositions will swarm all over your papers unless you are vigilant. Most dangerous is *of,* a creature that has to be as carefully screened out as the housefly. But also be on guard against *in, on, by, to,* and *with.* Here's how they operate:

Original: At the time *of* registration, students are required to make payments *of* their fees.

Revision: At registration time, students are required to pay their fees.

Better: At registration, students must pay their fees.

Original: Because of the increase *in* enrollments, some classes *in* sociology are closed by early *in* the morning.

Revision: Because of increased enrollments, some sociology classes are closed by early morning.

Eliminate the pesky prepositions by changing the noun following the preposition to a noun modifier as in the first example, or transform it to a verb form, as in the second.

You should also guard against some prepositional phrases. They come in clusters: the *fact* cluster, the *regard* cluster, the *reference* cluster and the *case* cluster are the main ones to watch out for. Here are three clusters in one monstrous sentence:

> Original: *With reference to* the library hours, *due to the fact* that many students will be preparing for final exams, and will *in most cases* be studying in the reading rooms, we will remain open from 7 a.m. to midnight.
>
> Revision: Because many students will be preparing for final exams and studying in the reading rooms, the library will remain open from 7 a.m. to midnight.

In reference to this subject and *in regard to* these prepositional phrases, and *in view of the fact that* you can improve your writing by eliminating most of them, why not do so?

4. Can I omit any *-ion* words? Unfortunately, the desire to impress others in writing often results in the piling up of the sonorous sounding *-ion* words. But they are all sluggish, overweight dreadnoughts likely to sink readers, sentence,

> Original: The chair made a recommendation that students be given an invitation to provide information to faculty members about proposed new courses.
>
> Revision: The chair recommended that students be invited to inform faculty members about proposed new courses.

5. Can I combine sentences and omit repetitious material? Using the techniques of sentence combining discussed on pages 76–81, you can combine a series of short sentences:

> Original: I decided to attend the university because of its fine academic program. The university has a good faculty. Athletics at the university are also excellent, particularly basketball. And the university has a lovely campus.
>
> Revision: I decided to attend the university because of its fine academic program, good faculty, lovely campus, and excellent athletics, particularly basketball.

6. Can I eliminate dead nouns and overworked verbs? Worn-out, meaningless nouns, such as *kind, manner,* and *nature,* as well as overworked verbs like *to be, give* and *make,* were listed and discussed on pages 92–94, so we will not bore you by repeating that information here.

7. Can I do away with deadwood? Although we have already classified six types of wordiness, many instances of wordiness elude these categories, so we have adopted a miscellaneous category termed *deadwood.*

Deadwood is so prevalent in freshman papers that it constitutes a serious fire hazard. We'd like to have a dollar for every time we've reduced the ponderous "in this modern world of today" to "today" or else crossed out the entire phrase. Why is it that expressions involving time bring out the wordiness in us?

> Original: At this point in time, we are exhausted.
>
> Revision: Now we are exhausted. (*or simply* We are exhausted.)
>
> Original: In this day and age of inflated prices, five dollars does not go far.
>
> Revision: In these inflationary times, five dollars does not go far.

And then there are those phrases using *number* ("five in number"), *color* ("blue in color"), *shape* ("round in shape"), and the like. Also on the deadwood list are certain unnecessary modifiers, particularly *very* and *really,* which can provide emphasis in speech but lose their effectiveness in writing. See for yourself:

> Original: You must work very hard on your article.
>
> Revision: You must work hard on your article.

The unnecessary modifiers have probably emigrated from advertising, a world of fat excesses. Another field, law, provides us with a different form of deadwood—doublets or synonym twins. *First and foremost,* you should be on the lookout for these, *anxious and eager* to eliminate *each and every* repetitive word. Naturally, this is not your *one and only* concern in hacking away at dead words and phrases.

Most deadwood defies classification. So you must become economy-minded, scrutinizing your sentences to strip away the waste. Naturally, you can't adopt a telegraphic style, but you can attack your sentences as if you were being charged for each word. Here's how one student reduced a sentence:

> Original: He contracted in his sociology course to fulfill the requirements for an A grade as established by his professor.
>
> First revision: He contracted in his sociology course to fulfill the professor's requirements for an A grade.
>
> Second revision: He contracted in his sociology course to fulfill the professor's requirements for an A.
>
> Third revision: He contracted to fulfill his sociology professor's requirements for an A.
>
> Fourth revision: He contracted for an A with his sociology professor.

Perhaps in some contexts, the pruning might have stopped at the second or third cutting. Sometimes, for stylistic or semantic reasons, all deadwood cannot be eliminated. For example, the third revision changes the meaning slightly in eliminating the word *course,* suggesting that the contract may have been made for independent study or for make-up work rather than for regular coursework. In the last revision, the omission of *to fulfill* and *requirements* could imply that the department, not the sociology professor, had established the contract requirements. (A further reduction of the sentence to "He contracted for an A" is even possible if the college, course, and teacher contexts are clear, and if such a short sentence is not awkwardly abrupt.) The point here is that sometimes you may change or obscure the meaning of a sentence or spoil its gracefulness by thinking only of eliminating words.

8.   Can I simplify my sentence structure? Often sentences become unnecessarily complicated. Simplifying their structure is another way to eliminate fat and weakness. Subject repetition in clauses, often signals wordiness.

> Original: While *he* was teaching the class, *he* noticed that there was a fire.
> Revision: While teaching the class, he noticed the fire.

Prepositional phrases can be recognized by their introductory prepositions, words that you should seek to eliminate as we have mentioned. Here's an example of how you can delete such phrases.

> Original: He accepted the award given *by the company*.
> Revision: He accepted the company's award.

Deciding what to cut is not easy, but usually long, involved phrases and clauses are good candidates for pruning.

Always be alert for wordiness. The eight questions, repeated here for your convenience, should serve as guidelines:

1.   Can I omit the relative pronouns *which, who,* or *that?*
2.   Can I remove the introductory *there is, there are,* or *it is?*
3.   Can I delete prepositions?
4.   Can I omit any *-ion* words?
5.   Can I combine sentences and omit repetitious material?
6.   Can I eliminate dead nouns and overworked verbs?
7.   Can I do away with deadwood?
8.   Can I simplify my sentence structure?

The key to achieving economy is your frame of mind. Remember that it's not the number of words you write that matters, but what you say. If you clutter your work with unnecessary words, you will annoy your readers and waste their time. So avoid padded prose; eliminate any unnecessary word. Doing so can be painful, but it will bring life and clarity to your writing.

APPROPRIATENESS

In selecting words and in revising your paper, you should be concerned not only with clarity, accuracy, and economy, but also with appropriateness. Although aware of this last quality in dressing and in speaking, you may sometimes forget your audience, purpose, and situation when writing. For instance, as we have pointed out previously (see pages 106–07), you would have little trouble knowing what type of clothes to wear to a beach party, college lecture, or formal dance. You would have little difficulty deciding how to talk about your college experiences to friends at a party, to colleagues at work, or to fellow members of a bridge, gourmet, or bowling group. In each instance, you would wear appropriate clothes and use appropriate language for the audience, purpose, and situation. Similarly, you should be concerned about appropriateness in writing. Specifically, you should avoid colloquial, pretentious, and awkward terms, and euphemisms, unless you deliberately choose them for special effects.

Colloquial Terms

When discussing the differences between speaking and writing in chapter 6, we pointed out that certain words and expressions acceptable in casual speech may distract readers. In talking, you might "gripe" about something; in writing, you would usually "complain," "protest," or "object"; and in more formal situations, you might "dissent" or "demur." In the same way, you would switch from the colloquial "uptight" to "nervous" or "anxious" and from "hang-ups" to "problems."

Of course, colloquialisms have their place, especially in writing dialogue or humor, as in the inscription "Deck them Halls" on a Christmas card. Otherwise, avoid language that you are unaccustomed to seeing in print. If you are uncertain, check the usage section at the end of this book. Or consult an up-to-date dictionary that designates words as *colloquial, slang,* or *informal.* Avoid items marked with one of these labels unless you are using them for special effect. And remember that special effects lose their effectiveness unless used sparingly. Just as you can overdress for a social event, so you can use words that are too fancy. Sometimes this results from deciding to use the longest and most impressive word you can find in a thesaurus. Why write "consider," you think, when "ruminate" is listed as a synonym? You'll show your readers that you know a thing or two! Yes, you'll show them all right—but not what you think. First, "ruminate" can be substituted for "consider" in only a few special instances! Second, this is likely to be as out of place as a tuxedo at a picnic.

Of course, we shouldn't blame the thesaurus for pretentious language. Pretentiousness stems from the writer's desire to impress others. Resist that impulse to show off—to use "remuneration" for "pay," "nuptials" for "wedding," and "ruination" for "ruin." Prefer the plain word to the pretentious one.

Awkward Terms

In chapter 11, we pointed out that awkwardness could result from faulty sentence structures. Word choice, too, may contribute to awkwardness. When trying to impress readers, many students resort to unnatural language, words and phrases that they would not say and do not hear or read.

Awkwardness may also result from your having read relatively little. If you do not read regularly you may be at a disadvantage in listening to your sentences while reading them silently to yourself. You may not have developed a sense of sentence rhythm and an ear for the way words flow together. Consequently, try to increase your reading. Look in your community or school library for interesting books, buy or borrow magazines with stimulating articles, and regularly read newspaper editorials.

Even without an experienced ear, you can alert yourself to two problems: faulty prepositions and careless repetitions. Because of their many meanings, prepositions can be especially tricky in our English language, as people not born and raised in our country attest. They are perplexed by idioms like the following:

> He cut down the tree.
> He cut up on the dance floor.
> He cut himself in on the profits.
> He cut it from the newspaper.
> He cut off a piece.
> He cut to the right.

But even some native speakers of English have difficulty with prepositions in some expressions:

> According (to, with) his instructions, ...
> He was an authority (on, about) skiing.
> They failed to comply (with, to) the regulations.
> She was equal (to, for) the task.

If you had any uncertainty about choosing the first answer in each example, you may need to be especially careful with prepositions. Whenever you have the slightest doubt, check for the appropriate preposition in a desk dictionary, preferably one that shows prepositions used in sentences.

Another type of awkwardness results from excessive repetition of words: If you repeat a *word* in a sentence, readers are apt to focus on the *word*, keeping the *word* in mind, and failing to pay much attention to other *words* in the sentence. (Right?) Sometimes, of course, writers repeat words deliberately, as in these two famous statements:

> Lincoln: "that government of the people, by the people, for the people, shall not perish from the earth."
> Roosevelt: "We have nothing to fear but fear itself."

Note how much weaker these would be without the repetition.

> that government of, by, and for the people shall not perish from the earth.
> We should not be afraid of fear.

However, word repetition in many student papers results from carelessness:

1. They should have questioned him about the first question.

2. Although they were eager to go to the game, they felt that the game would not be close.

Awkward repetition can usually be eliminated by using synonyms or pronouns, as illustrated here:

1. They should have *asked* him about the first question.
2. Although eager to go to the game, they felt that *it* would not be close.

Another form of awkward repetition occurs when the term at the end of one sentence occurs at the beginning of the next:

He knew that the folder was somewhere on the desk. The desk was piled high with papers, mail, notebooks, and candy.

This situation usually calls for sentence-combining, which might take this form:

He knew that the folder was somewhere on the desk, which was piled high with papers, mail, notebooks, and candy.

In this discussion of awkward repetition, we have talked only about words. Similar sounds may also be distracting:

You need not shed a tear because your concert seats are in the second tier of balconies.

It is easy to repeat words and sounds in writing a draft. But you should try to remove this awkward language while revising. Correcting the problem is usually easy; spotting it is not. Be alert.

Euphemisms

Euphemisms (or "prettifiers," as William Safire calls them) are words with pleasant or favorable connotations that are used to refer to unpleasant or unfavorable things or activities. Thus readers are likely to be misled and deceived by them. Politicians are unusually skillful at using them, referring to devastating missiles as "peacemakers," to tax increases as "revenue enhancements," and to the laying off of employees as "reduction in force (RIFs)." The military is not far behind with its infamous "terminate with extreme prejudice" being used for "murder," and "strategic movement to the rear" substituting for "retreat."

But euphemisms appear in all areas of life. Sometimes they serve a beneficial purpose, enabling us to avoid offending or upsetting people. To avoid one of the ugliest words in our language, we use "handicapped" or "disabled" instead of "crippled." We refer to "old people" as "senior citizens," "janitors" as "custodians," and "stupid children" as "slow learners." These substitutions and others like them, used not to mislead but to avoid offense, do no harm and make life more tolerable.

Whenever truth is obscured or tact is unnecessary, euphemisms should be avoided. Readers need no protection from reality under such circumstances. Thus we should write about women being "raped" rather than "criminally assaulted," and people being "poor" rather than "disadvantaged." The appropriate word does not mislead or misrepresent but presents life realistically.

SUMMARY

Writing clear, accurate, economical, and appropriate prose is no easy task. Usually you cannot achieve it while striving to express your ideas in a first draft. In revising your paper, however, you have an opportunity to scrutinize every word; then you can keep asking: "Is it clear?" "Is it accurate?" "Is it economical?" "Is it appropriate for my audience and purpose?" By doing so and following the suggestions in this chapter, you can do much to fulfill your writing commitment.

ASSIGNMENTS

For Discussion

1. We often think of specialized words as strange new terms, but sometimes they are simple words used in new ways. Here, for instance, are the opening sentences of a political editorial.

   > Congress may be getting ready to do a better job on the long-neglected task of legislative oversight. It would be a mistake to expect too much. Strong practical and institutional barriers remain. Nonetheless, new chairmen, new members, new rules and new grass roots pressures all push in the direction of an expanded oversight effort.
   >
   > —*Wall Street Journal*

   What does *oversight* mean to you? To the writer? If you do not know, see if you can figure out the meaning from the following sentence, which appears later in the editorial:

   > The new effort also stems from a belief that closer oversight of agencies and programs may help rebuild public trust in government, persuading many citizens that someone up there is at last fighting their battles.

   If you were writing the editorial, would you substitute another word for *oversight?* If so, what?

2. One of the most colorful and imaginative forms of slang is that used by short-order cooks. We were startled at breakfast one morning to hear our waitress cry out, "Wreck two and roast the English!" Soon afterward we received our two scrambled eggs and English muffins. Are you familiar with contexts where slang terms can be misleading to outsiders? In reproducing such terms in writing, what would need to be done so that readers would understand them?

3. Discuss the language of the following:

   > The word *love* has by no means the same sense for both sexes, and this is one cause of the serious misunderstandings which divide them.
   >
   > —*Simone de Beauvoir*

4. A pun is a play on words, often creating an effect of pleasure (or pain) from different meanings of the same word. For example, in *Romeo and Juliet,* the dying Mercutio quips, "Ask for me tomorrow and you shall find me a grave man." Do you know any pungent puns that illustrate how dual meanings can produce humor? Why should you be sensitive to such possibilities when you write expository papers?

5. Identify the specialized terms in the following sentences and explain how you would rephrase them for a talk to a club of retired people not familiar with current college slang?

   a. Students with a three-point average have developed good study habits.

   b. Some psych courses are snaps.

   c. One of the joys of the library is wandering around in the stacks.

   d. A few profs like to give pop quizzes.

   e. Many first-year courses are taught by teaching assistants.

   f. If we started Thanksgiving vacation on Tuesday, students would probably cut on Monday.

6. What is the meaning of the word *round* in each of the following sentences? What part does context play in each meaning change?

   a. He rounded off the bill at $23.

   b. The bout ended in the tenth round.

   c. The round trip cost $47.

   d. He bought chuck instead of round.

   e. He paid for the round of drinks.

   f. Just then he came round the corner.

   g. The earth turns round.

   h. He was a funny, round fellow.

   i. The library is open all year round.

7. What euphemisms can you substitute for each of the following?

   a. *dead, drunk, bar, places with toilets*

   b. *jailer, garbage man, barber, hairdresser, undertaker, psychiatrist*

8. Rewrite this statement sent by a telephone company to its customer and indicate what is wrong with it:

   If your service is interrupted, a restoral charge will apply.

9. In the light of the discussion in this chapter, rewrite the direction often found on envelopes:

   AFFIX POSTAGE HERE

10. Using each of the following homophones (words that sound similar), try to formulate a sentence.

*aid-aide   accede-exceed   capital-capitol   complacent-complaisant
comprehensible-comprehendible   hoard-horde   ingenious-ingenuous   peal-peel
peer-pier   sale-sail   taught-taut*

11. For comic effect, try to pun on the difference between the literal and figurative meanings of the following phrases:

Phrase: *to man something* Example: Can women man the lifeboats?

wolf down food	*play something by ear*
cry wolf	*the apple of your eye*
to go on a wild goose chase	*to go to pot*
to be down in the mouth	*to sell like hotcakes*

For Practice

1. Remove the unnecessary words from the following sentences and indicate the technique used—omitting the relative pronoun, removing the introductory words, deleting prepositions, avoiding the *-ion* word, combining sentences, eliminating dead nouns and overworked verbs, doing away with deadwood, simplifying sentences, or any combination of these.

a. There are two screws, which are included in the package, that attach the handlebars to the frame.

b. In some cases, students do not know whether they will have enough money to pay for registration at the university next semester.

c. The chairman received your letter in which you informed him that due to the fact that you were ill, you did not take the final exam.

d. I wish to invite you to the first meeting of the Philosophy Club this year. This meeting will be held in the conference room of the Student Center. It will occur on Wednesday, September 20, and start at 8 p.m.

e. He gave consideration to the recommendation that students should submit their applications before spring break.

f. In view of the fact that few women apply to the College of Engineering, there are few women students admitted.

g. It is the opinion of most women employees that the university is engaged in discrimination against them.

h. Many faculty members who have had extensive experience at other schools claim that discrimination of this kind also exists there.

i. The investigator conducted an examination of the records in a hurried manner.

j. The number of applications to the College of Education is on the decrease.

k. The president addressed the faculty with regard to this matter of decreasing enrollments.

l.   He was doing well in the course until the time during the semester when the research report was due.

m.   The bank set an all-time record yesterday in the number of free gifts given to new first-time depositors.

n.   He repeated again the advance warning that he had made at an earlier point in time.

2. Rewrite the following statement to make it more appropriate for an application to transfer to another college:

> I did poorly in my psych class because I goofed off instead of cramming for the exam. As a result, I flunked the course. But the instructor was really to blame; he was lousy, really a flaky dude who is far out. It's funny, but even though he teaches psych, he has lots of hang-ups. That's why his Psych 101 is no gut course.

3. Rewrite the following passage to make it clear to high school students:

> By examining situational differences that require special leadership skills, we do not imply that there are no commonalities in leadership abilities. It does mean that specifying the parameters of effective leadership and how to achieve it is a complicated equation involving components of leadership characteristics, population attributes, and context specification.

> —Adapted from S Sidney Ulmer, *"Leadership Is a Complex Equation"*

4. Select a verbose paragraph from one of your textbooks and rewrite it. Which of the eight techniques listed on pages 232–36 did you find most helpful in eliminating words?

5. Using current slang, write a short note to one of your grandparents. Then provide a dictionary entry for each word that they might not understand.

13

Special Topics |

As you move from the writer-based approach of personal writing to expository tasks that must take the reader more and more into account, you will need to give greater consideration to certain aspects of a more tightly organized paper: choosing titles, writing introductions, constructing an expository thesis, and formulating effective conclusions.

CHOOSING TITLES

Writers may begin with the first word of the first sentence, but readers start with the title—and sometimes go no further. If the title is not engaging or appealing, the reader may not go beyond it. Finding good titles is usually not difficult in personal writing; provocative ones generally grow directly and obviously from the subject matter, as our earlier examples indicate: "The Encounter," "Pond Creek," "Making a Statement with Blaring Boxes," "The Hunter." But reader-based writing, such as exposition and persuasion, may require that you give more thought to creating an effective title.

A good title is not indifferently slapped on. Just as creating an attractive, carefully coifed hairstyle dresses up a person, so can carefully crafting a title enhance a paper. Certainly, the title should provide a suggestion of the content—and it should be brief. Because each writing assignment is different, we cannot tell you precisely how to come up with a short, informative, and provocative title for each. But we can show you some types and examples, and offer some general advice.

Type	*Example*
The Question	"What's Wrong with Cocaine?"
Modified Saying	"Eat, Drink, and Be Thin"
What-to-Do + Surprise	"What to Do before the Crab Grass Comes"
Controversy	"The Student Football Ticket Dilemma"
Humanizing Nonhuman Things	"Keep House Plants Smiling"
Word Play	"Some Words about Words"
Imperative	"Don't Be a Cheerleader!"

You, your classmates, and your instructor may think of others that might be helpful. But whatever you do, avoid the single-word, general-subject title ("Ballooning") or its cousin that simply adds an article ("The Shopping Mall"). If you cannot think of a title that is short, snappy, and informative, then state your thesis in question or abbreviated form: "What Drives an A-Student?" or "The Driving Forces Behind an A Student." Never, no matter how exhausted you are, resort to "Essay I."

As you are probably aware, not all the words in a title are capitalized. For information about that tricky subject, see the Reference Guide.

WRITING INTRODUCTIONS

Starting a paper sometimes seems as difficult as shaking the first squirt out of the ketchup bottle. That's why it is easy to postpone writing until the deadline is imminent. But after you have worked through a prewriting exercise and perceived what options of content and organization are available, you should not find writing the first paragraph so formidable.

Although long articles and term papers may call for introductions of several paragraphs, short papers usually require only a one-paragraph introduction. Yet these introductory four or five sentences can be so frustrating to write that some teachers suggest you postpone them until you've completed your paper. You may do this if you're in a bind about getting started. But we've always liked the King of Hearts' advice in *Alice in Wonderland:* "Begin at the beginning, and go on till you come to the end; then stop." We find that skipping the opening paragraph and returning to it later is like starting a meal with the main course and eating the appetizer afterward.

What complicates the introduction are the challenges posed and the decisions required. Here are some questions you usually have to consider:

1. How can I get my readers' attention?
2. How can I interest my readers?
3. How should I handle my thesis?
4. Should I state the plan of my paper?

5. What voice should I employ?

6. What point of view should I use?

Let's consider these one by one.

How Can I Get My Readers' Attention?

The opening sentence is somewhat like the introductory "tease" in a television commercial: Both hope to attract people's attention so they will not turn away. Although advertising writers may rely on such standard visual devices as ravishing girls, virile athletes, appealing children, or breathtaking scenery, expository writers have none of these options. But they have others. One of these other choices may strike your fancy if your own inspiration fails. Here are some possible attention-getting approaches:

1. A controversial statement

    Some students swear that graduate teaching assistants are inexperienced, ignorant, and uninteresting; others insist that they are enthusiastic, friendly, and inspiring.

2. An element of surprise

    That slightly older guy, garbed in jeans and a sweatshirt, sometimes with beard, often with pipe, nearly always with a sack of books, who strides in late the first day of freshman class, is neither student nor professor but a peculiar species known as a graduate teaching assistant.

3. A note of contradiction

    Graduate teaching assistants are neither fish nor fowl, neither completely students nor teachers, neither really graduates nor assistants.

4. A short, dramatic statement.

    Beware of graduate teaching assistants.

5. The use of statistics

    Most of the two million freshmen entering colleges and universities this fall will be instructed by graduate teaching assistants.

6. A figure of speech (simile or metaphor)

    Graduate teaching assistants are like pilots on a new route: Each is capable, but each is unfamiliar with the course.

7. The use of quotation

    "Although they are inexperienced, most graduate teaching assistants are effective instructors because they relate well to their students," state the authors of *The Writing Commitment* (Adelstein and Pival, 8). [You would cite the source of this quotation in your bibliography. See chapter 21.]

8. A reference to a current event

    The recent debate in the freshman dorm about graduate teaching assistants was almost as heated as the one at the United Nations about the Third World.

9.   Proof of your authority

   Because I have been instructed by seven graduate teaching assistants in my
   first two semesters at college, I feel well qualified to discuss their strengths
   and weaknesses.

These nine opening statements may not all be appropriate for your subject,
your readers, or the occasion of your paper, but they do suggest some possibilities.
If not, here are three others to consider: the rhetorical question, the definition,
and the anecdote.

We separated these three from the others because they require some discussion.
The rhetorical question (see also pages 71–72) has been employed so frequently
that many readers find it condescending or trite. As we warned earlier, use it
sparingly. It can be effective on occasion, however, particularly when your subject
matter may be unfamiliar to most readers. As we suggested earlier, "Why" or
"What" questions are probably the most effective attention-grabbers. But if you
must resort to yes/no questions, it is often better to use a short series than to
gamble with a single question. If readers reply as you expect to the question,
you're safe; but if they don't you've lost them. Here's what we mean:

   Have you ever thought about what it would be like to have a graduate teaching
   assistant for an instructor?

Because most readers haven't thought about this—and don't see any reason why
they should—they might discard the paper instead of reading further. With a series
of provocative questions, however, the odds on hooking your readers' interest
increase:

   Should you sign up for courses taught by graduate teaching assistants? How
   effective are such teachers? Are they able to relate better to students than older
   professors?

The multiquestion approach does not always succeed; too many questions can
lose the reader's interest, particularly if they can be answered yes or no. A single
question that forces the reader to wrestle with a new idea can sometimes be more
effective:

   Why do many students prefer courses taught by graduate assistants?

   or

   What is a *graduate assistant?*

Another possible opener is a *definition.* There are some inherent dangers in
its use, however. Avoid the trite opening, "According to Webster. . ." or "The
dictionary defines _____ as. . . ." Also, definitions taken verbatim from the
dictionary can be deadening. For subjects needing a definition, try including it in
a provocative opening statement. For example:

   Patriotism is generally defined as love of country, but to Samuel Johnson it
   was "the last refuge of scoundrels."

The dictionary definition of a graduate teaching assistant as "a graduate student with part-time college teaching responsibilities" says a lot but explains little.

The third possible opening that warrants a word of caution is the *anecdote*. Although most people like to read about a significant or funny incident, these are effective only when they relate to the subject being discussed. In other words, the point of the anecdote must be closely related to the thesis of the paper. After-dinner speakers often violate this injunction with their "While I was coming to this meeting tonight. . . ." But after-dinner speakers have a captive audience. You don't.

Up to this point, we've been discussing ways to write an attention-getting introduction. Now we'd like to mention what not to do. Here are some ways to turn readers off:

1. The apology

   Although I don't know much about graduate teaching assistants, I thought that I'd write a paper about them.

   (Says the reader, "Then why should I read it?")

2. The complaint

   I started thinking about this paper after dinner and couldn't come up with an interesting subject because we were told that we could write about anything, but I finally decided to discuss graduate teaching assistants for lack of something else.

   (Says the reader, "I'm bored, too. What's on TV?")

3. The platitude

   Some graduate teaching assistants are good and some graduate teaching assistants are bad.

   (Says the reader, "Some papers are good but those that merely state the obvious are bad.")

4. The reference to the title

   The title of this paper, "Graduate Teaching Assistants," indicates that it is concerned with graduate students who are teaching in college while pursuing their own graduate work.

   (Says the reader, "So what else is new? Why waste time reading this?")

And there you have it—what you can do and cannot do to gain the attention of your readers. But do you always need to be concerned with getting their attention? No, not when you can assume that your audience will be highly motivated to read what you have written—as for example, when you address a controversial situation on campus or in your community that you know your readers are interested in. But generally you'd be wiser not to take your readers, especially your instructor, for granted.

How Can I Interest My Readers?

Let's assume you've written that highly important first sentence or so and are confident that it will get your readers' attention. Now to develop readers' interest in your subject. This requires answering these questions: Why is my subject important? Why should people read about it? How will it benefit them?

In our earlier discussion about selecting an interesting subject, we talked about the importance of appealing to readers. You may assume that most people would like to save time, effort, or money; to improve their knowledge, looks, and health; and to gain prestige, praise, and popularity. Does your subject appeal to any of these motivations? Or can you suggest why a reasonably intelligent person should be concerned about it? For instance, not everyone is interested in cats, but most readers have developed a fondness for some pet at some time in their lives. In writing about cats, you can build on this interest.

But keep your specific readers clearly in mind. If you were writing about graduate teaching assistants to a general audience of taxpayers, you would appeal to their curiosity in one way; to parents, in another; to entering college students, in a third. Unless you have your readers' interests at heart, why should they spend their valuable time finding out what you have to say?

How Should I Handle My Thesis?

In chapter 9, we discussed some concerns in formulating a thesis statement. We can now say more about how the thesis statement relates to the writer's purpose, where it belongs in the paper, and how it can be introduced.

In writing expository papers (except scientific or technical ones), experienced writers generally avoid a bald statement of purpose. And, unless trying to establish their authority, they also avoid explicitly stating an opinion, as in "I believe that. . .", or "In my opinion. . . ." Instead, they use word choice and sentence structure to make an implicit statement of their purpose and conviction.

Explicit Statement: *My purpose in this paper is to show how* surface-mining leads to many conditions that destroy the environment.

Implicit Statement: Surface-mining leads to many conditions that destroy the environment.

Free of the distracting and uninformative wordiness of the first version, the second still effectively indicates the writer's purpose: to show the cause-and-effect relationships of surface-mining to environmentally destructive conditions. The word *destroy* clearly indicates the writer's opinion about the subject.

Other sentences in the opening paragraph or paragraphs may also reveal the writer's purpose. In the following example of an opening paragraph, the purpose is made apparent in the word choice (*disproportions of wealth, peace, content, conflict, protest*) and in the contrasting examples expressed in the fourth and fifth sentences. The third sentence foreshadows the thesis, which is not explicitly stated until the final sentence.

The end of ancient shortage may mean a more peaceful world. Equally, we are not within sight of either. On the contrary, the present disproportions of wealth in the world community are themselves a cause of conflict. If everybody is poor, you may get the acquiescent peace of a tribal village. If everyone has enough, there is some chance of a more dynamic kind of content. But today the world suffers from contrasts between riches and poverty—internationally, regionally, and locally—which seem enough to incite the sufferers to the most violent protest.

—Barbara Ward, "The Balance of Wealth"

The example also suggests the answer to the question, "Where should the thesis statement appear?" Here it is included in the opening paragraph, but note that it is withheld until the subject has been introduced graciously. Sometimes the thesis statement is placed after a series of introductory paragraphs. Seldom should it be dumped on readers in the opening sentence, as if it were too hot to handle.

Ideally, your introduction should consist of three parts: (1) a hook or attention-getting device, (2) background information to explain the subject and to sustain the reader's interest, and (3) a statement of the thesis. In longer papers, writers often add a fourth part to the introduction: mention of the main points to be covered. By following this pattern, you start with an attention-grabber and then move on to the thesis, as in the following first paragraph from an advertising supplement that analyzes the reasons why companies encourage innovative employees. Because the essay deals with a coined term, the question "hook" prevents the reader from mistaking it for the more familiar "entrepeneur," and leads to the definition which provides the necessary background information:

What is an intrapreneur? Good question. Technically speaking, an intrapreneur is an innovator, a free thinker, an idea person—someone savvy enough to know that the surest and safest road to success is along a path paved by a parent company. More than ever before, *companies are looking to make major adjustments of resources and money in the start-up ventures of their own employees, main points with the dual expectation of a large return and increased employee productivity and job satisfaction.*

—*American Express Advertisement*

1. *Hook question*
2. *Background:*
   a. *Defines new term.*

   b. *"Success" interests readers*

3. *Thesis: Includes main points*

Should I State the Plan of My Paper?

Including all the main points in your thesis statement is not necessary in short papers. But in writing a long paper or one with a complicated organization, you would be wise to follow the lead of the two examples just given and indicate your organizational plan to your readers. This practice is helpful because the plan serves as a road map, showing readers where you are taking them. In the example by Ward, the writer's listing of three areas to be covered—international, regional, and local contrasts in wealth—gives the reader a framework for all that follows. Similarly, the "intrapreneur" paragraph from American Express indicates the main points to be explored: large returns and increased productivity. The order of the points leads readers to expect them to be discussed in that sequence—an important restriction to consider when you formulate a thesis statement (see also pages 182–85).

What Voice Should I Employ?

When you're introduced to a stranger—a friend of a friend, an acquaintance of your parents, a teacher, or the parents of the person you are dating—you usually adapt your manner to theirs. If they're polite, reserved, and detached, then you are too. But in writing, you call the shots. You must establish in the first paragraph, and to some extent in the first sentence, the voice that sets up the relationship between you, your subject, and your readers. We've already talked about this subject of voice several times, pointing out how it depends on numerous factors such as choice of words, sentence structure, verb form, and pronoun choice. In writing the introduction you will need to decide *which* voice to use. For example, the following opening sentences are arranged in order of increasing formality. Note how each launches readers into the subject in a slightly different way.

1. So you're getting ready to go on vacation.
2. If you want to make a clean getaway to your vacation hideaway, here is a way to do it.
3. The best-laid vacation plans need not go astray.
4. Before you go on vacation, you should spend some time planning.
5. Most people cannot wait to go on vacation.
6. Although people may differ in age and in their daily activities, nearly all engage in the ritual of recreation known as a vacation.
7. The preparations for departure on a vacation may be as significant and time-consuming as the planning for it.

Whichever voice you choose, maintain it throughout your paper. Decisions, decisions, decisions—that's what writing is all about. While you sweat over a few initial sentences, trying to establish just the appropriate voice, remember that the great historian Edward Gibbon rewrote the entire lengthy first chapter of *The Decline and Fall of the Roman Empire* three times before finding the tone of voice he thought appropriate.

What Point of View Should I Use?

In expository writing, as in personal forms, you can choose to "speak" in the first person (*I, we*), second person (*you*), or third person (*he, she, it, they*).

First Person—I Generally, the first-person *I* or *we* strikes a personal, intimate note, which is especially appropriate when you are relying on your own experience to lend authority or credibility to what you are saying about your subject. If your parents are divorced and you are writing about the effects of divorce on children, then by all means use *I* in referring to your own reactions. Take care, however, because (as chapter 3 pointed out) one *I* can lead to many *I*'s, annoying and distracting readers who may consider you egotistical or may turn away from the subject to speculate about you, the writer. To avoid *I,* some students resort to such bloated substitutes as "your reporter" or "the author of this article," which are usually more distracting. Although *I* is used less frequently in exposition than in personal writing, feel free to use it when doing so is the most natural choice. But be temperate.

The same cautions apply to *we.* Although the editorial *we* is acceptable in editorials, where it conventionally refers to publishers, it should be avoided elsewhere, particularly in situations where it may establish a condescending tone. Just remember the teacher who always annoyed you by saying, "We are going to do our arithmetic homework" or the nurse who insisted, "We will take our medicine now."

This warning does not mean that *we* is out. It can be perfectly proper and effective when used for two major purposes—to establish writer-reader togetherness:

We all struggle in writing the first sentence of a paper.

and to refer to an actual group:

As concerned citizens, we cannot allow our wilderness areas to be sold to the highest bidder.

The "togetherness" *we* establishes a natural, friendly relationship. The "group" *we* is generally more formal. Occasionally, a third situation calling for *we* arises: when two or more writers are collaborating—as we are in this book.

Second Person—You The second-person *you* is highly controversial. As you may know, many instructors forbid students to use it in their papers. We're usually on their side even though we ourselves use *you* throughout this book and accept it in some student papers. What's wrong with *you*? For one thing, it establishes a note that may often be too informal for exposition. Readers may resent being addressed as *you,* perhaps visualizing it as a finger pointing at them as in the old recruiting posters, "Uncle Sam wants YOU!" Then, too, the *you* viewpoint is closer to speech usage and is therefore considered less formal and acceptable than the third-person pronoun. Some instructors feel that students need the practice of writing in the more demanding formal style required in their work, in other courses, and often in business, industry, and the professions. Finally, *you* is subject to being "over-yoused" or to cropping up inadvertently in a paper having a different point of view. Like *I,* one *you* frequently leads to many more:

If you will take my advice, you will find that you do not have to spend much of your time studying for your final exam.

In defense of *you,* it is perfectly acceptable and effective when used sparingly and skillfully. It need not grab the reader ("Hey, you!"), but it can serve as a valuable impersonal or indefinite reference:

> As citizens interested in the community, you should inquire into the policies, practices, and politics of the zoning board.

In this book, we have employed *you* in this generic sense, hoping that you would find our textbook more personal than many others and that you could imagine yourself as a student in our composition course.

Third Person—He, She, It   The last point of view, third person, is the one used most frequently in expository writing. The subject itself—poets, garbage collectors, birth control pills, or organic farming—stands in the spotlight, attended by its appropriate personal or indefinite pronoun (*he, she, it, they, anyone, each, everybody,* and so on). The main problem when using this point of view is to avoid the stilted, deadly *one.* When one is writing exposition, one often wishes to impress others by showing how important one can sound. But after one has encountered this use of *one* in one's reading, one would plead with others to shun it entirely or else resort to it only when one is without any sensible alternative. You can see how *one* can drive a reader up the wall.

In recent years, many people sensitive to word connotation have become annoyed at the implied exclusion of women by the generic use of *he, his, or him* to refer to both males and females: "Everyone should be true to *his* principles," or "The duty of a dean is to speak for *his* faculty." Historically, the "masculine" pronouns were all-encompassing, embracing even *it and its,* as implied in the King James biblical line "The salt hath lost *his* savour." But for the last century or so, English has moved toward logical gender—*he, his, him* are masculine, *she, her, hers* feminine. So in a real psychological sense, the masculine pronoun does exclude the female sex. Because many find the use of the generic *he* insensitive, you would be wise to avoid constructions like the following:

> If a student wishes to make an appointment, *he* should see the department secretary.
> Anyone wishing a copy should write for one on *his* company's stationery.

In the last sentence, many people in talking use *their,* ignoring the problem of reference to a singular pronoun (*anyone*). This practice is generally unacceptable in expository writing. One way to correct both problems is to make both the nouns and their pronoun references plural.

> If students wish . . . *they* should see. . . . Individuals wishing . . . should write on *their.* . . .

In many situations like these, you can solve the problem simply by shifting to a plural. If not, try another of our preferred possibilities: changing an active sentence to passive, repeating the noun or substituting a synonym for it, or changing the pronoun to an article.

Example: The judge initially hears the case; *he* then determines its merits.
Passive: The case is initially heard by the judge, and its merits are then determined.

Example: A doctor should be called in such cases; only *he* can determine whether the patient should be hospitalized.
Synonym: A doctor should be called in such cases; only a *physician* can determine. . . .

Example: In deciding tenure, the department chair must consult *his* faculty.
Article: In deciding tenure, the department chair must consult *the* faculty.

Other less desirable solutions are to alternate feminine and masculine pronouns (as done by the student writer in the classification example on page 152) or to use the paired pronouns *he or she, he/she, him or her, him/her*. These practices are considered stylistically inelegant by many (including us). If no other options are appropriate, however, it may be better to sacrifice nicety of style to avoid offending many readers.

You certainly should use the appropriate pronoun when referring to a specific person; but avoid the offensive generic masculine in your writing.

A last recommendation about point of view: After establishing your point of view in the introduction, stick to it throughout your paper. Where point of view is concerned, consistency is not, as Ralph Waldo Emerson called it, either "foolish" or a "hobgoblin of little minds."

A Final Word About Introductions

After this discussion of getting readers' attention, maintaining their interest, stating a thesis, establishing a voice, and deciding upon a point of view, you should realize why a carefully written introduction is crucial. Although we recommend writing your introduction first, you should feel free to revise or replace it later. Because writing a paper is an on-going process, you may discover new ideas or approaches that necessitate a new introduction.

WRITING CONCLUSIONS

read

Many student writers fail to understand the dual significance of the term *conclusion*. A conclusion is an ending *and* a resolution or deduction. Consequently, a good conclusion is both functional and aesthetic—that is, it leaves the reader with a pithy final thought and with a sense of completeness.

The conclusion should not be long. Lingering goodbyes may be enjoyable with a loved one, but they bore readers. Three or four well-worded sentences are usually all that you need. In short papers that enumerate a series of reasons in climactic order, the most important being reserved for last, a conclusion may even be omitted.

You may look either backward or forward in these concluding sentences. In looking backward, you may return to some metaphor or other motif in the introduction, restate the thesis, or, in longer papers, summarize the main points. In looking forward, you may forecast the future, call for action, discuss implications, or point out the significance of the ideas. Here are some examples of these options.

Looking Backward
1. Return to the introduction (the italicized words refer to a comparison made in the introduction).

    Despite all these suggestions, finding a summer job may still be *as difficult as locating an inexpensive apartment near campus.* But at least you can be confident that you have gone about it efficiently and looked into all the possibilities. The rest is up to luck.

2. Restate the thesis.

    Looking for a summer job need not be a hit-or-miss process. If your search is conducted in a systematic, efficient manner, it should produce results. Almost always, it will.

3. Summarize the main points (only in longer papers).

    What is important is to start looking for a summer job early and to follow the specific suggestions noted here. You may not want to investigate all the possibilities—employers overseas, federal agencies, local or state governments, industries in other areas, and local businesses. But you should realize it is better to have too many opportunities than too few.

Looking Forward
4. Forecast the future.

    Despite these suggestions, you may not find summer work. The growing demand for these positions and the diminishing supply of them may mean that many unemployed young people will return to the campus to attend summer sessions. This could double present enrollments and produce a new phenomenon: the three-year bachelor's degree. If this happens, the regular job market will soon be glutted as well.

5. Call for action.

    Start looking for that summer job today. You can write letters to federal agencies, check into local and state government possibilities, get a copy of the *Summer Employment Directory,* and follow the suggestions about seeking work in local businesses. They who hesitate may be lost this summer.

6. Discuss implications.

    The implications of these suggestions should be apparent. Summer jobs will be more difficult to find this year than last. You can wait for Lady Luck to smile or you can roll up your sleeves and start searching for yourself. You may even decide to chuck the idea of getting a job—and enroll in summer school.

7. Point out the significance of ideas.

    Perhaps more important than following these specific suggestions is knowing that any undertaking—not just finding a summer job—can be carefully researched and planned. Some people go through life haphazardly, meeting problems with hastily conceived, last-minute answers. Other people antici- pate problems and study how to meet them. This second class of people is usually the more successful.

These examples suggest how the same paper might be concluded in various ways. Obviously, depending on the context, some would be more appropriate than others. Before concluding this discussion about conclusions, let us note a few rhetorical considerations brought out by the examples.

1.   Not one of the examples starts with the overworked words *In summary* or *In conclusion.* You should discard these feeble mechanical signals. They can be as monotonous to your audience as a repeated TV commercial.

2.   No apology is offered, no afterthought included, no extraneous note sounded. The conclusion should be like the favorable impression of a parting hand- shake: firm and brief.

3.   In several examples, short sentences end the paragraph. These are effective in snapping it to a close. Sometimes an uncommon sentence pattern is also helpful. Even punctuation, such as the dash in example 6, can be utilized to achieve a sense of finality.

4.   Another effective way to conclude is with a rhetorical question or with a catchy statement, as in example 5. A possibility not exemplified here is to use an anecdote. If you do, keep it short and make certain it is pertinent.

These suggestions should help you in writing the concluding paragraph of your paper. If you're stumped, look through them to find one that strikes your fancy and work it appropriately into your paper. After writing the paragraph, check to determine whether it conveys a sense of finality and leaves the reader with something vital to remember.

SUMMARY

In this chapter, we have offered suggestions for strengthening important aspects of an expository paper—the title, the introduction and thesis statement, the voice, the point of view, and the conclusion. All of these are important in creating a successful, well-written paper, one that will attract and hold your readers' interest. A weakness in any can mar the effectiveness of the whole; consequently, all deserve time and thought when you are rewriting.

ASSIGNMENTS

For Discussion

1.   Discuss a writing situation in which it would be unnecessary to attract the attention of readers.

2. What devices could you use to catch the interest of high-school seniors, professional people, or retired people in papers written about the following topics:

   Hypertension is deadly
   Safety tips for bike riders
   Jogging for health
   How to choose a hobby
   How to eat less and like it
   A review of no-fault auto insurance

3. Analyze the introductions to chapters in this book or in other textbooks you have with you in class. To what extent are they successful in gaining the reader's attention? Discuss, supporting your conclusions with reasons.

4. Evaluate the following introductions from student papers by considering their appeal, statement of thesis, voice, and point of view:

   a. The automobile, a four-wheeled transportation vehicle, was initially a great blessing. It was a source of pleasure for people and an indication of one's prosperity. Its invention has allowed society to become very mobile and distant places to become far more accessible. The auto industry has been a tremendous boon for the economy of the United States over the past one hundred years. Yet today it is a menace.

   b. There is always at least one television commercial on your set that will disgust you. When you come home after a hard day's work and flip on your TV set, the last thing you want to see is a lady caressing and singing to her box of detergent. I've watched people practically ram their feet through an expensive color portable just because a certain obnoxious commercial was on the air. The television commercial is an ineffective means of advertising a product.

   c. Even though freshman dormitory hours are a much debated issue among new students at the university, I feel they are essential.

   d. Surveys and statistics show that there has been an increase in the number of people who have experienced college life, and this is due in part to the fact that a college education has become more and more vital in succeeding in today's world. Because of the increase in recent college enrollment, more people have become informed about the Greek system and its advantages. People today realize there's more to get out of a college education than knowledge from books, and a fraternity or sorority helps a student to acquire this knowledge.

5. Compare your past instructions from teachers and your own attitude about the use of *I, we,* and *you* with the views presented in this chapter.

6. What are the two functions of the conclusion? Why are they both important?

7. Evaluate the following conclusions from student papers:

   a. Considering both the advantages and disadvantages of the automobile today, it is evident that the country needs to develop a mass transit system to relieve traffic in and around the major cities. This system will take years to build, and much time and effort will be needed to persuade people to use it. In the meantime, they will continue to curse at and be cursed with the automobile.

b. Insulting, shocking, and deceiving the public should not be effective ways of selling products. Yet products sell or else they would not continue to be advertised on television. Perhaps the continued use of these deplorable techniques says something about the American public. Perhaps people are not as intelligent as we would like to think they are.

c. For these reasons I feel freshmen should be required to be in their dorms at certain hours from the opening days of school until the Thanksgiving vacation.

d. According to a recent survey, there has been an increase in membership in social sororities and fraternities, so apparently more and more people have come to believe that the Greek system is good. Knowledge obtained from books is important, and just as important is the Greek system in promoting character, scholarship, and student involvement.

For Practice

1. Rewrite one of the introductions in Discussion Assignment 4 and the corresponding conclusion in Assignment 7. Add a statement explaining why your revision is more effective.

2. Write three introductory paragraphs, one for each of the audiences mentioned in Discussion Assignment 2, about any subject.

3. Write three different conclusions for a single subject, using a different technique in each.

4. Select one of the topics in Discussion Exercise 2 and write at least six opening sentences for it, each modeled after a different approach suggested in this chapter.

5. Choose one of the introductions in Discussion Assignment 4 or write one of your own on any topic. Restate the introduction twice more, using an increasingly formal tone, as exemplified on pages 114–16.

6. Based on the information supplied in the introductions in Discussion Assignment 4 and in the conclusions of Assignment 7, suggest a possible title for each of the original papers.

14

Rewriting
Strategies for
Expository Writing

Because the primary purpose of expository writing is to explain and clarify something to someone else, the rewriting step is more crucial in exposition than in personal writing, where your aim was to recreate an experience or impression. As you know from other situations in life, you need to take greater care if other people are somehow involved—particularly strangers. In dressing to go out to a gathering of strangers, for example, you take extra time to review your appearance—touching up your makeup or retying your tie, brushing a scrap of lint from your suit, making sure that accessories match. Few of us take such pains for ourselves or for close friends. Similar differences exist in our reviewing prose written primarily for an unknown audience and that written for close associates or for our own personal satisfaction.

Generally, failing to narrate or describe our personal experiences as well as possible has less serious consequences than failing to explain clearly. For instance, inadequately describing a place or ineffectively telling a story may inconvenience readers only slightly. However, failure to inform readers clearly and correctly how to drop a college course, open an IRA account, operate a word processor, or apply for accident insurance may cause serious problems. That's why you should take special care in rewriting an expository paper.

In chapter 7, we illustrated how a personal description, "Jekyll Island," was revised by changing the introduction, conclusion, organization, use of details, and other elements. As you revise expository papers, you should continue to be concerned with these same elements, examining your drafts from the perspective of the reader—someone who knows little or nothing of the subject and who expects to be enlightened. In the earlier descriptive paper, we concentrated on the steps of the revising stage; let's now focus on the editing process. (You may find it helpful to refer to the diagram of the writing process on page 4.) The following paper—on the effects of others' invading the parking spaces reserved for the handicapped—is a second draft, written after the revising steps had been followed. As you read through it, observe how, in editing, the writer has marked the draft, searching for ways to improve word selection, sentence style, paragraphs, spelling, punctuation, and mechanics.

A Problem for the Handicaped

∧ catchier title ?
sp ?

(People usually obey traffic laws.) They stop for
lights, signal when ~~they~~ turn_{ing}, observe ʃtop signs,
and [they do not // go over the speed limits.] The one
regulation they often ignore is parking in places
reserved for handicaped drivers. These places are
mainly in front of stores, particularly in
shopping centers.

Rewrite. Dull.
all lights ?
/ Redo—regulation not stated

all stores ?
only stores ?

¶   ~~You may want to know~~: What's wrong with
people parking there? Let's look at the problem it
causes a handicaped person in a wheel chair. (She)
may drive her van equipted with a hydrilic lift / to
a supermarket. When she arrives she cannot
park in the reserved spaces because other cars
without the special licence plates are parked
there. So she drives around, finally finding an
empty spot far away from the store. After she
shopped, she returned to her van only to find
that other cars have parked around her van.
Because a person in a wheel chair needs extra
space on the side to get into a van (or even a
car, she had to wait for the other drivers ~~in the other cars~~ to return, by that time her frozen
foods and ice cream had melted. The drivers
parking next to her should not be blamed. The
blame should be placed on the people who parked
ilegally in the handicaped spaces. Perhaps the
real blame / however / lies with the police who

∧ definite referent ?
sp ?

sp   What special plates ?

wordy
tense switch

rep

cs

rep
sp ?

give tickets and sometimes tow cars away when [*Do the police tow cars?*]

people ilegally park at basketball, football, or [*sp?*]

other games or concerts. Why don't they give

tickets and tow cars away from people who park

ilegally in spaces reserved for the handicaped? [*sp?*]

Why can't the police patrol ~~the streets looking at~~

patrol the streets looking

these places just as they ^look for traffic

violaters? [*sp?*]

¶ If the police enforced the law by ticketing

these people, towing their car, and soaking them [*which people? be specific*]

with large fines, then this ilegal parking would

soon stop. Instead, people know that nothing will

                                         a

happen when they park there. So they take ~~the~~ [*where?*]

handicaped space, usually right in front of a

excusing this violation

store, ~~telling themselves in a form of an excuse~~ [*/ wordy*]

    by saying   *B*

sometimes/that they'll be just a few minutes/ ~~but~~

                                         C

a few minutes here and there add up to a lot of

time and no time for a handicaped person. That's [*/ Rework. End on a stronger note.*]

a shame.

Reading through the marginal comments helps you realize that the writer has concentrated mainly on editing concerns. Faulty sentence structures, as in the last sentence of the second paragraph, have been flagged for rewriting. So, too, have misspelled words and punctuation problems, such as the comma splice (cs). But the comments show evidence that the student continued to search for revising concerns—the effectiveness of the opening and closing lines, vagueness of examples, and so on. In short, the editing step—although done separately—did not exclude further revising; the student sees the rewriting stage as an on-going process.

Read through the third draft of the paper that follows, comparing the results with the earlier draft.

Another Handicap for the Handicapped

Most people obey most traffic laws most of the time. They stop for

red lights, signal when turning, observe stop signs, and generally stay within the speed limits. Yet they often ignore signs reserving parking for handicapped drivers. These spaces are mainly found in front of supermarkets, movie theaters, and large stores, particularly in shopping centers.

What's wrong with people parking there? Let's look at the problem it causes a handicapped person in a wheelchair. A handicapped woman may drive her van, equipped with a hydraulic lift, to a supermarket. When she arrives, she cannot park in the reserved spaces because other cars with regular license plates are parked there. So she drives around, finally finding an empty spot far away from the store. After shopping, she returns to her van, only to find that other cars have parked around it. Because a person in a wheel chair needs extra space on the side to get into a van (or even a car), she has to wait until the other drivers return. By that time, some of her frozen foods and ice cream have melted.

The drivers parking next to her should not be blamed. The fault lies with those people who parked illegally in the handicapped spaces. The police are also at fault. They ticket people parking illegally at concerts and basketball and football games, and sometimes have their cars towed away. Why don't they do the same to people parking illegally in handicapped spaces? Why can't the police patrol these places just as they patrol the streets looking for traffic violators?

If the police enforced the law by ticketing people parking in these reserved places, by having their cars towed away, and by giving them stiff fines, perhaps $50 or $100, then this illegal parking would soon stop. Instead, people know that nothing's going to happen to them. So they take a handicapped space, usually in front of a store, sometimes excusing this violation to themselves by saying they'll be just a few minutes. But a few minutes by this person and by that person add up to no minutes for a handicapped person. That's just another handicap for the handicapped.

STRATEGIES FOR REVISING EXPOSITORY WRITING

The foregoing example suggests some of the ways you can edit your expository papers. But always keep in mind that editing is only one step in the rewriting process. The following checklist should help you in revising, editing, and proofreading.

Revising Checklist: Attention to Readers

1. What audience did I have in mind? In what ways could I better direct my paper to those readers?

2. What special interests might my readers have in the subject? Have I addressed those interests sufficiently?

3. Has everything been explained thoroughly? Are all necessary details given in the descriptions? Is each sequential step in the process clear? Are cause-and-effect relationships explained? Terms clearly defined? All subclasses accounted for?

4. In what ways might I improve the tone of the paper so that it is more appropriate for my readers?

Revising Checklist: Organization

1. Have I outlined the finished paper to find flaws in my original plan or in the written draft?

2. What changes are needed to make the organization more logical and more suitable to the subject matter and purpose?

3. How can I make my thesis clearer to my readers? If the thesis is implied, what do I need to add to help readers clearly discern my purpose?

Revising Checklist: Paragraphs

1. Do most of the paragraphs fit some variation of the SRI form? How should I revise those that don't?

2. Is the development (illustration) sufficient to explain the topic sentence? What appropriate paragraph development devices, such as examples, statistics, or authority, might I add or further amplify?

3. Do any paragraphs have only one level of modification? If so, what subordinate details, if any, would help to clarify and explain?

Revising Checklist: Introductions and Conclusions

1. How can I improve my introductory sentence so that it is a better attention-grabber?

2. What added background material in my introduction would increase my readers' interest and clarify what I'm saying?

3. Where is my thesis statement? Is this the most effective placement?

4. How can I rewrite my conclusion so that it is more effective in (1) reinforcing my thesis; (2) leaving the reader with a sense of completeness? Have I avoided introducing any topic not dealt with in the paper?

Editing Checklist: Language and Usage

1. What difficult, unusual, or technical terms have I failed to define sufficiently?

2. What words or phrases might be inappropriate for my particular readers and purpose?

3. What word meanings am I unsure of? Have I checked them in a dictionary?

4. Have I used words that might be considered pretentious or euphemistic?

Editing Checklist: Sentences

1. Where can I improve sentence structure for better emphasis or focus?

2. What sentences need clearer relationship signals?

3. What sentences might be written more economically?

4. Where can I eliminate unnecessary or wordy constructions? Superfluous relative clauses? *There is/are* or *It is* sentence openers? Any of the other unnecessary words and phrases discussed on pages 232–36?

Editing Checklist: Spelling

1. What spellings am I unsure of? Did I check them in a dictionary?

2. Have I made any typing errors?

Editing Checklist: Punctuation

1. Are any joined sentences connected only with a comma?

2. Have I confirmed in the text or the References Guide the correctness of all my uses of semicolons, colons, and dashes?

3. Where can I use hyphens to clarify compound terms? (See page 219 and the Reference Guide.)

Proofreading Checklist

1. Is my paper neat and legible enough for others to read?

2. Have I proofread the final draft slowly and carefully, looking for omitted and repeated words?

3. Have I double-checked for typographical errors or wrongly copied words?
4. Have I made sure that the words at the top of each new page follow correctly from those at the bottom of the preceding page?
5. Have I double-checked punctuation and capitalization?
6. Have I checked in the dictionary for the correct hyphenation of words split at the ends of sentences?

PART THREE

The Argumentative Voice: Persuasive Writing

Mastering the art of persuasion can be beneficial to you in your academic and social life, and in your career. In college, you will often confront controversial issues in class discussions, papers, and exams that require you to present effective arguments. In your social life, you will often want to stake out a position on significant subjects—politics, economics, arts, education. Less seriously, you may try to persuade your parents or friends to accept your judgment in such choices as films, clothes, restaurants, or television programs. In your professional life, no matter what field you work in, you will spend much time trying to sell people a product, a service, or an idea, perhaps urging them to accept an out-of-court settlement, to buy an annuity, to subscribe to a fitness program, or to contribute to a worthwhile cause. Skill in persuasion is demanded in all these situations.

Persuasion is a form of communication that attempts to change the attitudes or behavior of others through an appeal to their reason, their ethics, their emotions, or occasionally to all three. Of course, changing people's attitudes usually involves some informing and explaining—both expository skills. But in expository writing, informing and explaining are ends in themselves. By contrast, in persuasive writing, these and other methods, such as narration and description, are all subordinated to the primary goal of convincing readers to accept some proposal or spurring them to some action.

As you might guess, convincing readers and motivating them to act require tactics other than those used in merely informing them. In expository writing, when analyzing what readers need to be told, you are mainly concerned with deciding what they already know. But in persuasive writing, you must give at least as much consideration to how they *feel* about the subject. For example, in writing an expository paper to explain why local public schools are inadequate, you would have to supply your readers with information of various kinds, such as statistics on national test scores, comparisons with nearby school systems, drop-out rates, and so forth. In writing a persuasive paper to convince readers to accept higher property taxes to improve the schools, you would also include such information. In addition, however, you would have to take into account some emotional questions: what your readers' attitudes are toward public education, what appeals would best motivate them to pay higher taxes, what their objections might be, and how you could most effectively counter them.

In persuasion, the prewriting process of audience analysis is crucial. In urging readers to raise property taxes, for example, you would use a different approach for a particular group; parents of school children, young couples planning children, or retired people with grown children will respond to different arguments. On the other hand, in writing a newspaper editorial to reach a broad cross-section of the community, you should determine the approaches that appeal to all. As you can see, deciding on the best approaches for urging readers to act requires skillful planning.

But even the best planning will fail if the situation cannot be changed. Cold facts and strong predispositions may thwart even the most effective arguments. After all, you can't persuade your father to give you a million dollars if he doesn't have it. Nor can you talk an instructor into a better grade if you clearly didn't merit it. So a critical aspect of your planning involves considering both your proposal's feasibility and its merit.

Another concern is how best to project *yourself.* To be persuaded, your readers must have confidence in your knowledge of the subject, as evidenced by a thorough treatment of it. And they must respect your good sense and good character as projected by a courteous tone and a fair-minded analysis of the issue. If readers like, trust, and have confidence in you, they will respond positively—or at least with an open mind—to your views, just as you respond to your favorite newspaper columnist or TV newscaster. If readers react negatively to your projected personality, they will be hard to persuade.

All we have said here helps to explain why effective persuasive papers require more care in both planning and drafting than do other papers.

To help you master the complex art of persuasion, we will discuss in the following chapters the forms it can take, prewriting strategies for generating subjects and evidence, methods of organizing material, models for constructing logical arguments, uses and abuses of language and logic, and ways of crafting effective sentences and paragraphs.

As you read these chapters, remember that the study of persuasion is not unrelated to your life but is very much a part of it. To speak, write, and think logically, to analyze skillfully, and to reason effectively are skills you will need whatever your academic major and your occupation.

15

The Forms of Persuasive Writing

When political candidates want our vote, charities our donations, and companies our business, they try to affect the way we think or the way we act. In this process, although they may inform us, their primary aim is to persuade us. To do this, writers can use either formal or informal persuasion. The form they select is largely dictated by the demands of their subject matter and the characteristics and needs of their readers.

Traditionally, formal persuasion is referred to as argumentation. Although it may contain emotional appeals, it relies chiefly on appeals to the readers' reason. Typically, it consists of a claim or proposal urged by the writer, background material, presentation of the writer's arguments, confirmation of supporting arguments and refutation of contrary arguments, a summary, and an appeal. In this text, we present two types of formal persuasion: classical argument and problem-solution argument.

Informal persuasion, in a sense, is incomplete argument—lacking some of the necessary components of formal. Unlike formal argument, which relies heavily on logical reasoning, informal persuasion emphasizes emotional appeal—playing on people's sympathies, concerns, or self-interest.

FORMAL PERSUASION: CLASSICAL ARGUMENT

In writing to educated audiences about serious, controversial matters, you would generally choose the classical argument form. Centering on the contention or claim that you intend to promote, a classical argument relies on reasons, examples, facts, and logical reasoning to convince readers to agree with your proposition or to take action. And, because controversial subjects have more than one side, close attention must be paid to possible objections: arguments that counter your own.

Refuting counterarguments is an important aspect of classical argument because you cannot persuade people if you do not acknowledge and overcome their contrary ideas. In proposing that a speed limit be raised, for example, you need to realize that many readers will not accept your views unless you deal with their contention that auto fatalities have decreased since the limit was set.

Organization of Classical Argument

A classical argument, like an expository paper, has three main parts: an introduction, a body, and a conclusion. As in expository papers, the basic organization of classical argument is Subject-Restriction-Illustration (SRI). Its introduction contains a thesis that may indicate both the subject and its restriction. The body develops or illustrates; and the conclusion restates the subject and its restriction. In both kinds of writing, depending upon the subject and the writer's purpose, the order can be reversed (IRS), producing a climactic effect. Unlike exposition, however, effective persuasion requires the writer to establish explicitly some grounds of agreement—some assumption(s) shared by writer and reader—and to anticipate and refute views that conflict with those being advanced (counter-arguments).

Introduction   The introduction in classical argument is especially important. Regardless of how logically you present your arguments, you cannot effectively persuade people if you do not first establish rapport with them, pointing out your areas of agreement. For instance, let's say that you wish to persuade your readers of the beneficial effects of the NCAA ruling that requires all freshman athletes to score at least 15 on ACT or 700 on SAT examinations. You could reasonably assume that both the supporters and the opponents of the rule would agree on two points: that any college athlete can be exploited, and that college athletes of all races often fail to achieve a college degree. You might then use these points of agreement to refute an opposing argument that the ruling discriminates against some ethnic groups, before proceeding to your own stand on the issue.

Unless an IRS organization is used, the thesis generally appears in the introduction. Classical argument is centered on a thesis stated as a proposition: a conclusion reached about a controversial subject, a suggestion or recommendation for reform or action, or a strong personal stand on one side of an issue, as in these examples:

> Recent covert actions have greatly weakened U.S. foreign policy. (conclusion)
> The 55-mile speed limit should be raised to 65 on all roads. (recommendation for change)
> Life imprisonment is a worse punishment than execution. (strong stand on an issue)

But remember, a proposition reflects the convictions of the writer and, unlike a factual statement, may or may not be true or verifiable. A statement such as "The earth revolves around the sun" is factual; scientific evidence may be used to verify it. But a statement such as "The United States should not become involved in the internal affairs of other countries" is a personal conviction; the writer can only give reasons—can only present arguments that will logically lead readers to the writer's conclusion, which may or may not be right.

Body In the body of a classical argument paper, you present and develop your main points or arguments, perhaps comparing them with contrary arguments which are then refuted. To develop your arguments, you may use any of the writing methods we have studied: narrative examples, description, definition, classification, comparison, causal analysis, and so on. Chapters 16, 17, and 18 all offer useful advice on various strategies of persuasion.

Conclusion In the conclusion, you state or restate your proposition, perhaps summarize your own and contrary arguments, and make a strong, final appeal for action or change. In the following brief paragraph, the student writer restates his proposition, picks up a phrase from the quotation about the kaleidoscope that started his paper, and appeals to his readers' pride of community and home:

> With the proper planning of housing, we can surround ourselves with creative architecture and beauty. And, just as the mirrors of a kaleidoscope create beauty out of a jumble of pieces, builders can use planning to create beautiful neighborhoods and areas of housing that we can be proud of in years to come.

In the next example the student writer uses comparison-and-contrast to set up an *either-or* situation. Note that he, too, appeals to the readers' sense of responsibility and pride in country. By not overtly restating his proposition, he flatters his readers by allowing them to arrive at that conclusion.

> So there it is. The issue is laid out; sides have been chosen. One side represents life and the preservation of a fragile and beautiful world. The other stands for the exploitation of natural resources to the fullest extent, consequently supporting the destruction of the last wilderness in America. We, the people of America, are thrown into the middle to choose. We have the power to kill; we have the power to preserve. We have a responsibility to life and a decision to make: whether to preserve life or to destroy it. The balance rests in our hands.

REFUTING COUNTERARGUMENTS

Although important in all forms of persuasion, identifying and attacking arguments offered against your own is especially important in classical argument. Because refutation of counterarguments is so important, you need to be aware of its advantages and of some techniques for achieving it.

Advantages

If handled diplomatically and respectfully, refuting counterarguments can change the ideas and beliefs of readers opposed to your views. Also, because your knowledge of those contrary views establishes you as an informed person to your readers, refutation can make your own arguments and points seem more intelligent and thus more convincing.

Deciding where to place the refutation of counterarguments in your paper is sometimes a problem. Placement is largely up to you, though it will be determined in part by the writing situation. To gain full advantage from refutation, you need to consider the soundness and popularity of the opposing arguments. If they are illogical, unknown to your audience, or not strongly advocated, present them after you have thoroughly set forth your own arguments. But if the opposing arguments are sound and feasible, then your own arguments might have more force if you deal with all the opposing views first. In writing about highly controversial matters, on the other hand, you might find that contrasting each individual counterargument with one of your own is more advantageous.

Methods of Refutation

Although not all-inclusive, here are some methods used for refuting counterarguments or alternative proposals:

- Point out their logical weaknesses. If an opponent's claimed result does not logically follow from the proposal, point out the flawed reasoning. For instance, the argument that selling arms to a country which advocates terrorism will eliminate hostage-taking is illogical: the result does not automatically follow.

- Point out possible disadvantageous effects. These might include such matters as the high cost of a proposal or the greater future problems that could result, such as possible harm to individuals, society, or the environment.

- Create a scenario showing the proposal's impracticality. This method requires extreme caution, however. It works best with implausible arguments or proposals, but you should take care to avoid sarcasm. Otherwise, your attack may backfire and create hostility toward your own arguments.

- Question the truth of a counterargument. Again, this requires care and sensitivity. No one likes to be publicly called a liar or to be portrayed as a fool.

- Remember the Golden Rule of argumentation: Treat others and their ideas as you would be treated.

Tone in Refutation

Implicit in several of our suggested refutation methods is a concern for the kind of tone or voice projected by the writer. In refuting counterarguments, tone becomes crucial. To avoid alienating readers with opposing views, strive to create the tone of a person well-informed but not pompous; reasonable, not strident;

assertive, not obstinate. Readers should perceive you as a person logically convinced of the rightness of your argument, but also respectful of their views.

Perhaps the best way to control your tone in persuasive writing is to imagine a real audience that you admire and wish to impress in the best possible light. Remember, effective persuasion is not achieved by tirades, diatribe, or nasty ridicule of opposing views.

Organizational Model for Classical Argument

Here is an organizational model that accounts for all the rhetorical concerns discussed here and that contains most of the components of argument summarized in the opening paragraph of this section:

INTRODUCTION

Orientation: Introduction to your restricted subject. Why is it important to your readers?

Rapport: Attempt to establish common-ground agreements about the subject. What assumptions or opinions are all readers likely to share?

Thesis: Statement of proposition
Refutation of counterarguments (optional)

BODY

  I. First supporting argument
    A. Evidence or supporting material
    B. Evidence or supporting material
    C. Refutation of counterarguments for Argument I (optional)
  II. Second supporting argument
    A. Evidence or supporting material
    B. Evidence or supporting material
    C. Refutation of counterarguments for Argument II (optional)
  III. Third supporting argument
    A. Evidence or supporting material
    B. Evidence or supporting material
    C. Refutation of counterarguments for Argument III (optional)

CONCLUSION

Restatement of the proposition.
Appeal for action.
Refutation of counterarguments (optional).

Note that where you refute counterarguments in your paper is largely up to you and depends on the writing situation. You might consider counterarguments in your introduction to provide background material or to establish a common bond with your readers. With highly controversial subjects, you might more effectively take them up in the body of your paper to support and defend your own arguments and points. If discrediting counterarguments will enhance a final plea for action, you may save the refutation for the conclusion.

As we have indicated, not every persuasive paper will exactly follow this model. Some subjects may be so familiar to the readers that only a brief introduction to the subject is needed; others will require extensive background or history for orientation. Some propositions may require only one or two supporting arguments; others more than three. Some conclusions may benefit from an extended summary; others may need only a brief, dynamic statement at the end. Nor must you always deal with dissenting views. Less controversial issues require less attention to your readers' opinions than hotly debated ones. Also, you need not always state the proposition in the introduction. To achieve a climactic effect, you may save it until the conclusion. As you can see, this model is not intended as a restriction on your writing, but as a guide for structure.

To see how this model can be applied to written persuasion, consider the following example by a former education editor of *Saturday Review* for a publication addressed to a college audience. The paper is based on the proposition negatively stated in its title: Teaching needs higher standards to become a true profession. Our marginal comments highlight its specific-to-general (IRS) organizational scheme.

A Classical Argument

Schoolteaching Cannot Be Considered a Profession As Long As Its Entrance Standards Remain So Low
Paul Woodring

In their current demand for professional status, schoolteachers seek an elusive goal. The noun "profession" has always troubled lexicographers. The adjective "professional" is even vaguer. We speak of professional athletes, professional actors, and even of professional prostitutes and criminals. About all we are implying is that such people work for money and are good at what they do. Realtors, morticians, and stockbrokers are among the many others who now claim professional status. In our society of status-seekers, such striving is understandable, but according that recognition dilutes the concept of professionalism.

Introduction: **Defines term "profession"**

1. Points out ambiguities

Theology, law, and medicine have long been called professions. The faculties of medieval universities consisted of men who had been members of those professions before they became teachers. And, although they were bold enough to introduce their students to the pagan literature of Greece

2. Provides historical background

and Rome, most of the humanists in the Renaissance were Christian theologians.

By the 19th century, however, philosophers
who were not theologians, and scientists, mathe-
maticians, historians, and teachers of languages
and literature who were not members of one of
the traditional professions, were teaching at universities. A fourth profession had emerged, and its
members were the scholarly teachers who had the
responsibility of advancing knowledge, as well as
of disseminating it.

What distinguishes a profession from an occupation? High income is not the hallmark—some
professionals take vows of poverty. A license does
not identify a professional—physicians and lawyers
are licensed, but priests and college professors are
not. Indeed, a license is more characteristic of the
skilled trades—barbers, plumbers, electricians,
and bartenders.

Although the following criteria have not always
been lived up to, they can be useful in identifying
the professions.

- A profession requires a deep commitment
  on the part of all its members, going far
  beyond a desire for pecuniary gain.

- A profession rests on an organized body of
  scholarly or scientific knowledge.

- Members of a profession engage in work that
  improves the human condition.

- Members of a profession meet rigorous standards of education and selection.

Acting is not a profession, however much
talent is required of its practitioners—Shirley
Temple was a superb actress at the age of 4. Athletic achievement requires both natural talent and
a long period of training, but it does not rest on a
body of scholarly knowledge. Activities that stress
the importance of "the bottom line" are obviously
concerned primarily with financial gain, not service.

Is teaching a profession? Most college professors today assume they are professionals. In
general, they meet the four criteria, although
questions could be raised about the ones who join
labor unions.

What about school teaching? Most school-

3. Points out
distinguishing features
or criteria of
"profession"

Body:
1. Matches teaching to
criteria

teachers are deeply committed to their work, and none can be accused of having chosen a teaching career as a way of getting rich (an accusation often made about the career choices of some physicians and lawyers).

Teachers, regardless of the ages of those they teach, clearly are engaged in work whose goal is to improve the human condition. The primary-school teacher who teaches children reading and arithmetic may well be the most important person in the educational system, because all further learning depends on his or her success.

Teaching rests on a body of scholarly knowledge, including an understanding of the nature of the learner and the learning process, as well as of the subject taught.

It cannot be said, however, that schoolteachers are rigorously selected. The competency tests recently given to teachers in several states have revealed a substantial number of "fully certified" teachers who cannot answer questions that ought to be easy for a reasonably bright eighth-grader. To be sure, those who failed constitute a small minority, but they were the teachers of several thousand boys and girls.

While some very intelligent and talented young men and women enter teaching each year—and deserve more attention and credit then they get from critics who are denigrating the public schools—*it is still true that the minimum requirements for admission to programs in teacher education are much too low.*

Schools of education in many universities admit some candidates whose scores on the verbal section of the Scholastic Aptitude Test are a little over 400. Those scores are below the mean for high-school juniors who take the test, and they would not be high enough for admission to any other kind of professional program. When such students become teachers, they face classes in which more than half the students have greater verbal facility than the teacher.

Yet some professors of education go so far as to contend that the qualities measured by the S.A.T. are unimportant for teachers. It is true that effective teaching requires traits of personality and

2. Denies last criterion to establish basis of his argument

3. Thesis idea: Admission standards are too low. (italics added)

Provides statistics for support

Refutation: Refutes "personality" argument by attacking its logic

character not measured by standardized tests, and that some people with high test scores become poor teachers because they lack those traits. But it does not follow that a person with the right personality can become a good teacher without sufficient intelligence and without verbal competence far above the 400 level. So long as entrance standards remain this low, there is little chance that teaching school will be recognized as one of the learned professions.

In response to those who contend that raising standards would create a teacher shortage, I argue to the contrary that, just as has been the case in the traditional professions, high standards would in the long run attract to teaching a larger number of talented candidates. Raising standards might make legislators more willing to pay teachers higher salaries. It would surely improve the quality of teaching.

Conclusion:
1. Refutes "teacher shortage" argument
2. Uses refutation to make his final plea

Because he is writing for an audience of teachers who consider themselves professionals, Woodring chooses the specific-to-general organization (IRS). This permits him to define early and clearly his use of "profession," a term having many definitions. Thus, he opens with an extended definition, making use of such devices as negative definition to distinguish an occupation from a profession, giving historical background, and setting up criteria or distinguishing features. The criteria then become the basis for his argument, particularly the one that deals with rigorous standards. Not until he has established common bonds with his readers about their concept of teaching does he present his proposition that standards are too low. In the last two paragraphs, he refutes two possible counterarguments to enhance his own recommendation for change.

FORMAL PERSUASION: PROBLEM-SOLUTION ARGUMENT

As we indicated earlier, problem-solution argument involves the explanation of a current or future problem and the proposal of a solution. Any time you seek to change the way something is presently done, the problem-solution approach can be adopted. The basic outline for a problem-solution argument is simple:

I. The problem
    A. Explanation of the problem and its significance.
    B. Analysis of who or what has caused the problem.
    C. Discussion about why present policies will not solve the problem.
    D. Reasons for reader concern.

II. The solution
   A.   Explanation of the solution.
   B.   Discussion of how the solution will alleviate or eliminate the problem.
   C.   Reasons why the solution is practical and can be implemented.
   D.   Reasons why the suggested solution is superior to other solutions.
   E.   (If applicable) Ways to implement the solution.

Of course, you can modify this outline according to the nature of your problem, your readers, the situation, and your purpose. For example, if your problem is evident, such as the need for more student parking, then you will not need an extensive introduction. But if the problem is generally unknown, such as the necessity for making the campus more accessible for wheelchair students, then you should explain it in detail in your opening paragraphs. If you consider numerous solutions offered by others, you might present and refute them before you advance your own proposal, as we suggested in the model for the classic argument. The length of discussion you allot to each counterargument will depend on the writing situation. In writing designed for a limited space, such as a newspaper editorial or letter to the editor, you may need to shorten your discussion of counterproposals, saving valuable space to make a strong case for your own proposal as is done in the following newspaper editorial.

A Problem-Solution Argument

Get Smarter about Drunken Driving
New York Times

In New York and 41 other states, the 21-year-old drinking age law pays handsome dividends in accidents avoided and lives saved. But new evidence suggests that another popular tactic in the war on drunken drivers is based on false and naive assumptions. *It's time to challenge these assumptions and change these programs.*

Problem

Thesis: Proposal

One assumption is that first offenders are social drinkers who have had one too many. The reality, studies indicate, is that most are alcoholics or problem drinkers who got caught for the first time. Another assumption is that a few lectures on the dangers of drunken driving will deter it. Drunken drivers who are problem drinkers need medical treatment.

Refutation:
Flaws in current assumptions

These findings warrant more investigation. They imply the need for a new attitude toward drunken driving and a more rigorous approach to first offenders.

Among those pressing for a change is Judge

Albert Kramer of Quincy, Massachusetts, who has studied the issue extensively. "We're wasting our time in America on three-quarters of the hundreds and hundreds of thousands of people we arrest" for drunken driving, he told Matthew Wald of the *Times* recently. Of 1,252 people convicted of drunken driving in his jurisdiction between 1982 and 1985, 82 percent were found to be alcoholics or "problem drinkers." Only 18 percent fit the "social drinker" profile.

Support:
1. **Testimony of expert**

In most states, the legal blood-alcohol limit is 0.10 percent. The average blood-alcohol level for people arrested for drunken driving is 0.18 to 0.20 percent. To reach 0.20 percent, a 160 pound person would have to down 11 drinks of 80-proof liquor in one hour on an empty stomach. Only someone with a serious alcohol problem could do that and even remain conscious.

2. **Statistics**

Someone suffering from alcoholism is unlikely to be affected by a typical first-offender program. In fact, such programs may be triply wasteful. They squander the educational effort and the police exertion required to catch a single drunken driver—on average, 150 traffic stops. Most important, they do nothing to get alcoholics into effective treatment.

3. **Reasons for inadequacy of current plan**

New York's Department of Motor Vehicles already requires every participant in its first-offender program to be clinically evaluated as to drinking habits. About 20 percent are referred for further treatment. But if the experts are right, more should be. Whatever the actual figure, the new evidence compels nationwide study and action. After treating drunken driving too lightly for decades, Americans have been learning to get tougher. It's time now also to get smarter.

Solution: **Improve present system.**

Appeal:
For study and action

Although brief, this editorial follows a modified version of the outline suggested for problem-solution arguments. Early on, it states the problem (inadequacies of the present system for handling drunken drivers) and suggests a need for change. It then explains and analyzes the problem by pointing out weaknesses of the current system, using testimony and statistics, and showing reasons for its weaknesses (false assumptions, inefficiency, and inadequate controls). In the process, because of the space restrictions, the writer implies the advantages of the proposed solution. The concluding paragraph assertively states the editor's solution and appeals to readers to act.

INFORMAL PERSUASION

Informal persuasion may be viewed as incomplete argument, lacking one or more of the necessary components of formal argument. For instance, your purpose may be simply to argue a point without addressing or refuting the possible counterarguments, to simply "get something off your chest" without going into all the ramifications of the issue. Or there may be instances when you are more interested in pointing out the weaknesses of an opposing contention than in making a strong case for your own position. In writing about a significant societal problem such as prolonging life by artificial means, you may not have a proposal to offer, but wish to discredit someone else's view. Because informal persuasion often appears in newspaper editorials, TV commentaries, letters to the editor, and written appeals for charitable contributions, lack of space or time sometimes prevents a writer from presenting a full, formal argument. In such cases, the writer must decide which aspect of the argument is most important.

Unlike formal persuasion, which relies heavily on an appeal to reason, informal persuasion depends to a large extent on appeals to emotion, eliciting a response from the readers' desires, fears, compassion, or sense of justice. On occasion, bypassing formal, logical argument is advantageous, particularly with issues that are so controversial and emotionally volatile that readers are unlikely to be swayed by logical reasoning no matter how sound. On issues such as abortion, gun control, or capital punishment, people may already have rejected any logical argument you could put forth and will respond only to an appeal to their sympathies or religious beliefs. In such instances, however, be careful that you do not play on emotions irresponsibly; include only arguments that are grounded in commonly held ethical principles and that will not elicit a totally irrational response. Also, judicious word choice and careful organization can prevent an emotional appeal from becoming a "rabble-rousing" one.

Like classical arguments and many expository papers, informal persuasion is often organized in three parts: an introduction that establishes the issue and supplies background; a body that presents the writer's main points; and a conclusion that restates the thesis, perhaps making an appeal for action or change. In the following essay, the writer's main purpose is to point out the faulty logic of an argument contrary to his own, but in so doing, he indirectly argues his own case. Note that he strongly appeals to his readers' pride in American values.

An Informal-Persuasion Paper

Outlaws of the Western World
Sydney J. Harris

I wonder if the pro-handgun people in America realize what they are saying about our citizens when they repeat their familiar slogan, "Guns don't kill—people do."

Introduction:
Introduces issue

If guns don't kill, but people do, this makes Americans the most murderous population on the face of the earth. In 1980, for instance (the last year for which we have accurate international statistics), handguns killed 77 people in Japan, eight in Great Britain, 24 in Switzerland, eight in Canada, 18 in Sweden, four in Australia—and 11,522 in the United States.

What can this mean? If it is not the availability of guns here that is responsible for such a massacre, it can only mean that our citizens are by far the most vicious, violent, homicidal people in the world.

Do you believe this? Do you believe that Americans are so much worse than other people—so contemptuous of human life—that our death rate from guns is thousands of times larger than [in] those countries that have enacted civilized and sensible gun laws?

This is a terrible indictment to make about a nation that prides itself upon its decency and humanity, that likes to hold itself up as a model of democratic friendliness.

But this is what the pro-gun partisans would have us believe. That it is not the mere possession of firearms, but the people behind them, who are responsible for our appalling mortality, year after year.

It is by their own tortured logic that we must condemn, then, not the instrument, but the agent. And condemning the agent means that we condemn the American public, individually and collectively, for being brutally indifferent to the taking of human life.

Shifting the burden of guilt from the gun to the gunslinger inexorably marks our people as the outlaws of

Body (Refutation of Argument Contained in Slogan):
1. Uses statistical comparison

2. Draws a logical inference from the figures

3. Appeals to patriotic pride

4. Attacks logic of slogan

the Western world, who willfully or carelessly kill off one another in quantities that other countries find shockingly inexcusable.

I firmly believe that it is guns in the hands of people that kill, and not that we Americans are so much more murderous, by nature or training, than people elsewhere. *It is the easy availability of guns that accounts for our infamous death toll, not our vile dispositions.*

You can take your choice—blame the gun or blame the person. And if you blame the person, as the gun lobby prefers to do, you are indicting the nation itself for being the most bloodthirsty on earth.

I cannot believe this of our people, which is why I must blame the false conception of "freedom," which puts this weapon in their hands.

5. Introduces writer's own argument

6. States thesis strongly (italics added)

Conclusion:
1. Summarizes points made with choice

2. Restates thesis indirectly

Although effectively persuasive, our example is not a complete argument. Only one counterargument is refuted, and Harris does not openly state and support his own argument. And although he attacks the logical reasoning of his opponents, he relies heavily on emotional appeals—stimulating his readers' patriotic pride and then, from that emotion, eliciting an indignant response. Because he is writing about an issue that has become polarized, he is more likely to persuade readers with this kind of informal persuasion than with a formal, logically reasoned argument for gun control.

In addition to Harris's emotional appeals, he uses irony to enhance the persuasive power of his article. Although irony can be a useful tactic for all kinds of persuasion, it is most frequently employed in informal persuasion.

THE USE OF IRONY IN PERSUASION

Irony is a manner of speaking that implies the opposite of what it appears to mean. If, after a painful trip to the dentist, you tell a friend that "It was the most enjoyable hour of my life," you are being ironic. Both you and your friend know you really meant that it was the opposite. Often confused with sarcasm, which is a nasty, personal attack on an individual, irony ridicules human foibles or societal characteristics.

Sometimes writers include only an occasional ironic, "tongue-in-cheek" statement to enhance a specific point; at other times, they may use irony throughout a whole essay, creating a satire, as Jonathan Swift did in his famous work, "A Modest

Proposal." In it, he points out the brutality of Britain's treatment of the Irish by suggesting an ironic solution—selling the children for meat.

Because writing effective satire is a demanding task even for experienced writers, student writers generally profit more from using irony as an occasional device. Once you have mastered the techniques, then you might try your hand at satire. One further caution: You must be sure your readers have a context for recognizing an ironic statement. Consider the following pair of statements: the first a straightforward statement of fact; the second, ironic.

> Wildcat fans often display unsportsmanlike behavior. (straightforward statement of fact)
> Wildcat fans displayed their usual exemplary sportsmanship. (ironic statement—opposite is true)

As the reader, unless you happened to be familiar with the Wildcat fans' behavior, you would have no way of telling which statement was ironic unless the writer had provided clues elsewhere in the paper. Thus, unless a well-publicized situation is involved, you must supply the necessary context to use irony effectively; otherwise readers are likely to take your ironic statements literally.

Irony involves many complex tactics. Here we will discuss only those most frequently used and most easily mastered.

Tactics for Creating Irony

Exaggeration   Perhaps the tactic easiest to recognize is exaggeration. The trick in using it effectively is to make it so apparent that no one can miss your real intent. Note how Phyllis McGinley accomplishes this in her description of men's superiority:

> That men are wonderful is a proposition I will defend to the death. Honest, brave, talented, strong, and handsome, they are my favorite gender. Consider the things men can do better than women—mend the plumbing, cook, invent atom bombs, design the Empire waist-line, and run the four-minute mile. They can throw a ball overhand. They can grow a beard. . . .
>
> —*Phyllis McGinley, "Women are Better Drivers"*

McGinley's use of exaggeration includes attributing characteristics of some men to *all* and to listing undesirable or trivial accomplishments as if they were both desirable and important. The exaggeration is so obvious, so humorously written, that no reasonably intelligent person could read the passage literally, and few male readers could be offended by it.

Understatement   Understatement involves oversimplification: making a situation less complex or less serious or troublesome than it really is. Sydney Harris uses understatement in his article on guns when he sets up the *either-or* situation: "Blame the gun or blame the person." A parent who calls a child's destructive tantrums "youthful pranks" is guilty of understatement. Another way to understate is to negate the statement, particularly with a double negative: It was *not* an *im*possible situation.

Incongruity   A useful tool for creating irony is the unexpected joining of opposites, as in "Henry VIII was never reluctant to banish or execute his wives, but he loved women." Another kind of incongruity is the unexpected twist of a surprising, deflating, or shocking climax, as in these lines from an ironic argument contending that cannibalism might be a deterrent for murder:

> I asked myself why we, who scarcely blink at the wholesale burning alive of families [napalm victims], should yet quail and sicken at the thought of eating those we have not only killed but cooked. Such fastidiousness, it seemed to me, was far more curious and eccentric than cooking missionaries, especially *when I considered that the missionaries were usually killed beforehand.*
>
> —*Wendell Berry, "A Few Words for Cannibalism"*

Although few writers become expert at writing ironic essays, most of us can learn to use ironic touches in our persuasive papers to add interest and humor. Irony helps you to point out weaknesses and problems without sounding "preachy."

SUMMARY

Argument requires special organization and logical handling of the material. The organization of your paper should enhance your reasoning processes and your persuasive tactics. Supporting evidence can consist of statistics, authoritative quotations, analogics, facts, case studies, historical or social background, or explanation of causes. Along with the language you use, the way you order your material should help you develop your argument as forcefully as possible.

Whatever form of argument you use, your introduction must stimulate your readers' interest. The concluding paragraphs should both summarize the argument and restate the proposition. In addition, the conclusion should make an appeal to the readers for whatever action may be appropriate. This appeal can be emotional, capitalizing on the sympathy or indignation that you have stirred in readers. Or it can appeal to the decency and fairness of your audience. In some instances, you can present readers with a choice: Either this must be done, or this will be the consequence. Another effective way of concluding is to point out some benefit to your readers—how your proposition can affect them.

Because irony is particularly useful in persuasive writing, we have pointed out some of the primary ways of achieving it: exaggeration, understatement, and incongruity.

To be effective, persuasive papers must be based on sound logical reasoning. In the next chapters, we discuss some basic logical principles and point out some pitfalls to avoid.

ASSIGNMENTS

For Discussion

1. It is often necessary in a persuasive paper to provide factual information as support for your argument. Students sometimes find it difficult to design such material so that it is persuasive rather than merely explanatory. Examining the following pairs of examples and determining which is argumentative and which expository will help you with this writing problem. Determine the characteristics of each that influenced your identification.

    a. The usual explanation, that the stone giants were moved to their present sites on wooden rollers, is not feasible in this case, either. In addition, the island can scarcely have provided food for more than 2000 inhabitants. (A few hundred natives live on Easter Island today.) A shipping trade, which brought food and clothing to the island for the stonemasons, is hardly credible in antiquity.

        —*Erich Von Daniken, Chariots of the Gods?*

        One explanation for the Easter Island statues is that large numbers of people rolled the huge stones to their present sites. But it is believed that the island itself could not have supported so many people, nor could merchants from another place have brought food and supplies to the stonemasons on the island.

    b. The act provided that after every Indian had been allotted land, the remainder would be put up for sale to the public. But the loopholes with which the act was punctured made it an efficient instrument for separating the Indians from this land. The plunder was carried on with remarkable order. The first lands to go to whites were the richest—bottomlands in river valleys or fertile grasslands. Next went the slightly less desirable lands, such as those that had to be cleared away before they could produce a crop. Then the marginal lands were taken, and so on, until the Indian had left to him only desert that no white considered worth the trouble to take. Between the passage of the Allotment Act in 1887 and a New Deal investigation in 1934, the Indian had been reduced to only 56,000,000 acres out of the meager 138,000,000 acres that had been allotted them—and every single acre of the 56,000,000 was adjudged by soil conservationists to be eroded. At the same time that the Indians were being systematically relieved of their lands, their birth rate rose higher than the mortality rate, and so there were more and more Indians on less and less land.

        —*Peter Farb, Man's Rise to Civilization*

        The act provided that after every Indian had been allotted land, the remainder would be put up for sale to the public. But the many provisions in the act permitted the separating of the Indians from the land. The first lands to go were the richest—bottomlands in river valleys or fertile grass-lands. Next went the slightly less desirable lands, and then the marginal lands. Finally, the Indian was left with desert land that no one else wanted. Between the passage of the Allotment Act in 1887 and a New Deal investigation in 1934, the Indians retained only 56,000,000 eroded acres out of the 138,000,000 acres that had been allotted to them. During the same period, the birth rate rose higher than the mortality rate, so there were more Indians on less land.

c. All men are capable of procreation. Besides the power to think and will, man has the ability to create new life. These generative powers are possessed by all normal men and women for the purpose of perpetuating the human race. It is axiomatic that those who bring such life into existence should assume responsibility for it. And since this obligation is not a light one, mankind must be encouraged to assume it and be rewarded for doing so.

> —John S. Banahan, "What a Catholic Wishes to Avoid in Marriage"

Besides the ability to think and will, all normal people have the ability to procreate. However, human reproduction involves heavy responsibility.

2. Identify the tactic(s) of irony in each of the following:

a. All animals are brutes; only man is the perfect animal.

Some countries will go to war over which one wants peace the most.

Life is a terminal disease.

If you see a gunfight on the street, better get into it so you won't be shot as a bystander.

When it comes to giving, some people stop at nothing.

They sure get along like brothers—Cain and Abel.

> —Sam Levenson, "You Don't Have to be In Who's Who
> to Know What's What"

b. The neutron bomb is the greatest thing to come along since sliced bread. When set off, it produces high levels of radiation, cooking people, but leaving structures and buildings standing. Unlike present atomic weapons where blast and heat do most of the damage, the neutron bomb actually penetrates its target, frying anyone inside.

> —Art Buchwald

c. The Pentagon is very big and very noticeable. When it is driven along at 55 miles per hour, people can see it coming from miles away. It attracts attention. In short, it is a fat, easily detected target.

> —Russell Baker, "Universal Military Motion"

For Practice

1. Outline the following short arguments. What is the implicit proposition or proposed solution in each? The main argument? Does the writer appeal to the

readers' emotions or to their reason? Is there an attempt to show respect for the readers' positions? How is refutation of counterarguments handled? How effective is the conclusion? What kinds of evidence does the writer rely on?

a. Autos are the number one cause of air pollution, as well as energy wastage. They kill 50,000 to 60,000 people a year—needlessly, from unsafe design. Highways and parking lots drain available agricultural and industrial land. The exercise of which they deprive us (walking, bicycling) is a major contributor to death from heart disease. The 7.6 million [cars] we throw away each year, like beer cans, clog our landscapes and city dumps. The steel, rubber, glass, plastic and energy used in building eight to ten million new ones each year squander scarce resources.

Urban design, inadequate public transportation and physical health make automobile transportation a necessity for many Americans. We can't forbid their sale. But how about a ban on advertising cars? Isn't it incongruous for a nation claiming concern over energy to spend millions of dollars (especially on television licensed to serve "the public interest") encouraging the consumption of more and more thirteen-mile-per-gallon autos?

Half of all auto use is for distances under five miles. Bicycle sales (fifteen million a year) have already soared ahead of the sluggish auto market. Once the auto ads are banned, how about building on this citizen sensibility with a media campaign (à *la* World War II bond sales) to encourage further walking and bicycling—thereby saving our air and our health as well as our oil? (Reports and public-service spots on cars' gas mileage would be useful, too.) It worked (while we tried it) with anti-smoking spots on TV. . . .

—*Nicholas Johnson, "Ban Auto Ads"*

b. Ten years ago this month the U.S. surgeon general brought forth his Report on Smoking and Health. The report climaxed ten years of controversy over the relationship between cigarettes and lung cancer, and it precipitated a second decade of controversy on the same issue. The story merits a backward look.

In truth, the controversy over smoking and health probably dates from the time that Columbus first saw the Indians puffing their tabacas. Efforts to ban smoking can be traced to the edicts of James I against the "sot weed." From time immemorial, little boys have been warned against coffin nails. The cigarette has had many lovers, but very few friends.

Even so, it wasn't until the mid-'50s that statistical evidence began to accumulate on the cigarette-cancer relationship. By the time Dr. Luther L. Terry's study commission went to work, some 10,000 professional papers were available. From these papers—the commission did no independent research of its own—came the conclusion that heavy smokers are more likely to die of lung cancer than nonsmokers. Six additional reports have followed the first report of 1964, each of them identifying new perils and raising new warnings.

These cries of alarm have wrought considerable changes within the cigarette industry and within the advertising industry also. Back in 1963, the ten leading brands, headed by Pall Mall, included such non-filter labels as Lucky Strike and Chesterfield. Now Pall Mall has slipped to third, behind Winston and Marlboros; sales of Camels have dropped in half; Luckies and Chesterfields have disappeared from the top ten, and some new brands, relatively low in tar and nicotine, have taken their place. Cigarette advertising has vanished from radio and television; smokers are exhorted in public service announcements to "kick the habit" instead.

The anti-smoking campaign also has led to the ignored and familiar statement on every package and in every magazine ad: "Warning: The Surgeon General Has Determined That Cigarette Smoking Is Dangerous to Your Health." The decade has seen airlines divide their passenger compartment into sections for smokers and nonsmokers. The man or woman who lights up in public has become acutely self-conscious of the offense that may be inflicted on others.

Yet these years of intensive effort have had little effect on the smoking habit. Per capita consumption in 1963 amounted to 217 packs; last week it was 205 packs. Over the decade, cigarette sales have increased from 524 billion to 583 billion. Ironically, sales of cigars and pipe tobacco, thought to be less harmful, have significantly decreased in this period.

Why has the typical smoker been so indifferent to the warning and appeals? One answer may lie in the unconvincing nature of the evidence. After ten years, scientists have yet to identify what substance in the cigarette, if any, causes cancer. They have yet to demonstrate how smoke or tar or nicotine converts a normal cell to a malignant cell. The one major effort to prove that cigarettes cause cancer in dogs produced a publicity splash four years ago, but the experiment has run into professional criticism and has not been replicated.

The palpable fact remains that most smokers die from causes apparently unrelated to smoking. There may be lessons in all this, in terms of the power of government to control the personal habits of the people. Such a lesson should have been learned in the long, dark night of Prohibition. The nation even now is receiving instruction in such areas of the law as marijuana, homosexuality, and pornography; criminal sanctions may have some suppressive effect, but on the whole, not much. So, too, with tobacco: Men have smoked it for 500 years, and whole platoons of Surgeons General are not likely to dissuade them now.

—*James J. Kilpatrick, "Government Meddling Can Be Hazardous to Freedoms"*

   c. This new government regulation regarding waitresses' tips may be the best thing that has ever happened. Tipping is demeaning, patronizing. Our laws have long needed changing. Everyone should be getting minimum wages. It is little wonder we go to fast-food places. Most of us don't like to tip to pay someone for doing their job. We don't tip the checker in the grocery store or the service station attendant. We take for granted that these people are receiving an adequate wage. This idea of paying, plus worrying about how much to tip so as not to look cheap, is what is ruining not only restaurants, but beauty shops as well.

       Owners, get smart; advertise, tell your patrons that your prices reflect the living wage you are now paying. (No tipping please.) Point out in your ad that when their waitress smiles at them, it will be because she is glad they have come and wants to make this an enjoyable dinner for them, not because she feels if she doesn't, she won't make enough to pay her bills.

                  —Edith Bartsch, "Letter to the Editor"

2.   Choose one of the following topic outlines. Rewrite the parts, first as an organizational scheme for a classical argument, then as a problem-solution argument. State the thesis idea and the main points as complete sentences. Remember to select an audience before starting the exercise.

   a. Legalized gambling
      I. Alternative to increase income tax
     II. People always gamble
    III. Possibilities for revenue for charitable organizations

   b. Banning of automobiles in national parks
      I. Pollution damage
     II. Overcrowding
    III. Preservation of wildlife

   c. School busing
      I. Concept of neighborhood schools
     II. Integrated housing
    III. Fuel crisis
    IV. Educational advantages

3.   Determine which groups in your audience would be most likely to be hostile to your views about the subjects in exercise 2. What are some of their possible counterarguments that you might need to refute?

4.   Choose the outline in exercise 2 that you think best suited for an informal persuasion paper. Indicate how you would organize such a paper and discuss briefly the areas of agreement you could expect to share with your target audience.

For Writing

1. Assume that you are working in the public relations department of a major automobile company. Your manager has asked you to submit the copy for a full-page good-will ad persuading people to use their seat belts when driving. Write a 500–800 word statement to be run in college newspapers throughout the country. Using either a classical or a problem-solution argument, develop whichever topic you wish from the following fact sheet your manager gave you.

    a. Eighty percent of all automobile accidents causing serious injury or death involve cars traveling under 40 miles per hour.

    b. Three-quarters of all collisions happen less than 25 miles from the driver's home.

    c. Experts contend that almost half of all automobile occupant fatalities and many serious injuries might have been avoided if people had been wearing seat belts. They restrain people from being thrown about inside the car or from being flung clear of the car, which is almost always more dangerous than being trapped inside.

    d. People don't wear seat belts for many reasons: they are troublesome, wrinkle clothes, and are often uncomfortable. Many people also feel that they are careful drivers who won't have an accident. Many are fatalists.

    e. Drivers have the psychological authority to convince all passengers to wear seat belts.

    f. Company policy requires that everyone in a company-owned vehicle wear lap and shoulder belts.

2. Assume that you are the executive assistant to the president of a state university who has been seriously concerned about the problem of alcoholism on campus. The president has created an alcohol education program for students, staff, and faculty, and has required strict enforcement of the university's alcoholic regulations by the campus police, dorm advisors, and other administrators. Consequently, you can understand why she is upset this Tuesday morning after noticing that the latest cover of the alumni magazine portrays a young woman celebrating a basketball victory with an open bottle of champagne in one hand. The president asks you to stop the distribution of the 55,000 magazine copies, have the cover reprinted (even though it will cost $10,700), and write a statement for the first page of the issue, explaining why the publication did not appear on schedule. In the same article, she asks you to try to persuade readers to stop or reduce their own drinking, and to be especially careful about drinking before driving. Write a statement in problem-solution form that will satisfy her request.

3. Write a paper of about 750 words based on one of the outlines prepared for Practice Exercise 1 at the end of Chapter 17.

16

Prewriting Tactics
for Persuasive
Writing

The prewriting concerns for persuasive papers are similar in many ways to those for expository papers. A major difference is that greater attention must be paid to readers—their needs and attitudes. But more about the why and how of that concern later. For now, we'll review the prewriting process we outlined earlier, then examine a plan for following each of its six steps in persuasive writing: (1) selecting a subject; (2) generating ideas about the subject; (3) limiting the subject; (4) adapting the subject to readers; (5) formulating a thesis sentence; and (6) developing a plan. Remember that, although these steps might ideally be tackled in this order, you may change it to meet the demands of the writing task.

SELECTING A SUBJECT

Like expository writing, persuasive writing may often be assigned—either in your college classes or your job. But often it is self-generated: People or issues may provoke you into writing a letter to your campus or community paper or to some local, state, or national government official. You may have a grievance as a consumer of goods or services. Parents often must persuade their children and some-times children their parents. In all these instances, you normally would not need to search for a subject.

But assume that you've been asked to write an argumentative essay for an English course, to take issue with some current campus policy for an alumni magazine, or to state a position for a political campaign. What can you do? How can you come up with a subject? We'd like to suggest an activity that we call brainstorming. Our brainstorming plan calls for you to jot down any possible subject that comes to mind, no matter how absurd it may seem at the moment. To jog your mind, you might reflect on your interests, hobbies, gripes, likes, and worries. Then consider what you have argued about with your friends, members of your family, instructors or classmates, a coach, or anyone else you have talked to recently. Review recent class lecture notes and discussions that challenged your ideas. Recall television programs or films that dealt with controversial issues. And look through some magazines and newspapers for topics that you can agree or disagree with, preferably ones that increase your blood pressure.

After you've spent about thirty minutes writing down possible subjects, there should be at least three or four workable possibilities in your list. If you find a subject that generally interests you and that you are reasonably informed about, grab it. But avoid certain types of subjects. Eliminate arguments that can be proved or disproved purely through factual evidence. The resale value of used cars or the population of Soviet Russia and the United States, for example, can be resolved easily by consulting library sources. Instead, select subjects that involve judgments; for example, you might contend that used car dealers should list major defects in cars they sell or that the U.S. Navy is stronger than the Russian Navy.

Generally argumentative subjects involve the comparison of objects or ideas, or the analysis of proposals that the writer thinks should be accepted or rejected. Any comparisons, however, should be based on facts or objective criteria. Try to avoid such "no-win" topics as those involving personal taste. The contention that faculty members at small colleges are better teachers than those at large universities is not only a sweeping generalization but is based on personal opinion. After all, what evidence could you offer? But you might reasonably argue that one professor at your college should be given tenure, a teaching award, or some other honor on the basis of certain criteria that you could specify, such as student teaching evaluations, advising, publications, and college activities.

In addition to avoiding subjects that deal mainly with factual information or personal judgment, steer clear of those involving obvious or uninteresting ideas. Arguing that "students shouldn't cheat on exams" is likely to provoke a "so what?" response from your readers. Choose a subject that you believe will interest your intended audience; be wary of subjects that might elicit a "ho-hum" response.

Generating Ideas About a Subject

In previous prewriting chapters, we have discussed techniques for creating ideas about a subject (see pages 42–48 and 174–79). You can use any of these you like. In addition, you might try some of the following techniques:

Larson's Topics

Richard L. Larson has provided a long list of questions for writers to consider. These topics, as he refers to them in the tradition of classical rhetoricians, permit writers to anticipate questions that readers might ask. They also suggest avenues for exploration that may enable writers to discover overlooked ideas. The following are adapted from Larson's questions about propositions:

What must be established for readers before they will believe it?

Into what sub-propositions, if any, can it be broken down? (What smaller assertions does it contain?)

What are the meanings of key words in it?

To what line of reasoning is it apparently a conclusion?

How can I contrast it with other, similar propositions?

To what class (or classes) of propositions does it belong?

How inclusive (or how limited) is it?

What is at issue, if I try to prove the proposition?

How can it be illustrated?

What kind of evidence is needed to prove it?

What will or can be said in opposition to it?

Is it true or false? How do I know? By direct observation, authority, deduction, statistics, other sources?

Why might someone disbelieve it?

What does it assume? (What other propositions does it take for granted?)

What does it imply? (What follows from it?) Does it follow from the proposition that action of some sort must be taken?

What does it reveal (signify, if true)?

If it is a prediction, how probable is it? On what observations of past experiences is it based?

If it is a call to action, what are the possibilities that action can be taken? Is what is called for practical? What are the probabilities that the action, if taken, will do what it is supposed to do? Will the action call for work?

While many of Larson's questions will help with problem–solution arguments, the following questions might be more pertinent when some change is advocated in the present system:

What is the problem? Why is it serious? Why must there be a change?

Will it affect my readers? How?

What causes the problem? Is it caused by the system or the people administering it? What then must be changed?

How will the proposed solution work? How will it reduce or eliminate the problem? Will it create other problems? More serious ones?

Is the solution practical? Has it been successful elsewhere? Is its cost acceptable?

Are there sufficient people to implement it?

Why might people oppose it? What other solution might they suggest? Why is the proposed solution better than any others?

Although only some questions may apply to a particular subject, asking them will help you start an internal dialogue. By writing answers to the pertinent questions, you will be stretching your mind, seeking information that you might otherwise have overlooked. These questions, then, will help you answer the query that students have asked English teachers throughout the ages: What can I write about this subject?

Personal Dialogue

Another way to generate ideas is to set up a dialogue with a friend. This person should be someone eager to help you by taking a position opposite to yours. Talking out your ideas and responding to questions and objections can help to focus and clarify your points and explore counterarguments. Here's how such a dialogue might take place:

Friend: "So you're going to argue against a state lottery?"

Writer: "Yes, I realize that we need money. But a lottery is the wrong way to raise it."

Friend: "Why?"

Writer: "Well, first of all, it's gambling." (moral counterargument)

Friend: "What's wrong with that? Many people gamble."

Writer: "That doesn't make it right. And the state shouldn't encourage people to get something without working for it. The state shouldn't exploit the poor and uneducated." (ethical counterargument)

Friend: "The state isn't exploiting anyone. It's providiing some fun and some hope for people. People like lotteries."

Writer: "Hmmm. You've got a point. But while they may like lotteries, they aren't good for them. Did you know that the odds against winning state lotteries are higher than they are in other forms of gambling? The state is actually cheating people." (ethical counterargument)

Friend: "But the state will use the money for a good cause—for schools, health, and other programs. What's wrong with that?" (refutation)

Writer: "Nothing. But don't confuse means and ends. The means are wrong. The state shouldn't be in the gambling business."

Friend: "But the state makes money from horse racing and liquor, doesn't it? That doesn't mean it approves of betting and drinking." (refutation)

Writer: "Good point. Well, look. There's a difference. Your analogy doesn't apply. The state doesn't own and operate the race tracks and the liquor stores here. (I know it does in some states.) But the state would own and operate the lottery. It'd be taking money from the poor and from hard-working people who need it. Next thing you know, the state would be running gambling casinos or peddling drugs, all in the name of using the money for a worthy cause. What's wrong is wrong. The state shouldn't be a party to anything shady." (counterargument using analogy)

Friend: "Now you're getting carried away. You may be right. But anyway, it sounds like you've got some good ideas for a paper."

Of course, dialogue with a friend may not always be this helpful. But you will find discussing your views with a "devil's advocate" can expose you to some opposing arguments that you had not previously considered.

LIMITING THE SUBJECT

In persuasive writing, as in expository, you should restrict your subject according to your audience, your purpose in writing, and any word or time limitations. For example, if you were submitting a statement to the city council about architectural planning, you would be wise to confine yourself to public buildings or area development. And a restriction of 500 words might cause you to deal with only one area, such as the downtown. In general, as we advised previously: Be wary of a broad subject. There is comfort in selecting one, to be sure, but the danger lies in your inability to treat it effectively in a short- or medium-length paper. You will be wiser to cut your subject down to a size you can treat in great detail.

ADAPTING THE SUBJECT TO READERS

Only by being aware of your readers' opinions and possible reactions can you plan your argument skillfully. That's why you should try to have in mind a profile of your audience. The questions suggested for expository writing (see page 181) can be used for this purpose; but in argument, you should also consider the following questions:

To what extent should I reveal my knowledge, intelligence, experience, and expertise about the subject to my readers? What will be the effect of doing so?

Should I show good will toward my readers? How will this affect them?

Should I show a sense of responsibility toward my readers? How will this affect them?

Should I use an emotional appeal? What appeal or appeals will be most helpful in persuading my readers?

What examples, facts, reasons, statistics, testimony, or other evidence will be most helpful in persuading my readers?

What general principles or truths related to the subject will my audience accept?

What analogies, contrasts, or sayings might appeal to them?

You may feel that spending so much time thinking about your readers is overdoing it. But experts in the techniques of persuasion disagree. According to Kenneth Burke, "You persuade a man only insofar as you can talk his language by speech, gesture, tonality, order, image, attitude, idea, identifying your ways with his." And Carl Rogers concurs, stressing the need "to see the expressed idea and attitude from the other person's point of view, to sense how it feels to him, to achieve his frame of reference—to understand his thoughts and feelings so well that you could summarize them for him."

But you should realize that you may not be able to reach some readers. Think of your audience not as a people of one mind but as different individuals falling somewhere along this spectrum:

TARGET AUDIENCE OF PERSUASION

| Strongly in favor | Slightly in favor | Neutral | Slightly opposed | Strongly opposed |

Remember that strongly opposed readers may be unreachable. You may be unable to change their minds if your proposals are contrary to their best interests. It is doubtful, for example, that the tobacco farmers of North Carolina would accept an argument to lower the tobacco subsidy. About the best you can do with such readers is to enable them to understand your position and to recognize that it has some merit.

But while you certainly want to strengthen the convictions of those who strongly or slightly agree, you primarily need to focus on those who are undecided and who are slightly opposed.

FORMULATING A THESIS STATEMENT

As in expository writing, an argument paper develops and expands a statement that summarizes the main point or claim made. And like an expository thesis (pages 182–85), an argumentative thesis should be stated as clearly and concisely as possible. Generally, it is in the form of a strong recommendation that can double as a logical conclusion and is stated as a proposition with an auxiliary verb, such as *should, might, must, will,* as in:

Freshman English *should* be offered on a pass–fail basis.

In other instances, it may be a recommendation based on an assumption of universally accepted truth:

Society has the right to require people to fasten their seat belts.

For some purposes, you may need to qualify or limit your proposition. Here are some examples:

This country must avoid military spending *that will escalate the arms race.* (limits the subject)

Unless some teachers are rewarded for outstanding work, teaching in the nation's public schools will not improve. (sets up an alternate possibility)

Just as it is sometimes useful to offer alternatives, so too it is often advantageous to set up special conditions in your thesis. A conditional thesis is especially valuable in problem–solution argument, because it can reveal the problem and at the same time show the thrust of the recommended solution, as in these examples:

> *If Congress does not have checks on the powers of the CIA,* then the agency's autonomy endangers our democratic system.

> *Either we take steps to halt the loss of top soil,* or our agricultural production will seriously suffer.

Note that in the first example the writer would suggest ways to check the CIA's powers, thereby offering a solution to the problem of danger to the system. The same is true of the second example; the *either* clause provides a framework for offering solutions to the problem of eventual hunger.

As in expository writing, formulating an appropriate thesis is a demanding task. But the thesis in argumentative writing requires even greater planning because it becomes an integral part of the reasoning strategies necessary to produce an effective argument. We will talk more of this logical function in later chapters.

DEVELOPING A PLAN

In planning how to organize or arrange your supporting arguments and your evidence, remember that writers of argument do not merely lay out facts. Rather, they show that the evidence presented is relevant to their claims—that their thesis is actually a logical conclusion which a reasonable reader would arrive at from considering the discussion. You can best achieve this logical clarity if you shape your material so that the evidence (facts, reasons) has an explicit "therefore" relationship to your thesis. For instance, suppose you plan to write an argument on the issue of student aid. The conclusion you'll be arguing for (your thesis) might be this:

> Federal student aid funds should not be cut.

One supporting reason might be:

> Reducing student aid could result in a shortage of professional people.

To test whether this supporting statement leads logically to the conclusion, we can apply the "therefore" test:

> Reducing student aid could result in a shortage of professional people; *therefore,* federal student aid should not be cut.

As you can see, there is an implied cause-and-effect relationship between the two statements. Another way to test your evidence is to reorder the statements and join them with *because,* as in:

> Federal aid should not be cut *because* reducing it could result in a shortage of professional people.

You will find, as you work with these tests, that you may have to reconstruct your sentences several times before the relationship is obvious. But spending part of your prewriting time on this exercise can aid you in the final planning steps of constructing a suitable outline such as one of those we suggested on pages 185 and 187. You might also try writing a focused freewriting draft (pages 44–45) and then use it as a basis for an outline. In performing these steps, you will have solved many of the problems you may encounter in showing logical relationships in the paper itself—relationships necessary to effective argument.

Once you are satisfied that you have worked out the relationships of your evidence to your argument, you need to give some thought to the counterarguments some readers might raise. Using both the list you developed in generating ideas and the guidelines on pages 299–300, ask yourself these questions concerning the placement of these counterarguments in your paper. Will they fit best with one point that you want to make? Will your paper be more persuasive if you address them first or if you save them until after you present your views? Your decision should take into account your purpose in writing as well as the probable attitudes of your readers.

SUMMARY

Because persuasive writing makes many more demands on writers than any other form of writing, prewriting strategies are crucial to the effectiveness of the final paper. Shaping material to the special interests and attitudes of a target audience, anticipating possible counterarguments and deciding how best to refute them, constructing logical appeals, and establishing a conciliatory voice—all require careful planning. Time spent at this stage will pay dividends later.

ASSIGNMENTS

For Practice

1. Choose one of the following broad topics (or brainstorm one of your own) and apply the prewriting steps suggested in this chapter—generating ideas about it, limiting it, and so on. Construct an outline from your material, either in classical argument or problem–solution form.

   a. Student-aid programs
   b. Poverty in the United States
   c. The role of the media in government
   d. The effect of television on children
   e. Social change
   f. Seatbelt laws
   g. Drunk driving penalties

    h. Alcohol education for young people

    i. Mediocrity and American education

    j. Competition for grades

    k. Academic requirements for athletes

    l. Academic records—private or public information?

    m. Gun control

    n. Birth control for teenagers

    o. The role of government in the economy

    p. The energy crisis and possible solutions

    q. Merit pay for teachers

    r. Seniority versus affirmative action in lay-offs

2.   Select a subject of your own choice or use one of those in Assignment 1. Then complete the following exercises prescribed by your instructor.

    a. Write out answers to the questions listed on page 297. Remember that you may be unable to reply to every one.

    b. Engage in a quiet dialogue with a classmate, taking turns playing the writer–friend roles.

    c. Consider adaptability. Jot down notes about how you would write about the subject in a college newspaper, a newspaper going to people in nursing homes, and a community newspaper.

    d. Write three thesis statements, trying to illustrate the different types mentioned on pages 300–01. Decide which one of the three would be the most effective. Be prepared to justify your choice.

    e. Write a plan, showing how your conclusion logically follows from your evidence in a "therefore" relationship.

    f. Outline the main counterarguments your readers might raise. Explain why you plan to refute them either early in your paper during the presentation of your points or at the end of the paper.

3.   The following are thesis statements from argument papers. State each one as a straightforward and succinct proposition. What advantages does the writer of each gain from the printed version?

    a. We are precipitated into a war which, I think, cannot be justified, and a war which promises not a benefit, that I can discover, to this country or the world.

               —William Ellery Channing

    b. A great many folks admit that many of the people in jail ought to be there, and many who are outside ought to be in. I think none of them ought to be there.

               —Clarence Darrow

c. Legislation against manufacture and export of DDT, particularly in the United States, can bring a major international disaster: the return of malaria epidemics—suffering and debilitation from hundreds of millions of cases—deaths from tens of thousands of them.

—James W. Wright

d. It seems to me that our ideals, laws and customs should be based on the proposition that each generation, in turn, becomes the custodian rather than the absolute owner of our resources—and each generation has the obligation to pass this inheritance on to the future.

—Charles Lindbergh

17

Strategies of Persuasion

Effective persuasion requires a well-organized argument, but it also necessitates logical reasoning. True, eloquent orators have often played successfully on the emotions of an audience. And true, advertisers and others rely on similar appeals in print. But in most situations you would be wise to assume that your readers are as intelligent as yourself. That means you should mainly depend on logical reasoning, although you certainly may include emotional appeals if the subject and situation warrant them.

The basic study of logic is covered in a college course that deals with far more than we can touch on in this chapter. But we can consider some of the fundamental principles of logical reasoning that will help you in constructing sound persuasive arguments.

INDUCTIVE AND DEDUCTIVE REASONING

Arguments may be inductive, deductive, or, most often, a combination of the two. Induction and deduction differ in that they arrive at conclusions from opposite starting points in the thinking process. *In*ductive reasoning begins with an observation or an example—an *in*dividual *in*stance; *de*ductive reasoning proceeds from an already *de*termined generalization. To illustrate:

Induction

Individual Instance	This supermarket brand item is cheaper than its comparable name brand item.
↓	Each of these other seventeen supermarket brand items is cheaper than its comparable name brand item.
General Conclusion	Supermarket brand items are cheaper than comparable name brand items.

Deduction

Determined   Supermarket brand items are cheaper than comparable name
Generalization   brand items. (can be derived through induction)
                 Coffee X is a supermarket brand item.

Conclusion
about a   Coffee X is cheaper than comparable name brand items.
Particular

Which reasoning method is better? The answer depends on several factors, but in one sense inductive argument is weaker. Induction leads you to a conclusion that is *probable* but not *certain*. For example, in the illustration cited, unless you compare every supermarket brand item with every name brand equivalent you cannot know that all of the former are cheaper. Therefore, even though inductive arguments are certainly effective and carry great persuasive force, their conclusions should be stated with qualification and should reflect primarily the evidence examined. For instance, it would be more accurate to state the previous inductive conclusion in this form: *Usually,* the supermarket brand items in this store are cheaper than comparable name brand items.

Deductive reasoning, on the other hand, can result in more persuasive argument, leading to conclusions that are *certain*. However, these conclusions must be based on self-evident or accepted generalizations, and the argument itself must be constructed properly, as we shall discuss later. At this point, we want to explain only how inductive and deductive reasoning differ: Induction starts from individual instances, deduction from determined generalizations; induction leads to a conclusion that is probable, deduction to one that is certain.

Now let's look at each of these reasoning processes in greater detail, noting the forms and characteristics of each.

THE STRATEGIES OF INDUCTIVE REASONING

Whether or not you realize it, you practice inductive reasoning every day of your life. After comparing prices, for example, if you conclude that your bookstore charges more than your friend's, you are reasoning inductively. Or if you decide to eat at a particular restaurant because your friend, a connoisseur of good food, has recommended it, you are reasoning inductively. Or if you select a new book because you liked an earlier work by the same author, you are reasoning inductively. Or if you surmise that your healthy plant is doing poorly because it is the only one not getting light, you are reasoning inductively. All these examples may involve problems in the use of evidence, authority, analogy, and causal relationships.

Using Evidence

Whenever you reason inductively, you should make sure that your evidence is accurate, representative, and sufficient.

Obviously, your information should be accurate. Suppose you conclude from comparing prices that your college bookstore is more expensive than your friend's. In this instance, the accuracy requirement means that you should be careful in noting the prices of the books in the different stores. More difficult to grasp is the concept of representative information. What it means is that your sample should fairly take account of the different types of objects or people that you are investigating. Professional pollsters, for instance, must make certain that their sample includes people from different economic, educational, racial, religious, and ethnic backgrounds and that these groups are represented in proportion to their size in the population. Therefore, in our example, at a minimum your sample should include books from different courses and different class levels. Otherwise, your conclusion might be incorrect because your friend's bookstore might heavily discount certain kinds of books to attract new students into the store.

You can also achieve a representative sample by selecting randomly. You might, for instance draw the names of classes from a hat and then price the books required for them at both stores. Or, more systematically, you could select, say, the fifth course on each page of a schedule and survey its books.

But how many books should you sample? What number would be sufficient? The answer to this question is much more difficult because it depends on your purpose, your readers, and the number of objects or people being investigated. Purpose is important because it determines how precise you need your data to be. If it can be plus or minus 10 percent, then you can select a smaller sample than you would for greater precision. To be convinced, readers who already have some acquaintance with the data might not need as large a sampling as readers with little knowledge.

Finally, the number of objects in the groups being investigated (called *the universe*) would determine the number in your sample. Sampling the price of textbooks would require a more extensive survey than sampling the price of sweatshirts or running shoes. The precise number for a scientifically valid sample and how to compute it can be found in any beginning book on statistics. You would be surprised at how easy it is to calculate this figure and how small the number is. Yet your purpose or your readers may not necessitate your conducting such a scientific study.

Even though your sample is accurate, representative, and sufficient, your conclusion should be stated cautiously. After all, you have not examined all the evidence, such as the prices of all the books in the stores. Remember too that informants may not always be reliable in a poll, as the professional pollsters learned from the 1980 Reagan-Carter election, in which Democrats were reluctant to admit "crossing over," and from the 1948 Truman-Dewey election when large numbers of voters changed their minds at the last minute.

Using Authority

An inductive argument may also be based on evidence provided by an *authority*, a reliable person or source that is well informed about the subject and impartial about it. The chief problem with using authority is that we are prone to cite well-known individuals who may have some self-interest that causes them to be biased, or who may be authorities in some other field but know little of the subject under debate. For example, you should be wary about relying on assertions against cutbacks on defense spending by Pentagon officials, against strip-mining restrictions by coal companies, and against HMO's (Health Maintenance Organizations) by doctors. These people and organizations find it difficult to be impartial about such issues because their profits, salaries, lives, and futures are involved in decisions about them. Because the truth may be obscured by self-interest in any situation, relying on information from a particular source can be dangerous unless you know something about the source's relationship to the subject.

You should also be careful about using authorities outside their field of expertise. For example, athletes frequently provide testimonials in advertisements for products. But there is no reason why a professional quarterback should be a greater authority on razor blades than other men, or why a film star should know more about perfume than other women. Thus, in citing authority, you should both investigate the impartiality and competence of your experts and consider whether their expertise is relevant. You should avoid, for instance, assuming that a noted obstetrician can be used as an expert in a paper dealing with adolescent psychology. Even in cases where your authorities have some expertise, you should try to determine what their professional status is: Are they recognized as reputable experts by others in their field? The answer requires library time but is worth the effort if your argument is strengthened in the process.

The purpose of this discussion about authorities is not to discourage you from using them in your persuasive arguments. We want to stress only that you should be careful, checking to determine whether your authority passes the tests of being well-informed and unbiased. If so, then the use of authority can add great persuasive power to your arguments.

Using Analogy

Analogies are often used in inductive arguments to show that because certain previous circumstances have produced certain results, similar circumstances should produce the same results. For instance, if you select a new book because it was written by the author of one you previously liked, you are reasoning by analogy, calculating that something similar in one respect to what had pleased you before (same author) will prove similar in other respects (please you). We continually make assumptions on the basis of analogy.

But as you can realize from the book analogy, the conclusions are not certain. We may enjoy one book written by an author but not another. Businessmen may find a product may sell well in one region but not another. Coaches may discover that a 1–2–2 zone defense works well against one team but not another.

Analogies are often used cleverly in arguments to relate dissimilar things or circumstances. For example, it is often argued that because the United States placed a man on the moon, it should be able to eliminate poverty. Or, because the President is like the captain of a ship, he alone should determine the direction of foreign policy. Like all inductive reasoning, analogies should be checked and stated carefully. In the preceding examples, the analogies are faulty because the United States is not like a ship, and the social, economic, and political problem of eliminating poverty is not like the scientific problem of landing a man on the moon. Such flawed analogies may destroy the effect of your argument because intelligent readers can counter with the obvious differences.

Writers sometimes extend the analogies in proverbs to new situations. Take the old saying that "you can't teach an old dog new tricks," sometimes used to argue that old people cannot adapt to new ways of life or acquire new ideas. Nonsense. Dogs and people are not alike in their learning abilities. Folk sayings may be colorful, but their logical usefulness is questionable. Thus, you should be cautious about using them on your arguments.

As a writer, you should certainly use analogies because they have great persuasive force. But you should make sure that the two compared instances are similar in important respects and dissimilar only in unimportant ones. Thus, in chapter 15, Paul Woodring compares teachers with lawyers and doctors in establishing a definition of "profession," focusing on the common characteristic of service as the most important.

Here are some questions to ask about your analogies so that you can use them to best advantage:

1. How similar are the circumstances in the two cases being compared?

2. Which circumstances actually produced the result that interests me? (For instance, in the example above, was it the *authorship* of the first book that made it pleasing or something else?)

3. In the comparison I am suggesting, will the result be the one I claimed?

To sum up, analogies add interest, color, and punch to persuasive papers, often illustrating points effectively. Usually they have great persuasive power. But be aware of their logical limitations; an opponent can shoot down an argument if you try to base it solely on an analogy.

Using Cause-and-Effect

Cause-and-effect reasoning is so efective in persuasion that we rely on it frequently. In asking for contributions to combat various diseases, fund raisers are basing their appeals on causal reasoning, arguing that undesirable effects can be avoided by striking at their cause through contributions for research. The same reasoning might be employed to urge a change of diet for the average American. Recent studies have shown that too much animal fat produces cholesterol, which can contribute to heart disease and cancer. So a campaign to lessen the incidence of these diseases might focus on the beginning of this causal chain, on reducing the intake of fatty foods.

But causal reasoning is fraught with dangers and must be approached cautiously. Specifically, you should ask three questions before basing your argument on this logical form:

1. Is the stated cause true?

2. Is the stated cause the only one?

3. Is the stated cause direct or indirect?

Sometimes you may feel you have all the evidence to believe that a cause is true and yet be mistaken. So for many years doctors believed that the practice of taking blood from patients would cause them to recuperate and that chills and drafts would cause colds. Now we know that the former practice probably hurt rather than helped patients and that colds are caused by viruses. In these instances, inadequate knowledge was the culprit.

But often the villain is a tendency to ascribe a causal relationship to one that is merely temporal—because B occurred after A, then A must have been the cause of B (*post hoc; ergo propter hoc*—after this, therefore because of this). This logical fallacy (often called simply *post hoc*) is prevalent in many of our superstitions. If a student fails an exam on Friday the 13th, he might place the blame on the "unlucky day," rather than on the real cause—failure to study. Or if another student trips down the stairs and breaks an ankle, she might attribute it to having walked under a ladder earlier. To determine whether the causal relationship is truly a cause-to-effect situation or whether it is a mere coincidence of timing, try to find out if the cause *always* produces the result. Does Friday the 13th always produce bad grades, or is walking under a ladder always disastrous?

You also need to determine whether the stated cause is the only cause. Seldom is there only one. But people tend to oversimplify issues, often seizing on their pet complaint as the sole villain. Thus television is blamed for low national test grades, increased crime, drugs, and just about every other social problem. While television may be a cause, it is not the sole cause for these complex matters. So be careful in your own persuasive writings to check for other causes besides the one you have initially selected.

Even when you feel you have determined all the causes of an effect, you also need to consider which are the immediate or direct causes and which are only contributing, or indirect, causes. A direct cause is one that is primarily responsible for the effect; indirect causes are merely contributing factors. For instance, suppose you are driving through fog on an icy road as darkness falls, and around a blind curve an oncoming car with its headlights on high beam causes you to hit your brakes and skid off the road. How many contributing causes can you find in this situation? Yet, as any police officer on the scene would tell you, there was only one direct cause: You were driving too fast for the existing conditions.

Or, for example, you have a classmate who dropped out of school because of low grades—the direct cause. But her problems could stem from such indirect causes as working too many hours on a job, engaging in too many campus activities, or worrying about a family situation.

In many cases, finding the most important cause is a matter of interpretation and the writer's own convictions. For instance, in trying to find causes for increased teenage violence, one writer may feel that television is the most significant one; another writer may blame it on drug use; and still another may fault the breakup of the family.

What is important to you in writing persuasive papers is to realize that all these causes exist and that all are related to the effect. Then you can write persuasively without being vulnerable to attack for overlooking a contributing cause or its relationship to the effect.

METHODS OF DEDUCTIVE REASONING

To be effective in arguments, deductive reasoning must start from premises the reader accepts as true, and the reasoning process must be valid, following certain prescribed steps from the premises to a conclusion directly derived from the premises. Although *truth* is difficult to define, we assume that you have a common-sense knowledge of what is generally accepted as truth. If your premises in an argument are false, then even if your reasoning process is valid, your conclusion is likely to be untrue. We can explore this problem by looking at an example:

> All students who turn in typed papers automatically receive A's; therefore, all the students in Professor Brown's class who hand in typed papers will receive an A.

Here, the reasoning is fine: The conclusion—that all students with typed papers in Professor Brown's class will receive an A—can be validly inferred from the premise that all students who type their papers will receive A. However, the conclusion is *untrue* because it is based on a false assumption. Any reader would know that all typed papers do *not* automatically receive A's and would dismiss the argument as either stupid or dishonest.

As we have pointed out, you will usually have little trouble in recognizing the truth of your premises, but how do you test for valid reasoning? Some understanding of the way that logicians solve this problem may help you in writing arguments. Because space does not permit a full treatment of formal logic, we will deal here only with the forms of deductive argument most prevalent in writing.

The Syllogism

The most basic form of deductive reasoning is the *syllogism,* a term derived from Greek and literally meaning "a reckoning together." In classical logic, the syllogism consists of three statements: a major premise, a minor premise, and a conclusion with a "therefore" relationship to the first two statements, as in:

> All humans need love. (major premise)
> Todd Brown is a human. (minor premise)
> Therefore, Todd Brown needs love. (conclusion)

As you can see, the first statement—the *major* premise—sets forth a generally accepted principle about a need shared by all humans. The second statement—the *minor* premise—identifies a particular person (Todd Brown) as belonging to the class we know as human. The conclusion follows logically from, and is consistent with, these premises: Because Todd Brown is human, he shares the group's need for love. Thus, because we accept the premises as true and we see that the reasoning is valid, we find the conclusion sound. Although we may not be able to love Todd Brown ourselves, the syllogism would persuade us that Todd needs love.

Consistency, truth, and logical soundness, then, are necessary components of effective reasoning, no matter what form the argument takes.

We should make clear that rarely does a syllogism appear in such an obvious form in argumentative writing. Think of it as a skeletal form of a reasoning process much as an outline is an underlying framework for a finished paper. However, just as constructing an outline is useful in solving a rhetorical problem before writing, so too can the working out of syllogisms help you strengthen your ability to handle deductive arguments with force and conviction.

Since our purpose is to help you write better arguments and not to make a formal logician of you, our discussion of the syllogism will be brief and highly simplified. Using the following example, we'll show first the form a syllogism might take in a paper, then illustrate several ways of testing whether the reasoning is valid;

> Because all freshmen are required to reside in dorms, all the members of the tennis team are dorm residents.

Lying behind this sentence is a syllogism, the information in the sentence's subordinate clause acting as the syllogism's major premise. We can simplify the wording of the subordinate clause to conform to the proposition format required in formal logic:

> All freshmen are dorm residents.

The rest of the sentence contains the conclusion:

> All the members of the tennis team are dorm residents.

We can logically infer that the members of the tennis team are freshmen since they too reside in dorms. This, then, becomes the minor premise:

> All members of the tennis team are freshmen.

We can now put our three propositions or statements into a syllogistic form:

> Major premise: All freshmen are dorm residents. (general)
> Minor premise: All members of the tennis team are freshmen. (particular group of freshmen)
> Conclusion: Therefore, all the members of the tennis team are dorm residents. (combines the general and the particular)

Sometimes to test if reasoning is sound, logicians use circle diagrams. But circle diagrams are often confusing, so we'll use another form of diagram in the hope that it makes the reasoning process clearer:

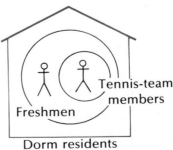

Our diagram shows first that the term "dorm residents" represents a whole group or *class*—other kinds of college residents are excluded. The first circle inside the "dormitory house" represents the whole freshman class; the second represents the tennis team, which is one part or subclass of the freshman class. As the diagram indicates, all freshmen, including the subclass "tennis-team members," are contained in the dormitory frame. Thus, the diagram has demonstrated that the conclusion is validly arrived at. And, if the premises are true; the conclusion is sound.

You should realize that our example is not the only form that syllogistic reasoning can take, but all forms of it involve the same reasoning processes. You should also realize that not all syllogisms exhibit sound reasoning. Deduction, like induction, has its logical pitfalls. One involves consistency: Generally, a logical conclusion stems from only three terms. In our example these are "dorm residents," "freshmen," and "members of the tennis team." Adding more terms leads to faulty reasoning. Suppose our syllogism had this form:

	1	**2**	
Major premise:	All freshmen are dorm residents.		
	3		**4**
Minor premise:	All members of the tennis team are college students.		
Conclusion:	Therefore, all members of the tennis team are dorm residents.		

Now the conclusion does not logically follow, because the term "college students" introduces not only a new class to be reckoned with, but one that is inconsistent with the major premise. Because not all college students are freshmen, it does not follow that all tennis team members are freshmen. So, in constructing a syllogistic argument, you should confine yourself to three terms having a close logical relationship.

A similar type of faulty reasoning occurs when the form of the syllogism confuses the members of a class and a subclass or indicates that sharing one characteristic presumes sharing all. Suppose our syllogism is in this form:

Major Premise:	All freshmen are dorm residents.
Minor Premise:	All members of the tennis team are dorm residents.
Conclusion:	Therefore, all members of the tennis team are freshmen.

Here the conclusion is unsound because the reasoning process was invalid. The predicate of the major premise shows "dorm residents" as the whole class in the syllogism. Yet the conclusion treats "freshmen" as the whole class. Because the syllogism does not stipulate that *only* freshmen live in dorms, the conclusion does not follow validly from the premises; and since upper-classmen could also live there, it does not follow that all tennis-team members *must* be freshmen.

Actually, the syllogistic form has created two separate groups of dorm residents: freshmen and tennis-team members. Here's how it would look on a diagram; compare it with our diagram of a valid syllogism on page 312.

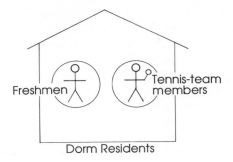

Although these examples of faulty reasoning do not comprise all the possibilities in syllogistic argument, they are the main ones that you will need to avoid in formulating deductive arguments. In the next chapter, we show you how these underlying forms are fleshed out in argument papers.

Conditional Deduction

In our discussion of the syllogism (known in classical logic as the categorical syllogism), we have pointed out that sound reasoning depends on a "therefore" relationship between statements made about classes—freshmen, dorm residents, goats, and so on. But other types of deductive reasoning may take the form of a single compound or complex sentence with a "therefore" relationship between one part of the sentence and the other. However, in these structures, a special condition must be met for the conclusion to follow logically, as in the *either . . . or* argument.

1. Either . . . or *Argument*

The *either . . . or* method of reasoning, sometimes called disjunctive argument, can also be highly persuasive, but it is especially tricky. On the surface, it seems that two alternatives are possible, but logically, the *or* means that only one can prove to be true. The other must be denied. Here are two ways that the disjunctive can apply:

Either the Common Market succeeds *or* Europe's economy fails.
The Common Market does not succeed.   (denied)
Therefore, Europe's economy fails.   (true)

or

Either the Common Market succeeds *or* Europe's economy fails.
The Common Market succeeds.   (true)
Therefore, Europe's economy does not fail.   (denied)

As you may have surmised, the *either . . . or* argument works best when alternatives are clear-cut, where there are in actuality only two choices: "You either live or you die," "Sink or swim." In discussing issues as complex as those in our Common Market example, however, the *either . . . or* form can weaken your position, because Europe's economy may fail for other reasons. If you neglect to account for those other possibilities, your readers may lose respect for your contention, and even question your knowledge of the subject or the validity of your reasoning.

When you present two conditions or positions as the *only* possible alternatives, disregarding others, you commit the *either . . . or* fallacy (sometimes called false dilemma). Although it can be highly persuasive, as in Patrick Henry's famous "Give me liberty or give me death!" you can put yourself out on a logical limb that can easily be sawed off by an argument presenting other alternatives. This happened in a community we know of, situated in a uniquely scenic area. The engineers and townspeople argued "Either build the dam or face yearly destructive flooding." Opponents of the dam pointed out other solutions, such as building a less expensive flood wall, and the dam was not built.

In your own writing, if you wish to present effective arguments, then recognize all the alternatives and discuss them. If you have done this, a concluding *either . . . or* statement based on plausible alternatives can add persuasive force to your argument, as in "Either we avoid nuclear war, or we face massive destruction and loss of life."

2. If . . . then *Argument*

Like the *either . . . or* form, the *if . . . then* or *conditional* argument states alternatives, but in order for the reasoning process to be valid, the conditions in the *if* clause must be met in order for the *then* clause to apply, as in such a statement as "If the stadium is finished, [then] the team will open its season there." Here the relationships between the two stated conditions is logically valid, as shown when we change the statement to a syllogistic form:

If the stadium is finished, [*then*] the team will open its season there.
The stadium is finished.
Therefore, the team will open its season there.

Or

If the stadium is finished, [*then*] the team will open its season there.
The stadium is not finished.
Therefore, the team will not open its season there.

As you can see, the result or conclusion logically follows from the condition established in the *if* clause. But when the conditions established in the argument are not scrupulously met—the second resulting logically from the first, then a flawed argument results, as in the ubiquitous teenage plea: "If I can't go to the senior prom (rock concert, road races, etc.), I'll die." Obviously, dying is not an inevitable consequence of missing an entertainment—maybe disappointment or temporary chagrin—but not death. Such irresponsible, fallacious argument has little chance of logically persuading others to your point of view.

Although the result you claim in an *if . . . then* argument must be a plausible one, it need not be the only possible one. Even though other results are possible, you can use the *if . . . then* argument to great advantage if you prepare your readers by refuting the other possibilities, if you support your contentions with specific examples, and if you indicate the reasoning processes that have led you to your conclusion. In the following example, John Ed Pearce uses *if . . . then* argument effectively in two closing paragraphs because his examples illustrate his contention that the public's acceptance of erroneous explanations for failed policies is a threat to democracy:

> There is a serious danger here. If a president, by skillful acting, can persuade people that failure is success, he need not take the hard and sometimes dangerous steps necessary for success. If he can, by grins and charm, deceive and mislead the people and still retain their support, he is under no pressure to be honest. If the people will accept Iceland as success and contras as George Washington, why should they be told the truth?
>
> Except that the alternative to truth is peril for democracy. For if a president can convince them that falsehood is truth, then the voters have no basis on which to judge or choose their leaders, and the world George Orwell envisioned in "1984" will not have to be forced on them—they will have chosen it.
>
> —*John Ed Pearce, Courier-Journal Magazine*

This argument is persuasively effective because even readers who might take issue with Pearce's points about failed policies will certainly respect the validity of his reasoning.

Deductive Arguments in Their Written Form

Syllogistic argument appears in almost everything we read each day: in newspaper editorials, in advertising, in public speeches, on bumper stickers, and even in poetry. But rarely is the syllogistic form obvious. The syllogism discussed earlier in this chapter is the "stripped down" form that professional logicians use; in written discourse, however, syllogisms can appear in many guises. With only a little practice, however, you can recognize them as *bona fide* logical syllogisms.

Occasionally syllogisms are complete; but often their three-statement form is disguised by some added explanatory material, or their conclusions are worded differently from the main premise, or their statements are arranged in an order that differs from the usual logical form. Most frequently, however, syllogisms are either shortened or expanded. Let's look first at a passage containing a complete, three-statement syllogism.

1. The Complete Syllogism

> Our society has moved illogically in this direction by virtually institutionalizing adultery; a growing number of spouses permit each other complete sexual liberty on the conditions that there shall be no "involvement" and that the extracurricular relations are not brought to their attention. It is beginning to institutionalize ritual spouse exchange.
>
> —*Alex Comfort, "Sexuality in a Zero-Growth Society"*

Here the form of the syllogism is hidden in a reordering of its essential elements: The terms of the major premise appear in the opening and closing sentences. Here's one way to put it into a tighter syllogistic form:

> A society that encourages ritual spouse exchange is a society that institutionalizes adultery.
> Our society is a society that encourages ritual spouse exchange.
> Our society is a society that institutionalizes adultery.

2. *The Shortened Syllogism and the Hidden Assumption*

On Washington's Birthday, a man interviewed by a roving reporter was asked if he thought George Washington was really truthful. His answer was, "Of course not, he was a politician, wasn't he?" This cynical reply was actually a shortened syllogism with the main premise missing—but easily supplied.

> Major premise: All politicians are untruthful. (unstated)
> Minor premise: George Washington was a politician. (stated)
> Conclusion: Therefore, George Washington was untruthful. (stated)

This is a common shortened syllogism, one in which the major premise is missing, but in spite of that omission it still carries logical force. In fact, one of the reasons that shortened versions occur so often in writing is that they frequently carry more persuasive power than complete, explicitly stated syllogisms do. This power stems mainly from their dependence upon hidden assumptions—the assertions missing along with the omitted statement. In this dependence lies both the strength and the danger of shortened syllogisms. These abbreviated forms can be persuasively effective because they flatter your audience: Your readers can demonstrate their knowledge and logical facility when you permit them to supply the missing part. But shortened syllogisms can also obscure premises or conclusions that are unsound or untrue. For instance, in our George Washington example, would you really be willing to accept as absolute truth the hidden assumption in the missing premise—that *all* politicians are untruthful? We hope not.

Hidden assumptions accompany all variants of the shortened syllogism. Let's look at some of these possibilities and their underlying hidden assumptions:

Shortened form	*Syllogism* (unstated premises italicized)	*Hidden assumptions*
Naturally, he's irritated; he's only human.	*All humans become irritated.* He is human. He becomes irritated.	Human beings share the same emotions.
"Folger's coffee is mountain-grown."	*Mountain-grown coffee is the best offer.* Folger's is mountain-grown coffee. *Folger's is the best coffee.*	All coffee grown in the mountains is superior to other coffee. (unproven claim)

| CAUTION: WOMAN DRIVER (bumper sticker) | *All women drivers demand caution. This driver is a woman driver.* This driver demands caution. | All women are dangerous drivers. (stereotyping) |

Although both the coffee and woman driver examples here are illogical because they are based on questionable or untrue assumptions, many hidden assumptions are not illogical. The first example represents sound reasoning because it is based on a plausible assumption and is logically related to the statements in the shortened syllogism.

3. The Expanded Syllogism

In a long, involved argument in which you need to make several statements that lead to the same conclusion, you can use an expanded syllogism. This not only eliminates repetitious "old" information but gives the argument greater persuasive force by making it more compact. Here's an example of a series of "minor premises" all sharing the same major premise and conclusion:

> The man who is not at peace with himself cannot be trusted to lead his fellowmen in the ways of peace. The unbalanced leader is certain to unbalance the society in which he functions. Even the leader who is intent on the side of the good but who is a fanatic will stimulate fanaticism in his followers, arouse dogmatism and bigotry, and induce oppression and cruelty. When he is on the side of evil, he will lead his followers into such excesses and wickedness as will shame all humanity, and which even the innocent will wish to forget as soon as possible.
>
> —Marten Ten Hoor, "Education for Privacy"

Here's the underlying syllogism:

Major premise:	A man not at peace with himself cannot be trusted to lead.
Minor premises:	The unbalanced man is not at peace with himself.
	The man on the side of evil is not at peace with himself.
	The fanatic is not at peace with himself.
Conclusion:	Therefore, these men cannot be trusted to lead.

Being aware of the many ways that syllogisms can appear in written discourse can aid you in adapting your own deductive arguments to various writing purposes. Often, in the prewriting stage, you'll find it helpful to construct an argument as a syllogism, then use it as a basis for a paragraph presentation. Or you can test the validity of paragraphs you have already written by putting them into syllogistic form.

ARGUMENT COMBINING INDUCTIVE AND DEDUCTIVE STRATEGIES

The strategies of inductive and deductive reasoning work well when you use either approach. But until recently, a satisfactory method for tracing the logical reasoning and relationships in arguments combining the two had not been devised. Stephen Toulmin, in his book *The Uses of Argument,* provided such a framework, and a number of modern rhetoricians have adapted it to help students write better persuasive papers. Like others before us, we have simplified Toulmin's terminology to make his method clear to undergraduate students with little background in formal logic.

Toulmin points out that most modern arguments are based on *evidence* of some sort—facts, findings of studies or experiments, historical knowledge, statistical data, and so on. This evidence is used to support the conclusion—what the writer wishes readers to conclude. But Toulmin also warns that merely presenting evidence does not always persuade readers. In order to use evidence to best advantage, the writer must provide a generalization or principle that links the evidence to the conclusion. We'll call such a generalization a *linking principle.*

For example, suppose you plan to write a paper arguing that the United States should limit its president to one term of six years. That, then, is your *conclusion.* In your prewriting stage, you have listed the following evidence:

1. Presidents X, Y, and Z spent most of their last two years campaigning for president.

2. To be reelected, President X tried to retain the support of special interests by vetoing important legislation.

3. Presidents Y and Z avoided controversial decisions to ensure the vote of the farmers and businessmen.

Note that we are describing essentially an inductive process that uses evidence acquired by research or observation to arrive at a conclusion. Now, we need to determine the linking principles behind these statements. Since the first involves *time* and the second *behavior* that could hinder leadership, these could be our linking principles. Here's how they could be stated and used to link the evidence to the conclusion.

EVIDENCE	LINKING PRINCIPLE	CONCLUSION
1. (time example)	Presidents waste time in campaigning rather than in providing strong leadership.	Presidential terms should be limited to a single, six-year term.
2. (behavior examples)	Presidents court political support for reelection rather than provide strong leadership.	Presidential terms should be limited to a single six-year term.

As you can see, we have increased the argumentative force, but we have now placed ourselves on a logical limb. We cannot expect all our readers to accept the linking principles we have provided; some may counterargue that it is part of the president's job to seek the support of the people or that campaigning time gives the president an opportunity to "take the issues to the people." Obviously we need to back up our linking principles to account for such counterclaims. Often, this backing involves refuting counterarguments or giving authoritative support for the linking principle itself. Backing statements have an underlying *because* relationship to the linking principles:

> Presidents fail to provide strong leadership in order to court political support for reelection *because* a strong stance on an unpopular issue can result in the loss of votes.

Another logical problem with linking principles arises when unforeseen, but possible, alternatives may change the situation. (You should be especially alert to such alternatives when writing a problem–solution paper.) If alternative possibilities exist, we can add a *reservation* to the linking principle; a reservation is often signaled by *unless*. Here's a possibility for our linking principle about time.

> *Unless* time restrictions on national elections are imposed, presidents will continue to waste valuable time seeking reelection.

Remembering that argumentative propositions are always controversial, we need next to consider what counterarguments might be made against our conclusion that a single six-year term is the answer. One counterargument might be that the nation would have no chance to reelect a particularly effective president or that a single term could create a "lame-duck" situation that undermines the president's ability to lead. Recognizing the validity of the counterclaims, we can qualify our conclusion:

> *Even at the risk of sacrificing potential leadership,* the United States should limit presidential terms to a single six-year term.

Obviously, this qualification would force the writer to discuss the counterarguments in the opening part of the paper.

Let's review our use of these new terms:

Conclusion:	The main point of the argument, usually stated as a proposition.
Evidence:	The data to support the main point.
Linking Principle:	The general truth, policy, rule, or belief linking the evidence to the conclusion.
Backing:	The reasons behind the linking principle.
Reservation:	An exception to the principle.
Qualification:	A restriction to the conclusion.

Now that you understand the terms and have seen them applied, we can review the basic components of combined inductive and deductive argument and the relationship involved.

The conclusion (the main point of the argument) is reached through the inductive process of generalizing on the basis of the examined evidence. This evidence then becomes the data used in the paper to support the conclusion. A causal relationship exists between the evidence and the conclusion (the conclusion is sound *because* of evidence 1, 2, 3). Since factual evidence alone does not necessarily carry persuasive force, it needs to be related to a widely accepted principle—the linking principle. Such principles must link the presented evidence with the conclusion; for example, the president's failure to lead in order to court political support links examples of avoiding controversial decisions to the conclusion about a single, six-year term.

Because many linking principles are not universally accepted, reservations are often necessary (*unless* X, then linking principle). Also, since conclusions (propositions) are controversial, they may need qualification.

If the argument is well constructed, the evidence and its linking principles together, like syllogistic argument, share a "therefore" relationship to the conclusion.

Besides giving you an understanding of the reasoning processes necessary for writing an effective argument that combines inductive and deductive reasoning, this model can help you "brainstorm" the material you need to consider in prewriting. It can also be used as a check on your reasoning procedures when you are revising. But remember that it is simply a tool, useful only some of the time as you look for ways to meet the writing commitment entailed by persuasive writing. Choose your strategy to suit your subject, purpose, and readers.

THE ROGERIAN STRATEGY

In his article on teacher standards (pages 278–81), Paul Woodring appeals to the teachers' professional pride and desire for respect before arguing that higher admission standards are needed. In so doing, he used a Rogerian approach: a persuasive tactic based on the principle set forth by the psychotherapist Carl Rogers that persuasion is more possible in a friendly climate than in an antagonistic one. By establishing such a climate, the writer reduces any possible tension or threat that readers with opposing views might feel. For example, in a paper arguing for the use of safety belts, the writer might establish rapport with the readers by first agreeing with those who find the devices uncomfortable. If such a harmonious atmosphere is established, readers will be less defensive, more willing to consider other ideas, more receptive to change.

How can you use the Rogerian strategy? Essentially, you should try to follow these four steps:

1. Present a fair and complete summary of the opposing argument to show that you understand and respect it.
2. Explain in what ways or under what conditions the argument has merit.
3. State your own position.
4. As much as possible, resolve the differences between your own and the opposing viewpoints, but show how the opposing argument would benefit if it included features of your position.

Let's examine first the reasons for using this strategy and then look at an example of its application.

By beginning with a fair and complete summary of the opposing argument, you show that you know the subject well, understand how others feel about it, and recognize certain good features of their position. Next you try to show how this argument might be acceptable under certain conditions. At this point, readers with these opposing views should regard you favorably because you have fairly stated their ideas. In addition, they do not feel threatened because they have not been attacked or belittled. Consequently, they are more receptive to your ideas than they would be otherwise.

In the same spirit of friendliness and respect for their views, you present your own. Next you show what your ideas have in common with theirs. Point out that even though you advocate different methods, their goals will be achieved. In this process, you should show how your argument is more advantageous, improving on the opposing one in certain ways.

The spirit that permeates the Rogerian approach is one of good will, cooperation, and respect. What underlies it is the realization that there may be an honest difference of opinion among intelligent, honorable people. Ridicule, sarcasm, belittlement have no place. Differing opinions are treated with respect.

The following example by William Raspberry illustrates how the Rogerian approach may be adapted to persuade a large national audience to accept the writers' views on a controversial issue. Because he is aware that his views may offend many young Blacks who regard their dialect as part of their ethnic identity, Raspberry spends much time trying to allay their hostility.

A Rogerian Argument

Poor English Is Barrier to Success
William Raspberry

WASHINGTON—In these days of rising costs and shrinking budgets, the one thing minority students have plenty of is free advice—not all of it from sources they would describe as friendly.

Shows sensitivity for youths' irritation over unsolicited advice

Still, on the outside chance that they may have time for one more piece of unsolicited counsel, I commend to them a front-page newspaper advertisement I came across the other day.

Cites a neutral source

"Shamed by your English?" the ad asks in bold letters, before going on to tout a course devised by a "world-famous educationalist."

Readers who take advantage of the self-instruction course are promised not only freedom from fear of "those embarrassing mistakes," but also the ability to "command the respect of those who matter . . . (and) to cut through every barrier to social, academic or business success."

What struck me about the ad was not its blatant appeal to the insecurity of those whose English is not as good as it might be, nor even the excess of its promise, but the fact that it appeared in the Manchester (England) Guardian.

Now I don't know whether the "educationalist's" correspondence course is worth the postage it takes to fetch it. And I certainly don't mean to imply that most minority students have reason to be "shamed" by their English. But the fact that the ad was addressed to the readers of a literate, upscale English newspaper ought to help drive home a point that often gets lost: Proper use of the language is routinely accepted as a mark of intelligence, the first basis on which we are judged by those whose judgments matter.

If it is true that poor English is a barrier to social, academic and business success for the readers of the Guardian, it is truer still for those Americans who grow up speaking the nonstandard dialects of the ghettos, the barrios or the rural outbacks.

I don't mean to underplay the importance of subject-content mastery. Obviously, skills and knowledge—competency—are vital to career success. But so is facility with the language. You may be quite a decent computer programmer, but few prospective employers will believe it if you speak poorly. You may have the skills necessary to become a first-rate manager, but if you can't write a decent memo—if your words are imprecise, your thoughts unorganized, your syntax muddled— you are likely to be thought incompetent. And it helps if commonplace historical and literary allusions don't leave you looking lost.

So while these ambitious youngsters are trying to figure out whether their future lies in computers or law, whether to head for the Northeast or the Southwest, or whether to

Shows sensitivity to possible reactions of students

Agrees with "content" position

Shows interest in students' desire for a good job

head for the job market or graduate school, my advice is that they also pay special attention to English.

The fact is, given the rapidity with which the job market is changing, young people will be hard-pressed to guess which fields will offer the greatest opportunities a decade or so down the road. But whatever field they choose, it's a safe bet that their skills will be in greater demand if they also are competent in reading, writing and speaking English.

It's such an obvious thing, when you think about it. We regularly make judgments as to the brightness, the competency and the intelligence of people we meet—not by giving them examinations in their specialties but by observing how they use the language. The lady over here may be an incompetent idiot, but if she speaks like Barbara Jordan, we'll give her instant credit for intelligence. The gentleman over there may be as smart as a whip, but if his diction evokes Mr. T, we will insist on some further evidence.

> Establishes a common ground: uses Black role models for comparison

That's true for all people. But it's doubly true for minorities who, too often, imagine that admonitions to improve their language are suggestions that they learn to "sound white."

> Deals sensitively with a common Black prejudice against "white" English

As the ad in the Guardian makes clear, the point isn't to sound white, but to command the respect that comes with sounding well-educated.

Raspberry's argument is made far more persuasive by his efforts to establish rapport with readers who may be opposed to his views. By using Rogerian strategies, he has established himself not as an older authority-figure preaching to young people, but as a person who treats them and their viewpoints with respect.

SUMMARY

In this chapter we have introduced you to some reasoning processes you can use to plan and write an effective persuasive paper. When you draw a conclusion for your readers about research data, you are reasoning inductively—generalizing from a sample. When you show how one event or condition will result from others, you are revealing the product of causal reasoning. When you use deductive, syllogistic argument, you are giving readers the results of your search for logical relationships between general principles and particular instances.

The same is true of papers using the Toulmin strategy. To illustrate, here is an outline of the classical argument in chapter 15, with labels to the right showing its relationship to Toulmin's system. We have used a classical argument, but Toulmin's system can also apply to a problem-solution paper or be modified for informal persuasion.

Classical	**Toulmin**
INTRODUCTION	
Orientation and rapport establishment } _____	Reservation: refuting counter arguments.
Thesis: Statement of proposition } —— CONCLUSION	
BODY	
Supporting arguments } ———————— LINKING PRINCIPLES	
Evidence or supporting material } ———— (Backing)	
Counterarguments } ———— EVIDENCE	

No matter how logically planned and constructed, your paper is not going to make an effective appeal unless you have established some common ground with your readers—a rapport achieved only by sincere respect for the readers' situation and views. Incorporating a Rogerian approach can help you find areas of agreement and mutual respect.

In this chapter, we have been concerned with generating, organizing, and reasoning about the material needed to write a persuasive paper. In the next chapters, we will suggest ways that you can handle the language, avoid logical fallacies, and write sentences and paragraphs that will effectively state your arguments.

ASSIGNMENTS

For Practice

1. In the following examples, determine whether the writers depend on inductive or deductive reasoning. Remember, induction comes to a generalization based on the evidence of individual instances; deduction arrives at a conclusion based on generalizations accepted as true.

   a. But just because war does go back to the first records of man, gloomy skeptics argue that there will always be war; that it is part of unchanging human nature.

   I reply that until 400 years ago, the time of Shakespeare, there had always been human sacrifice somewhere on earth. Until the early 19th century, there had always been dueling. Hamilton, one of America's founding fathers, died by a duellist's bullet. Until Lincoln's

Emancipation Proclamation in 1862, when my grandfather was alive, there had always been human slavery. Yet these barbaric curses have dimmed from the scene of mankind. To this extent, if human nature has not changed, it has come under control.

—Herman Wouk, "Must Wars Occur?"

b. Each year over four million Americans take "aptitude," "achievement" and "proficiency" tests. They include 1.8 million high school students who take the College Board exam required by most colleges for admission; 500,000 students seeking admission to graduate schools, law schools, and business schools; and people seeking certification or placement in more than 20 different occupations and professions—teachers, architects, auto mechanics, CIA agents, medical technicians and policemen. Their performance on these tests will determine, largely or in significant part, the schools they will attend and the professions they will enter.

—Ralph Nader, "Reports"

c. But if those skills were more than salable, if the study made them better citizens and made them happier to be human beings, they have not been cheated. They will find some kind of job soon enough. It might even turn out that those humanizing and liberating skills are salable. Flexibility, an ability to change and learn new things, is a valuable skill. People who have learned how to learn, can learn outside of school. That's where most of us have learned to do what we do, not in school. Learning to learn is one of the highest liberal skills.

—Robert A. Goodwin, "Should College Teach Salable Skills?"

Induction

1. Identify the inductive weaknesses (generalization from insufficient sample, weak analogy, unreliable information) in the following:

   a. Many students who dislike and fear courses in mathematics have learned to respect mathematical theory in logic courses. Therefore, students who are not proficient in languages might profit from a general linguistics course.

   b. Ralph Nader has quoted the president of the Educational Testing Service as saying that "charging the tests with bias against minority and poor students is like criticizing the bathroom scales because some people are fat and others don't get enough to eat."

   c. After interviewing the women on the third floor of the women's dorm, I concluded that most students drive home for the weekend.

   d. The Army Corps of Engineers and the law firm representing the investors in a proposed marina issued figures that "proved beyond doubt" that a new dam would be an economic asset to the state.

e. Every summer, the academically motivated new freshmen register early. Composition classes offered at prime times—9:00 a.m. to 12 noon—close out first. Therefore, these classes will have overall a higher grade average than classes offered at unpopular times.

f. Jobs for history graduates are almost impossible to find. My brother, who got a degree in history last year, hasn't found a job yet.

g. The president of a national fraternity reported that students who live in fraternity houses have a happier college experience than those who reside in dormitories.

2. Examine the causal relationships in the following passages. Identify the effect and the cause or causes. Does the writer consider all the causes, the direct cause, the only cause, or merely an indirect cause?

a. Ironically enough, this sinister and threatening phenomenon [over-population] has been caused by the beneficent and praiseworthy activities of medical science and public health in preserving life. It is the result of death control. Mortality has gone down, especially infant mortality, which not so long ago in many countries accounted for the deaths of a third or even a half of all babies born before they had reached the age of one. The expectation of life of a Roman citizen even at the height of the Empire was only 30 years; in tropical countries less than a century ago, it was often only 20. Today it is rising everywhere, and in some Western countries is over 70.

—*Sir Julian Huxley, "The Age of Overbreed"*

b. All the federal legislation in the world won't help this country if its citizens are not aware of their invaluable function to keep our communities safe. Many of you are aware of some strange trends which have developed in this country. There are people willing to overlook crimes which imperil us each and every day. Many shirk their responsibility for the crime rise by "scapegoating" the police and other law enforcement officers.

—*Congressmen Bill Chappell, "Some Call It Dissent"*

c. Clearly *Playboy's* astonishing popularity is not attributable solely to pinup girls. For sheer nudity its pictorial art cannot compete with such would-be competitors as *Dude* and *Escapade*. Rather, *Playboy* appeals to a highly mobile, increasingly affluent group of young readers, mostly between eighteen and thirty, who want much more from their drugstore reading than bosoms and thighs. They need a total image of what it means to be a man. And Mr. Hefner's *Playboy* has no hesitancy about telling them.

—*Harvey Cox, "Playboy's Doctrine of Male"*

d. Some say the reason bowling isn't covered by the print media is that the sport is a bore—just not exciting. Once you print the scores what else can you say? I don't buy that. After all, the number of people who bowl on a regular basis far exceeds the number who play tennis. I'm willing to wager that plenty of these keglers would find bowling exciting to read about, too. ABC has been televising the PBA winter tour for the past 21 years, and the program has been known to get higher ratings than the Masters golf tournament. Doesn't this say something about the enduring appeal of the game as a spectator sport?

—Joseph M. Arena, "My Turn: A Strike for Bowling"

Deduction

1. The following statements could serve as major premises in a syllogism. What kind or kinds of inductive reasoning—sampling, analogy, or causal generation—might have led to each generalization? Add a possible minor premise and conclusion to each to form a deductive syllogism.

    a. All public school teachers are people certified by state education departments.

    b. All cold-blooded animals are hibernating creatures.

    c. All West Point cadets are eligible for combat duty.

    d. Constitutional laws are those laws that ultimately can be approved by the Supreme Court.

    e. Disease can be eradicated by educating people about it.

    f. Undergraduate men's colleges tend to overemphasize sports.

2. Decide if the reasoning in the following syllogisms is valid and if the conclusion is based on true premises. If the reasoning is faulty, explain why.

    a. All human societies are doomed to deteriorate.
        America is a human society.
        America is doomed to deteriorate.

    b. All students are eligible for student government.
        No teachers are eligible for student government.
        No teachers are students.

    c. All barbiturates are drugs.
        Marijuana is not a barbiturate.
        Marijuana is not a drug.

    d. All rational people are believers in rule by law.
        Some rational people are college professors.
        Some college professors are believers in rule by law.

    e. All women are potential mothers.
        Betty is a potential mother.
        Betty is a woman.

    f. God is love.
        Love is blind.
        Homer was blind.
        Homer was God.

3. Decide if the reasoning is valid in the following deductive arguments. If you think it is faulty, restate the sentences to eliminate the fault(s). (First, identify the form of each.)

   a. Either we solve the problem of birth control or the whole world will starve.

   b. If nuclear waste is not controlled, then thousands of people will contract cancer.

   c. Recent studies have shown that more alcohol is consumed in "dry" communities than in "wet" ones. If the dry communities would permit the sale of alcohol, the rate of alcohol consumption would go down.

   d. When the battery is dead, the car won't start.

   e. Pesticides harmful to life must be banned or the ecology will be greatly damaged.

4. Using the Paul Woodring essay on pages 278–81, respond to the following:

   a. Referring to the discussion on pages 319–21, construct a Toulmin outline of the argument paper.

   b. Where in the article is there evidence of Rogerian strategy?

5. Analyze the reasoning in the following two letters written to the *Wall Street Journal* about the 1983 report by the National Commission on Excellence in Education. How could each benefit from using Rogerian strategy?

   a. Regarding your April 28 editorial "The Schools Flunk." Perhaps the sentence you quoted, "The educational foundations of our society are presently being eroded by a rising tide of mediocrity," says more about education than its authors intended. The National Commission on Excellence in Education needs to return to night school. Most teachers of composition there could point out the sentence's faults: (1) weak passive construction; (2) unnecessary use of *presently* for *now* (preferred usage is to restrict presently to the meaning of soon); (3) the cliche *rising tide;* but worse (4) rising tide *of mediocrity.* If something is mediocre, it is in the middle; as it rises, does it improve? The whole mixed metaphor is surrealistic: a picture of some kind of supports or piers being washed by an incoming tide somehow becoming nearer the middle of something (the root meaning of mediocre, middle of the mountain, confuses the image even more). But it does not take an etymological background to recognize a bad sentence. The schools flunk, yes, but so does the commission.

   —Patricia K. Hymson, National Defense University, Washington

   b. The report by the commission only confirms what is common knowledge. Yet the report completely fails to diagnose the root cause of the problem—compulsory public schools. Public schools are appropriate to Soviet Russia but they should never have gained a foothold in the Land of the Free.

   An inherent characteristic of any bureaucratic enterprise is that its primary purpose is to provide employment for bureaucrats and by this standard the public school system is a magnificent success though its performance is a disgrace. It provides an interesting paradox to realize that the American public thinks nothing of sacrificing the Detroit automobile industry because they favor imports but they will tolerate a deplorable educational system at a huge cost with barely a complaint.

6. Below are examples of shortened and expanded syllogisms. Complete the syllogisms and state the hidden assumption in each.

    a. Wars are not "acts of God." They are caused by men, by man-made institutions, by the way in which man has organized his society. What man has made, man can change.

                                             —Fred M. Vinson

    b. All those millionaires who pay no income tax can eat their hearts out; they won't get any rebate.

                                             —Newspaper filler

    c. Football coaches can't expect to hold the job forever. After all, they weren't elected by the people.

                                             —Newspaper filler

    d. Everything positive is accomplished in terms of negatives. You can become branch manager by not sticking your neck out. You can make it to the vice-presidency of the corporation by not contradicting and by not being too egghead grammatical. The man who knows says nothing controversial.

                         —Eve Merriam, "The Matriarchal Myth"

    e. But legislation which would funnel money to families who adopt [handicapped or retarded] children is not the right way of getting them into homes. People could start adopting children because of the money rather than because they really want a child. Children with special defects need special love and attention, and a subsidy from the federal government is not the way to get it.

                                   —Newspaper editorial

    f. "Milk-drinkers make better lovers."

                                             —Bumper sticker

    g. The company may discharge any employee whose conduct on the job is disruptive. Joe's conduct is certainly disruptive.

    h. Of course he was under surveillance. Anyone with a job in government who dates foreign women is suspect.

7. Choose one of the following syllogisms (or construct one of your own) and write a paragraph that incorporates the syllogism. Reword the syllogism so that it is not so obvious.

    a. The guarantee of a stable society is a desire of middle-class America.
        Enforcement of law and order is a guarantee of a stable society.
        Enforcement of law and order is a desire of middle-class America.

b. All people are members of the human family.
Blacks and whites are people.
Blacks and whites are members of the human family.

c. All forms of marriage are risky.
Contractual marriage is a form of marriage.
Contractual marriage is risky.

d. Protection of citizens is an obligation of all states.
Strict enforcement of drunk driving laws is a protection of citizens.
Strict enforcement of drunk driving laws is an obligation of all states.

e. All societies educate their children in compliance with societal values.
The people of the United States are a society.
The people of the United States educate their children in compliance with societal values.

f. If the United States and Russia fail to agree on arms control, nuclear war may be inevitable.
They have failed to agree.

18

Special Topics: Shaping Language and Logic to the Readers

LANGUAGE AND PERSUASION

You can achieve maximum persuasive force only after you have learned to express your logical reasoning in language that attracts your audience to the problem, convinces them that your viewpoint is valid, and appeals not only to their intellect but to their emotions and values. Especially for the task of persuasion, your writing commitment must add on an ethical commitment. Making use of persuasive tactics that appeal to people's baser instincts or that somehow deceive readers is dishonest. Unscrupulous politicians who deliberately play upon their constituents' racial or ethnic hostilities to sell themselves as candidates, and advertisers who exploit their readers' desires to be socially or sexually attractive, are using unethical persuasive tactics. Usually such appeals involve calculated and deliberate dishonesty.

But often there is a narrow distinction between honest and dishonest persuasion. You want to shape your ideas and language so that they best present your argument, but if you carry this too far, omitting or obscuring information, then dishonesty can be the result. You do want to appeal to the emotions of your audience—to foster sympathy, respect, or appreciation toward the subject of your argument—but too strong an emotional appeal may obscure the logical reasoning in the paper. The best way to make sure that your arguments are presented rationally and ethically is to be aware of the ways that persuasive language can be used and abused. In this chapter we will examine some of these ways.

Shaping Your Ideas to Your Audience

One tactic of persuasive writing is that of shaping your language and ideas in the way that your readers will find most attractive. Used wisely, language can help you to get your ideas across and perhaps persuade others to accept your views and proposals. Unfortunately, however, shaping can also be used unscrupulously, as shown in this exaggerated speech by a fictitious congressman. Which side is he really on? He slants his views so blatantly and dishonestly that his own stand on the issue is impossible to discern.

Congressman Oiley's Position on Whiskey

I had not intended to discuss this controversial subject at this particular time. However, I want you to know that I do not shun a controversy. On the contrary, I will take a stand on any issue at any time regardless of how fraught with controversy it may be.

You have asked me how I feel about whiskey.

Here is how I stand on this question:

If when you say whiskey you mean the devil's brew, the poison scourge, the bloody monster that defiles innocence, dethrones reason, destroys the home, creates misery and poverty—yes, literally takes the bread from the mouths of little children; if you mean the evil drink that topples the Christian man and woman from the pinnacles of righteous, gracious living into the bottomless pit of degradation and despair, shame and helplessness and hopelessness, then certainly I'm against it with all my power.

But if when you say whiskey you mean the oil of conversation, the philosophic wine, the ale that is consumed when good fellows get together, that puts a song in their hearts and laughter on their lips and the warm glow of contentment in their eyes; if you mean Christmas cheer; if you mean the stimulating drink that puts the spring in an old gentleman's step on a frosty morning; if you mean the drink that enables a man to magnify his joy and his happiness and to forget, if only for a little while, life's great tragedies, heartbreaks, and sorrows; if you mean that drink whose sale pours into our treasuries untold millions of dollars which are used to provide tender care for little crippled children, our blind, our deaf, our dumb, our pitiful aged and infirm, to build highways and hospitals, and schools, then certainly I am in favor of it.

This is my stand and I will not compromise.

Do you really know which side Oiley is on? No, because he has effectively kept his own position from you by exploiting to the fullest the connotative possibilities of words. Playing on their emotional effects, he employs words and phrases to support and heighten first one position, then the other.

In aligning himself with the temperance advocates, he woos their support by such words of condemnation as "devil's brew," "poison scourge," "misery and poverty," "evil," and "topples Christian man and woman from the pinnacles of righteous, gracious living." But to ensure the vote of his drinking constituents, he shifts to euphemism, or language of approval: "oil of conversation," "Christmas cheer," "when good fellows get together," "stimulating drink that puts spring in an old gentleman's step." Manipulating language to deceive is dishonest and irresponsible.

Argument, to be effective, must be shaped to your readers, but you should retain your own integrity in the process. Your aim, after all, is to convince your readers to accept your ideas, not deceive them about what you are saying. Responsible shaping involves (1) organizing your material—that is, selecting and arranging evidence and other support; (2) constructing your sentences so that their structure helps to emphasize your main points; and (3) choosing language that will set the mood and tone best suited to your audience and to the purpose of your argument.

In chapter 5, we talked of the importance of considering the connotations of words in writing vivid descriptions. In persuasive writing, you must be even more alert to the effect of words on your audience. In descriptive writing, you made word choices for aesthetic reasons—reasons that required no ethical decisions on your part. But in persuasion, there is often a fine line between using words responsibly to shape your ideas and irresponsibly twisting words to cater to the prejudices of the audience.

The following paragraphs from a newspaper demonstrate some of the degrees of shaping that are possible on a single controversial subject—in this case, the formerly proposed Equal Rights Amendment. The first is from an editorial:

> The equal-rights business just doesn't make sense when screened against tradition and mores and personal identity. But ERA agitators are hell bent for action, and as Alexander Pope said, "Oh woman, woman! When to ill thy mind is bent, all hell contains no fouler fiend."
>
> For the record, one does not quarrel with such ERA concepts as equal pay for equal ability. Nor does one take exception to the basic precept in the amendment's terse language: "Equality of rights under the law shall not be abridged in the United States or by any state on account of sex. . . ."
>
> What bothers us are the interpretations being placed on the proposition of equal rights and what this is doing and will do to our traditional way of life. Family, marriage, morality—these, for example, are threatened by libertinism already being practiced in the name of freedom.

Though colorful, these paragraphs are obviously biased in favor of the "woman's place is in the home" point of view. Words and phrases like "business doesn't make sense" and "ERA agitators are hell bent for action"; the derisive quotation from Alexander Pope; and the appeal to fears that the ERA threatens "our traditional way of life" are all unfairly and irresponsibly shaped. The highly emotive language begs for confrontation, not compromise. It seriously weakens the Rogerian attempt in the second paragraph to establish a common ground with opponents.

The second example, from a response to the editorial, still expresses a strong, biased opinion—this time on the other side of the issue. The language, however, is more neutral and responsible. The writers, a group of newspaper women, attack the editorial writer's contentions logically rather than relying on emotive language. The shaping is less offensive to readers, more dependent on content than on language. The language is generally neutral; no single word or phrase would be likely to elicit a strong emotional response that might interfere with the persuasive power of the logical arguments presented.

> [The editor] mentions "the best of all possible worlds" in reference to the traditional view of women. Some women prefer this, and we respect them for that, but some women today question whether they should have "easier jobs" because they are thought to be the weaker physically. We question the assumption that a physical job is harder than a nonphysical job.
>
> Most professional jobs are not easy jobs, neither are they physical jobs. They are jobs demanding integrity, ability to assimilate, innovation and imagination: a fine mind. We question the assumption that men's minds are of a higher quality than women's or vice versa. We concur that there will always be minds greater and lesser than all people's, but some will belong to men and others to women.

Here, the writers respond to the editor's concern about women's traditional role by expressing respect for a point of view that conflicts with their own—the preference of some women for that traditional role. Then they turn to another point that the editorial stressed—that women need to be excluded from certain kinds of "physical jobs" for their own protection. Generally, the writers' plea is rational: that men and women be hired according to individual ability instead of women's being disqualified because of their supposed inferiority. Thus these writers achieve responsible shaping by avoiding emotive language that derides or insults opponents, relying instead on rational, logical content and arguments.

As in this example, language use should be responsible and disciplined, showing sensitivity to the attitudes and feelings of the reader. Such language use enhances both the logical tactics of the arguments and the reasonable voice that writers should strive to project. You certainly may use emotive language, but it should appeal to the reasonable and humane instincts of your readers. It should not insult or taunt them, or appeal to their basest emotions. The latter tactics may occasionally have a dramatic impact. But their persuasive force is greatly limited, and with many readers they may backfire.

Ambiguous Language

In persuasive writing, clarity is of primary importance. In addition to defining any uncommon terms, you must also take care that each word has exactly the meaning you intend; words used in ways that permit more than one interpretation can weaken the force of your argument. Word ambiguity generally derives from using a term that has several dictionary meanings. If you also place it in a context that gives no clue to which meaning is intended, than your message is obscured, as in this sentence from a student argument paper:

> The want of independence is a common urge that often causes some people to act hastily and without proper thought.

Here the problem is with *want*, which can be a synonym for either *desire* or *lack*. Even if the content provided clues to the intended interpretation, the reader still might puzzle over it or be amused. In either case, your readers would lose some of the respect they may have for your position.

Unfortunately, not all word ambiguity is unintentional. Sometimes it is used purposely to confuse an issue—as Congressman Oiley does with his "stand." Deliberate use of ambiguous words is a common practice in unfair advertising; for example, consider a cereal advertised as "*the good part of any good breakfast.*" Since *good* could mean either "tasty" or "healthful," the ad implies a nutritional value that the cereal may not have. Tricks like unfair shaping should be avoided in responsible argument. Although they may have short-term effectiveness, they will in the long run harm the rational, fair-minded image you are trying to project.

Vague Language

Vagueness results from either the overuse of abstract language or the use of poorly defined words. These paragraphs from a paper intended to persuade students to seek a liberal education demonstrates both characteristics:

> The rags to riches ideology that Horatio Alger instituted in the 1900s has been perpetuated past reality. Climbing the "ladder of success" can no longer begin on the bottom if one hopes to reach the top. And a college degree is a means of starting in the middle. The increased technological advancements and growth of bureaucratic business have complicated our lives to the point that a specialized education is of paramount importance if one hopes to live with a certain degree of financial security and luxury.
>
> A student's primary concern is succeeding within America's economic system after graduation. Students, for the most part, are no longer interested in studying the humanities, but only what is able to qualify them for a good job. The purpose of education at the university level has been altered; the quest for knowledge is secondary and the quest for a degree is primary. In viewing a major university's faculty–student relationship one can see that education has been atomized and organized to the point that it has almost become a commodity.

Even though the paragraphs are potentially effective, the language is so vague that you might have had to read the material several times to get the message. Ask yourself whether an argument can be convincing if the reader is forced to reread and decipher meaning, in the meantime losing track of the point being made. Highly abstract terms such as *increased technological advancements, bureaucratic business, paramount importance,* and *financial security* combine with misused terms such as *humanities, atomized,* and *commodity,* producing a vague, weak statement and confusing the issue.

In this revision, we substitute more specific, concrete words wherever possible and provide some definition of specialized terms.

The Horatio Alger "rags to riches" concept has invaded the realm of college education. Unlike the Horatio Alger heroes, we can no longer start at the bottom rung on the ladder of success. Instead, we must start in the middle in order to reach the top. A college degree is a way of starting in the middle. But the demands of an <u>ever-expanding technology</u> and an <u>international</u> business system have forced many students to seek not a <u>liberal</u> education, but a <u>highly specialized</u> one. <u>Pre-med students, for instance, must specialize early in the natural sciences—chemistry, biology, anatomy—if they are to assimilate the number of scientific discoveries and techniques they will encounter in their graduate work.</u> Without a specialized education, there is little chance of <u>getting a professional job</u> and <u>making a decent living.</u> Therefore, to achieve financial security, students search out the <u>professional courses,</u> not the courses in <u>literature, music, philosophy,</u> and <u>language</u> that have traditionally been the core of the humanities. Thus, the purpose of education at the university level has been altered: The quest for knowledge is secondary to the quest for a certifying degree. Even faculty–student relationships reflect the change; instructors and students alike view education as a commodity—<u>a package of merchandise to be bought over the counter and resold in the marketplace.</u>

Notice that in the revision we have not altered the writer's meaning or strayed very far from the original wording. The "ladder of success" metaphor has been more specifically related to the topic; a specific example (pre-med students) has been provided; brief definitions have been added; specific courses have been mentioned to indicate what is meant by professional and humanities courses; the word *degree,* which could cover all college degrees, is now limited in meaning by the addition of "certifying"; and *commodity* has been explained by adding a descriptive phrase. Not only is the point made clearer, but the concreteness of the paragraph adds authority to the writer's voice. In persuasive writing, then, as in narrative and exposition, <u>concrete language generally better serves your purpose than words that are so abstract or so general that they mean nothing in particular.</u>

Defining Terms

As you may surmise from our discussion of ambiguous and vague language, defining your particular use of a term is crucial in all kinds of persuasive writing. Since argument deals with controversial subjects of one degree or another, the vocabulary of the subject matter may be open to many interpretations. For instance, *sexual harassment* has become a matter for debate both in the academic and business worlds. But there are all kinds of problems in defining it precisely. Should it include verbal as well as physical abuse? Should it apply to all relationships between the sexes—male–male, female–female, as well as to male–female? Does there have to be an element of power or threat of punishment involved? From this complexity, you should realize how crucial careful definition is to effective persuasion. If you fail to define your terms, you run the risk of persuading your audience to a position entirely different from what you meant to propose, and you will at least diminish—if not neutralize—your argument's persuasive force.

FOCUSING DEVICES AND THE AUDIENCE

You are probably familiar with the old story about the farmer who had much success in persuading his mules to perform their mulish duties. When asked his secret, he replied that there was no magic involved: Before telling the mules what to do, he hit them over the head with a stick to get their attention. Argumentative writing poses a similar challenge; but the "stick" is the collection of writing tactics you "hit them on the head" with. Your success in persuading your readers will be partly a result of your ability to capture their interest in your argument. But that interest must also be sustained. As stated previously, this requires supporting evidence—statistics, examples, authority, comparisons, facts—any material that can add to the persuasive force of your argument. Adding such information, however, can lead readers astray as the proposition may become lost in a mass of material. Mastering several devices for maintaining focus can help you to avoid such informational mazes, thus making your arguments more effective.

Using Paragraphs to Focus the Argument: Opening Paragraphs

Opening paragraphs in persuasive papers, like those in expository writing, should catch your readers' interest. But to be most effective, the paragraph should also contribute to the argumentative force of your paper. Sometimes this can be done by anticipating counterarguments and allaying your reader's possible hostility toward your subject. Or you might wish to start with a description or anecdote that appeals to the emotions. Examples can also be effective, as this opening paragraph from a student's problem-solution paper illustrates. Note especially how the examples add persuasive force to the depiction of the problem and also prepare readers for the solution presented in the final paragraph—the passage of the Alaskan Lands Act.

At one time in this country, many years ago, there lived an animal whose numbers were staggering; literally millions of them covered the Great Plains. Then came modern man with his rifle. Not only were they shot indiscriminately for food and sport, but often just the tongue and skins were taken from the dead animals. Skinned carcasses lay piled by the hundreds, left to rot in the sun. After twenty years of intensive hunting, this animal, the American bison, disappeared from the plains. Today, only a few private herds remain. Unfortunately, however, this is not the only example of ecological destruction resulting from human callousness. The bald eagle, the grizzly bear, the peregrine falcon, and the timber wolf are all perilously close to extinction in the continental United States.

But there is still a chance to preserve these species from man-induced pressures. At present before Congress is an act to set aside in Alaska an area of land the size of California for wildlife preserves and national parks. In order to preserve America's last true wilderness, the Alaskan Lands Act must be passed.

—*Carl Marshall*

As you can see, the student's lengthy description of the senseless slaughter of the bison appeals to his readers' sense of outrage both by offering specific details and by suggesting that the same kind of irresponsible killing has nearly wiped out the other animals mentioned. This appeal then helps to focus the problem and justify the need for legislation.

Using Paragraphs to Focus the Argument: Supporting Paragraphs:

In the body of the paper, you must concentrate on adding support, while at the same time, perhaps, dealing with counterarguments. Presenting so much material can make it difficult for your readers to keep their attention on your proposition or solution. This is particularly true when you attempt also to handle a demanding paragraph structure—showing causes and effects, making comparisons and contrasts, or drawing an analogy. All of these require careful attention to focusing devices. Here are some examples of each.

Cause-and-Effect Paragraphs   In chapter 10, we discussed some of the various ways that cause-and-effect paragraphs are used in expository writing. Cause-and-effect paragraphs used in persuasive writing are similar in form, but they can be shaped to enhance the paper's persuasive force, supporting the writer's points directly or refuting counterarguments. In the following example, from a paper contending that Americans must lower their material sights, the writer opens the paragraph with an *effect* of the shrinking of our resources—the discontent of middle-class Americans. He proceeds to explain *why* the situation will not improve.

Call it "middle-class discontent." It's demonstrably <u>higher</u> now than at any time in recent history. It will not lessen in our lifetime, not, at least, as a consequence of improved conditions. The cost of land will not diminish. The cost of money may diminish somewhat, but not to the levels that enabled millions of Americans to build their own homes in the years after the second world war. The value of the dollar will not increase. The cost of goods and services will not diminish, if only because the cost of fuel, a major production factor in every economic sector, will never return to previous levels. Populations will increase here and	Effect Causes

abroad, compounding problems of employment, education and maintenance.

—Leonard Gross, "Is Less More?"

The paragraph not only outlines the causes but is highly persuasive. The sentences containing the causes are couched as propositions: "The cost of land will not diminish." And the writer effectively uses parallelism—repeating the phrase "the cost of . . ." several times throughout—a device that not only adds persuasive power but focuses the readers' attention on his main argument.

Cause-and-effect paragraphs can move from effect(s) to cause(s) or from cause(s) to effect(s). In a long, complex argument, the effect may be introduced in a separate paragraph followed by a series of paragraphs, each dealing with a single cause. (For further discussion of cause-and-effect organization, see pages 160–63.)

Comparison-and-Contrast Paragraphs

Individual paragraphs in the body of a paper can follow the same comparison schemes that we discussed for expository papers in chapter 10 (see pages 163–64). The following paragraph compares two sides of America (A: the America of Lincoln and Stevenson; B: the America of Teddy Roosevelt). The author uses this scheme: Point 1: A, B; Point 2: A, B; and so on.

There are two Americas. One is the America of Lincoln and Adlai Stevenson; the other is the America of Teddy Roosevelt and the modern superpatriots. One is generous and humane, the other narrowly egotistical; one is self-critical, the other self-righteous; one is sensible, the other romantic; one is good-humored, the other solemn; one is inquiring, the other pontificating; one is moderate, the other filled with passionate intensity; one is judicious and the other arrogant in the use of great power.

—J. William Fulbright, The Arrogance of Power

Note that the focus of the comparison is maintained by the author's careful sentence structure: "one" statements refer to Lincoln's America; "other" to Roosevelt's. In the last sentence, the phrase "arrogant in the use of great power" pulls the reader back to the main argument of the book as revealed in the title.

Using Sentences to Focus the Argument

In chapter 4, we pointed out that the subject of a sentence contains the topic, often old or anticipated information, while the predicate's comment adds new material. With conscious effort, you can exploit these sentence functions to their fullest in persuasive writing. By reordering sentence elements, you can emphasize main points and create parallel structures—a highly effective device in persuasion, as illustrated by Martin Luther King's repetition of "I have a dream," or John F. Kennedy's "Ask not. . . ."

In persuasive writing, all sentence types are useful—simple sentences for stark emphasis; compound for listing causes, relationships, and proofs such as statistics; complex for indicating logical relationships, particularly those in which the clauses are joined by *if . . . then* and *either . . . or.* As certain sentence types may work better than others for a particular purpose, so too may certain signals of logical transitions and relationships.

Using Logical Transitions and Relationships

Experimenting with the placement of subordinators (see pages 76-77) to signal logical relationships can help you clarify and strengthen those relationships. Subordinators such as *if, because, since* and *unless* are frequently used in persuasive writing. As we have previously pointed out, moving them to the front of the sentence requires moving the whole subordinate clause:

Body gestures send significant messages to viewers *because* every adult act communicates.

Because every adult act communicates, body gestures send significant messages.

Placing the *because* first allows the *effect* (stated in the main clause) to have maximum emphasis at the end. When you wish to stress the cause, then reverse the order.

The placement of freely-movable conjunctive adverbs such as *however, therefore, consequently,* and *thus,* which are common to persuasive writing because they signal logical relationships, can also affect the force and clarity of your arguments. When you wish to establish the logical relationship between two sentences, the adverb usually works best in initial position because the relationship is made clear immediately:

Having nothing to say, the New Barbarians cannot interest others by *what* they say. *Therefore* they must try to shock by *how* they say it.

—*Daniel J. Boorstin, "The New Barbarians"*

In our next example, however, the first clause—"What has happened to privacy"—sums up a long discussion on changing attitudes toward privacy that has come before; consequently the writer's placement of *therefore* after this summing-up clause, at the beginning of the predicate, makes the new information in the predicate serve as a syllogistic conclusion to all the preceding statements:

What has happened to privacy, therefore, may be said to be less an invasion, than a corruption.

—*August Hecksher*

Reordering Sentence Elements

In the student paragraph on nearly extinct animals (page 339), the final sentence had originally looked like this:

The Alaskan Lands Act must be passed in order to preserve America's last true wilderness.

In the final revision, the clauses were reordered:

In order to preserve America's last true wilderness, the Alaskan Lands Act must be passed.

By reversing the order of the two clauses, the student achieved better transition from the ideas expressed in the rest of the paragraph (old information). But more important, he placed the proposition last in the sentence, taking advantage of the inherent climactic emphasis of this position, and giving his argument a clear, sharp focus.

A similar reordering opportunity occurs in the *if . . . then* sentence so commonly used in argumentation. Students often write this type of sentence as follows, thereby losing much of its possible force:

Many endangered species will become extinct if strict enforcement of the laws is not practiced.

See the difference in persuasive force when the sentence elements are reordered so that the proposition comes last.

If strict enforcement of the laws is not practiced, many endangered species will become extinct.

Using Passive Sentences

In an earlier discussion of the passive (pages 213–15), we pointed out that active sentences are usually more effective in narrative writing. In persuasive writing, if the passive construction is used carefully, it can help to focus on the topic. It can also be useful in other ways, as in the following sentence:

The journeywoman [in a union] *is given* less training [than a journeyman], her promotional ladder is shorter or nonexistent, and she *is paid* less.

—Marijean Suelzle

Note that this passive—especially with the omission of the "by" phrase that accompanies the passive—creates a subtle diplomacy: The writer can imply blame without placing it on a definite agent, thus avoiding a defensive reaction from the men in her audience—an excellent Rogerian device.

The following sentence demonstrates another advantage of the passage: the omission of the agent when it is unimportant to the point. This results in added emphasis on the reordered subject (the object of the underlying sentence).

But the mother's milk of party politics *can be defined* in a single word: patronage.

—James J. Kilpatrick, "Patronage Makes the System Work"

Used wisely and sparingly, passive sentences can be a valuable tactic for focusing, particularly when the agent is unimportant or unnecessary.

Using Cumulative Sentences

In your study of personal writing, you saw how cumulative sentences can be loaded with colorful details. But the structure of the cumulative sentence can also be advantageous in persuasion: The main clause at the beginning can carry an uninterrupted, emphatic statement of a point, which is then strengthened by the additional proofs or alternatives that follow in the sentence.

> Ask yourself what might happen to the world of tomorrow if there is complete automation, if robots become practical, if the disease of old age is cured, if hydrogen fusion is made a workable source of energy.
>
> —*Isaac Asimov*

The cumulative structure can also enable a writer to add descriptive details that qualify the stated point without breaking up the close grammatical relationships of the main clause:

> The treatments are worse than the sickness: insulin shock, electroshock, and even psychosurgery, during which the frontal lobes of the brains of unmanageable patients were quickly disconnected.
>
> —*Wesley C. Westman*

Using Periodic Sentences

Although the cumulative sentence can be an effective persuasive tool, its use in argument is limited. Of greater advantage for some persuasive purposes is the periodic sentence. Unlike the cumulative sentence, which presents the main statement first, the periodic sentence either places the modifiers at the beginning and the main clause at the end, or places the subject first, then the modifiers, and finally the rest of the main clause. This structure's value in argument is that its climactic effect can enhance persuasive force: It has the same advantages as specific-to-general organization. Note in the following examples how the message in the italicized material gains importance through the piling up of convincing details beforehand.

> As long as students whisper among themselves, look at their watches, read newspapers, and write letters in class, *little learning can take place*. (Main clause at end)

> *But the widely publicized estimates* that one in seven, one in four, or one in two of the seven million college students in America can be considered a "drug abuser" *are vastly exaggerated*. (subject at beginning; predicate at end)
>
> —*Kenneth Keniston*

The potential weakness of the kind of periodic sentence in the second example is that the interruption between the subject and predicate can make it difficult to read and comprehend. So use it only when you want the climactic emphasis it offers.

Using Balanced Sentences

As we pointed out in chapter 11, a balanced sentence often takes the form of two main clauses that are equal or similar in content, length, and grammatical structure, as in one earlier paragraph example:

We have the power to kill; we have the power to preserve.

Sometimes some sentence components may be omitted:

To err is human; to forgive, divine. (verb *is* omitted)

—*Alexander Pope*

Or the balance may be between a subject and a complement in the predicate:

The difference between tragedy and comedy is the difference between experience and intuition.

—*Christopher Fry*

The balanced sentence can be used to emphasize a point, as in the Fry example, or it can permit the counterbalancing of two opposite points, as in the following example:

Peace is conservation of life; war is waste.

A special value of the balanced sentence in persuasive writing is that its symmetry of form can lend an air of order and logic to the argument contained within. For this reason, perhaps, many writers use a balanced sentence to close an argument paper or to dramatize a central point.

FALLACIOUS REASONING AND THE AUDIENCE

In a world where you are constantly bombarded with advertising slogans and political speeches, you may well challenge our contention that valid logical reasoning, along with responsible shaping of your material, is the best way to persuade readers. After all, the public is persuaded to buy everything from disposable diapers to waterproof coffins every day—persuaded by argumentative devices that are fallacious. But such fallacies, despite their persuasive force, should be avoided in reasoned argument. They are the tools of the advertising con artist, the political demagogue, and the unscrupulous evangelist. Anyone persuaded by these tactics will sooner or later feel cheated and belittled—hardly the relationship you want to establish in persuading someone to your point of view.

Fallacious reasoning stems from a number of sources. Several that result from faulty inductive processes were discussed in the previous chapter: insufficient or inaccurate sampling, misuse of authority, faulty analogies, and *post hoc* reasoning. In our discussion of deductive reasoning, we pointed out that faulty reasoning stems from including too many terms in a syllogism, from ascribing the characteristics of a few individual items to a whole group, or from faulty logical relationships in conditional statements.

Fallacious reasoning can also result from the misuse of language and from dishonest appeals to people's emotions and prejudices. Although, as advertisements frequently illustrate, such fallacies may often be effective, they are generally avoided by writers who wish to be reasonable and fair. The following list can help you recognize these fallacies in your own and other people's writing.

Ad Hominem

Literally meaning "to the man," *ad hominem* attacks the person (personality, bad habits, behavior, appearance) in place of refuting the person's stand on an issue. Such an attack may be justified in instances where people's personal habits or personality might interfere with their performance in a responsible position. In writing a persuasive paper in which you take a stand against the qualifications of a presidential candidate, for instance, you would be justified in pointing out serious flaws in the candidate's decision-making abilities. But generally, an *ad hominem* appeal should be avoided in reasoned argument, even in politics. For instance, in a debate over how money should be apportioned for military spending, no useful purpose is served when a politician evades the issues and instead accuses the opponent of alcoholism.

Ad Populum

Ad populum ("to the people") is a direct emotional appeal to the crowd—one that plays on their prejudices, fears, or needs rather than addressing the merits of an issue.

Ad populum can be used responsibly in some circumstances: for instance, in a paper urging people to give up smoking tobacco you might make a rational appeal to people's fear of cancer. But to avoid alienating those immune to such tactics, you would need to supply evidence and statistics to justify the appeal and show the merits of your argument.

You need to realize, however, that *ad populum* is often used irresponsibly, deliberately appealing to people's emotions for the purpose of selling a product or persuading people to adopt unfair policies. Examples of this are advertisers who play on people's fear of cancer to sell a questionable cure, or the politician who campaigns on issues that exploit racial prejudice.

One kind of *ad populum* is *bandwagon,* the appeal to be like everyone else. Such appeals can be very effective, as many children realize when they persuade parents to buy them the latest craze in sports shoes because "all the other kids are wearing them." Similarly, many advertising slogans appeal irresponsibly to people's need to belong by urging readers to buy a product that will automatically make them like the rest of the population: the soft drink that allows people to join the "Now Generation," or the car that is "The Heartbeat of America." A slogan might instead appeal to the snobbishness or pride of a particular group: "The Car for People Whose Means Have Changed But Whose Values Haven't," "You've Come a Long Way, Baby," "For People with Discriminating Taste."

Begging the Question

You commit this fallacy when you arrive at a conclusion based on questionable or untrue premises that you present as absolute truth. Certain situations or subject matter can inadvertently trap you into using this flawed argument. When writing on religious and moral topics, for instance, you must deal with opinion and belief, not with demonstrated factual evidence. Since your readers will certainly not all share a single interpretation, presenting any one interpretation as a truth shared by all puts you in logical danger. For instance, abortion is a many-faceted moral problem, not a clear-cut factual one. Consequently an argument concluding that "Abortion is wrong, because it's murder" is begging the question because it is based on a premise not universally accepted as true in our society. If everybody agreed that it was true, then we would have no court cases trying to decide the issue.

The abortion example illustrates one of the most common forms of begging the question—the circular argument. The conclusion merely repeats the questionable major premise. Here's how it might look in syllogistic form:

Abortion, a form of murder, *is wrong.*

All forms of murder are wrong.

Therefore, *abortion is wrong.*

You can also beg the question and argue in a circle using an *if/then* form. In this statement from a letter to a newspaper editor, the writer both assumes that everyone accepts the truth of his reasoning and restates the major premise in the conclusion: "If God is left out of the schools completely, then the schools will be without God."

Glittering Generality

A glittering generality is a stock phrase that appeals to the pride we all feel in our country, our family, and our customs. Phrases such as "life, liberty, and the pursuit of happiness," "our constitutional rights," or "the great American family" stimulate certain predictable emotional responses from your audience. But such phrases often are not clearly defined, endangering the effectiveness of rational argument. Often they are *sweeping generalities*—generalizations arrived at from too small or nonrepresentative samples (see also pages 306–07). Phrases such as "the joys of motherhood" and the "American dream" assume that there is only one definition and that all readers know what is meant. In persuasion, this or any other device that is an oversimplification or solely an emotional appeal will not convince an intelligent audience.

Name-Calling

When Valerie Solanas wrote her *S.C.U.M. Manifesto,* her name-calling tactics helped to polarize the women's liberation movement.

> He [the male] is a half dead, unresponsive lump, incapable of giving or receiving pleasure or happiness; consequently he is at best an utter bore, an inoffensive blob, since only those capable of absorption in others can be charming.

Although colorful, this kind of verbal attack really persuades no one: It repels rather than attracts. Engaging in this kind of name-calling, however, may be less reprehensible than resorting to names intended to trigger an automatic negative response: *commie, gay, Nazi, fascist,* and racial and ethnic slurs—*nigger, kike, Cannuck,* and the like.

Non Sequitur

Non sequitur (Latin for "it does not follow"; pronounced "non se'kwitur") is evident in a statement like this: "X will make an excellent president because he's a good family man." Underlying this is the syllogism:

All good family men make excellent presidents.
X is a good family man.
Therefore, X will make an excellent president.

The problem lies in whether being a good president logically follows from the premise about family men. Knowledgeable readers may argue that the very qualities that make a good president—strong leadership, decisiveness of action, single-mindedness of purpose—might be disastrous to family relationships.

Stereotyping

This fallacy is a result of hasty generalization—coming to a general conclusion from insufficient sampling. It also assumes that all individuals of a group share the characteristics of the whole group. Many of our ethnic, political, and sexual stereotypes stem from this form of fallacious reasoning. For example, many Puerto Ricans are economically disadvantaged; however, this does not mean that *all* Puerto Ricans are poor.

SUMMARY

The purpose of our discussion on language and logic is not intended to make you a master of all the intricate devices of formal argument. Actually, we've touched on only a few. Instead, we have looked at some pitfalls to avoid: dishonest language shaping and irresponsible use of emotional argument—tactics that bypass or interfere with logical argument.

The strategies in this chapter for using sentences and paragraphs to provide support or focus can be added to your ever-expanding stock of writing skills. Because audience appeal is central to persuasive writing, you should attempt to gear all aspects of your papers to the particular needs of your readers, treating them as intelligent, discerning people. Being aware of responsible uses of language and logic and of the methods for focusing your material to help your readers clearly understand significant points can result in effective, persuasive arguments.

ASSIGNMENTS

For Discussion

1. In these examples, identify the words or phrases that signal the writer's opinions or bias about the subject.

   a. Grades are the play money in a university Monopoly game. As long as the tokens are offered, the temptation will be largely irresistible to play for them. Students are so busy taking notes, doing tests, and getting tokens that they have forgotten to ask: Of what worth is all this? Or perhaps they ask and the grade is their answer.

      One certainly learns something in the passive lecture-note-read-note-test process: how to do it all more efficiently next time (in the hope of eventually owning Boardwalk and Park Place). As Marshall McLuhan has said, we learn what we do. In this process most students come to view learning as studying and remembering what other people have learned. They assume that knowledge is logically and for practical reasons divided up into discrete pieces called "disciplines," and that the highest knowledge is achieved by specializing in a discipline. By getting good grades in a lot of disciplines they conclude they have learned a lot. They have indeed, and it is too bad.

      Such harsh judgment seems unjustified to many professors. From their viewpoint a great deal of thinking goes on; they generate most of it themselves and then hear their own echo, often disguised, on tests and papers.

      —Roy E. Terry, in "Dialog," Change

   b. Television must therefore always see its audience not only as an audience but as a market; what it presents is not only entertainment but advertising. Nothing can be done on television without consideration of both sets of conditions. Studies have shown that a program that requires too much thought, elicits too much excitement, or stirs up too much controversy is likely to make the viewer neglect the sponsor's message; the element of mediocrity thus has a certain importance in programming.

      —Russell Nye, "Television"

c. The murders within five years of John F. Kennedy, Martin Luther King, Jr., and Robert F. Kennedy raise—or ought to raise—somber questions about the character of contemporary America. One such murder might be explained away as an isolated horror, unrelated to the inner life of our society. But the successive shootings, in a short time, of three men who greatly embodied the idealism of American life suggest not so much a fortuitous set of aberrations as an emerging pattern of response and action—a spreading and ominous belief in the efficacy of violence and the politics of the deed.

—Arthur M. Schlesinger, Jr., Violence: America in the Sixties

d. A university, as a center of learning rather than as a manipulator of land, is a place of realism and ferment. Inevitably, performance of the academic mission has an effect on students who claim that knowledge has a moral force which dictates action. Naive as this claim is, it has led to a lot of earnest effort—if poorly planned and often bungled—toward changing the anteroom.

—William Ellet, "The Overeducation of America"

2. Identify the main weaknesses of the following sentences: vagueness or ambiguous language. Try to reword each so that the meaning you think the writer intended is more clearly expressed.

a. Many attempts have been made to force athletic teams to drop nicknames and mascots symbolizing the Indians.

b. The people are the church, but in their fear of involvement they have ironically used the church as a hideaway.

c. One reason for people's loss of faith is their inability to relate to the intangible.

d. Nurse Ratched is McMurphy's persecutor. She turns him into a vegetable but his essence still lingers on.

e. Almost all prejudicial views yield a lack of knowledge of the facts about prejudice.

f. Talking about sex in dealing with children, people and parents should be more open-minded.

g. I think that the highest appreciation should be given to parents, because what they have done for their children was done because they wanted to and not because they had to.

h. While there is accent on skills and methods, as there would be for any disciplined studies, the aims are to come to an understanding of language as fundamental to what it means to be human, and to the ability to synthesize and utilize that understanding in a variety of human concerns.

i. More schools have failed dropouts than dropouts have failed schools.

j. When these gun control laws failed to control crime, these groups, instead of looking toward the real cause of the problem, simply asked that more of the same type laws be passed as if the number of laws would aid in fighting crime.

3. What kind of audience is addressed in each of the following introductory paragraphs? Does the writer consider the audience neutral, supportive, or antagonistic? How does each writer appeal to the audience? Is any supporting information included?

a.   "What are your moral justifications for hunting?"

The man who asked me this is my neighbor, a well-educated and thoughtful newcomer to our little valley in northeast Vermont. He and his partner have just built a small house across the way. We want to be friends; there are going to be difficulties.

My first reaction is to trot out all the standard, unconvincing arguments about game management, about hunting as a last vestige of our primitive selves. It's easy, after so many years of assault, to feel defensive about this subject. Instead, I have a Socratic inspiration.

"What are your justifications for *not* hunting?" I ask.

So I get to listen to *his* standard, unconvincing arguments: the sacredness of life; the obligation not to interfere with its mechanisms; the storm of death; the suffering; the continuing evolution of man.

The hypocrisy of all this is staggering.

—*John C. Dunlap, "My Turn: In Defense of Hunting"*

b.   People of Yale University! What's happening around you? I'm becoming convinced that the rampant, out-of-touch intellectualism in which you immerse your daily lives is leading you down the path of inert oblivion. In the two and a half years I've been here, I have never seen so many people out of touch with themselves, their bodies, and maybe even life itself.

What good is your jammed-up intellectualism to you when you can't relate together the things that are happening around you, the things that are shaping your lives? I have never seen a place with so many talented people where inaction is actually valued, where people think that they can control their lives by thinking out something devoid of action. To think that this docile, jammed-up institution is to produce "1000 male leaders per year"! If so, then someone should seriously consider what it is that we will be leading.

—*Robert Wesley, "All About Production"*

4. The following are cause-and-effect paragraphs. Identify whether they move from cause to effect or from effect to cause. How is each focused toward the argument inherent in the paragraph?

a.   In the last month three national commissions have bluntly recognized the No. 1 problem: not one state system pays one public-school teacher even one penny extra for doing a good job. Why should we expect teachers to recognize and reward student excellence when we don't recognize or reward teacher excellence? Bipartisan support will pass the master-teacher program here and make Tennessee the first state anywhere to pay some teachers more than others because they do a better job. Guarantees of lifetime tenure and the refusal to accept evaluation ensure mediocrity in the schools. Teacher groups should realize that this issue has become a kind of competency test for their organizations in the minds of the taxpayers, and they are dangerously close to flunking it.

—Gov. Lamar Alexander, Tenn.

b. The pursuit of excellence in scholarship is inherently a lonely business and traditionally college life compensated by providing intimacy-producing relaxation, clubs, and other activities. As universities and colleges have grown at an explosive rate, creating an uprooted environment in the process . . . as they have become more depersonalized with television lectures, machine grading, and compulsory ID cards . . . as they have drawn more and more students from distant places . . . and as clubs have become less a part of the college scene, much of the old intimacy of college life has disappeared.

—Vance Packard, "Collegiate Breeding Ground for Transients"

c. In place of the traditional family has come the activist family in which each member spends the majority of his time outside the home "participating." Clubs, committees, and leagues devour the time of the individual so that family activity is extremely limited. Competition among clubs is keenly predicated upon the proposition that each member should bring his family into its sphere. Thus Boy Scouts is made a family affair. PTA, the YMCA, the country club, every activity, competes for total family participation although it demands entry of only one member of the family.

—Vine Deloria, Jr., "Indians and Modern Society"

5. In the following comparison-and-contrast paragraphs, identify the type of comparison scheme used.

a. The device used to limit competition is that of assigning different roles to the different groups within the American society. White males have assigned to themselves such roles as President of the United States, corporate executives, industrialists, doctors, lawyers, and professors at our universities. They have assigned to white women roles such as housewife, secretary, PTA chairman, and schoolteacher. Black women can now be schoolteachers, too, but they are most prominently assigned to domestic roles—maid, cook, waitress, and baby-sitter. Black men are thought to be good porters, bus drivers, and sanitation men.

—Shirley Chisholm, "The Politics of Coalition"

b.   Those who are for busing at all costs simply don't give a hang about the hostility, hatred, disaffection, and indifference generated among people who are expected to implement the educational and racial gains that are wanted: they are, typically, inclined to say that "at least we have an improved balance in the classroom." Consequently, they are miracle workers, do-gooders of the worst sort, who dream of transforming the country in accord with their entirely admirable vision, by means of cumulative but purely formal and administrative arrangements. Just bus them and the education of blacks as well as race relations will be improved—or, at any rate, a measurable gain will be added to previous, comparable gains, and the objectives will be brought a step nearer. Nonsense! On the other hand, those who are against busing at all costs simply don't give a hang for whatever deterioration appears within their own communities as a result of their imposed isolation, rigidity, and resistance to any but selected local concerns. Just throw the carpetbaggers out, keep the old traditions, let the neighborhoods manage their separate affairs, and education and relations between the races throughout the country will flourish in their most natural way. Again, nonsense!

—Joseph and Clorinda Margolis, "Busing"

6.   Discuss the effectiveness of the following conclusions. What kind of appeal is made? Is any syllogistic reasoning involved?

a.   From an argument for learning the history of black people in the United States:

We weep for the true victim, the black American. His wounds are deep. But along with their scars, black people have a secret. Their genius is that they have survived. In their adaptations they have developed a vigorous style of life. It has touched religion, music, and the broad canvas of creativity. The psyche of black men has been distorted, but out of that deformity has risen a majesty. It began in the chants of the first work song. It continues in the timelessness of the blues. For white America to understand the life of the black man, it must recognize that so much time has passed and so little has changed.

—William Grier and Rice M. Cobbs, The Shadow of the Past

b.   From an argument against the pursuit of status:

Finally, I think we must learn to transcend the pettiness of scrambling for the symbols of status. We should recognize the true strength that lies in being individuals who think for themselves and are independent in mind and spirit. We would all lead more contented and satisfying lives if we judged people not by the symbols they display, but by their individual worth.

—Vance Packard, "The Pursuit of Status"

c. From an argument that the space age can bring about a twentieth century spiritual and social renaissance:

The choice is ours, it must be made soon, and it is irrevocable. If our wisdom fails to match our science, we will have no second chance. For there will be none to carry our dreams across another dark age, when the dust of all our cities incarnadines the sunsets of the world.

—*Arthur C. Clarke, "Space Flight and the Spirit of Man"*

7. Identify the kinds of sentences below (cumulative, periodic, or balanced) and discuss their effectiveness in achieving the writer's purpose.

a. He calculated that if only one star in a thousand of these had planets at a suitable distance, and if an atmosphere developed on only one in a thousand of these, and if the right chemicals were present in the oceans and atmospheres of only one in a thousand of these, we would still be left with a hundred million planets suitable for life.

—*John P. Wiley, Jr., "Don't Bet Everything on the Big Bang"*

b. The earth rotates on its axis at one thousand miles an hour; if it turned at one hundred miles an hour, our days and nights would be ten times as long as now, and the hot sun would then burn up our vegetation each long day while in the long night any surviving sprout would freeze.

—*A. Creasy Morrison, "Seven Reasons Why a Scientist Believes in God"*

c. If one person alone refuses to go along with him, if one person alone asserts his individual and inner right to believe in and be loyal to what his fellow men seem to have given up, then at least he will still retain what is perhaps the most important part of humanity.

—*Joseph Wood Krutch, "The New Immorality"*

d. We no longer think of our life span as a steady, desperate accretion of money, but more as an arc, after a certain point tapering down into easy retirement.

—*Thomas Griffin*

e. There, for approximately a week, this teeming, milling mass of sun and sex worshippers swims, sleeps, flirts, guzzles beer, sprawls and brawls in the sands.

—*Alvin Toffler*

f. You are not in charge of the universe; you are in charge of yourself.

—*Arnold Bennett*

g. American parents, to the extent that they are Americans, expect their children to live in a different world, to clothe their moral ideas in different trappings, to court in automobiles although their forebears courted, with an equal sense of excitement and moral trepidation, on horsehair sofas.

—*Margaret Mead*

h.   To have a quiet mind is to possess one's mind wholly; to have a calm spirit is to command one's self.

—H. Mabie

8.   Identify the fallacious reasoning in the following examples.

a.   I was with the FBI for twenty years. My son can't be a bigot.

b.   The Imperial Wizard maintained in a newspaper interview that the Ku Klux Klan was the best organization in America—the only one organized for the purpose of maintaining Americanism.

c.   For too long the public schools have been run by the "elitists" or "experts" and the quality of education of our children has deteriorated to almost the point of "no return."

—Letter to the editor

d.   There is a certain kind of person who knows how to live. He knows how to get just a little extra out of every precious minute.

—Boat ad

e.   In this friendly, freedom-loving land of ours, beer belongs—enjoy it.

—Beer ad

f.   Middle America is concerned about law and order.

g.   Making [basketball] points wasn't always easy for a girl. But now you can do anything. Make the team or color your hair.

—Hair dye ad

h.   Bob True, in my opinion, is the best qualified candidate. I have known him since 1963, and in my opinion, he is an honorable, Christian man, an upstanding family man.

—Letter to the editor

i.   Men are all alike: selfish creatures who every weekend plant themselves in splendid isolation in front of a TV set. They substitute vicarious touchdowns, birdies, chip shots, and home runs for family participation and fun.

j.   The pinkos and weirdos at the state university naturally are against my legislative programs.

19

Rewriting Strategies for Persuasive Writing

In previous forms of writing, you did not need to worry about readers who might be unfriendly to your views. In persuasive writing, however, these readers and those who have not yet formed strong opinions or attitudes about your subject constitute your main audience. Naturally, you will also be concerned about those readers who agree with all or most of your arguments and points because you would like to reinforce their beliefs, but persuading the uncommitted or those opposing your views is your primary objective.

Consequently, in the first step of the rewriting process—revising—you should spend most of your time rereading your paper through the eyes of this audience. Then edit and proofread your paper, much as you have done previously. Because persuasive writing makes new demands on your revising skills, we have supplied a new checklist for that purpose. The previous editing and proofreading lists have been included here for your convenience.

FIRST STEP: REVISING

Revising Checklist: Attention to Readers

1. What is the nature of my audience? Their biases? Their interests? Their needs? Their educational level?

2. How have I tried to relate to readers who have opposing views?

3. How can I improve the tone of the paper so that it projects me as a concerned, informed, sensitive person?

4. What evidence have I supplied to support my claim? Is the evidence sufficient for the needs of my readers? What might I add or delete?

5. Are there additional counterarguments that need refuting? Where might I place the counterarguments to greater advantage?

6. How could I make clearer to my readers what action I am calling for?

7. How might I use a Rogerian approach to establish better rapport with readers?

Revising Checklist: Organization and Support

Classical Argument

1. How can I better present my proposition? How can I improve the focus, making sure that the proposition is evident throughout and restated in the conclusion?

2. In using specific-to-general organization, how can I make my point of view clear throughout the paper, leading up to my proposition in the conclusion?

3. How can I strengthen the "therefore" relationship between my supporting points and the main proposition?

4. Where have I used examples, analogies, or causal generalizations ineffectively?

Problem-Solution Argument

1. How can I more fully and clearly explain the problem to uninformed readers?

2. How can I improve my explanation of the seriousness of the problem?

3. How can I improve my explanation of how my solution will work and how it will reduce or eliminate the problem?

4. How can I better emphasize the solution's practicality?

Informal Persuasion

1. How can the argument thesis be more clearly stated? Have I used the organizational scheme most effective for my purposes? What are the advantages of the one I have chosen?

2. Where might I use emotional appeal more effectively? Have I overdone it in any place? Where might I include an ironic statement or argument?

3. How could I improve my final appeal so that it is more convincing and urgent?

Revising Checklist: Reasoning Tactics

1. In using inductive reasoning, did I check the following?
   a. Whether the stated evidence is relevant to my conclusion or proposal.
   b. Whether my analogies stand the test of the questions on page 309.
   c. Whether my causal relationships satisfy the questions on page 309.

2. In using deductive reasoning, did I check the following?
   a. Whether all my syllogistic reasoning is logically valid—with sound conclusions and true premises.
   b. Whether my conditional arguments meet the conditions set up.
3. In combining the two, did I check the following?
   a. Whether my evidence and linking principles lead logically to the conclusion.
   b. Whether I provided sufficient backing material.

Revising Checklist: Rogerian Strategy

1. How could I better summarize my opponents' positions to indicate my clear understanding of them?
2. What areas of agreement have I neglected?
3. How can I make my own position clearer?
4. What benefits to readers of my proposal have I neglected to include or explain clearly?

Revising Checklist: Organization

1. Did I follow a logically organized outline or would an outline reveal that my paper is logically organized?
2. Is my thesis sentence clearly stated or implied?
3. Do most paragraphs follow some SRI pattern?
4. Are my paragraphs fully developed with sufficient illustrations, such as reasons, examples, and facts?
5. In my introduction, do I attract my reader's attention, establish my credentials if possible, relate to my reader, and state my thesis, if appropriate?
6. Does my conclusion signal the end, review the argument, and appeal for action if appropriate?

SECOND STEP: EDITING

Editing Checklist: Language and Usage

1. What words needed careful defining? Could I improve the definitions?
2. What difficult or unfamiliar words do I need to check for meaning?
3. Where can I substitute clear, specific words for ambiguous or vague language?

Editing Checklist: Sentences

1. Where do I need to work on sentence structure to emphasize and focus my arguments?
2. Where might I use transitional or logical-relationship signals more effectively?
3. What sentences might be written more economically and clearly?
4. What sentences might be more effective if changed to periodic or *if . . . then* statements?

Editing Checklist: Spelling and Punctuation

1. Have I checked all questionable words in the dictionary?
2. Have I avoided connecting two sentences with commas?
3. Have I checked the punctuation I used with signals of logical relationships, such as *because, since, therefore, thus, so*?
4. Have I used hyphens when needed?
5. Have I checked my use of dashes, colons, or semicolons in the Reference Guide?

THIRD STEP: PROOFREADING

1. Is my paper neat and legibly written?
2. Have I made one last check for typos, spelling errors, words omissions, and repetitions?
3. Do I feel so confident about proofreading that I could send my paper, as is, to a newspaper or magazine editor?

PART FOUR

The Authoritative Voice: The Research Paper

Writing a research paper is much like writing a long expository or persuasive paper; it involves most of the same prewriting, writing, and rewriting skills. It differs from previous assignments in that it demands more sustained effort and organization. It differs also in that it requires you to learn how to use library sources, take notes effectively, and master the conventions of documentation. But little else is brand new.

Certainly the research process itself is not entirely new. You have already been engaged in research. You may have combed the classified ads while looking for a regular, part-time, or summer job. Or you may have consulted consumer guides and spoken to numerous people before buying a stereo, television set, or used car. In these and similar pursuits, you were involved in a small-scale research process: acquiring, interpreting, and evaluating information.

Just as the research process occurs outside of composition classes, so does the writing of research papers. In the semesters to come, if not the current semester, you will be investigating subjects or reporting on experiments in marketing, psychology, history, nursing, anthropology, science, or other courses. In your career beyond college you may often engage in research. Business people, lawyers, social workers, economists, engineers, architects, and many others do research, observing laboratory experiments, interviewing people, analyzing printed data, conducting surveys, and accumulating information in various other ways. And usually they must communicate the results of their work in writing to others. If they fail to convey their facts and ideas clearly, readers may discount or disregard important information.

In preparing a research paper for your composition course, you will be involved in this same process of gathering, interpreting, and communicating information, relying chiefly or entirely on library sources. The resulting paper may be either expository or persuasive. With an expository purpose, you will amass facts and opinions from many sources, sift and evaluate them, then organize and present your findings in order to inform your readers. You might explain, for instance, the vice-presidential selection process, new medical uses of the laser, or the causes of our deficit trade balance. On the other hand, you may investigate some subject, such as drugs in the public schools, to argue a point or advocate a solution to a problem. The investigative process is the same, but with a persuasive aim you will organize and present your material differently, perhaps in a problem-solution or classical argument form.

The research paper, then, has much in common with the expository and persuasive papers you have written. What may be new to you are the special skills involved in working with sources: using the library; recording, evaluating, and organizing the information gathered; and mastering the documentation conventions of scholarship—the proper use of quotations, citations, and bibliographies in order to give proper credit to others. These are skills that will serve you well not only in your college work but throughout your life.

Also, writing the research paper should be a rewarding—even exciting—experience in itself, particularly if you have a subject that you genuinely would like to know more about. The secret of success is to follow a systematic set of procedures that anyone can learn. In the following chapters, we'll show you how.

20

Prewriting Tactics
for Research
Writing

In previous modes of writing, prewriting consisted primarily of generating and limiting a subject; thinking of reasons, facts, examples, and other materials to develop it; and organizing your thoughts before writing about it. Although many of these steps are also involved in writing a research paper, a fundamental difference exists. The information for the research paper comes mainly from books and periodicals, not from your own head. Also, this paper is usually longer than previous writing assignments and involves much reading and note-taking; therefore, you will spend more time and effort in prewriting.

Usually there is less time available for the research paper than you would like. Whatever time you may have will vanish quickly. So you must get started as soon as possible, ignoring the comforting thought of that seemingly faraway deadline and the many pleasant distractions in your life. To begin, you should set up a schedule for the eleven-step process based on the time allotted. To provide you with an example, we offer here a tight three-week schedule for a short research paper. Of course, this is only an example; your instructor may suggest another schedule.

THE PROCESS	THE SCHEDULE (3 weeks) Days
Prewriting	
1. Subject Selection	1–2
2. Preliminary Reading	3–4
3. Preliminary Bibliography	5
4. Preliminary Plan	6
5. Note-Taking	7–10
6. Final Outline & Thesis	11
Writing	
7. First Draft	12–16

Rewriting
8.	Revising First Draft	17–18
9.	Editing First Draft	19
10.	Writing Final Draft	20
11.	Proofreading	21

By dividing the work for the research paper into a series of steps and by setting a deadline for each, you will probably write a better paper with less work. And you will sleep well the night before it is due. Let us examine the process step by step. We will cover prewriting in this chapter, writing and rewriting in the next.

STEP 1: SUBJECT SELECTION

Selecting a subject may be no problem. Perhaps your instructor will assign one or let you choose an interesting one from a list. Or perhaps you have some question already in your mind that you would like to answer and that would make an interesting paper of manageable length. For instance, you might wonder what has become of UFOs, or whether animals can be taught to communicate with people. Or you may want to explore some current controversial issue. For example, in recent years financial aid for students has been significantly reduced. You might be interested in investigating how and why this reduction came about, taking a position against the cuts or suggesting alternative ways for students to finance their education.

Subject Search

However, selecting a subject may be a problem. If your instructor wants you to find your own topic and you can think of nothing that seems promising, use some of the prewriting tactics we've examined in earlier chapters. Try freewriting for 20 minutes. If that is not productive, perhaps the viewpoint wheel (page 174) will be, or questioning (45), charting (46), listing (176), the perspectives approach (178), Larson's topics (296), and personal dialogue (296). If none of these procedures is helpful, here are three more possibilities: the course circle, the subject stairs, and the index search.

Course Circle

On a piece of paper, draw a large circle like the one in Figure 20-2. Then divide it into as many sections as you have other courses that might provide library research subjects for you. (If you are taking math, chemistry, or a foreign language, you may decide to exclude these courses as too technical. If you wish, you can add some of last semester's courses.) Now concentrate for about 15 minutes on each course, jotting down topic ideas in the space provided for them. Try to write down at least one idea before proceeding to another space. When you have finished, take a break; then return for a fresh look at the subjects you have generated. One of them may appeal to you.

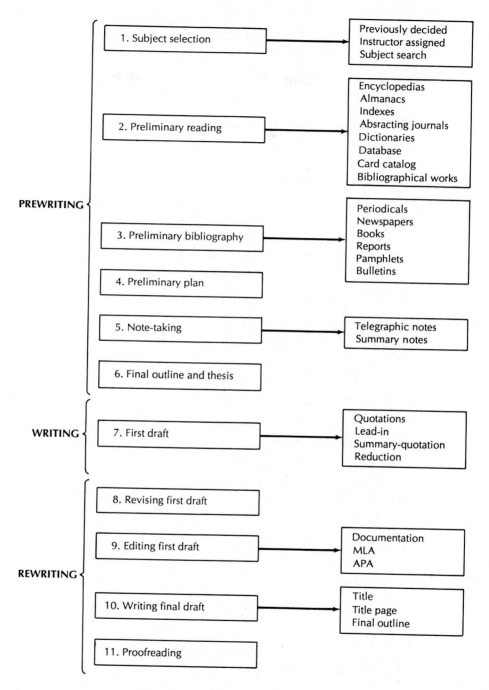

Figure 20-1. Flow Chart for the Research Paper

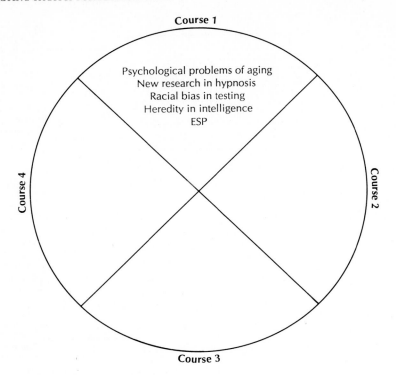

Figure 20-2. Course Circle

Subject Stairs

If you are unable to generate a subject from your courses, draw stairs like the ones in Figure 20-3 on a piece of paper. Above each step, write the title of a category, using the ones in the figure or others you think of. Then slowly "mount the stairs," writing ideas behind each step riser (as we have illustrated with the first few steps). When you reach the top, take a break and then, as with the course circle, return for a fresh look to see if something looks promising.

The Index Search

If the previous two methods have been unproductive, try the Index Search in the reference section of your library. Among the more helpful indexes that you will find there is the *Reader's Guide to Periodical Literature*, which classifies articles from over 150 magazines according to headings printed in bold type. At this point in your research, you are mainly interested in finding a topic, not articles, so you should merely skim the pages, searching these headings for subjects that might interest you. In addition to the *Reader's Guide*, you might try such specialized indexes as *The Education Index, The General Science Index, The Humanities Index,*

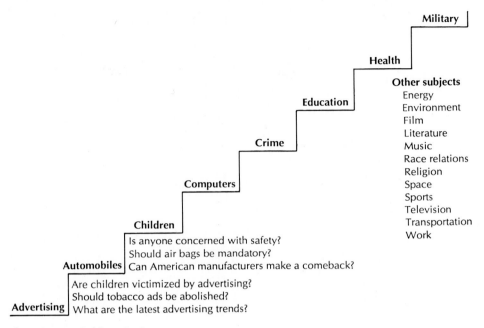

Figure 20-3. Subject Stairs

or *The Social Science Index,* all of which are discussed on pages 373–375. An encyclopedia index such as the *Americana* index may also suggest numerous possibilities, as you can see from the page reproduced in Figure 20-4. Skimming this page, you might decide to write about cancer, diet candy, or additives in canned foods, for example. You may also wish to check the index to the *Academic American Encyclopedia,* as well as the tables of contents in the yearbooks of the various encyclopedias, including the *Encyclopaedia Britannica.* Finally, you might skim the huge index volume *Subject Headings Used in the Dictionary Catalogs of the Library of Congress,* usually found near the library's card catalog.

Subject Criteria

Having found at least one interesting subject, you need to determine whether it is appropriate for a research paper and whether sufficient information about it is available.

An appropriate subject is one that will require your obtaining information from a variety of sources, certainly five or more, not solely or mainly from one or two. For example, a research paper about various species of dinosaurs might easily be based on material from a single book. But you would then be making little or no contribution of your own; you would merely be summarizing the information in the book. The paper would serve little purpose; readers could

Figure 20-4. Sample Entries From *Encyclopedia Americana* Index

just as easily turn to your single source themselves. You would have avoided one of the main objectives of the research assignment: to learn how to synthesize material from different sources by combining, analyzing, interpreting, and organizing information in order to make a statement of your own. This purpose could be achieved in a different research paper about dinosaurs, one based on your own investigation of various theories about their extinction and centering on your own conclusion about it.

Further, the diverse sources necessary for a worthwhile project must be *available to you*—and in printed form unless your instructor allows you to base your paper on personal interviews, surveys, and other nonprint material. For most college research papers, you will be expected to rely on library resources. That means you should avoid personal subjects (your grandfather's World War II experiences), local issues, or any events so recent that your library would not have a variety of published information about them.

Having tentatively chosen a subject which interests you and which you believe you will be able to find sources for, you are ready to proceed to Step 2.

STEP 2: PRELIMINARY READING

The purpose of your preliminary reading is to answer two questions: (1) Does your library have the sources you need? (2) Is there so much information that you should restrict your subject? While answering these questions, you will also be getting an overview of your subject, and you will almost surely glean some new ideas about it.

Reference Works

Your first stop in the library should be at the reference section. Here you will find a host of valuable sources: encyclopedias, almanacs, indexes, abstracting journals, dictionaries, bibliographical works, the card catalog and perhaps computers for a data base search. But most valuable of all are the librarians who work there. These trained professionals will be glad to help you with your research by suggesting specific sources for you to consult, by indicating where these works are located, and by identifying their strengths and limitations.

Encyclopedias An encyclopedia can be a valuable source of general information about a subject. But different encyclopedias are written for different readers. The *World Book*, for example, is written mainly for junior and senior high school students. Both the *Encyclopedia Americana,* which specializes in American subjects, and the *Encyclopedia Britannica,* which is the most respected general encyclopedia, usually provide fuller and more authoritative information. In using these works, particularly the *Britannica* with its *Micropaedia* and *Macropaedia,* be certain to consult the index first. You may also wish to examine the annual supplements published for both the *Americana* and the *Britannica.*

Biographies   If your subject is a person, you might find it most helpful to turn to biographical reference works. *Current Biography,* issued annually and in monthly supplements, provides information about living people, including their addresses and a list of articles and books about them. Another source of information about living people is the *Who's Who* series, which appears in different volumes according to classification, ranging from individual countries (*Who's Who in America*) to sex (*Who's Who of American Women*) to subject area (*Who's Who in Art*). Two other biographical sources that deserve mention are *Contemporary Authors* and *American Men and Women of Science.* Two of the most helpful works about people no longer living are the *Dictionary of American Biography* and *Supplements* (to 1981) and the *Dictionary of National Biography* and *Supplements* (British, to 1970). Both of these works are limited to individuals who died prior to the publication dates of the main volumes and supplements. *Notable American Women, 1607–1950, Who Was Who* (1952–1962), and *Who Was Who in America* (1607–date) are also valuable.

Almanacs   For statistical information, chronological listings, major developments in science and technology, and summaries of political events, almanacs are useful. Facts abound about athletics, climate, economics, employment, farm prices, famous people, foreign countries, and innumerable other subjects in these handy paperback volumes with their tissue-thin pages jammed mainly with figures, charts, tables, and lists. Two of the most helpful, the *World Almanac* and the *Information Please Almanac,* are published annually. The former probably contains more data; the latter has interesting articles, particularly its review of the year's events, and somewhat resembles the annual yearbooks published as supplements to many encyclopedias. Two other important sources of facts and statistics are *Facts on File,* a weekly summary of events, and the U.S. Census Bureau's *Statistical Abstract of the United States,* an annual goldmine of data about various aspects of American life drawn from the latest census (1980) and subsequent studies.

Dictionaries   A dictionary is far more than a spelling book, pronunciation guide, and source of definitions and synonyms; it is a storehouse of concise information about a wide range of topics—historical, biographical, geographical, scientific, medical, and linguistic, to mention just a few. Although limited, the information is quick and easy to find. If you needed the location of Pearl Harbor, a good desk dictionary would provide it. Or if you wanted some basic facts about Mahatma Gandhi, the dictionary would furnish at least his proper name and the years of his birth and death.

You certainly should invest in a hardcover college dictionary in a recent edition, keep it on your desk, and refer to it often. But remember that the unabridged dictionaries in the library's reference room, such as *Webster's Third New International,* not only contain more words, especially scientific and technical terms, than does a desk dictionary, but also provide more information about each word.

A useful dictionary for historical purposes is the *OED* (*Oxford English Dictionary*) with its supplements. This valuable work traces the meanings, spellings, and uses of words from the year 1000 to recent times. Anyone writing about eighteenth century literature or historical documents, for example, could find out what a particular word meant for readers of that period.

Among other dictionaries in the reference room are specialized volumes on slang, foreign languages, quotations, rhymes, clichés, and acronyms.

Bibliographical Sources

The reference works just described should give you some general, or background information about your subject and perhaps some specific data you can use. But you will need to find out more.

Bibliographies   If your subject is one on which much has already been written—for example, an important historical event or some episode in the life of a famous person—you may find that a bibliography (a list of works, with publication information) already exists. If so, you need to look elsewhere only for works published after the bibliography. To find these, check Eugene P. Sheehy's *Guide to Reference Books* (and its supplements) for the titles of guides to American, English, and Canadian works, or Albert John Walford's *Guide to Reference Materials* for English and European works.

Check also the bibliographies at the ends of pertinent articles in the *Bibliographic Index,* whose supplements appear four times a year and then are collected and published every four years. Listed there are bibliographies that have appeared in books and periodicals. If you are really fortunate, you may find an *annotated* bibliography, one that not only lists works but also comments on the value of each.

Indexes   Probably, you will not find a ready-made bibliography waiting for you, and will have to compile your own. In researching a relatively recent subject, one that would probably not yet be treated in books because they usually take a year or more to write and publish, your best bet is the periodical indexes. These valuable guides list magazine and newspaper articles by subject.

In dealing with material that is likely to be treated in popular magazines, start with the *Readers' Guide to Periodical Literature.* Among the more than 160 publications it catalogs are such magazines as *Time, Redbook, Sports Illustrated,* and the *Reader's Digest.* The abbreviated entries in this valuable work may seem baffling at first, but a short study of the sample entries in Figure 20–5, or of the introductory guide in each issue, will help you master them.

However, you should investigate sources other than the popular ones cited in the *Reader's Guide.* Some other indexes to check are the following:

Biography and Genealogy Master Index: a guide to about three million people listed in over 350 biographical works.

Biography Index: biographical information appearing in over 1,000 magazines, book, and newspapers. It complements the previous index.

Business Periodicals Index: a cumulative subject index to about 170 periodicals in accounting, advertising, banking, economics, finance, management, and taxation.

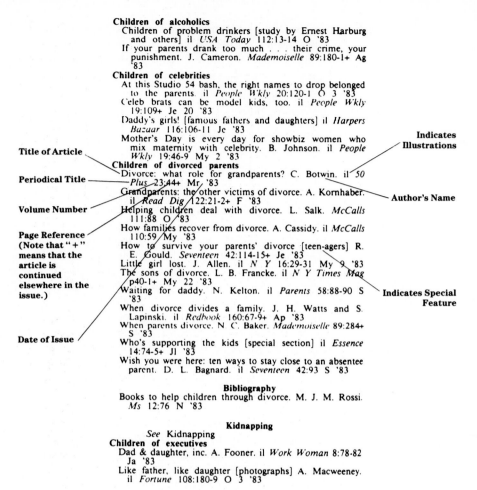

Figure 20-5. Sample Entries from *Readers' Guide*

Consumer's Index: lists of subjects covered in articles about the financial or physical well-being of consumers. Surveys about 100 periodicals. Includes test reports of products.

Environmental Index: a guide to articles about the environment.

Essay and General Literature Index: includes subjects treated in essays, chapters, or sections of books in the humanities and social sciences.

General Science Index: a guide to articles in astronomy, biology, earth sciences, environment and conservation, food and nutrition, medicine and health, and other scientific fields.

Humanities Index: catalogs 260 publications in such fields as archaeology, language and literature, folklore, history, philosophy, and theology.

Index to Periodical Articles by and about Blacks: a survey of major journals dealing with blacks.

New York Times Index: indexes news articles, speeches, editorials, reviews, and essays that have appeared in the *Times.* A highly valuable source of information.

Wall Street Journal Index: a guide to articles and other material appearing in this newspaper, which deals mainly with business news but contains many excellent articles about other issues.

Not listed here are numerous indexes in such specialized fields as art, biology, education, the humanities, science and technology, and the social sciences. Once again, your librarian can help you in your search for sources.

Abstracts   Similar to the index but often even more helpful is the abstract journal. Published mainly for scholars who do not have time to read all the articles in their field, the abstract journals provide summaries of articles. Among the ones you might find useful are the following:

Abstracts of English Studies: summaries of articles on literature in American and English periodicals.

America: History and Life: A Guide to Periodical Literature: summaries of articles on the history of the United States and Canada.

Historical Abstracts: summaries of articles on political, diplomatic, economic, social, cultural, and intellectual history.

Sociological Abstracts: summaries of national and international books and articles.

Psychological Abstracts: summaries of national and international articles, books, reports, and dissertations.

Women's Studies Abstract: summaries of articles pertaining to women.

Pamphlets and Government Publications   Finally, let's mention two other kinds of printed sources: pamphlets and government publications. The most inclusive guide to pamphlets is *Vertical File Index: A Subject and Title Index to Selected Pamphlet Material* (1932–date). Government publications are listed in the *Index to U.S. Government Publications,* the *Monthly Catalog of United States Government Publications,* and *Selected U.S. Government Publications.* The way that pamphlets and government publications are handled varies from one library to another. Once again, check with your librarian.

Database Search   The use of computers in libraries is increasing rapidly, making access to old sources easier and providing new sources as well, in the form of databases. If your library has computers for database searching, be careful how you use them. Because some libraries and most database suppliers levy charges based either on time or the number of items searched, the costs can mount speedily.

Especially useful for college papers is the Infotrac Database, which catalogs articles in business, law, technology, and the social sciences that have appeared in about 900 periodicals. More extensive and more up-to-date (with only a 30-day time lag) than *The Readers' Guide,* the Infotrac Database is simple to use. You merely type a key word (often called a *descriptor*) in the computer, press the "Search" button, and lo—in a few seconds, article titles which contain that key word or which are closely related to it appear on the screen. Press another button, and a nearby printer will type them out for you.

It is magical, but sometimes not as simple as it sounds. The trick lies in your selecting the correct key word (just as it does in searching in printed indexes and in card catalogs). Often the more general the term, the better. For example, if you are interested in learning what qualities are needed for success in business, the general word *management* will provide you with numerous other categories (see Figure 20–6), one being executive ability. Then, when you search again with this more specific term, you will receive the list of articles related to it (Figure 20–7).

The Card Catalog   We've left the card catalog for last in our discussion of library resources, not because you should consult it last but because you probably know something about it from your high school days. Even if you consider yourself an expert, you may benefit from a review. Furthermore, not all card catalogs are alike.

Your college library may have one card catalog, with all cards listed alphabetically, or two catalogs, one for author and title cards, the other for subject cards. If the cards are divided, you must decide where to turn first. For a paper on the geodesic dome, you would probably start with the subject catalog. However, to find a book by the dome's inventor, Buckminster Fuller, you might turn to the author-title catalog. But remember that if you wish a book *about* Fuller, not by him, you must turn again to the subject catalog.

If you cannot find a card for your subject in the card catalog, don't panic. Instead, consult the huge and thoroughly cross-referenced index volume *Subject Headings Used in the Dictionary Catalogs of the Library of Congress* to determine the heading (or headings) used for your subject. For example, if you were seeking books about writing, you would not find them in the card catalog under *Writing.* However, by looking up *Writing* in *Subject Headings,* you would discover a cross-reference to the heading that libraries do use, *Authorship.* Of course, if you are investigating a recent subject not yet treated in books, you won't find the subject listed in the card catalog at all. The guides to periodicals, such as *Readers' Guide* and *The New York Times Index,* will be your first resource (though the card catalog may tell you on a title card whether a particular periodical is available in your library and, if so, where it is shelved).

You are likely to find more than one card for the same book in the card catalog because at least two and often three or more cards (for multiple subjects or authors) are made for each book. These cards not only tell you where the book is shelved but also provide numerous other helpful hints once you understand the notations on the card. Look at the sample author-title card on page 379. What information does it provide? Let's list some points that may not be obvious.

1. The author is still living if the card is accurate (birth date but no death date). Biographical information may be available in current indexes.

```
>       MANAGEMENT
            see also
                ADVERTISING DEPARTMENTS
                ADVERTISING MANAGEMENT
                BANK MANAGEMENT
                BASEBALL MANAGING
                BUSINESS
                CAMPAIGN MANAGEMENT
                COMMAND AND CONTROL SYSTEMS
                COMPARATIVE MANAGEMENT
                COMPUTER PROGRAMMING MANAGEMENT
                COURT ADMINISTRATION
                CRISIS MANAGEMENT
                DECENTRALIZATION IN MANAGEMENT
                DELEGATION OF AUTHORITY


MANAGEMENT                                      InfoTrac Database
                                                  InfoTrac 3.23c

                                                    DATA DISPLAY
                EXECUTIVE ABILITY
                EXECUTIVES
                FACILITY MANAGEMENT
                FACTORY MANAGEMENT
                FARM MANAGEMENT
>               FINANCE DEPARTMENTS
                FOREST MANAGEMENT
                HOSPITALS--ADMINISTRATION
                HOTEL AND MOTEL MANAGEMENT
                HOUSING MANAGEMENT
                INDUSTRIAL MANAGEMENT
                INDUSTRIAL PROJECT MANAGEMENT
                INSTITUTION MANAGEMENT
                LINE AND STAFF ORGANIZATION
                MANAGEMENT BY OBJECTIVES
                MANAGEMENT COMMITTEES
                MANAGEMENT SCIENCE
                MANAGERIAL ECONOMICS
                MATRIX ORGANIZATION
                MIDDLE MANAGERS
```

Figure 20-6. Database Search—General Key Word

2. The number of pages (303—see "Descriptive information") suggests that the book treats the subject in some detail.

3. The date of publication indicates that the work is based on outdated materials.

4. The inclusion of a five-page bibliography suggests a scholarly treatment. This list of source materials could be helpful in your own further research.

5. The information marked with Arabic numbers in the "Tracings" indicates the main focus of the book (college attendance and school sites), the scope of the treatment (U. S. colleges only), and headings in the subject catalog under which additional material might be found (*College attendance, School sites, Junior Colleges*). Some catalog cards also give the reading level (not pertinent here). The entries with Roman numerals refer to additional cards for the same work (joint author card, title card).

```
EXECUTIVE ABILITY                          InfoTrac Database
                                           InfoTrac 3.23c

    =    aka Credit Union Executive             DATA DISPLAY
         12 Issues Per Year   $20.00
         Credit Union Nat'l Assn., Inc.
         P.O. Box 431
         Madison  WI  53791
    >    EXECUTIVE ABILITY
         see also
             DELEGATION OF AUTHORITY
             LEADERSHIP
             MANAGEMENT
             PERSONNEL MANAGEMENT
         --ADDRESSES, ESSAYS, LECTURES
    =        Marketers need many qualities to survive,
         Phillips executive says. (Charles L. Bowerman)
         j]  Oj]  Daily-Feb 20 '85 p5(1)
         --AIDS AND DEVICES
             The right organizer can make your day. by
         Edward Tenner   j]   Money  v14-Dec'85 p93(3)
         31K4170                               21R4246
         --ANALYSIS
```

```
EXECUTIVE ABILITY                          InfoTrac Database
  --ANALYSIS                                 Info Trac 3.23c

        --ANALYSIS                           DATA DISPLAY
    =        The evolution of cooperation.-(book
        reviews) by Robert Axelrod
      B    New Republic v190-May 21'84   p40(2)
        22H2974
    >=       Who is an intrapreneur? (corporate
        entrepreneurs) by Joel E. Ross and Darab
        Unwalla  j] Personnel v63-Dec'86 p45(5)
    =        Thinking and managing: a verbal protocol
        analysis of managerial problem solving.  by
        Daniel J. Isenberg  i]  Academy of Management
        Journal v29-Dec'86 p775(14)
    =        Succession planning. 1: senior management
        selection. (selection criteria for executive
        positions) by Paul Sheibar  j] Personnel
        v63-Nov'86 p16(6)
    =        The tasks of leadership, Part 2: setting
        an example.  by John W. Gardner  Personnel
        v63-Nov'86 p41(6)
```

Figure 20-7. Database Search—Specific

As you see, when you use the card catalog thoughtfully, you can learn a lot. It can save you time and effort by steering you to certain sources and away from others. It's all in the cards.

Microforms   Microfilm and microfiche, respectively reels and card-like pieces of film containing the printed materials such as newspapers and magazines that have

Sample Library Card

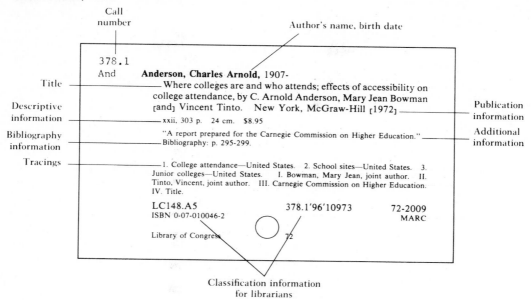

Call number

Author's name, birth date

Title

Descriptive information

Bibliography information

Tracings

378.1
And   **Anderson, Charles Arnold,** 1907-
        Where colleges are and who attends; effects of accessibility on college attendance, by C. Arnold Anderson, Mary Jean Bowman ₍and₎ Vincent Tinto.   New York, McGraw-Hill ₍1972₎
        xxii, 303 p.   24 cm. $8.95
        "A report prepared for the Carnegie Commission on Higher Education."
        Bibliography: p. 295-299.

        1. College attendance—United States.   2. School sites—United States.   3. Junior colleges—United States.   I. Bowman, Mary Jean, joint author.   II. Tinto, Vincent, joint author.   III. Carnegie Commission on Higher Education. IV. Title.

        LC148.A5   378.1′96′10973   72-2009
        ISBN 0-07-010046-2   MARC

        Library of Congress   72

Publication information

Additional information

Classification information
for librarians

been photographically reduced to miniature form, save libraries much-needed space. They also preserve perishable sources such as back issues of often-used newspapers and magazines, which would tear easily or even disintegrate in their original form. To read the microfilm or microfiche, you'll have to learn to use mechanical viewers, which are simple once you get the hang of them, perhaps with the librarian's help.

Results of Preliminary Reading

And now, having consulted many of the previously discussed sources, where are you? First of all, you should have a definite subject, one that has been properly narrowed down. Second, you should know that your library has sufficient material. By "sufficient material," we mean that you should have found at least five to seven substantial articles or five books, or some happy combination thereof.

Now you're ready to spend an afternoon skimming these sources. Doing so will be helpful in several ways. First, you'll find out where the sources are located, no simple task in some large college libraries. Then you will learn whether they are available. Otherwise, you may discover too late that your books have been checked out or that the periodical issues you need are not available because they are out at the bindery. Above all, you will find out whether your subject is really manageable and whether each source contains information pertinent to it. To find out, skim the books by studying their tables of contents, reading their prefaces, and looking at their indexes. Then, focusing especially on the opening sentences of paragraphs, flip through chapters (or smaller groups of pages) that appear to contain useful information. With an article, read the introductory and concluding paragraphs, and then read rapidly through the opening sentences of each paragraph.

Here's how this preliminary subject search and reading can be helpful. Let's suppose that you're interested in elections: the Electoral College, voting trends, primaries, national conventions, third-party candidates. A library check reveals dozens of books and articles about these and other aspects of the subject of elections. Obviously, the subject is too broad and must be limited. As you poke through the sources, you discover some interesting facts about American voting habits. For example, a smaller percentage of Americans vote than people in many other countries. You wonder why. Then you notice that only about 20 percent of our 18-to-20-year-olds said they voted in the recent national election. This surprises you. How could the figure be increased? As you read, you find several suggestions: postcard registration, registration at the polls on election day, weekend voting. You have a few ideas of your own. And so your research paper is born: "Getting Out the Youth Vote."

This example, however, may suggest that searching for a subject and material about it is always easy. It is not. Often it is exasperating and tedious. You may have an interesting subject but not be able to find information about it, or the information that you do find may be scanty or out of date. You may choose a subject and conscientiously narrow it down, only to find that you have to narrow it again and again. And in the process of finding a subject and information about it, you will almost certainly retrace your steps several times, going back and forth from finding sources to reading, to finding additional sources, and then later rereading some of the previously read sources. But by following our step-by-step process, you can cut false starts and repetition to a minimum.

STEP 3: THE PRELIMINARY BIBLIOGRAPHY

This step overlaps with the previous one. While you are skimming books and articles for information about your subject, you should also be working on your preliminary bibliography.

The Nature of the Preliminary Bibliography

The preliminary bibliography is a list of all the promising sources that you locate in the course of your research. It is distinguished from the final bibliography, which contains only those sources actually used in your paper. Because this final bibliography must be arranged in alphabetical order, and because information filed in this manner is easier to locate, most researchers use 3″ × 5″ cards rather than writing the sources on whatever pieces of paper are available. However, if you wish and your instructor permits it, you can substitute card-sized slips of paper.

Before this step, you primarily wanted to decide on a subject and determine whether sufficient material about it was available. Now, having done some reading, you'll want to evaluate the books, articles, or other publications so that you can select those you will use in your paper. Naturally, you'll also be on the lookout for additional sources. Remember to study the catalog cards thoughtfully, as we mentioned. In evaluating magazine articles in indexes and other bibliographical sources, note the date, title, and number of pages. Exercise some judgment. For example, a seven-page article in *Scientific American* about teaching chimpanzees to use language would undoubtedly be more informative than a four-page condensation of it in the *Reader's Digest* or a one-page account in *Newsweek*. You can learn something about the influence and biases of your periodical sources by consulting Evan Ira Farber's scholarly *Classified List of Periodicals for the College Library* or the lively reviews in *Magazines for Libraries*, 3rd ed., by Bill Katz and Barry G. Richards.

Also, be alert for mention of articles and books that you may have missed; these may turn up not only in discussions but in footnotes or endnotes. Often one good source will refer to others. Learn to snoop around a bit, play detective. Investigate related topics—for instance, the family and friends of your subject. For a paper on the presidency of Ulysses S. Grant, skim the biography of his wife. For one titled "General Patton—Hero or Heel?" check the indexes in autobiographies or biographies of Patton's fellow generals—Eisenhower, Bradley, Clark, Gavin, and Montgomery. For a paper on the pros and cons of state-operated lotteries, check into such related topics as the Irish Sweepstakes, state-run off-track betting, English soccer pools, and lotteries in European countries. A glance at the index of a book on a related subject can unearth a treasure of information.

Form of the Preliminary Bibliographical Entry

Whenever you find a promising article or book, jot it down, one title to a card. Although you may follow the precise form required for the final bibliography (pages 404–18), we suggest that you disregard that complicated form now; instead, merely be sure to record *all* of the following:

Book	*Article*
Author, editor	Author
Title and subtitle	Title and subtitle of article
Translator (if any)	Name of publication
Edition (if more than one has been published	Series number or name (if part of a series)
Number of volumes (if more than one)	Volume number (if published less often than bimonthly)
Series (if part of a series)	Date
Place of publication (first city listed, if several are given)	Page numbers
Publisher	Call number
Date	
Call number	

This information is generally available from the catalog card if the publication is a book, or the index entry if it is a periodical.

Three helpful hints about your preliminary bibliography:

1. Write the author's last name first to help you in alphabetizing later.

2. Copy the entire (yes, the entire) call number accurately. If you omit or are off a letter or a digit, you may be thousands of books or magazines away from the one you are seeking. And jot down the location if you might have difficulty finding the work later to check on something.

3. Write a comment or two about the work so you know what it contains and its strengths and weaknesses, as illustrated in Figure 20–8. This note may save you hours after you have examined many sources and forgotten what some contained.

STEP 4: THE PRELIMINARY PLAN

What you need now is a tentative plan to serve as a general road map for your paper, showing where you intend to go and how you think you will get there. You may later decide to depart from the plan by detouring here, staying longer there, skipping some places, and perhaps even changing your destination. But you need to begin with a plan. What is your purpose? Who is your audience? What is your thesis? How should you organize your material? By thinking about these matters now, you will save time in note-taking and in writing later. But remember, this preliminary plan may be changed.

Here is how to proceed. Let's say that you are concerned about the problem of attracting and retaining good teachers in the public schools. You think that one way to accomplish these goals would be to institute a system of merit pay, providing better teachers with salary increases and possibly with different ranks instead of their continuing on the present seniority system. After some preliminary reading, you draw up this tentative plan:

Purpose: To convince readers that a merit pay plan would attract and retain better-qualified people in the teaching profession.

Audience: Students in my class.

Thesis: A merit pay plan would attract better-qualified students into the teaching profession and would keep the best teachers in the classrooms.

I.   Failure to attract best students
   A.   Test scores and grades of entering education students
   B.   Appeal of other careers, particularly for women
   C.   Teaching's lack of appeal
II. Failure to retain best teachers in classroom
   A.   Promotion to administration
   B.   Resignation for other jobs

Library call number

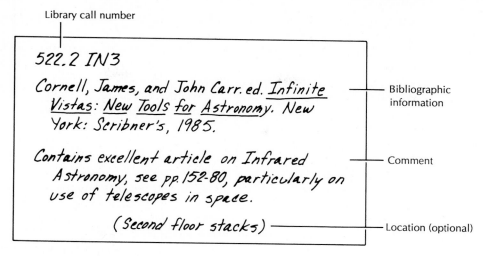

522.2 IN3

Cornell, James, and John Carr. ed. *Infinite Vistas: New Tools for Astronomy.* New York: Scribner's, 1985.

Contains excellent article on Infrared Astronomy, see pp. 152-80, particularly on use of telescopes in space.

(Second floor stacks)

— Bibliographic information

— Comment

— Location (optional)

Figure 20-8. Bibliography Card

III. Possible merit pay plans
    A. Plan 1
    B. Plan 2
    C. Plan 3
IV. Disadvantages of merit pay plans
    A. Difficulty of evaluating a teacher
    B. Effect on teachers' morale
    C. Impact on parents
V. Advantages of merit pay plans
    A. Incentive to better teaching
    B. Recognition and reward for good teachers
    C. Method of attracting better students
    D. Method of retaining better teachers

Your preliminary plan, as mentioned previously, is not a binding contract. It can be changed and changed and changed again. But it gets you started. And that is helpful because it is too easy to just keep reading about your subject and to postpone making a commitment. The preliminary plan pins you down and forces you to think about your purpose, your audience, your thesis, and your organization.

Another advantage of a preliminary plan is that it will help you in taking notes, the next step in the prewriting process.

STEP 5: NOTE-TAKING

Many college students recall the agony of a high-school research paper for which they first copied lengthy passages from their sources, then frantically tried to organize their mass of notes and half-formulated ideas during the last-minute nightmare of writing.

Sound familiar? If your research experiences were like that, lack of sleep was only one problem. First, however innocently, you may have plagiarized by failing to indicate that you were using someone else's words or ideas. (More about plagiarism later; see pages 385–86). Second, you were disorganized, having to scramble through pages and pages of notes as you searched again and again for information that you knew was there but could never find when you wanted it. Third, chances are that the result was mainly a mishmash of quotations rather than a coherent statement of your own *supported* by carefully integrated material from your sources.

If your experience was different, fine: You are better prepared than most of your classmates to tackle the research paper. Even so, you can benefit from a review of the techniques that numerous scholars have developed to save time and to improve papers. One of these techniques—essential for a well-organized, informative, and interesting paper—is skillful note-taking. Taking effective notes requires an efficient system and disciplined habits.

The Mechanics of Note-Taking

Taking notes efficiently enables you to achieve two objectives: to obtain information and to organize it. You can best accomplish both of these purposes by using 4″ × 6″ cards (unlike the 3″ × 5″ bibliography cards) or, if your instructor permits, slips of paper cut to 4″ × 6″ size. Avoid taking notes on notebook pages because it is impractical and cumbersome. Each card should contain a note from a single source on a single point. Later you can arrange these cards according to your outline and behold—you not only know where the pertinent notes are, but you have them already arranged in a useful order.

Writing one note to a card may seem wasteful, but in practice it saves hours. Let us show you how this system works. For the paper about a merit pay plan for teachers, you might have read that half of the teachers leave the profession within seven years. After writing this information on a note card (Figure 20-9), you would check your preliminary outline to see where it might fit. In our outline (page 382) the information belongs under IIB—"Resignation for other jobs." Therefore, as illustrated in Figure 20-9, you would write this outline heading, or a short form of it, on the card—"Resignation." If there was not an appropriate place, you would either revise your outline or decide that you had gotten off the subject and set the card aside in a "rejected" pile. However, it is a good idea to keep such cards in case you later have use for them after all.

Later, after consulting all your sources and taking your notes, you would sort your note cards into stacks according to their headings, arrange the stacks in the order of your revised outline, and begin drafting your paper. When you reach each section, such as the explanation of possible merit plans, all your notes on that subject will be ready, sitting in a stack, waiting for you.

With this note-card system, gone are the hours spent flipping through all those notebook pages, searching for a particular quotation or idea. Gone is the feeling

Heading

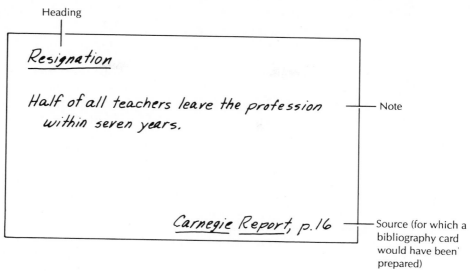

Resignation

Half of all teachers leave the profession
within seven years.

Note

Carnegie Report, p.16

Source (for which a
bibliography card
would have been
prepared)

Figure 20-9. Note Card

of being overwhelmed by the bulk of material you have amassed. Gone is the anxiety of not knowing how to start and continue and conclude. Instead, you are all organized, set to write.

For the system to work, however, you must be sure to include all the necessary information on your note cards. In addition to the heading and the note, you must provide the source. For a book or article by a named author, usually the author's last name is all you need write so that you can later match the note with the pertinent bibliography card. But if you are using two or more works by one author, or if two authors have the same last name, then obviously you will need to add a short title for each work or the first name of each author to prevent confusion. For a source without a named author, use the first few words of the title on the note card.

Remember, then, that your note cards must always contain three elements: (1) a subject heading from your outline, (2) a note, and (3) an identification of the source. And there is a further requirement: You must indicate whether your note is a direct quotation or not.

Plagiarism and Note-Taking

By being careful when you take notes, you can avoid plagiarism, which simply means using someone else's words or ideas without acknowledging the source. Regardless of whether it is intentional or accidental, this practice is considered dishonest, and the penalties can be severe. You will be guilty of plagiarism if you do any of the following *without crediting your sources:*

1. Use someone else's exact sentences or phrases.

2. Rephrase someone else's sentences.

3. Present someone else's ideas, methods, or approaches.

Generally, everything in your research paper should be documented if it is not based on your own knowledge and if it is not common knowledge.

What is common knowledge? If you were writing about the assassination of President Kennedy, the day, place, and time of his death is common knowledge, available in many sources. You would not be obliged to give credit to a source for this information. But once you began to deal with the details of Kennedy's death, such as the number of shots, you would have to cite your sources. A rule of thumb is to document any information that is controversial or questionable or is unique to one source in either substance or phrasing. This last criterion—unique phrasing—means that even items of common knowledge, if they are expressed in an original or distinctive way, must be credited to the source if you use the same phrasing. For instance, that Pearl Harbor was attacked on December 7, 1941, leading to America's declaration of war against Japan in World War II, is common knowledge which you could use freely; without citing any source, you could write that December 7, 1941, is a day many Americans will never forget. But if you were to refer to December 7, 1941, as "a date that will live in infamy," you would need the quotation marks and a citation to President Franklin D. Roosevelt, who used that ringing phrase in his speech to Congress and the American people the day after the attack.

Sometimes plagiarism is a legal offense; always it is a moral and scholarly offense. If the material copied or paraphrased without acknowledgment is copyrighted, you are legally liable. Even if it is not, you are still morally wrong because you have passed off someone else's words and ideas as your own. In most colleges, plagiarism is severely dealt with, the penalties ranging from—at the mildest—a failing grade on the paper to failure in the course and even expulsion from the college. Whether intentionally or not, the plagiarist has violated the code of scholars, who place great importance on acknowledging their debts to other scholars.

The Art of Note-Taking

When the language of a statement in a source is extraordinarily effective for your purposes, direct quotation may be your best bet. If so, be extremely careful in reproducing the quoted material *exactly* and in placing quotation marks around it when writing your note card. But remember that too many quotations can make your paper resemble a quilt—merely a stitching together of other people's material. A good research paper is more like a fabric that you have woven yourself. Some of the threads are drawn (with due acknowledgment) from the work of others, but the result is something new, reflecting your own views and expressed in your own style.

As you are taking notes, it is easy to convince yourself that there is no way to state the author's idea without using the author's words. But there is a way: Either use telegraphic style or summarize the material.

Telegraphic Notes   You probably are already proficient in telegraphic note-taking from your experience in lecture courses. Here's how to use it in working with printed sources:

Original passage

Another popular explanation for declining test scores is that desegregation has forced previously all-white schools to lower their academic standards in order to accommodate nonwhite students with fewer academic skills. But desegregation has been confined largely to the South and to a few big northern cities. Test scores, in contrast, have dropped off throughout the nation. In many cases the decline is even greater in the North than in the South. Both Iowa and Minnesota are more than 98 percent white, yet they report marked declines in high school scores. Whites cannot, then, blame their troubles on desegregation.

> —*Christopher Jencks, "What's Behind the Drop in Test Scores?"*

Telegraphic notes

Another explanation—declining test scores—desegregation. But desegregation largely in South—few northern cities. Test scores down nationally. Some declines greater in North. Iowa and Minn—98% white—test scores down greatly. Whites cannot blame desegregation.

From such telegraphic notes, you would find it relatively easy in your first draft to rewrite the ideas in your own words along the lines of the following:

Rewritten version

According to Jencks, lower test scores cannot be blamed on desegregation, which has occurred only in the South and in a small number of northern cities while test scores have declined nationally. Further, some scores have declined more in the North than in the South, and in two practically all-white states, Iowa and Minnesota, scores dropped significantly (21).

In the research process, instead of taking notes, you may decide to photocopy some pages from articles or books. If you do so, be sure you have made a bibliography card with all the necessary bibliographical information (page 381), and either make out note cards with references to the photocopied material or else write references directly on your outline at the appropriate subject headings. Such information might take this form:

II.   Potential of atomic energy
    A.   Soddy, 1904
    B.   H.G. Wells, 1914
    C.   Einstein, 1939
    D.   Sachs, 1939 (Rhodes, p. 156)

The Rhodes note refers to a photocopied statement by Sachs quoted on page 156 of a book by Rhodes, *The Making of the Atomic Bomb*. Such notes on your outline will remind you to consult your photocopied materials when writing the pertinent sections of your paper.

Summary Notes   When you are reading, summary notes take more time and effort to compose than do telegraphic notes, but they save time when you are writing because the work has been done. Read the material at least once, digest it, close the book or magazine, write the summary in your own words, and then check it for accuracy and completeness. It sounds time-consuming, but in the long run it is not because you can generally use the summary in your first draft either as is or with only a few changes.

The trick in writing a summary is to exclude all examples, secondary comments, unrelated references, and superfluous words, and to concentrate on the main idea. Here's an example of a summary note:

Original passage

Research has shown that it is all but impossible to develop mental fatigue by studying, even by studying hard. We get "tired" readily enough but this happens because we are bored with the subject, not because bodily wastes accumulate in the brain, or even in the muscles. You may push away a textbook with the comment, "I'm exhausted! I can't read another word," then casually pick up a magazine or newspaper and read avidly, without any signs of fatigue, for an hour or so. Obviously, we have confused *fatigue* with *boredom*.

—*Walter Pauk, How to Study in College*

Summary note

According to research, it is almost impossible to become mentally fatigued by studying hard. People think they get tired, but actually they become bored.

Observe that the summary is not a paraphrase, a sentence-by-sentence rewording of the original. Because a paraphrase requires nearly as many words, as the original, it offers little advantage; you may as well quote.

The summary, on the other hand, is shorter than the original and requires a thorough understanding of it. In particular, focus on the topic sentences, which we have italicized for you in the following example:

Original passage

Two things were outstanding in the creation of the English system of canals, and they characterize all the Industrial Revolution. *One is that the men who made the revolution were practical men.* Like Brindley, they often had little education, and in fact, school education as it was then could only dull an inventive mind. The grammar schools could only teach the classical subjects for which they were founded. The universities also (there were only two, at Oxford and Cambridge) took little interest in modern or scientific studies; and they were closed to those who did not conform to the Church of England.

The other outstanding feature is that the new inventions were for everyday use. The canals were arteries of communication: they were not made to carry pleasure boats, but barges. And the barges were not made to carry luxuries, but pots and pans and bales of cloth, boxes of ribbon, and all the common things that people buy by the penny-worth. These things had been manufactured in villages which were growing into towns now, away from London; it was a country-wide trade.

—*Jacob Bronowski, Ascent of Man*

Summary note

Bronowski points out that two unique qualities characterize the English canal system and all the Industrial Revolution: The inventors were practical people often with little formal education, and their inventions were designed to serve practical, everyday needs (163).

You could have worded this summary differently, of course; nothing is sacred about our version. But the point and the beauty of a summary note is that it forces you to read carefully and thoughtfully, requires that you write about the information while it is fresh in your mind, and results in your having written a statement that can be easily integrated into your paper later without your having to rewrite it them. But remember—even though the words are yours, the idea belongs to another. Consequently, you must indicate the debt by citing your source.

In short, then, writing a summary note is a five-step process: (1) read the passage; (2) digest the material, rereading it if necessary; (3) close the book or periodical; (4) summarize the material; and (5) check to see that the summary is complete and accurate.

Should you ever copy a passage down word for word? Yes, when using material from a literary work, such as an autobiography, play, or novel, or in special instances when the wording is particularly striking, memorable, or colorful. It would be a shame, for example, to redo Mary-Claire Van Leunen's cogent argument against overquotation:

When you are writing well, your sentences should join each other like rows of knitting, each sentence pulling up what went before it, each sentence supporting what comes after. . . . Quotation introduces an alien pattern—someone else's diction, someone else's voice, someone else's links before and afterward. Even necessary quotations are difficult to knit smoothly into your structure. Overquotation will result in something more like a bird's nest than like fine handiwork.

—*A Handbook for Scholars*

We agree. The fewer the quotations, the more readable the research paper. And especially, avoid long quotations. They may help you pad, but they bore readers. Remember the Golden Rule of Writing: Write unto your readers as you would have them write unto you. And just as you often skip over long quoted passages in your own reading (and may have done just that with our example), so you should be cautious about including them. The crucial time to decide not to use them is in note-taking. Later, when writing, you may not have the strength and time to resist inserting quotations to save yourself the work of absorbing the material and stating it in your own words. So—take notes in telegraphic style or write summaries, and save word-for-word quoting for irresistible passages.

STEP 6: REVISING THE OUTLINE

When you have completed a reasonable amount of reading and note-taking, retrieve your preliminary outline and thesis to change them as you deem best in view of what you now know about your subject. Think of this step as if you had planned a car trip, then heard from friends about new places you shouldn't miss, or others you should spend more time at, and you therefore revised your itinerary. Naturally, you may change the outline and thesis again as you write, just as you might change your trip if you find an interesting place. Stay flexible and loose, but have a sound reason for your changes.

SUMMARY

The preliminary tactics for writing the research paper—subject selection, preliminary reading, preliminary bibliography, preliminary plan, and note-taking—are time-consuming and complicated. By working carefully and precisely, however, you can save yourself hours of trouble and frustration. The prewriting work is much like preparing the soil before planting. The fruits of your labor will not become apparent until later. You will realize the benefits when you sit down to write your paper because all your notes will be organized for you, all your information will be where it is easily accessible, and all your efforts can be concentrated on the task of writing.

ASSIGNMENTS

For Discussion and Library Research

1. How appropriate would each of the following topics be for a research paper?
    The Recent Tax Changes
    Cheating at Your College
    Women's Athletics
    Child Abuse

Life Today Is Better
The Future of Nuclear Energy
The Impact of TV Advertising on Children
How No-Fault Divorce Works
Movies are Sexier than Ever
Affirmative Action in Your Community

2. How many of the following would you find in a standard desk (abridged) dictionary?

Months of the three principal calendars (Gregorian, Hebrew, Moslem)
Diagram of beef cuts
Table of alphabets (Hebrew, Arabic, Greek, Russian)
Currency of foreign countries
Geologic time scale
Diagram of car ignition
Manual alphabet for deaf-mutes
Proofreader's marks
Map of the United States
Books of the Old and New Testaments
Periodic table of chemical elements
Metric system
Morse code
Ship's bells
Zodiac signs
Radio frequencies
List of U.S. colleges and universities
Punctuation guide
Tables of weights and measures
List of capital cities of the United States

3. What information is missing from the catalog cards on pages 393–94? What facts can you glean from information on the cards?

4. Name some possible reference sources for material about the following subjects. Your instructor may also wish you to determine whether your library contains sufficient information for a research paper about one of them.

Mass transit
Day-care centers
Women in the clergy
Illegal immigrants
Gay rights
World famine
Polygamy today
Gambling
Hypnosis
Drinking on college campuses
Blacks in corporate America

American Mafia
Nuclear wastes
Campaign finance reform
Robots in industry
New U.S. political alignments
Fair trade laws
AIDS

5. Suppose the following people are coming this year to speak on your campus. As a student working in the public relations office, you have been asked to prepare biographical sketches of each. What sources would you consult? Your instructor may ask you to write a biographical sketch of one of the speakers.

Mortimer Adler
Woody Allen
Erma Bombeck
Art Buchwald
William F. Buckley, Jr.
Bill Cosby
Placido Domingo
Geraldine Ferraro
Jane Fonda
Ellen Goodman
Jesse Jackson
Coretta King
Toni Morrison
Garry Trudeau
Elie Wiesel

410
Bol
    Bolinger, Dwight Le Merton, 1907-
        Aspects of language / Dwight Bolinger. — 2d ed. — **New**
   York : Harcourt Brace Jovanovich, ₍1975₎

       xvii, 682 p. : ill. ; 24 cm.

       Includes bibliographies and index.
       ISBN 0-15-503868-0

       P106.B59   1975   410   74-25091
                                                   MARC

       Library of Congress   75

616.8
Fre
    Freud, Sigmund, 1856-1939.
        Sigmund Freud and Lou Andreas-Salomé; letters. Edited by
   Ernst Pfeiffer. Translated by William and Elaine Robson-Scott.
   ₍1st American ed.₎   New York, Harcourt Brace Jovanovich
   ₍1972₎

       "A Helen and Kurt Wolff book."
       Translation of Sigmund Freud, Lou Andreas-Salomé: Briefwechsel.

       1. Freud, Sigmund, 1856-1939. 2. Andreas-Salomé, Lou, 1861-1937.   I.
      Andreas-Salomé, Lou, 1861-1937. II. Pfeiffer, Ernst, ed.

       BF173.F85A43713   1972   616.8′917′0924   72-79922
       ISBN 0-15-133490-0   ₍B₎   MARC

       Library of Congress   73

340.07
Pac   **Packer, Herbert L**
New directions in legal education, by Herbert L. Packer and Thomas Ehrlich, with the assistance of Stephen Pepper. A report prepared for the Carnegie Commission on Higher Education.

xviii, 384 p.   24 cm. $10.00
Bibliography: p. 87-91.

1. Law—Study and teaching—United States.   I. Ehrlich, Thomas, 1934- joint author.   II. Carnegie Commission on Higher Education.   III. Title.

KF272.P3   340'.07'1173   72-5311
                                                      MARC

Library of Congress   72

Rutherford, William E
Modern English / William E. Rutherford. — 2d ed. — New York : Harcourt Brace Jovanovich, c1975-

v.   : ill. ; 24 cm.

Includes index.
ISBN 0-15-561059-7

1. English language—Text-books for foreigners.   I. Title.

[PE1128.R83   1975]   428'.2'4   75-10765
                                                      MARC

Library of Congress   75

21

Writing and Rewriting the Research Paper

Before starting to write, decide on some sort of schedule. How many days or hours do you have before the deadline? Will you have to work on your first draft into the wee morning hours or can you work more leisurely during afternoons and evenings? Naturally, you cannot know exactly how much time you will need, but a rough schedule, based on whatever you know about yourself as a writer, will be helpful.

If you are writing a long research paper, you might plan to work on your paper in sections. After some preliminary reading, you may decide to continue reading about one major area, then write about it, proceed to another major area, write about it, and so forth. For example, in a paper about freedom of the press, you might examine three problems: libel, prior censorship by government agencies, and protection of a news source. By dividing your paper into these three distinct sections, you might decide to follow the "read-and-write, read-and-write, read-and-write" approach instead of completing all the research and all the writing separately. When using this method, however, revise carefully, paying particular attention to cohesion by making sure that the main sections are effectively knit together.

No matter how you decide to work, start writing as soon as you reasonably can, perhaps even before you have finished your reading. One of the main problems for many writers is that they enjoy reading so much they postpone the moment of truth when they have to sit down before the blank page to write. Consequently, they always find something else to read, putting off the writing until the last minute.

Instead, think of writing as discovery. Use your first draft not only to get your ideas down on paper but also to learn what you know about your subject, what material you should recheck or reread, and what additional information you should obtain.

STEP 7: WRITING THE FIRST DRAFT

Starting to write is never easy. Most professional writers will attest to the numerous personal and social distractions they can find to postpone sitting down at their desks. And starting to write a research paper is harder than usual for most students because of its length. So beware of the "mental block" that is really an excuse, and of the temptation to read on instead of writing. Don't wait for inspiration or more information—get started.

Once started, resist the tendency to fuss with the opening sentences or paragraphs. It is safe and fun to keep playing with them, polishing them rather than venturing into the huge unknown lying ahead in your research paper. Later you will have time to rework your introduction. Now you have to get into the meat of your subject, the body of your paper.

On the other hand, you may have trouble finding a beginning. If so, forget about it and skip immediately to the first point in the body of the paper. Chances are that a good opening will occur to you as you work on the rest of the paper or after you have completed the first draft. Many experienced writers routinely save writing their introductions for last.

Quotation Techniques

Although, as we've said, overquoting is to be avoided, you'll surely have some material that should be quoted. The question, then, is how to keep such quotations short and readable. We offer three suggestions: (1) the lead-in; (2) the summary-quotation combination; and (3) the reduction.

Lead-In   Every quotation should be introduced with a lead-in phrase or clause instead of being dumped in the reader's lap. State the name of the person being quoted, the purpose of the quotation, or both. Here's what we mean:

Dumped:
Gay people are difficult to detect. "There are, undoubtedly, effeminate male homosexuals and masculine-type lesbians, but these constitute only a small minority of their population."

Lead-in:
Jeannine Gramick makes a similar point, stating, "There are, undoubtedly, effeminate male homosexuals and masculine-type lesbians, but these constitute only a small minority of their population."

In using lead-ins, avoid a monotonous dependency on the "So-and-So says" device: Gramick says. . . . George F. Will says. . . . Jane Bryant Quinn says. . . . Instead, strive for variety by using some of these introductions:

According to Gramick, . . .

Gramick has reported (confirmed, revealed) . . .

Support for these views comes from a study by Gramick. "There are, undoubtedly, effeminate male homosexuals and masculine-type lesbians," she reports, "but these. . . ."

Although Jeannine Gramick grants that "undoubtedly, effeminate male homosexuals and masculine-type lesbians" exist, she states that "these constitute. . . ."

Another practice to avoid besides dumping is the repetitious "tell 'em, quote, and tell 'em what you've quoted" technique. Here is an example of it, with a rewritten version using the more effective lead-in approach:

Tell 'em:

Dr. Bettelheim points out a more serious adverse effect of television on children. "They lose the ability to learn from reality because life experiences are more complicated than the ones they see on screen, and there is no one who comes in at the end to explain it all." This is another reason why Dr. Bettleheim is critical of television for children.

Lead-in:

Dr. Bettelheim points out a more serious effect of television. Children "lose the ability to learn from reality because life experiences are more complicated than the ones they see on screen, and there is no one who comes in at the end to explain it all."

Reduction   Another useful technique for reducing quotations involves using ellipsis dots. This punctuation device allows you to delete uninformative or irrelevant material by substituting three dots (. . .) to inform readers that words have been omitted. When the words omitted are those at the end of a sentence, the three dots follow a sentence period. In the Van Leunen example on page 389, for instance, we deleted this sentence: "(That's how I think knitting works.)" This parenthetical aside was unimportant so we substituted ellipses. In the following example, ellipsis dots are used to shorten a sentence:

Original quotation in source

Yet surely it takes only a little common sense to see that some sort of world history is the only way a college can do justice to students who live in a world where events in Asia, Africa, and Latin America are as likely to involve the United States in critical actions as anything happening in Europe or North America.

—*William H. McNeill, "Studying the Sweep of the Human Adventure"*

With ellipses

Yet surely . . . some sort of world history is the only way a college can do justice to students who live in a world where events in Asia, Africa, and

Latin America are as likely to involve the United States in critical actions as anything happening in Europe or North America.

Depending on your purpose, audience, and the number of other quotations in your paper, you might want to retain a sentence like McNeill's original. But you should realize that ellipsis dots can be used in this way to shorten and clarify.

When you use ellipsis dots, you should be careful not to distort the original. Such distortions occur frequently in advertisements for films, plays, books, performances, and the like. Here is an example.

Original review: The film is pretty silly, but it captures a certain scruffy, seamy side of big city life.

Ad with ellipses: The film . . . captures a certain scruffy, seamy side of big city life.

To avoid distorting quotations, copy them accurately. If you have legitimate reasons to omit words, use ellipsis dots, but make sure that the resulting sentence or paragraph accurately reflects the meaning intended by the author you are quoting.

In using ellipsis dots, follow these guidelines:

1.   For an omission *within* a sentence, use the ellipsis dots . . . with a space before and after each period.

2.   For an omission at the end of a sentence, use four dots, the first one closed up to the last word without a space, then the three spaced dots. . . .

Ellipsis dots are not used for an omission at the beginning of a quotation unless there might be some confusion. In this rare situation, use three spaced dots.

Additions in Brackets   Sometimes, you need to add words of your own to a quotation to clarify its meaning or explain its use. You can do so by enclosing your own addition in square brackets [ ]. For example, sometimes a quotation contains a spelling or other error. When this occurs, quote the original exactly and then place the Latin word "sic" (meaning "thus it occurred in the original") in square brackets after the error to show readers that it appeared that way in the material quoted and is not your mistake:

The young Prince of Wales wrote in his diary that he "did occasionally brake [sic] into the cabinet where liquor was kept."

A more common use of brackets is to enclose comments or other added information that might clarify a quotation for the reader. For instance, you can use brackets to insert the name of a person referred to by a pronoun:

Bate stresses that "however 'awkward' or 'strange' he [Johnson] might sometimes have seemed to others in his earlier years," the tics and convulsive movements dated from his twenties and were of psychoneurotic, not organic, origin (125).

Summary—Quotation Combination   The combination of summary and quotation consists of summarizing part and quoting part of a lengthy passage to capture its main point or flavor. This gives you the best of both worlds: You maintain the style and continuity of your own writing but provide some gems from your source. In the following example, note how the rewritten version preserves Ellen Goodman's ideas and much of her spark:

Original quotation

So, if we must have a draft registration, I would include young women as well as young men. I would include them because they can do the job. I would include them because all women must gain the status to stop as well as start wars. I would include them because it has been too easy to send men alone.

—*Ellen Goodman, "Drafting Daughters"*

Summary–quotation combination

Among others who would draft women is Ellen Goodman, who believes that they would perform well, that they should "gain the status to stop as well as to start wars," and that we should no longer rely on the easy decision to send only men.

Long Quotations   You might believe from all our warnings against long quotations and from our showing you how to shorten them that they are absolutely prohibited. Not so. You may certainly use some long quotations (more than four typed lines) from primary sources. These include such first-hand documents as diaries, letters, autobiographies, journals, interviews, or literary works (such as novels, poems, and plays).

Secondary works are usually writings about other writings. For example, Mortimer Adler's *Six Great Ideas* is a primary work, setting forth his philosophy. But a critical study of Adler's book would be a secondary work.

The decision to use a long quotation depends, of course, on your subject and purpose, but including a few long ones from primary sources can give readers a vivid sense of the person or work you are writing about. And occasionally you may find it desirable to quote a lengthy significant passage from a secondary source.

When you do insert a long quotation, be careful to use the appropriate format. In the Modern Language Association (MLA) style, which we are following in this section, such quotations are preceded by a regular double space, are themselves double spaced, and are indented ten letter spaces from the left margin but not indented on the right. (See the student example on page 425.) If the quotation consists of one complete paragraph or less from the source, you need not indent further as for a paragraph. However, if the quotation includes two or more paragraphs, indent the first line of each paragraph three additional spaces (thirteen spaces in all).

Indented quotations are not enclosed in quotation marks; the indentation serves the same purpose, showing that the material is quoted. Further, since no quotation marks enclose the quotation, any quotation marks appearing *within* it (that is, quotation marks used by the author of the source in quoting someone else) should be regular double quotation marks (") rather than the single marks (') normally used for quotations within quotations. Finally, a parenthetical citation for an indented quotation follows two spaces after the final punctuation mark rather than coming before the punctuation mark as it would in a quotation not indented.

```
It is not surprising that the philosophy expressed by

Henry David Thoreau became the credo of the 1960s

revolutionary movements:

          I heartily accept the motto—"That government is

          best which governs least"; and I should like to see

          it acted up to more rapidly and systematically.

          Carried out, it finally amounts to this, which also

          I believe—"That government is best which governs

          not at all"; and when men are prepared for it, that

          will be the best kind of government which they will

          have. Government is at best but an expedient; but

          most governments are usually, and some governments

          are sometimes, inexpedient. (6)
```

In using all the quotation techniques we have outlined—the lead-in, reduction, bracketed additions, the summary-quotation combination, and indented long quotations—remember that the goal is always the same: to weave the statements of others as smoothly as possible into the fabric of your own writing—as support, not a substitute, for your own ideas expressed in your own words. Strive for a smoothly woven texture of original and quoted material rather than a mere patchwork.

STEP 8: REVISING

You may try to perfect your blending of quotations while writing your first draft or merely insert them in place and wait to work on integrating them while you are revising. If you choose to do the latter, be sure when drafting to identify the source of each quotation by placing a note after it in parentheses so that when you have to document it you will recognize it.

Since research papers are either expository or argumentative, we suggest that, while revising, you turn to the checklists on pages 265–68 and 357–60 in the sections on these two kinds of discourse. Also, you certainly should be concerned with the major matters of organization, development of ideas, logic, and adaptation to the reader. But we want to call your attention to one special concern: continuity.

Because the research paper is usually longer than other papers and because it includes material from various sources, you may have neglected the careful linking of paragraphs and sections. Read through your paper carefully, therefore, asking yourself whether it flows smoothly. Should you add transitional paragraphs to carry the reader from point to point? Can you provide other signals that will help your readers understand how you have organized your material and what lies ahead for them? These signals provide maps, signs, and markers so that readers will know where they have been, where they are, and where they are going.

STEP 9: EDITING

Editing is the rewriting step that deals, as you know, with such matters as spelling, punctuation, word choice, and the improvement of sentences. In the research paper, there is also documentation. You may have encountered this convention in other papers, but here it is of more importance because the research paper relies heavily on source materials.

Documentation

Why do you have to document a research paper? First, you want to give credit to the persons whose words or ideas you have used. This acknowledgment not only is important for ethical reasons but also adds support and authority to your paper. Second, you want to allow readers to be able to verify the information in your paper and to learn more about some aspect of the subject if they wish. And third, by your care and concern for documenting your paper, you persuade readers to have confidence in its accuracy and thoroughness. When buying a used car from a person whose house or apartment is clean, neat, and attractive, you have confidence that the car has probably been well taken care of, too. Similarly, your readers will have confidence, because of your care in documenting sources, that you have treated your subject carefully.

Documentation includes all the information necessary to enable readers to locate the material you have used from your sources. This goal is accomplished through a system of parenthetical citations within the text, which refer to entries in a bibliographical section entitled "Works Cited" at the end of the paper. You may also add supplementary comments in the form of notes appearing just before "Works Cited." These are referred to in the text by raised numbers like this [1] right after the items in the text to which the notes apply.

One problem with documentation is that there is no single standard style for it, not even in a particular field like English or biology. But the form most frequently used in English and the other humanities is that of the Modern Language Association.

MLA Style

The documentation style of the Modern Language Association (MLA) was radically revised in 1984 and is set forth in two publications. The first, written for students, is the *MLA Handbook for Writers of Research Papers,* Second Edition, by Joseph Gibaldi and Walter S. Achtert (New York: MLA, 1984). The other, written for professional scholars, is *The MLA Style Manual* by Walter S. Achtert and Joseph Gibaldi (New York: MLA, 1985).

Parenthetical Citations When using someone else's words or ideas, you should acknowledge your source by stating the author's name and the page number in the source. Usually such citations take this form:

```
Iacocca points out that the Japanese are not only "shipping
us Toyotas . . . they're sending us unemployment" (320).
```

Readers understand from the citation that you have taken this quotation from page 320 of Iacocca's book. (Note that the parenthetical reference follows the quotation mark, contains no abbreviation "p" for page, and in turn, is followed by the appropriate sentence punctuation, usually, as here, a period.)

A number of variations exist for this standard parenthetical citation form. Here are some of the more common ones:

1. Author's name in the parentheses:

    ```
    One major American executive has complained that the
    Japanese are "sending us unemployment" (Iacocca 320).
    ```

    The author's name is not followed by a comma.

2. More than one author:
    a. Authors cited in text:

    ```
    Seager and Olsen make the point that women have held the
    top political position in other countries, but not in the
    United States (82-85).
    ```

    b. Authors cited in the parentheses:

    ```
    Women have held the top political position in other
    countries, but not in the United States (Seager and Olsen
    82-85).
    ```

If there are more than three authors, use the last name of the first author and the Latin abbreviation "et al.," which means "and others," for example, (Tillotson et al. 2222).

3. Title and author in text:

> In <u>A Celebration of Cats</u>, the definitive book about felines,
> Roger A. Caras observes that cats have never been as popular
> as they are today (167).

Use the title only if you consider it important. It is not essential in a citation (except in the situations described in 4 and 5 below).

4. Author of more than one source:

> In the central episode of the novel, a man performs a
> Caesarean on his wife without anesthesia (Everett,
> <u>Cutting</u> 1-7).

The title, shortened to its first significant word or phrase, must be included if the same author has written another work cited in the paper. Observe the comma after Everett's name.

5. Reference to anonymous work:

> Inexperienced canoers and kayakers will find that their
> crafts are available in a wide range of materials and prices
> ("Float Yourself a Holiday" 106).

A brief title such as this needn't be shortened (see comment on 4 above).

6. Reference to volume number:

> The ethical, religious, medical, psychology, social,
> economic, political, educational, and sociological
> aspects of happiness and pleasure are briefly discussed
> (Wiener, 2: 374-87).

With author's name in the preceding text, the form would be (2: 374-87).

7. Reference to a work appearing on nonconsecutive pages:

> In her article, "When It's Your Turn to Be the Boss," Jane
> Ciabattani offers sound advice to working women (109-14,
> 138-9).

These seven examples should help you with most of the parenthetical references you will use in your research paper. If they do not provide a model for all of them, consult either the *MLA Handbook* or *The MLA Style Manual* in your library for dozens of additional examples.

A final reminder: A parenthetical citation for a quotation appears after the closing quotation marks and before the appropriate sentence punctuation. A comma appears in a parenthetical citation only to separate an author's name from the title of a work or to separate nonconsecutive pages (see examples 4 and 7).

Raised Numbers and Endnotes   Sometimes in a research paper you may want to add information that might be unimportant to most readers but significant to some and that would interfere with the flow of your text if it were included there. Instead of presenting this information within the body of your paper, you may add it in a "Notes" section just before the bibliography ("Works Cited") at the end of the paper (see page 433) and indicate its presence there by using a superscript, or raised, number like this.[1]

Works Cited   As we have seen, citations in the text of your paper usually include only the author's name and the page number. How then can readers check your source? They can do so easily by turning to the end of your paper, where the "Works Cited" section furnishes a bibliography of all the works you have used. Note that it does not include other works, such as those you have consulted casually or ones that you have not used but might wish to list to impress your instructor. It includes only those sources referred to in your paper.

The "Works Cited" section consists of a separate page or pages, numbered in sequence with the rest of the paper, with the title "Works Cited" centered at the top (see page 434). The first alphabetized entry begins two lines below, flush with the left margin. If the entry is longer than one line, indent the second and subsequent lines five spaces from the left margin. Double-space the entire list, both between entries and within them.

Alphabetize the entries by the author's last name or, if the author is not indicated, by the first word of the title, ignoring the initial words *A, An,* and *The.* For example: "The Brightest and Closest Supernova" would be listed under the "B's," not the "T's."

The entries for your sources must follow the prescribed forms exactly. Since so many different elements are involved for different kinds of sources, we suggest that you avoid trying to memorize all the forms. Instead open this book to an appropriate model and adapt your entry to it.

For your ease in locating these models, we have arranged them in five categories: I. Books; II. Parts of Books; III. Periodicals (journals, magazines, and newspapers); IV. Other Printed Sources; and V. Nonprint Sources.

I. Books   The entry for most books has three parts—author, title, and publication information—each ending in a period and separated from the following by two spaces. The name of the publisher is shortened (see Figure 21-1). Here is an example of a basic entry.

Basic entry: a book by one author

Caras, Roger A. <u>A Celebration of Cats</u>. New York: Simon, 1986.

Observe the punctuation and spacing carefully: a period followed by two spaces between the main parts, and a period at the end; in the publication data, a colon and space between the place of publication and the name of the publisher, and a comma and space between the publisher and the date of publication.

Figure 21-1. Selected Shortened Forms of Publisher's Names

Appleton	Appleton-Century-Crofts
Barnes	Barnes and Noble Books
Columbia UP	Columbia University Press
Dell	Dell Publishing Co., Inc.
Doubleday	Doubleday and Co., Inc.
Farrar	Farrar, Straus, and Giroux, Inc.
GPO	Government Printing Office
Harcourt	Harcourt Brace Jovanovich, Inc.
Harvard UP	Harvard University Press
Heath	D. C. Heath and Co.
Holt	Holt, Rinehart, and Winston, Inc.
Houghton	Houghton Mifflin Co.
Knopf	Alfred A. Knopf, Inc.
Lippincott	J. B. Lippincott Co.
Little	Little, Brown, and Co.
Macmillan	Macmillan Publishing Co., Inc.
NAL	The New American Library, Inc.
Norton	W.W. Norton and Co., Inc.
Oxford UP	Oxford University Press, Inc.
Penguin	Penguin Books, Inc.
Prentice	Prentice-Hall, Inc.
Random	Random House, Inc.
St. Martin's	St. Martin's Press, Inc.
Scribner's	Charles Scribner's Sons
U of Chicago P	University of Chicago Press
Viking	The Viking Press, Inc.
Yale UP	Yale University Press

A. A book by two or three authors

Coles, Robert, and Jane Hallowell Coles. <u>Women of Crisis II: Lives</u>

> <u>of Work and Dreams</u>. New York: Dell, 1980.

Follow the order of names used on the title page of the book; reverse the name of only the first author. Also, give each author's name exactly as it appears on the title page; never abbreviate a name that is spelled out, and use initials if they are used on the title page.

B. A book by more than three authors; a revised edition

Blum, John M., et al. <u>The National Experience</u>. 6th ed. San Diego:

> Harcourt, 1985.

This book has six authors: Blum, McFeely, Morgan, Schlesinger, Stampp, and Woodward. Note that the added information about the particular edition is set off by a period and two spaces like the other major elements of the entry.

C. Anthology or compilation (book of collected works)

Anderson, Thayle K., and Kent Forrester, eds. <u>Point Counterpoint:</u>

> <u>Eight Cases for Composition</u>. San Diego, Harcourt, 1987.

For one editor, use "ed." rather than "eds." For the place of publication, use the first city given on the title page (or the following page) of the work. Many publishers have offices in several cities and list all of these in their books.

D. Two or more books by the same author or editor

Everett, Percival. <u>Cutting Lisa</u>. New York: Ticknor, 1986.

———. <u>Walk Me to the Distance</u>. New York: Tickno, 1984.

Hall, Donald. <u>Fathers Playing Catch with Sons: Essays on Sport (Mostly</u>

> <u>Baseball</u>). Berkeley: North Point, 1985.

———, ed. <u>The Oxford Book of American Literary Anecdotes</u>.

> New York: Oxford UP, 1981.

In listing two or more works by the same person (whether author or editor), give the person's name only in the first entry, and substitute three closed-up hyphens for the name in subsequent entries. Use a period (or, for an editor, a comma) after the hyphens exactly as you would after the name. List the person's books in alphabetical order by title. (Note in the second Hall entry how "University Press" is abbreviated.)

E. Book by a corporate author

Consumers Union. <u>Consumer Reports: 1987 Buying Guide</u>. Mt. Vernon:
Consumers Union, 1988.

F. Volume in a work of several individually titled volumes

Churchill, Winston S. <u>The Birth of Britain</u>. New York: Dodd, 1956.
Vol 1 of <u>A History of the English-Speaking Peoples</u>. 4 Vols.
1956-58.

G. Authored book with an editor or translator

Auden, W. H. <u>Collected Poems</u>. Ed. Edward Mendelson. New York: Random,
1976.

Proust, Marcel. <u>Swann's Way</u>. Trans. C. K. Scott Moncrieff. New York:
Random, 1928.

H. Paperback reprint

Hemingway, Ernest. <u>The Sun Also Rises</u>. 1926. New York: Scribner's,
1970.

The publication date of the original edition, 1926, is given after the title. All the
other information refers to the paperback reprint.

I. Book in a series

Fielding, Henry. <u>Tom Jones</u>. Ed. Sheridan Baker. Norton Critical
Editions. New York: Norton, 1973.

II. Parts of Books

J. Selection in an anthology

Young, Richard. "Invention: A Topographical Survey."
<u>Teaching Composition: 10 Bibliographical Essays</u>. Ed. Gary
Tate. Fort Worth: Texas Christian UP, 1976. 1-43.

Give the selection author's name, the title of the selection, and then the title
of the anthology, its editor, and the facts of its publication. Note that the pages
on which the selection appears are given at the end.

```
Derrida, Jacques.  "Force and Signification."  Writing and
     Difference.  Trans. Alan Bass.  Chicago: U of Chicago P, 1978.
     3-30.
```

Bass has translated this book of essays by Derrida.

K. Introduction, preface, foreword, or afterword

```
Hough, Graham.  Afterword.  Emma.  By Jane Austen.  New York: NAL, 1964.
     387-96.
```

The author and title of the part being cited appear first, followed by the title of the book, the name of the author of the book, and the publication data.

L. Article in a reference book

```
"Hess, Rudolph."  New Columbia Encyclopedia.  1975 ed.
```

Do not cite the editor of a reference work. When the articles are arranged alphabetically, do not include a page number and volume number.

III. Periodicals

M. Article in a journal with continuous pagination
A journal is a scholarly periodical, in contrast to a magazine, which is aimed at a nonscholarly audience and usually lacks documentation. A journal with continuous pagination is one that continues to number its pages throughout the year instead of starting each issue with page 1.

```
Keskinen, Kenneth.  "'Shooting an Elephant'—An Essay to Teach."
     English Journal 55 (1966): 669-75.
```

Like a book entry, the entry for an article begins with the name of the author, followed by the article's title. (In this example, observe that the article's title, enclosed in double quotation marks ("), happens to include another title, that of the essay the article is about. The essay title, therefore, is enclosed within single quotation marks (') as a title within a title.) Next write the name of the periodical, omitting initial words *A, An,* or *The.* Then comes the volume number, which is useful in locating the article in bound library volumes of the periodical. Finally, after a space, give the year of the publication in parentheses, followed by a colon, a space, and all the article's page numbers, not just the pages you used.

N. Article in a journal that paginates each issue separately

```
Clark, Thomas D.  "The Book Thieves of Lexington: A Reminiscence."
     Kentucky Review 5.2 (1984): 27-45.
```

Instead of just writing the volume number (5), add the issue number (2), separated from the volume by a period.

O. Article from a weekly or biweekly magazine

```
Adler, Jerry.  "Every Parent's Nightmare."  Newsweek 16 Mar.
     1987: 57-61.
```

Note that a complete date is given, the day appearing before the month. The names of all months except May, June, and July are abbreviated. No volume or issue number is necessary.

P. Article from a monthly or bimonthly periodical

```
Hitchens, Christopher. "Blabscam: TV's Rigged Political Talk Shows."
     Harper's Mar. 1987: 75-76.
```

Give the month and year without commas.

Q. Newspaper article

```
Geist, William E.  "Magazine Chaos: From Hot Tubs to Talking Birds."
     New York Times 20 May 1987, late ed.: B1.
```

Give the name of the newspaper, omitting the initial words *A, An,* or *The.* If the name does not include the city of publication, place it in square brackets after the name: *Courier Journal* [Louisville, KY]. The date is followed by the edition if applicable. (Most large daily newspapers issue several editions, moving or deleting certain articles to make room for others. Finally, a section designation appears either as part of the page number, as in this example, or before it with a colon: Sec. 2: 1.

R. Anonymous article

```
"Move Your IRA's As Often As You Like." Business Week 23 Feb. 1987:
     150.
```

S. Letter to the editor

```
Wayne H. Davis.  Letter.  Lexington Herald Leader 14 Mar. 1987, A23.
```

T. A review

Daniel Okrent. Rev. of Hardball: The Education of a Baseball
        Commissioner, by Bowie Kuhn. New York Times Book Review 8 Mar.
        1987: 11.

IV. Other Printed Sources

U. Pamphlet

Editors, Prevention Total Health System. Easing Aches and Pains.
        Emmaus: Rodale, 1986.

A pamphlet is treated the same way as a book.

V. Government publication

United States. Attorney General's Commission on Pornography.
        Final Report of the Attorney General's Commission on
        Pornography. Washington: GPO, 1986.

If the author is known, give that person's name first. Otherwise, begin with the
name of the government (national, state, or local), then (after a period and two
spaces) the name of the specific agency or department issuing the publication.

V. Nonprint Sources

W. Radio and television programs

Country Music Legends. PBS. KET, Lexington, KY. 12 Mar. 1987.

This is the basic entry: underlined program title, network, local station and its city,
provide state only to avoid confusion and broadcast date.

George Eliot. Silas Marner. With Ben Kingsley. Masterpiece Theatre.
        Introd. Alistair Cooke. PBS. KET, Lexington, KY. 23 Mar. 1987.

A series title appears after a program title. The title of a specific episode of *Silas
Marner* would have appeared in quotation marks before that program title. The
author's name is listed first only if the particular author is being emphasized, as in a
paper on George Eliot; otherwise, the author's name would follow the program
title like this:

<u>Silas Marner</u>.   By George Eliot.   With Ben Kingsley.   Masterpiece

     Theatre.   Introd. Alistair Cooke.   PBS.   KET, Lexington, KY.

     23 Mar. 1987.

As with the authorship, if the work of a particular director, producer, narrator, etc. is being emphasized, that information would precede the program (or episode) title. And such information can also be added after the title, in the order that best reflects the desired emphasis.

X. Film

<u>Platoon</u>.   Dir. Oliver Stone.   Orion, 1987.

This is the basic film entry: title, director, distributor, date.

Allen, Woody, writer, dir. <u>Hannah and Her Sisters</u>.   With Mia Farrow,

     Woody Allen, and Michael Caine.   Orion, 1986.

For special purposes, other film information may be added as in this example.

Y. Interview

Rapley, Gay.   Personal interview.   July 17, 1987.

For personal interviews, first give the name of the person interviewed, then the kind of interview (telephone, personal), and the date.

Z. Lectures, speeches

Jansen, William.   "The Rationale for the Dirty Joke."

     Distinguished Lecture Series, Arts & Sciences College,

     U of Kentucky.   Lexington, KY. 17 Apr. 1976.

Provide the speaker's name; title of the lecture and, if pertinent, the occasion; the sponsoring organization or institution; the city; and the date.

    As mentioned previously, this lengthy list does not include examples of all the kinds of sources. For others, see either the *MLA Handbook* or *The MLA Style Manual* in your library.

APA Style

    The documentation style most widely used in the social sciences—and it is very similar to the style used in many natural sciences—is that of the American Psychological Association (APA), set forth in the *Publication Manual of the American Psychological Association,* 3rd ed., 1983. If you have been using the MLA system in some of your courses, you need to be aware that there are important differences in the two documentation styles and you therefore need to check the examples carefully. In your English composition classes, you will probably use APA only when writing papers that are interdisciplinary. In the following discussion, we have concentrated on those documentation devices most frequently needed in undergraduate papers.

Parenthetical Citations

1. Author's name in the sentence

        Bettleheim (1987) stresses the importance of play in the lives

        of children.

Because the date of publication is almost always significant to scientists who look for the latest research, the year appears immediately after the author's name.

2. Author's name in the parentheses

        Leadership techniques for women managers are emphasized

        (Ciabattari, 1987, pp. 109-114).

The author's name, year of publication, and, if pertinent, page numbers all appear in the parentheses and are separated by commas. Note also that APA citations use "p." or "pp." before page numbers. In inclusive page numbers, all digits are given.

3. Two or more authors' names in parentheses

        The study was conducted in a psychiatric hospital (Zigler &

        Phillips, 1961, pp. 63-69).

APA style uses the ampersand (&) before the name of the last author. In citing books with six or more authors, the first author is mentioned and then followed by the abbreviated "et al." With books having three to five authors, all the names are given for the first citation, and subsequent citations are abbreviated as above: first author, et al.

4. Two works published in the same year by one author

        Bettelheim (1987a and 1987b) has written extensively about the

        importance of play in children's development.

Use small letters (a, b, c) after the year to identify the different sources. Follow this system in the "References" (bibliography) as well as in the in-text citations.

5. Direct quotation or paraphrase

```
Another consumer expert advocates buying used cars, pointing
out "the overall savings—in purchase price, insurance,
financing, operating costs, and depreciation. . . ."
(Tobias, 1987, p. 5).
```

As with MLA style, the parenthetical citation follows the quotation and is in turn followed by the sentence period.

References   The bibliographical section in APA style is called "References" and is similar to the MLA form illustrated in the student example. Here are some significant conventions of APA style that you need to be aware of as you prepare your bibliography.

1. *Indentation*   The second and subsequent lines of an entry are indented three spaces from the beginning of the first line.

2. *Author's names*   The names of all authors are inverted (last name first) with initials used for first names. All the authors' names are given, regardless of the number. Do not use the abbreviation "et al." allowed with in-text citations.

3. *Titles*   In titles of articles and books, only the first word is capitalized. (If there is a subtitle, its first word is also capitalized.) Quotation marks are not used for article titles.

4. *Publication dates*   The year of publication, enclosed with parentheses, immediately follows the last author's name and is followed by a period: Coles, J.H. (1980). If the month and day are pertinent, they are handled thus: Chiles, J.R. (1984, March 10).

5. *Pages*   "Page" and "pages" are abbreviated as "p." and "pp." when citing newspaper and magazine articles or anthology selections: pp. 65–70. With articles from professional journals, however, the abbreviation is omitted. (See page 416, entry N.)

6. *Journal volumes*   Volume numbers of journals are underlined; issue numbers (if any) follow in parentheses without an intervening space: *5* or *5*(2).

7. *Multiple works*   If two or more works by the same author are listed, the author's name is repeated for each work. The works are arranged in order of publication date, rather than alphabetically by title, as is otherwise the case. (See page 414, entry D.)

The following examples, used in the section on MLA style on pages 404–11, are converted to APA style. If necessary, you may want to compare the differences.

I. Books   The basic entry for books consists of the author and date, the title, and the place of publication and publisher.

Basic entry: a book by one author

Caras, R. A. (1986). A celebration of cats. New York: Simon.

A. A book by two or three authors

Coles, R., & Coles, J. H. (1980). Women of crisis II: Lives of work and
    dreams. New York: Dell.

Both names are inverted, and only first initials are used. The first word of the
subtitle, as well as of the title, is capitalized.

B. A book by more than three authors; a revised edition

Blum, J. M., McFeely, W. S., Morgan, E. S., Schlesinger A. M., Jr.,
    Stampp, K. M., & Woodward, C. V. (1985). The national experience
    (5th ed.). San Diego: Harcourt.

See the discussion in item 2 on page 413. Example B shows also how "Jr." is
handled when names are inverted.

C. Anthology or compilation (book of collected works)

Anderson, T. K., & Forrester, K. (Eds.). (1987). Point counterpoint:
    Eight cases for composition. San Diego: Harcourt.

D. Two or more books by the same author or editor

Everett, P. (1984). Walk me to the distance. New York: Ticknor.

Everett, P. (1986). Cutting Lisa. New York: Ticknor.

Hall, D. (Ed.). (1981). The Oxford book of American literary
    anecdotes. New York: Oxford University Press.

Hall, D. (1985). Fathers playing catch with sons: Essays on sport
    (mostly baseball). Berkeley: North Point.

"Lisa" in the second title by Everett is capitalized only because it is a proper name,
as are "Oxford" and "American" in the first title by Hall. Names of university
presses are spelled out.

E. Book by a corporate author

Consumers Union. (1988). Consumer Reports: 1987 buying guide.
    Mt. Vernon, NY: Author.

Corporate authors are alphabetized by the first significant word of the name, and the name is not inverted. When author and publisher are the same, use the word "Author" as the name of the publisher. In the title, "Reports" is capitalized only because "Consumer Reports" is the name of a magazine and names of magazines and journals (unlike titles of books) have all significant words capitalized. Place of publication includes state abbreviation if city may not be well known.

F. Volume in a work of several individually titled volumes

Churchill, W. S. (1956). <u>A history of the English-speaking peoples:</u>
   <u>Vol. 1. The birth of Britain</u>. New York: Dodd.

G. Authored book with an editor or translator

Auden, W. H. (1976). <u>Collected poems</u> (Edward Mendelson, Ed.).
   New York: Random.

Proust, M. (1928). <u>Swann's way</u> (C. K. Scott Moncrieff, Trans.).
   New York: Random.

H. Paperback reprint

Hemingway, E. (1970). <u>The sun also rises</u>. New York: Scribner's.
   (Original work published 1926)

I. Book in a series

Fielding, H. (1973). <u>Tom Jones</u> (Sheridan Baker, Ed.). New York:
   Norton/Norton Critical Editions. (Original work published 1749)

II. Parts of Books

J. Selection in an anthology

Young, Richard. (1976). Invention: A topographical survey. In G. Tate
   (Ed.), <u>Teaching composition: 10 bibliographical essays</u>.
   (pp. 1-43). Fort Worth, TX: Texas Christian University Press.

Derrida, J. (1978). Force and signification. <u>Writing and difference</u>
   (Alan Bass, Trans.). Chicago: University of Chicago Press.

The editor's and translator's names are inverted only when in the author position (compare item C, page 414).

K. Introduction, preface, foreword, or afterword

Hough, G. (1964). Afterword. In J. Austen, <u>Emma</u>. New York: NAL,
   387–396.

L. Article in a reference book

Hess, Rudolph. (1975). [Entry in] <u>New Columbia encyclopedia</u>.

III. Periodicals

M. Article in a journal with continuous pagination

Keskinen, K. (1966). Shooting an elephant—An essay to teach.
   <u>English Journal</u>, <u>55</u>, 669–675.

N. Article in a journal that paginates each issue separately

Clark, T. D. (1984). The book thieves of Lexington: A reminiscence.
   <u>Kentucky Review</u>, <u>5</u>(2), 27–45.

Only when each issue of a journal begins on page 1 (separate pagination), the issue
number appears in parentheses immediately after volume number.

O. Article from a weekly or biweekly magazine

Adler, J. (1987, March 16). Every parent's nightmare. <u>Newsweek</u>,
   pp. 57–61.

P. Article from a monthly or bimonthly periodical

Hitchens, C. (1987, March). Blabscam: TV's rigged political talk
   shows. <u>Harper's</u>, pp. 75–76.

Q. Newspaper article

Geist, W. E. (1987, May 20, Late ed.). Magazine chaos: From hot tubs
   to talking birds. <u>The New York Times</u>, p. B1.

Edition of newspaper goes with date. Complete names of periodicals are given,
including introductory *A, An, or The.*

R. Anonymous article

Move your IRA's as often as you like. (1987, February 23).
 <u>Business Week</u>, p. 150.

S. Letter to the editor

Davis, W. H. (1987, March 14). [Letter to the editor]. <u>Lexington</u>
 <u>Herald Leader</u>, p. A23.

Descriptive information added rather than quoted is placed in square brackets, with a period after closing bracket.

T. A review.

Okrent, D. (1987, March 8). [Review of <u>Hardball: The education of a</u>
 <u>baseball commissioner</u>]. <u>The New York Times Book Review</u>, p. 11.

IV. *Other Printed Sources*

U. Pamphlet

Prevention Total Health System. (1986). <u>Easing aches and pains</u>.
 Emmaus, PA: Rodale.

V. Government publication

United States. Attorney General's Commission on Pornography. (1986).
 <u>Final report of the Attorney General's Commission on Pornography</u>.
 Washington, DC: U. S. Government Printing Office.

Name of larger agency (in this case, United States) need be given only if the agency may not be well known to readers.

V. *Nonprint Sources*

W. Radio and television programs

Lickona, T. (Producer), & Menotti, G. (Director). (1987, March 12).
 <u>Country music legends</u> [Television broadcast]. Public
 Broadcasting System. KET, Lexington, KY.

Marks, L. (Producer), & Foster, G. (Director). (1987,

    March 23). <u>Silas Marner</u> [Television broadcast]. <u>Masterpiece</u>

    <u>Theatre</u>. Public Broadcasting System. KET, Lexington, KY.

The medium is specified in square brackets immediately after the title. Producer and director are the standard information required; other information such as actors involved, is worked into the text and omitted from "References" in APA style.

X. Film

Koppelson, A. (Producer), & Stone, O. (Director). (1987). <u>Platoon</u>.

    Orion Films.

Greenhut, R. (Producer), & Allen, W. (Writer and director).

    (1986). <u>Hannah and her sisters</u>. Orion Films.

Y. Interview

Rapley, G. (1987, July 17). [Unpublished personal interview].

Z. Lectures, speeches

Jansen, W. (1976, April 17). <u>The rationale for the dirty joke</u>. Lecture

    delivered in Distinguished Lecture Series, Arts and Sciences

    College, University of Kentucky, Lexington, KY.

At first reading, all these conventions may seem complicated. They are. But they have been designed to enable readers to obtain maximum information in minimum space and at the same time to avoid distracting readers who are not curious about sources. Just as baseball, backgammon, or bridge might have seemed impossible to understand when you first started to play but proved easier afterward, so, with practice, documentation makes more sense and gets simpler. You need not memorize or guess about documentation form. There is little excuse for errors except laziness or the unwillingness to look up the proper form.

Now it's time to move on to the next step in writing the research paper.

STEP 10: WRITING THE FINAL DRAFT

Three matters may be left for the final draft: the title, the title page (if any), and the final outline. This is not to say that these may not be attended to earlier if you wish, just that they may be postponed.

The Title

Although a research paper consists of a serious, scholarly investigation of a subject, it need not have a deadly title. Everyone enjoys a touch of wit, as in the following titles:

Fish, Stanley. <u>Is There a Text in This Class? The Authority of Interpretive Communities.</u> Cambridge: Harvard UP, 1980.

Juhasz, Susanne. "'Some Deep Old Desk or Capacious Hold-All': Form and Women's Autobiography." <u>College English</u> 39 (1978): 664–68.

Strasser, Susan. <u>Never Done: A History of American Housework.</u> New York: Pantheon, 1982.

The Title Page

In these days, with everyone trying to economize, it is natural that title pages, like free service station maps, should disappear. And so they have—MLA style no longer calls for one—as the first page of the research paper on page 424 will reveal. But we're old-fashioned enough to like them, and your instructor may be also, because they dress up a paper, giving it a touch of elegance. If you'd like to use one and know your instructor would not object, here's a form you can follow. The type is centered on the page both horizontally and vertically.

```
            Women Should Heed the Call to Arms

                     Becky Naser




                     English 105-6

              Ms. Dee Goertz, Instructor

                   17 January 1988
```

Notice that the title is in capital and lowercase letters (not underlined) and does not end with a period. Also, the title should be repeated at the top of the first manuscript page.

Although we think that a title page dresses up a paper and makes it look more attractive, your instructor may prefer that you omit it. In that event, include at the top of your first page the information shown in Figure 21-2, carefully observing the prescribed spacing, use of capital and small letters, and so forth.

Figure 21-2. Heading for First Page of Research Paper

```
Becky Naser

Ms. Dee Goertz, Instructor

English 105-6

17 January 1988
            Women Should Heed the Call to Arms


     Equal rights for women were set back when the Equal
Rights Amendment was not passed in June 1982, but equal
opportunities may be just around the corner.
```

The Final Outline

Some instructors may request that you hand in a formal outline with your final paper. This outline consists mainly of a revision of your preliminary outline. Be sure, however, that any changes you have made between your preliminary investigation and your completed paper are reflected in this outline.

STEP 11: PROOFREADING

You have put so much time and effort into your paper that you should proofread it carefully to avoid letting it be spoiled by careless mistakes. Plan to spend at least an hour or two to check for typing errors, to search for faulty notes and bibliographical entries, and to find the dozens of other things that can go wrong in a paper of this length. Patience in proofreading is a virtue. Practice it.

FINAL WORDS

We have treated this subject as completely as we think is necessary for most undergraduate research papers that you may write in English, economics, history, sociology, anthropology, political science, nursing, education, and other classes. But as graduate students, you may be required to follow some practices omitted or presented differently here.

The following student research paper should help you figure out how to deal with some typographical and other matters not specifically covered in this chapter. Refer to the paper as you write your first and final drafts. What we particularly like is that it is not cluttered with too many quotations as so many student papers are. As this statement implies, you should know your subject so well, have digested all the information so thoroughly, and be so filled with ideas about it that you can write freely without relying constantly on the words of others.

When you write "Notes" and "Works Cited," take care. A research paper, like a formal wedding ceremony, is steeped in tradition and protocol that must be followed to the letter. You may not like either, but you should show respect for both. Both are ceremonies of seriousness and importance that have evolved over the years. And despite the inconvenience they impose, both when completed bring joy, pleasure, and satisfaction.

The task of writing a research paper is demanding, but the achievement is fulfilling.

STUDENT RESEARCH PAPER

```
Becky Naser

Ms. Dee Goertz, Instructor

English 105-6

17 January 1988

                    Outline


Thesis: Women should select careers in the military.

    I. Women have a choice of many careers in the armed

       forces.

       A. Of 360 Army job categories, only 61 are

          unavailable to women.

       B. Of 230 Air Force job categories, only 4 are

          unavailable to women.

       C. Of 100 Navy job categories, only 14 are

          unavailable to women.

       D. The Marines, however, almost entirely a combat

          force, exclude women from 90 percent of

          occupations.

   II. The growing presence of women in the armed forces

       has dispelled several myths about women.

       A. Women are not more vulnerable to emotional

          breakdowns or suicides than men.

       B. Women do not have less stamina than men.
```

    C. Though women have less upper-body strength than men, they have greater dexterity and perceptual skills.

    D. There is little if any difference in leadership ability between men and women.

    E. The presence of women in a military unit need not adversely affect its field performance.

III. Women will encounter some disadvantages in the services.

    A. Women are more subject to sexual harassment.

    B. Women are not promoted as quickly as men.

    C. These disadvantages are also found in business, industry, and the professions.

 IV. The armed services offer college women attractive opportunities.

    A. Scholarships are available for up to four years.

    B. For non-scholarship winners, subsistence may be obtained for two years.

    C. Women are guaranteed a career with living expenses all paid.

    D. Women have an opportunity to serve their country.

Becky Naser   1

Ms. Dee Goertz, Instructor

English 105-6

17 January 1988

                Women Should Heed the Call to Arms

        Equal rights for women were set back when the
Equal Rights Amendment failed in June 1982, but
equal opportunities may be just around the corner.
Women are taking their place as surgeons, truck
drivers, astronauts, executives, lawyers,
accountants, postal carriers, and coal miners.
Indeed, today's women have a choice. They can
either opt for careers in the working world or they
can become mothers and homemakers. Often, they do
both.

        The mother of today's college student did not
have such a choice. Often she went to college to
earn her MRS degree rather than prepare for a
profession. Even though marriage may still be in
the picture, her daughter usually has different
ideas: she is interested in a career. She sees
herself as part of a new society in which women are
taking their place alongside men in nearly all
occupations, many formerly reserved only for men.

Naser 2

One occupational area which women generally overlook, however, is the military. To be sure, there are women in the armed services, but their numbers are relatively small. Yet there are many opportunities for women.

To show what women can do, let us look at their present military jobs. Robert Dudney and Jeff Trimble note that the Army has 380 job categories, only 61 of them unavailable to women, mainly because of the possibility of danger (30). Although no one can ensure that rear-line troops will be able to avoid casualties in future wars, Congress has decreed that women should not serve in combat and should not be stationed where there is an imminent possibility of danger.[1] And so reasonable precautions are taken to protect women. Consequently, emotional arguments like those raised by Eliot A. Cohen in the following questions should be ignored:

> What will Americans feel when they see on television mangled female corpses on the battlefield, when they welcome home the first female casualties who have had their faces sheared off by shell fragments, or when they read the first reports of the rape of female soldiers and the fates of their infants in prisoner of war camps? (38)

Lead-in and summary of quotation.

Raised-number reference to explanatory note.

Lengthy quotation indented 10 spaces; page reference two spaces after end punctuation.

Naser 3

Instead of being assigned to Army combat units, women are placed in combat support and combat service units. These are usually in divisions, which include maintenance battalions, missile and signal battalions, brigade level headquarters, and artillery units. Among other specific jobs that women perform are the driving and repairing of trucks and other heavy equipment and the maintenance of helicopters.

In this last position, women may come close to danger, as illustrated by the assignment of Captain Hope Jones, who was stationed at Palmerola in Honduras, "the closest thing to an active-duty base in Central America" ("Highest-Pressure Job" 38). There she commanded forty-five officers, many older than her 26 years, and supervised the maintenance of forty-five planes. Although assigned to this combat unit as support personnel, she once copiloted an Army recovery mission. In view of her work, she feels that the "Army ought to let women take the full responsibilities and risks any man is permitted."

In the Air Force, women serve in all but four of 230 positions. Among their many other jobs, women maintain aircraft, fly giant transport planes, and

Effective use of summary-quotation.

Anonymous article.

Source of quotation obvious.

Naser 4

serve with units responsible for intercontinental
ballistic missiles (Dudney and Trimble 32).

No need to repeat previous lead-in reference.

Like the Army and Air Force, the Navy is
restricted from exposing women to combat. So women
are not assigned to combat ships, such as carriers,
or to other vessels, such as oilers, that might be
in combat areas. However, women perform valuable
services on non-combat vessels such as destroyer
tenders, tugs, and hospital ships. Overall, women
in the Navy are eligible for 86 out of a possible
100 jobs (Dudney and Trimble 33).

Because the Marines are primarily a combat
service, women are restricted from 96 percent of
marine occupations. No unit of the Marine Corps is
allowed to contain more than 10 percent women
(Dudney and Trimble 33). Yet women do play an
important role in the Marines, and one woman Marine,
Gail Reals, was recently promoted to the rank of
brigadier general ("One Good Woman" 33). Although
she is the only woman who is a senior ranking Marine
officer, she joins eleven other female generals and
admirals in the armed forces.

Summary of anonymous article.

The growing presence of women in the military
services has dispelled several myths about them.
One former belief was that women are more vulnerable
to emotional disorders than men. However, Norma
Scott Kinzer, military personnel expert and

Naser 5

sociologist, claims that no verifiable studies exist
to prove that women in the military have a higher
rate of emotional breakdowns or suicides than men
("Interview" 34). She states that the idea of
women's being emotional comes from their greater
willingness to seek psychiatric help. She also
claims that because women are more open about
discussing their emotions, they are better prepared
to handle "the psychological pressures of active
noncombat participation in the war effort" (34).
These conclusions are supported by Kinzer's
references to U.S. Army Research Institute studies
showing that under simulated combat conditions,
women performed as well as men.

Another myth has been that women lack physical
stamina. But the services have learned that stamina
"depends on the individual's strength, not the
individual's sex" ("No 'Special Stresses'" 34). In
addition, Ellen C. Collier points that women will
not have to compete on the male level of physical
ability (4). Different criteria for physical
ability have been established for the two sexes by
the armed forces, and women are tested and assigned
to occupations accordingly.

Furthermore, though women may lack upper-body
strength, they compensate for it with other skills.

**Short title of
anonymous article i
"Interview."**

**Effective use of
summary-quotation**

**Quotation from
anonymous article.**

Naser 6

In areas requiring dexterity or perceptual skills, women actually outperform their male counterparts (Collier 5). Obviously, women are not equal to men in all skills and qualifications. In many instances, men are more suited to combat roles because of their physical strength. But women have other skills that are useful to the military; for example, a study of leadership ability at West Point showed that the differences between the sexes "was not great" (Rice et al. 896).

However, some questions have been raised about how the presence of women affects the performance of a military unit. The Army Research Institute, after studying mixed-gender units, has concluded that "the number of women in an Army unit has no impact on its performance in field exercises" (Shapely 16). Units with women performed as well as, if not better than, those without.

Although the armed forces are accepting greater numbers of women, and are realizing their potential to a greater extent, there are some disadvantages for women serving in the military. First is the problem of sexual harassment.

According to Levin and Miller-Goeder, sexual harassment accounts for the lower reenlistment rate of women, only 56 percent of them signing up for

Use "et al." for work by four or more authors.

Conclusion quoted from Shapely.

Lead-in with two authors.

Naser 7

additional service in the Army as opposed to
77 percent of the men (14). These writers claim
that this is a significant loss because women are
excellent soldiers, being "better behaved, more
polite, and more submissive to authority" while
female recruits are "typically more intelligent and
better trained" than their male counterparts (15).
Although Levin and Miller-Goeder admit that progress
against sexual harassment has been made, they doubt
that there will be a profound change in overcoming
the "fishbowl syndrome" (15).

They may be right. However, a study by Harold
E. Cheatham at the Coast Guard Academy suggests that
as men become more accustomed to working with women
in their military units, the men will accept them
more and harass them less (152). Cheatham found
that male attitudes at the Academy became more
positive since the first class of women was admitted
in 1976. (It must be granted, however, that men at
the Academy are selected for their officer potential
and so are better educated than average soldiers and
sailors in the enlisted ranks.)

Another problem involves the difficulty of
women's being promoted to top positions because the
military chiefly rewards individuals who are
directly involved in combat. The armed forces exist

Good use of
summary-quotation.

Naser 8

to wage war.   Those who are mainly engaged in this activity on the battlefields and on combat ships will naturally be rewarded better and faster than those who are occupied with relatively safe, noncombat assignments.   Thus men move faster through the ranks and into higher positions than women, as is illustrated by the example of Carolyn and Robert Deal, a husband-and-wife team in the Navy ("Officer and a Woman" 43).   Although she outranked him when they married, his career is on a faster track now because of his combat-related duty.

Reference to anonymous article.

But both of these problems--sexual harassment and the difficulty of obtaining promotions to top positions--are problems that women also experience in business and in many other fields. As men become more accustomed to working with women, it is reasonable to expect that these problems will decrease in civilian occupations, and so may they in the military.

Social change comes slowly, but it comes.   It will come in the armed forces in time.   Despite some disadvantages, which are also prevalent in business, industry, and the professions, the military offers many opportunities to women today.

Naser 9

These opportunities include lucrative
scholarships that pay for tuition and books and
provide money for subsistence. While each branch of
service offers a different program, all are
attractive. For example, the Army ROTC program has
a four-year and a two-year option leading to a
commission. All cadets in the advanced course of
the program receive a subsistence allowance of up to
$1,000 for each of the last two years (scholarship
holders excluded) plus pay for attending the six-
week advanced camp in the summer. And after
graduation, all cadets are guaranteed a career with
a salary and all expenses paid besides. These
students need not join the hordes of college
graduates seeking interviews and searching for jobs.

 There is no reason, according to Donald L.
Weinberg, for people these days to think that "men
are meant for war and women for hearth and home."[2]
There should be no inequality between men and
women. The American female has just as many
freedoms, privileges, and rights to defend as the
American male. Shouldn't she also heed the call to
arms by selecting an attractive career in the
military? By doing so, she can contribute to her
country's safety and security and also enjoy a
challenging, interesting, and productive life.

Documentation
unnecessary; common
knowledge.

Weinberg quoted in
anonymous article;
note clarifies.

Notes

[1]According to Dudney and Trimble, former Army Secretary Clifford Alexander, Jr., admitted that there will be a considerable number of women casualties in the next war, but in view of the expected increased bombing and the use of missiles, civilian women will probably also suffer more than in previous wars.

[2]Weinberg is quoted in "Draft Women?" an article that summarizes the arguments presented before the Supreme Court about the legality of drafting men and not women.

Naser 11

Works Cited

Cheatham, Harold E.   "Integration of Women in the U.S.
      Military." Sex Roles 11 (1984): 141-53.

Cohen, Eliot A.   "Why We Need a Draft." Commentary
      Apr. 1982: 34-40.

Collier, Ellen C. Women in the Armed Forces.
      Washington: Congressional Research Service,
      Feb. 1980. IB79045.

"Draft Women? The Arguments For and Against." U.S.
      News and World Report 3 Mar. 1980: 34.

Dudney, Robert, and Jeff Trimble.   "Women in Combat:
      Closer than You Think." U.S. News and World
      Report 3 Mar. 1980: 30:31.

"The Highest-Pressure Job." Newsweek 4 Nov. 1985: 38.

"Interview with Norma Scott Kinzer." U.S. News and
      World Report 3 Mar. 1980: 34.

Levin, Tobe, and Janet Miller-Goeder.   "Feminist
      Teaching in a Military Setting: Co-optation or
      Subversion?" Women's Studies Quarterly 12.2
      Summer 1984: 13-15.

"No 'Special Stresses' for Women in Battle." U.S.
      News and World Report 3 Mar. 1980: 34.

"An Officer and a Woman." Newsweek 9 July 1984: 43.

Naser 12

"One Good Woman." Time 11 Mar. 1985: 33.

Rice, Robert W., et al. "Military Cadet
    Leadership." Sex Roles 10 (1984): 885-97.

Shapely, Deborah. "Why Not Combat?" New Republic
    1 Mar. 1980: 16-17.

ASSIGNMENTS

For Discussion

1. Explain how you would document the following quotations or references within the text of a research paper:

   a. The following quotation from George Orwell's *Collected Essays,* volume four, pages 40–44, which were edited by Sonia Orwell and Ian Angus and published by Harcourt in New York, 1968: "Serious sport has nothing to do with fair play. It is bound up with hatred, jealously, boastfulness, disregard of all rules and sadistic pleasure in witnessing violence; it is war minus the shooting."

   b. A statement to the effect that one study of female networking in a business organization shows that women have not yet learned how to utilize networking skills in daily social contacts. This information came from an article by Sue Dewine and Diane Casbolt which appeared in *The Journal of Business Communication,* volume 20, number 2, Spring 1983, pages 57–67. The specific reference appeared on page 66.

   c. In a paper about the need for increased Federal support for the arts in the United States, you have written the following sentence: The establishment of the National Endowment for the Arts in 1965 is singled out by Gary O. Larson as the major turning point in the government's recognition that art was a democratic right. This information comes from Larson's book, *The Reluctant Patron: The United States Government and the Arts, 1943–65,* which was published in Philadelphia by the University of Pennsylvania Press in 1983. This information appeared on pages 264–69.

   d. In a paper about energy supplies in the Northeast, you have quoted Richard Asinof's statement: "James Bay embodies everything that is wrong with the way we produce, buy, sell, and consume electricity." This sentence was taken from his article "Deluge," which appeared in *Environmental Action,* volume 14, number 7, March 1983, pages 10–15. The sentence appeared on page 10; the magazine is published by Environmental Action, Inc., a national political lobbying group. In the same paper, you have previously quoted from another Asinof article.

   e. In a paper on the press and Watergate, you wish to document a point about the way that the Washington press handled the story. Your sources are the following: pages 69–82 of *All the President's Men* by Carl Bernstein and Bob Woodward, which was published in New York by Simon and Schuster in 1974; pages 75–83 of Edward Jay Epstein's *Between Facts and Fiction: The Problem of Journalism,* which was published in New York by Vintage Press in 1975; and pages 34–39 of Kurt and Gladys Lang's *The Battle for Public Opinion,* which was published in New York by Columbia University Press in 1983.

f. In writing about merit pay for teachers, you refer to a point made in two articles. The first, "The NEA in a Crossfire," appeared on page 13 of the June 13, 1983 edition of *Newsweek* and was written by Dennis A. Williams and Lucy Howard. The second, "Nine Proposals to Improve Our Schools," appeared on pages 59-67 of the June 5, 1983 issue of *The New York Times Magazine*. The specific reference came from page 63.

2. What errors can you find in the following entries from the "Works Cited" section of a research paper meant to conform to MLA style?

a. Alter, Robert. Rogue's Progress: Studies in the
   Picaresque Novel. Cambridge: Harvard University
   Press, 1964, pp. 80-105.

b. Baker, Sheridan. "Henry Fielding and the Cliché",
   Criticism, 1 (Fall 1959), pp. 354-61.

c. Baker, Sheridan. "Henry Fielding's Comic Romances."
   Papers of the Michigan Academy of Science, Arts,
   and Letters, 45 (1960, 411-19.

d. Braudy, Leo. Narrative Form in History and Fiction,
   Princeton: Princeton University Press, 1970.

e. Morris Golden, Fielding's Moral Psychology. Boston:
   Univ. of Mass. Press, 1966

f. Preston, John. The Reader's Role in Eighteenth-Century
   Fiction. London, England: William Heinemann, 1970.

g. Work, James A. "Henry Fielding, Christian Censor."
   The Age of Johnson: Essays Presented to Chauncey
   Brewster Tinker, edited by Frederick W. Hilles.
   New Haven: Yale University Press, 1949.

3. Which of the following statements should be documented?

a. Since its appearance in print in 1849, *Tom Jones* has been widely read.

b. Slippery Rock State College is located in Slippery Rock, PA.

c. An analysis of 40 prose nonfiction anthologies published between 1976 and 1980 revealed that of 2,529 selections, 10 percent were the same 45 essays, each of which had been published in at least four anthologies.

d. Charles Darwin delayed writing *The Origin of Species* for twenty years because he could not explain how evolution was caused.

    e.   Benjamin Franklin was a man of many roles: scientist, diplomat, author, journalist, publisher, inventor, humorist, and philanthropist.

4.   Explain the use of brackets in the following:

    a.   In January, 1604, he [King James I] ordered the principal clergymen of the Church of England to come to Hampton Court Palace to settle a dispute between the High Church and the Puritans.

    b.   As a boy, the future English king who would order thousands of men to wage war on the continent, wrote in his diary: "It seems silly for men to fight and be killed in a foriegn [*sic*] country, far away from their homes."

For Practice

1.   Using the works previously mentioned in For Discussion 1, write a "Works Cited" list in MLA style or a "References" list in APA style (whichever your instructor stipulates).

2.   Write a similar section for the following works used for a paper about Orwell's *1984*.

    a.   "Do It to Julia: Thoughts on Orwell's 1984," a scholarly article written by James Connors that appeared in volume 16 of *Modern Fiction Studies,* the 1970–71 edition, pages 463–73.

    b.   Irving Howe's *Nineteen Eighty-Four,* which was published in New York in 1963 by Harcourt Brace.

    c.   An article by George Woodcock entitled "Utopias in Negative," that appeared in volume 64 of *The Sewanee Review,* Winter, 1956, pages 81–97.

    d.   The New American Library edition of *1984,* which was published in New York in 1961.

    e.   George Orwell's *My Country Right or Left 1940–43* and his *In Front of Your Nose 1945–50,* which are volumes 2 and 4 of *The Collected Essays, Journalism and Letters of George Orwell.* This work was edited by Sonia Orwell and Ian Angus and published in New York by Harcourt in 1968.

    f.   Arthur Koestler's novel, *Darkness at Noon,* which was translated by Daphne Hardy and published in 1941. The edition used was a Bantam reprint, published in New York in 1966.

    g.   A newspaper story, "*1984* in 1983," written by Art Sullivan in the June 17, 1983 edition, page 23, of the *The Wall Street Journal.*

    h.   Shirley Kenney's "Big Brother Is Watching You Today," an article in volume 251, number 6 of the June 1983 issue of *The Atlantic,* pages 44–60.

3.   In a maximum of three or four sentences, write a summary note for each of the following passages:

    a.   Despite all of these difficulties, however, over the past twenty-five years there has been a gradual improvement in Soviet willingness to provide information, to negotiate details of on-site inspections—for example, in the 1974 Threshold Test-Ban Treaty—and to engage in the discussion of verification requirements. It has been a slow process, but it should not go unnoticed.

Although no arms-control treaties of significance have been ratified during the past decade, the numerical growth of nuclear forces has been somewhat restrained compared with what it might have been, because of limits in the SALT II agreement (even though it was not ratified) and the retirement of aging weapons. From 1978 to 1982, the number of strategic launchers actually decreased by about one percent for the Soviet Union and about 9 percent for the U.S. The total number of warheads and bombs deployed by the U.S. remained essentially constant during that period. The Soviet Union, completing its MIRV (multiple independently targeted re-entry vehicles) programs, did, however, increase its strategic warhead total by 60 percent, reducing the U.S. lead in that category.

The arms race in recent years has been not in numbers of weapons but in technological improvements. Both sides, for example, have greatly improved the accuracy of their forces. More improvements are to come. If new arms-control restraints are not negotiated, the next few years will see new weaponry incorporating even more remarkable technological changes: the building and testing of new bombers, new ICBMs, and new SLBMs (sea-launched ballistic missiles); the deployment of new cruise missiles on bombers, trucks, ships, and submarines; the attainment of absolute accuracy; and the development of anti-satellite weapons. Although many of these are planned replacements, there could be an increase of about 25 percent in numbers of weapons by 1990 if no agreements are reached.

—*The Harvard Nuclear Study Group, "The Realities of Arms Control"*

b.   Schools have also been affected by soaring divorce rates and an extraordinary increase in the proportion of births to unwed mothers. These social changes have resulted in almost one-fourth of all children being raised in one-parent or no-parent homes. Comparisons of children from one-parent and two-parent homes attending the same school usually show the former performing worse by almost every criterion: attendance, behavior, achievement. Several researchers have concluded that these differences tend to disappear after controlling for family income and other socioeconomic variables, but divorce and unwed motherhood usually have a huge negative effect on income. Currently more than half of the children in female-headed families are living in poverty compared to only 8% in husband-wife families.

Not only are more and more children being raised by one parent (predominantly the mother), but many children in two-parent homes find that both parents are at work away from the home during the day. Between 1960 and 1980 the labor force participation rate of married mothers with children under 6 rose to 47% from 18% and the rate for those with children 6–17 rose to 62% from 38%. Who takes care of small children when the mother works for pay? According to a special report based on the Current Population Survey, a surprisingly large number are said to be cared for by "child's parent in own home." When the mother works part time, 77% of white and 63% of black children ages three to six are reported as being cared for by "own parent in own home." Even when the mothers work full time, over 40% of the children are reported as being cared for in this way.

—Victor R. Fuchs, "Educational Reform Begins at Home"

4.   Write a paragraph using lead-in, summary quotations, and reductions to present the essential information in one of the following:

a.   An outstanding feature of recent times has been the growing independence of adolescents from the family, made possible by expansion and differentiation of the labor market. This has resulted in an increased dependence of the teenager on other adolescents. But peers do not take the place of parents as socializing agents: They have little or no investment in the outcome, are less likely to recognize deviant behavior, and, most important, do not possess the authority necessary to inflict punishment.

Moreover, research that looks directly at juvenile delinquents offers no support for the notion that they are economically deprived when compared to other adolescents in their immediate area. On the contrary, young delinquents are more likely to be employed, more likely to be well paid for the work they do, and more likely to enjoy the fruits of independence: sex, drugs, gambling, drinking, and job-quitting.

By looking directly at the family, we are thus able to resolve one of the minor paradoxes of our time, the fact that crime is caused by affluence *and* by poverty. General affluence to some extent weakens the control of all families. It especially weakens the control of those families in which the adolescent is able to realize a disposable income equal to that of his low-income parents (or parent) almost from the day he finds a job. Unfortunately, life for him does not freeze at this point. His earnings do not keep up with the demands on them. Most offenders eventually show up on the lower end of the financial spectrum, thanks to the very factors that explain their criminality. Individuals who have not been taught to get along with others, to delay the pursuit of pleasure, or to abstain from violence and fraud simply do not do very well in the labor market.

—Travis Hirschi, "Families and Crime"

b. It is evident, then, from what has just been said about the complexity of the writing process and of the task of teaching writing that there can be no real short cut to writing skill. That is, there can be no quick and painless way to develop a well-stocked mind, a disciplined intelligence, and a discriminating taste in language and fluency in its use. None of these can be acquired without hard work over a period of years, and it is preposterous to claim or to expect that any single course in either school or college, no matter how well taught or how intensively studied, can assure them. They are to a considerable extent the result of increasing maturity and of the total educational process acting on an intelligent mind. They are of course not absolutes which one either has or does not have; but in their higher manifestations they lie forever beyond the reach of many people, even some of those who attend the most highly selective college.

All teachers of academic subjects can help students to fill their minds, to train and focus their intellectual powers, and to make their use of language more exact; but English teachers and English courses have the opportunity to be especially helpful in moving students toward the second and third of these goals. More than other teachers and courses, they concentrate directly on the *quality* of written expression as well as the thinking embodied in it, on the principles that lie behind it, and on disciplined practice in applying these principles in written composition. But no one should expect a particular device or method or kind of subject matter in the English course to transform what must always be a slow and difficult process into one that is quick, easy, and unfailingly successful. The habit of good writing, like the habit of ethical conduct, is of slow growth; it is an aspect of a person's general intellectual development and cannot be greatly hastened apart from that development.

—*Albert R. Kitzhaber, from Themes, Theories, and Therapy*

PART FIVE

The Academic Voice: Writing Across the Curriculum

Good writers should be able to write well in all situations. If they have a sense of purpose and audience, a command of words and sentence structure, an ability to organize ideas and present them logically, and a knowledge of usage conventions and mechanics, they should be able to adapt their writing style to any particular assigment. This means that a good writer should be able to write effective newspaper copy, television commercials, condolence letters, instruction manuals, speeches, brochures, and the like. To a great extent, good writers can.

Yet, as you have noted throughout this book, different purposes make different demands upon the writer. Personal writing differs from expository, which in turn differs from persuasive. Although certain skills are basic to all writing, each situation calls for its particular strategies and techniques. Consequently, even experienced writers, when undertaking a new writing task, can benefit from a study of its special demands.

In the chapters ahead, we focus on specific assignments you can expect to encounter in your various college courses. Of course, most of what you have already studied in this book will be useful for such assignments. Most college writing is expository or persuasive, often in the form of library research reports, and so you may frequently have occasion to review Parts Two, Three, and Four of this book. Or you may be asked to write a book report for history, an analysis of plot devices for literature, a review of research for psychology, a laboratory report for biology, or an analytical report for business. All of these—which are the subject of Part Five—differ somewhat from the writing assignments previously encountered in the text. Each discipline imposes its own organizational and stylistic requirements.

Sometimes instructors give detailed oral instructions or distribute handouts with guidelines for researching and writing the papers they assign. Sometimes they refer students to scholarly journals so that the articles can serve as models. But often students are given little guidance; therefore, we have included this section on writing across the curriculum. Because of space limitations, we cannot deal with every type of paper. Instead, we concentrate on the assignments frequently encountered by most students in such disciplines as literature, history, sociology, political science, chemistry, biology, physics, and business.

22

General College Writing

In your academic career, certain types of writing assignments will be common to most of your courses. Because your success in college is largely dependent upon your ability to organize and write proficiently, this chapter will deal with two of the most frequently assigned writing tasks: the essay examination and the book review.

THE ESSAY EXAM

Although you may spend much of your college exam life filling in blank spaces, indicating T(rue) or F(alse), or selecting from among multiple answers, you almost certainly will have some essay exams, especially in your junior-senior courses. Consequently, you should learn some techniques to help you improve the way you write them.

Essay exams seldom allow you much extra time, but you can still follow the prewriting-writing-rewriting stages recommended throughout this book. However, you will have to spend most of your time writing. Careful planning can allow some extra time for the other two steps.

Prewriting

Avoid your first impulse to start writing immediately. Instead, spend a few minutes to size up the exam, understand the questions, and plan your method of attack. Here's how to go about it:

1. *Scan the questions.*   Read all the questions to obtain a sense of the exam. Note how many questions must be answered; if you have any choices, decide which ones to tackle.

2. *Plan your time.* Allow about 10 percent of the total time allotted for the exam for prewriting: reading the questions and jotting down some brief notes. Another 10 percent should be saved for rewriting. The rest of the time should go for writing, but even this time should be quickly planned. For instance, if one question is one worth 50 percent, you should devote about half of your writing time to it. When the value of each question is not indicated, organize your time so that you will be certain to answer every question.

3. *Decide on the order of your answers.* If you can answer the questions in any order, begin with the most important unless it appears highly difficult. If so, let it simmer in your subconscious while you answer the easier ones. Often while writing, you may think of points to use later in dealing with any difficult questions.

4. *Reread each question.* Before writing, reread each question thoughtfully, considering what information your instructor wants. Note precisely what the question calls for. Underline key verbs and be sure you understand their meaning. Some of the more frequently encountered key verbs follow:

   Explain: Usually, provide the reasons for.
   Define: Give sentence or extended definition.
   Compare: Usually, show similarities and differences.
   Contrast: Show differences.
   Illustrate: Provide examples.
   Trace: Show change or development in time.
   Analyze: Break into parts, consider different aspects, show relationships.
   Evaluate: Determine the value, importance, or worth of something. Justify
      your opinion.
   Interpret: Suggest a meaning and support your views.
   Discuss: This is a general instruction, usually calling for you to decide how
      to approach the subject.

5. *Write notes.* Before starting to answer each question, jot down your ideas either on the exam itself or in the margins of your paper so that you won't forget them later.

These five steps should take you only a few minutes, but may increase your grade greatly. They will help to ensure that you will answer the questions asked, use your time efficiently, and apply your knowledge effectively.

Writing

Writing an exam answer is much like writing a newspaper story: Both should begin with the most important information in the opening sentence or immediately thereafter. In journalism, this organizational plan is referred to as an "inverted pyramid" because it places the vital facts (who-what-where-when-why-how) at the top and then narrows down to other facts or details in order of decreasing importance. Similarly, you should begin your essay with a one- or two-sentence response that directly and clearly answers the question. You don't need an attention-getting opener or a paragraph about the significance of the subject. You do need to repeat some words from the exam question, but they can often serve as a thesis statement. Make your main point quickly and clearly. Then support it with additional points or with information and examples according to the question. Here's an example of how the inverted pyramid works in an essay answer. (Note how the question is incorporated into the thesis statement.)

Question: *Do prejudice and discrimination always occur together? Explain.*

Answer: Prejudice and discrimination need not always occur together. Prejudice refers to a state of mind, which is reflected in people's attitudes. Discrimination refers to a form of behavior, which is reflected in people's actions.

Probably, most prejudiced people do discriminate at some time. Also, most people without prejudice do not discriminate. Some people may be prejudiced yet not discriminate for one reason or another. Other people may discriminate but not be prejudiced.

If an employer who disliked men with beards hired one, he would be an example of a prejudiced person who is not discriminating. If a white homeowner without prejudice against blacks decided not to sell her home to one because it might upset her neighbors, she would be an example of a person without prejudice who is discriminating.

Note that the question is immediately answered, the terms are defined and further information is provided, and examples are furnished to complete the explanation.

In response to the following question, which calls for reasons, the writer using the inverted pyramid would mention all the reasons in an opening thesis sentence, then discuss them in order of decreasing importance as outlined here:

Question: *Why was the Battle of the Bulge crucial in World War II?*

Answer: The Battle of the Bulge was crucial because it resulted in the defeat of Hitler's major reserves, the end of his plan to win the war, and a psychological boost to the Allied forces.
(Discussion of first reason with supporting evidence.)
(Discussion of second reason with supporting evidence.)
(Discussion of third reason with supporting evidence.)

Not all questions lend themselves to this inverted pyramid arrangement. Some call for a chronological account or a spatial description, others for an order based on time or physical structure, comparison-and-contrast, or cause-and-effect. Because all these patterns have previously been described in detail, we shall merely refer you to those discussions.

As well as knowing what to do on an exam, you should know what not to do.

1. *Don't pad.*   You have studied hard for the exam, memorized a mass of material, and understandably would like to show your teacher everything you know. Stifle the impulse. Writing a lengthy, irrelevant answer can doubly penalize you. First, it uses up your valuable writing time. Second, because most teachers dislike reading through irrelevant material, they are more inclined to reward concise answers that directly answer the question.

   For instance, suppose that you've been asked why Clytemnestra kills her husband in Aeschylus' *Agamemnon.* Your instructor expects you to state three reasons: (1) she wanted to revenge the sacrificial death of Iphigenia, their daughter; (2) she wanted to protest Agamemnon's bringing home Cassandra as his mistress; and (3) she perhaps wanted to kill her husband before he could kill Thyestes, her lover. Instead of stating this answer directly, many students might provide a lengthy introduction including an explanation of the causes for the Trojan War, of the sacrifice of Iphigenia, and of the Thyestes' treachery. Few instructors will patiently wade through all this irrelevant material, searching for the answer.

2. *Don't write messy papers.*   You would probably have to practice diligently to make a permanent improvement in your handwriting. But there is much you can do to write neatly and legibly. Tiny, cramped letters are difficult to read. Instead, write reasonably large letters. Use a fine or medium pen point so that your letter strokes will remain distinct. Remember that your instructors must read numerous other exams. Any that require extra effort to decipher will be less favorably received than those that are neat and clear. Also provide ample space. If you double-space your lines and leave plenty of margin, you will find it much easier to make editing and proofreading corrections neatly and clearly.

Rewriting

Allow time to reread your answers, checking for omitted or misspelled words, for confusing or ambiguous sentence structures, and for wrong or inappropriate use of terms. You can write your corrections in the space above the line or in the margin. To indicate a substitution, insert a caret (∧) and draw a line through the material you plan to omit.

Obviously, someone who does not know the material cannot pass a course simply by following these instructions about taking essay exams. You can, however, make the most of what you have learned by going carefully through these prewriting, writing, and rewriting steps. And you can avoid the feeling that many students express when they state, "Well, I knew that but I just couldn't say it." Instead, you can feel confident that your essay exam represents your best effort and demonstrates what you have learned.

THE BOOK REVIEW

A common assignment in college courses is the review of a nonfiction book, an exercise that enables you to learn more about some aspect of your course work. The assignment demands much of you because you must describe and evaluate an author's contribution to a subject that you may know little about. How should you proceed?

Selecting the Book

Your instructor will usually offer some guidance about the book: a suggested list of books or some guidelines to follow in selecting a work. Generally, you should try to find a relatively recent work of about 200–350 pages on some aspect of the course that particularly interests you. Whenever possible, check your choice with your instructor to determine whether it is appropriate for the assignment and manageable for you.

Prewriting

While reading the book, take careful notes. These should include relevant ideas or quotations with their page numbers for easy reference (see the discussion of note-taking, pages 383–90). Taking notes can be more efficient if you use the following general outline of points to consider in writing a review:

1. Description
   A. Author
   B. Background
   C. Purpose
   D. Thesis
   E. Organization
   F. Summary
2. Evaluation
   A. Other reviews
   B. Scholarship
   C. Weaknesses and Strengths

In particular, be on the lookout for thesis statements, chapter summaries, striking quotations, discussions of methodology, conclusions, recommendations, and anything else you might want to consider later. If you question at times whether to take a particular note or not, remember that it would be wiser to err on the side of having too many rather than too few. Later you can always eliminate notes that appear unnecessary.

1. Description

A. *Author:* Some information about an author may appear on a book jacket or may be obtained or inferred from what is written in the preface. You should also do some library research into the author's present position, background, experience, and qualifications to determine to what extent he or she is an authority on the subject. Previously mentioned biographical sources (see page 372) will help you find this information. You need not write much, perhaps just a sentence, as in the illustrative book review by Carrie Carmichael (see paragraph 2, review, page 452); at most, you might include a short paragraph.

B. Background: Background information about a book consists of the historical, sociological, economic, scientific or other circumstances that may have influenced or contributed to its publication, if this information has some bearing on the book's importance or interest. In the illustrative review, Carmichael uses such background information in her first two paragraphs to catch the readers' interest in a common problem of modern society.

C. Purpose: Often the specific purpose of the book—to amuse, inform, persuade—will be apparent from the book's preface or introduction. Carmichael reveals the purpose in her first paragraph by pointing out the usual reaction of parents to the statement in the book's title.

D. Thesis: The thesis or central idea of the book will probably be stated in the book's introduction or conclusion. To gain an overview of the book that will help you realize its purpose and main ideas, read the preface and the introductory and concluding chapters first. In her review on page 452, Carmichael reveals the thesis by referring to the apprehensive reactions to the title and its implications.

E. Organization: If an outline of the book is not presented in the preface or opening chapter, a table of contents should provide you with one. You should check this outline to see that it is followed as you read the material. In our sample review, Carmichael outlines the organization in paragraph 4 (page 453) by pointing out the six stages experienced by mothers in dealing with their children's crises.

F. Summary: One of the most difficult parts of the review to write is the summary because so much depends on your audience. Are you writing only for your instructor, who has probably read the book or is familiar with it? Are you writing for your classmates who have not read it? Or are you writing for people not in the course who are perhaps entirely unfamiliar with the subject? Your instructor should inform you what audience the paper should address. Then you will be able to judge how thorough your summary should be, as well as whether or not terms should be defined and points explained in detail. In this connection, note how Carmichael uses examples effectively to give a sense of the book's contents and flavor to readers unfamiliar with it.

2. Evaluation

Up to this point, you have done research on the author and jotted down notes from your reading, along with page numbers. Your purpose has been to prepare for writing a description of the work. At the same time, you should be thinking about your evaluation of it. You should compare your evaluation with that of other reviewers, check on the writer's authority in the field, and consider the book's strengths and weaknesses.

A. Other Reviews: Especially in reviewing a book on a subject unfamiliar to you, you may wish to consult some published reviews of the book. You can find them by locating the following sources in the reference section of the library:

Book Review Digest.   This provides brief summaries from some reviews written during the year following a book's publication. For a book published in 1982, look under the author's name in the 1982 and 1983 volumes. (A work published late in the year might not be reviewed until the following year.) By reading the summaries, you can decide which of the original reviews to consult. The names and dates of the publications in which they appear are listed along with the important information about the number of words in the review. Normally, the longer the review, the more thorough (but not necessarily better) will be the critique of the book.

Book Review Index, Current Review Citations, Index to Book Reviews in the Humanities, and *Index to Book Reviews in the Social Sciences* do not provide summaries but do furnish other information about the publication of book reviews.

Of course, any ideas you obtain from these reviews should be documented— along with any quotations that you might wish to use. However, as we urged in the section on the research paper (pages 386–90), keep these and all other quotations brief.

   B. *Scholarship:*   You may find it difficult to judge the author's knowledge of the subject because of your limited understanding of it. But you can consider such matters as the use of sources (notes, bibliography), evidence provided, analysis of data, justification of conclusions, logic, omissions, bias, unsupported generalizations, and the like. These considerations usually do not require highly specialized knowledge. For example, someone reviewing a work entitled *War in the Falklands* would have little difficulty pointing out that this account of the 1982 war between Britain and Argentina is pro-British, with little information about the Argentine politicians, participants, and purposes. And someone with scanty scientific knowledge could still discern and perhaps lament the fact that in *The Youngest Science,* Lewis Thomas says little about his experiences as the dean of the medical schools of New York University and Yale.

   C. *Weaknesses and Strengths:*   You may find that your discussion of scholarship overlaps with your general discussion of the book's strengths and weaknesses. Never fear. In revising your review, you can eliminate any repetition of points. Plan to end with your general reaction: If favorable, deal with the book's weaknesses first; if unfavorable, its strengths first. Consider such matters as (1) the tone and style of the writing, (2) the importance of the book, (3) the soundness of the author's conclusions, (4) the value of the book for its intended audience, (5) the effectiveness of the argument, and (6) the practicality of the recommendations. Mention any particularly interesting or memorable points or passages, but use quotations sparingly. Also, be certain to support your opinions with specific references to the book.

   Note how effectively Carmichael uses examples from discussions in the book to point out omissions: "a daughter's lesbianism is addressed at length, but a son's homosexuality is dismissed in a short passage" (page 454). Note, too, that the reviewer discusses the weaknesses first and saves the redeeming strengths for her concluding paragraph.

In making your evaluation, you might reflect on how the book relates to your course. Consider what issues, ideas, or institutions the author criticizes or defends. Note the methodology used and evaluate how it shapes or restricts the topic. For example, if the author is a Marxist historian, how is the treatment of a period or problem affected by the writer's bias? Also, evaluate how well the author has added to your knowledge and understanding of the subject, particularly how it supplements the ideas in the textbook and the views of your instructor.

We have included the preceding discussion of points that might be discussed in a book review merely to help you generate ideas. Some points may be omitted. The order may be changed, with more important or striking matters appearing first. Although you might even begin with an evaluation under certain circumstances, usually the descriptive section appears first in nonfiction reviews, especially in scholarly journals. All these organizational decisions can be made in the planning step of the prewriting stage, after you have taken and reviewed your notes. A tentative outline is usually helpful, but you may wish to try a first draft to see what appears on paper before roughing out an organizational scheme for yourself. In any event, do not feel compelled to follow exactly the outline presented here.

A BOOK REVIEW

News That Parents Dread
Carrie Carmichael

MOTHER, I HAVE SOMETHING TO TELL YOU
By Jo Brans.
Research by Margaret Taylor Smith.
322 pp. New York: Doubleday & Company, $17.95

"Mother, I've got something to tell you" is not a statement that precedes announcements like "Gee, Mom, I just got accepted by Harvard" or "I've just been offered the job of my dreams." It is more likely to induce stomach-flipping, if not heart-gripping, apprehension. For that reason this book by Jo Brans, with research by Margaret Taylor Smith, is perfectly titled. It is about mothers whose children, as adolescents or young adults, developed what the author calls "unexpected" behaviors—a rather benign label for conditions that range from biracial marriage and homosexuality to eating disorders, drug addiction and suicide.

Introduction: Points out relationship of title to thesis and content of book

In original research supported by the Henry A. Murray Research Center at Harvard, Mrs. Smith studied mothers who principally described themselves as full-time parents for

Description:
1. Information about researcher and her study. Similar to information about author

whom "children were *the* career" and maternal successes, as one woman put it, were "told by the way your children turn out." Then when trouble, in its various forms, appeared the mothers initially blamed themselves.

"Mother, I Have Something to Tell You" puts surviving a child's crisis into the context of rebirth for the mother and the offspring. Giving birth is a hard task, but for some mothers, letting the child define his or her life and then taking charge of their own is even harder, particularly when the children make decisions that are hard for the mothers to accept.

2. Summarizes the book's content and organization

There are six stages of this "second birth," according to Ms. Brans and Mrs. Smith. First is the shock of finding out something is wrong. Second comes attention—along with asking whether she's to blame—followed by action. Whether or not the remedy works, the fourth stage, detachment, is essential for the mother's survival. It may involve admitting that you tried to save your child from suicide but could not. It may include cutting the child adrift to keep the rest of the family afloat. It may require taking a child partway to the answer and then letting him or her find the rest of the way alone. The fifth and sixth stages, autonomy and connection, are not reached by all. The mothers who attain them stand independent yet connected to the others in their lives.

a. The six stages

The mothers described in this book share two characteristics—energy and the ability to make assessments. These women were not ostriches, but brave combatants in the fight to save their children. They were anything but passive. Once they discovered something was in need of fixing they pulled out the stops. They called in experts but, sadly, not always the right ones.

b. Nature of the mothers

Crises with their children also forced the women to assess their men. One Southern mother of a delinquent realized that her husband had never been a positive force and, even with troubles, she was better off without him. Another woman sadly discovered that her husband chose to play backgammon rather than share an activity with their troubled boy.

c. Nature of their husbands

Male Rocks of Gibraltar do turn up in "Mother, I Have Something to Tell You." One mother, to whom appearances mattered greatly, found herself with a 14-year-old, pregnant daughter who chose to carry the baby to term and then place it for adoption. Says Joy, "My husband saved me. This is the man who took his nine-months-pregnant daughter to a restaurant for lunch on the day that the baby was born. . . . At the time she delivered the baby, she looked like she was about twelve." Anticipating trouble, he said to the headwaiter, "'We would like a table for three, please. And my daughter is not feeling well today. We would like a very comfortable table and very nice service today, because it's an important day to us.' And we walked through the crowd with our daughter big as a barrel. I couldn't have done it alone. He is the one who carried me through."

Although I found myself drawn into the worrisome lives of these families and touched by them, I was sorry that "Mother, I Have Something to Tell You" was limited by the nature of the research to white, middle-class, full-time mothers talking to each other. Children are in crisis all across the boards—ethnically, economically and socially. What about a black family? What chances does a troubled child have whose mother works? I would like to have seen more attention given to the problems of a mother facing her son's homosexuality. A daughter's lesbianism is addressed at length, but a son's homosexuality is dismissed in a short passage. Male homosexuality has not reached such social acceptance that most mothers can take it in stride. Moreover, the AIDS epidemic adds the threat of death to what might otherwise have been only socially upsetting news.

Evaluation: Strengths and weaknesses; evaluates usefulness to parents

"Mother, I Have Something to Tell You" is not a how-to book for the mother with a child in trouble. There is no self-help glossary in the back replete with toll-free numbers for referrals, but there is the compassionate record of experience. A mother can learn, perhaps, not to act precipitously, like the mother whose full-speed-ahead attempt to rescue her son from

the Moonies was badly botched. There is even
a lesson in another mother's decade-long fight
against her son's manic-depression, a state that
ended with his suicide. The *mother* survived.
Isn't that enough?

SUMMARY

In this chapter, we have suggested ways for you to adapt the writing skills
previously taught in the book to two common writing assignments: the essay
examination and the book review. With careful planning of your time, you can use
the three stages—prewriting, writing, and rewriting—to improve the quality of
your essay examinations. The techniques for writing essay answers can not only
help you succeed academically, but they can also carry over into many writing tasks
that you encounter in the professional world: writing summaries of reports or
drafting answers to questions you are asked in the course of your work.

Mastering the art of book reviewing can also be useful outside the academic
environment, most obviously in reviewing new books for local newspapers, trade
journals, or civic clubs or in discussing books with friends or colleagues. Even if you
never write another review after college, the skills you have learned can make you a
more efficient and more critical reader, better able to evaluate whatever you read.

ASSIGNMENTS

For Discussion

Essay Examination

1. What prewriting steps should you follow in writing answers to essay examination questions?
2. Find the key verbs in the following essay questions. Decide which rhetorical strategy or strategies you would need for answering each question.
    a. Discuss and evaluate the social and psychological advantages and disadvantages of the extended family concept.
    b. Trace the growing unrest of the American colonies in the pre-revolutionary period, giving some examples of the reasons for the unrest.
    c. What is meant by the term "nuclear fission"?
    d. Contrast the physical characteristics of Cro-Magnon and Neanderthal man.
    e. Explain the role of ionization in electrolysis.
    f. What are the major differences between Newton's theory of gravity and Einstein's?

g. Analyze the operation of the checks-and-balances system set up by the American constitution.

h. How do you interpret the change that takes place in Huck Finn's attitudes in Mark Twain's *The Adventures of Huckleberry Finn*?

The Book Review

1. In what respects is the prewriting stage of writing a book review similar to that of the research paper?

2. What aspects of a book should you consider in writing a review of it?

3. Using the Carrie Carmichael example (page 452), discuss the following:

    a. What information does Carmichaal give about the researcher?

    b. Book reviews usually provide a general narrative or descriptive account of what the book is about. How does Carmichael achieve this?

    c. How does Carmichael convey her evaluation of the book? What does she consider its strengths? Its weaknesses?

    d. How does Carmichael use case study summaries?

    e. What words indicate Carmichael's evaluation of the tone or style of the book?

23

Writing in
Literature Courses

READING LITERATURE

You may be asked to write book reviews in any college course. But you will probably be asked to write about literature only in certain classes, such as English, history, education, sociology, and anthropology.

Usually, book reviews in college courses deal with nonfictional works; literature papers involve fictional works, such as novels, short stories, plays, and poems. Book reviews are generally written so that readers unfamiliar with a work can decide whether they would be interested in reading it. (In college, of course, book reviews are written for professors, who want to know whether students have read and understood the book.) Literature papers are normally written for readers familiar with a book but interested in increasing their understanding of it and learning what others think about it. You can see, therefore, that book reviews and literature papers are both concerned with books, but they are written for different readers, have different purposes, and, in college courses, usually deal with different kinds of books.

A literature paper, as a form of literary criticism, may evaluate the strengths and weaknesses of a work, but it does not merely find fault. It tries to provide some insight and understanding into the work. In the process, a writer analyzes and interprets the work, developing ideas and judgments. These are based on standards that writers may either state or imply. If these standards are highly personal, there is a danger that readers may reject them. For example, some students favor stories with happy endings or romantic plots or young characters. Writing literature papers requires that you set aside your highly personal preferences so you can evaluate a work reasonably and fairly on its artistic merits.

Naturally, this evaluation will involve your personal opinion, but it should be based on generally accepted criteria and supported with examples and illustrations—just as in the other kinds of expository papers we have considered. For literature papers (unless argumentative, as some are) are expository, calling for the same skills and techniques as other exposition. They usually employ the expository process of analysis—in this instance, the taking apart of a novel, short story, play, or poem.

You may feel that such a process spoils literature. Yet you should realize that we appreciate a literary work just as we do other human achievements: We perceive the skill, artistry, and techniques necessary to accomplish them. In baseball, for example, we can admire a second baseman's artistry as we watch him go for a double play by taking the toss from the shortstop on the dead run, then pivoting for the throw to first while also dodging the oncoming base runner. Knowledgeable fans appreciate the game more because they realize what is involved in such situations as a double play, a hit and run, a pick-off, or a suicide squeeze. Less knowledgeable spectators may enjoy the game, but not to the same degree. Likewise, literary critics appreciate how writers handle point of view, scenes, character foils, foreshadowing, and other matters of craft. Readers who are unaware of these aspects miss much of the enjoyment of literary works. In analyzing a literary work, therefore, you can appreciate it better.

Analyzing a work also serves as part of the prewriting process: It is a method of data gathering necessary for writing literary criticism effectively and efficiently. But how should you begin? Perhaps the most helpful way is to use the *who-what-when-where-why-how* approach that we suggested earlier as a prewriting device. For literary analysis, it would take this form:

The questions	*The areas*	*The issues*
Who?	Character	The function, traits, and credibility of the people in the work.
What?	Plot	The series of related actions involving some problem that builds to a crisis and is resolved.
When?	Time	The time structure of the work and the period it is set in.
Where?	Setting	The physical location and the general environment, including the social, political, and other conditions affecting the characters.
Why?	Theme	The central or controlling idea that is conveyed mainly through the character and plot.
How?	Technique	The author's use of language devices to gain an effect.

This approach will suggest ways for you to consider a literary work and questions you can ask yourself to stimulate your thinking. In applying this method, we have limited literary works primarily to novels, short stories, and dramas, although many poems might also be analyzed in this way.

Character (Who?)

In life, we accept people as they are and try to understand them. In literature, we analyze to what extent they are lifelike or real and we try to understand them and their artistic function. In this process, we ask certain questions about the characters, such as the following:

1.   What kind of person is the character?
2.   Does the character change in any respect?
3.   What purpose does the character serve?
4.   How believable is the character?

Let us consider each of these.

What Kind of Person is the Character?   In formulating your opinion about characters, you should analyze them by considering what they say, what they do, what they think, what others say and think of them, and what the author may indicate about them. Modern authors generally do not directly reveal their opinions about their characters, often preferring to use one as a mouthpiece to convey their ideas. Earlier authors often describe a character's physical and moral nature, in addition to giving the character an appropriate name, as Dickens does to the obnoxious braggart and "bounder" in the novel *Hard Times,* Mr. Bounderby:

> He was a rich man: banker, merchant, manufacturer, and what not. A big, loud man, with a stare, and a metallic laugh. A man made out of coarse material which seemed to have been stretched to make so much of him. A man with a great puffed head and forehead, swelled veins in his temples, and such a strained skin to his face that it seemed to hold his eyes open, and lift his eyebrows up. A man with a pervading appearance on him of being inflated like a balloon, and ready to start. A man who could never sufficiently vaunt himself a self-made man. A man who was always proclaiming, through that brassy speaking trumpet of a voice of his, his old ignorance and his old poverty. A man who was the Bully of humility.

When authors do not provide such information, or even when they do, you may find it helpful to take some notes on the character's appearance, behavior, and interaction with other characters. For example, if you were writing about Brutus in *Julius Caesar,* here are some traits you could note:

1.   Foolishly trusting, naive (fooled by Cassius; tricked by Antony);
2.   Respected (all conspirators originally pay tribute to him; becomes leader);
3.   Irritable (quarrels with Cassius; peevish with poet);
4.   Tender, kind (loving husband to Portia; considerate of Lucius);
5.   Idealistic (duty to Republic; failure to plan for successor).

When you have finished, you will have to decide what all these qualities add up to. Is the character admirable or not? Sometimes, the answer is simple. Obviously, Fagin in *Oliver Twist* is a villain and Antony in *Julius Caesar* is a hero. But most main characters and some others are not pictured as black or white, all good or evil. Most are shades of gray.

Take our old friend Brutus, for example. What about this "noblest Roman of them all"? Do his honorable motives excuse his dishonorable act? What about the argument that he was sincere in what he did? Can his noble death atone for his ignoble deeds? The answers are not simple; great literary figures possess a complexity that intrigues and fascinates.

So, as judge and jury, you should find for or against the characters, viewing them as human beings, and arriving at conclusions about them based on evidence in the literary work.

Does the Character Change in Any Respect?   You may have assumed from this discussion of character traits that people in literature are the same at the end of a work as they were at the beginning. Not at all. Some characters, particularly most central ones, change as a result of their experiences. Young people initiated into the realities of life gain maturity and insight, as Gene (*A Separate Peace*), Henry Fleming (*The Red Badge of Courage*), and Frankie Addams (*The Member of the Wedding*) all attest. Older people, too, are altered—whether kings (Oedipus) or housewives (Nora in *A Doll's House*). Look for a change, determine how and why it takes place—or does not—and you will obtain more insight into the character.

Note, however, that some central characters do not learn from their experiences. One such is Harry Angstrom, the former high school basketball star, who is trapped in his marriage, his job, and his community in John Updike's *Rabbit, Run*. Like his nickname, Rabbit, he is more unthinking animal than responsible human, running away at the beginning of the novel only to return, wreck the lives of his lover and wife, and then run away again—no better, no wiser, no different—as the novel comes full circle.

What Purpose Does the Character Serve?   Fictional works revolve around principal characters, loosely called "heroes" or "heroines" and more correctly called "protagonists," who command our attention, attract our interest, and often arouse our admiration. We tend to identify with them and think about them as being among the people that have touched our lives and influenced us in some way. Among such fictional individuals are Oedipus, Antigone, Hamlet, Elizabeth Bennett, Heathcliff, Tess, Oliver Twist, Huck Finn, Holden Caulfield, and T.S. Garp. All serve the purpose of being an integral part of the central idea or theme of their respective works. But what about characters who do not play a key role?

They may have various functions, which you can best determine by asking what would be missing if they were not present in the story. Always remember that authors are creators, determining everything that appears on the printed page. Every character and every character's thoughts, feelings, works, and actions have been created by an author for some purpose. Being aware of that purpose will enable you to better understand the characters and the work itself. Exactly what do we mean?

Some characters serve as foils, whose actions, feelings, and opinions contrast with those of the central character, often in parallel situations that reveal much about both. So it is in *Don Quixote* that the practical Sancho serves as a foil to the impractical Don Quixote, and, in *Huckleberry Finn,* the clever Tom Sawyer to the naive Huck.

Other characters function like accessories, helping to portray the main character. *The Catcher in the Rye,* for instance, is populated with minor figures who reveal Holden's compassion for others. They range from the innocent and virtuous (the nuns) to the shrewd and vicious (Stradlater and the bellboy, Maurice). Unlike these characters who enter in one scene and later exit forever, other literary characters, like the slave Jim in *Huckleberry Finn,* appear throughout most of the novel.

Characters may also serve a plot function. The ghost in *Hamlet* causes the prince to suspect his uncle Claudius of murder; Mr. Mason in *Jane Eyre* stops the heroine's marriage to Mr. Rochester. These and other characters primarily create plot complications that add to the action of the story.

Characters can also function as spokespeople or representatives of the author's views. In *Crime and Punishment,* Raskolnikov's sister Dounia and his friend Dmitri personify the author's beliefs in salvation through love and generosity. And in *The Catcher in the Rye,* Mr. Antolini appears to express Salinger's ideas. However, reaching a conclusion that a character represents or speaks for an author should come only after a careful consideration of the reliability of that person and other evidence in the work.

Then there are background characters who add to the setting, providing an illusion of the real world. They are usually the common folk: the citizens in Shakespeare's *Julius Caesar,* the seamen in Melville's *Moby Dick,* the rustics in Hardy's Wessex novels. Such characters help to create a sense of place and atmosphere.

Somewhat similar are characters who perform solos, who provide a few moments of relief or laughter or interest, although they contribute little to the development of plot or an understanding of other characters. Among these characters, who are truly "characters," are the porter in *Macbeth,* many of the clowns in Shakespeare's other plays, and Dickens' eccentrics, notably Mr. Micawber in *David Copperfield.* Such characters contribute to the tone of a work.

Characters, in short, may play various roles: main figures, foils, accessories, plot functionaries, representatives or spokespeople for the author's views, and contributors to the setting or the tone. Determining how characters function will enable you to analyze a literary work with greater insight.

How Believable is the Characterization?   To paraphrase an old saying, God makes people but authors make characters. Consequently, one of your roles as critic is to determine how effectively authors have portrayed their characters. In doing this, you may consider numerous ways that a writer contributes to the reader's understanding of a character, among them motivation, consistency, and individuality.

Motivation   Readers must be able to understand why characters act as they do. And actions must stem from probable causes, not possible ones. Life is stranger than fiction partly because in life people's true natures are hidden. Several times a year, for example, we read about gruesome murders committed by quiet young men who have led exemplary lives as Boy Scouts and Sunday School teachers. In literature, such characters would be poorly conceived unless the writer provided reasons for their hostility and violence. Some modern writers, however, believe that people may act as a result of subconscious memories or irrational, incomprehensible urges and instincts. Characters in traditional literature, however, should be adequately motivated.

Generally, the crucial point for examining motivation occurs late in a work when a key character makes a decisive choice. At that time, we should not accept any sudden switch from dishonesty to honesty or selfishness to unselfishness. Certainly, people may change in life, but in literature this transformation should occur over a period of time, and the reasons should be plausible. That is why we can accept Arthur Dimmesdale's confession of adultery in Hawthorne's *Scarlet Letter:* We have watched him wrestle with his conscience until we know that he cannot bear his guilt any longer.

Consistency Although characters may change, we still expect them to be as consistent as real people. Generally, we know how our friends will respond in new situations. Similarly, we should be able to anticipate what characters will usually do. In *Sons and Lovers,* we realize that Paul Morel cannot marry either Miriam or Clara because of his strong attachment to his mother. To be consistent, Paul cannot love anyone but her. Although readers may prefer literature to end happily, it would have been out of character for Paul to marry Miriam or anyone else. Characters must be true to themselves: This consistency is necessary if they are to be effective.

Individuality If consistency is carried too far, characters will lack the complexity that makes them particulary interesting and appealing. This is not to say that consistent characters must be dull. Stereotyped or stock characters (the tough coach, the dumb jock, the sexy cheerleader) are all one-dimensional people who sometimes can be portrayed vividly. Tennessee Williams's Amanda Wingfield, the genteel Southern lady who lives in the past, is an excellent example of such a character. So too is Stanley Kowalski, the central character of Williams's *A Streetcar Named Desire*—a flat character with a single dominant trait. Stanley is all brute—hard, vicious, and cruel, lacking in kindness or compassion—but he exhibits a fierce vitality that makes him effective despite a lack of complexity.

Yet generally, memorable characters exhibit some complexity, revealing strengths and weaknesses, and undergoing some change or development in a literary work. Jay Gatsby (*The Great Gatsby*), Willie Stark (*All the King's Men*), and Holden Caulfield (*The Catcher in the Rye*) all begin as innocents, all change slightly or greatly, all exhibit vices and virtues, and all continue to appeal to generations of readers.

Literary papers may discuss any or all of the previously mentioned qualities in describing characters, comparing and contrasting them, analyzing their purpose, or evaluating them. For many of these tasks, however, it is helpful to have some understanding of plot.

Plot (What?)

When someone asks us what a literary work is about, we usually summarize its story—its plot. But in critical writing, you can assume that your reader knows something about the story, so you don't need to provide a chronological retelling of it. Instead, you analyze and discuss the plot's structure, explaining the *how* and *why* of one of its aspects. The following terms are useful for this task:

1.   *Exposition:* This refers to the background information provided in a work, especially at the opening, to acquaint the reader or audience with the characters, their relationships, the setting, and the time. You discover where you are, who these people are, and what physical, social, and cultural surroundings they live in.

2.   The *complication* often begins in the exposition because the audience needs to become aware of some problem or conflict early in the story. Something occurs or someone arrives to disrupt the routine and intensify the lives of the characters.

3.   *Rising action* is a term that describes the increased emotional effect created by additional incidents or the results of the original one. Tension increases; our interest rises. In *Romeo and Juliet,* the original complication of lovers from feuding families is intensified as Romeo kills Tybalt, the wedding date of Juliet and Paris approaches, Juliet swallows the potion, Romeo hears about her "death," and Romeo kills Paris.

4.   The *climax* refers to the decisive incident near the end in which the problem or conflict is resolved. It is the point of no return; once reached, the outcome must be settled. The central character usually makes a decision from which there is no escape. In *Hamlet,* the climax occurs in the dueling scene with Laertes.

5.   The *ending* may be presented in a paragraph, a page, a chapter, or a scene, depending on what is needed to explain the previous events and to account for what happens to the characters. It is used for tidying up, straightening out, unraveling. In *Hamlet,* the dead bodies (four) must be hauled away, the future King of Denmark indicated, and Hamlet's reputation clearly established. Every loose end is tied.

Naturally, all literary works do not fit neatly into the structure indicated by these terms. Episodic plots, for instance, consist of incidents involving a central character but have no single rising action or climax. Also, some narratives employ flashbacks, often starting with a climactic scene (like a courtroom) and then moving back in time to the beginning of the complication.

In addition to examining the structure of the plot, you might also consider how skillfully it is conceived. Your examination should consider such matters as foreshadowing, probability, and unity.

Foreshadowing   The word *foreshadowing* becomes self-explanatory when you think of the way that people's shadows can appear in front of them, alerting others to their approach. In literature, foreshadowing is a device to prepare readers for what follows. It may take the form of an ominous remark, a strange prophecy, or some foreboding note. In *Julius Caesar,* for example, the supernatural signs and warnings prepare us for his fate. In this way, foreshadowing removes some of the element of surprise from a story, making the unexpected more probable. At the same time, it may help create suspense by setting up an expectation in the reader.

Probability   Another factor to consider in evaluating the plot of a work is the extent to which authors manipulate the lives of characters. This may take the form of unusual occurrences (death, automobile accident, sudden fortune, and the like), or improbable coincidences (unexpected meetings, lucky or unlucky timing, discovery of unknown relatives, and so on.) Although we realize that these events occur in life, we expect a literary world to be more probable than the real world. If fact is stranger than fiction, then fiction must be more normal or probable than fact.

In particular, consider the ending, which should be natural, growing out of the conflict between characters or forces. Be wary of happy endings brought about by such violations of probability as the winning of a lottery, the killing of characters, or the unexpected conversion of a villain to kindly ways. Also question the use of marriage to resolve a plot happily. After all, how many weeks would you give Cinderella and the prince?

Unity   A third matter to consider in evaluating a plot is unity, whether all the episodes in a plot are necessary and contribute to its development. In popular escape literature and films, there is a tendency to add juicy sex scenes. We should ask whether they serve any function. Do they disclose something important about the characters involved, or are they included only to appeal to people's sexual instincts and thus to sell more copies or tickets? Generally, a work of literature should not contain digressions of any kind, unless included for some comic effect. The work should be as well unified as your papers.

In this section on plot, we have raised a number of issues to help you understand and write about plot structure. Let's summarize this information in questions that you should consider in analyzing the plot of a literary work:

1.   How effectively is the exposition handled?
2.   What is the complication? What issues does it raise?
3.   What other issues or problems are developed in the rising action?
4.   Are surprising events properly foreshadowed?
5.   Where is the climax? What is resolved and how?
6.   How probable are the incidents? How acceptable the use of chance and coincidence?
7.   Is the work unified? Are there unnecessary digressions?
8.   Is the ending logical and satisfying? Or, has the author resorted to chance or sudden character transformations to conclude the work?

Time (When?)

Time in a literary work is important in two respects: (1) the time sequence that the author uses to present the story; and (2) the historical time (day, year, period, century) when the characters live.

We have mentioned previously that writers may present stories either in straightforward chronological order or in flashback, beginning a work near its ending and then returning to a previous time.

Flashbacks may be used in other ways. Like the great epics, a story may begin *in medias res* ("in the middle of things") as *Wuthering Heights* does. After a dramatic opening scene involving the strange members of the household, the housekeeper relates in a flashback what occurred many years earlier, providing an explanation for the ghost-like figure at the broken window.

An even more intricate use of flashback occurs in other works when a character's memory is triggered by some association from the past. In Arthur Miller's *Death of a Salesman,* the characters during a two-day period recollect events that took place over an earlier sixteen-year time span. The study of how and why an author handles time may not always be as interesting or significant as it is in this play, but you should consider it in writing about a literary work.

The second important use of time involves the age or period when the action occurs. The time of the action in *A Separate Peace,* for example, is significant because Gene's aggression toward Finney parallels the aggression between nations in World War II, disrupting the peacefulness of the isolated prep school and affecting the lives of its students.

An author must decide how to handle time and at what time to set the action. Considering the following questions should help you understand the significance of each:

1. How does the author handle the movement of time in the work? Which of the two main time sequences is used—chronological or flashback? What are its advantages or disadvantages?

2. In what period of time does the work take place? What difference would it make if the work were set in another time? What is the significance of its being set at that time?

Setting (Where?)

A literary work takes place in a particular setting—that is, a physical place (house, community, region, country), and an environment consisting of the beliefs and values (social, political, economic, and so on) of the people there. In few works, if any, is setting insignificant, but its importance may vary considerably according to the extent of an author's belief that environment shapes or controls human lives or that a work should depict the manners and morals of the time or place.

On a simple level, literary works convey a vivid sense of realism resulting from the descriptions of the natural landscape, the architecture of a house, the decor of a room, and the clothes and physical appearance of a person. Setting can also create an atmosphere, establishing a tone for the work. Emily Bronte's moving description of the moors and their wild storms in *Wuthering Heights* provides a background conducive to the tragic, tempestuous love of Heathcliff for Catherine.

The setting of a work can serve an even more important function as a force in conflict with human desires and endeavors. In Hemingway's *The Old Man and the Sea,* for instance, Santiago fights nature and its creatures, while in Hardy's *The Return of the Native,* Egdon Heath destroys the people who live there, causing them to practice witchcraft and to succumb to the primitive emotions it evokes.

Setting is not confined to the physical location of a work; it also includes the human environment. Characters are born, raised, and live among other people. Their values may shape lives. In Fitzgerald's *The Great Gatsby,* Jay Gatsby is a product of his materialistic society; in another environment, he might have been a different person.

You might consider questions like the following in writing about a fictional work:

1. What is the setting? Does it serve *merely* as a locale for the plot or does it create an atmosphere? If the latter, describe it.
2. How does the setting contribute to the work?
3. Does the setting play an important role in shaping or controlling the lives of the characters?

Theme (Why?)

Authors may write for money, fame, self-fulfillment, or other reasons, but what they write expresses some idea about the human condition. This theme may be stated directly or indirectly; it may be philosophical, psychological, or social; and it may be revealed by the characters, plot, setting, or some other aspect of the work. The question "Why?" as it applies to literary analysis commits you to examine the ideas, particularly the main idea, in a work to determine what statement it makes about life. Does every work contain some such statement? If so, how do you discern it?

Even the simplest nursery rhyme or story has a theme: "Jack and Jill" shows how dangerous life's routines can be; "Little Red Riding Hood" indicates the need for vigilance against disguised evil. Every work, no matter how slight, contains some basic observation about the nature of people, the freedom of the individual, the opportunity for happiness, the role of society, the importance of love, the discovery of self, the existence of evil, the futility of war, or some other aspect of the human condition. On a simple level, if the central character finds happiness, then the view of life is optimistic; if not, it is pessimistic. But usually it is far more important to analyze *why* and *how* the work ends as it does rather than merely to note the ending.

The theme usually grows out of the ending—or, more specifically, how the ending resolves the conflict. Usually the theme is implied in a literary work because authors wish to *show* what people or life is like rather than state their views directly. But sometimes the central idea is expressed by a character, major or minor, who is favorably portrayed. Or, it may be stated ironically by an unattractive character. For example, when the odious Bounderby in Dickens' *Hard Times* argues strongly in favor of all work and no play, and also deplores anything appealing to the imagination, readers realize that the opposite is being advocated by the novel as a whole.

Whether or not an author has stated the theme through a character, you need to show that nearly everything else in the work points or contributes to this idea. For example, in Steinbeck's *The Grapes of Wrath,* Tom Joad seems to speak for the author when he talks to his mother about Casey. This Christ-like preacher had gone into the wilderness "to find his own soul" but also learned that "his little piece of a soul wasn't no good 'less it was with the rest, an' was whole." Tom Joad concludes from Casey's experiences that "a fella ain't no good alone."

This statement sums up the change in the novel from the Joad family's concern only for themselves to concern for others: first for the Wilsons, then for the people in the government camp, and finally in Rose's giving the milk of her breast to the starving stranger.

Just as you can check an answer in math, so you can check a theme in literature by seeing whether it applies to what occurs to the characters in the work. And sometimes a clue to the theme will be apparent from the title: *The Red Badge of Courage, Pride and Prejudice, For Whom the Bell Tolls.*

Asking yourself the following questions about a work may help you to perceive its theme:

1. What happens to the central character and why?

2. Was what happened the character's own fault or due to uncontrollable forces?

3. If it was the character's own fault, what weakness did it reveal?

4. If the character overcame the difficulty, what new realization or trait did the resolution require?

5. Did other characters have similar problems? What do their actions reveal?

6. If the central character's problem cannot be attributed to human weakness, what was it due to?

7. Can this force be overcome? If so, how? If not, how can human beings cope with it?

8. Are people portrayed as basically evil or good, selfish or unselfish, kind or cruel?

9. Do the characters find happiness? If not, why not? If so, why? How?

10. How does nature interact with the characters?

11. What statement, if any, does the literary work make about ethical, religious, economic, social, or political matters?

12. What insight does the work provide into psychological problems about sex, love, death, guilt, alienation, and so forth?

In determining the theme from answers to these questions, remember that a literary work may contain numerous ideas. But the theme is like a thread, tying together most of what occurs. *The Grapes of Wrath,* for example, contains numerous views about big business, charities, religion, private ownership of property, and the role of government. But only the theme of human community runs throughout and unifies the entire work.

The theme is not a Sunday School lesson, a moral, or a directive about how to live. Rather, it is a statement about life and people, an observation, a pronouncement, a verdict. For example, Ralph Ellison's *Invisible Man* is not a sermon telling readers to treat blacks better. Instead, it is a novel that points out how white people, failing to see blacks as human beings, use and exploit them.

As we read this and other fictional works, we experience the events as they unfold, much as we experience life. And just as we become wiser from the events in our lives, so we do from our reading of fiction. But the ideas we learn from literature are shaped and controlled by what the author has found significant and meaningful in the human experience. This central underlying idea constitutes the theme of a literary work.

Technique (How?)

No analysis of a literary work would be complete without a study of the writer's technique—the artistic devices that shape the content. We will limit our discussion here to three of them: point of view, irony, symbolism.

Point of View   In writing a story, the author must decide whether to tell it in the first person or in the third person, either as a character in the work or a story-teller relating it.

First Person   The first-person point of view is easily recognizable by the recurrent use of "I," the voice being that of a character, not the author. It is important to recognize the distinction between authors who write stories and characters who tell them. Clearly, Mark Twain is not speaking in *Huckleberry Finn* in these opening lines: "You don't know about me without you have read a book by the name of *The Adventures of Tom Sawyer;* but that ain't no matter." The person speaking is young Huck.

Like Huck, first-person narrators are characters and should be analyzed as such. But unlike him, first-person narrators need not be the main characters. Often an author uses a minor character to observe what occurs, as Fitzgerald does with Nick Carraway, who tells us about the central character, Gatsby. When such secondary characters narrate the story, you must determine the plausibility of their being present at various scenes and their knowing what they do about the other characters. For example, you might question whether Nick Carraway becomes everyone's confidant because he is so likable or whether Fitzgerald contrived these convenient relationships so that Nick could tell us the story.

You also need to question the reliability of the views of the main or secondary characters. Can they be trusted? Should you accept what they say? In the fourth book of Jonathan Swift's *Gulliver's Travels,* Gulliver becomes an unreliable narrator, one who is truly gullible, when he fails to realize that the horses, whom he worships and who live by reason alone, are flawed.

You should also realize that the use of first-person point of view conveys a sense of reality because the narrative seems to be autobiographical. Although authors gain from this advantage, they also lose; they are forced to restrict the work to what the "I" narrator can naturally see, understand, hear, and learn, either as the central character or a minor one.

Third Person   The third-person point of view is handled in one of two ways: the omniscient (all-knowing) or limited narrator. In the omniscient form, the godlike narrator describes all the thoughts and feelings of the characters and tells us what they said and why. Naturally, the actual words of the characters may be quoted, but third-person pronouns or proper nouns appear ("he felt," "she spoke to change the subject," "Bill was astonished.")

When omniscient narrators tell a story, you should not automatically assume that they represent the author. Often they do. But you should determine their reliability just as you would with other narrators.

This omniscient point of view is the oldest and most common way to tell a story. You would use it in relating a joke or anecdote in which you played no part. Its advantages are its convenience and freedom. As author, you can tell your readers whatever you wish—you can present the ideas, feelings, beliefs, motivations, and deeds of all the characters, without any limitations. Its disadvantage is that readers become aware that someone outside the story is telling it. As a result, some readers find it difficult to lose themselves in the fictional world, hearing always the voice of the storyteller telling the tale.

This disadvantage is eliminated in the limited third-person point of view. By telling the story through the mind and eyes of one character, authors allow readers to participate directly in that person's life, much as they live their own. So in Irwin Shaw's short story, "The Eighty Yard Run," you easily identify with the football player who "jumped for it [the pass], feeling it slap flatly against his hands, as he shook his hips to throw off the halfback who was diving at him." And you share the glory of that run and the later letdown.

Because Shaw continues from this first sentence to tell the story through the player's mind, the point of view is limited. If he had entered other minds, telling us what others were thinking, the point of view would be omniscient.

Sometimes authors have it both ways, combining point-of-view techniques, which can be disconcerting. In *Emma,* Jane Austen tells nearly all the story through the limited viewpoint of Emma, the central character, but switches in one chapter near the end to the viewpoint of a male friend. Understanding the purpose of these and similar changes, as well as being aware of the way that authors handle point of view in their stories, can lead to a greater insight and a better understanding of a literary work.

In dealing with point of view, you might consider these questions:

1. Has the author used the first-person point of view? If so, is the narrator a major or minor character? If not, has the author chosen the omniscient or limited form of the third-person point of view?

2. What is the function or particular effect of the point of view?

3. What personal traits and ethical standards does the narrator have?

4. Is it plausible for the narrator to know and see what he or she does?

5. Is the narrator reliable and trustworthy?

Irony   We mentioned in Chapter 15 that irony is achieved by incongruity—usually the inconsistency between appearance and reality. In literature, it may occur in statements (verbal irony) or in situations or actions (situational irony).

Verbal irony can be achieved through understatement, exaggeration, or other incongruity. For instance, a character might use words of praise to imply criticism, much as you do when you say to a boastful friend, "Don't be so modest!" However, effective verbal irony goes beyond sarcasm: It may indeed be biting or caustic, as in Mark Anthony's repeated "Brutus is an honorable man." It can also be comic, as when Hamlet wittily baits Polonius and other courtiers. Or it can be tragic, as when Romeo's friend Mercutio, mortally stabbed, answers Romeo's assurance that the wound cannot be serious in the understated "No, 'tis not so deep as a well, nor so wide as a church door; but 'tis enough, 'twill serve."

Situational irony grows out of actions or circumstances rather than statements. In Ibsen's *A Doll's House,* for instance, the irony results from the fact that Nora's loving sacrifice for her husband leads not to greater happiness for the two of them but to her disillusionment with him.

Dramatic irony is a special kind of situational irony. It occurs when the reader or audience knows something important that is unknown to a character. Sophocles' *Oedipus Rex* provides a stunning example. Relentlessly, Oedipus seeks to discover who killed his predecessor, King Laius. The murderer must be banished or slain to end a plague on Thebes and its people. Step by step Oedipus moves closer to the truth—the audience knowing at every step what he does not: Before the day is out he will dash out his own eyes in horror at finding out not only that he himself was the murderer, but also that Laius was his father, and that he had incestuously married his own mother and sired four children with her.

Irony is not always as central to literature as it is in *Oedipus Rex,* but when it is present in a work, it always contributes importantly to the reader's experience. Consequently, you should be alert for instances of irony.

Symbolism   Symbols are part of literature and life. A wedding ring, for instance, is more than a circular finger band of silver or gold; it represents the commitment of marriage with all its attendant values of love, companionship, fidelity, family, romance, and devotion.

In addition to such public symbols as wedding rings, writers create private symbols in their own works. The shark who battles the old fisherman for his catch in Hemingway's *The Old Man and the Sea* is more than a natural predator; it represents the forces of nature against which human beings must often struggle.

Occasionally in a literary work, a symbol will become a central, unifying force. In Conrad's *Lord Jim,* Stein's butterfly-collecting mania serves as the central symbol: the butterfly chase symbolizes the romantic striving for an elusive and unattainable ideal—the striving that brings about Jim's destruction. Thus the symbol is related to the novel's theme, depicting and reinforcing it.

Literary symbols must be well conceived. They should have some relationship to public symbols; otherwise, they may have meaning only to the writer. Also, as the butterfly chase and shark are, they must be integral, realistic parts of the story. Because of the prominence of a glove, newspaper, car, or other object in a story, you can recognize that the writer has used the object not simply as part of the setting, but as a symbol to convey a particular meaning. The recognition and identification of symbols add to the enjoyment and understanding of a literary work.

WRITING ABOUT LITERATURE

Prewriting the Critical Paper

The prewriting stage of a critical paper is much the same as for other expository or persuasive papers. If you have applied the *who-what-when-where-why-how* approach in your reading, you have already generated several ideas for a paper topic. Once you have determined your subject, you can again use this journalistic technique or another of the prewriting tactics suggested earlier to generate ideas about your topic. Papers about literature take the same forms as those about nonliterary topics. You may be writing comparison-and-contrast essays, character sketches, analyses, descriptions, arguments, or other types. Therefore, the organizational problems involved in writing about literature are basically the same as those for other subject matter, as we shall illustrate now.

Thesis and Support Like other papers, the critical paper needs a controlling thesis. This central idea indicates the kind of organization required and the support or evidence needed, as is illustrated by these student examples:

1. Thesis requiring a character sketch of a main character for support:

   > In *The Bridge over the River Kwai,* Colonel Nicholson's dedication to military discipline and duty saves the morale of the men but results in his treason to the British cause.

This thesis requires a cause-and-effect organization, showing first Nicholson's dedication to the bridge's completion, then its effect on his men's morale, and finally how duty becomes the fanatacism that leads to his treason.

2. Thesis requiring a comparison-and-contrast organization:

   > The language of the schoolboys both identifies the members of a group and excludes others from it in Kipling's *Stalky and Co.* and in Knowles' *A Separate Peace.*

This paper may be organized in these two ways:

PLAN A: I. *Stalky & Co.*
       A. Identifying language
       B. Excluding language
   II. *Separate Peace*
       A. Identifying language
       B. Excluding language

PLAN B: I. Identifying language
       A. *Stalky & Co.*
       B. *Separate Peace*
   II. Excluding language
       A. *Stalky & Co.*
       B. *Separate Peace*

Although both plans may be used, Plan B is preferable because it focuses on the language rather than the novels, thus emphasizing the subject of the thesis.

   3.   Thesis requiring analytical organization:

> The turtle in *The Grapes of Wrath* is symbolic of the Joad family and its fight for survival.

This paper requires classifying the numerous adventures and characteristics of the turtle to show how its plight is similar to that of the Joads. Like all papers about symbols, this one would require strong supporting evidence: citations from the work, evaluative comments by the writer.

   4.   Thesis requiring argumentative organization:

> Despite Tolkien's denials, *Lord of the Rings* can be interpreted symbolically as a Christian struggle between good and evil.

This argumentative thesis requires strong support from the novel, backed up perhaps by the opinions of reputable critics. Since the author himself denies the proposition, the student writer must prove that Tolkien's use of symbols, conscious or unconscious, leads the reader to this interpretation. Careful citation of such symbols is of course required to substantiate the proposition.

Audience   Because students usually write critical papers about a work that their fellow students have also read, discussed, and perhaps written about, they sometimes assume that all their readers know the work and need no explanatory materials. This assumption, however, can breed dangerous writing habits. Unless your teacher directs otherwise, you should write to your classmates, but should include among your envisioned readers some outsiders who may have only a slight knowledge of the book. Such an audience will keep you from boring your classmates with too much plot summary, but will force you to provide enough information to enlighten the outsiders. You should:

   1.   Identify the work and author early in the paper, as does the student example on pages 474–77.

   2.   Provide only enough plot information to illustrate the points you make. Resist the common trap of beginning the paper with an extensive plot summary before launching into your real subject. Unless the assignment is to write a plot summary, such detail can be kept to a minimum. The student example strikes a happy balance in this respect. Including details for the less knowledgeable readers also serves the purpose of providing specific evidence to support your inferences.

3.   Define or explain unusual terms or concepts. This is as necessary in critical writing as in other forms of writing. Use any of the methods of brief definition suggested previously (pages 155–57).

Writing

Just as the prewriting of the critical paper is similar to that of other papers, so is the writing. You should start early, follow whatever routine you find comfortable and convenient, and write to get your ideas down on paper, not worrying particularly about such writing matters as spelling, punctuation, word choice, and sentence structure. If you think of new ideas as you write, fine; but try to fit them logically into your organizational plan. Throughout, remember that your purpose is to complete a first draft, not a final paper.

Rewriting

The revising step of the rewriting process permits you to reconsider such major points as the organization of ideas and their development. You should examine how clearly and effectively you have supported the idea stated in your thesis. In this process, you may think of new points you want to make or examples to use. The revising step allows you to plug them into your paper, creating a new and better one, much as you may have done in your other writing assignments.

Editing   The editing step is also similar to the one you have become familiar with in your other papers, but two problems warrant your special attention: tense and the documentation of quotations.

Tense   In writing a critical paper, you may use either the present (called the literary present) or the regular past. Here are examples of your options:

Literary present:
In the opening scene of Hemingway's *A Farewell to Arms,* Lt. Frederic Henry, a young American, *is* attached to an Italian ambulance unit in World War I when he *meets* Catherine Barkley.

Past tense:
In the opening scene . . . *was* attached . . . when he *met* Catherine Barkley.

Most writers prefer the literary present because it makes the action more immediate and vivid. You may take your choice. But having once decided, you should not shift to the other tense in writing about the book. In other words, be consistent.

Documentation of Quotations   In critical writing, it is often necessary or useful to quote directly and frequently from a literary work. If you wish to support an analysis or interpretation, the author's own words normally carry more weight than yours. Sometimes lengthy quotations may be necessary to make a point, but you should bear in mind the warning made about them in the chapter on the research paper. You should also remember or review our discussion of inserting, reducing, and introducing quotations (pages 396–99).

Remember that after fully identifying a source in your first citation of it, you may document the following quotations from that source merely by indicating their page numbers in parentheses (as long as no other work has been mentioned in the meantime). Here's how it is done in the first reference:

> In Goldsmith's *The Vicar,* careless readers may overlook Burchell's referring to Sir William Thornhill as *he* and then switching to the first person, *I,* in the remark, "I have now found . . . (21).

The edition referred to would appear at the end under "Works Cited." Later references are handled like this as long as the source remains clear:

> After hearing his father curse, George reproaches him: "Hold, sir, . . . or I shall blush for thee" (151).

Note that the abbreviation "p." does not precede the page number, according to MLA style. Further, because the quotation is short and is therefore worked into the writer's own text, the sentence period follows the parenthetical citation.

The same convention is used for poems and plays. When quoting the passage about the Baron's "rape" of Clarissa in Pope's "Rape of the Lock," you should indicate the canto and line numbers in parentheses (3.125–54). Hamlet's explanation of why he fails to kill the kneeling Claudius ("Oh, this . . . is not revenge") should be documented by a reference to the act, scene, and line number (3.3.79). In referring to passages without quoting them, however, many writers prefer to use Roman and Arabic numerals: In *Hamlet* III.iii.79, Shakespeare explains. . . .

Proofreading The proofreading step in rewriting critical papers is no different from your former proofreading practice. Because you have spent much time on your paper, both in your reading and writing, you should take special care to see that you do not spoil it by careless typing or handwriting errors. The time you take to read your final draft slowly and intently is definitely well spent.

Example: Tracing a Central Theme Through Character Analysis

In the following paper, Gail Gardenhire, a student, demonstrates the most effective use of character analysis: not merely to describe a character, but to relate the character to a major theme in the work. In this case, Gardenhire develops a limited character sketch choosing only those aspects that support her inference thesis that a postwar conflict of values is a major theme in Ernest Hemingway's novel *The Sun Also Rises*. The organizational scheme is indicated at the side.

Jake Barnes' Loss of Values in *The Sun Also Rises*
Gail Gardenhire

One of the most overwhelming problems that Jake Barnes, the major character in Ernest Hemingway's *The Sun Also Rises,* has to face is adequately stated by a somewhat minor character in the book when Count Mippipopolous advises Jake, "That is the secret. You must get to know the values." Indeed, it seems that throughout this novel, Jake constantly searches to define his values and to see which ones will survive.

Perhaps the greatest influence on Jake's increasing loss of values is his "old grievance." There are, however, several possible interpretations of this phrase, the most obvious being Jake's impotence produced by an injury incurred "on a joke front like the Italian." Lady Brett Ashley might be another of Jake's "old grievances," which drags him farther and farther away from a definition of his values. Brett's "circle" of friends and even her very presence seem only to reinforce Jake's realization that he is incapable of enjoying or satisfying any physical "value" which he might hold, and this, consequently, leads him to seek superficial values as substitutes for human ones.

Also essential to Jake's search is his exposure to a varied set of values characterized by two types of people in the novel and to the transition that these values undergo as these people are introduced to new situations. Perhaps the best example of this idea is the abrupt change in the values of the peasants when confronted with a fiesta in which "everything became quite unreal finally and it seemed as though nothing could have any consequence." These peasants, with their pure and simple ties to the soil and the uncomplicated measure of values in yield of crops or animals raised, quickly lose their pure and simple values, though perhaps only temporarily, when they become involved in the fiesta. Before, "money still had a definite value in hours worked and bushels of grain sold," whereas,

Thesis

I. Jake's sexual impotence and his love for Brett contribute to his loss of values.

II. Shifting values of others in the novel contribute to his moral confusion.

"Late in the fiesta it would not matter what they paid nor where they bought." They have assumed the values of the city.

Similarly, Jake goes through some transition in what he thought to be things most dear to him prior to this fiesta. His enthusiasm for bullfighting had been most precious to him and served as his greatest emotional involvement. As the fiesta progresses, however, and Jake becomes involved in the decaying values of all those about him, he loses, due to his bitterness about inability to give Brett sexual satisfaction, the last of his "precious" values.

III. Jake reexamines his values.

As a result, Jake is forced to redefine his values in terms of money. Here lies the power he lost in his war accident. Here lies a way to satisfy his senses, through adequate food and plentiful wine to dull his inner awareness that these new values are meaningless. Jake reaches the conclusion that life is, after all, "just exchange of values." Everything that life has to offer must be paid for "by experience, or by taking chances, or by money," but "the bill" always comes. If you strive to "pay your way into enough things," then you'll eventually enjoy life and "get your money's worth."

IV. Jake redefines his values.

In essence, Jake has learned that in order to make friends, and in order to survive in this hopelessly "lost generation," one must value only things that can be replaced. Money can be replaced. Friends or acquaintances can be replaced through the use of money, and superficial needs can easily be satisfied with money. Jake has finally decided that he must *not* value his once-in-a-lifetime love for Brett or his enthusiasm for bullfighting, because these are values that cannot easily be replaced with a "simple exchange."

V. Jake exchanges his value system for that of Brett's "circle."

Sadly enough, any glimmer of hope for the survival of values honestly valuable to Jake is lost by the time the fiesta is over, and he succumbs to all of the "lost generation" by admitting that "I did not care what it was all about. All I wanted to know was how to live in it." He makes that final compromise, that final exchange of a life of substance for one of mere existence.

Conclusion: Restatement of thesis and the theme of values.

Note that Gardenhire not only works in significant quotations from the novel throughout her own prose, but effectively introduces her subject with one—a reference to the values that have thematic importance in the novel.

SUMMARY

In this chapter, we have presented a method for you to follow in analyzing literature. The "who-what-where-when-why-how" approach is certainly not the only one, nor have we discussed it fully. Yet you should have some idea now of what to think about and look for when reading fiction. And you should be better prepared to select a subject for a critical paper and to develop interesting and perceptive ideas about it. We have also discussed specific types of subjects and pointed out other considerations in the prewriting, writing, and rewriting of critical papers about literature.

ASSIGNMENTS

For Discussion

1. Consider the following passages, taken from literary works and representative of the narrative device used in each. Identify the kind of narrative point of view used in each.

    a. Gene's brow wrinkled again in irritation; he thought she was deliberately not helping him, whereas in truth she did not know he wanted her help.

    "The point is, Mother, I haven't the money to go."

    Now for something as important to him as this Ruth would never have denied him the money, and Gene knew it. But Ruth herself did not know it, though he thought she did. He thought not only that she knew it but that the long process of reasoning herself into it, which she always went through, was a method of reproaching him. She had nothing like reproach in her mind; though she did not know it she was providing her conscience with good reasons for giving this money to him.

    —*George P. Elliott, "Children of Ruth"*

    b. Yesterday afternoon the six-o'clock bus ran over Miss Bobbit. I'm not sure what there is to be said about it; after all, she was only ten years old, still I know no one of us in this town will forget her. For one thing, nothing she ever did was ordinary, not from the first time that we saw her, and that was a year ago. Miss Bobbit and her mother, they arrived on that same six-o'clock bus, the one that comes through from Mobile. It happened to be my cousin Billy Bob's birthday, and so most of the children in town were here at our house. We were sprawled on the front porch having tutti-frutti and devil cake when the bus stormed around Deadman's Curve. It was the summer that never rained; rusted dryness coated everything; sometimes when a car passed on the road, raised dust would hang in the still air an hour or more. Aunt El said if they didn't pave the highway soon she was going to move down to the seacoast; but she'd said that for such a long time. Anyway, we were sitting on the porch, tutti-frutti melting on our plates, when suddenly, just as we were wishing that something would happen, something did; for out of the red road dust appeared Miss Bobbit. A wiry little girl in a starched, lemon-colored party dress, she sassed along with a grownup mince, one hand on her hip, the other supporting a spinsterish umbrella. Her mother, lugging two cardboard valises and a wind-up victrola, trailed in the background. She was a gaunt shaggy woman with silent eyes and a hungry smile.

—*Truman Capote, "Children on Their Birthdays"*

c. But though my mother and I felt that I was fulfilling my part of the bargain all right, Lothar Swift's promise that I would go to Chicago with the band seemed far less reliable. There were rumors going around that he was having plenty of trouble raising money to move his horde so far, let alone to shelter them once he got them to the city.

Presently a form letter came for me. It said that band members had been put on either an *A* list or a *B* list, according to merit. While it was still the band's intention to pay travel and lodging expenses for all its members, it appeared necessary to ask that all *B* members sell two excursion tickets to "band supporters" who might wish to go along to Chicago. The tickets cost $47.50 apiece. Naturally, of course, I was on the *B* list.

—*R. V. Cassill, "The Biggest Band"*

d. Tom remembered that outside the hospital under the stone and brick carriage porch of the *Sanitarium,* on the newly curving and richly planted driveway which the old self-taught doctor had just had redone commemorating that his one son had just graduated from Harvard Medical School, the men had shouldered into their topcoats in the chilly September night and got into their cars, switched on their lights and pulled away. His father had been the last to pull away, in his brand new Studebaker. As he did, his wife, Tom's mother, had begun to sob and cry again. She had hated the old man, the grandfather, ever since she had first met him; and he had equally disliked and detested her. Tom and his sister had whispered together in the backseat about this new state of things where they were no longer grandchildren. They knew all about the active dislike between their mother and the grandfather, since she had told them over and over how miserable and unhappy he made her life having to live so close to him, so they did not put too much stock in her weeping and grief. They were much more interested in where people went when they died.

—James Jones, "The Ice-Cream Headache"

2. In his play *Desire Under the Elms,* Eugene O'Neill gives an explicit, detailed description of the setting he wishes for the play and for each scene. Here is the setting description for the opening scene, followed by the appearance of one of the main characters. What can you surmise from it about O'Neill's use of setting in the play?

> *Exterior of the farmhouse. It is sunset of a day at the beginning of the summer in the year 1850. There is no wind and everything is still. The sky above the roof is suffused with deep colors, the green of the elms glows, but the house is in shadow, seeming pale and washed out by contrast.*
>
> *A door opens and* EBEN CABOT *comes to the end of the porch and stands looking down the road to the right. He has a large bell in his hand and this he swings mechanically, awakening a deafening clangor. Then he puts his hands on his hips and stares up at the sky. He signs with a puzzled awe and blurts out with halting appreciation.*
> EBEN. God! Purty!
> *He spits on the ground with intense disgust, turns and goes back into the house.*

3. What kind of critical paper should result from each of the following student thesis statements: character sketch, comparison-and-contrast, cause-and-effect, argument, other? What key terms in the statements require discussion and support? What weaknesses do they manifest?

    a. The Joad family in *The Grapes of Wrath* possesses the same kind of unselfish love that the biblical Good Samaritan had.

    b. In the novel *The Bridge,* the baptism of Priest serves as a transitional link from the ending of one era to the beginning of a new one.

    c. In *Waiting for Godot,* Samuel Beckett explores Christian symbolism in the guise of garment and nature imagery to support the central themes in his play.

    d. In "Bright and Morning Star," Richard Wright illustrates the maturation of the protagonist by contrasting two rebels—one old and one young.

    e. In *The Secret Sharer* the young captain as an outsider struggles to overcome his external isolation by correcting his internal, self-imposed isolation.

    f. In *Matryona's House,* both Matryona and the narrator are quiet social rebels.

    g. In Salinger's *The Catcher in the Rye,* Holden Caulfield can be seen both as a social rebel and as a victim of society.

24

Writing in Science and Social Science Courses

During your undergraduate years, whether you major in some scientific field or not, you will take several courses in the natural or social sciences. Although your writing assignments may differ from those in the humanities, you will use many of the writing skills you have already learned. Your science instructors, like your freshman composition teachers, will expect you to write clearly, precisely, and objectively in the specialized writing tasks they assign.

Generally, you will encounter three types of writing assignments: book reviews similar in form to those discussed on pages 448–52; library reviews of research, which involve most of the same writing considerations as the research paper discussed on pages 395–402; and experimental or laboratory reports.

WRITING BASED ON EXPERIMENTATION AND OBSERVATION

Most of your writing assignments in courses such as biology, chemistry, and physics will deal with results of laboratory experiments or field observations. In either case, the data gathering precedes the writing stage and is an important part of the prewriting process, whether the information is collected by carefully recording the step-by-step performance of a lab experiment and its results or by meticulously documenting field observations.

Some courses, such as chemistry and physics, will emphasize lab experiments; others, such as botany, geology, and psychology, may combine lab and field studies. In courses like astronomy or sociology, where you must study phenomena not possible to duplicate in a laboratory, such as the movement of stars and planets in space or the behavior of human beings in societies, you will record your observations and then relate your findings to theories and hypotheses.

Often, too, you will need to acquaint yourself with the research already done in a certain area and to support your own findings with those of professional scientists. In a lab or field study report, for example, you might include a section that reviews the research already done in your area of study. Or a review of research may comprise a complete assignment in itself.

For such a study you may have to use specialized science libraries for gathering such data. There you may find that the bibliographical information has been computerized, requiring you to expand the library skills you learned in courses like English and history. If this is the case, seek help from the librarians in the science library; they are experts in the use of such research materials. Remember that even though you may use different means for gathering a bibliography in a science course, the other steps suggested in the chapters on the research paper (pages 365-66) remain essentially the same.

As you can deduce, the "three R's" in scientific writing are *research, record,* and *report.* Writing may result from primary research—your own observation or experimentation—or from secondary library sources. Unlike the personal writing and much of the expository writing you have been asked to do, scientific writing does not allow you to rely solely on your past experience and knowledge. The writing in your science courses will require you to research, absorb, and integrate new and often drastically unfamiliar information. In addition, because you are expected to record the data as a scientist would, you will need to become familiar with the forms of scientific writing and to become proficient in using the specialized vocabulary of the field in reporting your data. In the writing process itself, you will find that you can draw upon many previously acquired writing skills. As we discuss the various kinds of scientific writing, we will point out their relationships to other writing forms.

The Laboratory Manual

With each exercise, most laboratory manuals furnish a page or two of instructions for materials to use, steps to follow, and safety precautions to take, if necessary. In addition, there may be a data sheet for recording your results or calculations. Sometimes the manual may include questions about the experiment, which you should always answer with carefully constructed, complete sentences. And you may be asked to write a conclusion stating the generalizations you have drawn from your observations. Often in this, you will need to explain why your experiment did not obtain the expected results. Here's a student example written in a physics lab:

Conclusion:
    The experiment overall was very simple, but it demonstrated an important law. By measuring the amount of current (measured in milliamps, but converted to amps) and the potential difference (in volts), the resistance of the circuit can be calculated by Ohm's Law, $V = IR$.
    If we measured the accuracy of our procedure by the 90% differences in our values, part A was acceptable. The values were close, but a 9% difference was still produced. One possible reason was that it was hard

to get the needles (or current) stable. Part B should be done over, since a 58% error is unacceptable. However, we didn't have any special problems with this part, since it was exactly like the other part. The only difference was that the light bulb was added as an extra resistor.

Overall, the experiment was very helpful in demonstrating what we are now doing in lecture.

—Neal Mantick

As you can see, the lab assignment requires more than scientific techniques. Writing in clear, explanatory prose is an important aspect of scientific research. However, the lab manual is only part of the writing picture; in many courses, you will also be asked to keep a laboratory notebook.

The Laboratory Notebook

The laboratory notebook has much in common with the journals we have been urging you to keep for other kinds of writing. As we mentioned in Chapter 2, Leonardo da Vinci interspersed the entries in his journals with scientific observations that included detailed drawings. In a later time, Charles Darwin recorded in his journals the plant and animal life he encountered in his voyages, enabling him to develop his theory of evolution. Today, all professional scientists keep such journals, usually called laboratory notebooks. In these, they record every step of an experiment or observation, making careful sketches of equipment used or parts studied and recording the materials, methods, and results in as objective and clear a manner as possible, so that another scientist can duplicate the research. In addition, scientists often record questions they might have about their results or method, insights into the experiment's relationship to other scientific data or knowledge, and indications of further research needed. Importantly, all these are recorded during the course of the experiment or observation—nothing is left to memory.

Although individual instructors may give you specific directions for notebook format, generally you should apply the following suggestions. Many of these can also be used in completing the assignments in your lab manual.

1. Buy a separate notebook—one that will be easy to carry with you, but large enough to write in comfortably.

2. Make your entries in complete sentences because they force you to gain an understanding of the experiment and the reasons for it. They also help to ensure better recall of the process.

3. Write so that someone else at your level of expertise can duplicate the procedure.

4. Describe the experience according to the principles for analyzing a process given on pages 143–50. Generally a chronological sequence is required, but your material should not seem like a list or a bare outline. Make sure that you provide the logical transitions and relationship signals expected in any kind of expository writing.

5. Supply as many concrete, exact, specific details as possible. When you describe the equipment used, it should be in the form of objective description (pages 140–42).

6. Try to record everything carefully enough so that you will not need to make changes or additions. However, if you feel that some change is needed, make it before you leave the lab or observation site. Don't trust to memory or revise the material a day or two later. You may not remember accurately then.

7. If your draft must be recopied before you hand it in, copy it exactly without making substantive changes. Although you would be well advised to correct mechanical or spelling errors, don't change words or steps in the process unless absolutely necessary. Your original draft should not be discarded, but submitted with the rewritten version.

Remember that the laboratory notebook, like the lab manual, serves a double purpose: It helps train you in the scientific method of carefully recording data, and it serves as a tool for practicing scientific writing.

The Formal Laboratory Report

Unlike the research paper that relies solely on library research, the formal laboratory report draws most heavily on the research you conduct yourself in the laboratory or field. As we indicated earlier in the chapter, scientists have developed a rather tight, conventional form for laboratory reports. Like entries in the lab notebook, the format you follow is closely related to the scientific method itself, with the body of the report arranged in the chronological order of the experiment or observation. First comes a detailed account of the equipment used and the methods employed, then an analysis of the results or findings, and finally, a conclusion about the results.

In addition, scientists include a brief abstract or summary of the report, usually placed at the beginning. Also at the beginning of the paper is an introduction; at the end, a bibliography is provided if other research has been cited. When completed, the structure of most laboratory reports is as follows:

  I.   Abstract or Summary
 II.   Introduction
III.   Methods and Materials
 IV.   Results
  V.   Conclusions
 VI.   Bibliography of Sources Cited

Prewriting the Laboratory Report

Generally the subject for a formal laboratory report grows out of an assigned experiment or field study. If not, the prewriting technique of "brainstorming" (pages 295–96) is particularly valuable in finding a suitable scientific subject.

Furthermore, although the limits you put on your subject often are dictated by the nature of the experiment or the amount of time allotted for the field study, you may find the "perspective" technique (pages 178–79) useful in restricting a broad subject. However, it is always wise to consult with your teacher about your topic choice.

As with any research paper, part of the prewriting process involves the preliminary gathering of information or data. In the laboratory report, except for background information you might supply about other studies, your experiment or field study substitutes for library research. As you might guess, tabulating and recording the experiment in your lab notebook also serves a prewriting purpose. Analogous to the focused freewriting described on pages 44–45, it constitutes a first draft for your more extensive report.

As we indicated earlier, you may need to search in the library for information about studies related to yours. In this case, be aware of the specialized indexes and abstracts in the science fields. Space permits us to list only a few here; check the lists on pages 373–75 and the resource bibliographies in your own library to find others.

Abstracts of Mycology
Animal Behavior Abstracts
Applied Science and Technology
  Index
Aquatic Biology Abstracts
Biological Abstracts
Biological and Agricultural Index
Botany Subject Index
Chemical Abstracts

Cumulated Index Medicus
Microbiology Abstracts
Physics Abstracts
Science Abstracts
Science Citation Index
Social Science Index
Sources and Information in the Social
  Sciences

Like the *Psychological Abstracts* described on page **494**, the natural science abstracts contain indexes that include summaries of reports and articles, an author index, a general concept index, and an index of specific subjects. To use the library most efficiently, use the indexes first to gather a bibliography, then skim the abstracts to find reports that might be useful for your purposes. If you need help, ask the librarian; also, many libraries supply handout instructions on how to use the abstract indexes.

In taking notes, follow the suggestions we offered on pages 383–90. Your handling of quoted material in the report will be similar to those suggested for writing the research review paper (pages 497–98).

Adapting the Report to Your Audience

In college, most of your laboratory reports will be addressed to a science instructor or the other students in a science class. Therefore, unless your report deals with a subject not studied in class or your instructor specifies a general audience, your main concerns will not involve explaining concepts, defining vocabulary terms, or convincing your readers of the importance of the study. But this will not always be the case if you continue in a scientific field. If you someday write a report for a government agency, for industry, or for a research organization, you will need to concern yourself with these matters. And although you may restrict yourself to descriptive and expository techniques in class-assigned reports, you might need to use persuasive tactics in reports submitted to industry or to research foundations. Therefore, even though the format of a laboratory report is fairly rigid, the writing tactics you choose, as in all kinds of writing, will depend on your relationship with your audience and on the extent of their expertise in your field.

Organizing the Laboratory Report

Although the laboratory report requires a built-in, overall organizational scheme, don't be lulled into thinking that all your organizational problems will be solved by it. Because the way information is handled is different in each section of the report, you must consider how to organize each of these sections. For instance, the introduction may define some problem that led to the research, provide a history and analysis of previous studies, discuss some difficulties other scientists have encountered, or evaluate the work done previously. Deciding how to organize these matters requires careful consideration. Also, prior knowledge of what is expected in a report can help you in writing a laboratory report. In the following discussion we will point out the kinds of information and the writing skills each section demands.

Writing the Laboratory Report

Many scientific writers recommend writing the section of the report in the following order instead of in the order they will finally appear (see outline, page 484).

III. Methods and Materials

You should write the methods and materials section first for these reasons:

1. It is the most straightforward section of the report, using factual description and process description, usually organized in chronological order.

2. To a large degree, it has already been written. If you have logged your equipment and procedures carefully in your lab notebook and lab manual as you worked through the experiment or study, only minor changes in style and mechanics need to be made. (The precautions about substantive changes that we made in the discussion of lab notebook entries apply also to the laboratory report.)

3. Because accuracy is crucial, writing this section while the research data are still fresh in your memory is essential. Some scientists write it even before they gather information on previous research.

4. Even though you have already reached some conclusions about your findings, reworking the description of the research process often creates new insights.

What should be included in this section on methods and materials? To answer, ask yourself another question: "What would I need to include so that I can duplicate the study five years from now?" Obviously, you would need a complete factual description of all equipment used in the experiment (tubing, wiring, instruments), or the kinds of subjects studied (mice, rabbits, microorganisms), or both if both apply: Special equipment, such as an oscilloscope, should be specified exactly—by manufacturer, model number, size, or other pertinent identification. In addition to detailed description, scientists frequently include drawings or photographs of equipment or subjects.

Like entries in the lab notebook, this section generally is an accurate, factual analysis of a process as discussed on pages 143–50—moving in chronological order through step 1, step 2, and so on. Often, to clarify the process, scientists provide flow charts—drawings which show the mechanical setup of the experiment and the steps of the process. If you're not good at drawing, your instructor might permit you to take a photograph and label the parts and sequence. Almost any kind of graphic representation that helps explain your research design is acceptable. For instance, maps can be useful in pinpointing the location of observations made in the field. Instruction on how to construct the various kinds of graphic representations is usually given by the lab instructor.

IV. Results

The recommended second step is to write the results section, since it follows logically from the description of your research process. Be careful, however, not to draw conclusions about your study at this stage; you should merely report your results as factually and objectively as possible.

Even though you may indent and number the results, the section should not be a bare outline or list, but written like any expository, explanatory paper. As an example, here's an excerpt taken from a student report on a study of several stream locations to assess the water quality and the factors affecting it.

> Chloride concentrations were determined by titration in the lab. The highest count was, as expected, at the sewage treatment plant where chloride is used in sewage treatment. When chloride counts were correlated with snow and road salting, the two most urbanized stations showed the highest levels and station five (the third most urbanized) was third.
>
> —*Greg Shields*

In this section, your instructor may also expect you to include figures or tables to illustrate your findings. Although we cannot offer a complete course in how to construct these, we do make some suggestions later in this chapter on how they should be labeled and discussed.

II. Introduction

At this stage, it may seem logical to proceed to the conclusion section, but experts in scientific writing recommend that you write the introduction section next. Again, there are valid reasons for this suggestion. Your conclusion should reflect all the data you have collected, whether from your own experiments or the reports of others. Since your introduction contains important background information, often including references to other studies, it should contribute to the conclusions you reach. Writing the introduction before the conclusion may alert you to [or may reveal] new relationships between other studies and your own.

In introductory courses, most of your background information may come from your lab manual and your textbook. If so, you should paraphrase and summarize this material, not copy it. (If you need to review paraphrasing, see pages 386–90.) But even in freshman courses, you may be expected to seek out library references.

As in the rest of the laboratory report, there are rather strict conventions about what to include in the introduction. Your introduction should state your subject along with background information and your purpose in writing the report. You should also define key terms and indicate your experiment's scope and design.

Here's a student example of an introduction that makes reference to past studies, gives background information providing a reason for the present study, and states the specific purpose of it. Note that sources are carefully documented (in this case, in the style commonly used in biology).

Over the last 20 years a number of methods have been developed to assess water quality (Gaufin and Tarzwell 1955, 1956; APHA 1975). Originally, only chemical surveys were employed; however, it was recognized that chemical surveys indicate stream conditions only at the time of sampling (Farrell 1931; Wilhm and Dorris 1966; Wilhm 1967, 1972).

Survey of chemical research

Recently, emphasis has been placed on the biological diversity of water systems to indicate water quality because the living component of the system in question is indicative of both past and present environmental conditions. Even a short term exposure to water of poor quality may destroy intolerant organisms and change the community structure (Cairns and Dickson 1971). It is for this reason that aquatic organisms are being used more frequently to evaluate conditions in streams. Bottom organisms are particularly suitable for such studies because their habitat preference and low motility cause them to be affected directly by substances which enter the environment (Wilhm 1967; APHA 1975).

Background: Indicates importance of biological component; cites research

The importance of aquatic biota as indicative of stream quality does not diminish the importance of the chemical and physical parameters. There are certain important physical and chemical parameters such as pH, oxygen saturation, discharge, etc. that are highly indicative of stream quality. Knowledge of these parameters in the water system in question is essential in determining the water quality.

Discussion: Indicates the design of the study

Certain factors are known to influence the biological, chemical, and physical characteristics of a stream. Among these are degree of urbanization and stream order (see Horton 1945). The purpose of this study is to assess the effects of these two factors on the water quality of six streams in Fayette County, Kentucky.

Purpose and scope

—Ann Phillippi

As you can see, the student did not merely list the studies in chronological order. Instead, she classified the studies—first, those that were chemical surveys, then those that focused on biological diversity.

V. Conclusions

The conclusion of a laboratory report serves the same basic functions as that of any other paper: to summarize the discussion in the body of the paper and to restate the main idea (in scientific papers, generally a hypothesis). But the conclusion of a laboratory report may require other information. If, for example, your assignment repeats a classic experiment, then your conclusion should also report whether or not your results correspond with the original experiment. If not, you need to explain possible reasons for the unexpected results.

Also, because your conclusion will contain generalizations that you make from observation and experimentation, it requires that you indicate the thinking processes you used in analyzing the data. In comparing your results with others, you will need to use comparison-and-contrast; for pointing out possible reasons for your results, a cause-and-effect method will be necessary. (For a review of these writing tactics, see pages 163–64 and 160–63.)

Often, too, you will be expected to point out any weaknesses of your study or areas that need further research. Another tactic used in the conclusions of scientific papers is to include suggestions for other ways to research the subject. Be careful, however, that you avoid sounding apologetic or defensive about your own study. Make your case with as objective a tone as possible.

I. Abstract or Summary

In writing an abstract, the biblical adage applies: "The last shall be first." Although such summaries are usually placed at the beginning of reports, they should be written last. The reason is obvious: The abstract is a summary of your completed draft, either a brief description of the experiment or study (descriptive abstract) or a short explanation of the problems involved or of the results obtained (informative abstract). In either case, it should follow the same organizational pattern as your report. Although very short (150-250 words), the abstract must be a concise, clear summary of the material covered. Because a poorly written, badly organized, vague abstract can result in the rejection of a grant proposal or a research contract, abstracts are a highly significant part of any report.

The following abstract, written by a mining engineering student, summarizes his report, "The Technical and Economical Feasibility of Coal-Derived Methanol." This particular abstract is mostly informative, rather than descriptive.

Abstract

Coal has great potential as an alternate feedstock for methanol production. The basic process for manufacturing synthetic methanol consists of a series of chemical reactions which convert a feedstock into methanol. Methanol production from natural gas occurs in roughly this same basic process. A proposed process for deriving methanol from coal also uses essentially the same steps in this process, except coal must be mined and screened beforehand. However, this proposed methanol from coal process can also adapt to underground coal gasification. The construction of a coal-derived methanol plant using the proposed process would take six years. This construction is currently uneconomical because the predicted price of coal-derived methanol in six years is 19 cents per gallon greater than the predicted price of natural gas-derived methanol. However, several predicted trends indicate that coal-derived methanol may someday become feasible. These include drastically increasing natural gas prices due to its deregulation, greater demand, production stabilization, and desirable characteristics; mildly increasing coal prices due to its abundance, a mature mining industry, and increased production; and drastically increasing methanol demand due to the opening of new methanol markets, such as motor fuels. Experts predict these trends will cause production of methanol from coal to become economical as early as 1995. This economy of production will allow companies to supply the market with methanol derived from coal.

—*Robert Davis Stapleton*

VI. Bibliography

Like any other research paper where sources are cited, the laboratory report must include a bibliography. Because many sciences use the APA (American Psychological Association) format, you may need to refresh your memory on its conventions (see pages 411–18). Or your instructor may specify another format.

Appendix

Your report, especially one written for an introductory course, may or may not include an appendix. In this section, raw data are reported or results are shown, usually in the form of graphs or tables. Your instructor will advise you whether or not an appendix is needed and what should be included for a particular assignment.

Title

The title of a laboratory report should be informative. Generally, it will be longer and more detailed than the titles you would use for nonscientific papers. It should contain specific information about the purpose of the study, not simply state the subject. The title of the report from which we reprinted the introduction (page 488) is a good example: *The Effects of Urbanization and Stream Order on the Biological, Chemical, and Physical Characteristics of Six Streams.* This title is effective because it reflects the research design as well as the subject of the study. Note how much more informative it is than these titles from two other student reports in the same course:

1. *Limnological Study of South Elkhorn Creek Basin*
2. *Lab Report: Limnology*

The first title identifies only the type and site of the study; the second doesn't even indicate the site. Neither provides information about the nature and scope of the study. As you create your own titles, you would do well to remember your own frustrations in gathering a bibliography. Which of the sample titles would have been most helpful to you for finding sources on a similar topic?

Finishing Touches

A laboratory report usually has a separate title page. If your instructor does not specify a format, adapt the one suggested on page 419 or ask for special instructions on form. In a lengthy report, you should also include a table of contents with page numbers of the various sections.

Figures and Tables

Among the most common figures are graphs and charts. Line graphs are useful for demonstrating the behavior of two variables, such as temperature variations at different times of the day. Bar graphs, because they are easily read and interpreted, are a popular means of showing relationships among a number of variables. Figures should be numbered consecutively if more than one is included, and all figures should have captions. For an example, see Figure 24-1, a combined line and bar graph showing temperature variables.

Tables are especially useful for recording raw data or the results of observations. Tables are consecutively numbered separately from figures, usually with

Figure 24-1

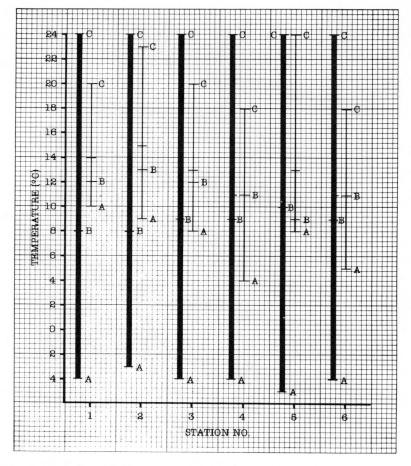

The temperature range (vertical lines) of the air (———) and the water (■■■) with actual values indicated by the short horizontal lines. Average values for each station are indicated by the red horizontal lines. A = 2/3/78; B = 3/10/78; C = 4/7/78.

Arabic numerals but occasionally with letters: A, B, C, and so on. Figure 24–2 is one type taken from a student report.

These examples represent only two of the graphic representations used by scientific writers. However, they are the most frequent ones expected of students in college courses. Because it is not our purpose to instruct you in graphics but in writing, we offer only a glance at them here. Our main concern is with the writing involved in their use.

When included in an appendix, these graphics need just enough written explanation to make them self-explanatory. When placed in one of the sections of the report, however, they should be discussed. But instead of merely describing in words what the graphic already shows, *comment* on the information: Compare

Figure 24-2

TABLE A

Results of 5-Minute Stream Invertebrate Collection, Shelby Branch, 2/24/81							
Taxon	Total No.	B1	B2	B3	B4	B5	Frequency per collection
Planaria	2	1	1	0	0	0	0.4
Helosoma	3	0	0	1	1	1	0.6
Goniobasis	93	38	19	10	14	12	1.0
Gammarus	17	7	1	4	4	1	1.0
Lirceus	135	24	24	27	50	10	1.0

your findings or results, generalize about the behavior illustrated in the graph, or classify the information in some way. For instance, the writer using our example Table A might divide the organisms into groups arranged from largest numbers to smallest in discussing his findings. Whatever you do in your analysis of the data represented in a figure or table, it should be relevant to your purpose in the report.

Some Stylistic Matters. Many scientific writers prefer to use the passive voice so that they can avoid "I" or "we," and although attitudes toward this practice are changing, the passive voice unquestionably is more common and more useful in scientific writing than elsewhere. For a discussion of both effective and ineffective uses of the passive, see pages 213–15. Whatever you may do in a particular case about the active-passive problem, don't solve the problem by using stilted phrases such as "this researcher" or "these investigators"; it is far better to use either the passive or the personal pronoun "I" with an active verb.

Rewriting the Laboratory Report

Even though you may have revised and edited as you wrote each section, you should still practice the three steps of rewriting the finished paper that we have suggested throughout the book. However, you should not revise extensively in the two sections that describe your experiment: "Materials and Methods" and "Results." In these, edit carefully, checking for sentence structure and clarity, eliminating excessive wordiness if it occurs.

In other sections, follow the advice given for rewriting the research review paper given on pages 497–98 and for the research paper on pages 400–20.

WRITING BASED ON LIBRARY RESEARCH

In many of your social science courses, such as psychology, political science, sociology, economics, anthropology, or education, you may be asked to investigate the published research on a given subject and to write a paper reviewing it. Like all writing assignments, the process of writing a research review paper involves prewriting, writing, and rewriting. To illustrate how these steps can be applied to such an assignment, we work through them in the context of a psychology paper; the same techniques, however, can be adapted to similar assignments in other courses.

Prewriting

As in any assignment based on library research, an important part of prewriting is to search out sources, engage in preliminary reading, and gather a bibliography. The discussion of these tasks in Chapter 20 should help you. Here we will focus on the four major steps of 1) selecting a subject, 2) adapting it to your audience, 3) taking notes, and 4) organizing the material.

Selecting a Subject

Selecting a subject may be easy or exhausting. Your instructor may provide one or a list of possibilities, your textbook may suggest some topics, or you may have some special interest to pursue, such as hypnosis, extrasensory perception, or intelligence tests. If you have a ready-made subject, count your blessings.

If not, try some of the numerous invention devices previously mentioned, such as freewriting, listing, brainstorming, or constructing a viewpoint wheel. In addition, flip through your textbook, looking at chapter headings and subheadings, and at the notes or the bibliography at the ends of the chapters or the end of the book to find topics that interest you and seem worthy of further investigation.

In addition, consider the major research areas by consulting an abstract index in the field, such as *Psychological Abstracts*. In that journal, the table of contents lists sixteen different divisions, among them general psychology, experimental psychology (human and animal), communication systems, developmental psychology, personality, social processes and social issues (marriage and the family, drug and alcohol use, and psychosexual behavior and sex roles).

If the general categories in the abstract index do not generate ideas, try the subject index, an alphabetical list of several hundred special subjects discussed in the articles. Placed at the end of the journal, this subject index will help not only in suggesting topics but in indicating whether sufficient information is available about that subject.

In addition to determining the availability of information, you should decide whether the topic is too simple or difficult—and too general or specific. Students tend to select subjects that are too general. Try to narrow yours by limiting the study to a certain age, type, or other group, or to some single perspective, such as behavioral, psychogenic, or organic, or perhaps to a comparison of two perspectives on a single issue. For example, the topic of autism is obviously too broad but you could narrow it to a paper about a particular approach to treatment of autistic children. Whatever you choose, you would be wise to check with your instructor after class or during announced office hours if you have any qualms about your subject.

Adapting the Paper to an Audience

Your concern about readers—as in planning most papers—is to determine who they are, what they know about the subject, how familiar they are with technical terms, and how they will use the information in your paper. Obviously, you would write different papers for your parents, your classmates, and your instructor, and it is also true that college papers are, in a sense, drills to prepare you for a variety of situations. So, even though your instructor may be your only real reader, you should find out what kind of audience the instructor wants you to write for. Only then can you decide what that audience needs to know. For example, if you are writing about transsexualism for a general audience, you would have to define the term. Your instructor, on the other hand, would need no such definition. Similarly, you might include the reactions of the clergy to the initiation of sex-altering surgery at Johns Hopkins Hospital in 1966 in a paper for a general audience, but not in a technical one for your instructor. Once again, knowing the needs of your audience is important.

Taking Notes

Review papers generally summarize information about methods, subjects, procedures, and the author's discussion of the results. Note how this information is used in the following example:

> Investigating the effects of therapist experience and general clinical ability in the treatment of schizophrenia, Tuma, May, Yale, and Forsythe 1978 studied 228 first admission schizophrenic patients without significant prior treatment. Patients received treatment from 38 residents or recently graduated psychiatrists by one of five methods (individual psychotherapy, ataractic drug treatment, individual psychotherapy *plus* the drug treatment, electroshock, and milieu care). The authors were able to find no evidence for the effects of therapist experience or general clinical ability on outcome. Differences which were found among therapists were related to length of time the therapists kept the patients in the hospital. An additional finding was that drug treatment tended to obscure or override these findings but did not eliminate entirely the effects.
>
> —*Jesse G. Harris, Jr., "Prognosis," pp. 38–39*

As this example illustrates, you need to take notes carefully, jotting down information about the methods, subjects, procedures, and discussion, and any other important facts about the study. All these details are significant because they provide the evidence for conclusions.

Organizing the Paper

Because the research review paper is expository, any of the organizational patterns previously discussed may be used. But the most common pattern is chronological, moving from a description of earlier studies to more recent ones. A paper about the causes of criminal deviant behavior, for instance, might begin with the nineteenth century work in phrenology by Johann Spurzheim and Franz Gall, continue with the twentieth century studies about physical stigmata, body types, the Jukes and the Kallikaks, including the work on chromosomal aberrations by Jacobs and others, and conclude with the reactions to the XYY theories by Montagu and later investigators who place greater emphasis on the environment.

Naturally, the chronological pattern cannot be used alone in all papers. Often cause-and-effect is also employed, as it might be in a paper dealing with the nature, causes, and treatment of migraines. In these examples, writers might arrange the material in cause-effect or effect-cause order, dealing first with a research review of the causes or conditions leading to migraines and then with ways to deal with or prevent them. Or, they could begin with preventive measures and then investigate causes and conditions. In other papers, comparison and contrast might be used—as in a study of how married women cope with the demands of their home roles (wife, mother, cook, maid) and their nonhome roles (student, employee, volunteer). Comparison-and-contrast organization is often also used in sections of a paper to compare related studies or to contrast the results of experiments with control and experimental groups.

Organizing a paper involves preparing a temporary outline to arrange ideas not only in the body of the paper but in the introduction and conclusion. The research review paper usually begins with a discussion, stating the importance of the subject, pointing out a problem concerned with it, or explaining the purpose of the study. For example, a study of body-build stereotypes in children might start by explaining the importance of this subject in social learning theory. Included could be a discussion of how fat children may be the victims of a self-fulfilling stereotype that describes them as stronger and braver but less attractive and more often teased than skinny children. Regardless of exactly how the study begins, it should include a specific thesis statement asserting exactly what you intend to do in the paper. For instance, the purpose of the preceding study might be threefold: (1) to determine whether body-build stereotypes of children exist; (2) to learn when children are influenced by them; and (3) to find out how children are affected by them.

The conclusion may summarize the main points of the paper if it is lengthy, but in any case it should contain your reactions to the findings. Among the questions you might consider are the following:

1.   What limitations do you perceive in the past studies?
2.   What inferences can you draw from the findings?
3.   What should be the direction of future studies?
4.   What changes or developments do you expect will occur?
5.   What aspects of your study did you find particularly noteworthy?

The following conclusion from a student paper on suicide by Edward F. Tipton illustrates how the answers to several of these questions might be used to end a paper:

> While a great deal of research has been initiated in the past twenty years, an even greater amount needs to be conducted for the detection and prevention of suicide. Certain signs and symptoms of suicidal individ-

uals have been delineated, but more accurate tests and scales need to be developed to determine more covert suicidal intent. In the area of prevention, much remains to be done. While Suicide Prevention Centers are revolutionary in concept and goals, many problems still need to be worked out. Also, more education is needed for the general public to recognize those people inclined toward self-destruction, and greater use of "gatekeepers" is called for. In addition, Suicide Prevention Centers should initiate some type of public relations campaign so that "high lethality" persons are more aware of services available to them and encouraged to take advantage of them. This seems especially critical because of the noted lack of participation in these programs by suicide victims. Overall, however, the outlook is bright, assuming as much progress will occur in the next twenty years as in the past twenty.

Writing the Research Review Paper

Our suggestions for writing the research paper (see pages 395–400) also apply to the research review paper. If you have drawn up a temporary outline and have keyed your note cards into it, you should be able to write a first draft without much difficulty. Remember, as we have pointed out previously, that it's important to get your ideas down on paper to see what they are. Later you can add, delete, modify, and rearrange them.

Rewriting the Research Review Paper

After you have completed your first draft, carefully go through the three stages of rewriting—revising, editing, and proofreading. As with the writing stage, the rewriting steps are similar to those suggested for research papers (see pages 400–20). Unless your instructor specifies a different style, follow the APA style of documentation described on pages 411–18.

In editing, check to make certain that you have followed the documentation style exactly, and also note whether you have avoided awkwardness in citing your sources. They may be mentioned in several ways:

Source as subject

> Fallik and Liron (1976) conducted a follow-up study on
>
> schizophrenic patients from different subgroups in Israel.

Source included in predicate

> One of the most vocal advocates of forensic hypnosis is Martin
>
> Reisser, a psychologist with the Los Angeles Police Department.

Source as object of preposition

Sources are often cited in prepositional phrases which also serve as transitional or parenthetical modifiers.

According to Aaron Katcher, associate professor of psychiatry at the University of Pennsylvania: "Perhaps pets are not substitutes for human contact, but [they] offer a kind of relationship which other human beings do not provide."

Source as citation

Recent research finds that the political drives of women are influenced by the self-esteem, attitudes and political drives of mothers rather than fathers (Kelly and Boutilier, 1978).

The main point to remember in using any one of these ways of citing is that it should fit smoothly and naturally into the sentence flow of your paper.

Another matter to consider in editing is your use of headings. Usually, the main and secondary sections of your paper should have them to help readers follow your organization more easily. The headings can simply be transferred from your outline to the paper but should appear in this form or a similar one:

Main Heading: Centered, Capitals and Lowercase

Second Level: Flush Left, Capitals and Lowercase, Underlined

This discussion of the research review paper should be valuable in introductory and advanced social science courses when experiments are conducted and the results are written up according to APA style. In these reports, a review of the literature about the subject normally appears in the introductory section, after the abstract. Following this review come sections about the methods used, the subjects who participated, the apparatus employed, the procedure followed, the results obtained, and the discussion of their significance. As you can see, the organization for this type of paper is standardized so you would be wise to consult the *Publication Manual of the American Psychological Association* or to follow closely the format of articles in an APA journal.

We highly recommend that you look at scholarly journals in a particular field before you write papers in any of the sciences. If you follow the style you find in the articles, you will satisfy your instructor.

SUMMARY

Two writing assignments frequently given in science courses have been discussed in this chapter: one based primarily on original research—experimentation and observation; the other based exclusively on library research. The first, the formal laboratory or field study report, is a highly conventionalized form used not only in science courses but in many fields of technological and scientific research.

Some form of the laboratory report is used in making routine progress reports in a number of industries, in submitting proposals for changes in production design, in reporting population studies, and the like.

The second writing form, the research review paper, can be assigned in many college courses, not only in the social sciences, but also in courses such as education, history, pharmacy, geography, and social work. A section dealing with a review of research is often included in laboratory reports, business reports, and graduate theses and dissertations.

Practice in these kinds of writing tasks, therefore, can benefit you in the writing tasks you may be asked to perform outside a college environment as well as those assigned in your science classes.

ASSIGNMENTS

For Discussion

Writing Based on Experimentation and Observation

1. What kinds of research might you expect to do for writing assignments in science courses? Give examples from your own experience in such courses.

2. What kinds of information might be included on a laboratory data sheet? What kind of writing is expected?

3. How do the laboratory manual and the laboratory notebook contribute to writing a formal laboratory report?

4. How does the writing in formal laboratory reports relate to the various forms of writing discussed in *The Writing Commitment*? Illustrate with situations in which each might be used.

5. Relate the steps involved in the writing process used in formal laboratory reports to the scientific method.

6. Evaluate each of the following student summaries according to these questions and instructions:
    What would you expect the paper to deal with? (subject)
    Does each summary primarily provide information or describe the methodology of the research?
    What kinds of research are evident?
    Outline the points you would expect to be made in a paper written from each.

    a. The fiber optics industry is beginning to mature as a result of the research efforts of the American Telephone and Telegraph Company. The process by which light is transmitted includes four main parts: a light source, a transmission medium, a signal repeater, and an optical detector. These parts work together to transfer data in several computer and telephone applications. The efficiency of the process produces economic advantages for ATT and for its investors. Recent trends in company policy strengthen the view that ATT stock will pay large dividends through the next decade.

b. The Medical Word Processing Center was installed in the 224 East Broadway building of NKC, Inc. during the June, 1981 expansion. Although the building was equipped for marginal off-hour operation, it was incapable of meeting the cooling demands of the Wang word processing system. Data gathered from the performa, air conditioning catalogs, and hospital personnel familiar with the situation were used to determine the individual unit that could maintain a room environment within the range prescribed by Wang. Due to economical and mechanical limitations, a direct expansion incremental unit proved best suited to serve the area. This system can also be interfaced with other systems to meet future requirements of the Medical Word Processing Center.

Writing Based on Library Research

1. How do the library research methods and materials associated with writing a library review of research differ from those discussed in reference to the research paper, pages 365–90?

2. How do the organizational problems of a research review paper differ from those of a term paper written on a specific subject?

3. What organizational functions are served by the conclusion section of a library review of research? Analyze the conclusion provided on pages 496–97 to help you with the answer.

25

Writing in Business and Business Courses

INTRODUCTION TO BUSINESS WRITING

In a sense, *business writing* is a misnomer, conjuring up images of the writing done only in stores, factories, banks, insurance agencies, real estate offices, and the like. Actually *business writing* is a term that applies to the writing done not only in business and industry but in government and the professions as well. Business writing occurs in such diverse places as universities, hospitals, social service agencies, military units, churches, and state and federal tax bureaus. It is performed daily by such different individuals as lawyers, engineers, accountants, realtors, florists, movers, museum administrators, farmers, and nursery school operators.

Generally, business writing occurs in the form of letters, memos, and reports. Usually, these communications require the same effective writing skills discussed throughout this book. In other words, if you can write well, you should have little trouble with business writing. But you should keep in mind that this type of writing places special emphasis on clarity, conciseness, and courtesy.

The need for clarity is obvious. A directive to the janitorial staff about a change of hours or to the sales force about a new travel allowance must be so clear that no one should be confused or misled. An error in the working world can be costly. A letter, memo, or report, therefore, must be written so that the intended readers cannot reasonably misunderstand it.

And because time in business is expensive, messages should be written concisely. Executives, administrators, and other professionals are swamped with papers that clutter their desks, requiring hours to read and digest. A three-page memo that could have been compressed to one page certainly wastes readers' time; in addition, it may irritate them so much that the message might be misunderstood or acted upon unfavorably.

Courtesy, the third important characteristic of business writing, is conveyed mainly by tone, particularly in letters and memos. A letter stating, "It's your fault," runs the risk of irritating a reader, thereby perhaps losing not only the controversy but that person's future good will. Interestingly, when we talk to people face-to-face, we usually are courteous, but when writing we sometimes take out our hostilities and irritations on our readers, failing to realize how our written words will affect them.

Business writers need to keep their audience constantly in mind, addressing not only their needs but trying to create a favorable impression of themselves and their organization. There's an old saying that every letter should be a sales letter, building goodwill. This applies even to collection letters because their purpose is not only to obtain payment of a delinquent account but to do so in such a courteous way that the customer will continue doing business with the store. Memo writers are also interested in impressing readers favorably in order to establish or maintain good relationships.

These concepts of clarity, conciseness, and courtesy (or appropriate tone) have been mentioned throughout this book, but we emphasize them here because people in the business world constantly complain that the writing of college students is weak in these respects. Of course, other qualities of good writing discussed previously, such as correctness (especially spelling), liveliness, and effectiveness are also important.

Our purpose in this chapter is to prepare you for the writing you may be expected to do in some business classes, in some part-time jobs, and in your later career. Our treatment will be brief, dealing only with the résumé, the letter of application, the memo, and the report. For further instruction and practice, consider enrolling in a business writing course.

RÉSUMÉS

As Richard Nelson Bolles states in *What Color Is Your Parachute?*, his popular book on obtaining a job, "He or she who gets hired is not necessarily the one who can do that job best, but the one who knows the most about getting hired." This knowledge includes mastering such matters as conducting a self-evaluation, selecting a career, searching for a job, writing a résumé and application letter, and preparing for an interview. We deal here with the résumé and the application letter, discussing the résumé first because it is helpful to write it first. After realizing and describing your qualifications in a résumé, you are better able to draft an effective application letter stating why you should be hired for a particular job.

A résumé, often spelled resumé or resume—sometimes called a data or qualification sheet, a *vita* or *curriculum vitae*—is an outline of a person's qualifications. Necessary in writing for jobs and in applying personally for them, it is used by prospective employers to screen candidates for present openings or to keep on file for future ones. Consequently, you should think of a résumé as an advertisement for yourself, setting forth positive information about your qualifications.

Although numerous résumé forms are acceptable, two types are generally preferred: the traditional and the functional.

The Traditional Résumé

The traditional résumé contains information about your education, work experience, activities, and personal interests. Essentially, your résumé outlines achievements in your life that would appeal to an employer, indicating why you would make a valuable employee. As illustrated in Samuel Senior's résumé (see Figure 25-1), it usually consists of the following sections: heading, objective, education, experience, references.

Heading   The heading of the résumé contains your name, address, and phone number. If you plan to leave your college address shortly, mention your departure date and provide another address and phone number where you may be reached (see Figure 25-1).

Objective   Below the heading, you should state the position you are seeking and your skills for it. For example, "A position in public relations to use my communication and creative skills." Or you may wish to state your short term and long term goals (see Figure 25-1). However, if you do not wish to narrow your choice to a particular position, you may omit this section.

Education   Unless your job experience is more impressive than your educational qualifications, the next section should deal with your post-high school education. List in reverse chronological order (most recent first) the colleges and universities you have attended, dates, degrees earned, and major field of study. If you will graduate soon, you can write:

Degree expected: B.A. in History, Michigan State University, May 1989.

If you have done well in your studies (over 3.0 on a 4-point scale), provide your grade point average. Or, if you have done well only in your major courses during your last year or two, show that fact as Sarah Ratley did (see figure 25-3). Another way to write about grades, which are important to employers, is to provide your class standing if you rank in the upper third or quarter of your class. However, if your grades are only fair or are poor, omit mention of them.

Depending on space and potential interest to employers, you might list special courses, research projects, internships, and other academic activities, particularly those that qualify you for your chosen career. If you have been active in campus organizations or won several honors, you might provide this information in separate sections with such headings as Extracurricular Activities, Memberships, Honors, Athletic Participation.

Figure 25-1. Traditional Résumé.

```
                       Samuel S. Senior


Permanent Address                College Address (until May 12)

533 Tenth Street, S.E.           1883 Edgewood Drive
Washington, D.C. 20003           East Lansing, MI 48824
Telephone: 202-544-2888          Telephone: 517-507-3156


OBJECTIVE               Sales, Manufacturer's Representative.
                        Eventual position in sales management.

EDUCATION               B.A. in History, Michigan State
                        University, 19___. Also completed
                        courses in business: economics,
                        accounting, marketing, and sales force
                        management.

EMPLOYMENT              Salesman, part-time (20 hours a week),
Fall 19___              Saks Fifth Avenue, Lansing. Sold suits,
to Spring 19___         slacks, sports coats, and accessories;
                        took inventory; worked as assistant buyer
                        from 19___ to 19___.

Summer 19___            Lifeguard, Fairfax Country Club,
                        Fairfax, VA.

Summer 19___            Counselor, Camp Navaho, Colorado
                        Springs, CO. Taught swimming, canoeing,
                        sailing, water skiing; in charge of
                        lake-front staff of five.

ACTIVITIES              Senator, Student Government, 19___ to
                        19___. Treasurer, History Club.
                        Member, Marketing Club.

INTERESTS               Water sports, reading, square dancing,
                        jogging, meeting people, travel.

PERSONAL                Excellent health, single, willing to
                        travel and relocate.

REFERENCES              Available with information packet from
                        Placement Bureau, Michigan State
                        University, East Lansing, MI 48824.
```

Employment   In this section, describe in reverse chronological order any full- or part-time jobs you have had, whether on a paid or volunteer basis. Each entry should include the dates employed, name, city, and state of employer, and a concise description of your duties and accomplishments. In describing them, write phrases with past-tense verbs, trying to omit the "I" subjects and other unnecessary words. For example:

> **Avoid:** I supervised four employees in the shipping department and I also logged and routed all incoming packages as well as directed and coordinated air freight pick-up and delivery.
>
> **Instead:** Supervised four shipping department employees; logged and routed all incoming packages; directed and coordinated air freight pick-up and delivery.

Because employers realize that young college graduates will probably have had little work experience, you should not feel embarrassed about mentioning menial jobs. These jobs suggest that you have probably acquired good work habits, realizing the importance of such qualities as punctuality, dependability, loyalty, and initiative.

Personal   This miscellaneous section, which can be divided into subsections, should include any other information about yourself that might appeal to an employer. Race, religion, marital status, and age can be omitted because employers cannot legally request this information. But you may provide it if you think it might be helpful. You might want to include memberships in and activities with any social, charitable, or civic groups. If you have been in military service, you should mention it here, stating the rank attained, dates entered and terminated, and main duties performed.

Other information might include an account of your hobbies, interests, travels, and sports. If you have received any honors or awards not mentioned previously, you might list them here. Also appropriate would be a statement about any special skills, certificates, languages, or internships. And mention of your willingness to travel and to relocate, if pertinent, may appear here.

References   Usually there is not sufficient space on a résumé to list the names of references. Therefore, mention that they will be furnished on request. If your college placement bureau provides them with your dossier, state that fact and give the bureau's name, address, and phone number.

Your references should consist of three or four people. If you have had some job experience, provide at least one work-related name. Other useful references would be at least one faculty member and one person from your home community. Be certain to obtain permission from all references before naming them.

The Functional Résumé

Although containing much the same information as the traditional résumé, the functional one is organized to feature or highlight the writer's skills and abilities. Note the differences between the traditional résumé, in Figure 25-1 and the following ones in Figures 25-2 and 25-3, particularly how the functional résumé places greater stress on the qualities that might appeal to a particular kind of employer. As you can see, this type of résumé is more flexible in structure than the traditional, allowing writers greater freedom to emphasize certain qualifications and to state their achievements in whatever way will best enhance their prospects.

Résumé Preparation

After typing a draft of your résumé, fuss with its appearance. As an advertisement for you, it should be well-designed, neat, and have a lot of white space on the page. Consequently, in revising, eliminate irrelevant material; hack away at unnecessary words. If you still have too much copy for one attractive page, you might type a second draft on legal size paper and consider having the final one reduced in size on a copier. But be certain it looks inviting to read. And be sure there are no spelling or other mistakes that might disqualify you from a job.

Then have your résumé typed attractively, being prepared error- and erasure-free on a good typewriter with a well-inked ribbon and then reproduced by offset or some other process that will provide handsome copies. Or, better yet, do it or have it done on a word processor with a letter-quality printer. Also, it pays to have résumés done on the best quality of white or off-white bond paper that you can afford. Remember that your résumé is a sales tool; it should look as engaging and professional as you do when you go for an interview.

Final Don'ts about the Résumé

1. Don't date your résumé. You may wish to use it for months.
2. Don't attach a photograph to your résumé.
3. Don't mimeograph or ditto your résumé.
4. Don't mention salary.
5. Don't be creative unless you are applying for a job requiring creativity (advertising, etc.).
6. Don't pad your résumé with irrelevant material.
7. Don't extend your résumé to more than one page unless you have had a lot of work experience.

Figure 25-2. Functional Résumé, Summer Job.

THOMAS A. BROADSIDE

14 Skipper Road, Katonah, NY 10536
(914) 768-3132

QUALIFICATIONS FOR SAILING INSTRUCTOR
AT CAMP SCHOONER

Experience with Young People

Assistant Scoutmaster, Troop 3, Katonah, 19____ to 19____. Supervised
25 boys. Directed overnight canoe trips.

Instructor, Sunday School, St. Paul's Church, Katonah, 19____. Taught
fifth grade Sunday School classes, 19____.

Assistant Coach, Little League Baseball, Katonah, summer 19____.

Sailing Experience

Owner, 19-foot sailboat, 19____ to present. Have sailed on nearby
lakes, Long Island Sound, and off Cape Cod.

Secretary, Rockland Sailing Club, Rockland, NY. Handled
correspondence, wrote and published monthly newsletter
with column on sailing instruction.

Yard worker, Mike's Dock, 15 Lake Road, Ithaca, NY 14850, summers
19____ to 19____. Painting, cleaning, repairing boats.

Education

Katonah High School, 19____ to 19____. Graduated in top 10%.

Completed sophomore year, Ithaca College, NY.
  Major: Physical Education. Courses: camping, recreational
planning.

Personal Information

Born: June 9, 19____. Height: 6'. Weight: 170. Health: excellent.
  Hobbies: reading, swimming, jogging, songwriting

References will be furnished on request.

Figure 25-3. Functional Résumé.

SARAH A. RATLEY
69 Graymoor Drive
Lexington, KY 40503
606-277-6712

OBJECTIVE

Work in public relations with future opportunity of becoming
public relations director.

EDUCATION

Case Western Reserve University, Cleveland, OH, 19____-19____.
B.S. in Journalism, University of Kentucky, Lexington,
KY, 19____.

COMMUNICATION SKILLS

- Contributed over 70 articles to Kentucky Kernel,
  university student newspaper, 19____-19____.

- As Director of Public Relations, Lexington March
  of Dimes, 19____-19____, wrote press, radio, and TV
  releases, appeared on radio and TV programs,
  handled correspondence, ran annual dinner for
  200 volunteers and others.

- Planned activities, communicated with parents,
  supervised children as head of Cub Scout troop
  with 37 members, 19____-19____.

- Served as Program Chair of Henry Clay High School
  PTA, 19____-19____. Wrote monthly newsletter,
  arranged for speakers, chaired panels.

PUBLIC RELATIONS SKILLS AND HONORS

- Receptionist, Department of Public Information,
  University of Kentucky, Lexington, KY,
  July 19____-May 19____. Welcomed visitors, handled
  phone inquiries, arranged receptions and media
  meetings, wrote copy.

- Winner of Best Article Award, "A Housewife Returns
  to College," Kentucky Kernel, 19____.

- Certificate for Excellence, Toastmasters Club,
  Lexington, KY

Figure 25-3. (*Continued*)

```
                                    SARAH A. RATLEY - Page 2


    • Certificate for Volunteer Service to Community,
      awarded by the Lexington Herald-Leader to
      12 outstanding women, 19___.


INTERESTS

    Family (husband and two teenage children), camping,
    gourmet cooking, gardening, tennis, golf.


EMPLOYMENT

    Secretary, Bush Insurance Agency, 245 Park Avenue,
    Lexington, KY 40502. Typed letters, policies; filed
    materials. January 19___-September 19___.


REFERENCES

    Academic transcripts and recommendations available from
    Placement Bureau, University of Kentucky, Lexington, KY
    40506.
```

LETTERS OF APPLICATION

When job-hunting, carry copies of your résumé to leave with employers. However, in pursuing a job by mail, always send a letter of application with the résumé. This cover letter identifies the position, emphasizes your interest and qualifications, and requests an interview. Address the letter to a specific person, not to an office (Director of Personnel); if necessary, phone the company to obtain the name of the person heading the division where you wish to work. Type the letter in the full- or modified-block format (see Figures 25–4 and 25–5).

Introduction

As with any form of writing, the opening sentence requires much thought and effort. Here are some suggestions about how to begin an application letter:

A Pertinent Name

Professor Peter Volker of our Accounting Department has suggested that I write you about a position as auditor. He thought that you would be particularly interested in the research in auditing that I did in his seminar.

Question

Where could you use an intelligent, articulate English major graduate who writes crisp, cogent prose and has had experience in public relations?

Summary

After putting my husband through law school and raising two children, I returned to college, earned a degree with honors in interior design, and now feel confident that I could be of value to your company.

New Development

Having read recently of your plans to enlarge your store, I felt that you might be interested in a hard-working young woman with a degree in sociology, an interest in working with people, and several years of part-time experience in department store personnel work.

Reader Accord

Many people in business today claim that college graduates can't spell, can't punctuate, and can't write. If that's the way you feel, then I'd like to show you I am an exception and that I could be a valuable employee for you.

Ad Reference

I believe I am that "hard-working, responsible, take-charge" kind of manager you are seeking in your advertisement of May 12 in the *Herald*.

Body

After engaging the reader's interest by your introductory sentence or two, you need to convince the reader that you are the right person for the job by providing specific information about your qualifications, by explaining your interest in working for his or her organization, and by discussing your skills and abilities. Note how the writer of the letter in figure 25–4 handles these objectives. And observe how, in passing, she refers to the enclosed résumé. Naturally, it will repeat some of the facts mentioned in the letter.

Figure 25-4. Letter of Application (Full-Block Format).

---

295 Fifth Street
Boston, MA 02125
April 1, 19____

Mr. Lawrence Byrd
Director, College Relations
Filene's Department Store
58 Commonwealth Avenue
Boston, MA 01915

Dear Mr. Byrd:

You will find me exceptionally well qualified for the position of assistant buyer advertised in the <u>Boston Globe</u>. My major in merchandising and my experience in women's specialty shops have provided me with ideal preparation for such a position.

I will graduate in May from Northeastern University with a B. S. degree, having completed courses in textiles, clothing, and merchandising. In my clothing course I designed and made a suit that won first prize in our annual year-end style show.

In addition, I have worked part-time at several specialty shops in the Boston area, as my résumé shows. The training I received at these stores has given me invaluable knowledge about dealing with customers and ordering clothes for their particular needs.

I have always admired Filene's, which I consider to be one of the leading department stores in the country. To work for such an organization would be an honor.

If my credentials interest you, Mr. Byrd, I hope that I may have an interview to discuss Filene's needs and my qualifications further. I would be glad to meet with you at your convenience.

Sincerely,

Sara Boggs

Sara Boggs

Conclusion

An application letter is usually written to obtain an interview. Thus you should conclude with some statement like the following:

May I have an interview to discuss my qualifications in more detail? I'll phone you Tuesday morning to arrange a meeting convenient for you.

If distance is a problem, you might deal with it in this way:

If you are interested in my qualifications, Mr. Regen, please write or phone me collect at 202-555-6711.

Importance of the Résumé and Application Letter

A well written, attractive, interesting application letter and résumé will not get you a job, but may prevent you from being eliminated from one. In the present buyer's market, employers can pick and choose. Often flooded with applications, they look for any excuse to eliminate someone. A single misspelling, a typo, a poorly worded sentence, or an offensive tone may very well cause them to toss a letter in the wastebasket. On the other hand, an effective letter and résumé will generally evoke a favorable response, assuming that an appropriate position is available and that the writer has the proper credentials for it.

You can realize now why you should spend plenty of time—perhaps several days—drafting your application letter and résumé. Show the drafts to people for their criticism, particularly someone at your placement bureau. Then be certain to proofread your final copy several times. Remember: Your future may depend on your making a favorable impression with your application letter and résumé.

MEMOS

Memos (or memorandums, memoranda) are messages written for communicating within a company, agency, or other organization. Handy because of their convenience and simplicity, they omit such parts of business letters as the sender's address, recipient's address, salutation, complimentary close, and signature identification. Also, they are efficient, enabling writers to state their ideas quickly and clearly, generally avoiding lengthy introductions and conclusions, as well as courtesy statements.

Among the numerous routine messages transmitted by memos are announcements, requests, instructions, acknowledgements, inquiries, directives, and informal invitations. They are also used to confirm telephone calls and important conversations, to publicize organizational news, to provide a permanent record, and to communicate short in-house reports.

In some instances, memos may be handwritten; usually, however, they are typed. Most memos are no more than one page, although they may run longer. Because they are sent to people in the writer's organization, they should be informal and friendly in tone unless the reader, purpose, and context demand otherwise.

Figure 25-5. Modified-Block Format.

1883 College Drive
Lexington, KY 40506
February 4, 1988

Mr. Andrew Dawson
2837 W. Logan Drive
Chicago, IL 60647

Dear Mr. Dawson:

If you have to write a business letter, here is a model, although its modified-block style is only one of several acceptable forms.

The heading in the upper right corner consists of the address and date. With printed stationery, only the date is typed. In typing the heading, you establish the top and right margins of your whole letter. The shorter the letter, the lower the heading and the wider the margins.

The inside address, spaced below the heading, includes the recipient's name, title, and address. Like the heading, it contains no abbreviations except those in a company name (Inc., Ltd.), common titles (Mr., Ms., Mrs., Dr.), and the two-letter zip designation for the state. Use no punctuation at the ends of the lines (unless an abbreviation ends a line).

The salutation, two spaces below, consists of "Dear" followed by a name, if known. If not, use a title ("Dear Sales Manager"), company name ("Dear General Motors"), or another form that seems appropriate: "Dear Sir or Madam," "Dear Sir," Ladies and Gentlemen," or "Gentlemen." End with a colon.

The body, two spaces below the salutation, is made up of single-spaced paragraphs with double spaces between. In a short letter, you may double-space with triple spaces between.

The complimentary close, two spaces below the last paragraph and aligned with the heading, often consists of "Sincerely" or the friendlier "Cordially," rather than the formal "Yours truly" or "Respectfully yours." Your signature follows, with your name typed beneath.

Cordially,

Peter Rose

Peter Rose

Format

Usually, memo forms are printed with headings and sometimes even action suggestions (see Figure 25-6). If no form is furnished, you may type a memo on a sheet of paper with the word "MEMORANDUM" typed in capitals near the top and the following four-part heading underneath:

```
TO:                             DATE:

FROM                            SUBJECT:
```

Or you may use this format:

```
TO:                             DATE:

FROM:

SUBJECT:
```

To preserve accurate records you should write people's complete names and titles. To personalize or authenticate memos, you may initial after your typed name on the "FROM" line. And to avoid or minimize introductions, you should state the subject as specifically as possible: for example, "Request for part-time secretarial assistance," not merely "Request for Assistance."

Style

Because the subject is stated in the heading, you should get to the point of the memo immediately instead of writing a sentence or two about its purpose. In long memos, you may use headings within the memo to mark different sections, much as they serve that function in this book.

Another device found frequently in memos is the listing of points to provide emphasis and ease of reference. By indenting and placing the words, phrases, or sentences that express your main points on different lines and highlighting each with a number, letter, or other mark (often a "bullet," an inked-in small *o*), you may be able to get your message across more efficiently and forcefully than in ordinary paragraphs. Note how this strategy is used in the memo in Figure 25-7.

Because memos are frequently short, you usually have ample space on a page for your message. This means that you can try to make the memo look attractive, arranging ideas in such a way that they will be as visibly clear and easy to read as possible.

In organizations, the memo is usually the most common form of written communication. For that reason, learning how to write effective memos can be crucial to your success. If you can make your memos clear, concise, and—whenever appropriate—friendly, you will establish a fine reputation for yourself in the world of work.

Figure 25-6. A Memo Form.

University of Kentucky
Inter-Office Exchange

Memo to .... from ....

Date..

TAKE ACTION INDICATED
NOT LATER THAN

SUBJECT { ....
( ) SEE ATTACHED SHEETS

Return to me .... ( )

See me personally .... ( )

Need not be returned .... ( )

Being sent for your
information .... ( )

Furnish data requested .... ( )

Take action indicated ...... ( )

Take up with .... ( )

Investigate and report to . ( )

Express your judgment .... ( )

Set time when we may
discuss this .... ( )
( )

PUT IT IN WRITING Written messages save time, reduce errors and prevent interruptions

Figure 25-7. Memo with List of Points.

MEMORANDUM

TO: All Managers   DATE: 17 August 19____

FROM: Walter Johnson, Vice President of Personnel *WJ*

SUBJECT: Excessive Overtime Work by Secretaries

    In recent months, payments for secretaries working overtime have been excessive. This problem not only affects us financially but also contributes to many secretaries' dissatisfaction with the long hours.

    To reduce or eliminate overtime, please follow these procedures with your secretary.

- Meet each morning to determine the priority of the work to be done during the day.

- Top priority should be given only to the number of items that can be reasonably completed during the day.

- Allow for interruptions. Do not overschedule.

- At 3:00 p.m., check with your secretary to make certain that all the top priority work will be done.

- If all the top priority work cannot be completed, let me know so that I can provide you with some clerical assistance.

    Please drop me a memo on October 1, telling me how you think this plan is working and whether we can improve it in some way.

Figure 25-8. A Short Memo.

MEMORANDUM

TO: All Employees   DATE: November 5, 19____

FROM: Doris Stockman, President   SUBJECT: United Fund Giving

Last year, 87% of our employees contributed $9,657 to the United Fund drive. This year the Fund needs 10% more to help our local organizations.

I'd like to see more employees give and more employees give more. As you know, you can have your contribution deducted from your salary checks or you can give it to your department solicitor, who will be around to see you this week or the next.

Remember that charity begins at home. The United Fund charities are all home-community charities. Please give generously.

REPORTS

Probably the most difficult kind of document to define in business is the *report* because the word refers to numerous types of oral and written communications, formal and informal. Depending on the job you have, you may be asked to write credit reports, product reports, sales reports, annual reports, feasibility reports, financial reports, and numerous others. These reports may contain information, analyses, or recommendations. They may be standardized in form like absence, trip, or accident reports. They may be written as letters or memos, or in other formats, some informal, some highly structured. They may cover various time periods, as do preliminary, progress, periodical, and final reports. And they may be written for various audiences inside an organization or outside of it—or both.

Headings

Despite this multiplicity of subject matter, forms, audiences, and purposes, most reports use headings for different sections. And often each section, such as "Recommendations," must appear in a specified place. Headings serve several purposes. They allow readers to find the particular sections that interest them without having to read the entire report. Also, headings make the reading easier because they function as transitions, signaling shifts from one topic to another. And by breaking up what would otherwise be massive blocks of print, they make the pages visually more inviting.

Headings benefit writers as well as readers, helping writers to organize their material by forcing them to decide on the order of the headings and their importance (major or minor). Finally, headings help writers unify their material: everything about a specific subject belongs in the section whose heading refers to that subject.

Various formats exist for headings, depending on the length and complexity of the reports. What is important is that the headings indicate the relationship of various sections as they appear in your outline, showing which are major, which minor, and which subminor. Here is a three-degree system of headings that shows the rank of these sections.

```
                        MAJOR SECTION

     All capital letters, centered on page, not underlined.


Minor Section

     Heading on separate line at left margin, initial capitals,

underlined.


     Subminor section: Heading run in on same line with the text and

indented, initial capital on first word only (as well, of course, as

any proper nouns), underlined.
```

Organizational Patterns

Some companies and agencies specify how they wish their reports to be organized. The advantage of this standardization is that writers are compelled to arrange information in the order the management considers most useful, and readers always know where to find various sections of the reports. Among the popular organizational patterns are the following:

Recommendation Report

   I.   Statement of Problem
   II.   Proposed Solution
   III.   Advantages
   IV.   Disadvantages (Optional)
   V.   Recommendation

Proposal Report

   I.   Abstract
   II.   Background
   III.   Problem
   IV.   Statement of Objectives
   V.   Procedure or Methodology
   VI.   Time Requirements
   VII.   Personnel Requirements
   VIII.   Budget Requirements
   IX.   Appendix

Formal Report

   I.   Preliminary material:
           Letter of transmittal
           Title page
           Abstract
           Table of contents
   II.   Body:
           Background
           Scope of report
           Definitions
           Methodology
           Findings
   III.   Conclusions and Recommendations
   IV.   Appendix(es)
           Bibliography
           Detailed charts, financial statements, etc.

Report Sections

These are only a few of the numerous organizational plans used in reports. Often writers must devise their own structures, or modify one of these (as the writer of the informal report in Figure 25-10 does with the recommendation report format). But in formal reports especially, the sections are often standard.

Letter of Transmittal

This letter from the writer to the person or organization that authorized the report provides a courteous introduction to the report, saying in effect, "Here's what you requested." In addition, it may include statements about problems incurred, expressions of gratitude for assistance received, suggestions for further research, and mention of special interest matters. Sometimes, the letter of transmittal also includes recommendations. Generally, it closes with a statement expressing willingness to provide additional information as the example in Figure 25-9 does.

Title Page

Similar to the title pages of research papers (see page 419), the title page of a report contains the full title; the name of the individual (perhaps a committee or research team) who prepared the report; the name and title of the person or group for whom the report was prepared; and the date.

Abstract

Often called a synopsis, summary, or executive summary, this important section should be a mini-report because it is all that some people may read. Written only after the report is completed, the abstract condenses all the information into one or several tightly written paragraphs that follow the order of the main points in the report. It should be as brief as possible, not more than 10 percent of the length of the report. Even for long reports, abstracts seldom are longer than 200 words. For additional information about abstracts, see pages 489-90.

Table of Contents

The table of contents is particularly valuable to readers of long reports because it provides the only guide to the material, showing what is covered and where it is located. This information is presented in the form of the specific headings in the report, which means that it should be written only after the report is completed. And just as these headings are typed in different formats to show their various levels, so they should appear in a similar style in the table of contents.

Body

The body of the report includes any pertinent background information necessary for understanding the report. Here would be presented an account of the

Figure 25-9. Letter of Transmittal.

Software Solutions, Inc. 1057 Fisher's Road
Tampa, FL 33612

Telephone (813) 789-2418

April 15, 19____

Mrs. Gertrude Dole, President
Academic Food Services Company
1221 Chinoe Road
Tampa, FL 33612

Dear Mrs. Dole:

Attached you will find the report that you requested
on December 23 about software packages and the means
for assessing the software needs of the company.

The report provides information about those software
packages that will help meet the company's needs for
recording pertinent company data, handling expanded
sales, and simplifying inventory and personnel record-
keeping. The report also suggests the criteria to be
used for selecting the software packages, the methods
for analyzing the company's software needs, and the
requirements to create an efficient computer center.

I would be glad to meet with you to review this report
or to answer any questions you may have about it.

Sincerely,

Jean Josephs

Jean Josephs
Administrative Assistant

Enclosure

situation covered in the report, a statement about any limitations of the investigation, definitions of special terms (if these are numerous, a glossary might be provided as an appendix), and a description of the methodology.

For instance, a report on customers' reactions to a new improved laundry bleach might begin by discussing the problems with the former product, mentioning the locations where the marketing research was conducted, stating the nature and size of the sample, and describing the way customers were approached and asked to complete the questionnaire.

The body of the report would also set forth and, if necessary, explain the findings of the investigation. In the bleach example, it would present the responses to the questionnaire and an analysis of this information.

Conclusion

The conclusion presents the results of the study. It might show why customers tried the improved product, what they liked about it, and what they disliked.

Recommendations

Frequently, management wants only information. On other occasions, it asks for recommendations. These should be provided in a section with that heading, and should logically follow the information presented in the preceding "Conclusions" section, unless organizational report policy calls for the recommendations to be placed on the first page. And sometimes conclusions and recommendations are presented in a single section: Conclusions and Recommendations.

In view of the many different types of reports, and their numerous sections, you would be wise to obtain previous reports from your own organization's files to see how they were written.

Report Tone

Reports present information, not feelings, emotions, hopes, or wishes. They are usually investigations into a problem or subject by subordinates, who then present their findings to their superiors. Consequently, the tone of reports is objective and usually impersonal, avoiding personal references, using the third person instead of the first (I, we) or the second (you), and omitting opinions unless necessary in the "Recommendations" section. Some organizations are more formal than others, however, and to some extent decisions about tone are always governed by the particular situation, by the relationship of those preparing the report to those who will read it, and by the purpose of the report. In any event, a report need not be dull; the writer should try to make it interesting, clear, and concise.

Figure 25-10. Short Informal (Recommendation) Report.

FLOWER POLICY AT BLUE GRASS COMPANY

Present Flower Policy

   In the past, individual decisions have been made about
sending flowers when any employee or member of an employee's
family has died or when an employee is hospitalized or is
suffering from a major illness or injury. Individual managers
have reviewed each case, decided whether flowers should be
sent, and if so, seen to it that they are ordered and paid for.

Problems with Present Policy

   Numerous problems have arisen. Some overlooked employees
have felt slighted. Others have complained that the bouquets
they received were not as handsome as those sent to friends. In
some instances, flowers were sent upon the death of a parent;
in other instances, they were not. Morale has suffered as a
result of the present policy of leaving decisions to individual
department managers.

New Policy Objectives

   To avoid continuation of these problems, the company should
establish a flower fund policy that will relieve
managers of making individual decisions and will ensure that
employees and their families are treated fairly and equally.

Proposed New Policy

   The following guidelines would meet these objectives by
specifying who is eligible to receive flowers, who will
administer the flower policy, and how it will be financed.

   Eligibility to Receive Flowers: Any company employee absent
from work because of being hospitalized or confined to home for
a major illness or accident is eligible to receive flowers.
However, these flowers will be sent only once even though the
absence may be an extended one.
   Flowers will also be sent on the occasion of the death of an
employee's parent, spouse, or child.

   Administration of Flower Policy: The Personnel Department
will be responsible for approving and ordering the flowers. No
more than $25 may be spent for each arrangement. An account
should be set up with one florist so that it would be familiar
with our policy and with our payment procedure.

   Financing of the Flower Fund: It is estimated that the cost
of flowers will not exceed $3,000 a year. Therefore, this
amount should be appropriated in the next budget and be
allocated to the Personnel Department. Any sums not expended in
one year shall be carried over to the next.

Report Audience

Usually a report is called for by one person who authorizes another to prepare it. Thus the writer should analyze the report writing situation and ask such questions as the following:

What does the authorizer want to know about the subject?
What does this person already know about the subject?
Is this report being written only for this person or will it be read by others?
If it will be read by others, what do they want to know and what do they already know?

Writing to a dual audience, as we do in this textbook to students and teachers is difficult, calling for careful judgment. But by keeping the interests and backgrounds of different readers constantly in mind, you can increase your chances of communicating effectively to them. In this way, you will enhance your value as an employee in a working world whose growing complexity demands ever more information, better information, and clearer information.

SUMMARY

Business writing—the writing done in business, industry, government, and the professions—generally takes the form of letters, memos, and reports. In style, it is characterized by clarity, conciseness, and courtesy.

People looking for jobs, either when graduating from college or when seeking a change of positions, rely on the application letter and the résumé—an outline of the applicant's qualifications that lists education, employment experience, and personal data. The traditional resume offers the benefit of a conventional structure that employers have come to expect. The functional résumé, more flexible in structure, offers the benefit of highlighting particular job-related skills and achievements. Usually restricted to one page for college students with limited experience, the résumé should be carefully written and its information attractively presented.

The letter of application identifies the position sought, emphasizes the applicant's interest, summarizes the applicant's main qualifications, and requests an interview. Since it serves as a cover letter, the application letter should be brief and refer the reader to the résumé for further information.

Because memos are usually messages written to others within the same organization, they omit many of the formalities of business letters such as salutations, courtesy openings, and complimentary closes. Generally, memos are typed on standard forms and are not signed, although the writers may pen their initials beside their typed names. Whenever possible, memos should be informal and friendly in tone.

Although reports take many forms and are used for numerous purposes, most are divided in sections with appropriate headings. Many companies and agencies require that their reports follow a specified organizational pattern. Often, however, writers may have to modify this pattern or create one suitable to a particular audience, purpose, and subject.

Despite all the forms and formats of business writing, it essentially requires the same skills and techniques that have been described in other sections of this textbook. Writers who choose their words carefully, who shape crisp and cogent sentences, who organize their ideas clearly, and who keep their readers' needs and interests constantly in mind will excel in business writing.

ASSIGNMENTS

For Discussion

Résumés and Application Letters

1. Why might it be better to write the résumé before the letter of application?
2. Describe the difference between the two types of résumés that were discussed. Explain which type might be more appropriate in applying for a position at each of the following: a bank, an advertising agency, a law office, city government, or a sales organization.
3. Why should you not obtain all your references from the faculty of your college or university?
4. Under what circumstances would you list your job experience before your education on your résumé? Why?
5. In writing an unsolicited letter of application, what do you gain if you begin by mentioning the name of someone who had suggested that you do so?
6. If you are applying for a job in a distant state, how can you request an interview?
7. If you wish to apply for four positions, will you have to ask each of your references to write four different letters? Explain.

Memos

1. Why are memos usually simple and effective means of communicating in writing within an organization?
2. Why do you suppose memos are seldom used to communicate to people outside the writer's organization?
3. Why is it important that the subject be stated specifically?
4. Where and why is a memo signed?
5. How does the beginning of a memo generally differ from the beginning of a business letter?
6. What is the advantage of listing? The disadvantage?
7. Why should a memo usually be friendly?

Reports

1. From your own experience, discuss some reports that you have seen, written, or completed.

2. Why do you suppose that except in lab courses, the report format described in this chapter is not usually called for in college but is required at work?

3. In what ways do headings help readers? Writers?

4. Explain the difference between a "Conclusions" section and a "Recommendations" section by using an example of a report about reducing long distance telephone expenses in a hospital.

5. What are the special challenges in writing to a dual audience? What difficulties do you think there are in writing to the dual audience for this textbook?

For Writing

Résumés and Application Letters

1. Write a traditional and a functional résumé for yourself.

2. Write a letter of application and a résumé for a summer job you would like to have. You may assume that it was advertised in your school or local paper, or that a faculty member called it to your attention, stating that you might use her name.

3. Assume that you are graduating this semester. Apply for a job that you might have learned about from your college's placement bureau, from a professor who stated you could mention his name, or from an advertisement in your school or local paper, or elsewhere. If you are replying to an ad, clip a copy of it to your letter. Make reasonable assumptions about your skills, education, and employment.

4. A new department store is going to open in your community. You would like a part-time job there during the school year. Write a letter of application and résumé; send them to Mr. William Cosby, Director of Personnel.

Memos

1. As president of the student government, write a memo to faculty members informing them about the Rent-a-Student plan for Saturday, April 6. Students will be available to clean, cut grass, wash windows, paint, and perform similar home chores. The charge will be $20 a student for their morning's work. Proceeds will go to a scholarship fund.

2. As manager of a local company, you have decided to pay the cost of tuition and books for all employees who take and pass the business writing course offered by a particular college or university in the town. The class meets on Tuesday evenings from 6:30 to 9:00 p.m. Inform your 79 employees about

this offer and try to persuade them to take the course. (If you wish, you may use the name of your own college or university.)

3. You are the chair of a student committee just established to reconsider the system by which students evaluate members of the faculty. Write a memo to other members of your committee, informing them of the date and place of the first meeting, persuading them to attend, and asking them to study the issues and prepare suggestions for improving the system.

4. As president of the student government, you have heard complaints from numerous students about faculty members scheduling final exams during the last week of classes. This practice imposes a hardship on many students and is contrary to the rules of your college or university, which specify that exams are to be given during a special period printed in the schedule distributed at the beginning of each semester. Write a memo to members of the faculty in which you try to persuade them to give final exams at the proper times.

5. As president of the student government, write a memo to students, informing them how best to add and drop classes at the beginning of the semester.

6. Assume that you are the manager of the Campus Homemade Ice Cream Company, which employs 27 students. Write a memo to them, pointing out that they are taking excessive time on lunch or dinner breaks, and that unless this practice is changed you will have to require them to sign in and out.

7. As chairman of a student committee on parking, write a memo to your college or university's vice president for business affairs, proposing a way to improve the parking situation for students.

8. As an older student returning to college after many years out of school, you have been asked by the registrar to recommend how the orientation, advising, and registration process might be improved for similar students. Write a memo to the registrar with your suggestions.

Reports

1. As head of the Student Consulting Agency, you have been asked by a local businessman, Mr. Robert Becker, to do a feasibility study for a tanning salon (or any other retail enterprise you wish to select) near campus. On the basis of student interest, competition, traffic, and other non-financial factors, write a recommendation report for Mr. Becker.

2. For admission to its summer internship program, Merrill Bache, a local stock brokerage company, has asked students to write a report, selecting five stocks that should increase greatly during the forthcoming year and providing reasons for their estimated rise. Write the report for Mr. E.E. Hutton, Manager.

3. Your college or university is about to celebrate the 100th anniversary of its founding. You have been asked to poll your friends and write a report to Mr. Stengel, Director of Public Relations, indicating what ceremonies, visits by celebrities, and other events should be scheduled to celebrate this event.

4. Mr. Ronald Bush, an alumnus of your college, has left an annual sum of $15,000 to be spent "to enrich the environment in which students live and to promote their appreciation of beautiful and lovely things." The money may be used for beautification of the campus, purchase of good and beautiful books, musical programs, works of art, lectures, and such matters. Write a report to Dr. Gary Monwood, chair of the Bush Trust Committee, with your recommendation about how the money should be allocated.

5. As chair of the Student Government Committee to Improve Student Academic and Campus Life, assume that you and your committee have studied one of the following campus problems: class attendance, registration, cheating, beautification or cleaning of the grounds and physical plant, library service, parking, sales of athletic tickets, sexual harassment, rape on campus, orientation of mature students, day care, summer orientation for freshmen, food, or student recruitment. (If some other campus issue interests you, check with your instructor.) Write a report to the president of your college or university recommending ways to solve or alleviate the problem.

Reference Guide

INTRODUCTION

Throughout, *The Writing Commitment* stresses that writers have many options, depending on the intended audience and on the purpose and occasion for writing. Those options include choices of diction, sentence and paragraph structure, organizational strategies, and levels of language. Chapter 6 discusses the different language styles available in written English, pointing out that writers shift from a casual to a more formal style when they move from personal to public writing, from a familiar audience to an unfamiliar. In the same chapter, we also point out that some usages from your spoken dialect can be effective in personal essays and narratives, but inappropriate in more formal writing.

As you realize, the style of English appropriate for personal writing—*Casual English*—has limited use: personal narratives and essays, dialogue in fiction, and personal letters addressed to friends and relatives. Here are its brief characteristics:

AUDIENCE	LANGUAGE FEATURES	VOICE
Familiar: close in some way to writer, mutual knowledge and experience.	Vocabulary: simple words, slang, and localisms: Sentences: short, simple sentences; fragments; compound, coordinate sentences. Punctuation: individualized and relatively free from conventional rules.	Subjective: personal, intimate, friendly tone; use of first-person pronouns and references.

Although you will continue personal writing in private life, most of your academic and business writing will be more formal in character—addressed to a more distant audience and dealing with less personal matters. In most instances, such writing will be in *General English*—a variety of almost unlimited use. You encounter it everyday in articles and letters appearing in newspapers and magazines, as well as in books appealing to a mass audience. It is the style expected in almost all your academic writing: term papers, nontechnical reports, argument papers, and written examinations. This table summarizes the characteristics of General English:

AUDIENCE	LANGUAGE FEATURES	VOICE
General: distant, but acknowledged. Audience needs informative details.	Vocabulary: generally recognized and current. Sentences: longer and more complex than in Casual English; coordinate and subordinate structures. Punctuation: tighter adherence to rules, less individualized choice.	Neutral: generally third person and impersonal *you.*

Those enrolled in technical or professional programs will learn to use the specialized writing formats and the technical vocabulary of their disciplines. For this style of writing, limited mostly to upper-division and graduate courses and the professional world, they will use *Specialized English* in technical or professional documents, in scholarly writing, legal drafts, business reports, and so on. Although closely akin to General English, it does have some added characteristics:

AUDIENCE	LANGUAGE FEATURES	VOICE
Select audience: distant, but sharing a specialized background with writer.	Vocabulary: specialized technical jargon; literary devices. Sentences: long and highly complex; high percentage of subordinate-coordinate structures. Punctuation: rigid adherence to rules.	Objective: highly impersonal and formal; third person; strict avoidance of personal pronouns.

Because you will be expected to write mostly in General English in your undergraduate courses and in your career, we will emphasize in this Reference Guide those usages most appropriate to General English.

SENTENCE STRUCTURE

sent
or **ss**   Grammatically, a sentence is a structure composed of a *subject* (S) that states the *topic* of the sentence and a *predicate* (P) that makes a *comment* about the topic. Together the subject and predicate express a complete idea or a unified statement

about a given topic. The predicate consists of a tense-carrying *verb* (V) and usually a *complement* (C), a word or words closely allied to the verb and completing the comment. A complement can be a *noun phrase object* (my mother, John); an *adjective* (sour, beautiful); or, in the sentence pattern Subject + *be* + Adverb, an *adverb* (there, in the morning).

All his fellow-students   like   John.
(Subject)   (Verb)   (Object)

Green apples   are   sour.
(Subject)   (Verb)   (Adjective)

The track meet   is   in the morning.
(Subject)   (Verb)   (Adverb)

For more details, see the discussion on pages 65–67.

Sentence Types

Sentences may be classified as simple, compound, and complex. Expansions or combinations of these can result in balanced sentences, cumulative or loose sentences, and periodic sentences.

simple sentences A simple sentence consists of only one SVC structure; sometimes such a sentence is called an *independent clause,* or *base clause* (See also page 67.)

Example: The cat slept. (SV)
Mimi bought a motorcycle. (SVC—the complement is an object.)
Mimi is extravagant. (SVC—the complement is an adjective.)

compound sentences A compound sentence is formed by joining two or more simple sentences with independent clauses in any of several ways (see also pages 75–76):

a. With a coordinating conjunction or a semicolon:

$$\text{SP,} \left\{ \begin{array}{l} and \\ but \\ for \\ or \\ nor \\ yet \\ ; \end{array} \right\} \text{SP}$$

Generally, when two independent clauses are joined, a comma is placed before the conjunction. The comma may be omitted, however, if the clauses are short or if a semicolon is used.

Examples: Mimi bought a motorcycle, *but* Oscar bought roller skates. (comma before the conjunction)

His heart pounded *and* he felt faint. (no comma needed in short sentence)

A great idea is often enough to open the door of opportunity; you may also need persuasive skills. (semicolon replaces conjunction)

b. With a correlative conjunction:

$$\left\{ \begin{array}{l} either \\ neither \\ not\ only \end{array} \right\} \text{SP,} \quad \left\{ \begin{array}{l} or \\ nor \\ but\ also \end{array} \right\} \text{SP}$$

The comma is often omitted with correlatives.

Examples: *Either* you study tonight *or* you go unprepared to the exam in the morning.
Not only did they buy a new car, *but* they *also* purchased a boat.

complex sentences   A complex sentence combines two or more simple sentences: an independent or base clause and one or more clauses that are dependent on the base clause for meaning. In the examples below, the joiners are italicized.

        Dependent   Independent
When the phone rang, I was in the bathtub.
            S   P S P

             Dependent   Independent
Before Hank went to college, he hitchhiked from Maine to California.
        S   P   S   P

                   Dependent   Independent
Malcolm, *who* used to be my best friend, is now my worst enemy.
        S   S   P   P

               Dependent   Independent
The movie *that* I saw last Saturday was exciting.
        S   S P   P

In the examples, the SP structures labeled as dependent clauses are logically incomplete without the independent clause. Used alone, they would be sentence fragments, as in:

Before Hank went to college.

balanced sentences   A balanced sentence is made up of two base sentences similar or parallel in content, length, and grammatical structure (see also page 218). Often they express opposing ideas and are joined with a semicolon, as in this example:

Love nourishes the soul; hate destroys it.

cumulative or loose sentences   In a cumulative sentence, the base sentence containing the main idea is placed first, with modifiers added at the end. (See pages 81–82.)

My view of the world is what I can see from my typewriter—a corner of the brick house next door, the upper branches of trees, a triangle of the street, one-third of a neighbor's shed, an occasional fleeting glimpse of a warmly dressed child on the tiny rectangle of sidewalk.

periodic sentences   A periodic sentence places modifiers before the base clause or places modifiers between the subject and the predicate. In either case, the main idea is not completed until the end. (Contrast with cumulative sentence.) Periodic sentences are most effective for creating a climactic effect. (See pages 216–17.)

Dreams of fame and popularity, hopes of love and admiration, visions of marriage and parenthood, of good deeds and daring exploits, these are the fantasies of youth.

Sentence Problems

dm   **dangling modifiers**   See discussion of misplaced modifiers, pages 220–22.

frag   **fragments**   Fragments are incomplete sentences. They commonly result from three main sources: 1) omitting one of the important grammatical sentence elements such as subject or verb; 2) breaking off a dependent clause; and 3) treating a relative clause as an independent sentence. Although common to Casual style, fragments should be avoided in General English unless they are needed for special effect.

Fragment: Being the only child in the family. (lacks subject and main verb)
Complete sentence: He was the only child in the family.
Fragment: Because he studied too hard. (dependent clause)
Complete sentence: Because he studied too hard, he suffered from nervous exhaustion. (independent clause added)
Fragment: Which is the reason for her poor health. (relative clause)
Complete sentence: She studied too hard, which is the reason for her poor health. (base clause added)

ro *or*   **run-on sentence**   Run-on sentences (sometimes called *fused sentences*) result from
fs   the omission or misuse of appropriate punctuation between two compounded
independent clauses.

> *Run-on sentence:*   Ralph's trousers are torn he should get a new pair.
>   (period or semicolon omitted)
> *Revised:*   Ralph's trousers are torn; he should get a new pair.

cs   **comma splice**   When a comma is used in place of a period or semicolon, it is called
a comma splice or fault.

> *Comma splice:*   Ralph's trousers are torn, he should get a new pair.
>   (comma separates two independent clauses)
> *Revised:*   Ralph's trousers are torn; he should get a new pair.
> *or*
> Ralph's trousers are torn. He should get a new pair.

/ /   **faulty parallelism**   Faulty parallelism results from joining unlike structures when
their grammar or meaning indicates they should be identical in form. It is often
caused by combining sentences whose subjects are not the same, as in:

> Gary is not a good track runner, and neither is his swimming.
> (*Gary* is the subject of the base clause; *his swimming* is the subject of the
> added clause)

A solution would be:

> Gary is not a good track runner, nor is *he* a good swimmer. (*he* refers to
> *Gary*)

In the complex sentences, faulty parallelism can result from using different
grammatical structures to express coordinate ideas. Here's an example of faulty
parallelism, followed by the effective, original version:

> We used to root for the Indians against the cavalry, because we didn't
> think it was fair in the history books *that the cavalry's winning was a great
> victory,* and *when the Indians won it was a massacre.*

> We used to root for the Indians against the cavalry, because we didn't
> think it was fair in the history books that *when the cavalry won it was a
> great victory,* and *when the Indians won it was a massacre.*
>
> *—Dick Gregory*

PARTS OF SPEECH

The terms *parts of speech* refers to specific word classes, such as nouns,
pronouns, verbs, adjectives, adverbs, prepositions, and conjunctions. Each of these

word classes fills a specific grammatical slot in the sentence as we indicated in our discussion of basic sentence patterns on pages 67–69. For instance, nouns can hold many positions in the sentence, among them: subject, object of the verb, object of a preposition, appositive, and so on. In fact, the placement of words in sentences is one of the clues that determine how the words function and that help to make sentence "sense." That's why the nonsense verse "Jabberwocky" seems to mean something:

> Twas brillig, and the slithy toves
> Did gyre and gimbel in the wabe . . .

You can infer from their position that *brillig* and *slithy* are adjectives; *gyre* and *gimbel* are verbs; *toves* and *wabe,* nouns. Without knowing their meaning you sense their relationships to each other in the sentence.

In addition to their function in a sentence, most parts of speech are characterized by a set of suffixes or endings that change their form. For example, the inflections *-ing* and *-ed* can be added to verbs, indicating different time relationships, as in these sentences:

> Jane laughed.   (*-ed* added to *laugh;* indicates an action in the past)
> Jane is laughing. (*-ing* added to *laugh;* indicates continuing action)

adj   Adjectives

Adjectives modify or describe nouns. They can also be recognized by the kinds of inflections they take and by the function positions they have in a sentence. Adjectives can occur before or after nouns, or follow verbs such as *be, seem, appear, taste, smell, become.*

> The *delightful* spring, *fresh* and *fragrant,* is *welcome.*
>   adj   adj   adj   adj

adj/ **adjectives: comparison**   One-syllable adjectives usually show comparison by add-
comp ing the inflections *-er* or *-est;* adjectives of three or more syllables take *more* or *most.* One-syllable adjectives ending in *y* substitute *i* for *y* before adding *-er* or *-est.*

> Bob is the smarter of the two.   (*-er* used to compare two items)
> Of the two, Bob is *more* knowledgeable.   (compares two items; more than two syllables)
>
> Maria is the happiest of the three sisters.   (*-est* used to compare more than two; *y* changed to *i*)
> Maria is the *most* imaginative person in class.   (*most* used to compare more than two; more than two syllables)

mm   **adjectives: placement and misplacement**   See pages 218–24 and *dangling modifiers* on page 533.

adv   ## Adverbs

Adverbs modify, qualify, or describe verbs, adjectives, other adverbs, or whole sentences. They generally indicate manner (*with great speed*), time (*then*), place (*at school*), or frequency (*constantly, occasionally*).

Verbs: He *easily* found her in the crowd.

Adjectives: They were an *exceedingly* handsome pair.

Adverbs: Mario sings *amazingly* well.

Sentences: *Unfortunately,* we heard of the plans too late.

Although many adverbs end in *-ly* (*easily, amazingly*), many are uninflected: *there, here, then, now.* Often prepositional phrases function as adverbs: *over the hill, within ten years, with malice toward none.*

Like adjectives, adverbs can show comparison with *-er* and *-est,* or *more* or *most.* The choice corresponds to their use with adjectives:

Sylvia carries herself the straightest of anyone I know. (one syllable; more than two compared)
Hannah does her work *more* conscientiously than Ruth. (more than two syllables; two compared)

adv/ adj   **adverbs: confusion with adjectives**   Many adverbs are formed by adding the suffix *-ly* to adjectives, creating the possibility of placing the adjective form in an adverb position, as in:

The man reacted *violent* to the situation. (misused adjective)
Revision: The man reacted *violently* to the situation. (adverb)

Some adverbs, like *well,* have a corresponding adjective (*good*). Others, like *fast,* are interchangeable as adjectives or adverbs:

He is a *good* runner. (adjective)
He runs *well.* (adverb) (*not* He runs good.)
That is a *fast* car. (adjective)
He runs *fast.* (adverb)

mm   **adverbs: placement and misplacement**   In spoken English, many adverbs, particularly *only, even, hardly, nearly,* and *most,* often occur before the verb and create little ambiguity; intonation indicates the meaning. But in writing, it may not be clear whether they modify the verb or some other material in the sentence. To avoid reader confusion, make sure such adverbials immediately precede the word or structure they modify. See also pages 218–24.

Ambiguous: He only anticipated a raise. (could mean that he merely *anticipated* or that he expected merely a *raise* and no other benefits)
Clear: He anticipated *only* a raise.

Ambiguous: The student who was running *frantically* yelled to the teacher. (*frantically* could modifiy either *running* or *yelled*)
Clear: The student who was frantically running yelled to the teacher.

art   Articles

Articles are a small but important word class: *a, (an)* and *the*. The singular *a* or *an* is synonymous with *one* and can be used only with a singular noun: *a* woman, *an* industry. Note that *a* precedes a consonant; *an* precedes a vowel. *The* occurs with plural nouns (*the* courses) and with singular nouns when we want to make them more definite (*the* woman). (See also agreement, page 545.)

Articles generally do not occur with proper nouns (*John, Winston, Connecticut*), nor with nouns indicating a mass of something, such as a substance like *glass* or *steel* or a product such as *wheat* or *rice*, when they have a general meaning.

_____ Glass is manufactured in Czechoslavakia.
An important American export is _____ wheat.

However, when we wish to make the "mass" noun more definite or specific we can use *the:*

The glass of Czechoslovakia is of high quality.
We harvested the wheat earlier than usual.

The use of articles in English is much too complex to discuss fully here. Trust your language instincts when using them. One caution: We all have a tendency to omit articles when we take rapid notes—which can lead to writing that sounds like a telegram. As you proofread your papers, check for omitted or misused articles.

conj   Conjunctions

Conjunctions are "joiners"; they connect elements of a sentence or join several sentences together. (See also pages 75-77.) Conjunctions are of two types: coordinate (*and, or, but, either . . . or*) and subordinate (*as, because, when, since*). *since*).

Gretchen *and* Peter are sister and brother. (*and* joins two elements)
Gretchen and Peter have the same parents *because* they are sister and brother. (*because* joins two sentences)

n   Nouns

Nouns have traditionally been defined as naming words. Most nouns in the language can show plurals, either by adding -*s,* or -*es* (cat*s,* match*es*) or by changing the form of the word (g*ee*se). Some nouns that are borrowed from other languages retain their original plurals (criteri*a,* indic*es,* alumn*i*), although many of these are taking on regular English plurals—for example index*es* rather than ind*ices*. When in doubt about foreign plurals, check the usage section of this reference guide or your dictionary.

When nouns can be made plural and can be preceded by numbers (one cat, twenty geese), they are often referred to as count nouns.

Mass nouns, however, refer to large masses or substances (*milk, coffee, cheese*) or to collective items or groups (*furniture, wilderness*). Many nouns can function as either count or mass: *government,* for instance: (See also *agreement of nouns and verbs,* pages 545–46).

> *Government* is necessary for people to live together in peace.
> The two *governments* were always at odds with each other.

Nouns can also be classified as common or proper, the latter referring to a particular person, place, or thing: *Margaret, Massachusetts, Senate.*

Noun plurals and noun possessives are often confused in writing, a confusion compounded by the two forms of the possessive, singular and plural. (Note that possessive nouns always have an apostrophe.) Here is a chart showing different classes of nouns, their singular and plural forms, and their singular and plural possessives:

SINGULAR	PLURAL	SINGULAR POSSESSIVE	PLURAL POSSESSIVE
character	characters	character's	characters'
deer	deer	deer's	deer's
woman	women	woman's	women's
furniture	—	furniture's	—
Jones	Joneses	Jones's	Joneses'

Note that even plural possessive take *'s* except when the nonpossessive plural form already ends in *-s.*

prep   Prepositions

Prepositions are words that take an object (usually a noun or pronoun) and that indicate some relationship to other sentence elements. Prepositional phrases (preposition + object) generally function as adverbs or adjectives, but, on occasion, as nouns. Some relationships indicated by prepositions are time, place, manner, and possession.

> *On* Saturday, the players *of* Michigan State beat
>   (time)   (possession)
>
> the team *from* Penn *with* comparative ease.
>   (place)   (manner)

Phrasal prepositions (*out of, in regard to, in spite of*) act the same as single prepositions, taking an object and showing similar relationships.

> *Out of* the darkness came a tall ship in full sail.
> (place)

pron   Pronouns

Pronouns substitute for nouns or noun phrases:

> *He* [Sam] jogs every day. (*He* replaces the noun *Sam.*)
> *She* [The woman who jogs every day in the park] is a lawyer. (*She* substitutes for the noun phrase in parentheses.)

Unlike nouns in modern English, pronouns show case functions; that is, they change form depending on their use in the language (see also *pronouns, personal*):

> *They* told me of *their* plans; *I* told *them* of *mine.*
> subject   object   possessive   subj   object   possessive

case   pronouns: case

In most forms of written English, pronouns acting as objects of prepositions should be in the objective case (*me, her, him, them, us, whom*). Usually, compound objects cause the most difficulty.

> They gave the award to *Carl* (*him*) and me. (both are objective case)
> Between you and *me,* Carl did not deserve the award. (both are objective case)

When in doubt about such constructions, test the second pronoun by removing the first; few people would say or write "They gave the award to *I*," or Between *we.*"

Although *whom* is the objective form of the pronoun *who,* many writers use the informal *who* in object positions in questions and relative clauses. In formal writing, use *whom.*

> *Informal:* Who did you write to about enrollment?
> *Formal:* Whom did you write to about enrollment?

> *Informal:* Bert asked Yvonne *who* she visited.
> *Formal:* Bert asked Yvonne *whom* she visited.

To check when to use the objective form, reorder the sentence, as: You wrote to *whom* about enrollment? She visited *whom*? In the first example, normal order reveals that the pronoun is the object of the preposition *to;* in the second, it is the object of the verb *visited.* In college writing, you would be wise to use the objective form in such situations. However, be careful to avoid such ungrammatical hypercorrections as:

Whom are you? (*Be* and other linking verbs take the subjective form.)

Whose is the possessive form of *who* and functions like any other possessive:

Whose gloves are these? / I don't know *whose* (gloves) they are.

Caution: Don't confuse *whose* with *who's* (who is)!

pronouns, personal Most personal pronouns substitute for nouns or noun phrases that refer to people. *It* and *its* refer to things and to animals (though pets are often spoken of as *he* or *she*). *They, their,* and *them,* can refer to people, animals, or things. As indicated under *pronouns,* above, pronouns change form to indicate case. Here's a diagram showing the form needed for each case or function: subject, possessive occurring before the noun, possessive used alone after the verb, and the form required when the pronoun acts as an object of the verb or a preposition. Note that possessive pronouns do not take an apostrophe as contractions (such as *it's* for *it is* and possessive nouns (*father's*) do.

SUBJECT	POSSESSIVE: BEFORE NOUNS	OBJECT	POSSESSIVE: USED ALONE AFTER VERBS
I	my	me	mine
you	your	you	yours
he	his	him	his
she	her	her	hers
it	its	it	—
we	our	us	ours
they	their	them	theirs

I told *her* that *my* secrets are *mine.*
subj obj   possessive   possessive
             before noun   after verb

pronouns, relative The relative pronouns (see also pages 78–79) *who, which,* and *that* substitute for noun phrases in relative clauses. *Who* is the only relative with case forms:

The man *who* was in the bank yesterday . . . (subject form *who* replaces the subject, *the man*)
The man *whose* name you forgot . . . (possessive *whose* replaces *the man's:* You forgot *the man's* name.)
The man *whom* you saw yesterday . . . (objective *whom* replaces the object: You saw *the man* yesterday.)

Who and its other forms should be used only to refer to humans; *which* only to nonhuman and inanimate items; but, *that* may refer to either. (See pages 219–20 for problems of ambiguity.)

demonstratives Demonstratives include *this, these* and *that, those,* which can substitute for noun phrases: "*This* is the situation," "*That* is the right answer." However, in these instances, the referent should be clear from the preceding discussion. Or demonstratives can frequently substitute for articles: "*those* Eskimo pies," "*that* situation." *This* and *that* are singular forms; *these* and *those,* plural.

pronouns, intensive and reflexive Intensive and reflexive pronouns are personal pronouns with the suffixes *-self,* or *-selves* added: *myself, yourself, himself, herself, itself, ourselves, yourselves, themselves.* When used for special emphasis (intensive), the pronoun is placed after a noun or pronoun:

> She *herself* dressed his wounds.

When used as a reflexive, the pronoun replaces the object of the verb, but it must refer to the same person or thing expressed in the subject:

> Jack shaved *himself* before dressing.

ref   **pronouns: reference** What a pronoun refers to should always be immediately clear. A common cause of vague reference is indefinite pronouns.

    The personal pronoun *they* and the demonstrative *this* are termed *indefinite* when they do not refer to a specific noun phrase, as in the gossip's standby "They say that. . . ." The reader or listener cannot know who is responsible for the gossip tidbit. *This* commonly creates unclear reference when two or three items precede it, making it difficult to discern whether all or only one is included:

> College freshmen often fail to follow a regular study schedule; they may miss key class periods and even hand in assignments late. *This* can result in academic failure. (What does *this* clearly refer to?)

Avoid indefinites in writing; they impede clear communication.

v *or*   **Verbs**
vb

    Verbs generally show action or state of being and indicate present or past tense by some change in their form. Most verbs show past tense by adding *-d* or *-ed;* they are called regular verbs. Others are irregular and change form in other ways, as in *grow, grew; choose, chose. Transitive* verbs generally are followed by noun-phrase or pronoun objects, *intransitive* verbs by adverbs; *linking* verbs link the subject with a noun phrase or adjective that refers directly to the subject. See also pages 67–69.

> Transitive verb: She *received* the package.
> Intransitive verb: He *whistled* merrily.
> Linking verb: She *seems* nice.

t *or*   **verbs, irregular** Most verbs in English are regular; that is, *-d* or *-ed* is added to
tense form both the past tense and the past participle (past participles are preceded by an auxiliary verb):

Present	Past	Past Participle
kick	kicked	(aux) kicked

But many verbs in English are irregular. They cause problems that are intensified by two factors: Many irregular verbs are used frequently; and many have more than one acceptable past or past-participle form. Even so, they do fall into certain patterns.

a. Past and past-participle forms are identical but differ from the present-tense form.

1. *-d* changes to *-t:*

Present	Past	Past Participle
send	sent	sent

2. *-ee-* and *-ea-* spellings change to *-e-*; present-tense vowel sound rhymes with *beet*; past and past-participle vowel sound rhymes with *bet*:

Present	Past	Past Participle
breed	bred	bred
lead	led	led
leave	left	left

3. Some irregular verbs following this pattern also add *-t* to the past and past-participle forms:

Present	Past	Past Participle
creep	crept	crept
feel	felt	felt

4. *-ou-* spelling in past and past participle (pronunciation varies):

Present	Past	Past Participle
bring	brought	brought
bind	bound	bound
seek	sought	sought
think	thought	thought

5. Past and past-participle vowel spelling changes to *-u-:*

Present	Past	Past Participle
dig	dug	dug
slink	slunk	slunk

6. Miscellaneous:

Present	Past	Past Participle
make	made	made
mean	meant	meant
win	won	won

b. A second class of irregular verbs consists of those with three different forms, the past participle adding the suffix *-n* or *-en:*

Present	Past	Past Participle
blow	blew	blown
break	broke	broken
freeze	froze	frozen
give	gave	given

c. A third set of irregular verbs shows a vowel change (in both spelling and pronunciation) in both the past and past-participle forms:

Present	Past	Past Participle
begin	began	begun
fly	flew	flown
see	saw	seen

d. Many verbs have more than one acceptable past or past-participle form, although their usage may vary. Some of the more common ones:

Present	Past	Past Participle
beat	beat	beaten, beat
broadcast	broadcasted, broadcast	broadcasted, broadcast
dive	dived, dove	dived
forget	forgot	forgotten, forgot
get	got	gotten, got
hide	hid	hidden, hid
kneel	knelt, kneeled	knelt, kneeled
prove	proved	proven, proved
show	showed	shown, showed

When in doubt about other verbs, use your dictionary.

verbs, compound   Compound verbs in English (sometimes called phrasal verbs) usually take the form of a verb linked to a preposition. Because of their peculiar behavior, they are often troublesome writing problems. And because they are complex, we will deal with only enough here to alert you to the problems. Most troublesome are those that are transitive—that is, those that take noun-phrase objects, as in "He gave up the ship." We can express this in two ways:

He gave up the ship. (*up* immediately following the verb)
He gave the ship *up*. (*up* is placed after the object)

When we replace the noun phrase with a pronoun, however, the preposition must follow it:

He gave *it* up. (*but not* He gave up *it*.)

Note that *give up* differs from a verb followed by a prepositional phrase, as in "He climbed up the ladder." Here, we can move the whole prepositional phrase to front position—an option we do not have with compound verbs:

Up the ladder he climbed. (*but not* Up the ship he gave.)

This brief discussion cannot alert you to all the characteristics of these problem verbs. However, you should realize that they are often the reason for a red "AWK" in the margin of your papers. You can't avoid using compound verbs; they are much too prevalent and too valuable. But you can use them carefully, reshaping your sentences when necessary to *pass* them *by*.

verb phrases

a. *Be*. Many American dialects omit the verb *be* as either a main verb or an auxiliary. Except in dialogue, these omissions are universally considered unacceptable in writing.

Jack *is* a good teacher. / They *are* going home.
Not: Jack a good teacher. / They going home.

Some dialects have two unusual usages involving *be* to express variant degrees of continuing time. Both are acceptable in writing only in a journal or dialogue.

His mother *is* working. (at this time) / His mother *works*. (all the time)
Not: His mother working. / His mother *be* working.

b. *Have* as an auxiliary verb. In both spoken English and in personal writing, we usually contract the forms of *have* (*have, has, had*) in verb phrases such as "I*'ve* never noticed that." This practice leads to two writing problems:

Deletion of *have* altogether: I been there.
Substitution of *of* for *-ve*: I should *of* known it. (for I should*'ve* known it.)

c. Passive forms. Modern English has two ways to show passive: The auxiliary *be* plus the past participle form of the verb:

She *was* seen by many people.

The auxiliary *get* plus the past participle (avoid its overuse in writing):

They *got* disgusted and left.

contr **verbs, contracted** See *verb phrases,* page 44.

subjunctive In earlier English, special subjunctive verb forms were used to indicate hypothetical or contrary-to-fact conditions: for example, to signal the difference between "that *is* the case," and "if that *be* the case." The latter is now obsolete, along with other subjunctives. Modern usage is "if that *is* the case. . . ."

In contemporary usage, particularly in formal English, the subjunctive is retained in only two constructions: *if* clauses and *that* clauses when third-person verb forms are involved.

1. In *if* clauses, only the verb *be* takes the subjunctive form, and then only to change *was* to *were.*

   If Liz *were* sure that she would be welcome, she would go.

2. In *that* clauses in written English, the subjunctive is used after verbs that carry a connotation of mandatory action: *demand, insist, request, command,* and so on.

   The NCAA demands that an athletic dormitory *meet* certain standards.

   The singular subject *dormitory* would be followed by the *-s* verb form in other contexts: The dormitory *meets* the standards.

   In less formal situations, a *to* + verb (*to meet*) or *should* + verb (*should meet*) can replace the subjunctive verb form.

   They insisted that an athletic dormitory *should meet* certain requirements.

AGREEMENT PROBLEMS

agr / Subject–Verb Agreement
s-v

nouns: problems of agreement with verbs Many agreement problems with nouns and verbs arise from the classification of the noun, whether it is a singular, plural, or collective noun. Singular nouns take a singular verb:

One girl *is/was* . . . One goose swims . . . One deer hides . . .

Plural nouns take a plural verb, even when no *s* is added to the noun:

Two girls *are/were* . . . Three geese *swim* . . . Four deer *hide* . . .

In American English, most mass or collective nouns take a singular verb:

> Glass *has* been used for windows for many centuries.
> The government *needs* dedicated leaders.

Many collective nouns, however, can take either a singular or plural verb, depending on whether, in the context of the sentence, the meaning is singular or plural:

> The team *is* leaving for its Tokyo tour tomorrow. (*team* is a single unit)
> Our basketball team *were* packing their college T-shirts to take to Tokyo. (*team* is a group of individuals, as indicated by the plural *their.*)

Nouns having only one form that seems plural take plural verbs; those seeming singular take singular verbs.

> Your trousers *are* pressed.
> Mathematics *is* a fascinating subject.

nouns: compound subjects   Another agreement problem arises with compound subjects. When any two nouns are joined by *and,* the verb is plural; when singular nouns are joined by *or* or *either . . . or,* the verb is singular:

> Jennifer *and* Pete *are* planning a vacation together. (Either) Jennifer or Pete *is* representing the group.

nouns followed by lengthy modifiers   A special problem in getting subjects and verbs to agree arises when a long noun modifier ending in a noun is inserted between the verb and the subject, and when this noun differs in number from the subject, as in:

> The introductory essays, especially on the literary Indian stereotype, *is* superb. (singular verb, *is,* erroneously triggered by *sterotype*)

> The introductory essays, especially on the literary Indian stereotype, *are* superb. (plural verb agrees with plural subject, *essays*)

noun substitute: expletive *there* (*There is/are*)   Sentences beginning with the expletive *there* often present tricky agreement choices. It may help to realize that such sentences can be reordered; omitting *there* and changing to normal order will reveal the real subject-verb relationship:

> There ___?___ some funny things going on in such sentences.
> Normal order: Some funny things *are* going on in such sentences.

pronouns: agreement with verbs   Pronouns follow the same conventions of subject–verb agreement that nouns do; singular third person pronouns take singular verbs; plural ones take plural verbs.

He/someone/everybody (sing.) *is* a nuisance.
We/they/you (pl.) *seek* a solution to the problem.
I/you (sing.) *seek* a solution to the problem.

Pronoun–Antecedent Agreement

agr/
p-a

pronouns: agreement with antecedent   Pronouns should agree in number with the noun or pronoun they refer to:

Each pronoun should agree with *its* antecedent. (Both *each pronoun* and *its* are singular)
Now is the time for *all good men* to come to the aid of *their* party. (*men* and *their* are plural)

For further discussion of agreement problems involving pronouns, see pages 550–51.

va *or*
agr/v

Verb Accord

Verb accord involves matching verb tenses throughout a sentence or paragraph. Usually, the main verbs are all present or all past, as these two versions of the same paragraph demonstrate:

Version A: All main verbs are *present.*

The other [girl] does stop just in time for Rosemary to get up before the tea *comes.* She *has* the table placed between them. She *plies* the poor little creature with everything, all the sandwiches, all the bread and butter, and every time her cup *is* empty she *fills* it with tea, cream, and sugar.

Version B: All main verbs are *past.*

The other [girl] *did* stop just in time for Rosemary to get up before tea *came.* She *had* the table placed between them. She *plied* the poor little creature with everything, all the sandwiches, all the bread and butter, and every time her cup *was* empty she *filled* it with tea, cream, and sugar.

—*Katherine Mansfield, "A Cup of Tea"*

ASSIGNMENTS: SENTENCE STRUCTURE AND AGREEMENT

1. The following student sentences contain faulty verb forms. Identify and revise them.

    a. The inspector opened the door, only to found himself coughing and gasping for air.

    b. The city must also possessed a bakery, because loaves of bread marked with bakers' stamps have been found.

    c. Last year, I drop math altogether.

    d. By the middle of the year, my talent growed even more.

    e. It would maked a stockyard smell like a bakery.

    f. I brung everything she told me to.

    g. We be using a new set of books at my high school.

2. These student sentences have faulty subject–verb agreement problems. Identify the source of each and revise.

    a. The only reasons I can think of for closing on Sunday is religious belief and custom.

    b. They was from a different school and really thought I was somebody.

    c. An infinite number of pants, shirts, socks, and shoes, along with the blankets from the unmade bed, was scattered about the room.

    d. There was all kinds of problems involved in the decision.

    e. Nobody in the two houses were hurt in the explosion.

    f. Each of the lawyers were given a chance to summarize the testimony.

    g. A hammer and a screwdriver is essential to every home tool kit.

    h. The size of planets are difficult to determine.

3. In the following sentences, choose the verb form necessary for subject–verb agreement.

    a. What reasons (*do, does*) she give for negotiating openly?

    b. The 1980s (*race, races*) along.

    c. Every one of the fishermen (*has, have*) practiced the craft for years.

    d. The salt marsh that edged the shores (*was, were*) like a great sea.

    e. The most basic difference between men and women (*is, are*) biological.

    f. Only students with uncommon talents or unusual drive (*is, are*) willing to study hard.

    g. One of the flawed premises (*state, states*) that quality (*suffer, suffers*) when profit (*is, are*) the goal.

    h. Few people in the world (*understand, understands*) the extent of the universe.

    i. A number of questions (*have, has*) arisen about the use of aspirin.

    j. The depressed economy of the troubled oil market (*appear, appears*) to be responsible for the political unrest in the country.

4. Supply the correct form for the irregular verb indicated. If necessary, consult pages 541–43.

    a. The tiger _____ up on the herd of impala. (creep)

    b. He had _____ his work early in the day (do)

    c. Although some of the birds had _____ south yesterday, most of the flock _____ out this morning. (fly)

    d. The paper carrier _____ my paper late this morning. (bring)

    e. The expedition had _____ Newfoundland by last Friday. (leave)

    f. He wasn't sure which car to _____, so he _____ the German model. (choose)

    g. The wind had _____ the papers all over the campus. (blow)

    h. Before he left home, he _____ the light timer. (set)

    i. The network _____ the show earlier than intended. (broadcast)

    j. The class should have _____ that an exam was scheduled. (know)

    k. John had _____ home before the program started. (go)

5. Some of the following examples are sentence fragments. Rewrite them to make complete sentences, adding material where necessary.

    a. The astronauts who manned the space shuttle.

    b. The person being closest to me in line.

    c. Because the appropriations for student aid were cut.

    d. Which averages thirty-five miles per gallon.

    e. Whenever I get a letter from home.

    f. The only man in the crowd without a hat was bald.

    g. To start another war like Vietnam.

    h. In spite of her writing a ten-page paper.

6. Choose the correct pronoun form in each of these sentences. Indicate the reasons for your choice.

    a. (*Him, His*) father urged (*him, he*) to study law.

    b. (*She, Her*) and (*me, I*) both knew the purse was (*her, hers, her's*).

    c. The professor warned (*her, hers*) students to do the project by (*themselves, theirself*).

    d. (*He, Him*) and (*I, me*) never agree on anything.

    e. (*We, Us*) always went to the movies with John and (*she, her*).

    f. For Christmas, my mother knitted sweaters for (*my, mine*) sister and (*I, me*).

    g. (*She, Her*) had a chocolate cone; (*my, mine*) was vanilla.

7. The following sentences contain faulty comparisons or adjectives used as adverbs. Correct and rewrite the sentences, making any other changes you think would improve them.

    a. You have to study intelligent to get the most out of school.

    b. Our basketball team played real good at last night's game.

    c. My roommate plays her stereo too noisy for me to study.

    d. The experience was the most strangest I ever had.

    e. Some relationships with friends are more better than others.

    f. You should read through an assignment as quick as you can.

    g. Most of my friends are usual flat broke.

    h. She telephones me frequent on the weekends.

    i. The bed was made so careful that not a single wrinkle was visible.

USAGE

**us *or*
usage**

Some Special Problems

negatives, multiple   Multiple negatives are generally unacceptable in all forms of written English except dialogue. Most acceptable negatives are formed by negating only one element of the sentence—subject, verb, or object. One negative rules out the need for any others in the sentence, as these examples show:

> *No* crisis was ever quite like it. (one negative element attached to the subject makes the whole statement negative)
> Harry *did not/didn't* understand the question. (one negative element attached to the auxiliary verb)
> He had heard *no* sound in the house. (one negative element preceding the object noun)

Sometimes a double negative is useful in producing a weak positive statement—when two items are slightly similar or when the truth might lie somewhere between a positive and negative statement:

> John is *not un*like his father.
> I am *not un*happy about it.

Double negatives resulting from negative adverbs such as *hardly* and *scarcely* used with *not* are avoided by most writers. (See *hardly.*)

possessives preceding nouns   Writing problems stemming from possessive usage are of several kinds:

1. One arises from the tendency of some social dialects to omit the noun possessive *-s* altogether: "*John* old lady house on fire." This usage is universally frowned upon in written English.

2. Another written taboo is substituting an object form for the possessive: *him* for *his; them* for *those.* That's *his* baseball. *not* That's *him* baseball. *Those* children are naughty. *not Them* children are naughty.

3. A third problem involves punctuation (see *aspostrophe,* page 565).

possessives with *-ing* verbals (gerunds)

1. *-ing* verbals as subjects. When an *-ing* verbal is the subject of a sentence, the noun preceding it is in the possessive case and needs an *'s*.

    John's leaving was unfortunate.

2. *-ing* verbals as the complement of the verb. When a gerund is the complement of the verb, the situation is more complex than when it is a subject. Some require the possessive case, some the objective case; in other situations, either case is acceptable.

    a. Requiring objective case:

    She taught *him* skiing. (not She taught *his* skiiing.)
    She taught *Mike* skiing. (not She taught *Mike's* skiing.)

    b. Requiring possessive case:

    John continued *his* shoveling (of) the snow. (not John continued *him* shoveling (of) the snow.)

    c. Either case acceptable, depending on meaning or emphasis intended:

    We heard *Jim/Jim's* singing.

split infinitives   Infinitives (*to* + verb) are verbal forms that can function as nouns, filling sentence slots such as subject, object, or complement of an adjective.

To pass a red light is against the law. (subject)
John did not want to leave. (object)
It is good to see you. (complement of adjective)

Like other verbals, infinitives can be modified by adverbs. Although many people view as unacceptable the splitting of an infinitive by placing an adverb between *to* and the verb ("to *readily* see"), this construction frequently occurs in the works of our most influential writers. Split an infinitive if you wish the force of the adverbial applied directly to the verbal; otherwise, don't. However, you should avoid the awkwardness of inserting a long adverbial phrase between *to* and the verb.

Avoid: They wanted *to* with the utmost sincerity and friendship *wish* him success. (awkward and unclear)

Usage Glossary

The term *usage* refers to the way we use language—the choices we make in vocabulary and grammatical structures in speaking or writing. As emphasized throughout this book, some choices are more appropriate than others in a given situation. Although practically anything is acceptable in the informal style of everyday speech, written General English is more restrictive. It requires a more careful language usage—a need which serves as our guide in this glossary. To ensure that your writing will be acceptable to a general audience, we offer the preferred form of the words or structures listed.

accept/except   As verbs, these two are often confused. *Accept* means to receive something, to approve or agree:

> The union *accepted* the terms of the contract.

Except means "to exclude" or "exempt":

> Juniors and seniors are *excepted* from obligatory dorm residence.

Only *except* can be used as a preposition. Its meaning is then essentially the same as when it functions as a verb:

> Everyone had a dessert *except* John and me.

advice/advise   *Advice* (rhymes with *ice*) is a noun meaning opinion or counsel:

> The physical therapist gave me good *advice* about health habits.

Advise (rhymes with *wise*) is a verb meaning "to recommend" or to "give counsel":

> The physical therapist *advised* me about health habits.

affect/effect   These words are often confused because they sound alike in speech. As a verb, *affect* means "to influence in some way":

> The disease *affected* him differently.

Usually, *effect* is used as a noun; *affect* as a verb.

> The *effects* of marijuana have not yet *affected* his ability to study.

Effect sometimes means "to bring something about":

> The doctors were able to *effect* a cure for his disease.

all together/altogether   *All together* is used to describe all members of a group gathered together; *altogether* is an adverb meaning "wholly" or "completely."

At last, we're all together under one roof. (all members)
The scene he encountered at the top of the hill was *altogether* delightful.
(wholly delightful)

allusion/illusion   *Allusion* and *illusion* are often pronounced alike, which leads to confusion of the two words. *Allusion* refers to a casual reference to something; it should be followed by *to*. *Illusion* refers to a false or fanciful impression and should be followed by *of*.

Women resent *allusions* to feminine frailty.
Napoleon retained his *illusion* of power even after his banishment.

among/between   Use *among* with three or more items that seem distinctly separate; never use it with only two items. *Between* is generally used with two individuals, groups, or when the meaning indicates two.

Carolina and Maria divided the candy bar *between* themselves. (two items)
The three decided *among* themselves to share the cost. (three—treated collectively)
The contractor planted trees *between* all the houses in the subdivision. (meaning is that the houses are separate, one to one)

amount of/number of   *Amount of* can be replaced by specific quantity words (*pounds, tons, gallons*) or *much*. Because it accompanies collective or mass nouns such as *rain, money, intelligence*, it takes a singular verb.

A large amount of tobacco *is* exported by the United States.
The amount of money in his account *was* small.

Number of can be replaced by specific numbers (*ten, one hundred*) or words that imply number (*many, most*). Because it is used with count words such as *dollars, chairs, answers*, a plural verb is needed:

A large number of forms *are* often required with income tax returns.

anyone/anybody   These pronouns take a singular verb:

The agent is not sure that anyone *has* bought the place.

The real usage problem with these pronouns is with another pronoun that refers to them. In spoken English, we often use a plural personal pronoun: "Did anyone lose *their* briefcase?" Although you should avoid the plural pronoun in writing, using the singular *his* creates a problem of sexist language. Modern writers have a number of solutions for the situation. One is to substitute *he/she, he or she, s/he*—all of which are stylistically awkward. For that reason, substitute, when possible, an article for the possessive pronoun or recast the sentence in the plural:

a. It is important that everyone accept *his or her* responsibility.
b. It is important that everyone accept the responsibility.
c. It is important that *all people* accept *their* responsibility.

as Because *as* is an overworked word, functioning in many ways, it is often difficult to choose the right usage (see also *as . . . as* and *like*). One of its most common uses is as a conjunction, joining two sentence elements:

I weigh the same *as* you do.

As a conjunction, it can also replace *because, since,* and *while;* therefore you should take care to avoid ambiguity when using it in certain constructions, as in this example:

Ambiguous: Ivan didn't hear the doorbell *as* he was playing the stereo. (Does *as* mean *while* or *because?*)

As also functions as a preposition with the meaning of "in the capacity of":

He acted *as* an envoy from the President.

as . . . as *As . . . as* is now considered appropriate for comparison in all kinds of writing, even in negative comparisons that traditionally demanded *so . . . as*.

Ralph is not *as* proficient in math *as* Nina.

In *as . . . as* comparisons, a special problem arises when the second *as* is followed by a pronoun and a predicate is implied but not stated. In most written English, the subjective case should be used.

Nina is as well qualified as *he*. (*he* is the subject of the implied sentence "*he* is well qualified")

But if the pronoun functions as the object of the implied sentence, use the object form to avoid ambiguity:

My mother loves my sister as much as *me*. ("as much as mother loves me")
My mother loves my sister as much as *I*. (ambiguous; could mean "as much as my mother loves *me*" or "as much as I love my sister")

When in doubt about such constructions, rewrite the sentence to avoid their use.

as if *See* like.

as/such as   Although in spoken English, *as* is commonly substituted for *such as,* you should use the full phrase in written English:

> They had many things in common, *such as* a love of music and an appreciation of nature.

as though   See *like*.

bad/badly   *Bad* is an adjective that functions as a noun modifier or as a complement for a linking verb. *Badly* is an adverb.

> Roberto stayed home because he felt *bad*. (Adjective after linking verb *feel*.)
> Francie performed *badly* on the exam. (Adverb modifying intransitive verb *perform*.)

barely   See *hardly*.

because/since   *Because* and *since* as subordinate conjunctions can be used interchangeably to show a cause relationship. However, use *since* carefully because it can also function as a preposition indicating *time*; thus, ambiguity may result:

> *Since* he left school, he has had difficulty finding a good job.

As you can see, *since* could indicate either a *time* or *cause* relationship.

because of   See *due to*.

beside/besides   Although often confused, *beside* and *besides* are not interchangeable. *Beside* is a preposition meaning "at the side of" or "alongside." *Besides* as a preposition means "in addition to" or "except."

> *Besides* the twins in the back row, she had two children *beside* her.

between   See *among*.

compare/contrast   Students often have a problem using prepositions with *compare* and *contrast*. Generally, use *compare to* to stress similarities and *compare with* to emphasize differences.

> Her paintings *compared* favorably *to* those of the great masters. (emphasizes similarities)
> In his paper, Tom planned to *compare* Hemingway's style *with* Fitzgerald's. (emphasizes differences over similarities)

Contrast as a verb takes the preposition *with*; as a noun, *between*.

The speaker *contrasted* the old New Orleans *with* the new. (verb)
He showed a *contrast between* the old and new New Orleans. (noun)

complement/compliment   Both *complement* and *compliment* can function either as a noun or a verb; however, *complement* means "completion" or "addition," while *compliment* is used to express admiration or flattery.

The accent colors *complemented* the room's color scheme.
One kind of *complement* is a direct object.
They *complimented* her taste in clothes.
Charles always found a way to *compliment* everyone.

contrast   See *compare.*

could of/would of/should of   These forms are often mistakenly substituted for the contracted *could have, would have, should have;* the punctuation of *could've* is a homonym to *could of.* Use *have* for most writing.

I would have done it. Or, I could've done it.
But not: I *would of* done it.

criterion/criteria   *Criterion* is the singular form:

One *criterion* for an *A* paper is the use of accepted grammatical structures.

Although *criteria* is frequently used as a singular form in spoken English, it should be treated only as a plural in written, General English. *Criterions* is also listed in recent dictionaries as an acceptable plural.

Several *criteria/criterions* have been established for an A paper.

data   Although often treated as a singular noun, *data* is the plural of *datum,* especially in writing for science and social science courses.

Those data were inaccurate.

different from/different than   Use *different from* when a noun phrase follows; *different than* before a complete clause.

The European cultural heritage is *different from* the American Indian's heritage. (*from* is followed by a noun phrase)
Today's Indian culture is *different than* it was prior to the European invasion. (*than* is followed by a complete SP clause)

due to/because of Although these are used interchangeable in speech, restrict *due to* to adjective positions after a noun or the verb *be* in writing:

> The team's poor game, *due to* a collective bout of flu, cost them the tournament title.
> The team's poor game was *due to* a collective bout of flu.

Use *because of* in adverbial situations:

> The game was cancelled *because of* rain.

effect See *affect*.

e.g. See page 579.

etc. See page 579.

except See *accept*.

few/less/little *Few* is usually restricted to plural nouns; *less* and *little,* to collective or substance nouns (those not generally pluralized):

> *Few* birds are now found in the swamps of Florida.
> *Less/little* animosity toward the administration is apparent on college campuses today.

former/latter *Former*—the first-mentioned item; *latter*—the second-mentioned item. They should be used only when there can be no confusion about which item in the preceding context each refers to.

> When it came to apples and oranges, he preferred the *former*, but liked the *latter* also.

Because of a tendency to mispronounce *latter,* it is often misspelled as *ladder.* Also, avoid confusing it with *later.*

> *Later,* if you have a choice between walking in front of a truck or under a *ladder,* choose the *latter.*

get *Get* is an overused verb and certain usages are strictly idiomatic or colloquial. Other verbs, more specific in meaning, can do more for your writing style. (See also passives, page 544 and overused verbs, pages 92–94.)

> Their political views really *anger* me. Not: Their political views really *get* me.

Avoid using *got to* for *must* or *have to:*

>   You *must* do it. Not: You have *got to* do it.

hardly/barely/scarcely   All three are weak negative adverbs meaning "not quite." Addition of another negative is considered a double negative and is generally avoided in writing.

>   Jim had *hardly* any appetite. Not: Jim didn't have *hardly* any appetite.

imply/infer   Colloquially, these words are often used interchangeably. In careful, written English, however, the traditional distinction is retained. *Imply,* meaning to "hint at" or "suggest," is always used in reference to the speaker or writer. *Infer,* to draw a conclusion from evidence or examples, applies to the listener or reader. The speaker *implies* something; the listener *infers* from it.

>   Roger *implied* that a felony was involved. (speaker)
>   Mary *inferred* from Roger's conversation that a felony was involved. (listener)

inside of/outside of/off of   When these words are used as prepositions, the *of* is omitted in written General English, as in:

>   *Inside* the building, people went about their business as usual.
>   Not: Inside of the building, people went about their business as usual.

When used as nouns, *inside* and *outside* require the preposition *of:*

>   The *outside of* the building was painted a drab gray.

irregardless   Although extensively used colloquially, *irregardless* should never replace *regardless* in written English.

>   *Regardless* of the situation . . ., but *not*
>   *Irregardless* of the situation. . . .

its/it's   *Its* is a possessive pronoun; *it's,* a contraction of it is. They cannot be used interchangeably.

>   It's (contraction) too bad that the dog hurt *its* paw (possessive pronoun).

latter   See *former.*

less   See *few.*

like/as/as though/as if   *Like,* when used as a preposition, ruffles no one's usage feathers:

> She *swims* like a fish. (preposition; universally accepted)

But when used as a conjunction replacing *as, as if,* or *as though, like* becomes controversial.

> He has never acted *as* he should.
> Avoid: He has never acted *like* he should.
>
> They act *as if/as though* they were the only drivers on the road.
> Avoid: They act *like* they were the only drivers on the road.

Because many people find the conjunctive *like* offensive, it is better to restrict it to personal writing and avoid it when writing to a wide audience. However, don't become so hyper-careful that you err in the other direction, substituting *as* for *like,* as in:

> As my mother, my roommate always tells me when to get up. (replacing, the preposition *like* with *as* creates ambiguity)

little   See *few.*

none   In current usage, *none,* whether used alone or in a phrasal construction, is generally treated as a plural when referring to persons:

> *None/None of them* were willing to volunteer.

However, when referring to things, *none* may still take a singular verb:

> Of all the movies I have seen this year, *none* has impressed me.

number of   See *amount of.*

off of   See *inside of.*

outside of   See *inside of.*

plus as a conjunction   There are no usage restrictions involving *plus* as a preposition:

> We invited all of Catherine's relatives to the wedding, *plus* Tom's family.

However, despite the fact that its use as a conjunction is becoming more widespread, substituting *plus* for *and* in a compound sentence is avoided in writing.

They spent a week on Oahu, *and* they took a tour to the other islands.
Not: They spent a week on Oahu, *plus* they took a tour to the other
islands.

proceed/precede   *Proceed* means "to go forward," in the sense of continued
action; *precede* means "to go before":

The army *proceeded* to the enemy camps.
She *preceded* her husband down the aisle of the theater.

Caution: Watch the spelling—*precede,* not *preceed*!

principal/principle   *Principal,* meaning first in rank, importance, or degree, can
act as a synonym for *head* or *primary.* A *principle* is an ideal, a rule of conduct, or a
doctrine.

The *principal* cause of divorce is incompatibility.
The right of free speech is a fundamental *principle* of our government.

raise/rise   The verb *raise* is transitive and takes an object; *rise* is intransitive:

Raise the flag at six o'clock.
From on deck, we watched the tide *rise.*

reason is that/reason is because   Traditionally, *reason is because* has been frowned
upon, and *reason is that* preferred. Even though the former is now widely accepted,
some readers may find the usage unacceptable.

The reason he didn't go is *that* (or *because*) his car broke down.

scarcely   See *hardly.*

should of   See *could of.*

since   See *because.*

seems like/seems as if/seems as though/seems that/seems like that   The use of
like as a conjunction, most commonly after verbs denoting sensation—*seem, look,
feel, appear*—is controversial (see also *like/as*).

He seems *like* an understanding person. (preposition *like*; accepted)
It seems *like* he doesn't know what's he's doing. (conjunction *like;* many
writers avoid)
It seems *as if/as though* he doesn't know what he's doing. (preferred by
many to *like*)

In many dialect areas, after verbs such as *seem, feel,* and *appear, like* may be paired with *that* in some situations, but should be avoided in writing.

> It seems *that* he doesn't know what he's doing. (Not: It seems *like that* he doesn't know what he's doing.)

sensuous, sensual Although these two words are close in denotative meaning (referring to sensory experience), their connotations make it important to avoid confusing them. *Sensual* carries a negative connotation of gross or sexual gratification of the senses; *sensuous* has more favorable connotations, referring to the senses in general.

> The Marquis de Sade devoted his life to *sensual* pleasures. (negative connotation)
> Walking in the woods in spring is a *sensuous* experience. (favorable connotation)

sit, set *Sit* is an intransitive verb without an object; *set* is transitive, taking objects. The past tense and past participle forms of *sit* are *sat, sat;* of *set, set, set.*

> They asked her to *sit* down. She *sat* down.
> She *set* the flowers on the table.

so/so that *So* is often overused in spoken English as an intensifier for emphasis, but generally this practice is avoided in writing.

> She looked *very* attractive in her new suit. (Not: She looked *so* attractive in her new suit.)

So that is a handy joiner, but you should make sure that it carries the meaning of "in order that," rather than merely substituting for *so.*

> The farmer plowed the new field in the late fall *so that/in order that* he could plant an early crop.

that, which, who See page 540.

themselves/theirselves; himself/hisself See page 541.

used to/supposed to *Use to* and *suppose to* are frequent misspelling of *used to* and *supposed to* in sentences like:

> He *used to* be mayor of New York. (not *use to*)
> Mary was *supposed to* graduate in June. (not *suppose to*)

The problem derives from the general practice of not pronouncing the final *d* before *t.*

while/although   Because the conjunction *while* can be used either to indicate time (when, during) or as a replacement for *although,* there is danger of creating ambiguity:

> *While* the rest of the family eats at five, she eats alone. (Does *while* mean *when* or *although*?)

-*wise* as a suffix   The adverb-forming suffix -*wise* has become an overused device of spoken English in the last decade, resulting in such stylistic monstrosities as "religion-wise," "marriage-wise," "politics-wise," and so on. Generally avoid this device in writing because it jars the ear.

> *Politically* speaking, the two-party system has stabilized the United States.
> but not
> Speaking *politics-wise,* the two-party system has stabilized the United States.

would of   See *could of.*

ASSIGNMENTS: USAGE

1. Rewrite those sentences containing unacceptable multiple negatives.
    a. You don't hardly ever see beauty like that in the eastern mountains.
    b. I never tried to beat nobody out of nothing.
    c. There wasn't scarcely enough food to feed the refugees.
    d. It was not an unlikely occurrence.
    e. The police don't want no trouble from anyone.
    f. Ain't no problem too big to solve.
    g. Hermits are people who live alone and don't go nowhere.
    h. Nobody in the world's got no problems like his.
2. The following sentences contain usages acceptable in spoken English, but generally avoided in academic writing. Identify them and rewrite the sentences, using the more appropriate items.
    a. It looks like the economy will be a long time recovering.
    b. The two cities had much in common, as an ocean bay and a large ship-building industry.
    c. The gait of trotting horses is different than pacers.
    d. The reason for much of the failure in college is because students have not developed self-discipline.

    e. Due to heavy showers, the baseball game was postponed.

    f. Anyone with average intelligence can solve most of their problems.

    g. Frank was put on academic probation because he failed courses this semester; plus he made two D's last semester.

3. The following sentences contain usages that involve some kind of confusion between two words. Identify and revise.

    a. The teacher preceded to lecture to the class.

    b. Early immigrants had the allusion that the sidewalks in America were paved with gold.

    c. The man finally excepted his fate.

    d. Congress was not able to affect a solution to the erosion problem in the West.

    e. One criteria is the ability to succeed academically.

    f. Hitler apparently had no principals.

    g. Smoke always raises.

    h. Farmers use to do most of their plowing with horse-drawn plows.

    i. When I left home, my father gave me good advise.

    j. My teacher inferred to the class that I am not a good student.

    k. He set down heavily.

    l. Taking a warm bath is a sensual experience.

4. The following sentences contain a number of noun and pronoun usages inappropriate for General English. Revise the sentences by using acceptable forms.

    a. *Boomsville* warns us that, unless we change ourself, we will continue to make our grandparents' mistakes.

    b. Anyone in business should be allowed to stay open by their choice.

    c. To have a best friend—a confidant with who you can share innermost thoughts—is something of great value to me.

    d. One criteria that they used was the ACT or SAT score.

    e. Less students are concerned with politics these days.

    f. My father always made those sorghum molasses in the fall.

    g. Because he wanted it done right, he always did it hisself.

    h. My parents always sent money to my brother and I while we were in college.

    i. Tobacco is the largest source of farm income in Kentucky, but cattle is becoming important, too.

    j. I never found out whosever boots they were.

    k. Each of his friends were happy to see him.

PUNCTUATION

p   For many reasons, punctuation is often a headache for even the most experienced writers. One is the seemingly arbitrary or illogical way punctuation marks
are sometimes used. Another is the inconsistent correspondence of punctuation to
intonation features of speech. A third is the possibility of using more than one kind
of punctuation for the same sentence function, making it difficult to decide which
to use in a particular situation. For instance, commas are often interchangeable
with dashes, as in this example:

> The subject which the author wished to explain—the concept of *net
> force*—is unfamiliar to most readers.
>
> —*Edward Corbett*

The sentence is just as "correct" when commas replace the dashes:

> The subject which the author wished to explain, the concept of *net force,* is
> unfamiliar to most readers.

Many puncutation problems have historical origins: Punctuation did not have
great importance until the advent of movable type, when typesetters—not
writers—decided arbitrarily where to place punctuation marks. Some of their seemingly whimsical conventions are still with us. As writing and printing have evolved,
punctuation has moved closer to having a correlation with the intonation devices
we use to make grammatical structures intelligible to our listener.

Years ago, the pianist-comedian Victor Borge devised a comedy routine in
which he used oral punctuation. He ascribed to each punctuation mark a verbal
equivalent—a grunt, a snort, a click. Borge was indicating in this comic fashion
that we need punctuation in speech, but obviously he was wrong. We do get along
without punctuation, but how? The answer is that in addition to oral vowels and
consonants, other vocal noises are present: oral devices for signalling important
syntactical structures and for indicating the boundaries of words. A brief discussion of these vocal noises might help you to understand some of their relationships
to written punctuation.

You are probably aware that you can change the meaning and function of
certain words in the language simply by shifting the stress to another syllable, as in
pérfect (adjective), perféct (verb). We can also rely on stress variation to signal
differences in sentence meaning.

> They are hunting *dogs.* ("They" are looking for dogs.)
> They are *hunting* dogs. ("They" are dogs that hunt.)

In addition to stress, we rely on pitch to signal our listeners. By varying the
tonal quality of our voices, we can affect the meanings of our sentences. By drop-
ping from normal pitch to a lower one, we can state, for example, "You're the

expert," without offending the hearer. But raising the pitch at the end can also raise the listener's temper:

You're the expert. ⟍ (falling pitch; statement of fact, compliment)
You're the expert. ⟶ (rising pitch; insulting or sarcastic question)

Another intonational signal is a pause. The dramatic effect that a pause can add to meaning is illustrated by an old linguistic joke. With normal question intonation, the question "What's that in the road ahead?" merely asks the listener to identify an object in the road. But when a pause is put before the last word, it indicates a second question mark, and the query then takes on a macabre tone: "What's that in the road? (pause) A head?"

Although our discussion of these complex intonational signals—stress, pitch, and pause—has been very brief, it should help you realize how we depend on these devices in spoken communication. They are the "punctuation marks" that Victor Borge jokingly found lacking in speech. To compensate for their absence in writing, we substitute punctuation marks. As you can see, a drop or rise in pitch at the end of a spoken sentence has close correspondence to end punctuation (periods, question marks, exclamation points). And pauses inside the sentence often relate to comma and semicolon placement. But you can't rely on intonation alone; you must become familiar with the conventions of our punctuation system.

Like universal traffic signals and signs, punctuation conventions help your readers follow approximately the same route you took in your thinking processes. Thus, even though you sometimes find them frustrating or foolishly arbitrary, choosing the appropriate punctuation devices is an important aspect of your writing commitment.

⟋ or

ap

apostrophe (')

a. With singular possessive nouns and compound pronouns

Janet's son   someone's car
the man's idea   nobody's business

Note that one test of the possessive is that an *of* phrase may be substituted: the son *of Janet*. Use the substitution test when in doubt about the relationships of time and value:

a dollar's worth (the worth *of a dollar*)
a month's vacation (a month *of vacation*)

b. With singular proper nouns ending in sibilants

One-syllable names ending in *s, z, sh, zh,* and *ch* add an apostrophe and *-s:* Strauss's waltzes. Two-syllable words add either the apostrophe (Janis' ruling) or apostrophe and *-s* (Janis's ruling); but be consistent.

c. With plural possessive nouns

1. Nouns with -*s* plural: Plurals such as *cats, dogs,* and *horses* add only the apostrophe (').

    the cats' food   the dogs' barking   the horses' manes

2. Other plurals: Words with plural meaning, but which do not add -*s* to form the plural, need an apostrophe and the possessive -*s.*

    men's attitudes   children's stories   the cattle's feed

d. With contractions (omitted letters)

    can't   she'll   here's

    Caution: Don't confuse *it's* (contraction of *it is*) with the possessive pronoun *its.* Possessive pronouns do not take *'s.*

    It's a useless car because *its* tires are flat.
    (it is)   (possessive)

e. Special use with plurals

    Traditional usage demands that *'s* indicates the plural of numbers, letters used as words, and abbreviated names of organizations. However, this usage has now become optional in some cases:

    with numbers: the 1970's or 1970s
    with abbreviated names: PhD's or PhDs

    But with letters the apostrophe is needed: your o's look like a's.

[ ]   **brackets** ([ ])   Brackets are mainly used inside quotes for adding information in the form of a brief definition or explanation, or to indicate a misspelling or other error in the original:
        Adding information:

        "He [Chris] needed to be alone."
        The Chinese Premier said, "We must stop Soviet hegemony [dominance]."

    Indicating a misspelling:

        "The elephants preceeded [sic] the giraffes."

    Caution: Don't substitute parentheses for brackets.

⁀ or ,   **comma** (,)   The comma is the most common internal punctuation mark. Its work is manifold, from handling rather easy syntactical problems in simple sentences to complicated ones in complex sentences. Comma use, perhaps more than with other punctuation, is often arbitrary, having little to do with structure or intonation. For instance, a comma is sometimes used and sometimes not after introductory words like *finally.*

Finally they left me all alone.
Finally, no one knew his name or where he was buried.

There is sometimes a slight intonational relationship: In the first, there could be little pause after *finally;* in the second, the pause would be longer and more perceptible. However, don't rely on intonation alone to determine comma placement; other factors, such as sentence length, might also be an influence.

a.   Separating elements in a series

1. With compound subjects and predicates

Oats, peas, beans, and barley grow.

In this example, a number of nouns make up the compound subject; the same punctuation is required for compound verbs:

He ran, danced, jogged, and sauntered his way through life.

Although the comma is occasionally omitted before the *and* in a series, it is usually preferred to ensure clarity.

2. With adjectives in a series

Adjectives in a series often present problems. If modifiers before a noun occur in normal order, commas are not necessary, as in:

The ten most-informed professional women in the United States attended.

The complete noun phrase, "the ten most-informed professional women," is a single group defined by the adjectives; therefore, no punctuation is needed. Also, the adjectives *ten, most-informed,* and *professional* cannot be shifted without creating awkwardness. However, in some noun phrases containing a number of adjectives, commas may be necessary, as the next example shows:

There was a loose, bulging, faded carpet on the floor.

Here, because the adjectives *loose, bulging,* and *faded* are independent of one another, they can be arranged in different orders. Thus commas are required. When read aloud, these commas "sound" like pauses.

3. With phrases in a series

The same rules that govern the separation of single-word items apply to phrases in sequence. The commas separate individual items from one another, keeping them in recognizable syntactic units. Note that pauses correspond with most of the commas:

I dressed as fast as I could, putting on *my best pair of jeans, a fresh shirt,* and *my newly polished hiking boots.*

b. With compound sentences

When long sentences are joined by ***and*** or ***or,*** a comma helps readers to recognize the two sentence units. The comma is placed before the conjunction:

One of these terrors is a dud, and the job of the dedicated worrier is to find out which one it is.

—*Ralph Schoenstein*

c. Comma splice (See also *run-on sentence,* page 534.)

Compound sentences are joined either by a conjunction (*and, or*) or a semicolon (;):

Sixty years ago I knew everything; now I know nothing; education is a progressive discovery of our own ignorance.

—*Will Durant*

Although commas are sometimes used to separate short compound sentences in fiction or personal writing, this practice is considered a comma fault in most college writing.

d. With complex sentences

Unless very short, introductory subordinate clauses are usually followed by a comma.

Because the weather was bad, he postponed his gardening.

Subordinate clauses following base clauses may or may not be set off with a comma, depending on the intended meaning.

I visited him in the city where he lives.
I visited him in the city, where he lives. (nonrestrictive; see *e* below.)

e. With nonrestrictive elements

The term *nonrestrictive* refers to any structure which provides additional information not specifically tied to the essential meaning of the sentence. Nonrestrictives, unlike restrictive structures, merely add descriptive or amplifying material; they can be omitted without damaging the sentence's meaning. The most frequently occurring nonrestrictives include: 1) appositives that do not identify or define a noun phrase, and 2) parenthetical structures.

1. Appositives   An appositive that adds nonessential information to the sentence is set off by commas:

The dog, which bit Tommy last week, won a blue ribbon in the obedience trials yesterday. (the winning of the ribbon is not dependent on the information supplied by the appositive)

Some appositive clauses, however, are restrictive; that is, they supply essential information. These are not set off by commas.

The dog that bit Tommy last week has rabies. (here the appositive identifies a particular dog; no commas)

Note: *That* can replace *which* only when the appositive is restrictive.

2. Parenthetical structures   Parenthetical information can serve as transitional material, as a written aside, or as further explanation:

Mr. Jones, on the other hand, could have driven his Ford. (transitional material not essential to the meaning of the sentence; set off by commas)

The situation, as any fool could plainly see, was hopeless. (an aside not central to the information in the sentence; set off by commas)

f. With reordered adverbs

When adverbs are moved to the initial position in a sentence, they are usually set off by commas from the rest of the sentence.

Time: At nine o'clock in the morning, we saw him sauntering across the square.
Place: At the corner store, many spectators had gathered.
Manner: Mysteriously, the woman had vanished.

However, this punctuation rule may not always hold. Frequently, writers will not use the comma if the sentence is very short and close to a basic sentence, as in this example:

From that day on I knew my power over my parents.

—*Lillian Hellman*

In most instances, however, a good rule of thumb for reordered adverbs is to use the comma if the adverb precedes the subject. This eliminates the possibility of ambiguity.

g.   With direct dialogue

1. Separating the dialogue line from a speaker tag.

"I'll only take forty for the lot," he said.

2. Setting off the speaker tag when it interrupts the dialogue.

"Thirty-five," I answered, "is my limit."

Note that commas punctuating the dialogue line are inside the end quotation mark.

:   **colon**

a.   With complex or compound sentences

A colon may replace a coordinating conjunction or a semicolon between two combined sentences, if the second amplifies or explains the first.

For her, the words were not "only words": they were horrifying things with their own terrible power. . . .

—*Thomas H. Middleton*

b.   With elements in a series

A colon may replace a comma or dash to introduce a series, particularly when the series is material that amplifies or explains the sense of the sentence.

It is the prototype of man-made meteors that can be directed to atomize any spot on earth: Moscow, London, Tokyo, Rome, cities that can become a series of figures.

—*Charles A. Lindberg*

c.   With documentation (See discussion on MLA style, pages 402–11.)

d.   With subtitles

When a book or article has a subtitle, it is separated from the title with a colon: "Walden: The Myth and the Mystery."

dash
or —

dash (—) The dash can replace any internal punctuation mark—comma, semi-colon, or colon. It is used freely in personal or informal writing, but it should not be overused. When typing your papers, use two unspaced hyphens for the dash.

a. With cumulative sentences, the dash usually replaces the colon:

I spent my whole summer's salary on nothing—candy, cokes, pool, games of pinball, hamburgers from McDonald's.

b. With compound sentences

In very informal writing, the dash may replace a semicolon or comma between two short combined sentences:

That's how I spend every Sunday morning—I go through the whole newspaper.

c. With parenthetical information

The dash may replace a comma in setting off parenthetical information or appositives for clarity or special emphasis:

Providing such an upbringing for children is the easiest and most efficient way to bring up children who will be persons first—individuals able to use their full potentialities—and members of one sex or the other second.

—*Margaret Mead*

excl
or !

exclamation mark (!) An exclamation mark is used after interjections, such as *Oh!, At last!, Eureka!,* and at the end of strongly emphatic commands, as in: *Stop killing the whales!* But otherwise, it should be used sparingly.

hyph
or hy

hyphen (-)

a. With compound adjectives

Adjectives compounded from a noun and a verbal form, such as *diesel-powered* truck, or from two or more nouns, such as *health-effects* research, often need hyphens to indicate their close grammatical relationship.

Diesel cars emit 30 to 70 times as many particulates as *catalyst-equipped gasoline-powered cars.*

b.   With compound nouns

Sometimes compound nouns are joined by hyphens. When in doubt about the punctuation for compound nouns, consult a recent dictionary.

At sunrise the local *dog-walkers* are out in force.

c.   With numbers

Hyphens are used to join numbers or modifiers involving numbers: *twenty-one* cousins; *six-day* hike; *350-cubic-inch* area.

d.   With prefixes

Many prefixes become an integral part of the word; however, when they are attached to a capitalized word, a hyphen is used:

un-American; anti-Communist; pre-Renaissance

Some prefixes are always separated from the base word with a hyphen: *co-, ex-, self-, all-:*

co-author; ex-governor; self-hypnosis; all-inclusive

Occasionally, adding a prefix creates a word similar to another, as *resign* (meaning to sign again). In such cases, eliminate the ambiguity by using a hyphen (*re-sign*).

e.   Dividing words into syllables

When breaking a word at the end of a line, you cannot arbitrarily decide where the division falls. Here are some easy-to-remember rules for dividing words into syllables:

1. One-syllable words cannot be divided.
2. Words cannot be divided so that one letter stands at the end of a line: *e-*. . . . *lectric.*
3. Words of more than one syllable should be divided at a syllable break: *tre*-mendously or *tremen*-dously or *tremendous*-ly. If you're not sure about syllables, check a dictionary.
4. Words can frequently be divided by cutting off a prefix or a suffix; *in*-different; indiffer-*ent.* If the suffix requires the word to double a consonant, divide between the consonants: *run*-ning; *clan*-nish.

( )   **parentheses ( )**

   a.   With added information

      When incidental information is added to a sentence, it is usually set off by parentheses.

      Virtually all lobster pots (or "pots," as they were once invariably called) are alike.

                                              —*Gordon A. Reims*

   b.   In citing sources   See discussion of documentation conventions on pages 402–11 (MLA) and 411–18 (APA).

⊙ *or* •   **period (.)**

   a.   As end punctuation

      The period is used at the end of a declarative or imperative sentence:

      A college degree is satisfying. (declarative sentence)
      Hand your papers in on Tuesday. (imperative sentence)

   b.   With indirect questions

      He asked *what I had been doing lately.* (Contrast with the direct question "What have you been doing lately?")

   c.   In ellipsis

      When material is deleted in direct quotations, three periods usually indicate the omission:

        In his Gettysburg Address, Abraham Lincoln ended with the hope that the country would be reborn and that the principles of democracy would not perish: "government of the people, by the people, for the people. . . ."

      Because this ellipsis comes at the end of the sentence, the writer follows the MLA-practice of three spaced periods plus the sentence period. Many contemporary writers prefer using only a period.

   d.   With abbreviations

      For most abbreviations, use periods:

      Mr.   Mrs.   Ms.   A.M.   M.D.   U.S.A.   ft.   mi.   hrs.

Sometimes, however, initials are used to form acronyms, as in corporation or organization names. In such cases, no periods are used.

IBM   UNESCO   NOW   CIO   IRS

?   **question mark (?)**

a. The question mark is the end punctuation for all forms of interrogative sentences.

Why don't you investigate it for yourself? (question form)
You call that a straight answer? (statement-form question)
You really meant that, didn't you? (tag question)

b. In direct dialogue with quotation marks, when a speaker tag follows the dialogue, the puncutation is as follows:

"How did you find that out?" my mother asked.

" "   **quotation marks (")**

a. With dialogue

Enclose the exact words spoken in quotation marks: "You know that isn't so," he said. But in indirect dialogue, they are not needed: He said that it wasn't so.

b. With quoted material

Quotation marks are necessary to enclose quoted sentences, phrases, or key words directly quoted from another source:

The senator said that the proposed limitation on health-cost reimbursement would be "catastrophic" for most families.

c. With words used as terms or definitions

Few people realize that the word "muscle" (term) stems from a Latin word meaning "little mouse" (definition).

d. With slang or regionalisms

On rare occasions, when you wish to use a word appropriate to your purpose, but which is perhaps too informal for the audience or tone of your paper, you may enclose it with quotation marks:

The farmers were forced to dump their souring milk during the trucking strike; they couldn't sell "blinky" milk.

e.   For special emphasis

This new awareness is reflected in the charge of "cultural fascism" that is being leveled at traditional English classes, where "Standard English" is taught to blacks and their nonstandard "Black English" is frowned upon.

—Olivia Mellan

Be aware, however, that when overused, quotation marks no longer signal special attention.

f.   With titles

Quotation marks are used to enclose titles of articles, essays, short stories, short poems, chapters of books, songs, speeches, and unpublished works, such as dissertations.

In his article "The Amerian Indian: Beyond the Stereotypes," Franklin Ducheneaux contends that the Indian still suffers because of the conflicting sterotypes that society holds.

g.   With quotations within quotations

When you quote from a work that contains quoted material, enclose the original quote in single quotation marks:

"A student had written on the wall, 'Life's a bummer, but hang in there!'"

h.   With other punctuation marks

1. Periods and commas go inside the quotation marks, as in the example of *a* and *f* above.

2. Colons and semicolons are placed outside the quotation marks:

You cited the quotation as coming from King's "I Have a Dream"; actually it came from "Letter from Birmingham Jail," an earlier statement of his position.

3. The dash, the question mark, and the exclamation mark are placed inside the quotation mark if included in the original version; outside, if applying to the whole sentence:

I enjoyed reading Ann Pincus' "Shape Up, Bionic Woman!" (Exclamation point is part of the title.)

You won't believe this, but he can recite all of Dylan's "Sad-Eyed Lady of the Lowlands"! (Exclamation mark belongs to the whole sentence.)

semi
or ;   semicolon (;)

a. With compound sentences

The most common use of the semicolon is to separate two (or more) complete sentences when they are combined without coordinating conjunctions. The semicolon replaces conjunctions such as *and, or, but, so.*

Liberty is not merely a privilege to be conferred; it is a habit to be acquired.

—*Lloyd George*

Some charge that testing is harmful to students; however, it need not be. (The transitional adverb *however* is followed by a comma; a semicolon precedes it)

b. With parallel sentences

A semicolon is also used when two joined sentences have a parallel structure, but part of the second sentence is omitted:

Hate is dehumanizing; love, humanizing. (the second verb *is* is omitted)

c. With phrases in a series

Items in a series usually require commas. However, when the series contains long involved phrases, themselves punctuated with commas, semicolons are often used to avoid confusion:

The shelves in the room displayed an array of collected items: pieces of pottery, some valuable and some sentimental junk; well-worn books— novels, poetry, and drama; treasured rocks and driftwood, gathered on memorable outings.

ASSIGNMENTS: PUNCTUATION

1. Supply the necessary commas for the following sentences:
    a. She pulled in the driveway parked in the carport and entered the house which was dark.
    b. If a company wishes to increase customer traffic sales volume and profit margin it should locate its retail stores in an attractive well-frequented shopping center.
    c. Planting seeds to reproduce forests is an inexpensive reliable method and small land owners can use it with confidence.
    d. At this time around 400 million years ago there was sufficient air to allow fish amphibians and other creatures to become land dwellers.

e. The team however will probably not miss its huge high-scoring center too much because it has recruited a seven-foot high school star who was selected for the *Parade* All-American team.

f. *Sixty Minutes* the award-winning popular television program which is aired Sunday evenings is an excellent example of hard-hitting uncompromising investigative reporting that appeals to people of all age groups income levels and educational backgrounds.

g. In 1945 after Germany signed an unconditional surrender which ended the war in Europe the United States could make an all-out effort against Japan which had lost most of its fleet in battles for the Philippines the Marianas Okinawa and Iwo Jima.

2. Correct the apostrophe problems in the following sentences where needed.

a. He could not decide which of the two movies had given him his moneys worth.

b. *The Chronicle of Higher Education* contained a letter by Harvards president explaining the universitys reluctance to take a stand on the worlds moral problems.

c. We do not understand it's significance; its too difficult.

d. Mens clothing in the 20th century is less ornate than womens.

e. The other students problems have nothing in common with your's.

f. Is Mark Hughes intent to show the poets use of metaphor's?

3. The following sentences exhibit faulty colon or semicolon punctuation. Supply the appropriate mark where needed.

a. Students should receive letter grades for at least two reasons to reward them for their achievement and to make the evaluation of their work apparent to others.

b. The Black English dialect may result from five influences African languages West African pidgin a plantation creole once spoken by southern slaves Standard English and finally, the isolation in the black urban ghettos.

c. A man may say that the moon is made of cheese that is an hypothesis.

d. We hold these truths to be self-evident that all men are created equal that they are endowed by their creator with certain inalienable rights life, liberty, and the pursuit of happiness.

e. Students with little academic talent are often forced to attend college therefore, they are doomed to failure.

4. Supply the appropriate punctuation for the following examples containing dialogue or quotations.

a. Ain't she cute Red Sam's wife said leaning over the counter Would you like to come be my little girl No I certainly wouldn't June Star said I wouldn't live in a brokendown place like this for a million

> bucks and she ran back to the table Ain't she cute the woman repeated stretching her mouth politely Ain't you ashamed hissed the grandmother

—Flannery O'Conner

 b. I have heard said he you will not take this place any more sahib What are you going to do with it Perhaps I shall let it again Then I will keep it on while I am away

—Rudyard Kipling

 c. How can I be a spendthrift he asked when I don't have any money to spend and I am not thrifty.

 d. The word imply means to hint or suggest the word infer means to deduce.

5. Supply dashes where appropriate in the following sentences.

 a. Students should receive grades for at least two reasons to reward them for their achievement and to evaluate their work in order to inform perspective employers, however, admission officials at graduate and professional schools are also interested in applicants grades.

 b. Many public figures have been afflicted with dyslexia a serious reading impairment.

 c. It was a typical school day rushing to dress for class, getting no breakfast, running up and down flights of stairs.

 d. Mr. Jones everybody but his mother called him "Jonesy" had the look of a man constantly recovering from a hangover.

 e. Albert Schweitzer was truly a humanitarian if there is such a thing as a true humanitarian.

MECHANICS

mech Mechanics—capitalization, abbreviations, numbers—are exclusively features of written English, used to help readers sort out items that might be confusing, such as whether a title refers to a story or a book, or whether an item is used as a special term. Like punctuation devices, they offer a set of universally understood signals. And like punctuation, the conventions of mechanics are often arbitrary and confusing; they also vary from one authority to another. This section should help you with the most common problems encountered in college writing. If you need information we have not provided, we remind you that all dictionaries include an extensive section on mechanical and editorial conventions.

ab **abbreviations** Unless you are writing informally to friends or trying to save space in some publication, avoid using abbreviations. They are generally accepted only in the following special situations:

a.   For common titles (*Mr., Ms., Mrs., Dr.*)

   Mr. Darcy   *Ms.* Farmer   *Dr.* Taylor

b.   For family, academic, or religious designations after names

   Howard Silk, *Jr.*   Thomas Swift, *Ph.D.*   Sister Treese, *O.S.M.*

c.   For dates (*A.D., B.C.*) and times (***a.m., p.m.***)

   468 *B.C.*   10:47 *a.m.*

d.   For certain common Latin terms

   etc.   from Latin *et cetera,* meaning *and so on.* Use only after a list of three or more items. Many writers prefer to substitute *and so forth* when referring to things, *and others* when referring to people. Note: never use *and et cetera.*

   e.g.   from Latin *exempli gratia,* meaning *for example.* This abbreviation appears in formal writing, but is usually replaced by *for example* or *such as* in casual and general English.

   i.e.   from Latin *id est.* This abbreviation appears in formal writing, but may be replaced elsewhere by its English translation, *that is.*

e.   For certain businesses and organizations (Periods are sometimes used, sometimes not. See also page 573.)

Except for these instances, do not abbreviate unless you are positive you should do so. In your papers, be certain to write the complete proper names of people, places, states, and countries (except D.C. and U.S.S.R.); measurement units (*feet, pounds*); time units (*hour, Thursday, February*); and book references (*page, chapter, volume*) except in documentation where they are omitted.

cap   **capitals**

a.   With proper nouns

The names of specific people or places, days of the week, months, companies, historical events, races, languages, and countries are always capitalized.

Mary Jones; Cambridge, Massachusetts; Prudential Insurance Company; Tuesday; November; Caucasian; English; Russia

When common nouns are used in special ways, they too are capitalized: the Church (church as institution a particular one, already mentioned); North (region).

b.   With titles

1.   Except when using APA style, the first letter of the first and last words and all other main words in titles of books, articles, television programs, movies, newspapers, and magazines are capitalized. Articles, prepositions, conjunctions, and the *to* in infinitives are not considered principal words unless they appear first in a title or subtitle.

The Tyranny of Words; "So You Want to Volunteer?"; *E.T.: The Extra-Terrestrial*

2.   Titles are also capitalized when used with the name of the person:

Colonel William Brown; Professor Lopez; Aunt Mary; Mr. Klein

no. *or* **numbers**   The problem in writing numbers is to know whether to use words or
num figures. Practice varies: Most writers prefer to spell out round or one-word numbers (sixty dollars, fifteen percent, thirty thousand students); otherwise, they use figures ($4.98, 24 percent, and 22,097 students). For large numbers they use a hybrid form: 24.5 million, $3.6 billion.

Only figures are used in the following situations:

a.   Sentences, paragraphs, or papers with many numbers

The football manager packed 15 footballs, 87 pairs of shoes, 167 jerseys, 84 helmets, and 91 shoulder pads.

b.   References to time or date

At 10:23 a.m. on the morning of May 12, 1980, he received his degree.

Note: When referring to whole hours, spell out the time: He awoke at four o'clock. He practiced for two hours.

c.   Addresses

You can write to her at 124 West 79th Street.

d.   References to volumes, acts, scenes, pages

Anthony's famous speech in Act III, scene ii, appears on pages 552–54.

Note: Capital and lower-case Roman numerals are used for acts and scenes; Arabic numerals for pages.

e. Temperature

The temperature was −2 degrees but the wind-chill factor was −37.

f. Proper names

DC-7   Channel 12   Interstate 75   Louis XIV

Do not begin a sentence with a figure. Either spell out the number or recast the sentence.

Not: 127 passengers boarded the plane in Rome.
But: In Rome, 127 passengers boarded the plane.
or
One hundred twenty-seven passengers boarded the plane in Rome.

ital *or*   **underlining (italics)**
ul

a. For titles

Underline titles of magazines or periodicals, books, plays, musical compositions, newspapers, pamphlets, films, radio and television shows, long poems published as a volume, and names of ships and aircraft. In print, these would appear in *italics.*

Newsweek   *The Courier-Journal*   *Idylls of the King*   *Carmen*

Use quotation marks for other titles, such as magazine articles, short stories, lectures, poems, film and play reviews, and chapter headings, and songs.

"Miss Brill"   "Save a Spot for Strawberries"   "Trees"   "Let It Be"

b. For words used as special terms (see also *quotation marks,* pages 574–75)

1. Terms to be defined:

Plagiarism can be defined as stealing.

2. Words used in unusual ways:

There are three *the's* in that sentence.

3. To show particular stress on a word:

You call *that* a proper meal? (Be careful not to overuse this in most writing.)

4. Foreign words not commonly used:

It was a time characterized by *Angst* and *Weltschmerz.*

ASSIGNMENTS: MECHANICS

1. In the following sentences, correct any errors in the use of abbreviations, numbers, or capitals.

    a. Among the notable books about world war two are Dwight D. Eisenhower's *Crusade In Europe* and Winston S. Churchill's *The 2nd World War,* which is published in 6 vols.

    b. One college offers awards ranging from five hundred and fifty dollars to twelve hundred dollars to students who rank in the top fifteen percent of their high school class and who score twenty-six or above on the ACT or one thousand and one hundred or better on the SAT.

    c. Sen. Edward M. Kennedy, chairman of the senate judiciary committee, was faced with the task of considering nominees for the one hundred and fifty-three new Federal judgeships created by congress in 1978.

    d. Marie Curie, recipient of the nineteen eleven Nobel prize, was encouraged in her scientific work as a young girl by her Father, a Professor of Physics in Warsaw.

    e. The new Doctor bought a mansion on Heritage St. on Tuesday, Oct. sixth, and moved in before six p.m. on Wednesday.

    f. 127 students signed up for professor Naomi Green's class in Ethics last spring, a 10% increase in enrollment over her previous course at the Univ. of N. Carolina.

    g. Although born in the east, he had lived for so many years in Ann Arbor, Mich, while studying for his m.a. and ph.d. degrees, that he considered himself a midwesterner.

SPELLING

sp   **Background**

Theoretically, English spelling should present no difficulties. Our writing system is alphabetic; if it were ideal, each letter would invariably represent a particular sound. Unfortunately, several historical developments have made our alphabetic system less than perfect. One influence was the introduction of the printing press in the fifteenth century. Thus, English spelling started to become conventionalized over 450 years ago, and since all languages undergo changes, especially in pronunciation, these conventions do not always reflect present-day pronunciation.

Since the fifteenth century there have been major changes in the pronunciation of English sounds, particularly the vowels. Many of these sound changes are not reflected in the spelling system; for instance, the spelling of *eye* (pronounced as *I* in modern English) is closer to the pronunciation it had when printing began in England; *eeyuh*. Some consonant spellings are also remnants from earlier pronunciations; the *gh* spelling in words like *right* represents a consonant sound no longer existent in the language; the initial *k* in *knife* or *know* was at one time pronounced.

A second contributor to modern spelling difficulties is our tendency to borrow words from other languages, retaining the original spellings. This trait has given us such spellings as the Greek *ps* in *psychology* and *pn* in *pneumonia,* and the French *eau* as in *bureau, beautiful.* The result of all these borrowings and changes in pronunciation is a spelling system that often seems chaotic. However, there is hope for baffled students. More than two-thirds of our words follow spelling patterns that can help you become a better speller if you learn them.

As with other conventions of the written language, there are good reasons for learning and applying these patterns. Our spelling system, imperfect as it seems, is recognizable throughout the United States and in other English-speaking countries. Also, it elevates no regional dialect over any other, but rather creates a leveled-off separate dialect. Last, and most important, many of the spelling conventions, although they seem unnecessary, prevent ambiguity: for instance, the spellings of the two words *pane* and *pain,* which are pronounced the same, but which for clarity, are spelled differently.

Tips for Improving Your Spelling

a. Make a list of all the words you misspell. Or better yet, write them correctly spelled on small cards; carry them in a pocket. During free moments, you can test yourself. Keep the cards in front of you as you write, and use the words often until you are sure you have mastered their spellings.

b. Try to analyze why you misspell certain words. Is the misspelling related to how the word is pronounced? Are you failing to note a general pattern in the spelling of several words that you consistently misspell? Are you unaware of the structure of the word, not realizing that some portions of it involve prefixes and suffixes that have fairly consistent spelling patterns? Making yourself aware of these weaknesses can help you master not only the spelling of one word but of others like it.

c. When in doubt, look up the word in the dictionary. Because many weak spellers have trouble finding a word, we have provided a chart on page 586 to help you determine the possible initial spelling of a problem word.

d. Make yourself aware of the variant spellings of the weak vowel sound (*uh*) that often occurs as the middle syllable sound. Any of the vowel letters—*a, e, i, o,* or *u*—can have this sound. Be especially vigilant in checking the spelling of words like dis*a*ppoint, en*e*mies, def*i*nite, hyp*o*crite, nat*u*rally.

e. You should also be aware that many words have more than one possible spelling, any of which may be acceptable; the word *judgment* for instance, may be spelled as it appears here or as *judgement;* the older plural of *scarf, scarves,* is rapidly being supplanted by *scarfs*. Again, the dictionary can help when you are uncertain.

f.   You can master the spelling of certain repeatedly troublesome words by using mnemonic devices. By associating the correct spelling of the difficult part of a word with something you can remember, you will find these devices invaluable. For example, thousands of people have finally learned to spell *separate* by remembering that it's *a rat* (sep *a rat* e) of a word. Here are some other examples of mnemonic devices:

accommodations: Usually couples seek accommodations. Hence the two *a*'s,*c*'s, *o*'s, and *m*'s before the *-tion*.
address: An *ad* for the place you *dress* is an *ad* + *dress*.
grieve: Did Eve gri*eve*?
marriage: To *marry* someone for an *age* is a *marriage* (the *y* naturally changes to *i*).
similar: People look somewhat similar because they have two eyes (*i*'s).

We could go on and on. But have fun and games with your own troublemakers. And the crazier or cornier the better, because you'll be more apt to remember them.

Spelling Patterns

a.   Single-Syllable Words

Despite the irregularities in English spelling, many single-syllable words have a one-to-one relationship between pronunciation and spelling. Poor spellers who make themselves aware of these patterns can drastically improve their skills in a short time. Not only do most of these single-syllable patterns occur with high frequency as complete words, but they appear again and again as syllables in longer words, although there may be a change in pronunciation. For example, *man* may occur as an individual word, patterning with words like *ran, scan,* and *stand*—all having the short *a* sound. As a syllable in a longer word, it may have the same pronunciation as in *man*ifest, while in *man*ipulate it is pronounced as if spelled *mun*. Despite this problem, however, making yourself aware of spelling patterns in English should help you to become a better speller.

1.   Rhyming words are often spelled the same except for the initial consonant. The spelling pattern for these is fairly consistent. Here are some examples:

cat, rat, mat, sat, splat, fat, frat, slat (*-at* is the basic spelling pattern)
ale, pale, sale, bale, male, scale (*-ale* is the spelling pattern)

2.   Words with the same vowel sound are frequently spelled the same, or may have two common spellings. Obviously, these often cause problems:

beet, meet, feet (*ee* is one spelling pattern for the vowel sound) beat, meat, feat, pleat, bleat (*ea* is another common spelling pattern for this sound)

We can't deal with all the spelling patterns in the language here, but often, if weak spellers become aware that patterns do exist, they begin to find them for themselves.

b.   Prefixes and Suffixes

About 75 percent of the words in English are created by adding prefixes and suffixes to a base (*kind + un + ness = unkindness*). Being aware of the spelling regularity of these word components can help solve spelling problems. Remember too that we have a limited number of these and we use them repeatedly.

1. Prefixes

With few exceptions, the spelling of prefixes is constant: *pro-, con-, re-, un-,* and so forth. Several prefix pairs, however, are almost homonyms (words that sound the same but are spelled differently). The following are sometimes confused: *pre-* and *per-, anti-* and *ante-*. Knowing the meaning of these prefixes may help to un-confuse: *pre-* means "before, prior to," *per-* adds the connotation of "throughout" or "thoroughly" to a base. *Anti-* is against, while *ante-* means before.

2. Suffixes

Generally, suffixes also have regular spelling patterns: *-ive, -tion, -ness, -ing,* and so forth. However, the spelling of a base to which the suffix is added often needs adjustment. For example, when *-ive* is added to *act,* there is no problem: *active.* But when added to bases like *attend* or *intent,* the suffix *-tion* creates a spelling problem. To avoid an awkward sequence of consonants, the final consonant of the base is dropped: *attention, intention.* A similar situation occurs when several suffixes are added to a base. Adding *-ity* to *active* creates activ*ei*ty, a spelling monstrosity. To eliminate the confusing vowel situation, the unpronounced *e* on *-ive* is dropped. If we dropped the *i* in *-ity* there would be confusion as to whether the resulting *-ty* is a suffix or the end spelling of a base.

An Aid for Finding Words in a Dictionary

Using a dictionary to determine correct spelling is a problem for those who can't guess the first few letters in the word. The following chart of the initial sounds with more than one common spelling should help. The omitted sounds have only one possible spelling; for example the sound *bee* is always spelled *b* when it is the first sound in the word. We do include sounds that have two consonants in the spelling.

INITIAL SOUNDS AND SPELLINGS

Initial Sounds (dictionary symbols*)	Initial Spellings (most common spelling first)	Examples
I. Consonants		
ch	ch	church
f	f, ph	feel, phone
g	g, gh, gu	give, ghost, guard
h	h, wh	hole, whole
j	j, g	jet, general
k	c, ch, k, qu	cat, character, keep, quiet
l	l, ll	love, llama
r	r, rh	red, rhetoric
s	s, c, sc	sent, cent, scent
sh	sh, sch, ch, su	ship, schist, charlatan, sure
t	t, th	time, thyme
th	th	thin
th	th	those
w	w, wh	wet, which (in some dialects)
z	z, x	zone, Xerox
II. Vowels		
$\bar{a}$	ai, a	aim, ate
e	e, a	ember, any
$\bar{e}$	e, ea, ei	eject, each, either
$\bar{\imath}$	i, ai, ey	idle, aisle, eye
$\bar{o}$	o, oa, oh	omen, oat, oh
oi	oi, oy	oil, oyster
ou	ou	out
yoo	u, you, yu	use, youth, yule
(as in but)	u, a, e	up, along, electric

*The pronunciation symbols are those used in *Webster's New World Dictionary,* Second Edition.

Spelling Rules

a. **Words ending in *-y***

   To form the plural or third-person verb agreement, change the *y* to *i* and add *-es:* curry to curr*ies;* carry to carr*ies.* The possessive ending does not require the change: fairy to fairy's wing, nor do words ending in *-ey:* journ*ey* to journ*eys.*

b. **Words ending in *e***

   Drop the unpronounced final *e* when adding a suffix that begins with a vowel: *-ing, -ed, -en, -ish, -er, -est, -able.* Lov*e* to lov*ing;* lov*e* to lov*able;* pal*e* to pal*ish.* Because the vowel in the suffix signals the pronunciation of the preceding vowel, *e* is not needed.

c. Words ending in consonants

Double the final consonant when adding a suffix that begins with a vowel. This rule applies only to words that have a single vowel preceding the final consonant: man, mann*ish;* but not *clean,* clea*nn*ing. Again, pronunciation is the key; doubling the consonant of a word like *mann*ish avoids confusion with man*ish* (like a *mane*).

d. Words with *ie* and *ei*

A general rule is *i* before *e,* except after *c* or when sounded *ay* as in n*ei*ghbor or w*ei*gh. This sentence contains most of the exceptions to the rule: Neither foreign financier seized either species of weird leisure.

Special Problems

a. Words ending in *-able, -ible*. Fewer English words end in *-ible,* but when in double, check the dictionary.

b. Words ending in *-ant, -ance; -ent, -ence*. The vowels in these suffixes are all pronounced the same. You had better check these before handing in a paper.

c. Words ending in *-ar, -er,* and *-or* (all pronounced as in w*or*th). Again, check.

d. Pluralizing words ending in *o:* Sometimes *-s* is added, as in halo*s;* for other words, *-es* as in hero*es.* For many of these words, either spelling is acceptable: fresco*s,* fresco*es;* mango*s,* mango*es.* When in doubt, check the dictionary.

e. Words ending in *-ous, -ious, -eous, -uous*. These syllables are pronounced so nearly alike that they frequently pose spelling problems. Pronouncing the word carefully can often reveal the differences. Try these words: riot*ous,* cur*ious,* right*eous,* ten*uous.* You should hear a "y" in curious; a *ch* in righteous; and "yu" in tenuous. These signal that the spelling is different from the *-ous* in riotous.

f. Words ending in *s, ch, sh, x*. In the plural, these words add *-es;* kiss, kiss*es;* church, church*es;* hash, hash*es;* hoax, hoax*es.* Pronounce them and you realize that the plural ending is pronounced as a separate syllable, thus requiring the vowel *e.*

g. Words ending in *-al* (leg*al*); *-el* (canc*el*); *-il* (penc*il*); *-ol* (capit*ol*); *-le* (rif*le*); *-ile* (fac*ile*). All are pronounced as *u*ll. When in doubt, check it out.

h. Homonyms. Many words in English sound the same but are spelled differently. They are easily confused and account for much misspelling. When in doubt about the spelling of such a word, check your dictionary for its meaning. Here are some common ones.

bread, bred	piece, peace
break, brake	principle, principal
cite, sight, site	stationary, stationery
coarse, course	their, they're, there
passed, past	your, you're

Then there are words that are confused or misspelled because they sound similar although they are not homonyms:

accept, except   eminent, imminent
advice, advise   lose, loose
affect, effect   moral, morale
chose, choose   personal, personnel
then, than   weather, whether
pen, pin   which, witch

100 Commonly Misspelled Words

Try to master the spelling of these words by having a friend dictate them to you. Analyze the words you misspell. Can you detect any patterns? If so, find the rule or way to master these and other words with the same spelling pattern. Also, keep practicing with other misspelled words until you have mastered them.

accommodate	courtesy	independent	privilege
ache	dangerous	interest	practice
acquaint	dealt	knowledge	psychology
across	decision	leisure	repetition
address	definite	librarian	racial
although	disappoint	license	recommend
analyze	divine	maintenance	receive
answer	disastrous	marriage	relevant
asked	embarrass	meant	restaurant
assist	equipped	missile	schedule
athlete	especially	misspelled	separate
beginning	excellent	muscle	similar
belief	familiar	niece	sincerely
believe	finally	ninety	sophomore
busing	foreign	obey	studying
business	fortune	occasion	succeed
category	friend	occurred	surprise
ceiling	gauge	odor	tendency
committee	government	optimistic	thought
conscious	grammar	origin	tragedy
consistent	guarantee	parallel	truly
convenient	handkerchief	perform	until
courageous	height	picnic	usually
criticize	hypocrite	picnicked	weight
curiosity	immediate	possess	writing

ASSIGNMENTS: SPELLING

1. A friend, a notoriously poor speller, has asked you to correct any misspellings in his paper, which follows:

Some specific experiments indicate that the affect of television on people is too place them in an alpha state. This condition generally occurs during some occasion when peole have the liesure to daydream, stair into space, or loose conscousness as they are beginning to fall asleep.

By studying a person's brain waves when television is turned on, scientists have gained knowledge of its immediate affect. The patterns recieved on amplifiers and compustors definately and consistantly indicate that television puts people into a non-thinking alpha state. A seperate study showed that a person was placed in this condition by three different commercals even though she beleived that one was booring, one relevent, and one irritating. This result surprised scientists, who thought that she would be sincerly involved in the annoying or intresting program.

When scientists analized they're results, they concluded that television is not only an excellant and convient source of information and entertainmint, but that it ansers a nead for some people. Just as some individuals can rock for hours in a familar seting or can sit accross from a fire, so others can gaze at a television screen for a long wile without a brake and without criticising what they see. Of coarse, this explains why people have the tendancy to watch terrible preformances night after night. They do not care to gage the quality of television; they simply need to watch something.

Because these studys of televisions affects on the brain are still speculative, psychologists are continueing there work and are writting up there researsh.

2. Proofread the following student paper, correcting only careless spelling, punctuation, and similar mechanical errors.

When living in a dorm, you give up all your privacy. It seems you are not alone for one minute. There is either someone talking at you or looking at you. This makes life difficult and exasperating at times.

Everyone likes to have the opportunity to do some studing sit and daydream undisturbed,or to have a private conversation with thier friends. The walls in the dorm, which are tissue-thin, conduct sound very well. This results in you're next store neighbor hearing all your most most valuable secrets. Besides accidental eavesdroping, there is the constant interruption of your thinking when someone plays there sterio or tv at full blast. Another difficulty is that guests always arrive at the most inconvient monent. At home they would call first. here they pop in whenever your a mess, at your worse.

Talking on the phone can also be a harrasing experence. There are no seperate lines, usually eight girls on a single one. And the same number on the other line. Providing you are lucky enough to get the person that you want to talk to to on the line, then the invasion of privacy begins. Every ten second one of the other fourteen people on the too lines tries to place a call, Or, someone sits near you, listenning, hopping you will hang up. You could go out of you mind?

That's not as bad as your date's being a topic of intrest and concern to all your dormitory friends. Take, for example, the "One O Clock Check-Up," which occurs on Friday and Saturdays nihgts when people return from their dats. Then the inspectors ually examine the new arrivals. They check for taletale signs such as drunken behavior, passion marks, overly red lips, wrinkled cloothing, messed hair, and and flushed faces. From this checklist they can detect what you did and what sort of time you had. You just cant keep anything a secret.

Usually the last stronghold of privacy is the bathroom, but in a dorm even this seems lost. The shower curtains do not insure privacy. they flap when the water is turned on, exposing all your fat and everything. Then there is the bathtub calamity. Every time you start you start daydreaming in a delicious, soothing, steeming tube of water, someone sticks her head in and tries to see if you are allmost done. Lying there, with faces peaking at your every few minites you want to scream.

Well, you finally realize that the privacy you had at home just isn't possible in the dorms. About all you can do is to expect the fact and enjoy invading the privacy of others. But then. if you get disparate, you can if you disire—go home again.

Copyrights and Acknowledgments

Index

similes, 22
simple sentences, 65-66, 531
sit/set, 561
situation and language use, 106
situational irony, 470
sketching (prewriting tactic for description), 48
slang, 113, 118
so/so that, 561
social communities and language, 108
social dialects. *See* dialects, social.
spatial organization
  combined with chronological, 61
  description, 61
  personal description, 18
  process analysis, 143
speaker tags in dialogue, 59, 570
Specialized English, 114-16, 118, 530
specialized terms in expository writing, 231
specific details in science and social science, 484
split infinitives, 551
spelling, 128, 360, 582-90
  commonly misspelled words (list), 588
  finding words in dictionary, 585
  tips for improving, 583-84
  patterns, 584
  rules, 586-87
  special problems, 587-88
spoken and written English, 112-14, 117-18
SRI (and IRS) form in paragraphs, 191-94, 196-97
statistics, 198, 247, 299
stereotyping, 348
style, memos, 514
stylistic varieties of English, 109, 114-18. 529-30
subject (grammatical), 66, 530
subject (of papers)
  adapting to readers, 180-81, 299-300
  limiting, 49, 173, 180, 299, 380
  See also subject selection.
subject selection
  expository writing, 173-80
  laboratory report, 484
  literature papers, 471
  personal writing, 43-50
  persuasive writing, 295
  research paper, 366-71
  research review paper, 494
subject-verb agreement, 545-46
subjunctive, 545
subordinate (dependent) clauses, 76-79, 223-24, 342, 532, 540
subordinators in persuasive writing, 342, 532

summary
  in book review, 450
  in classical argument, 278
  in conclusions, 256
  in literature papers, 472
  of opposing argument (in Rogerian strategy), 322
  in reports, 520
  in research paper, 386, 388-90
supporting arguments, 278
supporting evidence, 339
supporting paragraphs in persuasive writing, 340-41
surprise in openings, 247
sweeping generality *See* fallacious reasoning.
syllogism, 311-18
symbolism, 470
synonym dictionary, 232
synonyms and connotation, 98-99

table of contents, reports, 520
tag questions, 72, 574
tense of verbs
  in literature papers, 473
  irregular verbs, 541-43
  regular verbs, 541
  verb accord (tense agreement), 547
tense shift, editing, 129, 547
testimony in persuasive writing, 299
that, omitting for economy, 232-33
that, which, who See relative pronouns.
theme in literature, 466-68, 474
themselves/theirselves, 561
there is/are, omitting for economy, 233
thesaurus, 99, 232
thesis
  and attitude (tone), 24
  of book, in book review, 450
  in cause-and-effect analysis, 184
  in classification, 184
  in comparison-and-contrast, 185
  conclusions, restating thesis in, 256
  in definition, 184
  in essay exam, 446
  in expository writing, 182-85
  formulating thesis statement 23-24, 182-85, 250-51, 300-01
  in literature papers, 471, 474
  in personal essay, 23-24
  in persuasive writing, 274, 295, 300-01
  in process analysis, 184
  and purpose, 183-83, 250
  in research paper, 382
  in research review paper, 496
  and supporting evidence, 301, 358
  word choice in thesis statement 183

See also central idea; dominant impression.
time
  in autobiographical narrative, 14
  historical, in literature, 465
  signals, for paragraph cohesion, 55
  in Toulmin argument as a linking principle, 319
  See also chronological organization.
Time Magazine, "How to 'Write' Computer Programs," 147-50
title
  in bibliography. *See* References; Works Cited.
  laboratory report, 491
  page (laboratory report), 491
  page (reports), 520
  page (research paper), 419
  capitalizing, 246, 580
  choosing, 245-46
  italics in, 581
  quotation marks with, 575
  underlining (for italics), 581
  quotation marks with, 575, 581
tone (voice), 252, 529-30
  business writing, 501
  irony, 470-71
  memos, 514
  personal essay, 26
  in refutation, 276
  reports, 522
  sarcasm, 276, 286
  and thesis statement, 24
topic. *See* subject; *see also* topic sentence.
topic outline. *See* outline, topic.
topic sentence, 53, 56-57, 61
Toulmin argument, 319-21, 325
  as brainstorming device in prewriting, 321
  as check on reasoning during revision, 321
  compared with classical argument, 325
Toulmin, Stephen, 319-21
transitional devices, 53-56, 342,
  paragraphs, transitional, 204-05
  words, 53-56
  logical, 342
  place signals, 55
  time signals, 55
transitive verbs, 541

-wise as a suffix, 562
underlining (italics), 581
understatement, ironic (in persuasion), 287
  attitude and, 24

Reference Key to the Writing Process

(continued from front end paper)